D0553926

The Hoax of Freudism

A STUDY OF BRAINWASHING THE AMERICAN PROFESSIONALS AND LAYMEN

BY R. M. JURJEVICH, PH.D.
CLINICAL PSYCHOLOGIST

DORRANCE & COMPANY

Philadelphia

ALSO BY RATIBOR-RAY M. JURJEVICH

No Water in My Cup: Experiences and a Controlled Study of Psycho-therapy of Delinquent Girls. Libra, 1968.

Direct Psychotherapy, vols. 1 and 2: *Twenty-Eight American Origi-nals.* University of Miami Press, 1973 (editor).

Direct Psychotherapy, vol. 3: *International Developments.* University of Miami Press, 1974 (editor).

Freud's Phallic Cult: A Pseudoreligion Posing as Superior Psychology (in manuscript).

Freud's Non-science: Pitfalls in Clinical Thinking and Practice (in manuscript).

TO VERA

Who graciously accepted a part-time husband while this and related volumes were coming into existence.

"To me, psychoanalysis is a hoax—the biggest hoax ever played on humanity. By showing who analysts are, how they work, what they believe, and what they have done, I hope to show Freud as a fraud. If I succeed, I am idealistic enough to hope that the world may return to the belief in love, ideals, good taste and courtesy—the "books" that have been burned by the Freudian Inquisition."

Edward R. Pinckney, M.D. and Cathey Pinckney: *The Fallacy of Freud and Psychoanalysis*, 1965, p. 3.

"Hoaxers have thrived on human gullibility through many centuries. It is the author's hope that it will serve as a warning to potential victims so that they be fewer in number in the future than in the past. . . .

"More than anything else *Hoaxes* should serve as a warning to all of us on our beliefs, attitudes, opinions, prejudices and biases. . . .

"Many a hoax . . . has attained gigantic proportions of influence. Though exposed time and again, it has refused to die. . . . Whether the public likes to be fooled, as the Great Barnum declared, or is fooled for other reasons, it has always been. And it probably always will be. Nevertheless, knowledge of the nature and importance of many outstanding humbugs of the past may be insurance for the future. At least, let us hope so."

Curtis D. MacDougall: *Hoaxes*, 1940 and 1968. Preface to the second edition and p. VIII.

CONTENTS

Part I—ENCOUNTERS WITH FREUDISM

Chapter

Chapter

Part II—THE FREUDIAN PSEUDOSCIENCE

Chapter

ACKNOWLEDGEMENTS

I am obliged to the Staff of the Psychiatric Clinic, 3415 Dispensary, Lowry Air Force Base, without whose cooperativeness and assistance I could not possibly have finished the manifold chores connected with the first phase of this volume. Mrs. Annabelle Torre, secretary of the clinic, made the whole process of bringing the book to the final stage easier by her interest and patience. My two "chief clerks," Airmen Darrel D. Naasz and E. James Sidey, showed a stoic tolerance in typing and retyping three revisions of the "Anthology," as this and related volumes were called in the early stage, with no more complaint than a sigh and a smile. Airmen Terry "Kim" Mariner and George DePeyster were early co-workers on the Anthology, Airman Melvin Klein in the final phase. Airman James Soethy has rendered many useful services in checking references and correcting the manuscript.

My wife Vera, apart from lending her husband to this work, has performed many a chore connected with the work itself.

Professors O.H. Mowrer, Ph.D., Bernard Spilka, Ph.D. and John Vayhinger, Ph.D., were helpful in reading an early version of the Anthology and in providing appropriate suggestions.

My glad acknowledgment goes to Mrs. Marlene Chambers for conscientious attention to the manuscript, in eliminating many a foreign turn of phrase and introducing a better English style in the work. Jim Merrin, Ph.D., gave valuable help in editing a part of an earlier version.

The final form of the manuscript was read by B. Lynn Harriman, Ph.D., Mr. William Hart, William Matchett, M.D., and Dimitrije Pivnicki, M.D. and skillfully edited by Amy Shapiro of Dorrance. They provided many pertinent suggestions. The responsibility for the text remains fully with me as the author.

I acknowledge the kind permission to publish from the books and articles under their copyrights:

PUBLISHERS:

Academy of Religion and Mental Health; Aldine Publishing Co.; George Allen and Unwin, Ltd.; *AMA Archives of General Psychiatry;* American Humanist Association; *American Journal of Clinical Hypnosis; American Journal of Orthopsychiatry; American Journal of Psychiatry; American Journal of Psychotherapy;* The American Psychological Association; The American Psychopathological Association; Arlington House; Basic Books, Inc.; Beacon Press; George Braziller, Inc.; Brunner/Mazel, Inc.; Broadman Press; William C. Brown Co.; The Chicago Theological Register; Collier Books; Collins-Knowlton-Wing, Inc.; Dell Publishing Co.; The Denver Post; Doubleday and Co., Inc.; Dover Publications, Inc.; Duell, Sloan and Pierce; Duquesne University Press; E. P. Dutton and Co., Inc.; Farrar, Straus and Giroux, Inc.; The Fortress Press; Free Press, Inc.; *Genetic Psychology Monographs;* Grosset and Dunlap, Inc.; Grove Press, Inc.; Grune and Stratton, Inc.; Harcourt, Brace and World, Inc.; Harper and Row Publishers; Harvard University Press; B. Herder Book Co.; Hogarth Press, Ltd.; Holt, Rinehart and Winston, Inc.; Houghton Mifflin Co.; International Universities Press, Inc.; *Journal of Abnormal and Social Psychology; Journal of Clinical Psychology; Journal of History of Behavioral Science; Journal of Nervous and Mental Diseases;* Julian Press; P. J. Kennedy, Inc.; *Look;* Lewis Publishers, Ltd.; Liveright Publishing Corp.; Longmans, Green and Co., Ltd.; Macmillan; McGraw-Hill Book Co.; D. McKay Co.; Meridian Books; The Mosby Co.; Murray Publishers, Ltd.; *The Nation;* T. Nelson and Sons; *The New Physician;* New York University Press; W. W. Norton and Co.; Pantheon Books; Perma-Books; Philosophical Library, Inc.; Prentice-Hall Co.; Princeton University Press; *The Psychiatric Quarterly; Psychiatric Opinion; Psychotherapy: Theory, Research and Practice;* Regent House Publishing Co.; Henry Regnery Co.; Ronald Publishers; *Schizophrenia;* Schocken Books, Inc.; Science House, Inc.; Charles Scribner's Sons; Sheed and Ward, Inc.; University Books, Inc.; D. Van Nostrand Co., Inc.; Vantage Press, Inc.

INDIVIDUALS:

C. Anderson, M.D.; K. E. Appel, M. D.; P. Bailey, M.D.; F. Braceland, M.D.; Mr. Lurton Blassingame (Literary Agent for Mr. John Knight); J. V. Coleman, M.D.; J. Ehrenwald, M.D.; A. Ellis, Ph.D.; M. H. Erickson, M.D.; J. D. Frank, M.D.; Walter Freeman, M.D.; Eric Fromm, Ph.D.; Roy R. Grinker, Sr., M.D.; M. L. Gross; J. Haley; A. Hoffer, M.D.; H. K. Johnson, M.D.; Miss Elsie Junghans; J. G. Kepecs, M.D.; N. S. Lehrman, M.D.; S. Lesse, M.D.; J. H. Masserman, M.D.; J. A. M. Meerloo, M.D.; J. Moreno, M.D.; N. Morris; O. H. Mowrer, Ph.D.; T. Orne, Ph.D.; E. R. Pinckney, M.D. and Cathey Pinckney; Jerrold M. Post, M.D.; Helen W. Puner; Sandor Rado, M.D.; W. Sargant, M.D.; W. S. Taylor, Ph.D.; J. M. Vanderplas, Ph.D.; G. Weinberger, Ph.D.; J. C. Whitehorn, M.D.; L. Wolberg, M.D.; J. Wortis, M.D.; J. Zubin, Ph.D.

INTRODUCTION

I

My main theme is the *futility of Freudism* in its many aspects. *The Hoax of Freudism: A study of brainwashing American professionals and laymen,* represents the first of four volumes of criticism of Freudian theory, practice, and cultural influences. The other three volumes, which I hope will appear soon after this one, are *Freud's Non-science: Pitfalls in clinical thinking and practice; Freud's Phallic Cult: A pseudoreligion posing as superior psychology;* and *Freud and Christ: Irreconcilable adversaries.*

My intention in these volumes is to present to the public, both professional mental-health workers and intelligent laymen, what seems to me the best selection from various critics of Freudism, integrated by my personal and professional thinking and experience. The selections are meant to be representative, rather than exhaustive. Many other critics, not quoted in these pages, have expressed similar views about Freudian inadequate or fallacious logic, scandalous lack of scientific validation, and the corrosive influences of its unexamined postulates on both patients and the general public.

The Fraud of Freudism seemed a catchy title for this book but implied a more conscious deception than seemed present in the Freudian hoodwinking of professionals and the general public. Another title seemingly suitable for the book was *The Pretense of Freudism,* because in the analyses of many writers, the deep psychology, the vaunted psychotherapy based on it, and the "science" of Freudism are found to be mostly shams.

The Hoax of Freudism seemed to describe more accurately the main theme of the book, namely that the Freudian delusions were first indulged in by Freud and later induced in his students who then perpetrated them on others, with the confidence and zest of a secular sect. The "hoax" implies a deception in the form of a practical joke in which the agent participates skillfully and genuinely. The "hoax" is derived from the "hocus-pocus" of the old-line magicians, who put

1

their tricks over on the public by deft use of suggestion, clever maneuvers, and a show of confidence. This seemed to fit the ways by which Freudians put over their speculations ("insights," and "research") on the public.

It will be obvious from the forthcoming exposition that the Freudian hoax shows features of other deceitful or delusional operations: superstitions, myths, propaganda, advertising promotions, indoctrination, subtle conditioning, brainwashing. Superstitions were transmitted by assertive individuals playing on the credulity of their fellow men (which includes practically all of us). The essence of superstition transmittal is the claim to superior knowledge and experience on the part of a persuaded and persuasive individual, and acceptance of the rightness of that claim by a suggestible listener. Myths (in the sense of mistaken notions and concrete interpretations of spiritual realities) were spread by political and other leaders in all periods of history and were believed in by the larger part of the population to whom they were taught. The most notorious myths of our times were about Hitler's and Stalin's charismatic personalities and roles, and about the prewar Japanese emperors, whom Shinto-worship and ideology tried to deify. The propaganda efforts in China about Mao, in Jugoslavia about Tito, in Cuba about Castro, in Egypt about Nasser or in Greece about the dictatorship colonels, represent all the same effort of impressing the populace with the extraordinary and beneficial features of a leader. The advertising promoters in the United States utilize the same psychological mechanism of persuasion as the agents of authoritarian regimes. They rely on unconsciously or preconsciously acting suggestions to condition their subjects and insure the more or less automatic response of the kind desired by authorities or advertisers. The indoctrination through the press and other communication media insists that the correct views, the favored political or cultural doctrines, are *the* truth, and all the deviating views are ignorance and delusion, or worse.

Some of the subtlest ways of conditioning and indoctrination are found in brainwashing. The most notorious and efficient forms of brainwashing in our era are to be found in victims of police states in the Soviet Union and China. The old-time revolutionaries were broken down and were made to testify (seemingly freely) about their alleged despicable antirevolutionary activities during Stalin's purges. The enthusiasm shown by subjects of the Red Chinese "thought reform" camps for the convictions they evolved under the mentally cruel pressures of their "reeducation" shows how pliable human beings are if the right methods of terror, awe, and promise of delivery are unscrupulously applied. As we shall see, Freudians use modified forms of all these methods of persuasion to assert the superiority of their prophet over any other psychologists, to assume the authority of "deep," psychodynamic" interpreters of human psyche, and to usurp leading positions in psychiatry and allied fields.

The thesis of *The Hoax of Freudism* is relatively simple and straightforward. At the outset, Freud played the hoax on himself. In his late thirties and early forties he was suffering from aggravation of what Jung later called the middle-age neurosis. He was troubled by depressions, heavy moods and alternating periods of inability to work and feverish activity. His exaggerated hopes of making a brilliant university career were dashed by having to go into private practice. His family was growing, his income was unsteady and, what hurt him the most, he was not given the recognition by other gifted Viennese doctors to the extent that he thought he deserved. His letters to Fliess (4) testify to the pitiful psychological states he was experiencing at that time. He needed badly something to lift him out of neurotic instability. He found it in the hope of achieving fame through creating a new psychology. He confided to Fliess that it was useful for shocking and retaining patients to inject a generous amount of sexuality into their neurotic problems. His patients obliged him by producing dreams and feelings which could be easily pressed into the prefabricated "psychosexual" molds. Freud became a victim of his suggestible, hysterical patients as much as they were victims of his subtle brainwashing.

Alongside this clandestine conditioning of patients and obtaining back from them the supposed confirmations of his psychological notions, Freud conducted an extended self-analysis, the selected fragments of which were later published, mostly in *The Interpretation of Dreams*. He was caught again in the same trap into which he led his patients: Wishing to find confirmation of his theoretical suppositions within himself, he was blinded to the ubiquitous influence of suggestion and self-suggestion in psychological processes, and thus produced dreams in line with his theories. He wrote to Fliess that he sometimes

3

knew in advance what kind of dreams he would have at night; however, he failed to draw the inevitable conclusion that self-suggestion was molding his dream images, just as his own explicit and implicit suggestions were shaping the productions of his patients on the couch. Fliess recognized the subtle suggestive influences and communicated to Freud the suspicion that he (Freud) was getting back from patients what he had injected into them previously. However, Freud had invested so many hopes in the intellectual structure he had built that he did not dare accept the full implications. He rationalized and glossed over them, preferring to stay in the comforting fold of his unwitting hoax. Years later, as we shall see in chapters VIII and IX, he was compelled to partially lift the veil placed over suggestion, but never long enough to realize and admit that all the pretentious, speculative "demonstrations" of his theories were no more than an exercise in heterosuggestion and autosuggestion.

His admiring and uncritical pupils (see chapter VI) mistook this conglomeration of Freud's self-delusions and ambitious speculations as revelations about psychic depths. In this way, what could at most have been a disclosure about the psychopathological hangups of Freud and of his suggestible subjects—hysterics, and borderline psychotics—was made into a universal model of the human psyche. The indoctrination grew in geometric progression, particularly within the American culture: Freud's students transferred the traditions to medical and lay analysts; these, in turn, brainwashed their patients and wrote volumes of promotional articles and books; the fancies of many educated people, especially artists, were taken up, and the American scene was flooded and glutted by Freudianized writings. It became a substitute religion for many, alongside other viable fads. Emil Ludwig, a discerning biographer of many famous (and a few infamous) persons of modern history, was shocked not only to find the Freudianized jargon and attitudes among American progressive society women, but also to hear his car mechanic spout Freudian notions. He was pained to see what he considered to be one man's sick speculations growing into a psychological and moral epidemic in the United States. He felt concerned that Freudism had become an unofficial, secular sect, reinforcing in the American mentality the trends known historically as hedonistic, and psychologically as immature and irresponsible. Ludwig decided to write his warning against Dr. Freud (5) as his contribution to the mental health of the American people, who had generously accepted him as a Jewish refugee. Some of his expositions of what he perceived as the sick and sickening aspects of Freud and Freudism are provided in detail in my other volume, *Freud's Phallic Cult: A pseudoreligion posing as superior psychology.*

The quasi-religious features of Freudism are another aspect of the hoax. Freud never admitted publicly his ideological indebtedness to Jewish mystics. Only in his private correspondence with Fliess, Abraham, Pastor Pfister, and others did he speak of the Jewishness of his doctrines. It was only relatively recently that these unexpected sources of Freud's psychological illuminations were identified. It is somewhat shocking to find that the arrogant atheistic scientist and positivist Freud was mightily inspired by mystical fantasies of medieval and ancient Kabbalists. He unmistakably borrowed from them some of the central propositions of his theories and practices, such as the allegedly sexual character of psychic energies (libido), the exegetic method of dream interpretation (minute attention and associating to some symbols and words), wish-fulfilling motivation of dreams, etc.

In his exhaustive study of Freud's borrowings from *Kabbala,* and particularly the esoteric, mystical, and sexualized fantasies of *Zohar,* Bakan (6) demonstrated that Freud had studied these notions and had taken them seriously. Rabbi Grollman (7) had further confirmed Freud's utilization of quasi-insights of mystical medieval dreamers who were Jews by ethnic origin but were, like Freud, estranged from the prophetic mainstream of Israelitic positive religious traditions.

Again, Freud appeared to play this part of the hoax genuinely, determined by his "scientific" prejudices and superstitions, as well as his social and historical situation.

It would not be inappropriate in the context of familiar sexualized Freudian speculations to conjecture on the "deep," "psychodynamic" reasons for Freud's turning to this particular brand of mysticism. As happens with many depressive neurotics, Freud had lost interest in sexual experiences with his wife, as he wrote to Fliess. In the sexual mysticism of *Zohar* he found compensation and sublimation for his waning sexual promptings. Like many sexually inhibited individuals, Freud could at least talk and think sexuality. Be that as it may, it

5

would have been too much to expect Freud to admit that he, an avowed materialistic scientist, would seek the healing of his psychological turmoil in the quasi-religious intuitions and imaginations of unorthodox Jewish theosophists. These certainly were not the best representatives of the Jewish mind and spirit, just as Paracelsus, for instance, was not the best expression of European medicine, philosophy or mysticism. However, some writers misperceived Freud as a Jewish thinker. Even Jung was misled into the hasty generalization of contrasting Freud's "Jewish" psychology with the healthier Germanic psychologies. The best Jewish psychology is to be found in humble rabbis, in Buber or other humanists; Freud is only a low point of it. Machiavelli or the mafiosi are not the choice expressions of the Italian people, and the Spanish should not be caricatured by considering sadistic Inquisitors or ruthless Conquistadores typical of that fine nation.

Some of the recognized Jewish scholars have expressed vehement disagreement with the pansexual generalizations that Freud took over from some Kabbalists. Theodore Lessing, a philosopher of history, killed by the Nazis, called Freud's ideas "a monstrosity of the Jewish spirit." (8:299)* Alfred Adler wanted to dissociate himself from Freudism as "he came to believe that the whole process of psychoanalysis is inimical to the welfare of mankind." (9:66) I have already intimated Emil Ludwig's disgust. Victor Frankl (10) held three radio lectures in Austria about the dehumanizing and spiritually degrading implications of Freud's psychology. Later on, he published an even more scathing criticism, which spoke of the mutilation suffered by the human psyche when forced into the categories of the Freudian reductionism ("dynamic psychologism," as he called it). (11) Maslow rejected Freudism as a misshaping of human image, and developed a humanistic correction to psychoanalytic distortions. (12)

We shall see later on (chapter IV) that Freud had remarkable powers of repression of inconvenient memories. Bailey, an American neurologist, called him a "cryptamnesic sophist" in this connection, *i.e.* an intellectual acrobat relying mainly on a false amnesia for events

* The first number is of the reference found at the end of the volume, the second refers to the page of a particular reference beginning on page 467.

disturbing to his wishful thinking. Thus he concealed from himself and others the Kabbalistic sources of his theories. The clandestine religious features of Freud's theories and of the pseudoreligious movement he launched, are dealt with in detail in *Freud's Phallic Cult*.

The first adherents of Freud (and most of the later ones), suffering like their master from a religious disbalance in their psyche, bought the hoax wholeheartedly under the guise of "science." They perpetrated the beloved delusion in interminable praises to Freud the Magnificent, the New Moses promising to supply the refreshing springs to the dwellers in materialistic and naturalistic psychological wastelands. The psychoanalytic pretenses at science are considered in chapter VI.

Freud's adherents continued that aspect of the hoax which consisted in hiding the Jewish mystical sources of psychoanalytic propositions. Bakan mentions that *Zohar* is missing from Freud's library in New York even though a Jewish visitor had seen it among Freud's books in Vienna. One of the orthodox Freudians, writing on the foundation period of psychoanalysis, illustrates this particular attitude of concealment. Eissler (8) completely glosses over Bakan's demonstration of the Kabbalistic inspirations for Freud's most important ideas and presents the period of self-analysis in traditional terms, *i.e.* as if his insights were derived solely through analysis of Freud's own dreams and materials from the patients. He also presents Fliess, not as companion and security on the mystical "trip," but as a listener for lonely Freud. Perhaps the insight into the pseudoreligious nature of Freudism is offensive to his students; Eissler, at any rate, does not tire characterizing Freud as scientist, and Freudism as science.

As a genuine pseudoreligious movement, the Freudists fought other psychological and psychiatric sects, established themselves in the seats of the mighty in psychiatric schools, pushed out the unenlightened unbelievers, and suppressed, as well as they could, the opponents, their writings, and their influences. These undemocratic manipulations are exemplified in chapter I.

The medical and psychotherapeutic aspects of the Freudian hoax—the mediocre or harmful effects of psychoanalysis as therapy and as a way of thinking and behaving—are exposed in chapters II and III.

Only a few American doctors and others were able to withstand the subtle brainwashing pressures of Freudian "analyses." The hoax was played solemnly and insistently on their psyches too, and yet they did not succumb to it. They resisted the brainwashing to which a majority of psychiatrists, psychologists, social workers, and even Christian ministers, submitted docilely; the Freudianized subjects inhibited their critical thinking, as is appropriate for acolytes accepting any faith and a body of doctrines. The experiences of resisters are recounted in chapter V.

The bulk of Part II (chapters VI to X) deals with suggestion, as a basic promotional strength and fatal scientific flaw of Freudian theory and practice. Just as physicians before Pasteur misunderstood and misconstrued many biological phenomena because they did not recognize the effects of invisible microorganisms in illness and surgical complications, so Freud and Freudians missed the confounding influence of the *bacillus psychologicus*—the suggestion. Some of the scientific, experimental investigations of the unsuspected and pervasive influences of suggestion are described in chapter IX. The operations on the couch with highly suggestible hysterics, by means of which Freud misled himself into the hoax, are studied in chapter VII. The entertaining game of coming close to recognizing and then concealing the role of suggestion in psychoanalysis are exemplified in the mental acrobatics of Freud, Ferenczi, and Jones, in chapter VIII.

The inevitable conclusion of the preceding considerations is given in the final chapter, where Freud's method is recognized as most akin to brainwashing. A new term is proposed, Freudwashing, for the subtle transfer of Freudian ideology upon trainees, psychoanalysts and patients alike. Parallels are drawn with the arch-masters of brainwashing, the Communist jailers and investigators, as well as secret cults and societies, from ancient times to the contemporary era.

II

Although the term "Freudism" might sound somewhat irregular to those familiar with the more frequent "Freudianism," the shorter form was employed more often in earlier literature (*e.g.*, 3:37). The main reason for the choice of "Freudism" is that its connotations seem to convey better the cultish and undesirable aspects of the Freudian movement. Other undesirable ideologies are usually denoted by shorter terms: Stalinism, Hitlerism, Darwinism (as a biologizing philosophy of life). The shorter term, Freudism, standing for a biologizing psychology, also expresses better the approach of this book; the emphasis here is not on the theoretical refinements proposed by Freud's pupils, for which the term Freudianism might better be reserved. The main thrust of this work is toward the fallacious concepts and practices not so much of the disciples as of Freud himself.

It is not possible to state precisely what I had in mind when speaking of "Freudism." Just as socialism has many meanings, from Laborites in Britain to that of Maoists in Red China, or Christianity, from that of conservative Catholics to that of snake handlers in Tennessee, Freudism has acquired many faces in its development. For practical purposes, the meaning of Freudism and psychoanalysis is limited here to psychological and psychiatric thinking and practice holding loyally to the basic, more or less orthodox views developed by Freud.

I do not feel apologetic about this inability to speak of Freudism more precisely, for even the Freudians themselves have not provided an adequate definition. The official committee of the American Psychoanalytic Association concerned with the evaluation of psychoanalytic therapy, gave up the job, defeated by the hopeless task: "In order to evaluate a subject, one must know of what the subject consists, and since there are no two individuals on this Committee, nor in the society as a whole who would agree to a definition of psychoanalysis, the Committee was at a loss to know how they were to know just what they were evaluating."(1)

Zilboorg indicates that even the inventor of psychoanalysis gave up the trial to define his "science":

> ... even those who are earnestly initiated and professionally skilled are hard put to give a comprehensive definition of psychoanalysis. The point is that such a definition is really impossible without a number of qualifications, parenthetic insertions, and cross references. The reason for this state of affairs is that

9

psychoanalysis is not one thing, it is many things. Freud himself sensed this fact very clearly, and he seems later to have become convinced of it. (2:10)

Zilboorg fails to note that this conceptual vagueness was also useful in putting over the hoax on many intelligent but credulous individuals.

Many writers, even those sympathetic to Freudism, have pointed to the ambiguous features of psychoanalytic doctrine and practice. For purposes of illustration rather than definition, these aspects of Freudism are offered as salient in psychological theory and therapy:

1. Sexuality is presented as the basic drive of human beings. In the early writings sexuality was meant in its literal sense. Later on, to appease the philistines (the "squares" contemporary to Freud), an esthetic expansion was added, generalizing the sexual urge to love, Eros, and similar vague, mythological and philosophical concepts. To the end of his life, Freud remained adamant in insisting that psychic energy, libido (another mythologizing attempt), is sexual in nature. This exaggerated insistence on sexuality as the essence of psychological events was the main reason for Jung's and Adler's rejection of Freud.

2. The rich drama of human emotions, struggles, and values, was reduced to basic animal drives: sexuality and aggression. Sometimes, Freud would make verbal admission that he was examining only the basement of the human personality, but in practice he taught and behaved as if the crude promptings he discovered in the musty cellars were the only real functions of human beings. The noble features in him and in other humans, Freud explained away as derivatives, sublimations or other operations of "instincts." The "Oedipal" strivings of attempting to copulate one way or another with parents were announced as the basic formative influence and drive in *all* human beings, instead of being perceived as peculiarities of some neurotics and Freud himself. "Castration anxiety" was proposed as the prototype of all anxieties, and prudent avoidance of pain and conflict. Bisexuality was made into another pillar of Freudian conceptualizations of human nature—another example of quasi-mystical philosophical fancies, into which Freud was seduced by the alchemist-like fantasies of his friend Fliess. Many features of

Freud's credulity and unscientific temper are described in *Freud's Non-science*.

3. "Free" association, and fanciful interpretations of dreams, "resistances," and "transference," are considered the basic therapeutic tools. Freud's overriding interest in working with his patients was not to cure them—he expressly advised against therapeutic intent in analysis—but to use their subtly steered productions and sophist interpretations of them as alleged proofs of his theoretical speculations. Thus, Freud's needs imposed a futile therapeutic orientation and ritual upon himself and thousands of analysts indoctrinated by him and by his followers.

4. Freudism is essentially a translation into psychologese of materialistic philosophical preconceptions about the world and about human beings. Under the guise of "scientific" and atheistic *Weltanschauung*, Freud propagated his rationalistic and naturalistic presuppositions. He was not aware, or at least he never admitted it, that he was creating a nontheistic religion, a pseudoreligion, an inclusive world view and a particular set of values. The quasi-religious features of Freudism as a social and cultural movement are studied in *Freud's Phallic Cult*.

This description of Freudism is admittedly inadequate. Other elements of Freud's theorizing that have come to be considered his own by poorly informed psychological and psychiatric writers, are not peculiarly Freud's; they are borrowed from philosophers and psychiatric predecessors and contemporaries, as will be shown later in this volume, especially in chapters IV and VI.

The partial form of anthology was adopted here as a way of demonstrating that rejection of Freudism is not due to the peculiarity of an individual. At all times, even at the peak of Freudian dominance in the past thirty years, there have been psychologists, psychiatrists, men of letters and men of spirit, who have criticized the many debilities of Freudism. It is not a lonely psychologist howling in the Western prairies. There was a chorus of intelligent criticism in European countries and at home in the United States. Yet, like food fads and esoteric sects, Freudism has remained basically impervious to criticism. It pretends innocence, and continues to make claims of superiority, as it denigrates the nonbelievers.

PART I

ENCOUNTERS WITH FREUDISM

" . . . psychological establishment—the Freudian Mafia."
Sam Keen, Ph.D., *Psychology Today*, 1972, 5, (9), p. 44.

" . . . your American *crooks* . . . "
Sigmund Freud, referring to American psychoanalysts.
In Joseph Wortis, M.D., *Fragments of an Analysis with
Freud*, p. 110.

"Unfortunately in the field of mental health there have been relatively
few practitioners who wish to put their heads on the chopping block
by challenging orthodoxy. Some of these, while repeating the
catechism of accepted credos for the benefit of their associates, do
admit in off-the-record comments a disagreement with original
doctrines. But we are confronted too frequently with the frightening
spectacle of men so committed to their beliefs that they refuse to
relinquish them even when evidence proves that they are wrong."
Lewis R. Wolberg, M.D., in "Introduction," Adelaide
Bray, ed. *Inside Psychotherapy,* 1972.

Chapter I

The Nuisance of the Freudian Establishment

My brief maintains that psychoanalysis is guilty of reasoning unbecoming a candidate for scientific status, together with disorderly "logical" conduct injurious to the public mental welfare.
Joseph Jastrow, Ph.D., Professor of Psychology (1:177)

The ways in which psychoanalysis dominates psychiatry are myriad.
T.P. Millar, M.D., 1969 (49:427)

. . . at the present stage of psychiatric development, the influence of psychoanalytic institutes has certain potentially unfortunate implications.
Jerome D. Frank, M.D., Professor of Psychiatry, 1973 (69:177)

What a lesser breed are those . . . who run Institutes of Psychoanalysis from which a candidate can be certified only if he emerges with orthodoxy in his mouth and lead in his heart.
Sheldon B. Kopp, Ph.D. (60:132)

1. The need for a critical look at Freudism

The ideas of this book arose partly from my reaction to the psychoanalytic establishment in this country. The Freudian preconceptions, once a source of impetus to psychotherapy, an area in which I am principally interested, appear now more like a stultifying influence. The shell, formerly useful to the organism, needs now to be cracked and discarded to leave the body of psychotherapeutic practices free to develop a new stature.

Throughout this book, I will attempt to provide ample illustrations from literature of direct and implied criticisms of Freudism. Many others have observed the harmful professional effects of the Freudian establishment.

Grinker, a psychiatrist and psychoanalyst of considerable experience and training, expresses the following observation about recent trends in psychoanalysis: "For whatever reason, this brave outpost has become a crumbling stockade of proprietary dogmatism, to use George Kelly's phrase, by maintaining itself aloof from the progress of behavioral science and looking askance at conceptions of vigor." (2:371)

Frank, a noted psychiatrist, makes a practically identical evaluation in a milder form: " . . . psychoanalysis and its derivatives have had an invigorating and liberating influence that it would be hard to overestimate, not only in psychiatry. . . . Nevertheless at the present stage of psychiatric development, the influence of psychoanalytic institutes has certain potentially unfortunate implications . . . " (3: 11, 126)

Eysenck, a professor of psychology at the University of London, England, puts in a less circumspect form what Frank implies: " . . . the unsupported assumptions and theories of psychoanalysis have established a stranglehold upon psychiatric practice, and now are widely accepted in spite of the lack of experimental or clinical evidence in their favor." (4:IX)

Salter, an American psychologist and an early critic of Freudism, feels that, "Unfortunately, psychiatry and psychology have paid a heavy price for the Freudian sexual revolution, for psychoanalysis has left·behind only a dry and sterile wasteland. . . . " (5:13)

The conclusion is, then, that the outmoded Freudian concepts are interesting as historical remnants, but the current scene and accumulated psychotherapeutic experiences require fresh formulations and more efficient techniques.

As in any establishment, many in the psychoanalytic lead refuse to yield to more adequate approaches. To believers, the existing order is satisfactory; to unbelievers, it is a nuisance and nonsense. To unbelievers, Freudism in its orthodoxy and its variations has outlived its usefulness and should make way for less rigid, less vague, and more validated views and techniques. To make these latter more acceptable to professionals in mental health fields, it seems necessary again to point out clearly many of the often-demonstrated inadequacies of psychoanalytic theory and practice. The new techniques can hardly be practiced by those who still believe in psychoanalysis as theory and treatment *par excellence*. Physicians had to discard beliefs prevalent before Semmelweiss in order to start scrubbing their hands in chlorine solution; bloodletting was done as long as healers believed in the validity of that tradition. Haugen, Dixon and Dickel deplore the stifling of fresh approaches to psychotherapy by dogmatic Freudian prejudices:

> In spite of this dearth of scientific data to buttress our claim to knowledge, there has been for several decades, and is at present, a great reluctance to experiment with new theories of etiology and pathogenesis. Any theory that does not embody somewhere in it the concept of the "dynamic unconscious" is looked at askance. It is a minority of psychiatrists who swallows its Freud undiluted, but it is rare to find one who doesn't at least give lip service to "unconscious conflicts and repressions." (6:viii)

One of the purposes of this book and subsequent two volumes, is to suggest a saner and less inflated view of Freudism in its various aspects, particularly psychotherapy. An objective view reveals Freudism as an intellectual contagion infecting minds devoid of firm beliefs, those searching for new secular faiths and ideologies. Jacobson, a notable investigator of psychophysiological responses in man, and originator of Progressive Relaxation Therapy, criticizes these candidates for popular ideologies. He points out that, lacking definite convictions, they inevitably suffer from "addiction to ideas." They try to bind their insecurities by enthusiastic allegiance to political or philosophic leaders, to Marx, or Hitler, or—Freud.

> Man responds to allures of many varieties.... As might be expected "intelligentsia" everywhere are especially susceptible to *addiction to ideas.* One amazing example is the spread of Freudian ideas among many of the ruling classes of American universities and medical schools. Most members of these classes apparently do not fully comprehend the "ideal" basis of Freudian doctrine.... Addiction to such dogmata tends to dominate what is known as "present day psychiatry." (45:42)

Twenty-five years ago, Allers wrote that the purpose of his study, *The Successful Error*, was:

... not so much to convince psychoanalysts that they are in error, but to make those who are as yet but interested see psychoanalysis in the light of truth. There are but few conversions of psychoanalysts. They are too sure of having laid hand on the deepest truths of human nature. But one might hope to prevent the spreading of contagion. (7:VII)

The contagion was not contained. It spread even further, contaminating the greater part of the field of mental sciences. What Emil Ludwig wrote in the late 40s is still partly true in the early 70s: "The air is heavy with psychoanalytic dust which everybody is breathing." (8:120)

Such protests were conveniently disregarded by members of the Freudian establishment. It is only in the last few years that there appeared a possibility of reducing this pollution by the rise of behavior psychotherapies and humanistic, existentialist, and Christian approaches to psychology.

The question of why American culture showed so little resistance to *Bacillus Freudicus*, although intriguing in itself, will not be dealt with here. In a chapter entitled "Psychoanalytic Fantasies," Masserman provides an uncomplimentary explanation: " 'Americans are Jung and easily Freudened' wrote James Joyce." (70:31) The European tepid acceptance or outright rejection of Freud's speculations stands in sharp contrast to "Freudened" (Freud-happy or sexually titillated?) Americans. Masserman made a professional trip through many European countries and reported of practically universal disinterest and contempt for Freud's propositions. The report reads like a long list of declining notes to a party of an unpopular relative:

> *England, Oxford University:* ... psychoanalytic theory is an anathema at Oxford.... Outside the meetings of the psychoanalytic societies themselves, I encountered nearly everywhere a special dislike of Freudian metapsychology and analytic jargon— a semantic aversion with which, despite my own years of psychoanalytic training, I was quite in sympathy.... *France, Paris:* ... Aside from his aversion to Freudian analysis, Dr. Jean Delay, Professor of Psychiatry at Sorbonne.... *Denmark, Copenhagen:* The telephone directory in Copenhagen lists about a dozen

"psychoanalysts." None of them, I learned on inquiry, has had either medical or analytic training, but all are permitted to practice under Danish laws dealing with the regulation of extra-medical cults.... *Sweden, Stockholm:* The attitudes of most Swedish psychiatrists toward this specialty vary from strained tolerance (as Frey and Wolfart put it: "Some of us had that disease and have gotten over it") to the militant antagonism of Törngren who resigned (the analysts say was expelled) from the Analytic Society about five years ago, now classes all analysts with quacks, and wants a law passed to prohibit them from "misleading social workers and harming (*i.e.* treating) defenseless children."... *Norway, Oslo:* I found Professor Gabriel Langfeldt ... [appealing] to Dr. Evang (of the Royal Norwegian Ministry of Social Affairs) and others for national laws to curb the practice of analysis in Norway.... *Germany:* ... the general prejudice among German academicians to psychoanalysis.... *Finland, Helsinki:* Dr. Polaheimo, who had had two years of training in psychiatry and psychoanalysis in Baltimore and Boston ... since his return from America three years previously, ... had been only minimally successful in inducing either his psychiatric colleagues or the university faculty to accept modern dynamic approaches... (70:95-111)

The report was on Masserman's observations in 1952. He remarks that his subsequent contacts (the last one in 1965), did not show any appreciable change. My contacts in international meetings in 1963, 1968 and 1969 tend to agree with Masserman's impression: "European psychiatry is pretty much the same..." (70:115)

2. A personal equation and jarring experiences

As a social worker, before undertaking the study of clinical psychology, I felt a marked disaffinity for Freud's theoretical approach. The Freudian view of man was as alien to me as the Marxist and the Nazi-Nietzschean concepts. Psychoanalysis began as part and parcel of the anti-Christian movement in Europe, passionately bent on destroying traditional cultural values, morals, and beliefs. It never divested itself of the atheistic, materialistic views of its founder, neither in official pronouncements of the psychoanalytic associations, nor in the writings of its prominent adherents.

19

Like many European intellectuals during the last hundred years, I had to undergo a painful and critical struggle to free myself from the secular ideas offered as "science" in the universities, the lecture halls, and the press. Like many other Europeans, I also took ideas seriously, passionately, in contrast to the more pragmatic, uninvolved handling of intellectual issues by many middle-aged professional people in the Anglo-Saxon culture. Having taken ideas seriously, I felt the threat of materialistic and rationalistic views to my whole existence. I felt that my being could hardly remain vital, buoyant, and balanced if I incorporated these views into my personal philosophy.

It also seemed to me that some of my friends, suffering from spiritual disorientation and dis-ease, were being sickened by the prevalent cultural trends. I found good reasons to reject as sterile and existentially disturbing the prominent ideologies of European reformism: Marxism, Nazi-Fascism, emphatically secular democracy, Freudism, philosophical atheism, and numerous other cultural expressions of an anti-Christian orientation. They were of the same cloth as the "Comptean revolution" (Stern), a coarse attempt to supplant religion by a narrowly conceived scientism.

The European rationalists and naturalists were even more rabidly antagonistic to a religious outlook than many pointedly secular, "liberal" foes of Judeo-Christian beliefs in this country. They could not tolerate the traditional religion, as they had to spread their own religion of naturalism, based on philosophically naive misinterpretations of "science." Auguste Compte, the founder of one of these scientific imperialisms, repented in his spiritually more mature phase of life, rejected the school-boy philosophizing of his own positivism, and re-embraced Catholicism. Other less spiritually discerning minds got stuck in positivistic misperceptions, held to them with religious fervor and never reached Compte's final maturity of comprehension. Freud was one of them.

Upon coming to this country, it was an unpleasant shock to find that a great many psychologists and psychiatrists had accepted Freud's ideas wholesale, with timid modifications here and there. Psychoanalytic systems were presented in many colleges as the only reliable and "deep" teachings about the psychology of man.

Vanderplas regards the situation as unchanged in 1966, more than ten years after I first made my observations: "Freud's theory has gained such widespread acceptance within certain fields of psychology (notably the clinical areas) that many training programs offer course work in psychoanalytic theory (to the exclusion of other theories) as a basis for applied work in the field." (9:409)

At the time of my own studies in the 50s, Jung's psychology, more human and comprehensive than Freud's, was dubbed "mystical" by many leading psychologists and psychiatrists, with a sinister insinuation that he had ruined himself as a psychologist by showing vague sympathies with early Nazism. (This was not true, as we shall see in a later section, but the academic and professional community is subject to accepting unfounded versions of rumors like any other group of suggestible humans.) Glover, an orthodox Freudian, had by that time published his verdict, after re-reading Jung, "I have not detected in Jung's writings any desire for a religious conception," (62:9) yet the accusation of "mysticism" was maintained.

Adler was characterized as "superficial," in contrast to the "deep" psychoanalytic perspective. Rank was "incomprehensible." Stekel, whose writings are about equal in volume to Freud's and are clinically more varied and instructive, was hardly mentioned. Other less well-known rejectors of psychoanalysis were dismissed. The lists of required reading given to students consisted primarily of books and articles favorable or neutral to Freudism, while some of the objective and critical studies, like those of Ellis (10) and Orland (11), were ignored. Such neglect could hardly be explained by the ignorance of the instructors—the alternative was that they wittingly or unwittingly suppressed the negative evidence about psychoanalytic assertions.

Contemporary contributors to psychiatric treatment were dismissed as insignificant in comparison with those who were enlightened by Freud's doctrines. Sargant, for instance, mentions four of the creative psychiatrists who were pushed into obscurity or obstructed in petty ways by Freudians:

Dr. Manfred Sakel, who developed insulin-coma treatment, died in New York a disappointed man because his treatment was being so little used in the United States compared with other countries. Dr. Ladislas Meduna, an internationally famous and revered figure, who discovered convulsive therapy in Budapest, now lives without very much honor among his psychoanalytic colleagues in Chicago. Dr. Walter Freeman, also internationally famous, who did so much to develop lobotomy from 1936 on, had to face almost unremitting persecution in Washington by some of his fellow psychiatrists until he retired to California. And one can safely predict that the American psychiatrist Dr. Nathan Kline, one of the discoverers of a group of antidepressant drugs which have turned out to be especially useful to patients of good personality previously suffering from anxiety and phobic states, will find his path becoming more difficult for him in established psychiatric circles, though his fame now rings round the rest of the world. (43:4)

I remember the shameful and humiliating treatment accorded Eric Berne at one of the Group Therapy Seminars in 1960 at San Francisco. Berne was at that time struggling vigorously for recognition of his method of treatment, Transactional Analysis, which made him known throughout the United States a decade later. The chairman of the meeting, a psychiatrist convinced of the superiority of his Freudian faith, introduced Berne in a painfully inappropriate way, making light of what the speaker was going to say. During Berne's address, the chairman looked at him with a condescending smile as if saying: "You poor fool! Do you imagine you can improve on the greatest psychotherapist the world has ever known? You are only making an ass of yourself." Berne, struggling for his place in the psychiatric realm, took somewhat longer than the time allotted to him, so the chairman mumbled something that was obviously uncomplimentary. The remark created a pained and embarrassed pause on the part the speaker. He sat down angry and offended, with the chairman announcing in effect that there was little need to discuss such futile innovation any further.

3. *Arrogance with colleagues*

Apparently the arrogant domination of American psychiatry by Freudians was established at least twenty years before the Seminars. In 1939, a prominent practitioner and teacher of psychiatry, was irritated "by the very extreme statement of a psychoanalyst to the effect that practically all informed scientists accept psychoanalysis." (59:624) Meyerson knew that this was only a propagandistic assertion and he set out to investigate the state in the field. He sent a questionnaire to prominent neurologists, psychiatrists and psychologists, asking them to respond on a scale from complete acceptance to complete rejection of Freud's teachings. The results of the questionnaire, indicating a wide spectrum of responses, ranging from strong faith to profound scepticism, is not of primary interest at this point. What is of interest is that many of these professionals of established reputations did not dare state their opinion publicly for fear of embarrassment or other repercussions:

> ... a considerable number did not want their names given or to be identified, while others stated they did not wish to be quoted at all. Obviously, there was to some extent a distaste for or fear of the controversy implied in the whole procedure, so that it appears at once that a great deal of emotion is involved in any study of the psychoanalytic movement in a way which would undoubtedly not be found in a similar study, for example, which would involve the treatment of syphilis by arsphenamine or by fever therapy. This is confirmed by the fact that those who did not wish to be quoted belong mainly in the groups which, though friendly, do not completely accept and those which reject but are not unfriendly. (59:627)

Evidently, even before they established themselves as lords of American psychiatry in the 40s, 50s, and 60s, the Freudians were able to intimidate many of their psychiatric and psychological colleagues.

The persecution of non-Freudian professionals by members of the establishment can take quite brutal forms, leading to breakdown of more sensitive individuals, and embitterment of others. Meerloo, an experienced Dutch psychiatrist, who moved to this country after World War II, tells of the crisis the members of the establishment engendered in one of their coprofessionals:

> Not long ago a psychiatric colleague worked in a clinic where a different terminology was used, and the ideas of his former teachers, because they were expressed in terms other than those of the clinic, were criticized and even vilified. My colleague was a good practical therapist; yet he came to need psychotherapy himself, to counteract the utter confusion resulting from daily

contacts with aggressive adepts of a different terminology, just as much as some of our soldiers released from the Korean prison camps. (57:139)

My observations lead me to believe that the self-assured attitude of the already brainwashed teaching and training psychiatrists led to feelings of professional inferiority in students, which were hard to shake off in our later work with patients. Instead of using themselves as therapeutic instruments in a spontaneous way, the young psychiatrists and psychologists would harken back to the great Freudian technique as the only therapeutic way. They would hardly venture beyond the therapeutic activities circumscribed by Freudian precepts and examples. The whole training process was carried out with the vague image of the Supreme Therapist hovering in the background. It is only lately that mentors have come to the realization that keeping the Ideal Therapist before the eyes of trainees creates deep feelings of inferiority and insecurity, which hamper them in what should be a primarily human relationship with the patient. Ticho, a training analyst and supervisor at the Menninger Foundation's Topeka Institute of Psychoanalysis, finds that such an idealized image of a psychotherapist hinders the use of available personality resources of the trainee: "Our literature contains a good deal on the personality of the ideal analyst. . . . However, my impression is that the description of the ideal analyst, rather than the real, has an adverse effect. It is anxiety-provoking and does not promote a careful study of one's own personality traits."

Anderson, one of the few psychiatrists who were able to liberate themselves from veneration of Freud and psychoanalytically-stamped teachers, recalls the first phase of her servitude:

I came into psychiatry with no preconceived notions regarding behavior dynamics, probably because the year was 1931. I was taught the Freudian frame of reference by my significant authorities and, like any good child, I did not question because I had never doubted my parents; nor did I realize there might be anything else to believe.

I had been in psychiatry a dozen years before there was any conscious awareness that my current experiences seemed to have

24

little relationship to what I had been taught and was trying to practice. Up to this time, I had assumed that any discrepancy between my findings and the details of the master plan were due to my own shortcomings in perceptual acuity, in ascertaining the facts, or in making proper connections. (19:258)

In the beginning Anderson fitted herself into the mold of psychiatric conformity and believed all the "right" preconceptions. Like many a professional before and after her, she tried to make herself inconspicuous in order to blend with the group and belong. At the time of her writing she was approaching retirement and could be amused by the naive reaction of herself and other young conformists to the dominant school of thought:

My intention was never to be in the uncomfortable position of belonging to the out-group, whether in relation to Freud, or to "organicity," or any other position I have taken. However, the stress was no greater for me than for the stream of others who have found themselves in similar predicaments.

I have come to view the behavior of people in the in-group toward those in that out-group as merely corroborative evidence of the validity of my theory: whatever an individual learns which relieves him of a sense of helplessness and loneliness in any specific area becomes one of his right beliefs and guiding lights. When this sense of right belief can be reinforced through consensual validation, then he belongs to the in-group. Holding the accepted right beliefs of the in-group entitles him to feel smugly superior to others who are in error, *i.e.,* who do not see eye to eye with him, and to express a measure of contempt or benign tolerance toward them.

Many are the times I have smiled (with superior assurance) as I listened to young therapists who had been well taught by some other authority, as they invariably made the same repetitive response to the patient who had asked a question, "And what do you think?" Or I have noted their expressions of shocked superiority when they witnessed a therapist "being directive." It is not so much that we will not see as that we cannot. (67:260, 261)

A patient provides an apt illustration of the stultifying effects of such worshipful training. The exasperation of MacIver (12) in her psychotherapy with a Freudian analyst, though containing some elements of caricature, has enough resemblance to reality to serve as an indictment of the prevalent, essentially Freudian method of training. She describes in her novel *The Frog Pond,* how for five months she had been struggling on the couch with her many confusions; yet, her analyst had given her little "understanding," which, he told her in the beginning, was the purpose of therapy. She was desperate when he dropped her from "treatment" as he did not want to change the accustomed hour to accommodate her new conditions of employment.

Later on, she came to understand the frustrating experience better when she met one of the supervising analysts from an institute. Through him, she learned her analyst had been a nose-and-throat specialist who had switched to psychiatry. He had gone through the first part of training but was still completing control analysis. Now she could understand his odd behavior during her analysis. He had apparently been scared stiff to make any spontaneous reactions which might belie whatever stereotyped model had been imposed on him through training or conjured up by him in exaggerated veneration of classical psychoanalysts. Instead of meeting her legitimate questions, he had responded either by silence or by saying there was nothing to be said. She also understood why he had given belated interpretations of some of her dreams, when the context was no longer alive to her, and then only on Fridays. Apparently he had to wait to consult his control analyst in order to render *the correct* interpretation.

Brody, in a witty account of his attempt to make a living psychotherapist out of a "psychoanalytically oriented" automaton-technician demonstrates the stultifying effect of psychiatric training which worshipped a wooden Freud as a supreme model. The young psychiatrist, Dr. Novey, behaved in a spontaneous, humorous way in his group and found that his "non-professional" behavior had a marvelous effect on the group, but it was disapproved by more experienced doctors. He remarks wryly about them: "Every time you learn and use something new which can help you become more effective as a group therapist, expect some questions or criticism from more conventional colleagues." (47:479)

In the overblown reverence for Freudian suppositions, the interest of the patients may easily come to be considered as secondary. Spigel (44), for instance, reports how a Freudian supervisor forbade his trainee to continue hypnotic treatment of a patient suffering from hysterical pains, even though hypnosis abolished complaints. It was not important that the patient experienced pains again; the overriding consideration was to preserve the purity and the glory of Freudian therapy. Other harms to patients, perpetrated in the name of therapy, are described in the next two chapters.

The constricting effect of training in Freudian orthodoxy upon the professional understanding is illustrated in a therapist's reaction to treatment methods of the Synanon movement. These laymen, "unencumbered by the vast body of complicated and often conflicting theory and research found in professional therapeutic field," (68:794) achieved remarkable successes with addicts. Dr. Gold viewed these methods of treatment and remained unimpressed; even though they were more effective than any programs run by professionals, he could not see the factual results blinded by his theoretical prejudices:

> Professional criticism of Synanon often takes the form of what Chuck has called the "orthodoxy effect." Dr. Gold, described earlier by Reid Kimball, evidenced a typical professional response. He reacted negatively to what he considered to be an unorthodox method. He was more concerned with proper method than with results! Despite the clear, live evidence, in the person of Kimball and others, that the Synanon session was constructive, Gold believed that it was destructive because it was unorthodox. Perhaps professional therapy has reached the bureaucratic stage in which orthodoxy of method is more important than the achievement of concrete therapeutic results. (68:793)

The misdirection suffered by psychiatrists upon whom Freudian ideology had been imposed, is well illustrated by a statement of one of them to a *Saturday Evening Post* reporter:

> "Analytical training slowed me down for five years," Dr. David Vail, chief of Minnesota's mental-health program, says. "It's not only of little use in the world of everyday reality,—it can actually cripple a psychiatrist's ability to deal with everyday reality. It's like trying to survey ground for a highway by using a microscope." (33:42)

Yet thousands of physicians and psychologists were duped by their assumption that such an ineffective method is a superior psychotherapy. Psychoanalysts were victims of the hoax themselves before they victimized others. An irrelevant criterion was held out as bait to ambitious psychiatrists and psychologists: the length of training. "The psychoanalyst has acquired by virtue of the time spent in studying the field, the most prestige." (52:24) If psychoanalysis is only a glorified form of quackery, as a number of medical and psychological observers have asserted, then years of training remain just years of training in quackery. A trainee in Communist brainwashing institutions is not considered by outside observers to be any better off for longer periods of indoctrination or for being inalterably conditioned into a lifelong allegiance to the party.

4. *Freudian oppression of American psychiatry and clinical psychology*

The experiences in the two graduate schools which I attended are not isolated examples. A private polling of psychologists outside the establishment provides similar illustrations from other universities.

The power of the establishment might prevent many written expressions of discontentment. Three professors of psychiatry, speaking in 1968 before the American College of Psychiatrists about *Psychoanalysis in Present-Day Psychiatry,* explain how subtle social pressures from the establishment make it difficult to be objective and frank about psychoanalysis:

> ... this is a difficult task. For, the interpersonal intricacies and the individual and organizational vested interests relevant to such discussion are often important and delicately balanced. Indeed the first thing that must be said is that for a great many American academic psychiatrists, it has been almost impossible to say anything. For, candidly, our teachers, our friends, our colleagues, our personal psychotherapists, our wives' psychotherapists, our former psychiatric residents, and many of our government "site visitors" are all psychoanalysts. (34:53)

In spite of hesitation to express unfavorable reactions to psychoanalysis, a careful combing of literature reveals quite a number of them. Bowman, a professor of psychiatry, having in mind the aggressive Freudians, speaks of a "group who have religious fervor in trying to force the belief in what they consider to be the truth." By describing the relative inclusiveness of the University of California training in psychiatry, he testifies indirectly to the indoctrinating grip which Freudians maintain in many other schools:

> I feel that the Jungian and Adlerian theories should also be taught to all our residents. As you know now, we have a fairly strong group of Jungians here in San Francisco and they have teaching positions in the Department of Psychiatry. I would emphasize at this time that my idea is that all residents should be taught the varying theories of basic psychiatry and psychoanalysis, and that they should be exposed to teachers with different viewpoints. I feel very strongly that at the present time we have a group who have a religious fervor in trying to force the belief in what they consider to be the truth. I do not believe science should be taught in this fashion. We should try to teach our residents to think for themselves and not try to indoctrinate them with a particular point of view. (13:211)

Bowman's breadth of interest was certainly not exhibited by other professors of psychiatry. The reaction of Jones, "that unbending champion and teacher of Freudian psychology," (62:7) was unfortunately paradigmatic for most of his American colleagues. When in the Thirties Glover became "responsible for organizing the training of psychoanalytic students," he consulted Jones (then president of the British Psycho-Analytical Society), about his suggestion "that every candidate should be instructed in the systems propounded by the then most important psycho-analytical schismatics, Jung, Adler and Rank." (62:7) Jones brushed the idea brusquely: "Why waste their time?" and the training candidates were stuck into strictly Freudian molds.

When, in a clinical course in which I participated, a student suggested that a review be presented of A. Salter's *The Case Against Psychoanalysis* (5), the instructor exhibited such a pained, condescending smile, that the student felt embarrassed. The implication of that smile was that a graduate student should not be so naive as to give credence to the distorted thinking of a critic of the preeminent Freudian system.

Professors of psychiatry and coauthors of *The Three Faces of Eve*, C.H. Thigpen and H.M. Cleckley apparently experienced similar conflicts. They preface their questions on Freudian ideas to Dr. K. Menninger:

> In our experience it has been difficult to get from most Freudians and analysts of other persuasions answers that meet squarely the points we feel are pertinent and fundamental. When such questions have been posed in the past, we have usually encountered one of several responses: the first, like a complacent shrug of the shoulders, seems designed to dismiss the inquiry as if it were imprudent and undeserving of an answer. Secondly, we may evoke a sarcastic or supercilious comment, more or less personal, on the ignorance (or perhaps "resistance") of the questioner. A third type of reaction consists of requoting truisms that everybody had known for centuries. (14:258)

The troubles between responsible and scientifically oriented professionals and Freudian pseudoreligionists is nothing new. It has been going on ever since the inception of Freudian doctrines. Fifty years before this confrontation of Menninger by Thigpen and Cleckley, another physician, Friedländer, voiced similar objections. Speaking before the international medical congress held at Budapest, Hungary, in 1909, Friedländer said:

> "First, instead of the quiet demonstrations usual with scientists in their discussions, psychoanalysts make dogmatic affirmations punctuated by emotional outbursts; psychoanalysts are unique in equating Freud with such men as Kepler, Newton, and Semmelweiss, and for the vigor of their attacks on their adversaries. Second, instead of proving their assertions in a scientific manner, psychoanalysts content themselves with unverifiable statements. They say: "We know from psychoanalytic experience that . . . " and lay the burden of proof on others. Third, psychoanalysts do not accept any criticism nor even the expressing of the most justified of doubts, terming these "neurotic resistance." Friedländer quoted from Sadger: "The prudery of physicians in their discussions of sexual matters is due less to principle than to psychological background. . . . Rather

than accept themselves as hysterics, they prefer to be neurasthenics. Even if they are neither, they prefer to declare the whole theory invalid and condemn it a priori." Friedländer agreed with Aschaffenburg that such argumentation was unacceptable among scientists. Fourth, psychoanalysts ignore what has been done before them, or by others, thereby claiming to be innovators. It is as if, before Freud, no hysterical patient was ever cured, and no psychotherapy ever practiced. Fifth, sexual theories of psychoanalysis, are presented as scientific fact, though unproven, as when Wulffen says: "All ethical powers in the interior of man, his sense of shame, his morality, his worship of God, his esthetics, his social feelings, originate from repressed sexuality." Wulffen reminds one of Weininger when he said: "Woman is a born sexual criminal; her strong sexuality when successfully repressed easily leads her to illness and hysteria, and when it is insufficiently repressed, to criminality; often it will lead her to both." Sixth, Friedländer objected to the practice of psychoanalysts of addressing themselves directly to a wide lay public, as if their theories had already been scientifically proven; by so doing, they make those who do not accept the theories appear ignorant and backward. (46:802, 803)

Freudian intolerance for nonbelievers sometimes took the form of persecution. Some of the clinical psychology students of my days who failed to accept the dogma that psychoanalytic systems were the only ones deserving of scientific attention, had difficulty in arranging and completing their internships in training institutions dominated by analytically stamped instructors. Similar abuse was apparently present in the training of psychiatrists. Bailey, a psychiatrist, points out in a lecture given in 1956:

Yet those who call themselves psychoanalysts have moved into the seats of the mighty. Gone are the days when analysts were rejected. The disdained have become more intolerant than their predecessors. They say they agree that a man can be a good psychiatrist without having been analyzed, but they do not act as if they believe it. They have made the younger generation believe that if you have not been analyzed, you belong to a lesser breed. The youngsters believe that if they are not able to talk the special language of the system they are apt to have trouble with some of

31

the associate examiners of the Board of Psychiatry. It is not enough to speak dynamically . . . a candidate has a good chance to draw an examiner to whom dynamic psychiatry and psychoanalysis are synonymous. . . . Yet there is no proof that the system is true. It is an intellectually closed world . . . (15:38, 39)

Braceland, a former president of the American Psychiatric Association, registers several expressions of concern about the narrowing effect of Freudian dominance of psychiatry in the United States.

It is evident . . . that psychoanalytic formulations have captured the fancy of psychiatrists and expanded widely the potentialities of psychiatry: so much so that now we come upon expressions of concern regarding this current of psychodynamic enthusiasm. Cameron, for example, deplores the distortion that tends to creep into psychotherapeutic technique when the passive rather than the multidimensional role of the therapist becomes the focus of attention. Bartemeister, in his presidential address before the American Psychiatric Association, discussed other emerging dangers, notably that of viewing the patient as a bundle of psychological mechanisms and disregarding useful psychotherapeutic methods for a type of psychoanalysis entirely unsuited for a good many patients. A further hazard, in the opinion of Dr. Desmond Curran of London, is a tendency to overstate the possibilities of psychiatry and psychotherapy, to expand the borders of the specialty beyond the primary purpose of helping the mentally ill, to an unrealistic meddling in other fields on the assumption that any individual can be transformed, that his potentialities will be unlimited; indeed, that society itself may be revolutionized by the principles of psychiatry. (16:21)

Grinker (20) expresses his regret about going overboard with Freudian influences in the training of psychiatrists. Speaking before the 1964 meeting of the American Psychiatric Association, he accepts partial blame for participating in the mistaken direction of training the future psychiatrists. Other methods of helping emotionally troubled individuals were neglected in favor of the "psychodynamic" model. The psychiatric schools were selecting and training everyone as if he would be a psychoanalyst. Group therapy, family therapy, social psychiatry and other areas were neglected.

Thigpen protests against the Freudian blinders put on psychiatrists in training:

> Few would deny that the Freudian theories at present appear to dominate American psychiatric thought.... I question only the beliefs (which are as yet without proof) of some psychiatrists who are in highly influential positions and who I believe are, unwittingly and with good intentions, stagnating thought and research by indoctrinating and cluttering with rubbish the minds of young doctors. (14:250, 253, 254)

Such strong words of indictment of Freudian teachers for cluttering the minds of psychiatrists with psychodynamic rubbish might appear harsh, but they express well the oppression felt by those who could not join the dominating sect. More than twenty years earlier, Myerson and respondents to his questionnaire had seen the stultifying effect of Freudian orientation upon American psychiatry:

> ... I think that psychoanalysis has been the greatest block to the study and understanding of mental disease, and by this I mean insanity, that has happened since the time of Rush. All doctors in all institutions for the care of the insane that I have been in touch with in the United States were so saturated with the Freudian concept that real investigation of mental diseases was almost entirely excluded. (59:635)

Thigpen and Cleckley detest the narrow confines within which American psychiatry is contained by Freudians:

> One of the great dangers to psychiatry today rests in the fact that many who are devoutly convinced that Freudian theory has been scientifically established and proved beyond question have obtained high teaching posts and other positions of authority. Thus the Freudian theory is propounded as scientific gospel to the vulnerable, while other, and more modest, schools of psychological thought are ignored. By such means has the Freudian theory tyrannized American psychiatry. Those who express doubt of it are sometimes treated as heretics who would impede the progress of salvation. (17:102)

33

Masserman, in many ways a sensible and sensitive man, took a more moderate course in reacting to the superior stance adopted by Freudians. During his training in the late 30s, he had a satisfactory relationship with his supervisor at the Chicago Institute for Psychoanalysis, Franz Alexander. Being an ebullient personality and with a scintillating fantasy, Alexander would have impressed any student. The analysis itself did not enrich Masserman greatly, neither personally nor professionally. As a way of discreetly demonstrating the mediocre quality of his analysis, he cites protocols of dream interpretations while he was in training which are little more than a dilettante exercise. Apparently there was very little to show for four years of undergratified aspirations. When Masserman gained in professional stature in later years, and particularly as, with the departure of Alexander, the Chicago Institute assumed the drabness of other Freudian training establishments, Masserman tried to help gifted psychiatrists by tactfully directing them away from wasting their time and energy. He wrote frankly to a psychiatrist seeking the illusory elevation to the status of Freudian analyst, that he did not think that "the training given is currently worth a fraction of the time and expense involved." (70:74) Instead of letting the candidate get stultified through "approved" Freudian training, Masserman would rather see him go through broad psychiatric training, with a nonorthodox analysis and control supervision. He did not consider the approval of the American Psychoanalytic Association to be worth seeking. "Unfortunately," he adds, "some youngsters still do not believe this, but it is the most sincere advice I can give and [it is] what my own residents successfully follow." (70:74, 75)

5. *Freudian terrorism*

The terrorizing, maligning, and suppression of those rejecting the dominant ideology is a regular feature of all authoritarian regimes, Fascist and Communist alike. The Freudians apparently managed to do it to a surprising extent within the egalitarian climate of American society, establishing an almost dictatorial domination over psychiatric and psychological professions.

An observer from overseas, Eysenck, expresses a similar view of the psychoanalytic usurpation of power and the consequent brainwashing of the innocently trusting medical and other graduate students. He opens his article on "Psychoanalysis—Myth or Science?" with:

Psychoanalysis presents a rather curious dilemma to those who would evaluate it. In psychiatry it has become the leading school to such an extent that in some countries it is almost impossible to obtain a leading post, either in academic life or in private practice, without having undergone a training analysis and thus having been exposed to a most efficient form of "brainwashing" . . . indeed, to most people, psychoanalysis *is* psychology. (18)

Another observer from Britain, Sargant, a noted psychiatrist, is scandalized by Freudian domination of American psychiatry:

Most psychiatrists visiting the United States from abroad are *bewildered at the way the direction and control* of American psychiatry have been taken over since World War II by psycho-analysts, who are ideological followers of Freud and now sometimes call themselves "dynamically orientated" psychia-trists. (43:88)

Sargant notes the regular brainwashing of psychiatrists as a feature of beating the trainees into submission through mental oppression:

Despite the proved value of these varied types of new treatment in psychiatry, it has now, paradoxically, become increasingly difficult in only one country in the world, the United States, to obtain any high academic or university teaching post in general psychiatry, especially in a general medical school, unless one has first agreed to subject oneself to, or has already experienced, several years of personal Freudian "training" psychoanalysis on the couch. In the process, one must become *fully converted to the extremely circumscribed and purely philosophical tenets of the Freudian faith,* now well over fifty years old. For instance, one may still be expected to believe, if psychoanalyzed, that depres-sion is caused by breast frustration in infancy, despite the demonstrated fact that it can often be cured by a drug or a few electroshock treatments. And in a Freudian training analysis, one must also come to accept, *by a process akin to religious conver-sion,* the premise that the Freudian dogma and its philosophical

35

derivatives are still basic to the whole future development of psychiatry and that these methods should supplant in time—and, whenever possible, now—all the other more recent effective empirical methods of treatment. In fact, Freudian converts seem to become increasingly afraid of allowing any other methods of psychiatric treatment to gain any real recognition and acceptance in medical schools and university teaching centers.

Unless complete acceptance of the psychoanalytic faith comes about on the couch fairly quickly, the expensive training analysis goes on indefinitely, in an effort to dissolve what is called the trainee's "negative transference" to Freudian interpretations and theories. The trainee may see the cost of his training mounting higher and higher while he gets no nearer his goal of becoming an analyst and earning a good living in private office practice. This anxiety situation certainly helps some to speed up their "conversion." If the doctor on the couch happens to prove too resistant to indoctrination and continues to question the basic tenets of the faith desired of him, he may finally be pronounced unsuitable for acceptance as a trained analyst, and his money has virtually been wasted. (43:89)

Just as the brainwashed subjects from Communist institutions go to work diligently for Party causes, Freudian converts show faith and zeal in asserting their superiority in American psychiatry, in spite of the essential treatment failure of Freudian methods:

One of the greatest tragedies and strengths of a Freudian analysis seems to be that it can *completely brainwash even the most intelligent doctors, as well as many of their patients,* into believing that Freudian dogma holds the only key to the real understanding of mental illness. In England, for instance, we have had a very active Freudian school for more than forty years, but there are only about 250 Freudian analysts who practice this method alone, compared with 2500 other psychiatrists who are fully prepared to use and combine all methods likely to help any individual patient. It has generally been found over the years that psychoanalysis is a poor weapon to treat most forms of mental and even neurotic illness. (43:90)

Sargant observes that Freudian zealots have a strong predilection for the seats of the mighty:

The American National Institute of Mental Health, for instance, the main government agency dispensing many millions of dollars every year to promote research, teaching and the training of psychiatrists, recently had as its director someone who had been psychoanalyzed; the deputy director had been psychoanalyzed as well; and even the research director had been put on the couch. In the current climate of American psychiatry, it would otherwise have been virtually impossible for them to have obtained and held these influential and important posts. Most of the wealthier foundations, such as the Rockefeller and the Ford foundations, have also been advised, in recent years, to give by far the greater part of their very large grants to psychoanalytically orientated departments of psychiatry. And several of the most influential psychiatric journals in America are now being edited and directed by psychoanalysts. Yet we must ask ourselves just what has been the fruit of all this enormous expenditure of money when we look at American mental hospitals and compare the treatment of the less mentally ill in the United States today with that available in poorer industrial countries such as England.

There are, of course, other sorts of psychiatrists practicing in the United States. But only a very few of them have important and influential top professorial posts at universities and medical schools. New high professorial appointments are rarely given to the younger group of psychiatrists unless they have undergone analysis. Especially is this the case in those posts requiring the teaching of medical students. Some Southern universities and a few in the Middle West have not yet toed the line, and they find research grants much more difficult to obtain. (43:90)

Sargant's criticism is directed at the Freudian oppression of American psychiatry. Probably his ire had its roots partly in the scene at home. One of his colleagues writes (in 1966) against the idolatry of some of the British psychiatrists regarding Freud and the chief originator of psychoanalytic fantasies in Britain, Melanie Klein, as "an almost religious cult with Freud and Klein as group deities." (48:534)

The terrorizing pressure, as in other authoritarian movements, is felt not only by opponents but also by the loyal members. Fromm (63) described the predicament of a well-known British psychoanalyst, Balint, over the posthumous smearing of Ferenczi by Freud and his faithful. Jones reported in his biography of Freud that the psychoanalytic hierarchy had chosen to describe Ferenczi as a paranoid psychotic in the period of his apostasy from Freudian orthodoxy. Freud had, of course, concurred in this throwing of psychiatric diagnosis at one of his closest professional friends and co-workers. Balint, as Ferenczi's friend and executor of his literary estate, wanted to protest the smirching of his friend's memory. Yet he also had to be careful not to step on the toes of the most influential leader of the British Freudians, Jones. He compromised by writing a rather circumspect letter to the *International Journal of Psycho-Analysis*, attesting to his knowledge of Ferenczi's clear mind in the last days of his life. He did not dare face the issue squarely: either he, Balint, is right in his psychiatric observations, and Jones is wrong in his malicious gossip, or Jones is right, and Balint was diagnostically inept in his appraisal of the mental state of Ferenczi with whom he had maintained a close contact. Fromm considers Balint's ineffectual statement as:

> ... an example for the degree to which adherence to the organization twisted even elementary human responses. . . .
> If such a tortuous and submissive letter had been written by a lesser person than Balint, or if it had been written in a dictatorial system in order to avoid severe consequences for freedom or life, it would be understandable. But considering the fact that it was written by a well-known analyst living in England, it only shows the intensity of the pressure which forbids any but the mildest criticism of one of the leaders of the Organization. (63:9, 12)

One day an investigator might delve into reasons why Anglo-Saxon intellectuals should, in contrast to educated people in other civilized countries, be prone to cultish adoration of Freud, and possessed with the zeal to impose his teachings upon others as supreme psychological revelations.

If such subtle oppression of unbelievers and indoctrination of believers, as Sargant observed in American psychiatry and Fromm in British psychoanalysis, took place in a school of religion preparing ministers or priests for a particular denomination, it would be less reprehensible; such schools do not disguise their intention to teach a specific faith, and they can legitimately eliminate the bother of having to deal with dissidents. Dogmas are important for guiding the believers in matters of faith and morals, and they need to be presented authoritatively if they are to be of benefit to the faithful.

It is another matter if the supposed educators of psychiatrists and psychologists behave in this authoritarian way. They are not expected to engage in teaching a particular faith, even if paraded under the name of science. Exclusive and self-assured, speculative and unverifiable, psychoanalysis does not seem to deserve the name of science any more than various religious and philosophical or artistic schools of thought (see *Freud's Phallic Cult,* 36).

Shakow, a psychologist highly sympathetic to Freudism (he had subjected himself to two Freudwashings with two different analysts), criticizes the ideological dogmatism of Freudian institutes. He fears that their practices discredit psychoanalysis, make it look like "not being a member of the family of sciences." He describes Freudian institutes in a way reminiscent of religious and political training agencies:

> Another handicap of the independent institute is its hothouse atmosphere where lack of serious criticism is inevitable. In an environment where everybody holds essentially that same point of view, self-deception is easy. Counterfeit conceptual currency can pass easily from one person to another since for mutual self-protection there is tacit agreement not to examine the currency too carefully. (51:290)

Brody, another psychologist, damns Freudian institutes even more passionately:

> Primary responsibility belongs to the analytic institutes, surely among the dullest, most hide-bound educational institutions in the world. If analysis is to survive they must be turned from their Prussian stance to something much closer to the original, heterodox, and revolutionary spirit of psychoanalysis. Will they be communities of scholars or indoctrinating trade schools run for aspiring members of the professional establishment? Have they advanced the field or merely preserved it? Their model must be closer to the interdisciplinary graduate school, which strives for a new vision, rather than the authoritarian and elitist professional

school, which transmits a dubious technology. In this task more is to be expected from students than from established practitioners or entrenched faculty members, though no students are more conforming and seem more frightened than psychoanalytic candidates. They arrive at the institute pre-selected for conventionality and their survival is possible only if they produce the acceptable social and psychological attitudes to the profession and society as well as professional competence. Only if the training analyst has no influence on the students' evaluation and graduation can the field be expected to progress beyond the attitudes of the elders. No field of inquiry outside of theology has suffered more from the cult of personality than psychoanalysis. (52:23-25)

Stendahl had indeed depicted in his novel *Le Rouge et le Noir* the disservice done to religion in France of the last century by accepting into seminaries the candidates who were interested more in gaining power for themselves through the Church than in serving Christ and His flock. The dominant secular religion in the United States among intellectuals, in this century—the Freudian psychoanalysis—seems to provide a similar ticket to power, prestige and wealth for its trainees and faithful adherents.

Marmor realizes that the insistence on accepting Freudian doctrines on faith, has led to a decline in the scientific ability of trainees:

... these institutes became perpetuators and protectors of a tradition rather than open-ended scientific centers. Furthermore, the pattern of psychoanalytic training with its absolute control over the analytic candidate by a training analyst who is arbiter of the candidate's professional career as well as his therapist tended to limit the autonomy of the students and to discourage the skeptical questioning that is essential to the scientific spirit. (53:679)

No wonder that non-Freudian psychiatrists and psychologists are relieved by any signs of Freudian unpopularity. Anderson, an independent mind among women psychiatrists, expressed publicly the relief she felt as a psychiatrist at the recent abating of Freudian oppression of nonbelievers in psychoanalysis:

Some of us who have rejected the Freudian theories for as much as 10 to 20 years have often felt a closer kinship to the religionists than we have to the majority of our own colleagues in psychiatry. We rejoice at evidences that our profession is being unshackled from the chains that have bound us for half a century. . . . I might also add that it is moving away from many of its dogmatic formulations: from its previously held concept of the unconscious as some sinister force operating within each person; from the concept of repression with its emphasis on latent emotions; from expression of feelings as being curative of pathological behavior; from permissiveness as being preventive of emotional problems; and from instinctual drives as being the center and driving force of life. There was a time when one had to hold these ideas as essentially sacred or experience the almost brutal ostracism, which the group meted out to the nonbelievers, but this is less and less true. As one leaves Freudianism behind one has also left behind the feeling of belonging to a new religion in opposition to the old one. (19:294)

Another psychiatrist, trained in psychoanalysis, found that Freud's ideas did not correspond to data obtained in independent objective observation. There were more efficient ways of theoretical understanding of patients' dynamics and of acting therapeutically. These findings were ably expressed in the publications. The predictable reaction to such professional activity is described in a private communication to the writer:

I remember well the day I discovered I had been dropped from the teaching faculty of the school . . . When I discovered and inquired about it, I was told it would continue to be that way until I admitted that my concepts were not different from Freud's. The department head who made my sentence explicit was soon to be the President of the American Psychiatric Organization (Branch of ——————).

This psychiatrist was certainly not alone in suffering from the Freudian intellectual terrorism.

Grinker, although himself a trained psychoanalyst, attests to the usurping of medical schools by Freudians: " . . . most professors of psychiatry in university departments and directors of psychiatry in the

41

institutes of training are psychoanalytically trained since they are given precedence over those who are not . . . " (20:456) The insiders could tell us, if they dared, of many intrigues and dirty deals in such "precedence." In the same paper Grinker points out the stultifying effects of the Freudian invasion of American psychiatry and its antiscientific effects.

We are indebted to Grinker again for throwing some light on the internal dynamics of the Freudian takeover of American psychiatry:

> In this country, at least, psychoanalysts have always hoped to convince psychiatrists, who greatly outnumber them, that psychoanalytic concepts and portions of psychoanalytic techniques could benefit psychotherapy, and they attempted in their teachings and their psychotherapeutic work to infiltrate the techniques of psychoanalysis into psychiatry. The success has been much greater than anyone expected, and, now that practically all psychiatrists are using psychoanalytic concepts and some techniques of psychoanalysis, depending upon the problem at hand, psychoanalysts are fearful of the possible substitution of eclecticism for orthodoxy. (22:138)

Like any authoritarian party, Freudians have, in spite of these criticisms by competent professionals, remained firmly entrenched in a majority of psychiatric institutions. In 1968, a reporter found that "for all its limitations, analysis is still a powerful force in psychiatry. Half the heads of psychiatric divisions of medical schools are analytically trained." (33:42) Mann testifies that in Boston, Freudian psychoanalysts have done even better for themselves, capturing most of the important positions:

> There is only one Psychoanalytic Institute in this city and graduates of that Institute occupy most of the professional positions in the three medical schools, they are the directors of the important psychiatric hospitals and clinics, and better than ninety percent of them are engaged in teaching and consultative activities in addition to the private practice of both psychotherapy and psychoanalysis. (40:53)

Such assumed superiority of psychoanalysts over non-Freudian psychiatrists and psychologists naturally leads to discrimination in both professional relationships and employment. Strauss describes conditions as he saw them in the early forties. Those who know the mental health field will find that circumstances have changed little in clinical disciplines in the early 70s:

> ... both in this country and in the United States there are many posts in mental hygiene which are advertised with a clause limiting applicants to those who have undergone a personal analysis. This implies that we have reached a stage in our social evolution when a new kind of aristocracy, "the fully analysed," has appeared on the horizon, together with a novel sort of proletariat, those who have not done their drill on the psychoanalytical barrack-square and those who have seen fit to disassociate themselves from the Freudian chiaroscuro. (39:53, 55)

Low (21) surveying the psychiatric field in the early 40s and finding it preempted by Freudians in all important positions, and Sargant making the same observation in the 60s, may be marking for future historians of American psychiatry a period which could become known as "Thirty Years of Occupation by Freudian Militants."

6. *Freudism as a militant sect*

To an unsympathetic observer of Freudism, the promoters of psychoanalysis appear to be militantly propagating a faith announced by the great prophet Freud, with his writings as Scriptures, his pupils as lesser prophets, and his detractors as heretical deviationists.

Rieff, a moderate admirer of Freudism, also suggests a religious simile: "By January of 1914, when Freud sat down to write his *History*, a great part of the psychoanalytic canon already had been established, all from the hand of one man, Freud himself. It is as if Paul had composed the entire New Testament, or, more aptly, if Moses had composed the entire Pentateuch." (23, v. 1:11)

Another sympathetic observer is led to a similar comparison with religion while reviewing a book by a proper Freudian:

> Psychoanalysis is without question the Highest of our therapeutic churches. No other school of psychotherapy possesses so extensive and so codified a body of doctrine; ... Greenson's book

43

seems to announce itself on the side of orthodoxy. It is clearly meant to be canonical. (35:456)

Sixty years earlier, psychiatrists and other physicians observed the strong cultist undertones in Freudism. August Forel, one of the foremost Swiss psychiatrists, the author of a renowned book, *The Sexual Question*, wrote in 1911 that he agreed with other observers that Freudism reminded him of "sexual church," with its "Talmudic-exegetic-theological interpretations." (46:814)

Eysenck, commenting on the rejection of psychoanalysis on the part of many of those trained in scientific psychology, is characteristically blunt: " . . . psychoanalysis is a myth; a set of semi-religious beliefs disseminated by a group of people who should be regarded as prophets rather than scientists." (18:67)

Now that the psychoanalytic movement has achieved ascendance in this country, its sectarian arrogance is less likely to break into open aggressiveness. Messianic assurance can act subtly in discrediting opposition.

A few years ago, during a television interview of a group of psychiatrists, one was asked what kind of psychotherapy he practiced. He replied: "Psychoanalysis, of course, what else is there?" As he appeared neither ironic nor ignorant, his cockiness seemed the result of blind faith, apparently genuine belief that the only efficient therapeutic methods are those based on psychoanalysis. The salient aspect of his reply lay not in his firm and aggressive commitment to this faith, but in his failure to discern that he owed allegiance to a psychological and psychiatric cult, rather than to an undisputed science. It seems that Freudians fail to apply to themselves and their colleagues the art of analysis which they readily apply to their patients and outsiders. If they did, they would start wondering if their brashness might have something to do with unconscious insecurity about the Freudian dogmas.

Another psychoanalyst, with thirty years of experience, expresses doubt that Freudian therapy will endure much beyond this generation. However, in the next breath, possibly yielding to his indoctrination and implanted feelings of insecurity, he shows unwillingness to bury the ineffective Freudian therapy and imagines that "the big value of psychoanalysis will be for training psychotherapists, because they won't be able to help patients much unless they have had some psychoanalytic training—you really need analytic insight for supportive therapy." (42:198) It is not easy to see how a method of doubtful value for patients can be properly used to train future therapists. This illogical proposal was made in the 1960s, when volumes had already been written on poor therapeutic gains from psychoanalysis. Of course, deluded by their assumed superiority, most psychoanalysts read little outside writings of their clansmen, and the psychoanalyst in question was evidently not the exception to that rule.

Lehrman, a psychiatrist writing in the *American Journal of Psychiatry*, testifies not to the improvement implied by the psychiatrist quoted above, but to the coarsening and worsening of personality of the physicians who go through the process of Freudwashing:

> I have known several analysts both before their training analyses began and since they have finished them. It seems to me, as an observant friend, that most of them are stiffer, less courageous and less human after their supposedly successful analyses than they were before. Some are members of the "authentic" American Psychoanalytic, and some are not. From my own small sample (hardly enough for a hypothesis, and certainly not for an assertion), those who have been "authentically" analyzed by training analysts of the "approved" New York institutes seem, in general, to be less warm, less spontaneous, less human and far more arrogant than those friends whose analyses were conducted under the aegis of one or another of "the shoddy perversions and dilutions that usurp the name" of psychoanalysis.
>
> If classical psychoanalysts wish to make a secular religious cult of themselves, nobody can stop them, even if the consequences affect our entire society. (58:1102)

In a vein similar to Lehrman's, Masserman remembers the disturbing influence of Freudian analysis on another gifted psychiatrist: "Norman Cameron, brilliant and literate . . . after his analysis became remote and retiring to the point of inaccessibility." (70:25)

The cocksureness of psychoanalysts may then not be only a compensation for insecurity about their own Freudian experiences, but may also arise for some out of the moral support enjoyed through membership in an exclusive guild. For many professional Americans, forced to "sell themselves" by their standing in professional associations, this may be an important support to be achieved even at the risk of impairing scientific and academic integrity. Abroms, Miller, and Greenfield point to the differences between professional guilds and science proper and how the guild reassures the practitioner so that he would not even ask about the lack of scientific status of favorite guild traditions. Almost unwittingly they classify behavior of Freudian psychoanalysts as members of a professional union rather than of a scientific community:

> What is so uncomfortable about this form of education, which derives from the guild or apprenticeship tradition, is that it contrasts so sharply with the Western scientific ethos, in which the contest of opposing viewpoints is valued for its own sake and where the skill and scholarship with which an idea is advanced, not its content, form the basis of a student's accreditation. So, the psychiatrist who is both psychoanalyst and academician is saddled with competing, and at times, incompatible loyalties. As a member of an academic medical discipline, the psychiatrist gives intellectual assent to the value of scientific research. As a member of a guild, he takes the existing craftmanship as a given, always in danger of being degraded by modern influences. In short, the guild tradition is hostile to the innovating scientific spirit. . . . in the strong apprenticeship tradition of psychoanalysis, even 30- and 40-year-old men and women are judged to be too busy polishing up an intricate craft to legitimately worry about its scientific underpinnings. From the point of view of a medical scientist, however, this long training period during which a tradition is learned rather than questioned is very troublesome indeed. (34:42, 43)

The three authors explain as insiders of psychiatry, why the unscientific guild practices were not thrown out of medical schools:

> One must ask, "Why did academic psychiatry so often acquiesce in this domination of a guild craftmanship tradition over its own research and scientific mandate and commitment?" It has been

suggested that academic departments "looked elsewhere" because psychiatry was the youngest and least established of the medical disciplines during the second twenty-five years of the twentieth century; that it was "an insecure, low status division" within medical schools. The early academic departments of psychiatry had few scientific trophies to set against the extravagant claims for understanding or for results described by psychoanalytic writings.

In short, a common enemy may have served to produce the kind of climate of passive acceptance, the generally neutral gear, "see, hear, and speak no evil" characteristic of the relationship between organized psychoanalysis and educational institutions. (34:44)

Even though this explanation might be knowledgeable, the sectarian arrogance of Freudians is not much easier to take. It is felt by the non-Freudians from a number of directions. We shall look at Freudian forms of book censorship, and book burning in particular in later sections. Now we shall turn to an illustration of Freudian meanness—the vilifying misrepresentation of Jung.

7. The smearing of Jung

The smear campaign against Jung illustrates one of the sordid activities of the Freudian fraternity. Apparently, the psychoanalytic community is no less prone to attempt character assassinations and strangling maneuvers against its critics than the Communists or Nazis or any other demagogues. The method, proven successful on many victims, is quite simple: dropping hints or asserting guilt by association. The village gossips have used it effectively for centuries.

The totalitarians have been masters of it. The unfair tactics used lately against Solzhenitsyn in the Soviet Union are reminiscent of the Freudian campaign against Jung. Solzhenitsyn survived the Siberian prison camp to which Stalin's police sent him and found that he had to face an even harder struggle for survival against the oppressive regime outside the prison after release. His fight for freedom of the artist to create according to his conscience did not place him in a favorable position with post-Stalinist rulers. When he won the Nobel prize for literature in 1971, he did not dare travel to Stockholm to receive the prize in person as he feared that the political authorities would not let him come back into his home country. In the meantime, the stooges of the Communist party started spreading rumors to vilify the brave and uncompromising writer. Word was passed around about some alleged disloyal behavior during World II, although Solzhenitsyn had acquitted himself well as a Russian officer. His literary works were unfairly criticized in the periodicals of the party-approved writers' association, yet his novels were proscribed from publication, so that the public could not judge the case. Suggestions were made through both official and unofficial channels that Solzhenitsyn should not be invited to lecture before any learned bodies as he was suspected of holding grossly erroneous views. Everything was done to blacken him and stifle his voice. The Freudians did as much as they could within the free American society to denigrate and suppress Jung and his ideas in an analogous way.

Even though I was not a psychologist in Europe, I had learned that Nazis had denounced both Freud's and Jung's works as unsound from their point of view. When I arrived in this country in the early 50s, I was surprised to learn that Jung was in disfavor here because of his alleged pro-Nazi activities. This puzzled me somewhat, knowing from personal contacts with Swiss citizens that they had contempt for Nazi ideology and brutishness. In the schools of psychology and psychiatry, I found that there was a reticence about and neglect of Jung's manifold contributions to modern psychology. He was passed over as mystic, incomprehensible, and irrelevant to psychological science. Again that puzzled me, since I knew that Jung had devised the Association Experiment, one of the earliest projective tests, and had elaborated a theory of psychological types that was well respected in Europe as one of the early systems of personality classification. In contrast to Jung, Freud had produced mostly vague speculations, scientifically untested or untestable; yet, Freud's "science" was extolled by many American college teachers and writers. In my later psychological studies I understood how this irrational state of affairs came about.

Jung was never liked in Freudian circles. Freud's original disciples, being practically all Viennese Jews, rebelled against the place of honor Freud was giving Jung in the few years of their cooperation. The jealous hostility of the disciples was barely held in check by Freud's expedient maneuvers to use Jung as a bridge to the non-Jewish and predominantly anti-Jewish European culture.

Jung joined the Freudian movement as a previously established psychologist. He was interested in and remained appreciative of some aspects of Freud's theory throughout his life, but was not willing to buy Freud's speculations in toto. During their ocean voyage to America in 1909, Freud and Jung had a chance to clarify their views. Freud was pained at Jung's rejection of his assumption that psychic energy, "libido," is essentially sexual; Jung held to a more comprehensive view of the human psyche. However, when Freud and Jung broke up their association, the disciples, and to some extent Freud himself, reacted to Jung as if he were a despicable renegade from their movement. With gusto they distorted the situation in which Jung found himself with the rise of Nazis to power; they made him into a Nazi ideologist, anti-Semite, and a sympathizer with fascist doctrines.[1]* They accused him of " 'playing along with the Nazis,' as has more than once been charged." (32:224)

Even though initially skeptical of these vituperations and insinuations, by hearing them repeated by word and some publications, I came to suspect that Jung must have shown some failure of judgment which was now standing in the way of his being recognized as a significant psychologist, as I believed he truly was. Only lately have I realized that I was a victim of an unscrupulous smear campaign by Freudians against Jung, after I came across an objective exposition of the facts, published more than twenty-five years earlier.

My running into outright prejudice against Jung is paralleled in the experience of an American psychologist, Elkind.

> . . . In researching an article on Jung for *The New York Times Magazine*, I was amazed to find no evidence to support the many stories I had heard, as a student and afterwards, about Jung's Nazi sympathies.
>
> Despite the fact that I was unable to turn up any factual evidence to support the contention that Jung was a Nazi sympathizer, many colleagues remained unconvinced. After the article was published, I received letters from numerous people,

* Numbers in brackets refer to Notes at end of each chapter.

including some influential and well-known Freudian analysts, asserting that Jung was an ardent antiSemite. However, to this date, no one has been able to bring forward any new evidence to support this widely held belief. I was pleased, therefore, that Ellenberger after much more extensive research than I had undertaken, came up with a similar conclusion; namely, that there is no factual basis to support the claim that Jung was anti-Semitic. If an elaborate positive mythology has grown up about Freud, it appears that an equally elaborate but negative mythology has grown up about those who broke with him. (56:58)

As we shall see in chapter IV, Freud's pupils were prone to aggrandizing Freud beyond reason, and denigrating his opponents beyond decency.

Harms, a Swiss compatriot of Jung, has tried to turn the tide of the strange fury against Jung by writing a well documented paper, "Carl Gustav Jung—Defender of Freud and of the Jews." It was published in a reputable periodical, *The Psychiatric Quarterly*. Yet it was of no avail, as my previous misorientation on the matter indicated, and as Reik's prejudice shows. Reik, one of Freud's favorite pupils, shows in 1969 that he had not been able to overcome the insidious lies about Jung. One can wonder about the power of prejudice, this time Semitic prejudice against a gifted Western European, which remained in the "fully analyzed" Reik. The interviewer asked him what he thought of Jung.

Reik: I didn't like him, but Freud liked him very much.
Freeman: Why didn't you like him?
Reik: Because he was too goyish.
Freeman: Too goyish? In what way?
Reik: Oh, he talked very loud, and very decisive, authorita-tive. He was blond and tall. . . . I think he (Freud) was attracted to him originally, because Freud was small, you know, and Jewish-looking, don't forget.
            Jung was prejudiced against Jews. It seemed as though he had given it up entirely when he came to Freud, but that was not correct; . . . Jung was the son of a pastor, and that had an influence upon his teaching. He did not give up his anti-Semitism.
Freeman: How did Jung's racial prejudice manifest itself?

Reik:	I don't know anything about that; but later he welcomed Hitler and became dedicated to the Nazis. He thought there was a Jewish psychology and a German-Christian psychology....
Freeman:	And did he say what the difference was?
Reik:	Yes, he said that psychoanalysis, in the sense of Freud, is Jewish psychology. And he, Jung, represented the German-Christian psychology, so to speak.... (55:50)

As we shall see from documents quoted by Harms, Reik's ideas are only distortions and low level professional gossip. Harms speaks of "a wave of misinformation" and numerous "misstatements" that have "swept through professional periodicals and popular informative literature." (32:199) He mentions "fanatic followers of Freud" as chief fabricators of distortions about Jung. Harms sounds a note of hopelessness as to the success of his attempt to stem the tide of prejudice against Jung, warning that "the presentation here is made for sound and humanly adjusted minds and not for psychopathological personalities." (32:224) In retrospect, it seems the latter predominated among Freudians. The dark forces of human prejudice, fear for one's own interests, rage against those who are different, and the irrational aggressivity that sent Socrates, Christ, and innumerable prophets and noble minds to their deaths, could not be brought to reason by facts. Such behavior is natural to mobs and tyrants, but is unexpected in those who pride themselves of having penetrated the depths of the human psyche, and thereby, supposedly having brought the primitive passions under control. As we shall see in other sections of this book, the claim of the Freudians that they had liberated themselves from human irrationalities by illuminations reached on the couch, is another aspect of the hoax played on them and on others. The facts brought up by Harms, and the distortion of the facts by Freudians, seem to illustrate my contention convincingly.

Harms reviews the history of the relationship of Freud and Jung, showing that even Freud appreciated Jung as an independent scholar and not a convert to his ideas as his other disciples were. In his writings and in his papers at the international psychiatric congresses in the first decade of our century, Jung had publicly stated that he accepted only a part of Freud's ideas. Yet Freudians continued to diminish Jung's stature by presenting him as supposedly only a dissident from Freudism.

Even though maligned by Freud's disciples, and to some extent by the master himself, Jung had enough of an honest and un-opportunistic character to pay his tribute to Freud at a meeting of the International Association of Psychotherapists at Bad Nauheim, Germany, in 1934. The Nazis had already spread the anti-Semitic terror, so it required a high level of integrity and courage to say at that meeting that Freud constructed "the first medical theory of the unconscious." (Jung had shown the same courage in cooperating with Freud for a number of years, at a time when Freud was considered a charlatan by his psychiatric colleagues in Vienna and at German universities.) The Nazi press responded with a flood of vilification against Jung, finally banning his works from their territory.

Harms deals in detail with "many inaccurate and untruthful statements" calculated to "convey a distorted and misleading picture" about the alleged Nazi leanings of Jung. The detractors of Jung presented him as the Nazi-appointed head of the Medical Society for Psychotherapy. The truth of the matter was that Jung had attempted to save the international psychotherapeutic association, and particularly its German branch, from destruction by Hitlerites. The Nazis were strongly suspicious of any international groups, and Jung cooperated in decentralizing the international association by creating a federation of national societies. He accepted the presidency of the federation and saved the *Zentralblatt für Psychotherapie,* the principal periodical of European psychotherapy, from extinction by becoming its editor. It was Jung's proposal to reorganize the international organization that enabled the German Jewish psychiatrists, who were thrown out of the German association under Nazi orders, to join the supra-national federation as individual members. Jung, as president of the Swiss association, had no part in the Nazi-controlled German national association of psychotherapists, which was headed by Dr. U.H. Goering, a relative of the Nazi henchman. Yet, in the frenzy of anti-Nazism, Jung was misidentified as the chief of the German-speaking psychiatrists, operating with Hitler's blessing. Harms shows that sympathizers of Freud were no less irrational than the Nazi anti-Semites. He quotes "in careful translation the pages [of a paper by Jung] which have been widely circulated in misleading abbreviations and translations, and from which extracts have been pieced together in a fashion which distorts their meaning." (32:216)

In this paper, Jung denies that neurosis is an illness with universal characteristics, which could, if that were the case, be cured by a technique. Rather, he conceives neurosis as a disturbance of the whole personality, which includes the particular national background and culture of each individual. He points out that both Freud and Adler were endowed with that peculiar sensitivity of the Jews to human foibles and dissimulations. He considers this capacity for penetration under the surface behavior and under rationalized pretenses a function of the much older Jewish culture, in comparison with which the national psychological traits of Western Europeans can be considered barbaric. He writes about the German psyche, in which he shared, as rooted in the primitive unconscious sources, more pregnant with novel thrusts, but also less civilized than the Semitic psyche. He defends himself against the imputation that he has anti-Semitic bias, by pointing out that he should not be considered anti-Chinese if he observes specificities in the Far-Eastern psyche. (Jung's critics at that time did not yet have at their disposal the letters to Pfister, Abraham and others, in which Freud himself admits the broad Jewish character of his psychological notions.)

Much was also made in depicting Jung as an admiring pro-Nazi, by misinterpreting his statement about "the mighty apparition of national socialism which the whole world watches with astonished eyes." (32:221) Anyone living in countries surrounding Germany remembers with shivers the display of German brute force. I was in Switzerland just before World War II, and I remember the fear and hatred of the Nazi specter in that peace-loving country, and its resolute preparation to beat back any German military encroachment. The word Jung used for "mighty," *gewaltig*, particularly in its Swiss usage, as Harms points out, conveys the feeling one has watching horror movies.

The other equally distorted implication of Jung's meaning was achieved by misinterpreting the "astonished eyes" (*"erstaunten Augen"*), as a positive evaluation of the Nazi spectacle. Jung and we, his contemporaries, certainly looked at the terrifying scene with astonishment, but there was no admiration in it. When Czechs looked at Hitler's tanks rolling down the streets of Prague, and when thirty years later they saw another brute force display its might on their streets, they were undoubtedly "astonished," but not in a welcome way.

In defending Jung against the Freudian calumnies, Harms quotes a letter which Jung wrote in 1934 to a Jewish pupil and friend, who was at the time in Europe and later settled in America. This physician apparently did not want his name mentioned even though he agreed to the publication of the letter out of loyalty to Jung. (One may speculate about the terror the Freudians established over the psychiatrists in this country, when this physician did not want to experience the criticism and ostracism which would have come upon him for not joining the anti-Jung chorus.)

Jung mentions to his Jewish friend the vile fabrications spread against him:

I need hardly mention the other rumors. It is a downright lie to quote me as having said that Jews are dishonest in analysis. Anyone who believes that I could say anything so idiotic must think me extraordinarily stupid. Neither have I addressed Hitler over the radio or in any other manner, nor have I expressed anything in regard to politics. (32:228)

Jung tells his Jewish colleague that he had experienced attacks for his supposedly anti-Christian views, just as he had been maligned for his supposedly anti-Semitic views. He traces part of the anti-Semitic imputation to Freud: "As you know, Freud previously accused me of anti-Semitism because I could not countenance his soulless materialism." (32:229) Jung sees pathological implications in such reactions as Freud's, misrepresenting the criticism of an individual as supposedly being directed against that individual's ethnic group. He says that the English, Americans or French are not prone to such misinterpretations; among the Europeans, he had only found Germans to be so pathologically sensitive.

In the conclusion of the letter, Jung expresses his feeling that he is living among madmen:

Finally I want to inform you that my new book *"Wirk-lichkeit der Seele,"* had appeared. I have included in it a Jewish author on the "Psychology of the Old Testament" in order to annoy the Nazis and all those Jews who have decried me as an Anti-Semite. The next thing they are now going to invent about me is that I suffer from a complete absence of convictions and that I am neither an anti-Semite nor a Nazi. We happen to live in a period which overflows with lunacy. *"Quem deus perdere vult primum dementat."* [Whom God wants to destroy he first makes him insane]

With kindest regards,

Yours,

C.G. Jung,

"et semper idem"

[and ever the same] (32:230)

8. *Book censorship (the Freudian way)*

Writing in 1969, at a time when some professionals had the impression that Freudian oppression was easing, a British psychiatrist protests against the nuisance of psychoanalytic censorship in professional journals:

> We are in an era when the sine qua non of publication in many a psychiatric journal is a dynamic formulation of the problem in oral, anal or oedipal terms. Under these circumstances the psychiatrist who accounts for his observations without resort to this model risks being considered untrained and unread, as well as uncomfortable to have around. The fact that his formulation may account for the facts in a logical and parsimonious way may not enhance the possibility of publication. Indeed there is scarcely room among the papers analysing fairy tales, literary characters, historical greats, and such crucial concerns as the dynamic relationship between commemorative postage stamp choice and patient pathology, for the clinical case reports that please the editor, let alone those that make him uncomfortable. (49:427)

Part of the Freudian censorship is carried on by means of supposedly objective reviews of articles and books. Kaplan's protest

55

against an unfair review by F. Auld, Jr., of Kisker's book *The Disorganized Personality* details the tactics employed. The title of Kaplan's note, "Pain, Auld, and Kisker," refers to the pain caused by imperious assumptions of those who have climbed on the bandwagon of the Freudian establishment and who deliberately or inadvertently disparage the works of other professionals because they do not agree with their dogmatic views. The letter reads in part:

Kisker's eclectic consideration of many viewpoints, with a prominent and sympathetic role assigned to psychoanalytic theory hardly seems to deserve the severity of Auld's charge of prejudice. Granted Auld's contention that Kisker "nearly always speaks of a psychoanalytic hypothesis as a 'hypothesis,' 'a controversial idea,' 'an assumption.' "

Such caution might, with charity, be called objectivity, it is not necessarily prejudice.

... Auld's conclusion reminds me of the politician with the sign on his wall: "Don't disturb me with the facts, I got my mind made up."

In the last paragraph of his review, Auld says, ... "For Kisker has striven valiantly to avoid bias (though he hasn't quite succeeded), and it certainly can't be said that he pushed psycho-analytic views. ..." Why should Kisker *push* psychoanalysis? Kisker is an eclectic who *presents* psychoanalysis sympathetically as other points of view. ... Auld's phrasing implies that Kisker is guilty of something bad, something that I shall call un-Freudianism, something almost as bad as un-Americanism. How does Auld ferret out Kisker's heresy? It is a simple case of guilt by association. Because Kisker treats with respect several cultural and biological theories that are independent of psycho-analysis, then Auld suspects that Kisker is secretly against psychoanalysis. God help Kisker if he had dared to oppose psychoanalysis openly!

... I believe that abnormal psychology is a field where we can be confident that psychoanalysis is not the final, total answer.

I think it is a shame that Auld's review requires a man to search his conscience and to screw up his courage before he dares to state what ought to be simple truism. ... It is Auld who ... says he is pained at professors whose distaste for psychoanalysis makes them fail to correct deficiencies in Kisker's book. I have a pain in the same place but for a different reason. I am pained because professors who are sympathetic to psychoanalysis are left unprepared by Auld's review to examine the benefits of Kisker's text. (24)

Among other points, Kaplan has put his finger on one of the Freudian methods of censoring non-Freudian books: make them appear unobjective, prejudiced, unscientific, so that others would not care to read them or adopt them for classroom teaching.

Freudian psychiatrists are no more tolerant of their non-Freudian colleagues than the psychologist mentioned in Kisker's letter. In 1956, Johnson (29) published a short critique of a psychoanalytic book which treated Beethoven as a homosexual on the basis of magnified psychoanalytic "clues." Johnson protested such psychological cartooning in the name of objectivity, decency, and a nonmaterialistic philosophy. He indicated that psychoanalysis is essentially an atheistic and misanthropic ideology. Two psychiatrists (30) wrote angrily to the editor of the *American Journal of Psychiatry*. They felt that the editorial board had been incompetent in allowing the appearance of such articles, "full of misinformation." As usual, they assumed that Freud's fantasies about bisexuality are a proven fact, "clinically demonstrated time and time again. Also it is a basic tenet for the understanding of human behavior." (30:466) They seem oblivious to the unreliability of clinical guesses and to the fact that bisexuality is a "basic tenet" only of the Freudian cult, and not of scientific psychology. Yet, they assert that Johnson "confuses scientific information with judgment statements." Again, they hoist the favorite Freudian placard, "This is Science," and impute arbitrariness to those who reject that "science." But, as Johnson (31) remarked in his reply, his two colleagues carefully skirted the issue of psychoanalysis as a psychiatric sect which enjoys the financial support of the government and favors from the public by presenting itself under false pretenses *i.e.,* pseudoreligion disguised as medicine. He also points out that they ignored the painful issue of psychoanalysis as a detrimental psychology, leading to suicides among its physician-adherents.

The suppression of non-Freudian writings also operates through Freudian editorial consultants. They influence publishers, by unfavorable reports, to reject independent writers. Brandwin mentions that

Kaiser's book of essays, *Effective Psychotherapy*, was rejected by twenty publishers before finally being accepted for publication. Though trained in psychoanalysis, Kaiser's independent mind discarded Freudian ceremonials in psychotherapy and started a more natural and more humanly suitable approach to treatment. His penalty was to have his proposals pronounced "unprofessional" by Freudians entrusted to evaluate the book's publication merits, and as therefore not worthy of the publisher's interest. In reacting to an unfair review of Kaiser's work, Jones protests that it may "dissuade some readers from Kaiser's only publication." Jones states that he and his colleagues from Brandeis University have found Kaiser's contribution to psychotherapy impressive. He points that the reviewer's bias is apparently the same as that of those publishers' consultants who had advised rejection of the book's publication. "Brandwin prefers to see this as a merited consensus of critical judgement rather than an index of the psychoanalytic community's resistance to free inquiry." (26)

Though wary of generalizations, I submit that these few cases are typical of treatment meted any publication which seems to threaten Freudism.

A similar suppression of the critics of Freud and psychoanalysis may be operating in the selection of library books. Trying to obtain Emil Ludwig's study *Dr. Freud: An Analysis and a Warning*, from two large university libraries, I was offered about fifteen other books by Ludwig—on Bolivar, Goethe, Napoleon, Mussolini, Beethoven, German history, happiness, and others—but not one on Freud. Was this title missing because those professors responsible for recommending library acquisitions did not want students exposed to a book which was devastatingly critical of Freud? Or was it unavailable because, as Cowles (25) asserts, an association of psychoanalysts attempted to buy off and destroy the edition? Neither possibility attests to a liberal attitude on the part of the psychoanalytic fanatics.

A similar subtle bias might be manifest, for instance, in the absence of Adlerian periodicals from local university libraries. Neither the *Journal of Individual Psychology* nor the *Individual Psychologist* can be found, though the shelves are well stocked with Freudian periodicals.

The censorship of non-Freudian publications and activities does not always take such relatively benign forms. It operates much more viciously in some cases. The president of the American Schizophrenia Association (a group of medical men and laymen dedicated to breaking the stranglehold Freudians have over psychiatry in this country), reports examples of psychoanalytic machinations against its opponents. After relating how the Freudians tried to break the Schizophrenia Association by interfering with its sources of income, he turns to the cunning games played against physicians and psychiatrists unfriendly to Freudism:

But the hallmark of the mental health establishment in the U.S. is an almost paranoid incapacity to tolerate new ideas or criticism, and it has always been so, since Freud. The New York Times recently quoted Dr. Fritz Redlich, dean of the Yale Medical School, as saying that the analysts "have created a tightly controlled shop through a careful system of educational supervision and control. One would almost speak of censorship. The boundaries are tight. There is little room for the doubter, the critic, the maverick." This doesn't come from someone with an ax to grind, but from one of the best known and respected psychiatrists in the country.

The call for censorship of the *ASF Newsletter* is only one of a long series of attempts at suppression of information.

Dr. Walter C. Alvarez [an internist, writer of articles and books on psychosomatic problems] informs us that one of the newspapers carrying his syndicated column discontinued it under pressure of local analysts after he wrote an article critical of psychoanalysis. . . .

In 1967, King Features Syndicate, a newspaper feature supplier, asked Dr. and Mrs. Pinckney to author the daily column "Mirror of Your Mind." For nearly a year, the Pinckneys prepared answers to commonly asked questions about mental problems and mental health. Sometimes they were critical of psychoanalysis. According to Dr. Pinckney, "All of a sudden we were told that certain questions and answers would not be sent out to subscribing newspapers. We were also quite pointedly told not to write anything against Freud or psychoanalysis any more."

When the television station of a major university decided recently to do a show on schizophrenia and the ASF, the analyst-dominated Department of Psychiatry at the university's hospital objected and forced the station to cancel the show. (41:10, 11)

The chicanery and double dealing through which a lay critic of Freudian "therapy" went is worthy of a Hollywood script:

A peculiar chain of events also preceded publication of the book *In Search of Sanity* by Gregory Stefan. From the time that Stefan's agent first began to send the manuscript to publishers, in Jan., 1962 the book got the run-around, and was turned down by 10 publishers until it was finally accepted by University Books in 1966, over four years later. The book, highly critical of psychoanalysis and the mental health establishment, was sent successively to Simon & Schuster, University of Michigan Press, Harper's, David McKay, Grove Press, Braziller, Macmillan, Crown, Ballantine Books, and University Books.

The agent reported to Stefan that "Simon & Schuster returned your manuscript with an enthusiastic report concerning your personal story but a so-so report as to your medical theories." Grove Press had it for three months, and then decided that though the book "is most probably publishable, we have decided that *we* should not be the ideal publisher." The responses followed a pattern: the reader, editor or editor-in-chief would express great interest in the book, and sometimes high enthusiasm; but after a long wait for a decision, it would finally be rejected. The agent reported that the editor of Ballantine Books was "much interested" but he then proceeded to hold onto the manuscript for *eight months* before finally saying "no."

But most extraordinary of all was the great interest expressed in the manuscript by the editor-in-chief of Crown. On May 6, 1964, Stefan's agent reported that "I am cheered by having found at lunch on Friday that the editor-in-chief at Crown Publishing, Millen Brand, is tremendously interested in the idea of your book." She added: "He (Brand) has a wide personal acquaintanceship amongst doctors in the field and seems to know a great deal about the biological approach to schizophrenia. *As I say, he feels about all this as you do,* and I have sent all the material I have to him." But on June 19, the agent reported: "I have had a talk with Millen Brand of Crown Publishers, and he tells me that after a lot of discussion, Crown is not going to offer to publish it. *They feel that although their sympathies are definitely with biological research,* the sales angle is not promising, as they see it, because the sum of the argument is that much research remains to be done."

What Stefan did not know at the time was that Millen Brand, the editor-in-chief of Crown, was himself an author, that he had written the screenplay for *The Snake Pit,* and that he himself was writing a novel stoutly defending the same Freudian establishment which Stefan's book was attacking. Brand's novel, *Savage Sleep,* was published last fall, by Crown, amidst much advance publicity; and it confirmed Brand's position as the Chief Propagandist for the Freudian-psychoanalytical school in the U.S., though his position is daily being challenged by a legion of novelists and playwrights who have profited, far more than their readers and the ill people have, from this fiction. (41:10, 11)

9. *Book burning (the psychoanalytic way)*

I might mention a personal experience in this connection. By the end of 1967 I had obtained over fifty papers from originators of non-Freudian psychotherapeutic approaches from both this country and Europe, Asia, and Australia. I edited the collection as *The International Handbook of Direct and Behavior Psychotherapy.* For more than two years I could not find a publisher for it. I wrote to more than forty trade publishers and two dozen university presses. Most of them appreciated the professional standing of contributors and the efficacy of the therapy they proposed, but would not dare undertake the risk of publishing a large volume going counter to psychoanalytic superstitions, which were dominating the field. A few of the publishers quoted the opinions of their reviewers which led them to reject the manuscript. These opinions appeared irrelevant, superficial, and prejudiced against the methods proposed in the *Handbook.* The reviewers were apparently comfortable with their position in the mental health establishment and did not care to have intruders and innovators challenge the "psychodynamic" dominance. One reviewer was frank enough to say that he did not like the Foreword by Professor H.J. Eysenck, reputed to be one of the arch-enemies of psychoanalysis. One publisher practically accepted the volume, with provision that a mail survey would be used in making a final decision. I was informed of the quotas they consider crucial in undertaking publication. Through a telephone inquiry I learned that the two most important groups, psychiatrists and psychologists, responded better than the required percentage of returned orders. I thought I had finally succeeded in placing the volume. Two weeks later I was informed that the *Handbook* was rejected. The reason given for rejection was that two other sampling groups—general practitioners and hospital administrators—responded with less interest than required by the quotas. The reasoning seemed faulty in view of the principal groups for the volume having shown an encouraging response; GPs and administrators are only tangentially important as buyers of a volume on psychotherapy. I was left wondering what Freudian protestations went on behind the screen to discourage the publisher. I continued making the offers and being rejected. I divided the volume into two portions in order to avoid the excuse of the *Handbook* being too bulky for commercial considerations. It was practically three years after I started contacts with publishers that the two volumes were accepted for publication as *Direct Psychotherapy Vols. I and II: Twenty-eight American Originals* (37) and *Vol. III Direct Psychotherapy: International Developments* (38).

A few months had elapsed after I had written the above lines. I argued with myself on a number of occasions about omitting my conjectures that Freudians had anything to do with my troubles in publishing the *International Handbook*. Then I learned of the troubles that were caused to another exposer of Freudian abuses by the same publisher at the time coinciding with the abrupt rejection of my *Handbook*. *The Newsletter of the American Schizophrenia Association* reports:

> Another physician, Dr. Edward R. Pinckney, of Beverly Hills, Calif., author of *The Fallacy of Freud and Psychoanalysis*, reports that the publisher, Prentice-Hall, discontinued the book despite the fact that it was selling extremely well. According to Dr. Pinckney, an internist and former teacher of psychiatry, Prentice-Hall initially approached him to write a critical book on psychoanalysis. Dr. Pinckney and his wife then spent several years researching and writing the book. "Everything was going along swimmingly," he says, until the head of the textbook department read the galley-proofs of the book and "persuaded Prentice-Hall officials that publication would hurt the sale of the company's textbooks."

Dr. Pinckney says that a Prentice-Hall official then flew out to California and told him that the publishing company wanted to get out of publishing the book because of a fear of a boycott of its textbooks by some college professors. But the Pinckneys insisted on fulfillment of their contract, even though they were told that there would be no advertising or promotion of the book. The first edition of the book, out in 1965, sold out in a short time, and was praised in many medical journals. A second edition was printed to fill orders, Dr. Pinckney says, but then suddenly bookstores and individuals who wrote directly were told the book was out-of-print. (41:10) [2]

Such suppression of an already printed book is more akin to Nazi bookburning than even to censorship. The intolerance and hatred for disliked ideas is behind it, if the manner is (appropriately) psychoanalytically more subtle.

When *Direct Psychotherapy: Twenty-eight American Originals* was published, some representatives of the Freudian establishment still tried to stifle it. They refused to accept the two volumes into the professional book clubs' lists as they did not like my outspoken rejection of psychoanalytic superstitions. And this in spite of my accepting the publisher's suggestion that some strong expressions of criticism be omitted!

My difficulties in finding a publisher for this and related volumes of criticism of Freudism were even greater than for *Direct Psychotherapy*. I wrote to more than four score of publishers without finding acceptance. Some explained that their programs were limited for psychological works although they soon produced Freudian books. Others complained that their budgets were insufficient, yet they published sizeable psychoanalytic volumes. Some candidly said that it would not make sense for them to publish my volume as they have already heavy investment in pro-Freudian books. When I read of Eissler suggesting that "if someone wants to become well known these days and to obtain a quick success, he has only to write against Freud," (61:2) I wondered how one could develop such a misperception.

The Freudians have attained power and have been no more scrupulous than industrialists trying to suppress Nader or CBS their particular critic who threatened to depict them as *The News Twisters*.

(64) What happened to Miss Efron had, knowingly and unknowingly happened to many a Freudian critic. She exposed the machinations in *How CBS Tried to Kill a Book*. (65) In following other Freudian tactics we have become familiar with the "democratic" book-burning technique:

Even before *TNT* was officially published, CBS undertook a massive and expensive publicity campaign designed to discredit the book before it could be read by the public.

HOW CBS TRIED TO KILL A BOOK is an analysis of the well-oiled CBS campaign of smear and vituperation directed at *TNT* and its author. The book was written, according to Miss Efron, to help the reader "learn ... about the mental processes of the executives in those CBS news offices as they checked their own broadcasts against *TNT*'s charges ... exactly what they feel so guilty about; why every strong challenge to their fairness scares them into fits; and why a pioneer bias study was such a threat to them they had to cry conspiracy in order to deal with it."

It is easily predictable that this very important and readable new book will leave any fair-minded reader shaken and enraged. Shaken, to see the lengths to which an organization whose purpose is to objectively report news will go in order to twist and distort facts to its own ends; enraged, by their cynical disregard of intellectual honesty and fair play. One professor at an Eastern university wrote to Miss Efron in astonishment: "CBS is not a company—it is some kind of Mafia." To which Miss Efron reponded " ... Personally ... I have a higher regard for an ordinary gangster than I do for educated men with the mentality of book burners." (66)

In concluding this chapter on the nuisance of Freudian psycho-analysis and its cultists, we might admit that their behavior is commonly human, even though in a primitive way.

It is in the nature of sects to proselytize and to belittle other sects. [3] The Freudians disparage or ignore the good results achieved by other therapeutic theories and methods. Their sectarian arrogance could be considered an amusing human foible if it were not causing a serious imbalance in psychotherapeutic training and practices in this country. Overly impressed by the theoretical imaginativeness of psychoanalysis and by the assumed efficacy of psychotherapy based on Freudian models, many psychotherapists deprive their patients of more efficient methods of help. Furthermore, their professional growth is impeded by a fearful clinging to Freudian therapeutic technique and an unquestioning attitude before the psychoanalytic assertiveness. Narrow training makes the devout Freudians unwilling to venture beyond the officially sanctioned precepts and examples. "The new, the liberal, the radical of one generation becomes the conservative, the traditionalist, the dogmatist of the next." (15) The deterioration of psychotherapy under Freudian influence is the subject of the next chapter. It is the most damaging aspect of the Freudian hoax.

Notes to Chapter One

1. Glover (62:147-152) exhibits the hostile imputations practiced by Jung's detractors. He plays fair at the opening by quoting Jung's saying: "As a Swiss I am an inveterate democrat; yet I recognize that the nature is aristocratic, and what is more, esoteric." Then Glover invites the reader to compare it with Hitler's reference to "the basic aristocratic principle in nature." This trick should mislead an uncritical reader to conclude that Jung and Hitler shared the same ideology. By the same logic some Americans jump to conclusion calling a socialist a "Commie," or a patriot and anti-Communist a warmonger.

Then Glover, as if to prove his insinuation, goes on to quote a number of passages in which Jung seems to present in an impressed way the electrifying effect National Socialism had on German people. He could not help seeing what any observer could not miss: the German masses were imbued with enthusiasm, social conditions had improved, they were full of pride, anticipating to reach peaks which Hitler had repeatedly promised.

I remember my own experience in 1938 in Germany. I had gone there to learn the language, staying with an impoverished German family. They were Christians and looked askance at the pagan frenzy expressed by the majority of their compatriots. They had a daughter my age (early twenties), an unusually shy and inexpressive girl. One day the two of us went for a bicycle ride on country roads. We had to stop on the side as we met an armored column on some sort of maneuvers. The girl waved enthusiastically to the young soldiers, tears in her eyes, whispering reverently, "Unsere Wehrmacht! Unsere Wehrmacht!" (our defense forces). Witnessing her uplift, I felt both awed and depressed. I was awed by the inspired state reached by this ordinary girl, realizing that this was happening to millions of Germans; I was depressed with fear of what would happen to me and my people when one day this psychological and military might turns on us Jugoslavs, as one of the yet unsubjected neighbors.

The Swiss must have had the same feeling about the mighty spectacle of Nazified Germans, as I saw them building fortifications and antitank barriers on all the approaches to their country. Yet, Glover chooses not to make the reader aware of the subtlety of the situation in which Jung found himself. As a Swiss democrat he was revolted by the Nazis and as a psychologist he was astounded by the demonstration of the irrational archetypical might, the basic postulate of his theories which he saw potently expressed in the German happenings. Glover, remaining consistently unfair, leaves the reader in suspicion and uncertainty but concluding: "Further comment is unnecessary."

2. Dr. E.R. Pinckney had subsequently contributed all suppressed copies to the American Schizophrenia Association, 56 W. 45th St. New York, N.Y., 10036, from whom the copies may be purchased by donating $3.00.

3. The sort of oppression exercised by the Freudian establishment also exists in other groups. *The Velikovsky Affair* (27) reveals a similar primitive censorship practiced by a group of scientists dealing with far less emotional matters—the astronomers. The editor, A. deGrazia, writes in the Foreword:

> In 1950, a book called *Worlds in Collision,* by Dr. Immanuel Velikovsky, gave rise to a controversy in scientific and intellectual circles about scientific theories and the sociology of science. Dr. Velikovsky's historical and cosmological concepts, bolstered by his acknowledged scholarship, constituted a formidable assault on certain established theories of astronomy, geology, and

historical biology, and on the heroes of those sciences. Newton, himself, and Darwin were being challenged, and indeed the general orthodoxy of an ordered universe. . . .

What must be called the scientific establishment rose in arms, not only against the new Velikovsky theories but against the man himself. Efforts were made to block dissemination of Dr. Velikovsky's ideas, and even to punish supporters of his investigations. Universities, scientific societies, publishing houses, the popular press were approached and threatened; social pressures and professional sanctions were invoked to control public opinion. There can be little doubt that in a totalitarian society, not only would Dr. Velikovsky's reputation have been at stake, but also his right to pursue his inquiry, and perhaps his personal safety.

As it was, the "establishment" succeeded in building a wall of unfavorable sentiment around him: to thousands of scholars the name Velikovsky bears the taint of fantasy, science-fiction and publicity.

Whatever the scientific substance, the controversy itself could not be avoided or dismissed by behavioral science. The politics of science is one of the agitating problems of the Twentieth Century. The issues are clear: Who determines scientific truth? Who are its high priests, and what is their warrant? How do they establish their canons? What effects do they have on the freedom of inquiry, and on public interest? In the end, some judgement must be passed upon the behavior of the scientific world and, if adverse, some remedies must be proposed. (27:1, 2)

In American psychiatry and clinical psychology it is clear that the "high priests" who "determine scientific truth" at this time are the members of the Freudian establishment. They have no warrant, yet they damage consistently the patients and the public interest.

Chapter II

Freudian Practice: Failure and Worse

I ask again, how much damage is daily done the minds and souls of men in the name of psychoanalysis.

Emil Ludwig (24:240)

But after 40 years of social inoculation and when generations of medical men have grown up with active psychoanalysts writing, talking and working, the professional prejudice would have been broken down if results were overwhelmingly clear and valuable.

I state definitely that as a therapeutic system psychoanalysis has failed to prove its worth.

Abraham Meyerson, M.D. in 1939 (61:624, 640)

The trouble is that a war of ideas, like a war of armies, is really not a concern of reason or reasons. Rather it is, as it probably always shall be, a true war—a combat which is considered really finished only if one of the combatants is destroyed or brought to his knees to ask for mercy.

Gregory Zilboorg, M.D. (1:35)

The most important question to any psychotherapist, whether a psychologist or a psychiatrist, is "What happens to the patient in my care?" The question is not at all easy to answer in an objective way. Most therapists take for granted that their methods are salutary. How else could it be, particularly for traditionalists like Freudians? The great teachers are presumed to have proved that the therapeutic methods of psychoanalysis were beneficial to patients, and professors at medical and graduate schools perpetuate this impression. Although moderately helpful to professional psychotherapists, the faith they place in the authority of revealed Freudian knowledge often blinds them to what they actually find in their experience, and restricts them to useless healing rituals, which assume more importance than the

68

patient's needs. Such effects, crippling to the professional function, are likely to be more pronounced after dogmatic schooling in psychoanalysis than after training in less rigid approaches. Some enlightened non-Freudian teachers actually train students to be skeptical of their methods, to observe the patient's reaction more carefully than to worry about the sacred rules. The patients of such therapists are less likely to be sacrificed to the "scientific" shibboleths of a Freudian school.

1. *Needed: more professional modesty*

It is in the nature of men and particularly in the nature of insecure practitioners to overlook or rationalize their failures. When a dam breaks down, the engineers who built it are likely to have all sorts of explanations for the collapse, except that their skill was insufficient or their calculations at fault. Captains of losing teams offer ingenious explanations for their defeat, rationalizations which usually do not include the poor quality of the team's performance. When a patient dies subsequent to surgery the catastrophe is often explained by everything but the limited human ability of surgeons to intervene successfully in all cases. Very little can be found in the voluminous medical literature about mistaken diagnoses, wrong prescriptions, and improper treatment, although the matters come up often enough in private professional conversations, and even laymen get an occasional glimpse of medical errors. [1]

Psychotherapists, and particularly psychoanalysts, are no more eager to recognize their failures or blunders than any other profession. Marcuse (not related to the pro-Communist philosopher) offers an amusing comment on this reluctance (probably referring to *Failures in Psychiatric Treatment*, by Hoch, 3): "A textbook on failures in psychiatry, one of very few known to the author, has for its contributors top men in their field. These persons spend a great deal of time and pages in this text on failures describing their very many successes, for the idea that we can learn by failures as well as by successes is not very popular." (4:118) In a recent book (47) on therapeutic failures, the consideration of them is considerably toned down by blowing up the successes beyond scientific warrant.

A lay inquirer impugns psychiatric terminology as a defense against criticism:

The cryptic character of psychiatry regarding its methods and treatment techniques, intentional or not, created justifiable doubts in the minds of interested inquirers. It is difficult enough for them to translate the language of psychiatry without being fooled in the end by an apparent attempt to cover up what has the earmarks of a reluctance to admit ignorance. (5:9)

The professionals in mental-health fields guard their public image of omnipotence as keenly as space-flight engineers or missile technicians. It is therefore difficult to speak of the Freudian psychotherapeutic failures or harm to patients except in terms of either limited personal impressions or a few published reports.

A psychiatrist tried to discuss in 1964 the harm done to patients by psychiatrists, *i.e.* the iatrogenic (doctor-induced) problems in psychotherapy. He protests the assumption that psychotherapy would do no harm if it does not do any good for the patient. He complains: "So little has been written on this subject that at this stage it is only possible to ask questions, cite examples and hope for wider observation and writing about this topic. . . . The good of psychotherapy has been evangelically proclaimed. Its possible dangers have been left unmentioned." (43:23, 24) He apparently experienced disapproval of his colleagues, who preferred to keep the matter under wraps:

> Those psychotherapists who have tried to deal with psychiatrogenic aspects of psychotherapy have sometimes been looked upon as fifth columnists within the movement or as persons who "need more therapy to work through their ambivalence about psychotherapy." Those who have tried to tackle the ungrateful task of dealing with psychiatrogenic aspects of psychotherapy have more often had diagnoses thrown at them than compliments. (43:24)

Chapman hopes that consideration of psychiatric failures would produce the appropriate modesty in therapists: "A frank consideration of the psychiatrogenic problems in psychotherapy will lead to more humility in all of us who practice psychotherapy." (43:29) It is doubtful that he had much success with his idealistic proposal.

2. *Psychoanalytical Butchery*

Apparently Chapman was mainly concerned with the mental troubles produced by Freudian therapists. He does not explicitly say so, probably assuming that all American psychotherapists tend to harm some of their patients by slavishly following Freudian precepts of inducing neurosis as supposed curative expedient:

> Most experienced psychotherapists have had the unpleasant task of examining patients who after years of psychotherapy left the treatment with painful unresolved feelings about the previous therapist. It is of little value to point out that if the patient had persisted in treatment his transference problem might well have been solved. The fact remains that the bonds or practicalities of treatment were not such that the patient did remain to solve his transference problems. Their aftermath in the patient must be frankly recognized as a psychiatrogenic problem which deserves more systematic attention in psychiatric thinking and writing. Much has been written about the cause, the meaning and the desired utility of transference neuroses. . . . Much more attention should frankly be given to their prognoses, both in treatment and those instances in which treatment is interrupted before the transference neurosis is resolved. (43:28)

The empirically and statistically documented inefficiency of psychoanalysis will be discussed in the volume *Freud's Non-science* (25); at the moment we are concerned with some diffuse but no less pernicious influences of Freudism in current psychotherapy.

The principal cause of harmfulness of Freudian orthodox and "psychoanalytically-oriented" therapy is the crude and ruthless handling of the fine psychical apparatus. It is often a senseless analysis, tearing apart psychological structure beyond the possibility of putting it back together again. It is not unlike biological explorations of rats in the laboratory which leave them maimed and sick. Some Nazi physicians tried such unscrupulous experimentations on prisoners, creating wounds or bringing human bodies under stresses of ice packs or poisons, just to prove how much the human organism can stand. Freud and his students dealt with the psyche almost equally unscrupulously. They would bring out of it or inject into it all destructive, depraved, animal irrationalities, creating psychic infections from the disbalancing unconscious materials and then busying themselves with saving the endangered psychic system. Freud's chief interest was analysis, "research" on the psyche, and not primarily the healing of its malfunctions, although he conducted his psychological vivisections under the guise of therapy. Driven by ambition to prove his psychopathological fantasies and intuitions by obtaining them from the subjects on the couch, he subtly indoctrinated them with overattention to all sorts of ugly, immoral, and insane promptings in them. This was essential to his purposes. He needed to induce guilt and anxiety in them to keep them on his bench long enough to undergo the brainwashing process to the fullest extent and "prove" his theories right.

What was "research" for Freud became psychotherapy for his pupils. They continued infecting their patients with notions intended to cause psychic stress of guilt and anxiety, and then proceeded to "cure" them from such iatrogenic ailments. Other, more sensible, psychologists shuddered at such coarse handling of whatever level of psychological adjustment a patient may have. Pavlov (see 40) warned in his writings against making patients conscious of their negative feelings and fears; he considered focussing on patient's weaknesses as clearly antitherapeutic. He considered such emphasis on negative psychological developments particularly harmful when they are emphasized by such an awesome authority figure for the patient as his psychotherapist.

These two men, Pavlov and Freud, were basically different in their attitudes to life and human nature. Pavlov, the son of a Russian Orthodox priest, remained basically a believer in Christian concepts of reality. In spite of his experimenting with animal organisms as guided by reflexes, and later generalizing some of his conditioning experiments upon some human behaviors, he approached psychic life as an image of God in man, with which he did not dare tamper irresponsibly. Freud, a rabid atheist, handled psychic mechanisms without basic respect, showing no more inhibition to interfere with it than animal experimenters have for organisms of laboratory dogs, cats, and rats. Speaking of the two poles of scientific endeavor, science and service, Lazarus announces a guiding principle under which Freud could be indicted: "Technicians, be they physicians, surgeons, or psychotherapists, should operate rigorously, making as much use as possible of applied scientific principles but without forgetting that their function is to alleviate suffering rather than to advance knowledge or satisfy their own curiosities." (41)

The basis of psychotherapeutic failure and the inefficiency of Freud's approach to therapy is his obsession with "analysis," *i.e.,* finding out real or contrived "causes" of mental troubles. Freud was misled by cathartic cures early in his career to believe that patients have to come up with true or fancied "traumas" in their childhoods before they are able to overcome their neurotic entanglements. The successful therapeutic work of direct psychotherapists (50, 51) with thousands of patients makes Freudian delusion clear. What the patients need in order to function better is not to concentrate on their minute psychopathological features and traumas of the past, but to have their coping capacities strengthened, their faulty habits re-trained, and their goals redirected away from the points on which they got hooked. A detailed previous analysis of traumas is not a pre-requisite for liberation from neurotic involvement, as Freud claimed. Yet, millions of hours were wasted by his followers in overprotracted and overexpensive analyses with little benefit to the patients. The results amounted more to an abuse than a treatment.

Forty years ago, Jastrow, a prominent professor of psychology, wrote of unscrupulous interference of some psychoanalysts in the lives of their patients. If psychoanalysts allowed objective research into their procedures and the effects of their treatment, Jastrow's report could be duplicated many times over in contemporary data. One such report will be included at the end of this section. It confirms in 1963 what Jastrow saw as the harm to patients by Freudian method:

The possible menace of psychoanalytic exploration cannot, should not, be overlooked. That it has been taken up by the "idle rich," lured to the novel by the attraction of a fashion, or espoused by prurient and unstable personalities as a thrill in sex or narcissism is but one side of the picture. Tales from Vienna* recount cases of distracted American husbands resorting to extreme measures to save their wives from psychoanalytic "transferences"; and of patients, bullied into admissions irritating rather than healing to emotional wounds, and of others driven to despair by emotional upset. These tales can be duplicated ad lib. in New York or wherever psychoanalysts have appealed to the same type of clientele. It is quite too easy for a practitioner to spend a few months in Vienna and on his return announce himself as a psychoanalyst ready to tamper with the holy of holies in the lives of bewildered patients. From unwisdom to indiscretion to scandal, and again from wicked lives to suicide, the unsavory rumors accumulate. More than any form of practice that has sought scientific sanction, is psychoanalysis open to the abuse of confidence,** to the sex-degradation that is mistaken for enlightenment, and even more seriously, to the complete undoing of deserving patients neurotically tortured and psychoanalytically crucified.

One such tale in my correspondence will suffice: The writer is a woman who had had tragic marital troubles and had procured a divorce from her husband. She writes: "My physician in whom I had implicit confidence, persuaded me to try analysis. I felt no need for it, but not knowing anything about mental troubles I accepted his suggestion to my lasting despair. I was analyzed over a period of a year. It not only cost my family thousands of dollars, but as a result I became extremely ill; in fact one of the shocks which resulted from the analysis so unbalanced my mind that I became suicidal."

To revert to the patter of the analyst, why should the discovery of a "psychic trauma" be considered beneficial in a depression case? They tell you that depression is a "flight from reality" and then proceed to make reality worse than it had ever been.

* George Seldes: *Can These Things Be?*
** Dr. Tannenbaum has printed an instance, which, if reprinted here, might bring upon my publisher embarrassing censorship. (6:267, 268)

The sexual exploitation of patients by some Freudian therapists, hinted at by Jastrow in the preceding quotation, might be even less rare in the contemporary generation of therapists reared in the enlightenment of our thoroughly freudianized culture. It is evidently frequent enough to prompt a psychologist to raise the question at a national convention in 1972:

> Psychotherapist Arthur Seagull of Michigan State University, in a talk prepared for the convention of the American Psychological Association in Honolulu, bluntly asked a question that rarely surfaces on official programs: "Should a therapist have intercourse with patients?" He answered it in the negative: "I think having intercourse with a patient is destructive, is an acting out of an adolescent fantasy on the therapist's part, and never helps the patient." (52:16)

It is certainly not morally insignificant that Seagull assumed that "other therapists may think differently." (52:16) Such cynical attitudes could be expected from professionals trained into seeing sexuality as a primary and profound function of human beings, and expression of sexual drives as a way to "mental health" or genitality, as Freudians are rather apt to call it.

A psychiatrist reports of another abuse of patients by "therapists" steeped in Freudian tenets. Schmideberg, at that time a prominent psychiatrist in New York, wrote to the editor of the *American Journal of Psychiatry* about mismanagement of patients' lives by Freudian psychoanalysts. The editor titled it Iatrogenic Disturbance—the illness created by the physician; a more proper title could have been psychiatrogenic, or, even more precisely, freudiatrogenic disturbance. The letter reads:

> Sir: A colleague who used to relate his cases to me became, at times, very upset because he could tell when his patients started to become psychotic. At first, I reassured him by saying that he was not to blame, until one day he asked me to see one of his patients. After that, I could reassure him no longer.
>
> Miss R., a Jewish lower middle class woman in her early 30's had gone into therapy with the hope that it would aid her in getting married. (Therapy has now become a sort of magic that helps us to achieve everything we desire.) Dr. X., in his attempts to cure her "inhibitions," tried to "get out her aggression," with

the result that the domestic situation steadily worsened. So, Dr. X persuaded Miss R.'s sister, with whom she lived, to go into therapy with a colleague. Since he also tried to get his patient's aggression out, the quarreling now became violent. Dr. X also tried to remove the patient's sexual inhibitions, so that she became promiscuous and lost all self-respect. Furthermore, he told her not to allow her boss to "exploit" her and she consequently lost the job she held for over 10 years which had stabilized her and given her social standing. She became aggressive, depressed, anxious and agitated and was finally hospitalized by her therapist, who was unable to cope with her. After 6 months, with the help of shock treatment and general care, she had calmed down somewhat and was discharged.

When I saw her, she had gained 20 pounds as a result of the insulin and her mental and physical condition was such that it precluded any possibility of her getting married. She was neither willing nor able to work and was living on the meagre allowance her brother, who could ill afford it, gave her. I could give her no advice.

A woman, applying to me for a secretarial position, confided to me that her little daughter had developed a neurosis and was receiving psychiatric treatment. The attempts to get "her underlying jealousy out" were so upsetting for the mother, that she too had to undergo treatment and was now looking for a job in order to finance her treatment and that of her child. She could not understand why I, a psychiatrist, was not eager to engage her since she so ardently believed in psychiatry and was making such sacrifices in its behalf. I refrained from telling her that, if they both dispensed with treatment, and the mother devoted more time to the family, the child might feel less jealous and be happier.

Not every maladjustment is neurotic. And not every neurosis is caused by suppressed aggression or cured by an indiscriminate release of aggression. There are cases of very timid, inhibited patients who could be helped by expressing a moderate amount of aggression in a socially acceptable manner. But unlimited and indiscriminate expression of aggression and sexual impulses is harmful to the patient's self-esteem and often has disastrous social and family consequences. (42:899)

An emeritus professor of psychiatry and a training and supervising analyst thus depicts the plight of psychoanalytic victims:

> I should like to speak of a series of cases in which the patients were seen after they had had between 600 and 900 hours of classical psychoanalytic treatment—mostly five days per week on the couch—conducted by a number of *experienced analysts.* The patients showed striking similarities in their complaints: Each was depressed and anxious, with a sense of failure and a frightening loss of self-confidence. In each instance the *patient was almost impossible to live with at home or work,* was deeply embittered, and felt his self-control threatened. *Each wished bitterly that he was as he had been prior to treatment.* (46:119, 120, emphasis added)

3. *A design for psychotherapeutic failure*

In a satire of psychotherapy under Freudian dominance, Haley (39:338-342) counsels professional healers about how to assure failure of their efforts. Contrary to prevailing opinion, to fail in psychotherapy is not an easy matter. One half or more of patients recover spontaneously without professional help anyway, so that a therapist has a good chance of appearing successful, without doing anything. If he follows some wise rules, derived primarily from Freudian precepts, he has an excellent chance of leading his patients into a worsened mental condition.

It is disconcerting to us who were trained in the belief that Freudian techniques lead to superior therapeutic results, to see them presented as the conditions for therapeutic ineffectiveness. Some of the treatment histories presented in this and subsequent chapters vindicate Haley's prescriptions for failure. Here are some of the negative counsels for avoiding therapeutic benefits à la Freud:

> 1. Insist that the problem which brings the patient into therapy is not important. Dismiss it as merely a "symptom" and shift the conversation elsewhere. In this way a therapist never learns to examine what is really distressing a patient.

2. Refuse to directly treat the presenting problem. Offer some rationale, such as the idea that symptoms have "roots," to avoid treating the problem the patient is paying his money to recover from.

3. Insist that if a presenting problem is relieved something worse will develop. This myth makes it proper not to know what to do about symptoms and will even encourage patients to cooperate by developing a fear of recovery.

Given these three steps, it seems obvious that any psychotherapist will be incapacitated, whatever his natural talent. He will not take seriously the problem the patient brings, he will not try to change that, and he will fear that successful relief of the problem is disastrous.

4. Have no theory, or an ambiguous and untestable one, of what a therapist should do to bring about therapeutic change. However, make it clear that it is untherapeutic to give a patient directives for changing—he might follow them and change. Just imply that change happens spontaneously when therapists and patients behave according to the proper forms. As part of the general confusion that is necessary, it is helpful to define therapy as a procedure for finding out what is wrong with a person and how he got that way.

5. Insist that only years of therapy will really change a patient. This step brings us to more specific things to do about those patients who might spontaneously recover without treatment. If they can be persuaded that they have not really recovered but have merely fled into health, it is possible to help them back to ill health by holding them in long-term treatment.

6. As a further step to restrain patients who might spontaneously improve, the therapist should focus upon the patient's past.

7. As yet another step with that aim, the therapist should interpret what is most unsavory about the patient to arouse his guilt so that he will remain in treatment to resolve the guilt.

8. Perhaps the most important rule is to ignore the real world that patients live in and publicize the vital importance of their infancy, inner dynamics, and fantasy life. This will effectively prevent either therapists or patients from attempting to make changes in their families, friends, schools, neighborhoods, or treatment milieus. Naturally they cannot recover if their situation

does not change, and so one guarantees failure while being paid to listen to interesting fantasies. Talking about dreams is a good way to pass the time, and so is experimenting with responses to different kinds of pills.

9. A continuing refusal to define the goals of therapy is essential. If a therapist sets goals, someone is likely to raise a question whether they have been achieved. At that point the idea of evaluating results arises in its most virulent form. If it becomes necessary to define a goal, the phrasing should be unclear, ambiguous, and so esoteric that anyone who thinks about determining if the goal has been achieved will lose heart and turn to a less confused field of endeavor, like existentialism. . . . To be human is to err, and inevitably a few deviant individuals in the profession will attempt evaluation studies. They should be promptly condemned and their character questioned. Such people should be called superficial in their understanding of what therapy really is, oversimple in their emphasis upon symptoms rather than depth personality problems, and artificial in their approach to human life. Routinely they should be eliminated from respectable institutions and cut off from research funds. As a last resort, they can be put in psychoanalytic treatment or shot.

10. On the wall of every institute training therapists, there can be a motto known as *The Five B's Which Guarantee Dynamic Failure:*

Be Passive
Be Inactive
Be Reflective
Be Silent
Beware

In the light of these wise precepts we can better understand some of the professional bungling described in the forthcoming treatment histories.

4. *Was this patient (mis-, mal-, non-) treated?*

A foreign-born woman in her thirties was referred to me after the psychiatrist whom she had been seeing for a year left the city. He was a quiet, conscientious man. She related to the new therapist in a friendly, uninhibited way and the transition from one therapist to

79

another seemed accomplished successfully, partly because the new therapist was also a "foreigner." I was encouraged to think she would continue without a break in the healing process I imagined was initiated by numerous interviews with the previous therapist. She spoke of her depressions, of pains in the abdomen and of headaches, of longstanding emotional coldness between her and her husband. She seemed worried about her inability to decide whether to live with him in an unfriendly relationship or move toward divorce.

Having primarily listened throughout the session, I thought I had understood her situation sufficiently to say at the end of the interview: "I imagine you are coming to see that the unpleasant relationship with your husband is one of the sources of your unhappy feelings. Once you make the decision either to break up the marriage or work toward improving it, you might get to feel less uneasy." She suddenly straightened up in her chair, became agitated and flushed in the face, and shot back, angrily and fearfully: "How do you expect me to get hold of this situation so quickly? That's impossible. I can't decide on things so quickly." Her voice trailed off and angry tears appeared as she struggled with the imagined threat from her "unsympathetic" therapist.

I was taken aback by my misjudgement of what this woman wanted from therapy or had learned to expect from it. With my other patients I usually handled therapy as collaborative problem-solving, [2] but apparently the woman before me wished to maintain her painful situation, extracting a secondary benefit from the sympathetic attention of a male.

I only partially reassured her: "I'm sorry that I gave you a wrong impression. I did not say that you have to reach a solution next week or next month; I implied only that you will decide when you want to start getting yourself off the hook which you feel is hurting you." She gave me a reproachful glance upon leaving. Apparently she was disappointed when she compared me to the "nice man" whose interviews had always made her "feel better afterwards."

In the following interviews, what she called her "hypochondriacal complaints" became worse. An almost permanent headache on one side made her fear brain tumor. I agreed with her plan to obtain a medical checkup; when she did, no organic cause was found. "This might make it easier for you, as you will be less worried about health and freer to examine the emotions which are leading to your uneasiness," I told her, only to discover I had said the wrong thing again—she gazed at me askance and sighed. Taking the warning, I let her talk of innocuous matters.

Some of her history was obtained in the next two or three interviews. The younger of two siblings, because she was quiet and compliant, her mother preferred her to her older sister. The mother used the patient's good manners and good school performance to berate the elder daughter. The patient played with dolls, alone, did not make friends in school, spent time reading. Once, however, she got in such a rage with her sister that she chased her with a knife. This was the worst childhood action she could remember. Then, at fourteen, came the big shock of her life—her parents were divorced. She lived alternately with her mother and father, both of whom had remarried shortly after the divorce. She left school, worked as a seamstress, joined a military organization from which she was discharged for anxiety reaction. A romance with an older man broke up over religious differences and she married her present husband "for security." Things went wrong from the beginning: although married for the second time, he was sexually clumsy and began the first intercourse without preparation, leaving her frustrated when he turned his back to her and fell asleep. Her hatred and contempt for him had remained at an almost constant level for the ten years of marriage. She complained of his limited interests, his self-centeredness, and his lack of warmth.

If I had seen her a few years sooner, the two of us would have had a royal time hunting all possible insights to discover how her past was disturbing her present. She was intelligent, literate, and sensitive; such a hunt would have been "delightful brainpicking," as Ellis (7:5) called it. At that earlier time I was awed by so-called mental illness as an insidious process of early traumas leading to inevitable personality "sickness." In the course of time, though, I had liberated myself from the medical and particularly the Freudian model of psychopathology, and had begun to see the "illness" essentially as an unwillingness to take responsibility for oneself and others.

In the sixth interview I again tried to lead her toward finding her

81

role in her troubles. I consistently led her to "objective reviewing" of her stress, as Alexander (8) called it. I asked her how she was responding to her husband. She told of avoiding physical contact with him, condescending to have intercourse with him every few weeks, at his insistence. She could find nothing interesting to talk to him about, nor did she think it would do any good to bring him to talk with me as I had suggested. I rejoined with calculated tactlessness: "I guess your husband is as discouraged by your rejection as you are by his." She appeared pained by such brashness. After a pause of about two minutes she said, "I do not know what to do," and her words sounded as if uttered more as passive resistance to the demands implied by my remark than because she actually wished to do anything. "As we go along," I told her, "you might consider what you can do to make things less unpleasant for the two of you. You might also want to join the group of married couples with whom I am working. They can help you, and you can help them."

The patient did not appear for the next interview. An hour later she called to tell the secretary that she had not slept well the night before, had taken a nap at noon, and overslept. She added that she felt the doctor was not helping her, anyway, so she would not see him anymore. She inquired about consulting another therapist.

Had this case occurred while I had respect for psychoanalytic precepts in therapy, I would have felt guilty of a technical mistake, of mismanaging the situation, of damaging the patient's interests. Expecting such an unpleasant reaction in myself, I would not have dared displease the patient. But having discarded the accumulation of "insights," even emotional ones, as the primary method of psychotherapy, and considering the frank confrontation of the patient with the maladaptations in the present situation as the main therapeutic agent, I felt only slightly uneasy about the situation. A probable source of my assurance was the positive outcomes of a controlled study I had made of fourteen severely maladapted adolescent girls. (9)

I felt that the patient was brought closer to more efficient response to her situation, even though she currently rejected it, than if she had spent months musing over her troubles as if she had nothing to do with their occurrence. Like her previous therapist, who had thoroughly

82

absorbed his psychoanalytically oriented training and apparently departed little from it in his subsequent practice, I could have kept the patient by endlessly commiserating with her. [3] Such insipid practice seems to me an abuse of the professional role and a reinforcement of the dependency and masochistic pathology out of which the therapist is supposed to lead the patient, even though it might not be listed as unethical in the official code. If a physician did not warn a patient about harmful diet or the effects of smoking or loss of sleep he would be remiss in his duty. Equally at fault is the psychotherapist who sees the insidious effects of entrenched emotional misdevelopments but only continues to listen to the patient, instead of actively offering help in the struggle against the pathogenic habits. [4] Yet this failure is the almost inevitable result of "permissive," nondirective or interminable therapies and dragged-out psychoanalyses.

5. *Useless Freud-aping*

A clinical professor of psychiatry (44) reveals indirectly the reasons for ineffective Freudian handling of a patient's problems, for what I would call the practice of no-therapy. He discusses causes of failure in psychoanalytic psychotherapy and conceptualizes them in exactly the opposite way from non-Freudian therapists: he considers the therapeutic zeal and active focussing on patient's problems as the ground of therapeutic failure. Luckily for the reader of that book, another contributor to it criticizes severely the passive, "analytic" attitude of nonchalant Freudian therapists, urging them to translate insights produced on the couch into concrete applications to patients' life situations: " ... the emphasis on a too exclusively sexual theory of personality and of the etiology of the neuroses distorts perception of these other forces. Because of this persisting historical bias, other forces and relationships are perceived but not appreciated or effectively used in treatment." (46:122)

A few years after my experience with the woman spoiled for therapy by training in the Freudian slow-motion therapy, I found support for my criticism of psychoanalytic approach to treatment in the observations by Shepard and Lee. Throughout their book they see the chief reason for "psychodynamic" inefficiency in therapy in mistaken concentration on feelings instead of on actions of the patient; feelings being elusive and profuse, the poor patient dwelling on them is likely to bog down in years of analysis:

> Therapists interested in altering patient-behavior must know much about P's [patient's] activities; they must locate those inter-actions which might be amenable to change. Behavioral therapists are more concerned with what the patient does, whom he does it with, and what the other person does in return.
>
> Nonbehavioral therapists are apt to forget or overlook the importance of activity and to lapse into the role of pseudo-philosopher or emotional historian, devoting unnecessary time to the study of feelings and their place in the life of man. Regardless of what patients bring to their therapeutic sessions, the antiaction therapist, feeling safe in the rut of his classical training, invariably directs the discussion to one of emotional reaction. . . .
>
> Players of *Tell Me Your Feelings* are able to avoid head-on collisions with reality-situations, and to hide ignorance of solu-tions interminably by sticking with the discovery and analysis of emotional phenomena. (26:58, 59, 60)

Allied to overemphasis on feelings, Shepard and Lee see the *why* questions in therapy as another block to helping the patient change his behavior:" . . . the *Tell Me Why* therapist is not interested in the facts. He is concerned with proving that he is one step ahead of the patient. He can hide his ignorance of life-solutions by relying on a long analysis of *Why,* rather than launching into *What* and *What-to-do-about-it.*" (26:62)

The Freudian therapists appear to forget that "when your car breaks down and you take it to a mechanic you do not want a dissertation on what made it develop mechanical trouble as much as you want him to take whatever action is needed to make the necessary repair." (26:182)

Grinker brings out a similar criticism. He had extensive experience in training psychiatrists and was apparently troubled by the distorting effects psychoanalysis produced in the trainees:

> In all of these experiences I have had to struggle against the deep impressions made by the psychoanalytic model on youngsters

barely beginning their training in psychiatry. It was easily observed that their goals included uncovering significant dynamic processes during long-term treatment with the desire for cure or so-called "complete reorganization of the personality" which they held out for themselves in their future personal analyses. In the young therapist this involved long periods of passivity and length of relationship often induced a serious regression on the part of the patient, the development of a transference neurosis, and serious countertransference problems. In imitation of the psychoanalytic model, these youngsters called for and encouraged the recounting of dreams which they could not understand or interpret. Lack of understanding forced them to defend themselves against anxieties stimulated by communications from their patients and by frustrations of their failures to understand or to make progress, thereby further handicapping their therapeutic effectiveness. They tried to imitate the analytic imperturbability, but instead only achieved attitudes of coldness and "objectivity," concentrating entirely on the content of the patient's productions. Some of them, without attempting to understand the patient's needs of the moment, developed the notions of furnishing a "corrective emotional experience" by playing artificial roles, which were easily penetrated as play-acting by anyone with a modicum of intelligence.

Even though many of these students were but shortly out of their internships, they very quickly and easily forgot their roles as doctors whose goals are to help their patients. They lost the human capacity of helping patients in serious life situations when these required temporarily stepping out of the therapeutic chamber. I was confronted by quotations from supervisors who were involved in the students' other cases and learned how many considered the psychotherapeutic process to be almost identical with psychoanalysis. I have never ceased to marvel at how quickly the seed of the psychoanalytic model sprouts and how difficult it is to uproot it once it had gained a footing. (27:134)

Very few of the mistrained students were able to liberate themselves from the model imposed on them early in their education. Parlour was one of them. "Finally, about 1960," he says, "my impatience with what I was doing and my self-confidence simultaneously reached a point where I increasingly disregarded psychoanalysis and began a search for some other meaningful approaches." (32:1) He developed treatment teams, consisting not only of professionals but also of members of the patient's family, ministers, and neighbors. The treatment is active, confronting the patient with his behavioral inconsistencies and creating contracts to be followed by everyone involved. They work on the real-life situation, instead of being guided by theoretical precepts and therapeutic fictions.

There is almost a built-in ineffectiveness in Freudian psychotherapy because of the belief that the healing process has to be slow and extremely long. Jacobson is scandalized by the ineffectiveness and unscrupulousness of some Freudian healers:

> ... Patients often go to analysts for many years—perhaps an hour daily on six days per week—failing to attain results satisfactory even to the analyst. I know of such costly futility in cases so treated as long as seventeen years! The patient as if hypnotized continues too impressed to break away from the futile treatment. Addiction becomes profound. (33:43)

Forty years ago, Jastrow wrote critically of this:

> ... the simple talking cure of Breuer which, however, has grown into months and years of rating and magnifying the simplest incidents to a fictitious significance.
>
> The protracted analysis, which has become the support in more than one sense of the analytic profession, is a cultist contribution. By what revelation has it been determined that the analysis must consume months and even years of confabulation and the payment of fees by the hour? Naturally this procedure raises a suspicion whether science is so generously favorable to revenue. But as I write, I am informed that in the Viennese citadel of psychoanalysis, curtailed periods of analysis have been sanctioned in deference to the prevalent [economic] depression. Science is not as inconsiderate in its demands as it is rated. (6:252)

A recent report (62) from Britain illustrates the wasteful practices of Freudian psychiatrists. The wife of a physician describes the travails she had to go through in seeking treatment for her adolescent schizophrenic son. The years of psychoanalysis did not alleviate her son's condition, yet the typical Freudian interpretations of the supposed role parents have in the serious mental illness of their offspring only aggravated her agony.

An American counterpart of this British tragedy is the travail of James A. Wechsler, editor of the New York *Post,* and his family. Their mentally ill son killed himself at the age of twenty-six after unsuccessful treatments with eight psychiatrists for nine years. The parents wrote their account as a memorial to him. The reviewer of the book sees it as a monument to " 'professional' intimidation and iatrogenic effects of conventional psychiatry's darkness." (57:3) Inasmuch as American psychiatry, particularly in the East, is thoroughly Freudianized, the criticism is pertinent to the thesis of this volume—that psychoanalytic therapy is mostly a hoax.

The reviewer, Mendelssohn, disagrees with Dr. Karl Menninger's whitewashing the outrage by expressing the hope that the book would provide "comfort" to others who had to go through a similar agony. "On the contrary," exclaims Mendelssohn,

> . . . sharing the atrocity story of Michael's treatment (or mistreatment) by eight of the "best" therapists that money could buy, at five of the "best" psychiatric facilities in the East, is less likely to comfort than to arouse fear, despair, and—hopefully—the public outrage necessary for meaningful change in conventional psychiatric practice.
>
> While Mr. Wechsler acknowledges that Michael's illness was not created by the therapists, it would be difficult to ignore the implication that a nine-year series of conflicting theories and techniques may in fact have contributed to Michael's ultimate deterioration: "Sometimes, as in the Thorazine treatment . . . , he was required to defraud the doctors in trying to save himself from becoming a 'vegetable.' By the time he had reached Dr. Eighth, he was once again being subjected to the Freudian rituals that Dr. Seventh had so plainly, and with at least temporary success, ruled out as a futile round of reverie and recrimination."
>
> Berating himself for losing confidence in his capacity to intervene in the treatment process and being awed by "psychiatric dogma that too often proved irrelevant or inconsistent," Wechsler retains a remarkable degree of respect for the practitioners he encountered, notwithstanding their isolation and

mystification of him and other family members. We can agree here with Dr. Menninger (in a letter to Wechsler) that "it's a wonder to me that you have any tolerance left for doctors at all (or any money)." (57:3)

6. *In support of non-Freudian treatment*

Considering psychoanalytic inefficacy, no wonder a woman psychologist, perplexed with anxiety over a program she set up in a commercial company, would tell Ellis after she experienced the Rational-Emotive Method: "I think I've learned more in these three sessions with you than I did in my four whole years of analysis." (7:167) In his article in *Direct Psychotherapy: Twenty-eight American Originals*, Ellis (11) has described another case treated in twenty-nine sessions, after four and a half years spent in psychoanalysis without a resolution of the problems.

Other therapists, contributors to *Direct Psychotherapy* also, discuss the futility of Freudian ritual. The cases of the little boy, Aaron, and of the V.A. hospital patient, Roy, and others described by Glasser (12) amply illustrate the failure of a passive, psychoanalytically based, uninvolved role for the therapist.

To the colleague who consulted her on the case of the passive-aggressive, possibly paranoid, nun, Anderson (13:286, 287) suggests that he was not treating her, *i.e.,* moving her toward solution of her problems, but was merely being used to gratify an immature woman's need for attention. Anderson would rather concentrate on "what needs to be done" than on the patient's hurt feelings. Otherwise the therapist degenerates into a baby-sitter.

Discussing the prevalent emasculation and self-seeking nature of our culture, King (14) disputes Freudian concepts of therapy: "We are concerned with solving problems, not learning how to live with them."

Mowrer (15) recommends a deemphasis on emotions in therapy and a stress on actual behavior. He warns against making the patient complacent and comfortable, instead of leading him to better behavior. Mowrer's *Morality and Mental Health* (16) also contains several articles making a similar psychotherapeutic emphasis.

Storrow (17) tries to turn his patient's fixation from self-pity to an active struggle with his problems, to bring him to a realization that his own behavior is causing his difficulties.

Patients are likely to respond better to active, direct therapy by showing more improvement and by responding with satisfaction to the therapist's practical help. Sometimes patients even indicate a desire for such help. A patient of mine, an excitable, hypomanic, twenty-year-old man, was seen in both group and in individual interviews. As usual, I was passive in the first few interviews, trying to obtain an undistorted impression of what the patient was like when not involved in active interaction with the therapist. The patient was uneasy, wondering loudly why I responded so little to his excited talk: "Are you angry with me? You seem gloomy. I have a feeling you do not like me." Apparently he was trying to encourage the therapist to handle him in the ways he sensed would be helpful in changing his personality reactions. Throughout this passive phase of treatment, the patient remained fidgety, apprehensive, and tremulous, with such unsteady ego control that he evoked several laughing comments in group sessions due to his inappropriate reactions.

I began to point out his nonsensical precipitousness in talk and behavior, and to suggest reactions that could be more useful to him. I also explained how he was passively opposing his work supervisor, as he had his overbearing father. The implication was: I expect you to fight your established reactions, to stop exciting yourself over imaginary threats, to stop maltreating yourself by these unstable reactions. He calmed down considerably, and became more active in bringing his difficulties into the open in individual sessions. He assumed a more assertive role in the group therapy. He continued in treatment for about three months. In one of his last few interviews, he said: "I went for a year to that psychoanalyst, or whatever he was. He let me talk. It was good. I had a chance to solve my problems, but it did not take me far. I stayed the way I was, except I knew more about it. Here I find each session leaves me with a challenge, something I have to try to do. This is a better and faster way." Reflecting upon this treatment, I feel that the most important ingredient of it was my implied and indirectly conveyed attitude that he can and must take an active stand toward his symptoms. The passive therapists play into the hands of neurotic fatalism—the conviction that the patients are victims of psychological misdevelopments—and cannot but be prey to such neurotic fate—, as inexorable growth of traumas is a firmly embedded notion of the Freudian model of psychopathology; thus, they unwittingly reinforce the patient's neurosis.

The failure of many patients to progress through passive therapy has been remarked upon, even by Freudians. Menninger, himself a Freudian analyst, seems to agree with "the accusations of unsympathetic outsiders who allege that what certain patients want is not cure but treatment and that what some psychoanalysts want to do is to treat rather than to cure." (18:110) Lou Andreas-Salomé, had a chance to observe early psychoanalysts in Vienna. She notes about one of them, Sadger: "He presumably enjoys his analysands more than he helps them or learns anything from them." (34:41) Frankl (28:54) tells of a case which certainly justifies such an indictment. When a patient, who had been "treated" for six years six times a week, wanted to interrupt such futile "therapy," her psychoanalyst protested that the analysis had only begun!

One of the hazards of Freudian psychoanalysis is that its passivity often carries over into life, making many patients languid and disorganized. The early observers of Mesmer's treatment noted that convulsions induced in hypnotic trance were continued by patients as a learned behavior long after the treatment was over. Freudian treatment trains the patient in the passive submission to irrational, illogical processes in the hope of learning what is supposedly in the psychic depths and early memories of the patients; it induces a pernicious state of abulia, a lack of will or direction, so that the patients have to be treated for years for psychoanalytically induced personality ailment. Jones strongly objected to this abuse and misdirection of patients in suggestive hypnotic treatment, Freudian analysis being only a clandestine subvariety of it, as we shall see later:

> ... suggestion develops automatic and subconscious activity, and diminishes the last voluntary efforts. This indifference, this renunciation of all personal control is most dangerous, and increases in no small measure the fundamental abulia of these patients. In a word, suggestion, like all dangerous drugs, is useful in certain cases ... but outside of this it is extremely harmful, for it can only increase the mental disaggregation, the underlying cause of all the accidents. (35:249, 250)

The Freudians have been allowed too long to use their "dangerous drug" on their patients, under the protection of medical immunity. In the atmosphere of ethical indifference ("neutrality") which they have helped create in social sciences, they discredit the traditional human values which in the not so distant past used to undergird the moral stamina of everyone, scientists and nonscientists alike, and are still a source of strength to those unaffected by naturalistic preconceptions. Even the "scientific" moral relativists cannot deny that an efficient coping with life, the "strength of will," is superior to a languorous, abulic, or hedonistic existence, induced through Freudian ideology and practice.

In *Freud's Phallic Cult: A Pseudoreligion posing as superior psychology* (36: ch. VI, "Pathogenic emanations of Freudism") I have described the "unsavory fruits of Freudian idolatry," not the least of which is the high rate of suicides of the generation of American psychiatrists indoctrinated and sickened by psychoanalysis. In his *The Doctor and the Soul* (29) Frankl reports from Freud's native Vienna a number of clinical observations of destructiveness to patients of Freudian preconceptions regarding psychotherapy. A number of American writers have published their conclusions about the detrimental consequences that the obsession with the Freudian model of psychotherapy had upon treatment both in private settings and the American mental hospitals. Only with the waning of psychoanalytic dominance have more effective methods of treatment been applied. (Some of these writers will be quoted later in this and the following chapters.) As to the institutional treatment, Treffert (31) reviewed the annual reports of state hospitals and found that little progress was made: the reports of a hundred years ago mention the same unsolved problems as those of today. The lack of results of fifty years of Freudian enlightenment imposed on American psychiatry and psychology, seems to point to another aspect of the psychoanalytic hoax.

Storrow, having in mind the therapeutic disinterestedness of many Freudians and their fellow travelers, urges therapists to throw off their "scientific" apathy and engage themselves in problem-solving with the patients:

"The great end of life," said Thomas Henry Huxley, "is not knowledge but action." No group of professionals forget this

91

more often than psychotherapists. We prattle about insight, introjections and instincts. Stumbling along in a fog of words we lose sight of the reasons patients come to see us. A man calls for an appointment because he can't hold a job; a teen-age boy shows up at the office because he has just run afoul of the law; an elderly spinster appears accompanied by a friend because leaving home alone terrifies her. Our job is to help these and other patients change behavior patterns that are causing trouble for them and often for others as well.

Theories and techniques are secondary. Any ethical approach that yields lasting results merits our attention whether or not it fits a favorite set of assumptions. As intellectuals we are perfectly free to enjoy the stimulating luxuries of speculation; as therapists we must look for results. (19:76)

Müller-Hegemann, professor of psychiatry from Berlin, East Germany, reports on deleterious effects of Freudian treatment on a patient in the contemporary European culture. He starts with considering "the problem of prolonged psychotherapy." He suspects that "prolonged psychotherapy might cause iatrogenic [caused by the healer] harm to the patients." (38:233) He points to the shorter methods developed by Stekel, Horney, Sullivan, and Fromm, as more therapeutically efficacious. (A reading of numerous case histories reported by Stekel leaves a clear impression that he was a far more effective and flexible clinician than Freud.)

The patient was a young Frenchwoman suffering from severe depressions, suicidal preoccupations, and a personality deterioration bordering on psychosis. Two years before she came in touch with Müller-Hegemann she had been made worse by the orthodox Freudian analysis. The short description of her treatment would sound technically comical to an experienced therapist, if it did not involve the sickening of a person through Freudian rituals. The analyst had apparently been trained in awe of Freud's own method and applied it confidently and insistently, as she had no doubt that she was practicing the most beneficial method of healing a neurotic. The victim reported on the senseless psychological torture imposed upon her:

That analyst had treated her with some interruptions for 18 months, mostly six times a week for one-hour sessions. She

92

described the analysis as "terrible," because she longed to get advice but was always told that she ought to give way to her associations, as new strength would emerge from the subconscious. As she responded progressively less during the analysis, the analyst questioned her concerning all details of her sexual experiences and asked her also to report all associations relating to them. All her remarks had been given a sexual interpretation and all her complaints had been related to her immature sexual development. For this reason she had had several affairs, with the result that she became progressively anxious and rigid during attempts at sexual intercourse which she thus had never experienced in a normal way. Her relations to . . . [her lover] had also been broken off in the course of this kind of existence. Subsequently she felt completely incompetent and lonely.

Two years prior to my seeing the patient, the suicidal preoccupation had increased, especially when she looked at an open window (her aunt had thrown herself out of a window) or in the subway where she had the urge to throw herself under a train. Thereupon she had urged the analyst to give her real help. The analyst had interpreted the open window which played a great role in the patient's fantasies, as the "introitus vaginae" and had advised her to submit completely to her associations and experiences of anxiety. Subsequently the patient's condition had become so intolerable that she had cut her wrists; this had occurred about 20 months before the onset of our therapy. She was admitted to a psychiatric hospital in Paris where she was treated with insulin and drugs. After three months her condition had improved to such an extent that she could be discharged. However, she was still desperate and lonely. She then decided to go abroad and came to Leipzig to continue her studies. (38:236-237)

Müller-Hegemann had no doubt that her neurosis was "exacerbated by the period of psychoanalysis she had undergone." The patient herself knew that too and dreaded that her new therapist would torture her further through Freudian procedures. "The reassurance, in answer to her repeated questions, that no psychoanalysis would be carried out calmed the patient." (38:237) She was helped by what Müller-Hegemann calls "rational therapy," a combination of several direct psychotherapy methods including autogenic training, hypnosis, reassurance, wakeful suggestion, problem-solving, therapeutic tasks, and guidance. "On the basis of these reports her tendency to expect failure was discussed during every session; likewise, her small successes were discussed and she was given detailed advice on how to improve her performance." (38:239) Instead of misdirecting the patient's attention to the supposed faults of her parents, and real or imagined maltreatments by them, Müller-Hegemann avoided that favorite Freudian stratagem, and led the patient to appreciation of her deserving mother, liberating her in that way from misperceptions about her childhood, which were liberally encouraged by her former Freudian healer. Her new therapist was successful in leading her out of the morass of her own maldevelopments and those induced by psychoanalytic ceremonials, precisely because he was free of Freudian blindspots. Müller-Hegemann disregarded Freud's dictum "that no secret of neurosis can be solved by efforts of will or of attention, but only by patiently following the rule of psychoanalysis which dictates the elimination of criticism against the subconscious and its derivatives," (38:242) and was able to help his patient. According to Freud's formula, he acted untherapeutically, using the "efforts of will or of attention," and dealing only peripherally with the "subconscious." Yet, the outcomes were therapeutic. His report demonstrates that Freud's prescriptions are not sacrosanct, as they are considered by many well-freudwashed American psychotherapists, and that Freud's principles have only a limited application. And all this was achieved in less than thirty sessions, contrasted with hundreds of hours wasted in Freudian exorcism.

In view of the psychotherapeutic futility of psychoanalysis with many patients, it is hard to understand how a clinical professor of psychiatry could publish a statement in 1972: "Psychoanalytic psychotherapy ... is ... a very effective form of treatment." (44:37) As if to reflect the confusion in the Freudian camp, another contributor to the same volume begins his paper by admitting: "In the research literature ... one finds a growing disenchantment with psychoanalysis and psychotherapy based on psychoanalytic principles. The arguments have essentially followed this pattern: ... psychoanalytic psychotherapy in general and orthodox psychoanalysis in particular are hopelessly inefficient methods ... " (45:71)

7. *Pfister failed to teach Freud*

Fifty years ago, Pastor Pfister drew Freud's attention to the advantages of active participation by the therapist. Apparently Pfister had combined psychoanalytic ideas with the common sense of pastoral counseling and was obtaining better results than the passive orthodox analysts. He refers to what Freud had called "the unsolved problem of therapy;" to put it less euphemistically, the therapeutic failure of psychoanalysis. In their private correspondence, Pfister might have been less guarded, and Freud perhaps less defensive and freer to consider views other than his own; however, he was already convinced about his superiority as therapist, and he could not absorb the validity of pastor's better method.

Pfister tells Freud that "F. gained no lasting help from analysis in Vienna. He describes that therapeutic success as minimal...." (20:111) F. was apparently an intelligent individual, grasping that all he got from numerous sessions was, as he called it, "theory"—*i.e.* coaching in how to think in Freudian idiom. Pfister brings another case to Freud's attention to indicate the therapeutic futility of the Master's method. He tells of an unintended experiment in which the patient served, so to speak, as his own control: he was first treated with no improvement by an approved Viennese analyst; then he was treated in an unorthodox way by Pfister and obtained durable relief from his migraine headaches. Pfister's method was apparently a melange of what would today be called relationship therapy, rational counseling, friendly support, and smatterings of Freudian preconceptions, too diluted to do much harm to the patient.

The patient in question was Harold Schjelderup, a professor of philosophy and psychology, whom Pfister considers "brilliant." He had written the first Freudian-permeated textbook in his native Norwegian, a translation of which (in German) was to be published that year. The poor professor labored on the psychoanalytic couch for seven months. The only result—"his agonizing weekly migraines grew worse and worse." (20:111) (Freud could not have been surprised as he had suffered from the same ailment, psychoanalytic illumination notwithstanding.)

Schjelderup interrupted the useless ordeal as he had to return to Oslo. Then, that summer, he came to Pastor Pfister.

We analyzed hard, and the last, much milder, attack took place after a fortnight. After that we went on analyzing for about another three months, but the originally violent pathogenic repressions made no further appearance, and after three weeks we broke off. Then, without our doing any more analysis, after the Locarno congress he accompanied me to Zermatt. Since the beginning of July the migraines have disappeared completely. (20:111)

No wonder that the patient's attitude to his former (orthodox) analyst was "predominantly negative." He wrote a grateful letter to Pfister about the great difference between the two ways of analyzing. In this indirect way Pfister tried to show Freud the weakness of his approach: passivity; impersonal, "humiliating" relationship to the patient; fragmenting of patient's life experiences and leaving him stranded in the "therapeutically" created shambles, instead of integrating him into wider and deeper aspects of life as a whole, of existential wisdom. In Schjelderup's words (to Pfister):

The whole nature of your analysis is much more active and effective. There was something unsatisfactory about the whole analysis in Vienna, and something humiliating to one's ego feeling as well. When an unpleasing instinctual impulse or infantile wish appeared, I was left with no idea what to do with it; the fact was simply noted. But you laid emphasis on your own attitude and on its connections with the whole. It seems to me that only if that is done can inappropriate attitudes be really disposed of. Thereby the humiliating element in the situation largely disappears, and a healthy transference is made possible. . . . I have the definite impression that the short time I spent with you was of much more practical value than the seven months' analysis in Vienna. The migraine has gone—I hope for ever." (20:111)

Pfister describes to Freud the way he works with his analysands and how he avoids the disadvantages of too strong a transference (dependence). The major difference lies in not regressing the patient toward irrationality, helplessness, artificially heightened abnormality, but rather establishing a measure of human involvement. Pastor Pfister, coming out of a religious orientation to reality, apparently knew more about "psychodynamics" than the founder of it, and he introduced traditional values to counterbalance the sickening process: "... according to my observations, it is also important that the analyst should transmit values which over-compensate for the patient's gain from illness or guilt feelings." (20:112) Freud had no viable values to transmit and had no alternative to leaving his patients in a moral lurch.

Pfister also understood where the strength of his approach was and the corresponding weakness of Freud's: "... I do not completely break the link with the patient, but only *cleanse the transference of all unreality.*" (20:112, emphasis added)

Pfister also reveals what saved him from becoming a futile orthodox analyst: "... my being always ready to be of assistance in making use of every kind of human value in regard to which the patient is not always able to help himself, because that is my duty as an educator and a minister..." (20:112)

The therapeutic superiority of Pfister to orthodox analysts lies in his not fostering "transference" to pathological intensity. Maybe he could afford to do that as he did not have to earn his living by tying the patient to himself in irrational ways conducive to extended payment of fees. He describes the healthy allegiance of the patient to himself without the regressive submission imposed by Freud:

> With the exception of a few cases which ended unsatisfactorily, I have never experienced dependence or lasting overaffection on the part of my patients, but only a certain attitude of gratitude and liking, which seems to me healthier and more natural than just a cold leave-taking from a person to whom, after all, one has so much to be grateful for. After all, behind the personal relations springing from the transference in the narrower sense for which there is no justification in reality, there must be real relations based on the real characteristics of the two persons concerned. Should the attitude to the analyst not be a pattern for what it should to other people. (20:112)

All this sensible demonstration of better therapeutic methods made little impression on Freud. Having established an impersonal and infantilizing way of working with the patient, on the basis of his own unloving, inhibited personality, he does not disapprove, but fails to see the therapeutic advantage of a decent human relationship. He writes to Pfister:

> On the question of therapeutic technique I must express myself plainly. You as a minister naturally have the right to call on all the reinforcements at your command, while we as analysts must be more reserved, and must lay the chief accent on the effort to make the patient independent, which often works out to the disadvantage of the therapy. (20:113)

Apparently Freud is impervious to the positive experiences of other therapists with their patients. He assumes the role of a superior therapist who can be taught little by other lesser healers, mistaking his own personality predicaments, which made him act detached, for undoubted therapeutic axioms. Like the absolutistic ruler Louis XIV, to whom the saying *L'état, c'est moi* (I am the state) is attributed, Freud assumes here the attitude "I am psychotherapy." He does not even care to think consistently in answering Pfister. As we shall see in other instances, he asserts an obvious untruth at the end of the above quote, and supposedly dismisses Pfister's psychotherapeutic wisdom with it. Freud says that he acts aloof with patients to make them "independent." The fact known to any observer of psychoanalysis is that the therapist's lack of real involvement with the patient leads to a regular pathological dependence on the analyst ("transference").

8. *Putting a lid on the id*

Post proposes to "put a lid on the id" as a useful counter-therapy for patients who have been overtreated and regressed in Freudian therapies. This is done by deliberate neglect of the pathological verbalizations of feelings, and concentrating instead on healthy interests and goals and by focusing on the tasks presently facing the patient. These are corrective measures to counter Freudian obsessive delving in unconscious, immature, and irrational elements which only tends to sicken the patient further.

Post describes a woman of thirty-four who had been previously "treated" for eight years by five therapists (three of whom were in training at that time). She came to the hospital trying to be admitted on an emergency basis. She had evidently been well brainwashed regarding the current "psychoanalytically oriented" fads, apparent from her own report: "I have no sense of identity because my mother has always considered me an extension of herself.... because of crucial events at the age of three I want to go to bed with my father and kill my mother." She had difficulties "establishing meaningful heterosexual relationships." One of the previous therapists told her she had "an oral fixation." She showed she had absorbed the lesson: "I have discovered that my sexuality has been transferred from the appropriate place to my mouth. I learned that when I developed positive feelings for my therapist and told him 'I could eat you up.'" (21:475)

In spite of such advanced indoctrination she could not concentrate on current difficulties, and always returned to some experiences of her childhood, like "sibling rivalry." She "was so busy talking about the past that she could not consider the present nor the future." (21:480) The therapist helped her deal with current problems, and acted like a "village idiot" when she reverted to her Freudian jargon.

Another patient whom Post tried to extricate from the cobwebs of Freudian practices was a twenty-three-year-old man who had spent six years in a psychoanalytically oriented private hospital. The referral note said that he felt very worried about his homosexual tendencies and his sexual desires for his mother. Apparently he was made into the proper model of psychopathology so that he could be at length duly cured of it. He was also steeped in the Freudian psycho-mythological categories. (We shall see later that part of the Freudian cure is to brainwash the patient into acceptance of the superstitions of his therapist.)

It was implicit, and the patient later confirmed this, that the therapist not only had not attempted to help the patient suppress these feelings, but had encouraged their elaboration. The patient later complained that the doctor seemed only to be interested in sex and didn't seem very interested when he spoke about work. (21:478)

The patient spoke blandly of masturbation as one of his recreational pursuits, and of various colors and shapes of breasts. When the new therapist asked why he spoke this way, he explained: "Aren't you supposed to say anything that comes to your mind?"

The therapist corrected the patient's Freudian misdirection and instructed the nurses in the dayroom not to respond to his talk about homosexuality, but to show an interest in his future plans for employment and readjustment.

Post points to the ego deterioration in these patients which had passed for therapy. They were "so caught up in free associating that they were unable to consider current difficulties, speaking and behaving as if the normal censorship processes were no longer effective." (21:480) Because of the blind spots imposed on therapists by Freudian theory, "an overtreated patient can be extremely seductive in leading a therapist down the garden path of primary process." (21:480) Post wanted to stop such therapeutic nonsense.

I still vividly remember my first encounter with Freudian oddities in handling a patient, even though it happened fifteen years ago. While serving as a psychological intern at a psychiatric ward of a general hospital, I attended a staff meeting with psychiatric trainees, nurses and the head psychiatrist. I absorbed with awe anything the official authorities had to say, as I was without previous experience in a mental hospital. Even so, the head psychiatrist offered a warning on this occasion that sounded somehow unbelievable and devoid of sensibleness. He admonished the psychiatrists in training to prevent the sort of terrible psychotherapeutic mishandling that had occurred with a patient that morning.

A psychiatric aide had been accompanying a young schizophrenic male to another ward for medical examination, when the patient suddenly developed an urge to masturbate. The aide would not tolerate it and ordered the patient to stop. The patient obeyed, but became so disturbed that the aide was reprimanded for his non-therapeutic behavior. Other staff members nodded in deep understanding of how wrong it is to interfere with the sovereign sexual urge. I felt confused, unsure how to take the profound revelation of the Freudian psychiatric principles. I wondered who was really crazy in this situation, but I suppressed the blasphemous thought.

Now, after years of study and observation, I know that my suppressed insight was correct. Psychiatrists of Reality Therapy or of various behavior therapies would praise that psychiatric aide and look scornfully upon the stereotyped Freudian reaction of that head psychiatrist.

The examples of Freudian irrationalities and the resulting misguidance of patients reviewed here contain one element in common: the patient's interests are not promoted, and may even be harmed by the application of Freudian doctrines and precepts. The products of Freudian treatment leave the impression that original psychopathologies have only been supplanted by Freudian ones.

It should be of concern to the medical profession as well as the general public to ask whether it makes sense to allow the Freudians to supplant a patient's real maladaptive pattern with a pathological model of their own. Distracting the patient by transforming his actual psychopathology into a Freudian one might produce some changes, even some improvement; but it is questionable whether replacing one maladjustment with another can be considered a cure at any time. In the past doctors have abandoned medical treatments with undesirable side effects: quicksilver, arsenic, lobotomy, etc. When will they discard Freudian superstitions?

9. *Freudian travesty of psychotherapy*

In concluding this section on Freudian abuses and misdirection of treatment, Ellis' (22) summary of the harmfulness of psychoanalysis is appropriate.

> Probably the greatest harm that psychoanalysis does is its tendency to sidetrack patients from what they have to do to get better and to give them a "good" excuse not to work hard at curing themselves. . . .
>
> Psychoanalysis sidetracks the health-seeking individual verbally by encouraging him to concentrate on innumerable irrelevant events and ideas: such as what happened during his early years, how he came to have an Oedipus complex, the pernicious influence of his unloving parents, what are the meanings of his dreams, how all-important are his relations with the analyst, how much he now unconsciously hates his wife, etc. These may all be interesting pieces of information about him; but they not only do not reveal, they often seriously obscure, his simple basic irrational philosophies that originally caused, and that still instigate, his aberrated feelings and behavior. Being mainly

diagnostic and psychodynamic, analysis is practically allergic to philosophy, and therefore often never gets around to the basic ideological assumptions and value systems with which humans create their symptoms.

To make matters much worse, psychoanalysis is essentially a talky, passive, insight-seeking process which encourages the patient merely to lie on his spine or sit on his behind in order to get better. . . . The poor analysand, who probably has remained disturbed for most of his life largely because he will not get off his ass and take risk after risk, is firmly encouraged, by the analytic procedure and by the nauseatingly nondirective behavior of the analyst himself, to continue his avoidant behavior. He now, moreover, has the excuse that he is "actively" trying to help himself by being analyzed; but this, of course, is a delusion if anything like classical procedures are being followed; and he consequently tends to become more passive, and hence more sick, than ever.

Most patients are overly-dependent individuals who are afraid to think and act for themselves and to risk being criticized for making mistakes. Psychoanalysis is usually a process which greatly fosters dependency. . . .

Because it heavily emphasizes free association, dream analysis, and the involvement of the patient and therapist in transference and counter-transference relations, psychoanalysis inevitably puts a premium on the expression of feelings rather than the undermining of neurotic and psychotic ideas. This tendency of the patient to "feel better," however, frequently sabotages his potentiality to "get better." . . .

In the expression of hostility that psychoanalysis encourages, the situation is even worse. Starting with the assumption that it is bad for the patient to feel hostile and to hold in his hostile feelings—which is a fairly sensible assumption, since there is empirical evidence to support it—psychoanalysts usually derive from this view another, and rather false, assumption: that the expression of hostile feelings will release and cure basic hostility. Nothing of the sort is probably true; in fact, just the opposite frequently happens. The individual who, in analytic sessions, is encouraged to express his hatred for his mother, wife, or boss may well end up by becoming still more hostile, acting in an overtly nasty fashion to this other person, engendering return hostility, then becoming still more irate, etc.

Expression of hostility, moreover, is one of the best psychological cop-outs. By convincing himself that other people are awful and that they deserve to be hated, the patient can easily ignore his own maladaptive behavior and his self-loathing and can nicely avoid doing anything to look into his own heart and to change his irrational thinking and his disordered acts. One of the main functions of an effective therapist, moreover, is to help the patient minimize or eliminate his hostility. . . . By (a) failing to show the patient how to change his anger-creating views and by (b) encouraging him to become more hostile in many instances, it seriously harms probably the majority of analytic patients (or should we say victims?).

The analyst himself, rigidly-bound as he usually is by the orthodox rules of the therapeutic game he is playing, and self-condemned by following these rules to be a non-assertive, undaring individual himself, tends to set a bad example for the patient and to encourage him to be a reactor rather than an actor in the drama which we call life. . . .

Instead of helping the patient with this kind of cognitive, semantic and logical analysis, psychoanalysis provides him with many unverified premises and irrationalities of its own. It usually insists that he must be disturbed because of past events in his life, that he does have the need to be loved and to become angry when thwarted, that Oedipal feelings and other sexual confusions are at the bottom of his nonsexual problems, that he has to have years of intensive analysis in order to change himself significantly, that he must get into and finally work through an intense transference relationship with his analyst, etc. All these assumptions—as is the case with most psychoanalytic hypotheses —are either dubious or false; and the analysand is given additional irrationalities to cope with over and above his handicapping crooked thinking with which he comes to therapy. In innumerable instances, he becomes so obsessed with the analytic *mishigas* that it becomes his religious creed and his be-all and end-all for existing; and though it may somewhat divert him from the nonsense with which he first came to therapy, it does not really eliminate it but at best covers it up with this new psychoanalytic mode of "positive thinking." Rather than, through analysis, becoming less suggestible and more of a critical thinker he very frequently becomes worse in these respects. . . .

To make matters much worse, analytic therapy leads in most instances to such abysmally poor results that the patient is highly discouraged, is convinced that practically all the time and money he spent for analysis is wasted, that there is no possibility of his ever changing any longer, and that he'd better avoid all other types of psychotherapy for the rest of his life and adjust himself, as best he may, to living with his disturbances. An untold number of ex-analysands have been utterly disillusioned with all psychological treatment because they wrongly believe that psychoanalysis is psychotherapy, and that if they received such poor results from being analyzed nothing else could possibly work for them. If the true facts in this regard could ever be known, it is likely to be found that analysis harms more people in this way than in any of the other many ways in which it is deleterious. Just the number of people in this country who feel that they cannot afford any more therapy because they fruitlessly spent many thousands of dollars in psychoanalysis is probably considerable. . . .

Human beings—in contradistinction to the analytic assumptions—do not basically modify their thoughts and behavior by insight into their past, by relating to a therapist, or even by understanding their present irrational assumptions and conflicting value systems. They change mainly by work and effort. They consequently have to be helped to use their insights . . .

Even if it were a good method of psychological analysis (which it actually is not), it is an execrable method of synthesis. It does not notably help the individual make himself whole again; and it particularly does not show him how to live more happily when he has to some degree stopped needlessly bothering himself. Because it implicitly and explicitly encourages him to remain pretty much the way he is, though perhaps to get a better understanding of himself (and often to construct better defenses so that he can live more efficiently with his irrational assumptions about himself and others), it frequently does more harm, by stopping him from really making a concerted attack on his fundamental problems, than the good that well might come to him if he received a non-analytic form of psychotherapy or even if

104

he resolutely tried to help himself by reading, talking to others, and by doing some hard thinking for himself.

Psychoanalysis in general and classical analysis in particular are fundamentally wrong in their assumptions about why human beings become emotionally disturbed and what can and should be done to help them become less anxious and hostile. Consequently, analytic therapy largely wastes considerable time teaching the patient mistaken theories about himself and others, which happen to be highly diverting and diversional, and which consequently at best help him to feel better rather than to get better.... Although ostensibly an intensive and ultradepth centered form of psychotherapy, analysis is actually an exceptionally superficial, palliative form of treatment. Because it deludes the patient that he is truly getting better by following its rules and because it dissuades him from doing the simple but difficult reorganizing of his underlying philosophic assumptions that he has to do to radically modify his thinking and his behavior, psychoanalysis usually (though of course not always) does more harm than good and is contraindicated in the great majority of instances in which it is actually used. (22:16-24)

This verdict of psychoanalysis as worthless or harmful procedure is not only an American observation. Many European psychiatrists have voiced negative opinions of Freudian "therapy." A prominent British psychoanalyst, who is a writer in many psychiatric periodicals and handbooks, resigned lately from two psychoanalytic associations because she did not intend to disregard any longer the antimedical effects of Freudian method:

In a letter published recently in the *British Journal of Psychiatry,* Dr. Melita Schmideberg of London claimed that "the psychoanalytic situation is an abnormal one, and necessarily abnormalizes." She said that analysts "aim at breaking down the personality, hoping it will afterwards build itself up again in a more satisfactory manner." She asked: "But does it?"

Dr. Schmideberg contended that "the constant dwelling on painful pathological and irrational aspects, the minimizing of and undermining of rational thinking and objective achievement, the attacks on social values, and the isolating of the patient from

105

ordinary people can only be harmful and warp the personality. . . .

"I myself have been connected with psychoanalysis for the greater part of my life. I have been a practising analyst for many years, and I was a member of the British Psycho-Analytic Association until I resigned. I have treated many failures of psychoanalysis, and I have gradually dissociated myself from psychoanalysis because I have come to the conclusion that it is harmful both for the patient and the analyst." (57:3)

10. *Irresponsible diagnosticians*

The misdirection of treatment and misdiagnosing of the patient's pathology may sometimes have grave consequences in the lives of defenseless patients, as illustrated by the case of a young airman sent to me for an interview regarding his alleged homosexuality. He denied any homosexual contacts and interests. He had been "going steady" with a girl for two years, had enjoyed sexual intercourse with her, and was planning to marry her on his next leave.

I could uncover no significant psychological abnormalities in him, although he did not seem to hold back information. He had been a student of engineering for three years. He had done well at first, but had neglected his studies in his last year to engage in excessive partying, so faced being drafted as a failing student. He had had no wish to carry a gun in Viet Nam, so he had enlisted in the Air Force where he would have the opportunity to use his technical knowledge. He had done well in electronics training, and had no serious difficulties with military discipline. He enjoyed the city and the mountain country surrounding it. He had a girl friend here, enjoyed having a good time with her, but liked the "steady" girl at home better. He expected to finish the technical school in two weeks and looked forward to his assignment to a Texas base. All this was brought into jeopardy by his psychiatrist's allegation in his records that the young fellow was a homosexual. Any intimation of homosexuality is taken quite seriously by the military, particularly for those serving in highly sensitive technical areas. If the charge of homosexuality were sustained, the airman would be released with an undesirable discharge, a permanent handicap in obtaining responsible positions later in life.

How did the charge of homosexuality arise? The young fellow was puzzled about the psychiatrist's statement. He had gone to him to obtain a certificate about his inability to study at that time because of alleged emotional trouble, to avoid a failing grade and obtain an "incomplete" instead. The psychiatrist had fished for personality weaknesses. The airman denied that homosexuality had been mentioned in that interview. The only odd behavior he remembered having mentioned was that when he was sixteen, four years earlier, he had not been able to stand for anyone to grab him by the neck from behind and squeeze it. Apparently this was enough for the psychiatrist, brainwashed in the Freudian tradition, to make the usual diagnostic jump to the favorite sexual aberration. He had apparently not read a psychoanalytic study of homosexuality (30) which considers Freud's concept of bisexuality, (the ground doctrine for readily imputing homosexuality to everyone) as erroneous both biologically and psychologically. Certain that he was following in Freud's footsteps, the doctor's mind was not conditioned to seek other explanations of the boy's peculiarity. He did not consider that the patient was rather small and might not do well in horsing around with bigger fellows. The doctor disregarded another possible explanation, that his patient was intellectually oriented and somewhat withdrawn and did not care for sports, for close bodily contacts with peers, and for physically competitive activities. If he were not over-trained to think primarily in Freudian categories, the psychiatrist could have seen an actual counter-indication of homosexuality in the dislike the patient felt for the attack expressed in that particular form of horseplay, rejecting it just as he rejected overt homosexuality. This psychoanalytically conditioned "mental health" professional was taught that homosexuality is a basic tendency in human beings, and he could not believe in the genuineness of any rejection of homosexuality. He apparently had so little doubt about the mythology with which he had been indoctrinated that he transformed Freud's unproven hypothesis into a diagnostic fact and did not hesitate to seriously jeopardize his patient's current situation. He would be surprised to be accused of acting in a medically irresponsible way. We shall see later (chapter V, 2) that Campbell, a psychiatrist, also was scandalized by irresponsible diagnoses made on loose Freudian presuppositions.

Riess describes another case of irresponsible diagnostic action. A young man, effeminate, shy and severely dependent, was jolted out of his precarious adjustment by the psychiatric rejection from military service. He had no conscious homosexual leanings or fantasies, yet the induction board psychiatrist read homosexuality into his ineffective artistic personality and classified him as undesirable for service. "The allegation of homosexuality panicked him." (48:224) The brash diagnosis brought a crisis into the frail personality, with aggravated self-doubts, increased apprehensiveness with females and much neurotic suffering. He had to seek therapy to regain some balance. The therapist did not discover any homosexuality, covert or overt, except for vague resemblance to the personality pattern of some homosexuals. The psychiatrist had thoughtlessly created trouble where there was no sickness visible before. The iatrogenic trauma proved to be very hard to overcome in therapy:

> With all this seeming improvement, there was one area which appeared to defy change. This was in the sexual field. Any image, situation, or off-color joke which mentioned homosexuality triggered an intense anxiety reaction. Relations with girls were entered into with fear and an expectation of rejection both for not being the ideal American male and for the homosexual picture which he was sure he projected in the minds of girls whom he dated. Repetition of this theme was endless. For months, each session was begun with a query or a dream-recital in which fear of homosexual attack or overture were central. John dug into Kinsey, Ellis, and other so-called authorities on homosexuality to find out whether his body-build, esthetic interests, and family background were similar to self-identified homosexuals. As the therapist I tried to make him see the relationship of the fantasied attacks and fears as distortions of the hostility and guilt centering on his father and mother. The elaborate and repetitive working over of these problems and their patterned projection in behavior had no effect in reducing the anxiety nor in facilitating easy-going heterosexual contacts or even man-woman friendships. (48:226)

He was not well after several months of psychoanalytic therapy. His therapist describes the troubled state of mind: " . . . more and more hostility, despair, concern with body-image, homosexual panics, gradual withdrawal from social life, and increased questioning about the value of treatment." (48:227)

It is a legitimate question whether these homosexual concerns would have been as stubborn with a therapist less impressed with Freudian presuppositions about ubiquitousness of homosexuality.

The trouble with overdiagnosis of homosexuality comes from the semantic confusion which started with Freud. He labeled any warm, friendly feelings for a person of the same sex as homosexuality. He wrote a treatise on Leonardo da Vinci describing him as homosexual even though there is no record of homosexual experiences. Leonardo thus became one of the victims of Freudian pathography. Eissler in the same vein speaks of "a man who like Tausk, had serious homosexual conflicts," (49:329) even though Tausk had the reputation of being a "ladies' man" and there was no homosexual involvement of which he was ever suspected.

Freudian obsession with psychopathological states and the sophisticated skill in imparting sick implications to common human reactions, reduced in some respects American psychiatry to a laughingstock. The readers of some American newspapers were scandalized and bemused lately to read of the farce of diagnosing sane people as insane. A Stanford University psychologist who is also a teacher of law, devised the experiment of checking on diagnostic biases of professionals in mental hospitals. He and seven other sane individuals (four psychologists, a psychiatrist, a pediatrician, a painter, and a housewife) feigned schizophrenic symptoms to gain admission in twelve hospitals. The hospitals were located in five different states; some were old, some new, some research-oriented; some well-staffed, others not; one was university-supported, others run on state or federal funds.

As soon as they were admitted, these eight pseudopatients started behaving in a sane way, and tried to convince the staff that there was nothing wrong with their minds. None of them succeeded. The staff, trained to interpret behavioral phenomena as defensive operations, simply could not see what was under their noses. Other patients, with vision uncluttered by Freudian precepts, perceived the normality of the experimenters. They took notes of all they observed, and this was taken by staffs as special indication of their being sick, presumably paranoid. The staffs put them under medication, prescribing 2100 tranquilizing pills during their stay in the hospitals, which averaged nineteen days. It took the experimenters seven to fifty-two days to get extricated from hospitalization they did not need, and even then they were discharged as "schizophrenics in remission."

The writer reports that the chief experimenter discerned that the bias toward psychopathology was one of the important reasons for such gross diagnostic misperceptions: "The psychiatrists' failure to recognize sanity, Dr. Rosenhan believes, may be attributed largely to the physician's inclination to look for illness rather than good health." (60:78)

11. *What happened to this psychiatric team?*

Taking part in a staff meeting of a large mental health clinic, I viewed another instance of the subtly insidious influence of psychoanalytic views upon clinical practice. Psychologists, psychiatrists, and social workers were about equally represented among the eight staff members. One of the reports under review concerned an eleven-year-old boy who had been referred to the clinic for evaluation and help because of persistent fighting with other children on the school playground and in the neighborhood. He had tried to join the games of older boys, became involved in many fights with them too, and settled into the role of a sullen loner and a bully. The psychologist, who had worked with delinquent youngsters in the past, reported that the behavioral and verbal expressions of the boy in the testing period left no doubt that a serious character disorder was in the making. The social worker who had interviewed the parents described them as suburbanites; both working full time, social climbers with only a superficial contact with the boy. They were annoyed at their son for throwing a shadow on their social image. The mother was, as is often true in such cases, domineering, demanding, efficient, and cold. The father was withdrawn, submissive to his wife, and failed to assume the role of a supportive male adult to the boy. The parents had expressed interest in doing something about their boy.

One psychologist, who was not a Freudian adherent, recommended in view of the chronic shortage of time at the clinic that at least a few interviews be tried with the father. The plan would be to lead him to see that he was letting the boy down, that his son could develop into a juvenile delinquent unless a closer and more active relationship was established between them. The heads of some of the staff members shook with dismay as the psychologist outlined this plan. After a short discussion, the staff agreed not to go further into the case, except to

110

send a report to the school principal, and to follow the boy if he got into worse trouble.

Why was such a negligent decision made? At the same meeting, less serious cases were assigned continuing professional attention; the shortage of staff time was not the explanation. The recommendations of the psychologist had been accepted as guidelines in other cases, so that this rejection could not be ascribed to the absence of professional regard for his opinion. The most feasible explanation was that the clinical thinking of the dominant staff members was too deeply steeped in and clouded by Freudian concepts. Their training compelled them to reject any common-sense intervention as useless in such a case. Somewhere in the dim regions of their professional unconscious, they were certain that such formidable emotional forces were called into action that nothing but very "deep" and terribly long therapy would be of any use. Who could blame them for withdrawing from the assumed abysmal depths of a mother's penis envy, a father's and a son's castration fears, a boy's primordial sexual yearning for his mother, the awesome complications of the Oedipal triangle, oral aggressiveness of the father and the murderous anal aggression of the mother, and other terrible psychodynamic demons? Only a person uninformed about these Freudian phantoms would enter such a den of wild beasts and hope to bring a semblance of order without a patient and demanding struggle, in which only the heroes, the well-trained psychoanalysts, could succeed. One must grant the reasonableness of retreat from a cave full of dragons and witches, crawling insects and vampire bats. (The metaphor might be closer to ascertainable facts than many of the "scientific" Freudian myths. Freud and Freudians have made fantasy a legitimate basis for psychological "science.")

Not sharing their belief in the fatality of the demonic evils of Freudian lore, the psychologist had naively assumed that there might be enough power of reason left in these three tangled beings to straighten out the instinctual mess. The more psychoanalytically enlightened staff members had given him a tacit lesson in psychodynamic wisdom, which discards the obvious and rational, fixing its gaze upon the unseen, atavistic ground of the human psyche. After all, it was their venerable teacher who had established that "it is common sense which produces all the ills we have to cure." (23:18)

111

How much different and more responsible reactions can be shown by those working outside Freudian preconceptions is evident from a similar treatment case described by Parlour and associates. (32) The family situation was far more deteriorated: the wife had accused the husband of incest with his daughter and was suing him for. divorce; other children were brought to the attention of juvenile authorities; the mother was apparently depressed, unkempt, disorganized; and family life was chaos. Yet, Parlour and associates did not shrink from the sick situation, worked with the family for four and a half months and helped them settle into a more satisfactory and human way of living.

12. *Twisting children into Freudian molds*

Weinberger (53) provides an incisive discussion of the confusion into which the Freudian preconceptions led many professionals in child psychiatry and psychology and the damaging effects on children and parents coming for help to psychoanalytically run clinics. He lists the fallacies adopted from Freudian presuppositions, and suggests reformulations:

1. The child and the family applying for help are automatically cast into a sick role, which is unavoidable for those trained in Freudian obsession with psychopathology, in readiness to interpret any minutiae of behavior as proof of sickness and abnormality. "It is very rare indeed that a family is told their child is normal and once the 'disturbed' label is attributed, they cannot win. . . . " (53:149) The realistic and common-sense considerations of parents are cast into categories of denials and resistance. The parents who are able to keep rejecting the Freudian distortions, experience a conflict at the clinic and may leave without receiving any benefit. This does not bother the professionals involved, as they rationalize parental behavior as "resistance" to the therapeutic role of the clinic, and it just confirms what they knew in advance—that the family was "disturbed." Weinberger suggests that the child should be understood as reacting to some realistic stresses in the family and school, that it should be given credit of reasonably sensible behavior, and that the family should not be considered mentally troubled at the outset.

112

2. The Freudian theoretical hangups of clinical workers further muddle the approach by leading them to assume that the children are invariably "victims." The actual possibility that children are capable of influencing the behavior of parents is disregarded and the usual one-sided search for Freudian antecedents to psychopathology is instituted:

Depending upon the sympathies of the therapist, the villains may be either social forces (poverty), other institutions (the schools), or the favorite scapegoat, the parents and their marital problems. Little time may be spent in delineating the nature of the child's problem and how the parents have tried to cope with it, but a great deal of time will invariably be spent upon the parents' marital relationship, especially in the sexual area. Since the child's problems are seen only as symptoms, one need not linger too long upon them, even though that is exactly why the parents sought help. If the parents should insist on doing so, this is treated as resistance on their part. (53:149)

Weinberger suggests corrections to Freudian superstitions: the child should be considered "an active participant in his problems" and "responsible for his actions." Having discarded the Freudian blinkers, Weinberger perceives the trap into which psychoanalytic thinking leads the professionals:

Because adults prefer not to see children as acting deliberately or with malice of forethought, the child is often exonerated from being responsible for what he does. Children are very quick to grasp this belief. Even though they are not always as skillful as adults, they do become quite adept at denying intent, denying knowledge of the consequences of their behavior, and denying awareness of what is troubling them. In this way they hope to avoid unpleasant consequences, and in fact, they often do. They become skillful at statements of reformation, expressions of sorrowful affect and repentance, and projections upon others as being responsible for what they themselves have done. Often their parents accept this, or fear not to, and become quite intimidated by their children. It is crucial that the therapist not do the same. Instead he should consistently confront the child

113

with how he avoids accepting responsibility for his behavior. (53:151)

3. Weinberger objects to the practices designed to control the questioning parents by preventing them from talking with the child's therapist directly and sending them back to their own "therapist." This is one of the many manipulative tricks to keep the patient in submission; these will be amply illustrated in later sections dealing with the relationship of Freudian analysts to their subjects (see especially chapters V, VII, and X). Weinberger wonders at the brainwashing effects upon parents: "It is a constant source of amazement how intimidated parents are, and how many will stay in treatment for long periods of time without ever getting any direct feedback on how their child is doing and how this therapist sees the problem." (53:150)

4. Freudians miss many therapeutic opportunities by following their model of unconscious sources of behavior. They take it for granted that the child is not "aware of the real problem":

> Since he is presumed to be unaware of the real causes of his problems, it is only the therapist who, with his superior expertise, can perform the necessary and delicate operations designed to resolve the unconscious conflicts. Thus the child is placed in a situation where, often without knowing why and over his strenuous objections, he follows the lead of the therapist who presumes to act on his behalf without ever involving him directly and actively in the therapist's conception of the problem and goals of treatment. One might speculate as to how many children would consent to come if they were given a choice. (53:150)

Weinberger ascribes such ineffective "therapeutic" behavior to Freudian training. Most traditional child clinicians operate from a psychodynamic viewpoint in which the child is seen as beset by unconscious and intrapsychic conflicts which have been internalized from his relationship with his parents. The focus of treatment is to resolve these underlying conflicts which are visible only through their behavioral or emotional expressions. Since these behaviors are considered as being merely symptoms of the "real" problem, and the emotions as merely expressions of the "real" problems, they are often ignored. Unfortunately this often excludes from therapeutic consideration the child's interpersonal transactions (except for transference), his self-evaluation, goals and expectations, and especially his own participation in his difficulties. The child is not viewed as an active participant in his problems, not as being aware of the consequences of his behavior. Rather, proceeding from the aforementioned conceptualization of the child as victim, he is seen as helplessly driven and controlled by unconscious forces, and thus exonerated from being responsible for what happens to him. (53:150)

Weinberger treats the children as capable of perceiving their own and their parents' behavior; lacking experience, they may not be able to understand what they observe, and they need the therapist to provide guidance to better understanding of and dealing with circumstances. This is quite a different kind of therapy from that based on Freudian preconceptions: "If a therapist sees the child as a naive and innocent babe he will avoid raising potentially upsetting issues for fear the child is either unaware of them or too upset to deal with them. Viewing the child as so fragile and easily hurt not only impedes treatment but confirms for the child that certain issues are taboo, perhaps bad, and certainly at best left alone." (53:151)

Readers familiar with Glasser's (12) account of his first steps toward Reality Therapy, as a more effective therapy than the one imposed upon him by his Freudian supervisor, will remember that Glasser, like Weinberger, stopped playing games as the alleged therapy. Instead, he talked with and told the child which way he needed to behave, and the child started improving after many months of futile psychoanalytic "treatment."

13. *The psychoanalytical joy ride*

In 1950 there appeared an article under the above caption in the none too conservative weekly *The Nation*. It described the sickening influence of psychoanalytic "treatment" upon an individual and his family. In retrospect, the essay could have been more appropriately titled "A wife crying in the Freudian wilderness." She opens her story with the family breakdown induced by Freudian "therapists" and the myths they had helped build among the public about the superior worth of their ideology and practice:

> My husband and I were recently divorced upon the suggestion of his psychiatrist. Several weeks later my husband voluntarily entered a sanitarium to be treated for depression. I, too, am depressed; I'm also angry. In our lives there was no mother-in-law, no "other" man or woman. But there was always a psychiatrist.
> When I first met my husband six years ago, he had been seeing his analyst five times a week for eighteen months, which was then considered about the average course of treatment for persons with ordinary problems. His trouble derived primarily, as far as I could judge, from a bad experience in his first marriage. Jim was a social-work executive in daily contact with psychiatry. To him it was something everyone could use, a panacea for many ills. He said that in his profession to have had an analysis was as desirable as to hold an advanced academic degree. (54:183)

Jim, like most of his social work colleagues in the 1950s and 1960s, was thoroughly Freudwashed. He had fully absorbed the Freudian "viewpoint and vocabulary which he applied to all situations . . . ; the theories appeared reasonable and enlightening." (54:183) Yet, in all this reasonableness there was the telltale sign of Freudian unreasonableness—the hatred of the parents, fanned in psychoanalytic subjects as regularly as the hatred of "capitalist exploiters, imperialists and warmongers" among Communist brainwashees. "I couldn't help being surprised at the intensity of Jim's resentment against his mother, who had been dead for many years." (54:183) We shall find in the next chapter Mowrer reporting that a similar mother-hating was induced in him as part of the supposed healing on the Freudian couch. Mrs. Ferman, unencumbered by psychoanalytic presuppositions, voices a conclusion at which many professional therapists were to arrive only twenty years later. She felt that the seething rage of her husband toward his mother and his first wife "should have been ameliorated after some 360 sessions with an analyst. I wondered vaguely whether the problem of the analyst and his effort to remove guilt feelings from the mind of his patient had not needlessly emphasized old grievances better left forgotten." (54:183)

Jim was in a regular infantilized relationship with his analyst, in "deep transference," as it is fondly named. "Throughout our courtship I was uncomfortably conscious of another presence. I felt that all the nuances of our relationship were being carefully scrutinized by both Jim and his doctor. Sometimes it struck me that my young man's remarks were quotations from his analyst. Once when he was coming to see me, I found myself setting out three glasses for cocktails." (54:183) However, the analyst did not play the role of demon as in some other reported Freudian analyses; instead of disrupting, he blessed the relationship and Jim accepted his bride as another psychological crutch in his life and declared himself "happier than he had been in many years." He considered his prospective marriage happiness as his "diploma from psychoanalysis." As in many other Freudian treatments, the diploma proved to be only a certificate of having gone through many grades in the school of psychoanalysis, the school being so arranged that graduating is almost impossible.

His psyche being lacerated and injected with irrational components in his Freudian treatment, Jim was not able to handle sensibly his problems on his job and in his marriage. He was apparently hooked on analysis and he "kept going back for more and more psychotherapy. His dependence on psychiatric aid had become such a habit that he seemed unable to act decisively without it." (54:183) His reliance on the therapist apparently helped him avoid the challenge of intimacy and emotional sharing with his wife, but his analyst was not interested in building up the marriage. He kept aggravating his patient's tensions. Under his guidance Jim "magnified those problems beyond their actual importance."

Mrs. Ferman, apparently a sensible and emotionally stable woman, had achieved satisfactory relationships within the family, getting along well with Jim's children, and with "a stimulating group of friends" in the new community. Jim showed a brave face to outsiders, cheerful and confident, but continued to play his childish role with his wife and his analyst: "It was exclusively for my benefit and that of his psychiatrist that he relaxed into morbidity." (54:184) Jim had become a psychological hypochondriac, overreacting to minor strains and reversals. "He would have been among the first to recognize and discourage overdependence upon a parent. Personally, I can't see that a mother's apron strings are much worse than a psychiatrist's couch." (54:184)

Another strain on the marriage relationship and a psychological upheaval was brought about by Jim's moving to take a job in another town. "The transition from one doctor to another was again a painful process." (54:184)

As could be expected, the Freudian "therapy" produced further trouble for the couple: "Eventually an analysis for me became a big issue in our lives." Mrs. Ferman could not see what could be gained by her entering into a process that had only sickened her husband. In order to purchase this questionable help she would have to give up housekeeping and care of children and go to work herself. That made no sense to her as Jim could not point out any personality weaknesses in her that could be strengthened by psychoanalytic operations. She realized that what he wanted was basically to "initiate me into his cult."

Jim's demon was unrelenting; he was determined that his wife would embrace his faith or he would abandon her. The wife could not put herself on the Freudian Procrustean bed and their marriage was destroyed. The distortions of married relationship, common to Freudism, helped dissolve yet another family. Looking back, Mrs. Ferman shows wisdom and an unusually clear perception of the limited perfectibility of human nature:

> At the end Jim told me that if I had submitted to analysis our marriage would have been saved. There are times when I wish I might have embraced the faith. Then I remember that Jim had been prostrating himself before the altar of mental health for seven years and still seems a long way from what passes for "normal." In recent years I have known dozens of men and women in one stage or another of psychoanalysis. Before, during, and after, they have one thing in common with the rest of mankind: they are full of foibles, even as you and I. With or without psychiatry there seems to be little perfection on this planet. I will not say that psychiatry failed to help my husband solve his problems. I do say that he grew a new crop of them in spite of psychiatry, because he happens to be problem-prone. (54:184)

Having had numerous contacts with contemporary mind-doctors,

Mrs. Ferman has little admiration for most of them. They have given her contradictory explanations and recommendations regarding her relationship with Jim. She sees them without the halos and make-ups with which many promotional ventures had invested them:

Each doctor described the situation as he saw it and it became obvious to me that with years of scientific training behind them psychiatrists are, nevertheless, just people, with varying degrees of insight and varying skill in straightening out human relationships. Their understanding, like that of everyone else, is colored by their own childhood, their own education for life, their own emotional and sexual experiences. Among them two or three marriages are not uncommon. Maladjustment and even suicide are as frequent among mind doctors as the rest of the population. In a jest that was at least part truth, one famous analyst said that if psychoanalysis were a more exact science, half the doctors now practicing it would be prohibited from doing so by their own personality disorders. Yet under the rules of the medical profession no layman can get help in distinguishing the skilled from the fumbling. Consequently, the position of power accorded the psychiatrist by the *mores* of our time seems dangerous to me and frightening. (54:184)

Mrs. Ferman suggests that the caution needed in dealing with exaggerated claims of charlatans should be no less exercised toward the officially sanctioned mind-healers: "Doctors who are critical of patent medicines might recognize an analogy. They tell you it is dangerous for the public to depend on nostrums which often fail to live up to their advertising. So it is with psychoanalysis. Superbly effective in many cases, it seems useless and even harmful in others." (54:184) She perceives correctly the source of psychological harmfulness of Freudian treatment: regressing the patient to infantile functioning and worshipful dependency on the analyst:

My husband's retreat into dependency under the influence of psychoanalysis is not, they say, uncommon. Theoretically the psychiatrist does not give advice or make decisions for his patient—he merely helps him to make up his own mind. The extent to which this is true depends of course upon the personality of the analyst. The skilful practitioner is supposed first to gain

119

his patient's complete confidence and then, hundreds of sessions later, at just the right moment, untie the bond, leaving the patient immediately capable of helping himself. Obviously, this is not always successfully accomplished, and the patient is left weakened, not strengthened, by psychiatric aid. (54:185)

Mrs. Ferman also antedates by twenty years the criticism of psychoanalysis as socially wasteful practice voiced lately by community psychiatrists and psychologists:

Only those who can afford to pamper themselves receive the full psychoanalytical treatment, and it is merely an accident if these include the people who need it most. Appointment books are crowded with the names of men and women who consume countless hours of doctors' time with matters formerly resolved by simpler methods. And it is common knowledge that most of our mental hospitals are understaffed and overcrowded. I look forward to a future when these wasted hours may be spent on research that will make psychoanalysis a more reliable science, or devoted to the treatment of the truly sick. (54:185)

In the following number of *The Nation* two psychiatrists responded to Mrs. Ferman's criticism of the psychoanalytic joy ride. Their reactions were fundamentally opposed, illustrating Mrs. Ferman's thesis that psychiatry is at this stage based more on individual opinions than on incontrovertible facts. Dr. Wertham, a reputable professional and a writer of a number of psychiatric books, considered Mrs. Ferman's criticism of Freudian therapy fully justified; he characteristically titled his paper "What to Do Till the Doctor Goes." Dr. Zilboorg, an equally capable psychiatrist and writer, and a fan of Freudian analysis, completely disagreed. He pronounced both Mrs. Ferman and Dr. Wertham ignorant and titled his paper "Ignorance—Amateur and Professional."

Dr. Wertham wished he could dispute the criticisms of psycho-analysis, as that would please his professional ego; however, he could not disregard the observations made in his clinical practice: "What she writes rings true. In fact, I have encountered literally dozens of similar cases." (55:205) He expressed an unequivocal opinion about the therapeutic futility of the Freudian procedure: "From many years'

120

experience in clinics I have come reluctantly to the conclusion that eight out of ten orthodox psychoanalyses are not indicated, and that six out of ten are more harmful than helpful." (55:206)

Dr. Wertham sympathizes with the suffering of a woman caught in the Freudian "hocus-pocus of the divorced-from-life couch-ritual." (55:206) He quotes another wife who wrote to a columnist about her husband who only grew worse through more than a year of analysis. Dr. Wertham takes exception to the defense of psychoanalysis by the columnist who criticized the woman for expecting "speedy, miraculous, and magic changes." The columnist echoed the typical Freudian line: "Psychoanalysts cannot erect a beautiful new edifice with a solid foundation out of every ramshackle structure, weakened by the furious emotional storms that have battered it about, which is figuratively tossed on their couch." (55:206) Dr. Wertham responded to this: "But there are many 'personal difficulties' which do not develop out of anything that happened in earliest childhood. To refer them to this stereotyped first cause is often only an evasion. The threat, equally stereotyped, that the wife's assertion of her existence might 'reactivate the mother-child relationship' was pure speculation." (55:206)

Dr. Wertham corrected the assumption expressed by Mrs. Ferman that "five-day-a-week, eighteen-month psychoanalysis" is needed for solving ordinary life problems; he would rather see it applied to "definite and serious disorders." He blamed psychoanalysts for misleading the public: "To use it [psychoanalysis] at random for almost everything, as is done nowadays, is a sign not of progress but of the opposite. Yet mass advertising for this kind of decadence goes on in the guise of enlightenment, in such forms as the radio program 'Psychoanalysis in Daily Living,' sponsored by a psychoanalytic society." (55:206)

Dr. Wertham proposed that psychoanalytic fantasies need be tempered by realistic concerns which were traditionally the province of social workers. However, he also noticed that social work practices are perverted by Freudian infiltration: "Psychiatric social service, with which I have had daily contact for many years, is indispensable. But psychiatric social service is increasingly becoming psychoanalytic social service, and more and more even the 'social' is being left out, until only psychoanalytic service remains. That doesn't help people with real social and family problems." (55:206) He sided with family members of psychoanalytic victims who "feel that the analyst makes life revolve around the analysis instead of the analysis serving life." (55:206) He observed that apart from "mishandling of the emotional life of the marital partner," psychoanalysis induces undue strain upon most families by imposing financial hardships on them. He agreed with Mrs. Ferman that "the psychotherapy has been bad" because it did not help the patient handle better the realistic problems, it only increased anxiety within the family, and did not improve their coping ability. The fault lies in the Freudian obsession with psycho-pathological elements and disregard of healthy functions:

> . . . old-style psychoanalysis has not yet learned to let people rely on their own resources or helped to mobilize their resources. I know of hardly any instance of an orthodox psychoanalyst telling a person that he did not need psychoanalysis, although Freud said that very definitely to a number of people who consulted him. Orthodox psychoanalysts see no need to classify diseases and therefore have no scientific yardstick with which to determine when analysis is indicated. Their glib concept of a sick, neurotic society makes them find almost everyone sick and in need of psychoanalysis. (55:207)

Dr. Wertham discerned that in this kind of Freudian treatment the interests of the patient were sacrificed to Freudian misperception about what is therapeutic. "The formula triumphed over the facts." He agreed with Mrs. Ferman about the "dangerous and frightening power" of Freudian psychiatrists devoid of responsible and socialized orientation to values:

> Lacking a social frame of reference which would fit them to give patients good advice or honest encouragement, they extol methods according to which no advice or encouragement is given. They have their patients lead a double existence—half lying on a couch and half standing up to life—and are unable to unite the two existences constructively.
> Their advice on marital problems, as Mrs. Ferman noted, is contradictory because they see a social institution like marriage from an over-individualistic point of view. (55:207)

Dr. Zilboorg, on the other hand, took the usual Freudian party line in handling the embarrassing situation. We shall meet in later chapters other examples of the cynical handling of opponents by Freudian adherents. Instead of dealing with their criticisms squarely and objectively, Dr. Zilboorg took recourse to disparagement and irrelevant rhetoric. He first classified both Mrs. Ferman and Dr. Wertham as ignorant. As someone said, if you cannot answer an argument, the next best thing is to call the opponent a fool. He first pretended to sympathize with poor "Mrs. Ferman [who] is an unfortunate, unhappy, bitter person." He categorized all critics of psychoanalysis as psychological misfits and mean hypocrites. He charitably described them as "hundreds of thousands of people whose neuroses lead them to carry an olive branch on their lips and a stiletto on their tongues, so that they both kiss and kill psychoanalysis with the self-righteous bitterness which is the lot of people who walk around this world like 'true normals' but who are actually wandering, lost, and not a little confused." (56:207)

Dr. Zilboorg then made the usual Freudian assertion that those unenlightened by Freudian teachings are subject to twisted and prejudiced thinking: "One does not have to be 'insane' to be the victim of a number of the illusions and delusions of which our society is full. It is more than pseudopious triteness to insist that they be understood for they know not what they are doing." (56:207)

Abandoning the pose of magnanimous pity toward the poor, misdeveloped Mrs. Ferman, Dr. Zilboorg took a more clearly aggressive stance: "Our sympathy for Mrs. Ferman's misfortune ought not to blur our sight. There is no getting away from the fact that Mrs. Ferman has troubles of her own." (56:207) Her main trouble was, according to her critic, that she presumed she could render psychological help to her husband. Such superior operation is the province of the extremely subtle skill of a psychoanalyst, and the common human reasoning and relationship is of no avail; to think so "is so foolish or, if done seriously, as neurotic as for a good housewife to want to be a substitute surgeon for her husband's appendicitis." (56:208) Of course, Dr. Zilboorg begs the question here whether psychoanalytic skill is even remotely comparable to a surgeon's precision and reliability.

Dr. Zilboorg tried another psychoanalytic trick often applied in arguments—the scapegoating. He asserted that the failure of Mr. Ferman's psychoanalysis should not be blamed on the Freudian method, but rather on the "instability of our middle- and upper middle-class hedonistic civilization." (56:208) (He probably is right here, but that is beside the point. The real question is why the Freudian analysts, with their assumed deep understandings, have not admitted that they cannot treat the unmanly American men, instead of accepting them into lucrative "treatments.") Then he added another customary defensive maneuver to his argument: the psychoanalysts or Freudian psychiatrists who failed to help her husband must have been incompetent and ill-trained. Dr. Zilboorg apparently could not conceive that a rigorous application of Freudian principles would only more surely lead to therapeutic failure. The emphasis on unconscious promptings, irrational associations, and psychopathology, and a corresponding disregard of spiritual and moral values, and of healthy potentials, can be expected to weaken rather than strengthen the functioning of any personality.

Another scapegoating Dr. Zilboorg used was blaming the frivolous public for showing lack of appreciation of psychoanalysis as a great form of psychotherapy. "It takes a long time," he concluded his condemnation of ungrateful people who attack psychoanalysis, "for the public to become humble and submit to knowledge in exchange for its garrulous and gullible ignorance." (56:208) Mrs. Ferman was, of course, part of that garrulous and ignorant crowd, together with Dr. Wertham.

In the end Dr. Zilboorg turned upon his colleague. He assumed a slyly respectful attitude; he wanted to spare the reader the embarrassment that would be caused if he said openly what he thought of Dr. Wertham: "It is interesting and at the same time melancholy to observe how confused the best minds and the most charitable hearts become when they engage in attacking a science for the fads which the public makes out of it, and for the prejudices which it weaves into our misconceptions of the science." (56:209)

It appears that Dr. Zilboorg had heard neither Mrs. Ferman nor Dr. Wertham about the important objections they voiced against psychoanalysis.

Twenty years later the confusion regarding psychoanalysis is no less prominent among psychiatrists than in Dr. Zilboorg's and Dr. Wertham's time. Writing in 1972 in a superior professional periodical (the *International Journal of Psychiatry*), two psychiatrists talk past each other, no less senselessly disunited than their seniors in 1950. One of them, like Dr. Wertham, sees personal psychoanalysis as a useless exercise for therapists, detrimental to patients and corrosive to family relationships:

> Many people become distant from their spouses, parents, and extended kin in the course of what are considered to be successful psychoanalyses. I find that these people, although well-analyzed, are chronically depressed. Their parents and their spouses are also sometimes chronically depressed. The lack of explicit direction for maintaining open relationships allows some family systems to get into these mutually distant, depressed states as a result of the analysis of one member. (58:16)

The other discussant, like Dr. Zilboorg, remains oblivious to the misguidance of trainees through Freudian psychoanalysis and psychological harm to patients, and insists dogmatically:

> Perhaps Guerin, too, is skeptical about the value of psychoanalytic therapy, which may appear to him to involve merely viewing one's parents "as the malignant cause of my shortcomings."
>   It is my opinion that a personal psychoanalysis is of paramount importance for anyone who does psychotherapy, whether it is individual, group, or family-oriented. (59:16)

Notes to Chapter Two

1. I came across an exception recently and wish to cite it as a worthy professional example. It is to the credit of the American Medical Association that it cooperated in the inquiries on the wide extent of medical failures. (2)

The dangerous deficiencies include medication errors,

anesthesia incompetence, hospital-bred infection, faulty diagnostic workup, blood transfusion errors, unnecessary or poor surgery, inadequate nursing care, inappropriate therapy and negligence . . . Cesarean sections where there was no need; out of 60 hysterectomies, in more than 20 cases there could not be one possible cause for doing them. . . . Errors in judgment or technique concerning anesthesia or surgery, or a combination of the two, contribute close to 50% of mortality in the operating room. . . . It has been reliably shown, says *JAMA,* that an essential therapeutic measure, blood transfusion causes death in approximately one out of every 150 transfusions in persons over 40 years of age as a result of serum hepatitis. . . . In one reputable Florida hospital alone, they unearthed the annually projected 51,200 medical blunders. . . . A five-hospital survey of seven common operations (including ulcer and ovary surgery) showed, by hospital average, that 24% of their surgery should have been scrupulously avoided.

2. Years later I came across a similar therapeutic approach by two psychiatrists, McGuire and Sifneos on "Problem solving in Psychotherapy." They report that:

> . . . certain patients improve rapidly when they learn this technique. This improvement is obtained without any appreciable understanding of the so-called deeper conflicts. In turn this finding suggests that with certain patients the deeper conflict itself may be less important than the fact that they do not have the capacity to resolve the derivative of the conflict. Moreover, the fact that this deficit seems to be as much cognitive as it is emotional, simply underscores the point that patients are unable to look at themselves in a manner which they find useful to initiate change. (37:673)

3. After all, priests have for centuries heard many futile, basically insincere confessions, but have never viewed such pretenses of repentence as an efficient method of caring for one's soul.
4. One of the psychoanalytic reformers, Alexander, expresses a similar view:

In general, of course, the present is always determined by the past; still, many contemporary analysts believe that there is an unwarranted neglect of actual life circumstances. The patient comes to the therapist when he is at the end of his rope, so entangled in emotional problems that he feels he must have help; the analyst should never allow the patient to forget that he came to him to resolve these problems. The interest in the past history at the expense of the present is a residue of the historical period when research in personality dynamics was, of necessity, a prerequisite for developing a rational treatment method.

Alexander and Selesnick quote Sandor Rado's comments:

The patient must learn to view life, himself, and others in terms of opportunities and responsibilities . . . even when the biographical material on hand reaches far into the past, interpretation must always begin and end with the patient's present life performance, his present adaptive task. The significance of this rule cannot be overstated, . . . The goal of both Rado and Alexander is the same: to minimize the danger of encouraging undue regression and evasion of the current adaptive tasks. (10:326-329)

Chapter III

Freudian Corrosion of Civilized Values

I certainly do not agree with all that Freud has to say and feel
that some of his followers are of a low order.
Tracy J. Putnam, M.D., Professor of Psychiatry (19:631)

Freudian Psychoanalysis taught us much about the unknown
motives which guide men's actions. It promised to explain everything and ended up explaining everything away.
Sheldon B. Kopp, Ph.D. (20:13)

... he got an impression of Freud as a wicked disrupter of family
life ... And herein lies Freud's pernicious, evil influence on our
society, on our laws and the institutions established from time
immemorial to protect our society.
Martin D. Kushner, M.D. (15:78, 151)

1. *Freud, an anti-Moses*

Freud suffered, among other psychological maldevelopments, from
a messianic complex. He aspired to be the new Moses who would lead
humanity out of the alleged wilderness of repressions, neuroses,
sexual misperceptions and all kinds of unwisdom. He deluded himself
that he would be the founder of scientifically acceptable morals,
whatever they might be. In the process he unwittingly created a cult, a
new sect, disguised under the cloak of science. His sect proved to be
more destructive than salutary. In retrospect, Freud appears as
anti-Moses. The religious implications of Freudism, the corroding
antireligious religion he launched at the world are dealt with exten-
sively in my volume *Freud's Phallic Cult*. (14) Here I shall deal briefly
with destructive influences of Freud's doctrines upon family life,
children's upbringing, decadent orientation of art, deteriorating
morals and manners.

128

Many Western intellectuals have adopted an almost reflex reaction of accepting readily even preposterous reformist proposals if they are considered new, and rejecting as thoughtlessly the wisdom of existing social traditions. Freud rode on the wave of this unthinking reformism and became one of its paragons. A more thoughtful person would question the wisdom of changes for the sake of change. An educated man would remember from history that philosophical destroyers of moral and religious traditions had sometimes contributed to the downfall of their own countries, Rome being one of the widely recognized examples. The warning of "all that glitters is not gold" seems to apply well to Freud's views and their consequences described in this chapter.

Freud injects a special value-orientation into his followers. They glory in debunking and destroying moral and attitudinal certainties, spiritually crippling themselves and their believers. Many thoughtful observers, free from the facile revolutionist hangups, have objected to the cynical moral negativism of Freud and, even more, of his less balanced pupils. They smack of sociopathy. Jung was troubled by the Freudians' crude, reckless, and disrespectful treatment of beliefs and values that sustain our culture. He objects to their sexualized "interpretations," finding them akin to witticisms entertained by immature and uncouth individuals:

> I cannot avoid mentioning how often it happens that otherwise serious physicians, in complete disregard of all the fundamental tenets of scientific conscience explain psychological material by means of subjective conjectures—conjectures of which one can really make nothing, except that they are attempts to find that particular obscene witticism through which the material under investigation could be in some way related to an anal, urethral or other sexual abnormality. The poison of a devaluating interpretation has infiltrated the very marrow of these people, so that they can no longer think at all except in the infantile perverse jargon of certain cases of neuroses which are characterized by the special features of Freudian psychology. It is really too grotesque that the physician himself falls into that way of thinking which he rightly objects to as infantile in others, and therefore would like to cure. . . . But if the physician's thoughts

129

overtly or silently are as negative and devaluating as the patient's, and are equally desirous of pulling everything and anything into the infantile-perverse morass of an obscene wit-psychology, one must not be surprised if the latter's soul becomes a barren waste and he compensates for this barrenness by an incurable intellectualism. (16:220)

A contemporary observer reacts to Freud's distortions of ethical behavior in a way similar to Jung's protest:

> The prevalent psychodynamically-oriented view of kindly and generous behavior tends to question its sincerity. Friendship is not listed in the index of Otto Fenichel's standard text on psychoanalytic theory. Generosity is often interpreted as a maneuver for placating the more powerful and attempting to escape injury; it is seen as a sign of weakness and neurotic dependency. Tenderness is interpreted either as aim-inhibited sexuality or is suspect as reaction-formation against sadistic trends. At best, kindliness may be credited with the status of a sublimated libidinal urge. But even then its sincerity is brought into doubt by the belief that its roots are in the id. Behind these interpretations of kindliness, generosity, and the like, there seems to be an assumption of an irreconcilable opposition between one's own interests and those of others. (17:1)

Haronian discerns clearly that Freudian ethical views are based on an animalized model of the human psyche and human life. Having lost the belief in the genuineness of noble human promptings, Freudians see only the ignoble reactions, the animal moral insensibility, and the "wolf eat wolf" aspects of human condition. They cannot help, therefore, aggravating the situations their patients bring to them for amelioration.

2. Freudian poisons sold as antidotes

Lehrman, a psychiatrist, describes one of his experiences with psychotherapy in marital problems which indirectly reflects the pernicious influence of Freudian superstitions upon "treatment" of patients. He reports in the section of his paper entitled "Personal help, family harm":

130

Some time ago, the mother of two teenage girls came to see me, anxious and guilt-stricken because her husband had left home to live with a woman of dubious reputation. The wife had learned of the affair a few months ago, had become quite agitated and had sought psychiatric help. The psychiatrist calmed her but did nothing about the cause of her condition: her husband's continuing infidelity. At no time did he try to see the husband, or to influence him in any way, other than to indicate that he too was "disturbed" and should also get treatment—from another therapist. This the husband refused to do. Since the wife's psychiatrist saw the husband's affair as symptomatic of his "disturbance," it was indicated that she should tolerate it, and make neither scenes nor demands upon him about it.

She tried earnestly, but found herself unable to suppress her resentment completely. But when the husband later left home, blaming her failure to "understand" him, as recommended, she became intensely guilt-ridden and came for help.

I immediately telephoned the husband to suggest that he come in. Shortly before I called, however, he had himself started treatment with one of New York's leading psychoanalysts. Having already started his own treatment made him reluctant to come to my office, and his analyst supported his reluctance. With the wife's agreement, I suggested she might see his analyst, but this proposal was also rejected by both husband and analyst. At no time were the husband and wife ever seen, alone or together, by the same physician. The breach between them, widened by the interventions of mental health professionals, was never healed.

A few months after entering the situation, I met the husband's analyst at a professional gathering. I again raised the possibility that one of us might see both husband and wife, to try to re-establish the family unit if at all possible. He replied that he saw his role as assisting the husband alone to find what he really wanted, and then helping him to achieve it. He therefore felt he was obliged to be neutral toward the integrity of the family unit, and, by extension, "neutral" concerning any moral questions which might be involved.

The husband's easiest course, for the moment at least, was along the road once called primrose path. This path was approved by the analyst, despite his protestation of neutrality. Perhaps he saw the effort to change from wrong to right as too upsetting for the husband to manage, or perhaps he regarded ideas of right and wrong as merely authoritarian remnants of the pre-Freudian era. (1:59, 60)

Lehrman ascribes such socially irresponsible handling of the marital situations to the morally immature views of the dominant Freudian sect in psychiatry:

The tendency to avoid moral issues is widespread and deep throughout the world of mental health, in a great measure because its primary orientation is individualistic. This in turn is largely the result of at least two fundamental scientific errors made by Freud and subsequently carried over into the entire field. These errors are the confusion of harsh enforcement of the moral codes with the existence of the codes themselves, and the belief that individual needs stand in permanent, irreconcilable, conflict with social law. (1:60)

Lehrman's concern for patients exposed to the misleading influence of Freudian assumptions, leads to a proposal to reexamine current values:

The present situation in mental health clearly warrants some fundamental revaluations. More attention to the moral codes of psychiatry and mental health might seem preferable to some of the present hoop-la for bigger clinics and more organizations. If the overall medical effectiveness of already existing clinics is dubious, what is the use of new ones? And when they do help individuals, how often do they do so by making immorality more comfortable? (1:61)

It is not only American Freudian psychoanalysts who unwittingly or for "therapeutic" reasons loosen the moral stance of their patients. Frankl reports a case from Vienna. A neurotically labile woman had tried psychoanalyses with two well-known Freudians without much benefit. She describes the only consequence of her therapy: "Psycho-analysis freed me gradually from my self-reproaches and guilt feelings and drove me to try affairs with other men." (10:65) This therapeutic gain must have been all the more significant as the woman was married!

These and similar reports from psychiatric practice, raise an important question: can we allow members of a profession to place themselves above moral principles which motivate a majority of other members of society? Are Freudians licensed to disregard the long-standing values of our society? Should they be made responsible for the moral and social damage caused by their cynicism?

3. *Freudians, natural moral cynics*

Pinckney, a professor of psychiatry, shows that Freudians cannot but behave destructively when dealing with social values, as they are encased in a cynical, thoroughly pathological view of human situations.

> One doctor reported to a medical meeting that if you have a woman patient who happens to tell you her husband is wonderful, you can pretty well assume that woman patient is a neurotic. Furthermore, this same doctor predicted that whenever a woman feels her husband is great, and talks about it, the marriage will break up within a year or so. He concluded his diagnostic education for his fellow therapists with the assertion that married women patients are probably normal only if they feel their husbands are "inconsiderate slobs!"
>
> This doctor's publicly expressed viewpoint, along with the admitted fact that "marital" problems far outweigh any other psychoanalytic situation, could well be responsible for many of the nearly half million divorces that take place in the United States each year . . . (7:113)

Pinckney shows the destructive consequences of Freudian "therapy" for the family of a physician:

> . . . let us look at what happened to a doctor's wife who went to a psychoanalyst because she began to have some doubts about her adequacy as a mother and mate. Mrs. C. had been married nearly 20 years. She and her husband had four lovely children, all of

133

whom had expressed no "problems," at least through their school work since they were at the head of their respective classes and were well liked by their classmates. The doctor-husband was considered "outstanding" in his community and by his professional cohorts—as well as being financially well off. In many instances the couple even worked together, she applying her artistic talents to some of his scientific work. To the outside world, at least, there was no evident conflict.

As the children grew older, and as the confining responsibilities of being a mother and housewife lessened, Mrs. C. began to express certain doubts as to her place in the society of her home. One might rightfully assume these anxieties to be a normal phase of any adult development. One of the people to whom Mrs. C. expressed her feelings was her own mother. And it must be stated here that Mrs. C.'s mother had, only a few years prior, completed six years of her own psychoanalysis. The immediate and persistent response of the mother (as seems to be the case with virtually everyone who has been psychoanalyzed) was to point dogmatically to psychoanalysis as the only way to resolve such a "terrible situation," and to pressure her daughter to follow in Mother's footsteps.

In this particular case, however, the wife first mentioned the idea of seeing a psychoanalyst to her husband, who, trying to be understanding, suggested she initially consult a general psychiatrist whom they both knew, and solicit his opinion. The psychiatrist, after discussing the matter with both parties, strongly advised against psychoanalysis, saying, without hesitation, that such a fear-provoking adventure could precipitate trouble that did not actually exist either at the moment, or even in one's real past. Despite this admonition, and on the insistence of her mother, Mrs. C. did pay a visit to a psychoanalyst.

What followed was fairly typical of the woman who, with some real doubts about her marriage, succumbs to psychoanalysis. The first visit stretched into half-a-dozen consultations, all of which, like the Chinese finger torture, entrapped Mrs. C. more and more, no matter how she struggled to escape the analyst's contention that she needed psychoanalysis to resolve her problem. As Mrs. C's analysis went into its second year, even the children began to comment, innocently to be sure, "What's the matter with Mommy?" Through the ensuing months everything took on a hidden meaning. If one of the children spilled milk, the incident became a magnified tragedy—as Mrs. C. described it, "A deliberate provocation to show up my inadequacies." When Dr. C. was late for dinner because the surgical procedure he started that afternoon revealed some unexpected prolific disease that had to be attended to at that very moment, his wife did not hesitate, in front of the children, to accuse him of philandering. Her "excuse" for any outburst was to stress her analyst's advice that she never be afraid to express herself whenever and wherever she felt like it.

One day, during the third year of Mrs. C.'s psychoanalysis, she came home and demanded her husband undergo psychoanalysis. It was interesting to note that her analyst happened to have a young friend who was just starting out in his own practice, and this friend was supposedly the only analyst suitable for Dr. C. Mrs. C. applied the threat of immediate separation—regardless of the children's emotional welfare—if her husband did not seek psychoanalytic help. So the good doctor adjusted his own professional schedule and for four mornings each week lay on the analyst's couch and said whatever came into his mind. Obviously, the main mental preoccupation of the doctor was his wife's actions and reactions toward him and their children.

After several weeks of trying to uncover why his wife had "changed," only to be refuted with some references to his own infant sexual experiences and desires, Dr. C. could take it no longer, and quit. The very next day he came home to find all his clothes, and a few other personal belongings such as his medical books and his hi-fi set, out on the lawn and the front door bolted. It took the police to get him inside his own house. To his utter amazement, he found his wife in bed—with her mother!

From this point on, things became progressively worse until Mrs. C. actually filed for divorce and obtained a court order (with the help of her lawyer and psychoanalyst) prohibiting Dr. C. from entering the premises. The husband, having no choice at the moment, took an apartment nearby, and spent several months working through the courts, and pleading with his wife, trying to effect a reconciliation—if for nothing more than the children's sake.

When the case finally came before the judge, it was the psychoanalyst's testimony that led to the divorce decree, which also gave custody of all four children to their mother. Dr. C. protested against divorce, even at this point, asking the court to allow him and his wife to work out their problems together, without outside interference. Dr. C. was allowed to see the children once a month, but they had to be brought to him, as he was forbidden by law ever to interfere with his former wife's welfare by even seeing her.

Unfortunately, this true story does not end there. A few months after the divorce, at the insistance of Mrs. C.'s analyst, the older son was sent to another psychoanalyst (by court order) since he became, in the words of his mother, "hostile, unmanageable, and dangerous." The school work of all the children became so inferior that two of them had to repeat certain grades, and the present outlook is certainly not promising for them—as children, or later as adults. Mrs. C. is now in her seventh year of psychoanalysis, still living, and, sleeping, with her mother. Dr. C. has closed his office and is now working for a pharmaceutical company (primarily to support his children as well as furnish his wife's alimony). And even Mrs. C.'s mother is professing unhappiness at having to devote all her time to taking care of her daughter. In all, six lives which were once fairly normal have been ruined by one psychoanalyst, who over and over again kept saying to Mrs. C., "Why do you stay married to your husband?" No, that analyst may not have actually said "get a divorce," but he left his patient no other choice if she was to "understand herself better."

In this particular instance, no matter what words were used, the analyst actually recommended divorce. To be sure, through his actions he did not directly advise the permanent legalized separation; he merely provoked the woman into making the decision. While psychoanalysts in general deny they ever recommend *anything* to their patients, the patients themselves insist that their analysts virtually demand the divorce. (7:114-118)

Being themselves disloyal to the positive social and Christian values of our society, Freudians are naturally destructive in their work with patients who come to them for counseling. Out of their socially estranged minds they can only give a socially disturbing counsel:

Only one woman out of the several hundred I have talked with regarding psychoanalysis and divorces, told me her analyst insisted on her staying married. She also added that her analyst reached this decision after questioning her as to the source of her income. On learning that her lawyer had said she probably would not be entitled to monetary maintenance during the separation period before divorce, or alimony afterward, the analyst told her that since she needed the financial income in order to complete her analysis, and that, since he could not continue to listen to her free of charge, it seemed the lesser of two evils to live with the source of her problems for another few years until she understood herself better. While analysts may claim they do not advise or direct their patients, in this instance it cannot be denied that "money talked" more than the patient.

In most interviews with psychoanalysts on this very subject, however, the overall impression I received was that divorce itself is not at all important, nor does it enter into the picture. In fact, on a radio program in which a psychoanalyst discussed psychoanalysis with two women patients under his care—both in the process of divorce—the analyst dismissed this environmental and social influence on the lives of his patients as irrelevant to their problems. To the psychoanalyst, the immediate problem of the person lying on the couch began in infancy, and adult relations are really meaningless until the basic sexual obsession that began during the first few months of life, is resolved. One analyst stated that, in essence, marriage can have no meaning to someone who has not been psychoanalyzed.

But what about the fact that quite a few divorced patients emphatically state that their analysts pushed them into divorces —many of which were later regretted. Are those patients making up the story to excuse their inexcusable actions? While this is the retort of some psychoanalysts (which really makes no psychoanalytic sense, since after analysis the individual should not need to forge excuses), one analyst summed up the situation in a more comprehensible, if not illogical manner. He flatly stated that in many cases psychoanalysts *do advise*—be it divorce or digression from standard moral values. . . .

What is even more unfortunate, however, is that analysts actually encourage infidelity—one more approach to avoiding the normal moral responsibilities that have long proven the most successful basis for a happy life. They seem to encourage people to do the things which will make them feel guilty, and they then spend years curing the guilt that they caused. If you happen to be

137

talking with someone entering a divorce, and that person shows no remorse or no doubt that it might have taken two to break the marriage just as it took two to make one, you can be fairly certain that that individual is going to an analyst to have him justify his divorce, rather than making even the slightest effort to keep the marriage together. . . .

Marriage counselors who have a high rate of success in rejoining so-called "broken homes" have told me that, in their practical, actual experience, psychoanalysis does more to defeat marriage than the original, seemingly intolerable situation which initiated the conjugal dissolution. The end result is inevitable—that what starts out as a "cold" war must necessarily become "hot" in the hands of a psychoanalyst.

Freudian psychoanalysts do not hesitate to blame the "childish" American attitude that combines love with marriage as a major factor in our ever-rising divorce rate. One analyst stated flatly that marriage was designed by society in order to compel people to live together after their love illusions had vanished. The same analyst decrees that love, no matter what form it takes, is temporary and always ceases to exist after a short period of time. Can someone with such firm beliefs against marriage really help a helpless marriage? Should they even be permitted to intervene? (7:118, 119, 126, 127, 129)

In another section (chapter V, 5) we shall consider another testimony of a patient who suffered at the hands of Freudian healers, and whose marriage was systematically destroyed by them. As natural moral cynics, they are bound to play the role of moths in the moral fabric of society.

4. *Decivilizing direction of hostility*

The social irresponsibility of Freudians is also expressed by their disregard of another injunction of socialized and civilized behavior, namely, that we should control and dissolve our hostility instead of directing it at others. According to Freudian therapeutic gospel, hostile feelings toward others should be expressed. Religions have taught that the inner hostility should be resolved in the individual through prayer, forgiveness, forbearance, doing good to those who anger him; Freudism sanctions a return to jungle law, urges us to bare our teeth and growl in all irritating situations. Such is the decivilizing influence of this antireligion. With what results?

I remember the case of a colleague who was undergoing a Freudian analysis. From a pleasant, cooperative, civilized individual he became a boorish, arrogant, biting fellow. The expression of his anger did not seem to make him any more relaxed or any less hostile. But he believed what his trainer had taught him: that expression of hostility is good for one's soul!

Wertham, well acquainted with deteriorating influences of Freudian analysis upon the character of patients, making them more self-centered and undersocialized, notes that they "often become individualistic; their philosophy becomes aggressive; some of them become over-introspective, unaltruistic, egotistical." (11:39)

Mowrer gives two examples of the results of this "therapeutic" policy:

> ...one of the standard forms of "treatment" dictated by this classical Freudian presupposition is that the victim should be encouraged to express his annoyances and hostilities outwardly, openly, instead of "turning them inward." Recently another psychologist, told me of a woman who had come to him about her husband, a dentist, who a short time ago, because of depression, consulted a psychiatrist and received this advice. The woman is now afraid her husband is going to lose his practice, and end up in a mental hospital as well, because he is being so intemperate and aggressive with other people.
>
> But I don't need to cite only hearsay evidence in this connection. When I was having my last "spot" of psychoanalysis, some sixteen years ago, I was strongly encouraged, as I frequently had been before, to regard my parents as primarily responsible for my difficulties (since it was from them that I had received my supposedly too severe superego). And since only my mother (in her late seventies) was then living, I gradually formed the design, under this mischievous tutelage, of writing to her and, once and for all, "telling her off." This, in due course, I did. My mother never replied to that letter but went ahead, instead, writing me as if she had never received it. However, after her death, a year or so later, I learned from my brother how deeply distressed she had been by this action on my part. Repressed aggression, indeed!

The aggression we are thus encouraged to express is far more likely to be the source of mental anguish than the cure. (2:6)

Mowrer describes the only benefit he had from his protracted Freudian instruction:

But as I have gotten back on my feet again, emotionally, I have developed a fairly ruddy glow of resentment against psychoanalysis itself, and have had a rather delightful time "expressing" it. This of course, is not precisely the direction which one's anger is supposed to take, to be maximally "therapeutic;" but I believe history will show that we today have far greater justification for distrusting and resenting the ideas embodied in Freudian psychoanalysis than those which most people, including "neurotics," have traditionally learned at their mother's knee—or over their father's. (2:6, 7)

Pinckney also found that psychoanalyzed individuals are typically inconsiderate and uncivil:

... the one most outstanding accomplishment of psychoanalysis seems to be that it takes someone who is covertly obnoxious and makes him overtly obnoxious. The next time you run across an individual whose obvious manifestations of rudeness and forsaking of social amenities figuratively slap you in the face, ask that person if he is in, or has been in analysis. Unfortunately, the chances are great that, if you can get by the challenging, retaliative, "WHY," you will find yourself facing a self-deluded victim of regular psychoanalytic sessions. (7:157)

Psychoanalysts take pain to dissolve feelings of family obligations, loyalty and gratitude toward parents, creating thereby the half-civilized specimens of unbridled egotism:

He [Freudophile] does not limit his invectives merely to the people around him; he has a session with his psychoanalyst, the Freudophile's mother looms large in the picture. Within a few months after starting psychoanalysis, the Freudophile shows an increasingly visible contempt for all the problems caused by his mother's desire to keep him alive and well when he was a child. Evey time the Freudophile remembers how his mother gave him some sort of special attention (e.g., to keep him from catching cold; to avoid trouble with the law; to relieve some school problem, etc.), he relives what he now calls overprotectiveness, as if it were some sort of deliberate plot to emasculate him. The fact that his mother did keep him alive and well is completely forgotten. (7:163)

Adler's views, in contrast to Freud's, emphasized the need of the neurotic to integrate himself in the community, to let the social feeling take the upper hand, to renounce the "private [egoistic] intelligence." Aggressive reactions, instead of being expressed, were to be modified with altruistic feelings. Adler, having grown up in the same culture as Freud, had apparently progressed much further toward social maturity. While Freud remained a prisoner of his "Oedipal" reaction, in rebellion against the limiting agents of existence, Adler found no serious conflict between the individual and his group and culture, and saw integration in the community network of relationships one sure sign of mental health and satisfactory personality development. In comparison with Adler, Freud was an undersocialized egotist.

Another psychiatrist who refused to buy Freudian dogmas, Glasser, also shows disagreement with inciting the expression of hostilities through psychoanalysis. "We never encourage hostility or acting out," he says of Reality Therapy, which he developed, "for that only compounds the problem." (18:580) Countless other wise and decent human beings, of the past and at present, would side in this matter with Adler, Glasser, Mowrer, Wertham, and Pinckney, rather than Freud.

Freud and Freudians are caught in the Western delusion that man should *express* himself. This is proposed in rather indiscriminate ways, as if human beings had no obligation to others, as if an individual living with others could be law unto himself. These modern worshippers of "self-expression" disregard the understandings of other generations that built civilization with the clear realization that living with others requires repression and restraint. An otherwise sharp thinker and debater, Eissler seems to slip into romantic irrationality when handling this favorite Freudian topic. He first,

141

expresses the conviction that "the works of such thinkers as Nietzsche and Freud contain the seeds of a new ethic." (21:300) The seeds of Nietzsche's "ethics" were partly expressed in the beastly behavior of the Nazis; those of Freud have been shown as unsalutary in many respects. Eissler hopes that Freudism will lead to "freedom" of expressing without restraint any feelings, no matter how negative or disturbing to others, at least in words if not in actions: "Man will be granted the right to feel (and to express his feelings?), in accordance with his own inner processes. The ethical opprobrium that is still attached to some feelings will have been lifted, and man will perhaps be able at last to hate and to rage, without incurring a feeling of guilt." (21:301)

Eissler, however, does not follow his precept of full self-expression himself. He is apparently too civilized to do it. Under the current standards only small children and lunatics express themselves without regard to other moral and social considerations. Eissler wrote this book prompted by anger at someone who, it appears to him, maligned his hero, Sigmund Freud. The book with its massive argument must have taken hundreds of hours to research and write—a good index of annoyance he had experienced against Freud's detractor. Yet he does not call him a fool, a scoundrel, a pig—which could more directly express his feelings. Instead, he uses literary insults, which are only a mild distillate of his rage. He speaks of Roazen's "truly embarrassing emptiness of his psychological understanding" (21:43), calls his book a "wild construction" (21:2), a "pasquil" (21:87), "a travesty of psychoanalytic theory" (21:335), and a few other similar civilized hostile remarks.

5. *Capitulation to psychopathology*

Here I gather various observations about how Freudian practices foster psychopathology instead of reducing it.

Phillips (3) offers several illustrations of how the psychoanalytically (mis)trained workers in mental health clinics harm children and parents by wearing the Freudian blinders provided by their instructors: they disregard everyday problems and reactions, discarding the patient's reality as "superficial," transpose everything into some mystical "deep" pathology, refuse giving advice which the troubled parents seek in order to start correcting their blunders. They ask why patients misdeveloped, and no decisive answer can be given. They do not ask more practically important questions: *how* the patient causes his problems and *what* attitudes and situations bring about the troublesome symptoms.

Smith describes how "Freudian oriented colleagues advised strongly against the patient's revealing her transgression to her husband" (4:122) in Integrity Therapy—a procedure which effected a dramatic improvement in the treatment of his hysterical patient. His colleagues were therapeutically wrong exactly because they were right in terms of the dominant Freudian superstitions.

Ellis has observed that the "depth-centered prejudices" keep the psychoanalytically brainwashed professionals blind to what is "under their noses." (12:174) Anderson (13) gave examples of how some therapists become blinded by their training. Some therapists like to imagine themselves indispensable, and they adopt the corroborating superstition that the patient is a slave to his symptoms. A patient provided for me and for others in that group psychotherapy meeting a clear illustration of the capacity for self-cure blatantly neglected by Freud and his students.

A man close to forty, participated with his wife in therapy for about six months. He had come alone initially, complaining that his wife had been unfaithful to him while he was on one of his business trips. He was almost sure that she had deceived him with the garbage collector. He and his wife were invited to participate in the group. It soon appeared that the patient had been in one of his psychotic episodes and had hallucinated the whole affair in an attempt to dislodge his wife from her, as he put it, "queen's throne" in their marriage. Their conflict about leadership was still unresolved when he reported to the group:

Something rather strange happened to me last weekend. Agnes had proposed that we take a vacation of three days and drive to a mountain resort about 200 miles from here. I agreed to it outwardly, but I felt I had had enough of her bossing me in this marriage. I could not bring myself to tell her this, so we left. She was driving, and I was sitting on the front seat, feeling more and more irritated as the miles rolled by. I developed a headache, my

whole body was tense, my arms were aching. I still could not tell
her that I didn't go along with her proposal, even though I had
started on the trip. Her usual driving with a foot on the clutch
irked me badly. I felt like screaming or hitting her. Then I asked
myself: "Why shouldn't I go along with her? I can sometimes do
what she wants, without having always to follow her desires. If
she wants to drive with her foot on the clutch, why should this be
important to me?" As I gave up my anger, my headache disappeared, and my arms relaxed. I suggested that we stop and eat
because I know she likes that. I offered to drive when she got
tired, and she seemed glad to let me. We had three good days
together. But, oh man! what a fool I would have made of myself
if I hadn't worked against that anger. Am I glad I didn't mess up
everything as I wanted to in the beginning.

In contrast to this man who was influenced by his psychotherapist
to control his "symptoms" or to tolerate them, look at the results of
Freudian "therapy," encouraging a surrender to one's pathological
trends and even fanning them up with interpretations:

A young author was having more than the usual amount of
marital problems. The basic cause of conflict was his new wife's
desire to continue her acting career—in contrast to making a
home. He came to me, first as his doctor for an intangible
backache, later as his friend for an apparently interminable
heartache. Physical therapy cured the back pains, but the patient
would not admit that he could possibly be partially at fault concerning his domestic disease. When I asked him to bring his wife
in so that we might discuss the problem from all sides, he flatly
refused, saying that at the suggestion of friends he had sought
out a "specialist for this problem"—a psychoanalyst.
After six months of analysis, he filed for divorce. One year
later, well into analysis, he had lost his job—in addition to his
wife. Still another year after his divorce, and now thoroughly
"Freudwashed," his savings ran out and his analysis ended. At
about that time I happened to run into him. The sum and
substance of his analysis was that he could never live with any
woman, since all women reminded him of his mother, whom he
really hated. That he could have swallowed this line seemed
impossible to those of us who knew that his mother had died

when he was seven months old and he had been brought up by his physician-father. Even when you reminded him of the fact that it would be virtually impossible for him to remember his mother at all, he would reply, "Dying was the same as her going off to work; she abandoned me."

This is a typical case of psychoanalytic indoctrination. The author is now an admitted homosexual; secure in the belief that homosexuality is the best way for him to master his infantile sexual frustrations. The case is called typical because it incorporates most of the psychoanalytic principles, to wit: blamelessness on the part of the Freudophile, sex at the root of any and all problems, and almost always related to the parent of the opposite sex; and, of course, the literal licensing of illicit love. This is the kind of thing of which very few people have any awareness. This is the kind of thing that should be stopped. (7:169-170)

The almost inevitable worsening of patients' both psychological functioning and responsible behavior under the unmodified Freudian "treatment" became quite plain to me as I worked with a middle-aged woman. We were in about our fiftieth interview and her neurotic psychopathology was clearly delineated, largely through her own effort, as she was highly intelligent, sensitive and introspective. She was widowed some ten years earlier and had progressed to the position of a successful minor business executive. She had raised her two sons in a wholesome way and they had started their families and their promising professional careers. By this time she was living alone in a home she had bought after her husband's death. She came to me when she became troubled by recurring depressions, probably triggered by menopausal stresses. She was still an attractive woman, but she had apparently renounced her sensual and affective needs, sublimating them into fantasy outlets through reading and music and some philanthropic work.

Her psychopathology lent itself beautifully to Freudian constructions. Her memories were filled with what could easily and superficially validly be built into castration anxieties, Oedipal conflicts, incestuous drives, lack of identity with maternal "object," dammed sexuality, overstrict superego, and much more. Her childhood paradise was shattered at the age of three with the arrival of a younger

145

brother. She felt unbearably neglected and deprived. If I cared to do it, I could have subtly coached her and obtained from her a very real case of penis envy, hatred for mother, infatuation with father and decided incestuous fantasies. I felt a distinct possibility that I could flood her with all sorts of depraved wishes and fantasies if my image of the human psyche were built on Freudian ugly presuppositions. I could sicken her more by injecting (allegedly discovering) despicable cravings into her psychic reality. This would be akin to the "analysis" practiced by inquisitors on accused witches.

Having felt rejected by her mother, she had turned to her father for emotional security. He was a weak, ineffectual man, given to drinking sprees. When sober he would talk about books with his gifted teen-age daughter and the two of them became close. The arthritic, ailing, and embittered mother was probably jealous of the relationship between father and daughter, as the marital experience was riddled with reproaches and disappointments for both of them. One day, when the father came home drunk, the mother went into her customary tirade. He was speechless with guilt. His wife wanted to annihilate him in front of the children, throwing at him the accusation that he had no love for anyone in the family or he would have refrained from drinking for their sakes. My patient must have said something in defense of her father and the mother turned upon her: "He does not love you either. He has no love for anyone. Ask him if he loves you, if you do not believe me." The terrified daughter looked at the father for reassurance but he was too guiltridden to say anything in front of his family. My patient felt shattered again and her trust in her father was never repaired. She assumed an emotionally aloof role toward all members of her family.

It is patent from the above events that I could have easily led this imaginative woman to produce for me a mighty Oedipal drama, with all the incestuous implications, schemes and yearnings that are appropriate to the Freudian lore. It would not have been any problem to impute sexualized meanings to the memories of the scared, neurotic youngster that she was, trying desperately to maintain hope and self-control under difficult family circumstances. I could have also fanned up her repressed sexual drives, constructing Oedipal transference out of the turmoil I could have aroused in her. She would

146

be frightened by my demonstrating moral depravities in her, she would get even more depressed and her therapy with me would lengthen into the usual Freudian "interminable analysis." In the name of curing I could legitimately (according to Freudian "therapeutic" premises) drive this decent human being into self-loathing and deeper depression. I could thus undermine her religious discipline by making a spectacle of her impurity, increasing her cynical propensities, and poking holes in her self-respect. I could sicken her under the pretense of psychotherapy. She had by this time become quite attached to me and I could also easily build a grand case of sexualized "transference" out of it. I almost shuddered at the power I had over her current and future psychological development. I realized that I could twist this basically healthy and efficient person into sick Freudian molds. I could maim her for life by shaping her thinking into prevalent Freudian psychopathological forms. I did not slip into that "correct" procedure as both my and her values demanded a spiritually positive approach. Instead of scratching and squeezing her small psychological sores till her whole psyche became infected, I dealt sparingly with her "instinctual" promptings and the childish, dependent, and insecure needs and mild delusions. We did not neglect them, in fact I refocused her attention upon her immature demands upon others and upon herself on a number of occasions, but I primarily dwelled on her mature strivings, needs and achievements, as only these could maintain her at the level of responsible functioning, self-approval and hopefulness. Instead of trying to ennumerate the inexhaustible weaknesses in a human being, I rather chose to reinforce her strengths and help her establish supremacy over her liabilities. I emphasized her value as a mature human being: she had fulfilled her responsibilities of working hard and devotedly for her family and for her business firm, she had lived a morally and culturally dignified life, she had behaved lovingly, and was being loved by her children and friends. I urged her to think of her many fine achievements when neurotic tendencies arose to make her feel worthless and ungratified. She regained balance and used her fortified self-image to ward off depressions and handle her childish aspects without repressing them nor yielding to them. She had come to me, as she said, "because, as a non-Freudian, I knew you would not un-

147

dermine my religious and moral convictions, but help me master my weaknesses," and I believe I had not failed her as I surely would have done if I followed the prevalent Freudian precepts.

6. The widespread infection

Landis, professor of psychology at Columbia University, describes the saturation of American culture by Freudian categories and jargon:

> That psychoanalysis had permeated the thought and the systematic formulation in the social sciences is self-evident—clinical psychology, sociology, cultural anthropology, political economy, advertising, motivational research, unconscious motivation, oral and genital types, the mental mechanisms of catharsis, identification, transfer, rationalization, isolation, etc. are commonplace figures of speech in the parlance of the educated man. Just as the educated citizen speaks of cosmic rays, atoms, protons and $E=MC^2$, without really knowing what the terms really mean, so he also talks about Oedipal fixation, free-floating anxiety and inferiority complex in the same blind ignorance. (5:59)

A more recent observer notes how thoroughly Freudism had pervaded the popular American culture, to become itself vulgarized in the process:

> For the last 40 years, psychoanalysis has been largely an American product enjoying a cultural influence, scientific interest, and political power that it never attained in Europe nor even dreamed of in its native Vienna. Freud and Freudianism have become American ikons rivaled only by technology in their appeal to American sensibility and faith. It is the classical American success story: the harassed and impoverished refugee arrives on these golden shores, works faithfully, multiplies, prospers mightily, and within a generation adopts the values and attitudes of his neighbors. What began as a revolution led by Jews and foreigners had become another technology offering adjustment and success to analyst and patient. (24:8)

Pinckney expresses the view that Freudism had coarsened and deteriorated American morals, an opinion with which most of the critics would agree:

> The United States has accepted Freud blindly, reflecting our increasing lack of responsibility that many critics have observed in our society....
>
> Since the advent of that doctrine, our culture and even our daily activities have been penetrated to the point where morality is not only outmoded, immorality is virtually licensed. With each passing year that the personal philosophy of Sigmund Freud has been foisted upon the "average" individual, the level of what were once ideals has dropped one notch. Today, we live in a society where virtue is tolerated for the few "Victorians," and where freedom of expression—both physically and vocally—must dominate common courtesy and consideration for others supposedly to prevent mental illness. (7:53, 56)

Sokoloff, a physician and a biologist, educated in France and a cancer researcher in the United States, echoes other intellectuals, immigrants into this country like Ludwig (9), and Allers (23), and Kushner (15), in his concern about the pernicious effects of Freudism upon the moral health of American society. He attributes "the chaotic state of this country" (22:7) to Freudian infection primarily.

In his introductory note to the chapter on the contribution of permissiveness to the rise of crime in this country, he writes:

> For more than three decades, American intellectuals, the flower of our society, have been subjected to the influences of Freudian doctrine and ethics. As was said, and we hope was proved, the basis of the Freudian movement is extreme permissiveness, directed first of all against Society or The Establishment. Without exaggeration, one must acknowledge the phenomenal success of Freudian permissiveness in all aspects of American life: crime, narcotics, family, education and campus riots, sex, and even in the Supreme Court decisions. Many intellectuals call the present permissiveness drive a revolution, one which, according to them, would open new horizons and a new era for the American people. (22:109)

149

LaPierre finds that the profession of social work (like that of psychology, psychiatry, sociology, and education) in the States is overrun by Freudians. Again we see the effects of a defective view of man upon professional practitioners:

Many of the teachers in these schools [of social work] are dedicated Freudians, and the rest are at least sympathetic toward the Freudian view of man. The students are, as a consequence, indoctrinated rather than simply trained. They are indoctrinated into the theroy and practice of what is termed "case work" but is actually a sort of lay psychoanalysis for people who cannot afford the more extended and intimate type of professional analysis. The people so trained usually secure positions in the private agencies; and since these agencies have been relieved of the major burden of charitable work by the rise of public welfare organizations, they deal with a highly select clientele in a markedly Freudian manner. The underlying assumption is that whatever may seem to be the matter with the client—poverty, illness, inability to get or hold a job, desertion by husband or wife, abandonment by parents, or the infirmities of old age—the real difficulties lie deep within the client's unconscious. Such being the case, the simple manipulation of environmental factors is obviously futile. What is needed is diagnosis of the underlying psychological causes of the apparent difficulties and therapy to modulate the effect of these causes.

So the really professional social-welfare worker does not trouble herself with crass and practical matters. She (sometimes he) interviews the client over and over. These are "depth" interviews and may run for an hour or two. The reports on these interviews, dictated by the case worker in a sort of free-association manner, run to many pages. And if the client hangs on long enough, his complete and intimate life history will eventually be assembled and his case will be ready for diagnosis. The character of this diagnosis and of the therapy that will finally be prescribed is predetermined by the doctrine upon which the entire operation is based: the doctrine that man is an unhappy victim of the conflict between his nature and society. His troubles may seem to stem from occupational incompetence, the irresponsibilities of an unfortunate wife, or the physical disabilities that often come with advancing years. But the real trouble lies far deeper: he is psychologically insecure, he suffers from a sense of guilt, he has never outgrown the infantile stage of narcissism. (6:74, 75)

A professor in a school of social work pleads with a critic of Freudism to turn his attention to social workers and save them from serfdom:

> In closing I would like to add that I wish Dr. Johnson would bestow his literary talents to the field of social work which for the past three decades probably has done (and is still doing) more than any organized profession to promote Freudian psychology in the United States. If some of his critical views were published in a social work journal I feel that the shock treatment might be highly therapeutic for some social workers and I hope not too traumatic for others. (8:467)

Dr. Johnson, however, is rather skeptical about his ability to do anything for the thoroughly brainwashed social workers:

> This would accomplish nothing. For it is my general impression that most social workers believe what they are told to believe. If by some cosmic freak the school faculties were dynamically reoriented overnight to Zen Buddhism, there would only be the mildest susurrus of protest in the classrooms. (25:469)
> Advertising has also become permeated by Freudian "insights":

> The motivational researchers have become, it would appear, a considerable power in advertising and related circles. An increasing proportion of advertising is slanted towards such "unconscious" motivations as the need for emotional security, ego gratification, guilt release, and inevitably thwarted sexual desires. Whether the new appeals actually fool the buying public is debatable, but the fact that the advertising fraternity believe they do suggests that advertisers have taken over the Freudian idea of man and have made the public in its image. (6:77)

The permissive, overindulgent, unrealistic upbringing of children in the United States is plainly one of the results of Freudian brainwashing of the public. Instead of preparing the children for the world of hard knocks in which they would perform responsibly, parents have been persuaded by Freudian psychiatrists, psychologists, and educators that children should not be frustrated, should not be held down to certain universal rules of behavior, but should be allowed free "self-expression." Such distorted views of training children flow, of course, from Freud's distorted representation of society as an oppressor of the individual. The positive role of social guidance, supports and restrictions is completely disregarded.

The advocates of the permissive mode of child rearing are, in effect attempting to validate the Freudian ethic, although it is doubtful if any of them are aware of or comprehend the social implications of their endeavor. They propose that the infant and child be treated as though man were in fact what Freud's fancy made him to be. They hold, with Freud, that as a consequence of his biological nature, the individual is an exceedingly delicate organism and that any attempt to teach him to behave in accordance with socially designated rules of conduct will make him into a complex-ridden, guilt-ridden neurotic. Unlike Freud, they seem to assume, further, that if the individual is from birth showered with love and affection, granted his slightest whim, and never in any way guided or constrained, he will grow like a butter-fly from its cocoon to stretch its lovely wings and soar gracefully through life. (6:102)

When these children, untrained in respect for rules, grew up, many turned towards socially disorganizing behavior: delinquency, crime, divorce, promiscuity, child neglect, cynicism, purposeless rebellion, and other expressions of self-centered, unintegrated personalities. Some professional workers are now swinging back towards a less indulgent approach to child rearing. LaPierre (6) notices that the 1957 edition of the most popular book on child raising, Spock's *Baby and Child Care,* is less permissive than the 1946 edition. But the public usually lags behind the professionals, and we can expect that Freudian superstitions will dominate or at least influence the field for the next decade or two.

The Freudians have infected other areas of social activity, particularly education and penal practices, producing conceptual confusion and practical ineffectiveness. It would take us too far afield to deal with these problems here. LaPierre (6:110-176) provides a telling summary of the Freudian corrosion.

Pinckney points to the crude overemphasis on sex and the degradation of American women to almost exclusively a sexual object as a consequence of Freudian ascendance in the entertainment and artistic media:

If you think that because you have never been directly enveloped by the psychoanalytic octopus, you are not a captive of one of its tentacles, you are sadly mistaken. Virtually every man, woman and child in the United States (and a fair amount of citizens in other countries) has felt the effects of the Freudian fallacy. The most flagrant example of this morbid invasion of our lives can be seen in the entertainment image of the modern American woman. There is very little disagreement that all too many of those who write about the American woman (in the theater, motion pictures, books, etc.) are post-Freudian analyzed homosexuals. Such indoctrinted authors use the entertainment medium as their whipping post to obtain revenge against all womanhood.

Writers of all sorts in the last 20 to 30 years seem to be preoccupied with psychoanalysis. Certainly there can be no denial of the spate of sordid sexual novels, plays and films that now prevail. Every form of sexual sensation, response, deviation and perversion has been examined by writers for the "entertainment" media, to the point where simple wholesome love, of which sex should be only an integral part, is shunned. Authors of books, plays, films and television dramas have so related psychoanalysis to our society that this kind of thinking has become accepted as normal. People in all walks of life sport psychoanalytic jargon without even realizing the implications of what they are saying.

Homosexuality has become so overt, due to analytical thinking and writings which have wholly accepted Freud's belief that everyone has homosexual tendencies, that what was once an attitude to be ashamed of, is now influencing our lives. Women have been told by homosexual dress designers to dress more like boys—to obliterate the difference between men and women. Men are encouraged to take an equal interest in fashion, with women. Men's clothes are becoming more effeminate, and hairdressers for men are gaining wide acceptance. (7:137, 138)

153

Chapter IV

Freudism: A Promotional Success

Now it is vain to expect apostles to display a sense of scientific responsibility. Their primary allegiance is to their creed.

Edward Glover, M.D. (54:18)

... psychiatry—by which I mean psycho-analysis...

M. Royden C. Astley, M.D. Professor of Psychiatry, in 1962 (80:56, 57)

The assurance of Freud and the gullibility, and want of criticism, in his followers is truly astounding.

A. Wohlgemuth, Ph.D., Professor of Psychology (1:56)

Ernest Jones, official biographer of Freud, mentioned that some of Freud's friends suspected that he himself did not believe in some of his own sensational postulates. He used them to stir the attention of the public to his work. There is no question that Freud was an excellent promoter of his own teachings.

Boris Sokoloff, M.D., Ph.D. (74:35)

Nowhere has psychoanalysis flourished more than in the United States and nowhere have Freudian theories had a greater impact on child rearing, psychiatric training, literature, and arts.

Modern man in distress is like the aborigine who looks to the witch doctor for powerful magic.

Hans H. Strupp, Ph.D. (82:35)

1. *Lessons from propaganda*

The techniques of brainwashing and propaganda practiced by totalitarian masters may throw some further light upon the predominance of the psychoanalytic cult in American psychiatry and psychology.

In Communist propaganda, Stalin was admired and praised as one of the greatest men of history, both in the USSR and among Communists abroad. A great many capable and intelligent people spoke and wrote of him in the 1930s and 1940s not only as an unbelievably gifted political leader, but as a man with the utmost compassion for the "sufferings of the oppressed masses," a genius of an industrial organizer, a brilliant military strategist, a profound thinker, writer and historian, and even a talented scientist. The image of the murderous ruler stared from walls in factories, schools, reading rooms, and all government offices, from huge processional banners and from the pages of newspapers, in schools and in clubs. Millions of Americans were duped into belief about "good old Joe" [1] by wartime propaganda, not to speak of millions of Russians who trudged in droves to pay homage to one of the most vicious mass murderers in human history. This incredible deception was achieved by constant drumming about the great qualities of the leader and by raising in the background the specter of capitalist plotters, imperialist warmongers, vile reactionaries and despicable local traitors.

In a similar camp, the Nazis erected an idealized effigy of another brute. He was portrayed as the gift of providence to the German people, destined to lead them to the Teutonic millennium. His heart was described as bleeding for injustices and injuries of even the lowliest German. His leadership, based on pure blood and Germanic honor, was destined to regenerate the German *Volk* and overcome the corruption engendered by Jews, Masons, Marxists and other allegedly depraved groups. Germans believed it and went to their deaths by millions to fulfill his messianic plans. Again the spell was cast and the frenzy of admiration maintained by a steady conditioning stream of newspaper articles, broadcasts, speeches, books, pictures, etc.

2. No limits to human gullibility (suggestibility)

It would be an example of a self-perpetuated hoax if we thought that the above examples, being drawn from totalitarian countries, do not apply to us living in a free society of the United States. In his comprehensive study of many kinds of hoaxes, MacDougall (78) collected several hundred innocent or fraudulent deceptions which fooled many Americans. The educational level of the subjects to hoaxes seems irrelevant; learned individuals may be no less prone to being taken in than simple folks, as Freudians have amply demonstrated.

In chapter IX I shall review some experimentally verified demonstrations of how extremely suggestible human beings can be. Here I shall draw on MacDougall's rich collection of tricks that have been readily and successfully played on humans in the American culture. He reviews in separate chapters the reason why we suspend our critical thinking, why we do not disbelieve: indifference to an objective appraisal of the hoax; ignorance and superstition in the matter of the hoax; readiness to be fooled ("suggestibility"); and the prestige of the hoaxer. He has seven chapters on the "incentives to believe," among them: financial gain of both suggester and the subject; vanity; promoting a cause; allegiance to pet theories; the thirst for vicarious thrills; and cultural climate. We have already seen some of these incentives operating in the Freudian hoax, and others will become obvious in further exposition.

MacDougall starts with gullibility demonstrated in some simple experiments taken from Gardner and Lois Murphy's *Experimental Social Psychology:*

> For instance, one professor sprayed pure water about a schoolroom, telling the students to raise their hands when they detected an odor; 73 per cent did so. Of 381 children shown a toy camel and told it would be seen to move when a windlass turned, 76 per cent said they saw the motion. A coin about the size of a fifty-cent piece was passed around a class of forty-eight boys from fourteen to seventeen years of age with instructions to examine it carefully. At the end of the class period the instructor asked each boy to draw a picture of the coin, indicating the position of the hole in it. Although there was no hole, all but four of the forty-eight indicated one, some even drawing two holes. Of the four only one, the bad boy of the class, unaccustomed to obeying orders, was positive that there was no hole. (78:29)

Reading MacDougall's book is both amusing and terrifying. It is hilarious to see sane people accept preposterous propositions; yet there is reason to be seriously concerned with the readiness of many to be fooled. The reader interested in the matter might well turn to this book for telling illustrations. I shall provide only three or four here.

156

In 1906, a journalist given to stunts, revived the old story about the "Jersey devil." The original fantasy was to be found in an old book, telling about the wish of a blasphemous mother that her seventh child be a devil, which came to pass. Immediately after birth the little devil flew up the chimney and disappeared. The journalist reported that an (invented) farmer's wife had seen the devil again after nearly a hundred years since its last appearance. Even the Associated Press reported the item.

From then on accounts agree. Reporters gathered, plaster casts were made of footprints in the snow, reports poured in of prominent citizens who staggered home in dilapidated condition as the result of meetings with the creature, women were found in hysterics on lonely roads.

And the devil was seen. Reputable citizens described in detail his horrific form, the great wings, the frenzied countenance, half human and half animal, the long tail, the eleven feet, the deadly vapors which were exhaled in a mixture of fire and smoke. The fiend was ubiquitous. He was seen all over the southern part of the state. He was seen in the rural parts of Pennsylvania, Delaware and Maryland, all on the same night.

It was impossible for the learned to avoid being drawn into the controversy. An expert of the Smithsonian Institution said that the appearance "bore out his long cherished theory that there still existed in hidden caverns and caves, deep in the interior of the earth, survivors of those prehistoric animals and fossilized remains. . . . " The devil, he concluded, must be a pterodactyl.

As the terror spread, several mills in Gloucester closed because their female operatives were afraid to go home after dark. Phil Nash, noted theatrical manager, who had leased the Broadway Theater in Camden, was compelled to close for several nights. When the devil was reported seen in California on the same night that it also had appeared in New Jersey, Professor Samuel P. Langley, of aviation fame, was consulted. He examined descriptions of the wing spread and opined that the beast easily could fly the distance in a night, considering the difference in time. (78:32, 33)

As our focus here is on the hoax aspects of Freudism, it is worth noting the reactions of the learned dupes of this practical joke. The learned people, of course, would not accept the plainly superstitious aspects of the devilish creature. They could be fooled only in their peculiar way: the nonsense had to fit their favorite theoretical fantasies and predilections. In a comparable way, many learned psychiatrists and psychologists had taken over from Freud his theoretical phantoms, the "scientific hallucinations," as Jastrow had diagnosed Freud's special intuitions. To begin with, they were trained to accept Freud as the authority about psyche. This accomplished, they were ready to accept any other fantastic presupposition. Having bowed once to Freud's reputation, they would easily believe any other of his irrational derivations.

The prestige of the hoaxer has an overriding influence upon evidence of the senses and the sense of the subjects.

Pitirim A. Sorokin, Harvard University sociologist obtained the cooperation of 1,484 human guinea pigs, 32 of whom he tested individually and the rest in twenty-one groups ranging in size from 4 to 299. To them all he played two phonograph recordings of Brahms' Opus 68, Symphony No. 1 in C minor, Part VI. Preceding each rendition, the statement was made that musical experts had selected one (sometimes the first, sometimes the second) as the better. Purpose of the test, it was announced, was to determine if laymen agreed with critical opinion.

Although actually the same record was repeated, 95.6 per cent accepted the dogmatic suggestion that the two playings were different. The judgement of the supposed critics was accepted by 58.9 per cent. In part summary of his findings in the March, 1932, American Journal of Sociology, Sorokin wrote:

Thus a mere dogmatic statement, bluntly put, that the records were different dimmed their sense of discrimination and led them to an entirely wrong conclusion, in spite of the contrary evidence to the reality—the real sound stimuli. . . . on a large scale, and in thousands of forms, facts of this kind happen daily in social life, especially on various political platforms, in discussions, clubs, various lectures, and so on. (78:41)

When Freud was established as the most profound investigator of the human psyche, he attained the power of prestige to put any partial or complete nonsense over his students, patients, and readers. They were all astonished to find in themselves the evidence of Oedipal complexes, castration fears, mighty or perverse sexual promptings, and many other phantoms of psychoanalytic theory.

The cultural climate greatly facilitates the acceptance of any foolishness as revelation of truth. Dr. Jordan announced jokingly in *Popular Science Monthly* that he had succeeded in photographing the mental processes of persons contemplating a cat and produced the faked photos. The minute description of the process in scientific, technical terms deceived many an educated reader.

The learned members of the Authors Club of New York played a hoax on literary critics about a (nonexistent) great Russian author, Alexis Sarrovitch, who was so unjustly neglected by men of letters. They arranged for a commemorative meeting at which speeches were given on various aspects of the famous writer, and these were even published in the form of a book. Many a learned critic was taken in before the hoax was revealed, as the hoaxers were well-known college professors and literary gentlemen, whose erudition was beyond question.

Artists, a group given to preponderantly emotional reactions, are particularly easily fooled by their preconceptions:

In the field of art several attempts to show up modern cults whose adherents have high-sounding Freudian explanations of how they put their souls into their work have been such as to make lowbrows chortle. At the 131st annual exhibition of the Pennsylvania Academy of the Fine Arts in 1936 in Philadelphia for instance, Margaret Gest won a prize for her painting "Pink Lilies," despite the fact that it was hung upside down. In the same year B. Howitt-Lodge, portrait painter, smuggled "Abstract Painting of Woman" into the International Surrealist Exhibition in London. Signed D. S. Windle, it was a phantasmagoria of paint blobs, variegated beads, a cigarette stub, Christmas tinsel, pieces of hair and a sponge. The composer explained that he had painted the worst possible "mess" as a protest against "one of the most warped and disgusting shows I ever attended." The stock answer of the so-called modernists who believe in the Emersonian principle that art is its own excuse for being, even though it communicates nothing because its vocabulary is gibber-

159

ish, was: "He may think it's a hoax but he's an artist and unconsciously he may be a surrealist. Aren't we all?"

To the 1938 spring exhibit of the Art League of Springfield, Massachusetts, a local conservative painter, J.P. Billings, sent "Opus No. 1." When it was accepted he promptly resigned, explaining that he had attempted deliberately to paint the worst picture of which he was capable. (78:266)

An artist, critical of the modernist quasi art, jokingly started the movement of Disumbrationism, which was praised as a breakthrough by American and French art review critics. He painted a few canvases in careless and deliberately disgusting (to him) ways, signed them with a foreign name and was accepted as the talented leader of the new Disumbrationist School.

Jules Masserman, a trained but not brainwashed psychoanalyst, played a similar trick on his audience of physicians. He playfully reported to them, in the proper Freudian technical jargon, of a new mental aberration he had discovered, the onychoneurosis, the neurosis of the stubbed toenail. He was shocked to be congratulated later on for his perspicacity as a Freudian researcher. This hoax on a learned audience, ready to buy any nonsense if couched in mystifying Freudian terms, is reviewed fully elsewhere (*Freud's Non-science*, 61).

MacDougall concludes: " . . . Indifferent, ignorant, vain, suggestible, awed by the real or feigned prestige of those who speak with authority, man believes what he wants to believe. . . . and disbelieve[s] what does not square with preconceived ideas." (78:146, 88) He attributes the proneness to be deceived to the childish component of human personality which is never completely overcome by anyone: "In fact there is no reason to be amazed because the ordinary person believes anything. Belief is natural and pleasant. The child begins life by believing everything. He has to be taught skepticism before he will doubt that there is a Santa Claus, or that the moon is made of green cheese." (78:5)

As we have seen and shall further see, the basic Freudian procedure is to reduce both trainees and patients to a level as close to infantility as possible. This is the supposedly "therapeutic regression." Reduced to childish phases of personality functioning, the Freudian subjects, if integrated into the process, are ready to receive anything coming from

160

the psychoanalyst as revelations from on high.

A final item in this section on human gullibility concerns MacDougall himself. This clever exposer of hoaxes was himself caught in one. He seriously suggests that "the careful investigation of the psychology of swindler, forger or imposter is to be undertaken only by a psychoanalyst"! (78:VII)

3. *Freudian hero worship*

Following the natural pattern of any enthusiastic and credulous group, the psychoanalytic movement carried on a process of idealizing Freud and mythologizing his role. Undoubtedly, Freud was an exceptional man. He was highly gifted, hardworking, consciously honest, responsible, morally strict, and imaginative—a persuasive thinker, talented writer, sometimes astute clinician, and capable teacher. Many other fine things can be said about him. But some of his disciples went overboard displaying frenzied admiration and religious fervor for their Messiah. They projected him into the greatest psychologist in history, a phenomenal seer into the psyche, the first real scientist in matters of human nature, the solver of enigmas of unconscious depths, the originator of the first psycho-therapeutic system founded along scientific lines, the destroyer of centuries-old misconceptions about the human mind, the savior from rationalistic superficiality, the prophet of liberated sexuality, and so on *ad infinitum*. These admiring comments are repeated piously in lectures, supervisory sessions, books, articles, and in conversation. Ellenberger observes that the two hundred years of dynamic psychiatry from Mesmer's animal magnetism to Freudian dominance were characterized by hero worship. Freud's partisans seem to have gone into it with the utmost abandon. Ellenberger analyzed in detail the legends and myths which the admirers built around Freud:

A rapid glance at the Freudian legend reveals two main features. The first is the theme of the solitary hero struggling against a host of enemies, suffering "the slings and arrows of outrageous fortune" but triumphing in the end. The legend considerably exaggerates the extent and role of anti-Semitism, of the hostility of the academic world, and of alleged Victorian prejudices. The second feature of the Freudian legend is the blotting out of the greatest part of the scientific and cultural con-

161

text in which psychoanalysis developed, hence the theme of the absolute originality of the achievements, in which the hero is credited with the achievements of his predecessors, associates, disciples, rivals, and contemporaries.

The legend discarded, we are permitted to see the facts in a different light. Freud is shown as having an average career of the contemporary academic man in central Europe, a career whose beginnings were only slightly hampered by anti-Semitism, and with no more setbacks than many others. He lived in a time when scientific polemics had a more vehement tone than today, and he never suffered the degree of hostility as did men such as Pasteur and Ehrlich. The current legend, on the other hand, attributes to Freud much of what belongs, notably, to Herbart, Fechner, Nietzsche, Meynert, Benedikt, and Janet, and overlooks the work of previous explorers of the unconscious, dreams, and sexual pathology. Much of what is credited to Freud was diffuse current lore, and his role was to crystallize these ideas and give them an original shape. (65:547, 548)

Not unlike his hysterical patients, Freud helped the legends along by exaggerating his woes with critics, with colleagues and with the public. He enjoyed the role of a misunderstood genius, of a rejected savior and an ostracized Jewish savant. Alongside the messianic complex, Freud apparently had a martyr complex too. Taking point by point, Ellenberger unmasks the pretenses and falsehoods: the Vienna doctors were not blindly unreceptive; the public was not "shocked in their philistine puritanism." Contrary to the usual assertion, his publications did not meet with the icy silence or the disparaging criticism that are said to have existed. (65:455)

Writing fifty years ago, Dunlap, professor of experimental psychology at the Johns Hopkins University, ascribes the lack of objectivity about Freud to ignorance of psychology, in which, as we shall see, the pupils were following their master:

In an equally naive way the Freudians deduce from time to time other important "discoveries" from the Freudian principles. The great importance of sex in human life is something which is supposed to have been entirely unknown until pointed out by Freud. It is a constant surprise to disciples of the Vienna physician that a psychologist may recognize, and even emphasize, the fundamental role which sex ideas and sex activities play in mind and conduct and yet not be a Freudian. Even the principles of the association of ideas, are, by frequent implication, products of psychoanalysis. The fact that all details of conscious conduct are causally directed by the results of previous experience was, according to psychoanalysis, never surmised until Freud's *Psychopathology of Everyday Life* appeared. Students unacquainted with psychology, who get their first knowledge of commonplace psychological facts from Freudian sources, necessarily look upon Freud as the founder of modern mental science. (2:94)

In order to build up their hero even further and to show with what terrible cultural odds he had to struggle, they falsified the cultural scene in Vienna and Western Europe at the end of nineteenth century. People were supposed to be prudes, repressed, blushing at the slightest mention of sexuality. Into such darkness Freud brought the light of knowledge and healthy views. Ellenberger learnedly and patiently reveals such falsifications as nonsense. Both Vienna and Paris were known as capitals with the loosest morals. The four volumes of Stekel's (68, 69) case histories of frigidity and impotence are full of examples of men and women engaging in extramarital and other affairs.

The so-called Victorian spirit, which had reigned mostly in England until the middle decades of the century, had declined everywhere, and little of it remained in continental Europe. On the contrary, books, journals, and newspapers were filled with erotic preoccupations, though with slightly more restraint and more subtlety of expression than today. The abundance of obscene literature was such that Jules Claretie, in a review of the year 1880, wrote the epitaph "Here rests the pornographic year 1880." Eroticism dominated literature from the very top in the refined works of men such as Anatole France and Arthur Schnitzler down to the trashiest publications for the uneducated. (65:282)

The learned people produced "a flood of literature" on sexual problems. A yearbook on sexual matters published in 1903 had 1368 pages. There was a spate of books in German, French, Italian, designed to enlighten on sexual problems. Freud's misperceptions notwithstanding, the Catholics were not shutting their eyes in horror before sexuality even in children:

> While physicians generally considered child sexuality as a rare abnormality, it had been taken for granted for a long time by priests and educators. Father Debreyne, a moral theologian who was also a physician, insisted in his book upon the great frequence of infantile masturbation, of sexual play between young children, and of the seduction of very young children by wet nurses and servants. Bishop Dupanloup of Orleans, an eminent educator, repeatedly emphasized in his work the extreme frequency of sex play among children, and stated that most children acquired "bad habits" between the ages of one to two years. Similar ideas were brilliantly expounded by Michelet in some of the works that he wrote for popular education. In *Our Sons* he warned parents against the dangers of what would be called today child sexuality and the Oedipus complex. (65:295, 296)

Apparently, Freud's promoters had a special prism through which they viewed their master and the surrounding culture. Restraint and objectivity were not characteristic of their approach.

4. *Freud the Magnificent*

A whole volume of admiring quotations and biased comparisons of Freud with other psychologists could be gathered from worshipful statements of Freud enthusiasts. A few examples may give their flavor.

Alexander and Selesnick describe Freud as "one of the most important and influential figures in the history of psychiatry, and indeed in the history of Western civilization." (3:181) Those of us who disagree could only say the eulogists stood too close to their great man, and too far from other great men in the Western world. The disproportionate place they give to Freud in comparison with other great contributors to the advancement of psychiatric knowledge would have made it proper to subtitle their *History of Psychiatry:* "As Viewed Through the Freudian Prism."

164

The section they prefer to call "The Freudian Age" includes reviews of Adler, Jung, Bleuler, Binet, Piaget, Rorschach and Meyer. Apparently their merits in psychiatry and psychology were primarily that they happened to live and work in the era of Freud; that some of them stood against Freud's dogmas seems to be of secondary importance (although recognized in one subtitle). Freud and the faithful occupy forty-four pages, the Dissenters get twenty-six pages, including those devoted to disparagement of their work. There is a chapter with the suggestive title of "Freud's Scientific Evolution," with fourteen pages, while Bleuler is alloted one, Meyer three, Horney one, Sullivan one-half, Pavlov and the behaviorists two, while the existentialists are lumped with Zen on four pages. J. H. Schultz, the doyen of German psychiatry, is not mentioned at all, in spite of his great productivity and influence; Frankl, with fourteen books and almost three hundred articles on Logotherapy and other psychiatric topics is also omitted. Behavior therapy, although one of the chief rivals to psychoanalysis, is not mentioned at all, nor is the name of Eysenck, its chief early proponent. Although a psychologist, Rogers is rated better and is given a little less than a page, but Ellis, Kelly, Mowrer and other psychologists critical of Freudism are considered unworthy of mention. Bandura, Wolpe, and Salter [2] are only named along with one publication each. By way of dismissal, the authors claim that "these therapeutic designs practiced by some psychologists are not based on theories of unconscious motivation, nor do they consider internal subjective experience, and have not been adopted by psychiatric and psychoanalytically oriented practitioners." (3:331) None of these assertions are quite true, but they do show the authors' characteristic slant in disposing of competing systems: Wolpe is a psychiatrist; the subjective experiences are considered in typical behavior therapies; some advanced psychiatrists had already reported on their work in this non-Freudian direction before the publication of the *History*.

Ellenberger, with a much deeper sense of fairness and proportion, rejects such unbalanced appreciation of Freud. He provides a telling historical analogy:

In every textbook on the history of Greek philosophy, the chapters concerning Plato, Aristotle, the Stoics, and Epicurus are about the same length. This length bears no relation to the relative size of each school. Plato's academy and Aristotle's lyceum had few members compared to the Stoics and Epicureans. The Epicureans were as dominant as today's Freudians. In every Mediterranean city a group of Epicureans met each month to feast under the master's portrait and to celebrate his doctrine, his life, and his legend. What would you make of a book on Greek philosophy that devoted two or three pages to Plato and Aristotle, a hundred to Stoics, and eight or nine hundred to Epicurus? (83:53)

The propagandistic bias of Alexander and Selesnick becomes evident when the judgement about what is important in psychiatry is compared with someone who does not have the Freudian ax to grind, Ellenberger for instance. Ellenberger's *The Discovery of the Unconscious* (65) covers the history of modern psychiatry in a much more comprehensive and objective way. Compared with 153 pages assigned to Freud (including the exposition of accumulated falsehoods), Janet gets 87 pages, Jung 92, Adler 85, and the forerunners of dynamic psychiatry 330 pages!

Stranger than the bias of Alexander and Selesnick, the two psychiatrists engulfed in the Freudian *Zeitgest*, is the reaction of some well-known psychologists. As a rule, psychologists in this country are better trained in objective thinking and are less prone to buy assertions by alleged authorities in a wholesale manner. Yet, Freud's popularity in this country has apparently swayed some leading psychologists into overreverence for Freud's ideas. Roeckelein reports on an investigation of the number of references to the names of influential psychologists in eight most widely used American textbooks of introductory psychology, "in which presumably most of the basic facts of psychology reside." (84:657) If the emphasis is on psychological "facts" in these textbooks, then it is hard to understand how Freud's name could be given the prominence Roeckelein discovered. Freud's apparent psychological "facts" are alluded to 409 times. Adler and Jung had far fewer "facts" for selection by these American teachers of psychology (35 and 34 respectively). Similar counts could probably be obtained if one surveyed the political texts in Germany in 1933-1945 for mentions of Hitler and President Roosevelt, and in Soviet Russia for references to Stalin and Churchill.

166

Other psychologists who contributed ascertained or ascertainable facts to psychology fared no better in these American textbooks than Freud's rivals, Jung and Adler. Pavlov, the founder of what appears the closest to an ideal scientific investigation of behavior, has only 113 mentions. Watson, the founder of American behaviorism, gets 59, and Skinner, who advanced the behavioristic approach to its most systematic expression and effective application, got 118 references. Allport, the best-known American theoretician of personality, had only 59 mentions. The same number of references went to Carl Rogers, who not only theorized fruitfully but also, unlike Freud, verified many of his suppositions experimentally. Piaget, who contributed so much to developmental and cognitive psychology, was referred 134 times, little more than twenty-five per cent of Freud's number of references. Köhler made many important systematic contributions through applications of Gestalt psychology, yet he got no more than 30 mentions. Kurt Lewin, who constructed scientifically applicable formulations in psychology, was mentioned 23 times. Maslow, for all his raising of psychological conceptualizations of human nature out of the reductionistic, scientistic formulations, did not receive more than 47 references in all the eight textbooks. The founders of scientific measurements of sensory and memory functions, Wundt and Ebbinghaus, were mentioned only 37 and 47 times respectively. Clearly, the bandwagon mentality was significantly present among American psychologists of our period.

The promotional drive of Freudians to aggrandize their master and to belittle his critics and competitors for fame is manifest even in the pages of the *Encyclopaedia Britannica*. The *Encyclopaedia* can usually be relied upon for a balanced opinion, but not in the case of Freud. When the number of pages assigned to Freud and psychoanalysis is compared with those of other important psychologists and with sensible proportions of a study like Ellenberger's, it is obvious that the members of the *Encyclopaedia* board were overimpressed by Freud's fans. In the 1970 edition, Freud and psychoanalysis is allowed seven pages, while Jung, Adler, Janet and Mesmer have only one-fourth page each, A. Meyer and psychobiology one-half. No space is devoted to individual or analytical psychology as systems, nor to Frankl or Schultz.

The editors of the *Encyclopaedia* have even swallowed the

customary Freudian pretenses to "research" and "therapy" in allowing Hartmann to insert this piece of pure propaganda in his article: "His [Freud's] method of free association is essential to the therapeutic technique and also a powerful tool of psychological research." (72:930) The short statement contains two untruths patent to any objective examiner of Freudian practices. The method of free association is essential only to orthodox Freudian treatment, and Hartmann did not write "*his* therapeutic technique" but "*the* therapeutic technique." The majority of contemporary psychotherapies do not use free association. Probably Hartmann, like other disciplined Freudians, assumes that non-Freudian treatments are not psychotherapy. Also, Freudian free association has little to do with what is known as psychological research. One can readily admit that it is a powerful tool for proliferating speculations in Freudian "research," which bears little resemblance to objective psychological investigations, as will be shown later in Part II, and particularly in *Freud's Non-science*. (71)

If such a balanced and objective publication as the *Encyclopaedia* can be swept into a biased judgment as evidenced above, how much more pronounced inobjectivity can be expected from individual Freudian enthusiasts. Nelson, for instance, shows a serious loss of historical perspective when he proposes "that the Twentieth Century go down in history as the *Freudian Century*." (4:9)

Ehrenwald, too, perpetrates the Freudian historical bias, assuming that Freud has preempted the field of psychology to such an extent that others can hardly say anything new and important that he had not already discovered. In his discussion of Adler, Ehrenwald demonstrates the arbitrary treatment afforded psychologists who stand for ideas diametrically opposed to Freud's. It is obvious from Ehrenwald's exposition that Adler diverged so fundamentally from Freud that he can be subsumed under Freudism only by forced and biased reasoning:

> Despite differences, Alfred Adler's individual psychology ranks as one of the major subclasses of the Freudian model. Thus it is not by coincidence that it purged itself with equal zeal of all remaining vestiges of magic and myth. Even more than the Freudian system, it has aspired to become a therapy of "pure reason"—if not of ordinary common sense. Individual

168

psychology has a frankly didactic purpose. At the same time, it has substituted Freudian determinism with a consistently teleological, Thomistic system of explanations. It maintains its link with biological aspects by calling attention to the part played by organ inferiority and its compensation. By contrast to Freud's libido theory, it minimizes the importance of sexuality in the origin of neurosis. If Freud tends to sexualize the individual's quest for power, Adler reduces the power of sex to the point of insignificance or turns it into one of the tools in the quest for power. Thus individual psychology has developed an explanatory system essentially based on one single variable. Nevertheless, some of its propositions can easily be converted into Freudian terms. Adler's inferiority feeling bears close resemblance to Freud's concept of castration anxiety. His "masculine protest" can roughly be translated into Freud's penis envy; the Oedipal conflict is viewed as the pampered child's need to vie for or to monopolize father's or mother's love and attention. The Freudian unconscious, on the other hand, is turned into the stepchild of Adler's psychology; it is simply that of a person's mental content which he does not care to recall or to look at. Dreams, slips of the tongue and neurotic symptoms reflect a person's "style of life." The Freudian superego, instead of being derived from introjected authority, is projected back into the outside world and designated as the feeling of social responsibility of *Gemeinschaftsgefuehl*.

Based on these more or less loosely knit general propositions, Adlerian therapy aims at reducing inferiority feelings, at correcting faulty habits of thinking and increasing social cooperation. Thus Adlerian therapists specifically subscribe to the principle of learning theory but have no use for psychodynamics in the Freudian sense. (5:196, 197)

It is hard to see how with these many differences, Ehrenwald can subsume Adler's psychology as a "major subclass of the Freudian model." With such reasoning, one could confound Christianity with Mohammedanism, Egyptians with Israelis, and mystics with junkies.

Writers less eager to shove famous psychologists under Freud's umbrella, find that both Adler and Jung are so different in their approach to psychological reality that it would be unreasonable to pigeonhole them with Freud. Introducing the chapter on Adler in his superbly documented book, Ellenberger suggests that "when studying Adler, the reader must temporarily put aside all that he has learned about psychoanalysis and adjust to a quite different way of thinking. . . . individual psychology is not just a deviation of psychoanalysis, but radically differs from it." (65:571, 636)

Ellenberger also protests similar annexation of Jung to the Freudian model; he wants to "definitely refute the current stereotype that Jung's system is merely a distortion of Freud's psychoanalysis." (65: X)

An amusing Freudian slip expressing the imperious spread of psychoanalysis might be involved in Ehrenwald's mentioning in another publication the psychodramatic techniques, developed by an anti-Freudian, Moreno, as "psychodynamic techniques such as role reversal, role playing, doubling . . . " (5:30) Moreno had disclaimed in 1946 any liking of "psychodynamics": "I am an outsider and an opponent of psychoanalytic philosophy." (70:19)

Unfortunately, these Freud-aggrandizing operations have caused confusion even among the learned people, not to speak of the general public. The confusion is evident even in the thinking of the permanent secretary of the Swedish Academy, the Nobel-Prize awarding body. In the presentation address for the award for literature to Hermann Hesse in 1946, the learned gentleman made a misstatement: "Sick and bed-ridden, he sought a cure in the psychoanalysis of Freud, eagerly preached and practiced at that time which left lasting traces in Hesse's increasingly bold books of this period." (73:234) If Hesse had undergone a brainwashing on the Freudian couch, his creativity would have taken quite a different turn, and possibly his life, too. He would not have become an idol of the generation searching for wider inner and outer horizons in Europe and in the States in the sixties, fifty years after his analysis. Actually, he was analyzed by Jung, who offered him a very different therapy than a Freudian would have. The permanent secretary of the Swedish Academy was apparently so impressed by Freudian assertiveness that he inferred factuality.

Jones (6:69, 100, 101, 121, 150) provides several examples of extravagant eulogies of Freud before venturing some of his own. One panegyrist exalts Freud over Einstein: "Sigmund Freud had no Newton before him. If Einstein's theory of relativity is said to be the greatest feat of human intellect, it is difficult to find further words for the attainment of Freud." Apparently neither the writer nor Jones took into account that Einstein's theory still stands as one of the bases of modern physics, while Freud's ideas were found wanting by psychologists of the stature of Jung, Adler, Horney, Fromm, and a host of others.

Jones is well aware of the vulnerability of the psychoanalytic position to detractors. In discussing Freud's influence on contemporary psychiatry, he admits: "I cannot think of a single statement I could make about it that would be non-controversial." Yet he chooses to display the selective vision of a devotee. He quotes the eulogies of another writer: " ... changes in the fundamental categories in terms of which we interpret the world and each other, with the very framework of our thought and language, are rare in history, and more rarely still can we attribute such a change to one man. But about Freud, the inventor of psychoanalysis, there can be no doubt." Apparently, though, Jones has some doubt, and feels a certain compunction about siding with such an obviously uncritical view. He begins the next sentence, "I am myself inclined to doubt that estimate, ... " then quickly recovers the posture of adoration to finish, " ... although in time to come it may well prove to be justified." Jones continues with the same abandon: " ... his name will become imperishably engraved as one of the greatest benefactors of mankind. ... As to his work, it remains forever as a gift to mankind, whose recognition of its value can only increase with the passage of time." Even if the thoughts of Freud's opponents about the doubtful value of the "gift" and benefactor are disregarded, only a victim of historical myopia would rank Freud among the "greatest benefactors of mankind," who might include Christ or St. Francis, Hammurabi or Socrates, self-sacrificing medical investigators, and idealistic political reformers.

One contemporary historian of medicine, writing in a Freudian periodical, expresses amazement at the distortion of facts by Jones. She protests Jones's thesis of "the loneliness of Freud's achievement" (60) by which he tried to aggrandize his master. He claimed Freud's psychological concepts were "essentially the product of his own intuition and personal experience." Veith shows that there were many predecessors to Freud's ideas; it was only his neurotic drive for fame through assumed originality that made him and his disciples oblivious

171

to forerunners. As we shall see later in this chapter, Jones followed Freud in this falsification of Western culture. Veith respectfully applied the term "unusual" for such machinations by Freud and his pupils. Indeed, an unusual description for self-interested dishonesty.

Veith's article illustrates how difficult it is for even a modern historian to view Freud objectively. Freud had obviously deceived himself by pretending that he believed his alleged nonacquaintance with his predecessors in philosophy and literature would protect him from being accused of plagiarism. This piece of false reasoning Veith describes as "novel." On another page, she discusses Freud's pretense about his being indifferent to fame, which she finds is contradicted by some other expressions of Freud indicating delight with recognition when he received it. Veith circumspectly wonders if "he himself was aware of these ambivalent reactions." (60:248) After this realization of Freud's genuine "sour grapes" reaction to fame, the historian starts the next sentence with "Most assuredly, Freud was second to none in self-awareness and self-criticism"! The Freudian power to strike back is still considerable, and Veith was seemingly careful not to cause too much offense.

5. *Artists, an easy prey*

Artists, being impressionable and prone to react emotionally, welcomed Freud as their kind of psychologist. Of course, they can be credited with ability to recognize good literature, and they found it in Freud's works. Unfortunately, they mistook it for psychological science, for supposedly objective findings about the psyche. They enjoyed "psyching" each other (7:74) and creating Freudianized characters in their works. Though their opinions did not carry much weight with scientifically trained psychologists, they were in a position to popularize Freud as a new Columbus.

The "psyching" of the 20s and the 30s has apparently continued in some quarters, under the influence of some professors of literature who are still hooked on Freud and have their students brainwashed with the Profound Doctrine. A psychiatric reviewer calls them "innumerable horde of successors" to Freud's own dabbling in literature. The reviewer is apparently nauseated by the slavish emulation of Freud's fantasies and naive overinterpretation of slight clues into big Freudian findings:

> There seems to be a tacit assumption that each element of the work must stand for something else and that it is the critic's task to ferret this out, to tell us what it *really* means. . . . I am not arguing against the presence of "hidden meanings," only against their needless proliferation. Most of the essays in *Psychoanalysis and Literary Process* are overlong, clotted, and tedious owing to the author's compulsive need to find a phallus in every exclamation point. (67:25)

Among literary men, as might be expected, there is no dearth of praises to Freud. An exhaustive treatment of their admiring misperceptions would easily fill a book. Their statements might also be used as examples of Freudian transference, a childish enthusiasm for the immeasurably wise father. The otherwise gifted writer and biographer Stefan Zweig, a contemporary and friend of Freud, even claimed that Freud was the discoverer of the soul!

Sherwood Anderson, unaware that he was dealing with the psychological fancies of a troubled man, considered Freud's writings as a source of deep knowledge of human nature. He wrote in *Dark Laughter:* "If there is anything you do not understand in human life, consult the works of Dr. Freud."

Theodore Dreiser was even more impressed by Freud's mysterious revelations:

> I shall never forget my first encounter with his *Three Contributions to the Theory of Sex,* his *Totem and Taboo,* and his *Interpretation of Dreams.* At that time, and even now, every paragraph came as a revelation to me; a strong, revealing light thrown on some of the darkest problems that haunted and troubled me and my work. And reading him has helped me in my studies of life and men. I said at that time and I repeat now that he reminded me of a conqueror who has taken a city, entered its age-old, hoary prisons, and there generously proceeded to release the prisoners of formulae, faiths, and illusions which have racked and worn man for hundreds and thousands of years. The light that he has thrown on the human mind! Its vagaries and

destructive delusions and their cure! It is to me at once colossal and beautiful! (8:329, 330)

Apparently he, too, was deceived by one of the darkest nightmares about human nature, to receive it as a visionary discovery of what the psyche is like.

The exaggerated status of Freud in psychology led to uncritical acceptance of his theories irrespective of their arbitrariness and lack of proven validity. Cohen's criticism of Freud's outlandish ideas in *Moses and Monotheism* discusses the dilemma most readers would experience when resisting the fancies Freud had spun:

> If anyone else had written this book, we should have been justified in dismissing it as a work of an opinionated crank who is more interested in his tortuous speculation than in getting at the verifiable facts. Freud, however, is the discoverer of an extensively used method of mental therapeutics and the inventor of what is claimed to be the science of psychoanalysis, which has swept over our popular literature and the conversation of those who call themselves sophisticated. A very large number thus regard him as the infallible source of profound and even scientific truth. Moreover, he not only possesses an extraordinary gift for making the most fanciful hypothesis seem plausible, but admits the inadequacy of the evidence to support his conclusions. Nevertheless, he does claim certainty for propositions for which there is no evidence at all—for instance, that Moses introduced circumcision. He unhesitantly dismisses the identification of the Habiru of the Amarna tablets with the Hebrew invaders of Palestine and also waves aside the sole known Egyptian reference to Israel, because they do not fit into his chronologic scheme. He is certain that the Priestly Code did not adopt any new tendencies, that religion is a neurosis and only thus can it be understood, that all children and primitive people are neurotic, and (contrary to all experience) that tradition is less subject to distortion in time than a written text. While, therefore, no careful student of the subject is likely to be misled by a work which has so little sound foundation, the general public is likely to get the impression that a new and substantial contribution to the understanding of Jewish history had been made on the basis of psychoanalysis. (9:139, 140)

Kazin offers an explanation for artists flocking to Freud: "it helped them imagine that their fantasies were scientific." Freud "brought, as it were, the authority of science to the inner prompting of art, and thus helped writers and artists to feel that their interest in myths, in symbols, in dreams was on the side of 'reality,' of science, itself." (10:19)

Some of the swooning pronouncements of Freud's delirious pupils are reminiscent of a boy's bragging about his mighty father. They seem to have lost all historical perspective, forgetting that in the past some very impressive and talented people have dazed their contemporaries into ascribing to them an extraordinary importance. Hegel's writings, now known only to philosophical specialists, were praised in his heyday as the most significant contribution to philosophy ever produced. Schopenhauer, Nietzsche, and Dewey were considered by impressionable contemporaries as peaks of philosophical thought. The following generation saw them in a more sensible and more modest perspective.

As far as the current adulation of Freud is concerned we are far from attaining a sensible appraisal. Two statements which came to my attention in 1971 reflect the transitional stage of evaluations of Freud. One is by Clifton Fadiman, one of the editors of the Book-of-the-Month Club. In trying to sell a biography of Einstein, Fadiman apparently hoped to achieve better sales by linking Einstein's greatness to Freud's:

> There will always be argument as to the definition of greatness. By certain relaxed criteria Roosevelt and Churchill, though neither generated any ideas of permanent importance, are great men. By more rigorous criteria Gandhi is great, perhaps the only great politician of the century. But few would deny that, of all the towering figures of the last hundred years, the pair that continue to be thought of, almost automatically, as truly great are Freud and Einstein. (62:34)

Another, completely opposite statement came from a publisher to whom I had offered this volume: "Five years ago, we might have been interested in your book, but right now it does not seem feasible because from all the evidence Freud is on the way out." Which of the two is better informed? Probably each represents one of the poles in reaction to Freud. One is accepting the traditional overvaluation, the other is more aware of the idol's clay feet. Objectively, Fadiman represents the majority, if a dwindling one, as the voices of depreciation are swelling. Brad Dorrach, for instance, rejecting Irving Stone's (63) biography of Freud as voluminous but insignificant, characterizes Freud as "the Great Destroyer," and expresses the current depreciation of the hero:

> Though only 32 years have passed since his death, that impact now seems largely spent, and Freud himself sometimes appears little more than a joke saint of pop cult. Many of his ideas have been openly repudiated by the new humanistic psychologies, and some recently published evidence indicates that the apostle of emotional honesty carried on a tatty affair with his wife's younger sister. What Freud could use right now is a major revaluation by a responsible and generous biographer. No such luck. He has fallen into the hot little hands of Irving Stone. (64:91)

Ellenberger, a reliable historian of psychiatry, does not see such a deserved demise of Freudism and concludes about the scene in 1970: "Freudian and pseudo-Freudian ideology pervaded cultural life." (65:868)

6. *Freud deplumed*

Some readers will remember the fable of the haughty bird strutting along to be admired for its beautiful feathers. It had collected the best plumage of other good-looking birds and put them on. One day the other birds became annoyed with the braggart and each bird took its own feathers. There stood the pretender, disgraced in its own ordinary plumage.

Historians of philosophy and psychiatry have looked more closely at Freud's ideas and have found that they have been picked from other writers, wittingly or unwittingly, under the same or different label. Giving the matter a hard, nonpartisan look, Ellenberger reports: "In fact, many of Freud's theories were known before him or belonged to contemporary trends. Freud drew from his masters, his colleagues, his rivals, his associates, his patients, and his disciples." (65:534)

The place his adherents assigned to Freud in the development of psychological concepts appears, for instance, quite different after considering the following statement of Janet, written sixty years ago:

Charcot's lectures on the traumatic neuroses and my own studies [on "disaggregated"—repressed—ideas and disturbing memories]... were the starting point for a remarkable theory of neuroses and of a new method for the treatment of these diseases. I refer to the work of Sigmund Freud of Vienna and his pupils, to the system known as Psychoanalysis... Freud's earliest writings on this subject, published in 1893 and 1895, acknowledged as their starting-point the studies of which I have just been speaking anent happenings which have aroused emotion and which have left dangerous memories. He agreed with the view which I myself took as to the part these memories played in causing the actual neurosis. I must admit that at first it did not seem to me that the studies of Breuer and Freud differed much from my own, and I was simple enough to regard them as an extremely interesting confirmation of my own researches. "I am delighted to learn," I wrote, "that Breuer and Freud have recently verified the explanation I gave some time ago of the fixed ideas of hysterics." In fact, these authors showed by aptly chosen instances that certain hysterical symptoms were due to traumatic memories; and I was glad to find that their observations tallied so closely with mine. At most these authors changed a word here and there in their psychological descriptions. They spoke of "psychoanalysis" where I had spoken of "psychological analysis." They invented the name "complex" whereas I had used the term "psychological system" to denote the totality of psychological phenomena and the movements whether of the limbs or of the internal organs which were associated to constitute the traumatic memory. They spoke of "catharsis" where I had spoken of the "dissociation of fixed ideas" or of "moral disinfection." The names differed, but the essential ideas I had put forward, even those which were still subject to discussion (like that of the psychological system), were accepted without modification. Down to this very day, if we disregard hazardous speculations and confine our attention to the accounts of traumatic memories published by Freud's pupils, we shall find descriptions closely akin to those I published long ago. When we consider these primary doctrines and these cases of traumatic memory, we find it difficult to understand how it is that psycho-analysis can be supposed to differ so much from psychological analysis, and difficult to discern the novelty of the psycho-analytical contribution to psychiatry. (11:600-602)

Is it any wonder in view of the above explanation that, as Freud says, he was accused by French writers "that I had listened to [Janet's] lectures and stolen his ideas"? (61:91) [3]

Professor McDougall also observed Freud's tendency toward plagiarism, overt or covert. He found that Freud restated one of his ideas as his own, "mixing it well-nigh inextricably. . . . Now I am sure that Professor Freud did not mean to steal my theory . . . [It was] the venial error of subconscious plagiarism." (61:91) Subconscious perhaps, but certainly not the only one, as we shall see.

Dalbiez (12, v. 1:88) quotes de Saussure, whom he considers "one of Freud's best pupils," as finding that, apart from the method, Freud made no startlingly new discovery.

Riese (13) and Bry and Rifkin (14) provide an objective summary of Freud's acknowledged, and sometimes unconscious, assimilation of the philosophical and psychological traditions. Harms (15) speaks of Tissot, who died a century before the publication of Freud's major works, as "the Freudian before Freud." Allers shows how closely interwoven Freud's thought was with the cultural climate of his day—with the ideas of Herbart, Fechner, Feuerbach, Schopenhauer, Nietzsche and others. Some of the most "Freudian" concepts had apparently been elaborated by Herbart:

The psychology of Freud uses terms which were originally Herbart's. This philosopher made a curious attempt at developing a mathematical psychology which was definitely dynamic in its principles. The contents of consciousness were conceived as due to the interplay of forces adhering to ideas. The notion of cathexis is indeed already implied in Herbartian psychology, as are those of repression and inhibition, of the threshold of consciousness and of ideas pushing upwards from the unconscious. Herbartian is also the notion of quantities of energy and of the relation of emotional states to the forces at work in the mind. (16:226)

Fechner was also an important source of theoretical concepts of psychoanalysis: "Freud took from Fechner the concept of mental energy, the 'topographical' concept of the mind, the principle of pleasure-unpleasure, the principle of constancy, and the principle of repetition." (65:218)

Taylor provides a list of psychodynamic ideas proposed long before Freud:

When we survey not only the Freudian current but the entire psychodynamic stream, we find that most of Freud's good emphases had been or were being explicated by other workers, often with more penetration and discrimination.

Male hysteria, also hysteria in little girls and in women past the menopause, had been described explicitly in all its principal forms, by Le Pois. His description, together with an essentially psychological interpretation, was published in 1618. Through Le Pois and perhaps other sources, hysteria as occurring in both sexes was known to Willis, Sydenham, Cullen, Whytt, and many other physicians in western Europe, including Freud's teacher Charcot.

Conflict and repression from the higher into lower consciousness were set forth clearly by Leibniz (1924, orig. publ. 1714), and especially by Herbart (1895, orig. publ. 1824). Further, Herbart developed the idea of complexes and the relatively unified as compared with the divided personality. Similar ideas were presented by Macnish (1834), Ribot (1882, 1894, 1898, orig. publ. 1881, 1883, 1885), and other students. What we now call lapses, rationalizations, and various defenses were emphasized by Schopenhauer (1896, orig. publ. 1819).

Dreams have long been interpreted more or less magically through "dreams books," of which perhaps the first appeared in Egypt about 2000 B.C. More scientific interpretations were developed by Hippocrates about 400 B.C. Rightly interpreted, he said, dreams can help explain many a patient's difficulty. Eminently psychological examples of symbolism in dreams were presented by Artemidorus about 150 A.D.; and Ibn Sirin, about 700 A.D., seems to have found out important facts in the lives of individuals through interpreting their dreams. Cullen, Rush, Pinel, Macnish, Janet, Prince, and many others contributed to the psychology of dreams, though none of these men stressed psychotherapeutic dream interpretation as Freud did (Taylor, 1954).

Apparently most persons now concerned with psychodynamics do not realize that Pierre Janet (1859-1947) showed that many psychoneuroses can be cured through discovering their experiential, motivating factors through direct conversation, hypnosis (1886), automatic writing (1886), dreams (1892) or some combination of these factors, together with observation of symptoms, and through breaking up the fixed ideas and "setting the memories in order" so that the patient can assimilate or adapt to the disturbing factors (Goldsmith, 1934; Janet, 1925; Schwartz, 1951; Taylor, 1947).

Morton Prince (1854-1929), like Freud, studied with Charcot and Bernheim; but Prince studied also the work of the other important predecessors and contemporaries in psychodynamics. In his 40 years of studious practice, Prince verified much that others had done and added important observations of his own. His range of cases was more significant than Freud's, in that he included more extreme psychogenic cases and a gamut of sexual abnormalities, from frigidity to frank perversions; and he treated many of these cases with a success unknown to Freud. Prince was, indeed, an extraordinarily successful therapist. (17:785, 786)

Whyte's study (18) traces even the most meritorious concept of Freud, that of the unconscious, to his predecessors.

Substantially the Freudian view of "the unconscious," including the supposed sexual core, was developed perhaps first by Schopenhauer, whose work, *The World as Will and Idea* (1896, orig. publ. 1819), was widely read. Another author, von Hartmann, produced *Philosophy of the Unconscious* (1931, orig. publ. 1869). This was a compendious work, historical, speculative, and observational, and went through 10 editions by 1890. Von Hartmann's picture of "the unconscious," however, was less dark than Schopenhauer's and Freud's; for him the unconscious was resourceful and creative, more like Jung's view (Jacobi, 1952). Publications by Carpenter, by Maudsley, and by others also emphasized subconscious phenomena and influenced Freud's teachers (Whyte, 1960). Charcot used the concept of repression by "the ego." (17:787)

Yet, a well-known trainer of psychoanalysts, still writes in 1956 about "Freud's discovery of the unconscious mind." (54:19)

A British psychiatrist, Stengel, wondered why Freud did not acknowledge his indebtedness to the "father of British neurology," Hughlings Jackson. Stengel found that Freud referred to Jackson only twice in his works, even though the "close similarities between certain Freudian and Jacksonian concepts suggest that Jackson's influence on Freud went far beyond the field of the aphasias and contributed to the foundations of psychoanalytic theory." (81:349) These "close similarities" involve some of the fundamental concepts of Freud's theories: repression of tendencies and memories, resistance to change in mental states, "psychodynamics."

> The concepts of psychodynamics goes back to Jackson, who spoke of the "dynamics of the nervous system."
> The close resemblance between Jackson's and Freud's dynamic theories, which has astonished a number of writers (Jones, Grinker, M. Levin, Ey, Angel, and others) can now be understood as the result of Freud's encounter with the ideas of Hughlings Jackson. It may be asked why then Freud did not acknowledge his indebtedness to Jackson. (81:351, 352)

Stengel's question sounds rather rhetorical; he knew that Freud suffered from "unconscious plagiarism" and his disciples only followed the suit.

Even Freud's cardinal concept of libido was not genuinely his. Strauss notes that the concept of the unconscious driving power can be found in the writings of St. Augustine and St. Thomas Aquinas. (55:40) What Freud contributed was a thorough sexualization of the unconscious. Choisy traces the origin of the idea of libido even further back to Plato. (56:68) The most famous German philosopher of the nineteenth century, Schopenhauer, spoke about it under a different name. He called it the Will, the blind but powerful drive toward pleasure and mastery. Moritz Benedikt, a Viennese physician, had used the term libido repeatedly in his publications thirty or forty years before Freud. In 1868, he explained hysteria as a "disorder of the libido," and he meant sexual frustration. The feature on which Freud insisted as special discovery, that libido is basically sexual in nature, he apparently borrowed from Jewish medieval mystics. [See *Freud's Phallic Cult*, chapters I and III. (57)]

Ellenberger (65:212-215) reveals that Freud was antedated regarding sexualized nosology of personality disorders by Ideler by at least sixty years. In 1835, Ideler, in his *Grundriss der Seelenheilkunde* (*Outline of Psychotherapy*) ascribed the development of abnormal psychological reactions to frustrated sexual drives. When Freud was only three years old, another German psychiatrist, H.W. Neumann, published this textbook of psychiatry emphasizing the role of frustrated drives in the formation of psychopathology. He stated there the insight which Freud's adherents ascribed to the master's psychological sharpness: "The drive which cannot be gratified becomes anxiety."

Neumann also had, before Freud, the psychodynamic insight that unconscious sexual motivations are behind many seemingly puzzling and unconnected clinical manifestations: cleanliness or uncleanliness, compulsive washing or smearing of the body, dislike of clothes or tearing them, calling female attendants whores, morbid religiosity, exaggerated interests in divine service or in the pastor. Other students of emotional disorders before Freud were also fascinated with the possibility that emotional troubles might be associated with unrelieved sexual tensions. Peyer, a Zurich physician, writing in 1890, quotes a dozen physicians agreeing with him regarding his hunch that neurotic troubles are caused by irregular sexual practices. He even found that a form of asthma was caused by interrupted intercourse. It seems that Freud just joined the superstitions of his culture, instead of being the discoverer of supposedly sexual roots of neuroses, as his disciples imagined him to be.

Even the oversexualized dream symbolism was not a Freud original. In 1861, Scherner preempted that claim. "A dozen pages in Scherner's book are devoted to symbols related to the sex organs. As male symbols he mentions high towers, pipes, clarinets, knives and pointed weapons, running horses, and fluttering birds being chased; among female sex symbols Scherner mentions a narrow courtyard and a staircase that one must climb up." (65:305)

Freud's operations in deciphering dreams were employed by students before him. "The mechanism of displacement and condensation had been described under other names by many authors. The term 'dream work' (*Traumarbeit*) was used by Robert. Much of Freud's theory can be found in Maury, Strümpell, Volkelt, and particularly Delage," (65:493) who predated Freud by decades.

Benedikt realized before Freud that hypnosis is ineffective with hysterical patients and published his recommendations in 1891 that conscious states should better be employed in psychotherapy. Freud acknowledged Benedikt's ideas in one of his early writings, an indication that even abandonment of hypnosis and introduction of "free" associations was not completely his original idea.

Rozenzweig (20) points out that Freud did not acknowledge that a number of important psychoanalytic concepts, like "sublimation," "autoeroticism," and an intimation of "narcissism" were proposed by Havelock Ellis even before Freud wrote his major works. Probably not caring to detract from the exaggerated image of the master, Freud's disciples did little to suggest his indebtedness further. Perhaps they feared the consequences suffered by the proud bird.

"As a result of my researches," states Bailey, "I came to the unexpected conclusion that hardly any of Freud's early ideas were completely new." (27:32)

After picking out what were not Freud's ideas in his body of work, Ellenberger finds that only four might be ascribed as his originals: "the psychoanalytic situations with the basic rule, free associating, the analysis of resistance and transference." (65:549) Even these four are vitiated by the hoax aspects of Freud's theory and practice: the basic rule of saying whatever comes to mind was rarely possible on account of "doctrinal compliance" to the analyst's theoretical framework; free association was recognized even by Freud as being "free" only in an idealized way; and resistance and transference, were not only what Freud said they were, but also the struggle of the analyst to convert the patient to Freud's peculiar ideology.

Obviously, dynamic psychiatry did not begin with Freud, as some adulators would like us to believe. In fact, the many psychiatric and philosophical forerunners of Freud make us ask: what are the truly original findings of Freud? Wohlgemuth (1) applies, with justice, J. H. Voss's epigram to Freud's work:

Dein redseliges Buch lehrt mancherlei Neues und Wahres,
Wäre das Wahre nur neu, wäre das Neue nur Wahr.

[Your loquacious book teaches us things new and true:
Only, if the true were new, and the new were true!)

7. *Freud's pretended modesty*

The master himself did not want to jeopardize the fulfillment of his neurotically determined wish [4] for making outstanding contributions to "science." He was fired with ambition to make a name for himself in science one way or another. In 1896, in his study *Zur Aetiologie der Hysterie,* he compared his findings about the causation of neurosis by sexual traumatization in early childhood to the discovery of the sources of the Nile. Several years later he had to retract this famous blunder. The whole episode only served to disclose Freud's motives for developing a unique science. For the same self-aggrandizing reasons, he implied that all his "discoveries" and notions were strictly his own. He asserted that he was greater than Einstein because there had been no Newton in his own field to prepare the way. He did not hesitate to compare himself to Copernicus and Darwin. (There might be a flaw in this argument, as Wohlgemuth points out. Copernicus and Darwin were ignored or attacked by men outside their fields. In Freud's case, it was his colleagues, psychologists and psychiatrists, who criticized and rejected his psychology.)

Freud's pupils were apparently confused about what was really great about their master. They could not, for instance, accept his modest disclaimer about himself in a letter to Marie Bonaparte, "I have restricted capacities, and talents, nothing for mathematics, nothing for anything quantitative." This realistic evaluation of himself and his failure as a scientist in work done after his fortieth year, was inadmissible by pupils who wished to view Freud as more than a gifted speculative thinker and artistic visionary.

Freud, often self-contradictory, says in *The Interpretation of Dreams:* "I am not, so far as I know, ambitious." Yet in the same work he analyzes dreams that clearly reveal his strong desire to become a full professor at the University of Vienna, a very high achievement, and his resentment for finding that success closed to him. Thus Freud reveals in his dreams what he did not admit even to himself when awake. Zilboorg, a historian of psychiatry who was quite sympathetic to Freud, reveals what the originator of psychoanalysis preferred to cover up: "There is no doubt in anyone's mind, friend or

184

foe of Freud, that Freud was an ambitious and intensely sensitive person. He hoped for world fame from the very outset of his career. He wanted greatness and recognition, and he hoped for a permanent place (immortality) in the history of human thought." (21:39)

I shall deal later with Freud's ostensible distaste for reading other authorities and the apparent reasons for it. At this point it suffices to illustrate how the idolatry of Freud was unconsciously encouraged by his example.

In his *History of the Psychoanalytic Movement* Freud declares of his concept of repression, one of the two pillars of his theory, "I certainly worked [it] out independently." (22:939) Then in the same paragraph he continues:

> I knew of no influence that directed me in any way to it, and I long considered this idea to be original until O. Rank showed us the passage in Schopenhauer's *The World as Will and Idea* where the philosopher is struggling for an explanation of insanity. What he states there concerning the striving against the acceptance of a painful piece of reality agrees so completely with the content of my theory of repression, that once again, I must be grateful to my not being well read, for the possibility of not making a discovery.

Freud's evasion of the issue here by making a witty remark about the benefits of his not being well read hardly conceals his strong motivation to be considered the independent originator of the concept. A man anxious to be fair would have admitted to having forgotten the source of his idea, even though this would deprive him of originality. Freud still does not say that he ever read Schopenhauer; however he has testified elsewhere to his strong interest in philosophy, and it is difficult to imagine that he would not have read the most influential philosopher of the period. In fact, Dorer (23) shows that Freud was acquainted with Schopenhauer's writings on sexuality and repression. Schopenhauer, like Freud, was obsessed with sexuality. Both were sexually undergratified because of their neurotic inhibitions, and both apparently sought compensation in sexualized philosophizing and theorizing. Either of them could have written this aphorism about the allegedly basically sexual nature of man: "Man is incarnate sexual instinct, since he owes his origin to copulation and the wish of his wishes is to copulate." It happens that Schopenhauer is to blame for such hasty generalization, but Freud theorized in the same short-sighted direction. Schopenhauer also preceded Freud in the concept of the unconscious; he proposed a model of personality comparable to earth and its crust: the conscious mind is represented by the relatively thin crust, while below it is magma, the unformed bowels of our planet corresponding to the unconscious, which is filled with passions and irrationalities. Yet Freud prefers to think of himself, as the originator of the notion which was apparently quite popular in his cultural domain. Faithful to the hysteroid pattern of presenting himself according to his emotional needs, Freud asserts tht he had "carefully avoided contact with philosophy proper. This avoidance has been greatly facilitated by constitutional incapacity." (24) Yet, he could write to Fliess in 1896, "When I was young, the only thing I longed for was philosophical knowledge." In another letter of the same year. Freud speaks of philosophy as "my original ambition, before I knew what I was intended to do in the world." (25:162, 141) Why all this hedging about philosophy? My guess is that Freud still wanted to be considered a "scientist" so intensely that he pretended he despised philosophy as an allegedly useless pursuit from which he could not obtain ideas for his "scientific" theories.

Zilboorg reports that "an intimate and ever loyal disciple of Freud" told him: "Freud had a remarkable capacity for forgetting some sources of his ideas." (21:37) The irony of it all is that Freud misled both himself and others, failing to see that his "science" was little different from certain other imaginative philosophical efforts in the realm of psychology. It is not surprising, that one of the experts contemporary with Freud, the famous professor of psychiatry at the University of Vienna, Wagner-Jauregg, considered Freud a charlatan. [5]

In a further defensive maneuver designed to enhance his reputation for originality, Freud confesses that he denied himself the pleasure of reading Nietzsche, "with the conscious motive of not wishing to be hindered in the writing out of my psychoanalytic impressions by any preconceived ideals." Freud taught his neurotic patients to look for their unconscious motives, but he did not care to recognize his own promptings—a consuming wish to overcome his depressive self-doubts by imagining that he was producing immortal psychological doctrines out of whole cloth.

Freud maintained this pretense of originality consistently and seemingly irrationally. The game is unmistakably revealed in a meeting of the Vienna Psychoanalytic Society (58:358-360) when two of the prominent members pointed to considerable affinity between Nietzsche's and Freud's ideas. Adler "stressed" that of all the great philosophers, "Nietzsche is closest to our [Freudian] way of thinking." In a former study he had also tried to show the affinity of Freud's and Schopenhauer's ideas. Federn joins Adler in pointing that Nietzsche had announced concepts which later appeared in Freud's psychological theories:" he was first to discover the significance of abreaction, of repression, of flight into illness, of the instincts—the normal sexual ones as well as the sadistic instincts." (58:359)

In response, Freud plays the innocent plagiarist, distancing himself by the same maneuver from "nonscientific" philosophical pursuits. He first denounces philosophy, whose "abstract nature is so unpleasant to him." He still pretends that "he does not know Nietzsche's work." Finally he performs a logical *tour de force* giving "the assurance that Nietzsche's ideas have had no influence on his work." (58:359-360)

In the next breath, as if the truth will out, Freud revealed unwittingly the dynamics of his forgetfulness: he could maintain it as long as it served his purposes. He told his disciples how he had become oblivious to the fact that Charcot, Breuer, and Chrobak had independently communicated to him the assumption about "the sexual etiology of the neuroses." Freud had apparently considered this idea as his own till "only later when, faced with the [general] repudiation of this concept he attempted to justify himself." (58:359, 360) As it happens with self-serving repression, it was removed when Freud found it useful to himself.

A very sympathetic writer on Freud and psychoanalysis wonders in this connection about the master's puzzling forgetfulness: "Freud denied ever having been acquainted with the writings of Schopenhauer and Nietzsche. Yet as early as 1905 Hitschmann, one of the first adherents to psychoanalysis, read a paper in Freud's presence and at

187

Freud's house on the very subject of Nietzsche's ideas as compared with some of Freud's theories." (59:70)

It is of some interest at this point to remember that Nietzsche did actually speak of repression, in such a way that even throws some light on Freud's motivations: " 'I have done this' says my memory. 'It is impossible that I should have done it,' says my pride, and it remains inexorable. Finally, my memory yields." (12, v. 1:27) The unconscious must have played some such trick on Freud again, or he could not have written in 1925: "I named this process repression; it was a novelty, and nothing like it had ever before been recognized in mental life." (24:30) Freud somehow repressed the point repeatedly brought to his attention by Rank, Adler, Federn, and Hitschmann, and overlooked that Nietzsche described the same concept, using the term inhibition. Freud did not care either to admit that the concept of id came from Nietzsche (via Grodeck), and that Nietzsche described conscience as the depository of influences of early authorities much the way Freud conceived the superego.

Nietzsche also described the concept of sublimation (16:19), and Freud conveniently preferred not to recognize that either. "For those acquainted with both Nietzsche and Freud, the similarity of their thought is so obvious that there can be no question about the former's influence over the latter." (65:276) Jung was also greatly influenced by Nietzsche, but he admitted his indebtedness without hedging. The title given Freud by Bailey, the "cryptamnesic sophist," (27) appears well deserved. According to his biographer Robert, Freud was ill at ease regarding thefts of ideas:

> The few violations of the scientific code of which he was guilty, out of ignorance, thoughtlessness or weariness, were in themselves of no great consequence, but they weighed heavily on his scrupulous conscience to judge by the frequency in his work and especially in the dreams he relates of themes more or less concerned with the theft of ideas." (26:156)

Freud's pretenses were apparently impenetrable not only to early disciples, but also to some later sympathizers. Zilboorg is, for instance, misled into a belief in Freud's (unlikely) ignorance of important philosophers—psychologists of his day: "It is true, of course, that despite the apparent similarity of some of Freud's ideas to those of Herbart, Schopenhauer, and Nietzsche, Freud did not read those philosophers till sometime after his basic ideas had been formulated." (28:33) Zilboorg as a historian, of course, knew that Freud studied psychology with Brentano, and was passionately interested in philosophy in his undergraduate years. Yet he seems to suspend his psychiatric perspicacity when he falls under Freud's spell.

8. *Example more powerful than words*

Most of Freud's disciples followed the behavioral precept of the master rather than his pretended verbal modesty. Ferenczi, although a persistent admirer of Freud, was still objective enough to mention that one of his most troublesome notions, that of infantile sexuality, was part of Freud's professional milieu and had even been published by a Hungarian pediatrist in 1879, almost twenty years prior to Freud's announcement. In contrast to Ferenczi, later Freudians lost sight of the cultural context which prompted some of Freud's ideas. Their unconscious seems to operate in their writings as in their psychoanalytic investigations; in both instances objectivity gives place to transference distortions. A member of the child therapy faculty of the Chicago Institute for Psychoanalysis, observes that contemporary Freudian analysts have not yet grown out of that attitude. Erika Fromm writes: "An unfortunate characteristic of orthodox psycho-analysts today is that they deify Freud and as a group have not overcome their Oedipal feelings toward him. Many do not dare to progress beyond Freud or to admit to themselves and their colleagues that they do." (29)

In their eagerness to aggrandize their leader, the disciples tend to ascribe to Freud expertise which he did not have and did not claim. Kline draws attention to one such false assertion:

> Contrary to implication by Thompson (in *Psychoanalysis: Evolution and Development*) that Freud had considerable experience with experimental as well as clinical hypnosis, there is little to indicate that he himself ever worked intensely with hypnosis, apart from induction and use in suggestive and cathartic therapeutics. (30:51, 52)

Erikson (31) essentially agrees with Kline. He considers the developing of Freud's method of "free" association the result of his having been a poor hypnotist. Freud himself stated in one of his later writings that hypnosis remained an "enigma" to him; yet, his disciples had taken his earlier pronouncements on hypnosis as gospel, and remained aloof from and discouraged others from this useful therapeutic adjunct.

Bailey provides another example of the hysteriform lack of objectivity Freud's adherents show in exaggerating his merits. Having read in Weiss and English (32) that supposedly "No work on psychosomatic medicine could have been attempted without the biologically orientated psychology of Freud," Bailey reacts:

> That did it. How could anybody make such a statement who had read Dejerine [(33)] and Hack Tuke [(34)] or even Dr. William Sweetser [(35)], who, in his book on mental hygiene, published in New York in 1843, remarked, "Few, we imagine, have formed any adequate estimate of the sum of bodily ills which originate in the mind." Psychosomatic medicine is as old as the hills. (19:30)

The German psychiatrist Heinroth had used the concept in 1815, but Freudian devotees do not care to take such facts into account. Even Plutarch quotes the "psychosomatic" insight of a student of human nature, who preceded him: "If the body sued the mind for damages, the mind would be found to have been a ruinous tenant to its landlord."

Freudians seem to suffer from that ahistorical malady which Sorokin has found in a number of American writers in the social sciences. He writes of the scientific foibles of the previous twenty-five years:

> The first defect of these sciences has been a sort of amnesia concerning their previous history, discoveries and achievements. ... The younger generation of sociologists and psychologists explicitly claims that nothing important has been discovered in their fields during all preceding centuries; that there were only vague "armchair philosophers" and that the real scientific era in these disciplines began only in the last two or three decades with the publication of their own researches and those of members of

190

their clique. Claiming to be particularly objective, precise and scientific, our social and psychological Columbuses tirelessly repeat this delusion as scientific truth. Accordingly, they rarely make any references to the social and psychological thinkers of the past. When they do, they hardly veil the sense of their own superiority over the unscientific old fogies. ... As a result, the indexes of their books list none or very few of the thinkers of preceding centuries, in contrast to the long list of "researches" belonging to the author's Mutual Back-Patting Insurance Company. (36:3, 4)

Sorokin calls them the "business men of science," *"docta ignorantia,"* the learned know-nothings. He mentions the example of Parsons, his former student, who incorporated many of Sorokin's ideas in his sociological writings, without giving credit to the source.

Bailey had felt similarly discouraged about half-baked practitioners in neuropsychiatry: "Of such a half-educated generation what can be expected? Unless one adopts the attitudes of another of the starry-eyed youngsters who, when I asked him whether he had read anything of Janet, replied, 'Why do I need to read all that stuff? Have I not been analyzed?' " (19:31)

9. *Denigrating the opponents*

Concomitant with blowing up the master's image, the disciples also deflated the image of other psychologists. Just as Freud is considered infallible, they are considered untrustworthy. As an example, in the chapter on Dissenters—Adler, Jung, and Rank—Alexander and Selesnick say that "it is only fair to point out that their later philosophical speculations so abrogated rigorous adherence to systematic scientific observation that they vitiated whatever impact they may have had on psychiatric thought. In our view Freud, in contrast, rarely departed from scientific orientation." (3:252)

Alexander and Selesnick appear to have forgotten that Freud admitted late in his life that his "discoveries" about Eros and Thanatos were announced more than two thousand years earlier by the Greek philosopher: "The theory of Empedocles which specially claims our attention is one which approximates so closely to the psychoanalytical theory of the instincts that we should be tempted to

191

maintain that the two are identical, were it not for this difference: the Greek's theory is a cosmic phantasy, while our own confines its application to biology." (28:349)

Freud begs the question here if the application of a "cosmic phantasy" to biology makes a science of the phantasy.

One wonders whether these two historians of psychiatry, claiming an unbroken allegiance to Freud, came across a document published about Freud's patently unscientific fantasy about Moses. In writing his warning against Freudism, Ludwig had contacted H.S. Yahuda, professor of Biblical history and an expert in both Hebrew and Egyptian. The professor sent the following statement:

> First of all, Freud's work cannot be regarded as scientific because he himself states that he is not competent and believes must be supported by other authorities.
>
> Being ignorant of the question, Freud repeatedly contradicts himself, yet asserts that his deductions are correct.
>
> The worst is that he utilizes his sources only as long as they support his theories, and drops them when they contradict him.
>
> His principal source to the effect that monotheism was not created by Moses but by Ikhnaton is James Breasted, whose statements have been proved falsifications by the inscriptions of Ikhnaton himself. In reality this king not only acknowledged a number of other gods but also made himself divine and sacrificed to his own image—so much of a monotheist was he!
>
> The comical thing, however, is that Freud discovered two Moseses, a genuine one who was an Egyptian and an imposter who was a Hebrew. He also discovered that the Egyptian was murdered by the ungrateful Hebrews and the imposter equipped with the ideas of the murdered man. This was derived from Professor Sellin, who twenty-five years ago formed the murder thesis on the strength of a wrong interpretation of a passage in the Bible. Ten years later, he admitted his error!
>
> In 1938, I advised Freud to recall his words as Sellin had done, demonstrating that the assassination story was all wrong. Freud did not argue, but replied quite calmly, "And yet it might be true, for it fits so well into the frame of my thesis." (37:245, 246)

One might also question what is scientific about Freud's "anthropological romance" (as Dalbiez called it), the "pseudo-anthropology" (as Herberg called it, 39:145), science fiction fantasy of the primal horde of sons killing the father to possess the females, which even Freud called a "scientific myth"; or Eros and Thanatos as basic cosmic forces which find expression in humans as sexuality and aggression—Kardiner calls them "philosophical constructs" (38:5); or about viewing religion as a neurotic illusion—all of which belong to Freud's later writings.

With this and other Freudian pretenses at science in mind, Bailey concludes: "It now seems strange to me that I did not realize earlier that many of Freud's writings are not scientific treatises but rather reveries—a sort of chirographic rumination." (19) In another lecture Bailey (40), in contradiction to the two reputed historians, presents the period 1873-1897 as the only "scientific period" in Freud's activities, *i.e.* before he developed the more recognizable features of psychoanalysis. Looking at Freud's productions twenty years after his death, Jaspers (52:149), the renowned psychiatrist-philosopher, places Freud among psychological philosophers, alongside Fechner. This probably will be the classification with which future historians will agree.

In contrast to Freud's fanciful theorizing, one of the "unscientific" dissenters, Jung, was gathering observations not only from dreams and analytic sessions, which are inevitably contaminated by the analyst's suggestions, but was seriously studying primitive and other art, religious symbols, mystics and alchemists, all in order to gain a comprehensive picture of the universal unconscious expressions of past and present humanity. This painstaking, creative, empirical scientific work, when compared with Freud's armchair speculations of the same period, can be called "philosophical" only by a complete distortion of terms.

Contrasted with the estimates of others, even by friends of psychoanalysis, Menninger's impressions oppose those of the two historians: "Freud's early work was predominately inductive; his later work predominately deductive" (41) *i.e.* philosophical and nonscientific. Frenkel-Brunswick reports a similar impression: "While at the beginning of his psychoanalytic explorations Freud kept close to data, . . . he later became more speculative . . . to the extent which may be considered controversial." Rado, a nonorthodox Freudian, puts it even more plainly: "In Freud's psychoanalytic work, the artist eventually defeated the scientist." (42, v. 2:106)

193

Murray, the developer of the TAT test and professor of psychology at Harvard, sees Freud's psychology as only a speculative system: "Freud was attempting to bring order out of chaos by pure thought; for at no time did he review the simple facts, subjective and objective." (43:162) Murray compares Freud with alchemists: trying to order elements, and mixing many personal fantasies in their schemes. He considers that Freud disregarded many important human drives and overemphasized the sexual drive. Such a distortion is easily made by an armchair psychologist.

Hendrick exemplifies the Freudian scientific innocents. He speaks of Rank's secession from Freudism in terms which solemnly assert Freud's scientific merit as opposed to the unscientific work of those who disagree with him: "With each new publication he departed further from the empiricism and determinism of Freud and finally repudiated scientific methodology. His final views appeared to analysts to be based on a philosophical concept of freedom of the will and the volitional control of neurotic wishes." (44:337)

Jones went even further in denigrating the nonconformists in Freudian ranks. He considers Ferenczi and Rank to have become mentally ill in the period when they tried to amplify the official canon of psychoanalysis. Commenting on this kind of revengefulness, Fromm (45:11) implies that Freud and Jones might be considered mentally deranged on the same basis.

Mowrer, having crossed swords with Freudians on many occasions, hints at one of the motives for the Freudian establishment's denigration of its opponents:

> My perception of the nature of mental illness, if valid, has broad implications for both "diagnosis" and "treatment;" and it does not in the least surprise me when I hear that some persons who have made heavy investments—in time, money, and personal involvement—in training along other lines are threatened by this alternative way of looking at the problem. Small wonder they wish to dismiss and discredit my views and similar ones by saying that anyone who subscribes to them "must be crazy." Perhaps what they are saying, more exactly, is that they feel that if they themselves were to subscribe to such views, they would be "crazy." (46:3)

10. *A successful mission fizzling out*

The campaign of singing praises to Freud and reviling his opponents, like much propaganda, achieved the desired effect: Freud was enthroned as the Supreme Psychologist, and his detractors were made to appear ludicrous.

Zilboorg (47:1), for instance, comments that Jung and Adler are best known for their controversy with Freud, although he does not deny their importance to psychology in their own right. Their seeming lesser stature as psychologists is only relative, based on the overvaluation of Freud beyond all reason.

The band of the faithful grew, and they went to unconverted regions as salesmen-missionaries. They spread their reverent attitudes in medical schools and universities, artistic circles and the press, notably in the United States. The new faith met with some opposition, but it ultimately carried the field, as zealous proselytizers are likely to do: sometimes by sheer persistence, sometimes by cunning and scheming, sometimes by arrogance. They created considerable turmoil in psychiatric meetings with "narcissistic megalomania," which, Menninger suspects, operates in psychoanalysts:

> It was inevitable that, in a young and growing science such as psychoanalysis has been, there would be great zeal and intensity and almost evangelistic defensiveness. ... The mysteriousness of psychoanalysis and the closed group principle have offended many scientists, who find it difficult to accept our explanations of why this is necessary. But perhaps to an extent larger than we realize some of us are guilty of just plain bad manners or, to speak more psychiatrically, of poor self-control and arrogant truculence. Some analysts seem to assume that having learned about the unconscious of a dozen patients, we now *understand* human nature—and understand it *our way*. It has been remarked by numerous observers how much more friendly and congenial the meetings of neurologists, internists and other colleagues frequently seem as compared with meetings of psychoanalysts. However much more interesting we believe ours to be, theirs are certainly less hectic. Do our preoccupations with the unconscious and our zeal in undertaking to clarify the unconscious of other people foster some pathological degree of narcissistic megalomania in us? (48:93)

Perhaps the reason for Menninger's perplexity over psychoanalytic meetings being more hectic than those of neurologists and internists lay in his starting from the unproven postulate that psychoanalysis is a science. If he were to take psychoanalysts for what they are—not scientists but believers in a peculiar cult—the difficulty would be resolved and the reason for the differences clear. Neurologists and internists deal with objective subject matter, while the Freudians traffic with the articles of faith of an "esoteric system," as Meyer (49:229) called it. Murray, ordinarily sympathetic to psychoanalysis, discerns the features of a theocratic sect among psychoanalysts:

> . . . creative thinking is prohibited. Calvin's theocracy seems clearer to us now. The analysts' sacerdotal attitude may be due in part to the illegitimate displacement of feelings and aspirations belonging to the realm of value that were set adrift when they gave religion, and all that savors of it, its quietus. The orphaned sentiments found lodgment in the ark of the new covenant, Freud's collected works. (43:172)

The rest of the story, according to one of the early psychiatrist-observers, Harrington, can be explained by the salesmanship of the Freudians and the credulity of the public. The spread of Freudism is paralleled in many aspects by the spread of many other hoaxes, described by MacDougall. (78) Harrington, a psychiatrist, analyzes it:

> Now it may be laid down as an axiom that, whenever there is something which can be sold at a good profit, there will be found someone to sell it. So, when Professor Freud produced so highly salable a commodity as psychoanalysis, it was inevitable that he should presently have gathered about him a group of enthusiastic disciples eager to help him sell it. Of course, in making this statement, I do not mean to imply that men who go in for the practice of psychoanalysis are actuated merely by the love of gain; their motives—which they themselves do not understand— are mixed and vary more or less with the individual. A powerful motive in many cases is the desire to be a pioneer worker in what looks like a new and highly dramatic field of scientific endeavor, the desire to be a psychological discoverer and penetrate into the deep recesses of the human heart, or to be a great healer and guide to suffering humanity.

196

A factor of considerable importance in the rapid formation of a large professional group of psychoanalysts is to be found in the fact that this vocation is one which really calls for very little in the way of technical knowledge or training. To understand the ailments of the body, one must understand the principles on which the body works. He must know anatomy and physiology; and before he can understand these, he must know something of chemistry and physics. In the medical school, the student finds a long course of preparation required, before he is allowed to touch the problems of disease at all. This discourages all but a limited number of serious students. But, to treat the ailments of the mind by the Freudian procedure, one need not have any preliminary knowledge of either psychology or medicine. In fact, it is doubtful if such knowledge is not to be looked upon as a positive detriment, since it results in the setting up of resistances that stand in the way of the acceptance of psychoanalytic doctrines and methods.

It will not seem strange that so little technical knowledge is necessary for the successful practice of psychoanalysis, if we bear in mind that psychoanalytic treatment is a form of suggestion therapy and that, therefore, it really makes little difference what explanation the analyst offers of his patient's symptoms provided only that he is able to induce his patient to accept his explanation as the right one.

It was inevitable that the salability of psychoanalysis should result in the development of a strong professional group, and as a result of the development of this group, we have another very important factor brought into play. People generally, especially in matters that are of no great personal concern to them, believe what they are told. They follow the tide of popular opinion, assuming that what everyone says, or what the majority say, must be so. But what determines the direction in which the current of popular opinion will flow? As a rule it is determined to a large part at least, by the activities of a vociferous few. If a limited number of people are sufficiently interested to carry on an active propaganda in favor of some belief or course of action, they are likely to have their way unless they collide with some counter interest as strong and active as their own. Now, in psychoanalysis, we have such a strong vested interest. Psychoanalysts as a body are vitally interested in spreading the doctrines of their cult, for it is only as these doctrines become widely known that they can hope to get practice. If an analyst is to attain prominence, if he himself is to be a successful practitioner of his art, he must make himself known, and this he can do best through talking and writing, through telling as many people as possible of the wonders of psychoanalysis and the marvelous cures which he himself has wrought by means of it. So we have a vigorous propaganda, a strong advertising campaign, going on all the time, which cannot but carry the public with it unless it meets with opposition of some sort powerful enough to offset it.

Where, however, is such opposition to come from? The majority of our psychologists and physicians have never bowed the knee to Freud; but, of these men who do not accept the psychoanalytic gospel, there are few who feel strongly enough in the matter to raise their voices against it. Few people will exert themselves for long in any direction unless they find sufficient profit in so doing to justify the effort expended. Most of us are too busy taking care of our own personal affairs or advancing some cause with which we are identified to spare much time on the thankless task of trying to pull down other people's houses. There have been a great many who have been vitally interested in building up a belief in psychoanalysis; there have been few who would reap any great personal profit from pulling it down; so for the most part, those who could not see their way clear to accept psychoanalysis said little about it, while those who espoused it sang its praises, and the general public, hearing a loud and constant chorus of ayes and only an occasional no, have assumed the vote in its favor to be practically unanimous. The effect of this has been to carry over to psychoanalysis all of that great group of people who turn their faces in whatever direction the crowd seems to be going, and to silence the not inconsiderable number who lack the courage to express an opinion in support of what they conceive to be an unpopular cause.

Apparently the time has now come, however, when the tide is beginning to swing in the opposite direction. Psychoanalysis succeeded because it was salable, because it appealed to the popular imagination. Now, however, the general public, always fickle and chasing after new fads, is losing interest in psychoanalysis. This means fewer auditors for psychoanalytic lectures, fewer readers for psychoanalytic books, and fewer patients for psychoanalytic practitioners; which, in turn, of course means fewer people making a living out of psychoanalysis and fewer voices in the psychoanalytic cheering section. A little longer and psychoanalysis will be well on its way to oblivion to join the fads and follies of yester-year.

I am sorry to have found it necessary to discuss here thus frankly these psychological factors responsible for the success of psychoanalysis. I see, however, no way in which such discussion could have been avoided. By all odds, the most potent argument for psychoanalysis with most people today is that afforded by its popularity: it has, we are told, been generally accepted, therefore it must be sound. Obviously, it is impossible to weigh the merits of such an argument without going into the question of the causes to which this popularity is due. The psychoanalyst himself, of course, has never been squeamish about impugning the motives of those who disagree with him; as a matter of fact, his habitual way of carrying on a debate has always been to ignore the arguments advanced against him and discuss instead the motives to which, in his opinion, his opponent's "resistance" is due. He should therefore not take offense if the motives or desires lying back of his own beliefs are also subjected to scrutiny. (50:126, 131)

Harrington wrote before the great influx of psychoanalytically trained physicians who fled Hitler's persecution in Europe in the 30s and 40s. They created a fresh force of able propagandists who stemmed the tide of disfavor regarding Freudism and achieved a virtual takeover of American psychiatry and clinical psychology. Not until the 1960s were there fresh indications of a large-scale abandonment of Freudism by mental health professionals. Surveying the field in 1968, Marmor wonders at the "striking paradox" of the prestige of psychoanalysis waning in spite of its broad penetration into many fields:

The contributions of psychoanalysis to American psychiatry over the past 60 years have been impressive. Most major medical schools in America now accept psychoanalytically oriented psychodynamics as the foundation of their psychiatric teaching, and postgraduate psychoanalytic training institutes have been established in a number of them. In psychosomatic medicine, in child psychiatry, in the psychotherapy of the psychoses, in the neuroses of war, in social casework, in individual and group psychotherapy, in research, education, sociology, anthropology, and the arts, the impact of psychoanalytic theory has been enriching and rewarding.

Yet we are faced with a striking paradox. In the past ten years—despite all of this impressive impact—the prestige of psychoanalysis in this country appears to have dropped significantly in academic and scientific circles. (75:679)

Marmor explains the lack of enthusiasm for psychoanalysis by its being a "movement" rather than "an open-ended scientific theory." Retaining some residual devotion to Freudism, Marmor does not hint that the explanation might be even more in disenchantment with psychoanalytic fantasies. Announced with great fanfare, they did not stimulate scientific progress in any of the fields into which they were injected, except increasing the verbiage and compounding the confusion.

Brody, reviewing a study of psychiatrists in 1971, observes a similar decline of Freudian prestige:

Psychoanalysis offers an unusual example—perhaps unique in the world of science—of a small, elitist group with a shocking, heterodox ideology (and heresies to match) assuming an undisputed intellectual power with all the bureaucratic benefits of quasi-political success, now possibly entering a period of decline, and all within a hundred years. (76:22)

Brody's explanation of the beginning downfall in prestige of (predominantly Freudian) psychiatrists is that they simply could not deliver what they were confidently prophesying:

Twenty years ago the psychiatrist was considered by all but the most hard-nosed or hopeless as providing not only therapeutic help and the theoretical underpinnings for all the social sciences and humanities but as a social prophet and personal paragon as well. Today he seems to many more like a spoiled priest. (76:22)

Another psychologist, Sherman, sees that in 1971 the wind has gone out of Freudian sails. All that is left are the husks of an outmoded cult:

200

Psychoanalysis has fallen upon evil days. From times of daring innovation and creative intensity it has come to narrow refinements and a suffocation of the spirit. . . . particularly within the boundaries of orthodoxy, psychoanalytic innovation and new theoretical horizons have become conspicuous by their absence. Ego psychology has come to a blind alley, problems of technique no longer attract even discussion, much less change, and little vitality appears to be left except for the superficial functions of formal professionalism. (77:15)

The disaffection is more marked among psychologists than among psychiatrists, for psychiatric schools are still largely dominated by Freudians. However, a moderately disenchanted Freudian, Kepecs, sees definite signs of the diminishing status of psychoanalysis and its becoming "a rather lonely island":

Psychoanalysis in the United States is today suffering a decline in prestige and popularity, having reached the high point of its influence in American psychiatry in the 1950's. Many young psychiatrists then believed to be really first class one had to become an analyst. In many residency programs, particularly in analytic training centers, almost all the residents applied to psychoanalytic institutes. Acceptance was a great event and rejection was treated as shameful. Young candidates who had been dropped from training because they were regarded as not suitable felt stigmatized and a pall of second-class citizenship was cast over their careers. Some psychoanalysts, by this turn of events placed in positions of great power over the careers of others, became afflicted by a distressing spirit of arrogance and pride. By certain sectors of urban, middle class society, psychoanalysis was also regarded with great respect and often illusory hopes existed about its effectiveness as a means of treatment. When I became interested in psychoanalysis in the 1930's, it was a new, venturesome, small, exciting movement. After World War II it expanded rapidly and eventually became a more organized, more structured, and hierarchical social organization. Now in recent years with the rise of popularity of community psychiatry and other innovations, psychoanalysis no longer possesses the golden key to professional and academic success.

201

Even in large cities many residents no longer feel that their hopes of success depended upon becoming a psychoanalyst. (51:161)

A similar indication of the waning influence of the Freudian hoax in psychiatric circles is reflected in a report from the University of California at Los Angeles, Department of Psychiatry: "Ten years ago at UCLA, 60% of a group of beginning residents completed psychoanalytic training. In the present residency group, only one sixth would be considered 'analytic,' while the remaining would be characterized as 'eclectic.' " (66:3) And they find that the residents are rated consistently higher now than ten years ago. These phenomena of decrease of psychoanalytic dominance and improvement in the quality of trainees, might not be unconnected, in view of the low scientific demand upon adherents of the Freudian system.

Notes to Chapter Four

1. The long-lasting effects of the large-scale American brainwashing are probably reflected in the bias of the *American Heritage Dictionary*. Stalin is described there as "Russian revolutionary statesman" and Mussolini as "Fascist dictator of Italy." Yet, brutalities of the "statesman" far outreach those of the "dictator."

2. I would like to contribute to the already large literature of Freudian slips. Salter's name is turned into Slater by these friendly historians.

3. Freudians achieved a posthumous revenge on Janet for slighting their Master. This unfairness to Janet is a telling comment on sectarian narrow-mindedness of Freudians. By the time Freud's centenary of birth came around in 1956 the Freudians had attained a sufficient grip in French psychiatric circles to bring about placing of a plaque at Salpêtrière hospital, commemorating Freud's frequenting Charcot's lectures there for about six months. Yet, when 1959, the centenary of Janet's birth, came around, no commemorative appreciation was organized. This travesty of professional evaluation is inconceivable under any scientific or professional considerations. Evaluated objectively, Janet showed much more scientific discipline

than Freud (in his psychoanalytic phase). He was a careful and painstaking investigator, avoided going beyond the observable behavior of patients, wrote what have by now become classical studies in dynamic psychiatry. He spent not six months as a visitor, but worked for years as director of the psychological laboratory at Salpêtrière, investigating, teaching, and healing. Yet, in his own country he was not accorded recognition given to a less deserving foreigner.

4. Some readers might be puzzled by my referring to Freud's neurosis. It might appear incongruous to them that the allegedly most effective therapist for neuroses would himself suffer from them. I have dealt in more detail with aspects of Freud's neurotic troubles in *Freud's Non-science* [chapter V, 2, "Science out of Freud's neuroticism," (71)]. Suffice at this point to quote a staunch defender of Freud, Eissler, on a list of neurotic troubles in the master. He starts with Freud's neurotic symptoms evident in letters to Fliess: "... swings of mood and psychosomatic symptoms." Even after the supposedly successful self-analysis, "He suffered from anxiety about missing trains ... migraine headaches, and at times from a superstitious-like preoccupation with numbers referring to the age at which he expected to die; all his life he suffered sporadically from constipation. ... was unable, against all medical warnings to abstain from smoking ... even though smoking had caused cancerous changes in the oral cavity ... occasional stubbornness in clinging to a doubtful—or even more than doubtful—theory as well documented. ... Freud was probably a mildly compulsive character." (79:234-236) The reader may or may not agree with Eissler's conclusion: "Freud's neurotic symptoms, taken together do not amount to all that much. Phobias, headaches, and superstitions are the usual triad one finds in intellectuals." (79:236). I for one do not agree with it. Well-integrated individuals, psychoanalyzed or not, do not show such neurotic traits as a rule. Eissler is apparently too lenient in presenting Freud's neuroticism. He also failed to mention some aspects of moderate sociopathy in Freud, like his experimentation with cocaine (which he even recommended to his family members for upset stomachs), lack of identification with established moral standards, some misanthropic reactions, suspicious and accusing attitude, regularly warming up and cooling off toward friends, and other human foibles.

5. During a recent visit to Vienna, I became acquainted with an old

physician who was a student of medicine at the University of Vienna about 1918. He told me of how he and a few other students went to Freud's lectures. "Freud was not yet a professor then. He used to put us together to analyze each other."

"Why didn't you specialize in psychoanalysis in that case?" I asked him.

"It was not so good in those days. Wagner-Jauregg, who was the professor of psychiatry at that time, would not let us get through the medical exams if he knew we were going to Freud's lectures. He would say: 'If you go to that charlatan, you're not worthy of being medical men.' "

Chapter V

Some Balked at Brainwashing

...the brainwashing process implicit in psychoanalytic
training...

W. Sargant, M.D. (15:95)

...those numerous Renans, raised within the bosom of the
"Freudian Church."

H.K. Johnson, M.D. (1:322)

The book (in German), entitled *The Rosicrucian in his Naked-
ness,* published by Master "Pianco," an ex-member of the
society, in 1782, was a violent attack and exposé of the
Rosicrucians; but the delusion continued to flourish.

Charles W. Heckethorn (19:230)

[To a psychiatrist who had suffered the indignities of psychoanalytic training]...I am glad you are recovering from the
Procrustean wounds of the Chicago Institute,...

Jules H. Masserman, M.D. (18:442)

We shall turn later (chapter X) to the understanding of psychoanalysis as basically a manipulation by subtle suggestion or, to put it
more plainly, a concealed brainwashing process. As with brainwashing, very few people could successfully resist Freudwashing. Here
we shall review two training analyses—one performed by Freud on
Wortis (2) and another carried out on Campbell (3) by a recognized
teacher of psychoanalysis—and a failing analysis of an intelligent and
"resistant" patient, Natenberg. The games played by Freudians on
both doctors and patients are described by two former analysands,
Sheppard and Lee. The subsequent section demonstrates the irresponsible undermining of a mental patient's psychological and
existential situation by superimposing Freudian categories on his sick
mind in the name of therapeutic influence. And finally, not to be
one-sided, there is a review of a successful analysis with Freud.

205

None but one of the analyses was "successful." Both trainees refused to accept psychoanalytic interpretations on faith, and did not concur in predetermined interpretations of their dreams, thoughts, and other reactions if they felt their understanding of themselves did not vouch for it. They struggled to keep their eyes open and they later made devastating reports of their experiences. The analysis of Natenberg resulted in an angry book denouncing Freudism as presumptuous quackery. The two analysands see psychoanalysis as a futile game. The mental patient started getting better spontaneously, or by mega-Vitamin therapy, but in any case after he discarded psychoanalytic wisdom and submitted himself to the healing effects of religion and morally mature living.

1. *A skeptical American and Freud*

Wortis spent four months in didactic analysis with Freud in 1934. The process was stormy, upsetting, and so unconvincing for Wortis that he did not want to cash in on it by becoming a psychoanalyst. Instead, upon his return from Vienna, he introduced shock therapy in this country. There were apparently no incontrovertible facts by which Freud could convince him, and he failed to develop a devotion to his trainer which would have helped him build a faith and accept the revelations. He experienced most of Freud's interpretations as arbitrary, farfetched, and dogmatic.

After the first interview he sensed that he was in for trouble, not only because his aroused feelings might interfere with other postgraduate psychiatric studies, but also "because there was the unpleasant prospect of developing what Freud called *Wiederstand,* or resistance, against him, my present lord and master; who sat in quiet judgement while I talked, like a stern Old Testament Jehovah, and who seemed to take no special pains to act with hospitality or reassurance." (2:22)

Apparently, Freud was deliberately and freely using his cold, authoritarian manner to prepare the subject not to resist the mental modifications that were to be demanded of him later. Wortis refused to be cowed: "I said to Freud that it was impossible, I thought, to let my thoughts flow freely, since I was undoubtedly influenced by Freud's presence, and what he brought to mind: sex and neurosis." (2:22)

206

Wortis kept his end up for a while. After the fifth session he noted: "Freud was irritated that I should air independent views, somewhat at variance with his own, and that I should, moreover, explain away my own problems to my own satisfaction." (2:29) Apparently he correctly observed that what was expected was to adopt the role of a believer, not a cothinker. "Freud now proceeded to give me my first real lesson in analysis. Other things were hidden from me because of my preconceived scientific opinions or prejudices." (2:34, 35) A convert to a new, strict faith would be exposed to a similar treatment if the priest were at all conscientious.

Freud attempted on many an occasion to teach Wortis how he should view his inner events through special psychoanalytic mirrors:

> One of the feminine elements in my dreams, according to Freud, was the symbolic entry of the line of servants into the house. This, thought Freud, might represent a mother's womb with my brother and sisters issuing from it. Similarly, the dream of little animals sucking my finger might have represented female elements (since little animals always meant females) sucking at the breast. (2:39, 40)

When Wortis reported a dream in which he was playing truant from school, Freud strongly suggested as an enlightened guess that what Wortis had in mind was to stop the analysis and use the money (supplied by a Foundation) for his own needs. It did not matter much when Wortis protested that such an idea had never crossed his mind. (Such personalized distortion of meaning also appears in Freud's accusation that Jung—who wanted to see some archaeological relics near Bremen—entertained a death wish regarding Freud. Paranoiacs abound in such intuitions.)

Freud told Wortis in no uncertain terms: "You want to learn more about human nature because you are ignorant and I am here to teach you. An analysis is not a chivalrous affair between two equals." (2:50) In other words, the role of the adult trainee was reduced to that of an ignorant first-grader who should accept unquestioningly the teacher's ideas.

Freud tells Wortis later in analysis: "You must learn to absorb things and not argue back. You must change that habit. Accept things that you are told, consider them, and digest them. That is the only way

207

to learn. It is a question of *le prendre ou le laisser*—take it or leave it."
(2:114) Just like religion: you can only take it or leave it! Annoyed,
Wortis shot back at one point: "You act as if psychoanalysis stood
high and perfect and only our own faults kept us from accepting it; it
does not seem to occur to you that it is simply polite to reckon with
one's own prejudices too." (2:49) Wortis apparently just could not get
it into his head that it was unthinkable to Freud that the student's
view of his own psyche could be correct if it diverged from that of the
Professor.

In spite of his resistant attitude, Wortis showed signs of wearing
down. He was being slowly browbeaten, and the brainwashing
pressure began to tell on him. He developed uneasy moods, was
bothered by guilt feelings. "I had moods of self reproach for being so
resistant a subject during analysis." (2:81) He praised Freud for his
extraordinary contribution to science as a trial at reconciliation and
submission. He said humbly: "I must say again that I am sorry if I
have been stubborn and superior, and make slow headway in
accepting your ideas. Conceit is an unpleasant quality . . . I should be
perfectly willing if you treat it as a bad symptom and cure it if you
can." (2:50, 51) Two days later he repeats: "I promised again to be
good . . . I will do what I can (*ich werde mein Möglichstes versuchen*)."
The German meaning is quite strong: "I'll try all I can, my utmost!"

The trainer did not let up the pressure: "Freud again began to
speak with vehemence and I could think of nothing better to say than
that I was very sorry I seemed so proud; I did not want to be, I
recognized it was unpleasant, and it might later make for unhappiness . . . I felt depressed and discouraged again when I left."
(2:82) The following day: "I thanked Freud for his pains . . . and left
in some distress because I did not believe in his psychoanalytic theory
of dream symbols." (2:83)

Obviously, Wortis was showing the beginnings of a surrendering
attitude. This process of breakdown and perplexity is a regular
feature of all induced mind changes and is particularly prominent in
Communist or other totalitarian "reeducation" or "thought reform"
camps, as will be shown in the last chapter on Freudwashing. Wortis
experienced it as part of his unsuccessful initiation in the Freudian
movement: "My mood at this time began to be [one] of scientific
bewilderment, because I could not accept many of Freud's con-

clusions and was essentially out of sympathy with his attitude." (2:95)

However, his self-reliance was shaken. When Wortis in his vacillations began to praise psychoanalysis, Freud seemed to want to test the strength of his apparent conversion by reminding him that he had not talked that way at the beginning of analysis. Wortis struggled valiantly, turning now upon himself, now upon the peculiar thought system that was being forced on him. On one occasion he reported:

> I did what associating I could, but nothing came out. If I continued associating long enough, I told Freud, no doubt something would turn up which could be appropriately used. Freud said it was inadvisable to force an interpretation, and that I had best talk on. With due apologies, I resumed the discussion of my attitude. I refused to concede that I was rejecting parts of analysis merely for reasons of personal pride. My "narcissism" did not seem to be a general phenomenon: I stood in real awe of Ellis, for example, and trembled in his presence. (2:120)

Of course, the reason for this different reaction is simple: Havelock Ellis did not try to foist his opinions on the young doctor. [1]

The analytic situation developed into a meaningless alternation of yielding and arguing back. Wortis found that his "free" associations were somewhat of a farce, as he had to make an effort to produce them: "I suggested a sexual interpretation, I told Freud, just to show how honest I am, and to show I have no *Wiederstand*. That makes me feel there is never a completely free association; there are always elements of motivation in what occurs to me and that ought to be taken into account." (2:126) Naturally, Freud could not take Wortis's comment into account as it threatened to make nonsense of his procedure and his theoretical "discoveries." The "wish-hunting in the unconscious" (4) had to proceed according to hallowed precepts, safe to Freud's blindspots.

An observer of this tortured analysis can hardly fail to notice two features of the situation. One is that psychoanalysis, even in the hands of Freud, has no validated facts. If the procedure dealt with validated facts, let us say the rate of learning certain verses or galvanic response to suggestive pictures, there could be no argument; the disagreement would be settled by recourse to measurements. But Freud operated with psychological hypotheses and used his own authority and his

209

logical and intuitive guesswork to deny the validity of any other hypotheses the analysand would dare make in an independent way. The course of this "analysis" points strongly to the hollow core of psychoanalysis as a system of unconfirmed and mostly unverifiable propositions, a philosophic and mystical system, rather than a science. One has first to believe in the oracular authority of the analyst before accepting his Freudian guesses. Though despising religion, Freudians thus fall into an essentially religious procedure. In my view, there is nothing in itself reprehensible in the procedure of arriving at and holding fast to religious beliefs; when they are propagated under the guise of science, however, they become onerous.

The second observation to be made from Wortis's experience is that psychoanalysis operates as unsuspected reeducation, hidden persuasion, and suggestion. Again, I find nothing improper in helping people correct twisted perspectives by these methods unless the subjects are fooled into the belief that it was not the analyst who put the idea into their minds, but they themselves supposedly discovered it, in the disclosed materials. It is remarkable that an astute individual like Freud could be blind to the real nature of his procedures. It is a sad example of compartmentalized thinking, for which one readily excuses lesser minds.

It is ironic that a psychologist of Freud's reputation, who unmasked various pretenses and rationalizations in his contemporaries, should require such defenses. Before the start of his analysis, Wortis had expressed fears that he might not always agree with him. Freud reassured the young man that he need not fear the loss of his independence. (2:17, 18) The subsequent course of analysis shows that this was only one of Freud's rationalizations. Freud failed to discern that his analytic procedure moved in a quite different direction. He could not see behind the myth he created. Toward the end of analysis, Freud encouraged Wortis to express his anger. The latter replied that Freud's "methods of arguing were intimidating and coercive, and that he did not allow me enough freedom of discussion or opinion." Under attack, Freud resumed the role he had consciously adopted earlier, showing new patience, and even asserted that he "would rather have me be skeptical and cautious." (2:137)

At one point, in the last quarter of analysis, Freud tells Wortis that he has acquired only *Schmarren* (trifles, traces) of psychoanalysis and

210

tries to shame him into acceptance of his "science": "A serious scientist should inform himself on the subject first; you should read books on the subject in this case, my books—and let yourself be convinced." (2:129) In the interview before the last, Freud says earnestly that "analysis tries to avoid every kind of suggestive influence," (2:163) seemingly unaware of the incongruity of this statement with what had gone on in analysis with Wortis for four months. Natenberg calls attention to Freud's "unrivaled capacity for delusional thinking." (5:VIII) [2]

We shall return to look at the lack of objectivity in Freudian methods and the use of suggestion in psychoanalysis in later chapters (VIII to X).

2. Another psychiatrist refuses blinders

Head of the Department of Psychiatry, School of Medicine, University of Oklahoma, until his death in 1957, Campbell summed up his disillusionment with psychoanalysis in the title of his book: *Induced Delusions: The Psychopathy of Freudism.* (3)

Campbell had been a psychiatrist for seven years before submitting to subtle pressures from those who were already on the Freudian bandwagon and who directly or indirectly implied that the only effective and worthwhile therapy is through psychoanalysis and that any self-respecting psychiatrist should be trained in it. Yielding to these influences, he arranged for a training analysis with a competent, recognized analyst, and experienced 170 painful and irritating hours. Although struggling against the concealed brainwashing, he was overcome by it, and practiced psychoanalysis for four years on about thirty patients. Only one improved, and that amelioration Campbell attributed to spontaneous recovery. He describes two cases in which psychoanalytic narrowness led to considerable harm and loss to patients. (3:20-22) He had enough courage to abandon the "elite" form of therapy.

Several years later he wrote to M. Natenberg, another victim of psychoanalysts, and author of *Freudian Psycho-Antics* (5): "You and I are brothers under the skin. I underwent a training analysis some sixteen years ago and like you, have made fairly satisfactory recovery." (3:VI) In his preface to Campbell's book, Natenberg conjectures that Campbell wrote in order to rid himself of "weird Freudian delusions"

211

emotionally, although he had won intellectual freedom much earlier.

Campbell's story shows a pattern of haughty and arbitrary handling of the analysand similar to that experienced by Wortis. The first session lasted fifty minutes instead of one hour as Campbell expected. The second session started ten minutes late, the analyst claiming that Campbell was waiting in the wrong room, and Campbell suspecting that the analyst came out of a meeting. This inevitably cropped up in the process of free association.

Apparently my doubt of his veracity irked him but, instead of dealing with the actual issues involved—the proper accounting of time—he obscured matters by suggesting that I was repeating certain emotional reactions originally pertaining to my father in relation to the primal scene and to his scolding me for watching our cattle being mounted. Obviously this was an arbitrary assumption, indicative of the way analysts evade current issues and make their interpretations on illogical suppositions. Yet in the peculiar aura of psychoanalysis, one accepts such interpretations in a half-believing way. (3:5, 6)

In the next session the trainer attempts to inject himself into the mind of his victim:

I recalled a dream about operating on my father with unsterile instruments and under unsterile conditions. A dirty rag for packing the wound worried me in the dream; "womb" was associated with the word "wound"; I decided to sterilize by pouring water into the wound; and this evoked recall of scalding a pig too long when working as a butcher's helper as a boy.

A lengthy interpretation followed. The analyst accused me of violent hostility, of calling him a pig, and of harboring intense jealousy toward my father. These interpretations followed the pattern he had established during the previous seance and were made again on wholly illogical assumptions after short acquaintance. The somewhat paranoid character of analysis is obvious. The sexual recollections, the figure of my father, the boiling water and the pig, all were interpreted by the analyst as pertaining to himself. In other words, he was suggesting that I was involving him in my psychic life, whereas it was just the opposite: he was interjecting himself into the situation.

212

Obviously such interpretations, made to a novice who is lying on a couch and who by virtue of training requirements must respect the interpreter, constitute an exceedingly bizarre interpersonal relationship. To submit such illogical conclusions under the guise of training is a travesty upon logic and indeed a travesty upon science itself. (3:6, 7)

The solemn farce of "deep" interpretations continued. A rich emotional life was autocratically distorted to fit predetermined theoretical conceptions, dead forms imposed upon the exuberant mind of the analysand. Indeed, his mind was put on Procrustes' bed while he lay on that couch. The badgering of the recalcitrant patient, the authoritarian certainty of making diagnoses from slight clues, and the reckless attack upon the trainee's self-understanding is clearly in evidence:

> ...mention of a sexual rivalry was interpreted as a continuation of my jealousy toward my father. In accordance with the analyst's already established opinion, jealousy toward my father was tantamount to jealousy toward him, for according to his several interpretations he was playing the role of father in my mind. Mention of my harelip which followed was interpreted as holding my father to blame for it, which supposedly justified my jealousy or resentment toward him because he was somehow responsible.
>
> Such was my uncertainty of mind and confusion that, although I was unable to accept these interpretations, neither could I emphatically reject or refute them. I left the session unable to see any connection between the analyst and my father.
>
> My conscious thought processes could not accept these interpretations, but I listened because I was in the role of a trainee and paying so much a minute for the training. At the same time I was also a physician, already trained in science, mathematics, philosophy, and other spheres of learning, and accustomed to the right to question anything I could not understand or accept as true....
>
> These interpretations of my envy toward the analyst I somehow partly accepted because I wished to proceed with the analysis in order to complete my training. I was beginning to realize that if I were dubious about his interpretations he would persist on and

213

on to make his point and then the procedure would never end unless I concurred.

In retrospect, it now seems rather odd how the analyst could make interpretations of envy, jealousy, and so on but overlook evidence of other emotions and feelings which did not fit into his scheme of things. . . .

As can readily be ascertained, psychoanalysis is chiefly a method of drawing inferences of a far-fetched nature. Dreams are the greatest source of material from which such inferences (interpretations) are drawn. My dream of a man ascending a ladder while carrying on his shoulder a person with a pot in his hands, evoked the following associations: pot—toilet receptacle; man climbing ladder—two psychiatrists I disliked. The interpretation my trainer rendered was that the dream revealed resistance; that the man carrying the pot dealt in dirty matter; and that climbing the ladder without help indicated my resistance to both the analyst and the analysis.

These interpretations and/or constructions illustrate the ease with which an analyst can make his own associations fit the material so as to clinch further his interpretations of competitiveness, jealousy, hostility, or other motives. [3]

Another display of his interpretive magic was performed when I related of having a dream of sexual intercourse with a young woman, during which she suddenly gave birth to a baby. In the dream, I told her the child was not mine because of our brief acquaintance, but I delivered the child and tied off the umbilical cord. The analyst concluded the dream was a grandiose representation that I could make a baby instantly, that I emphasized potency and that the woman in the dream represented himself.

In another dream fragment, as an expert witness I defended a paranoid man from his wife. The analyst interrupted to assert that my free associations proved the paranoiac was myself and that I had wronged a paranoid patient in order to defend myself against my own homosexuality. [This is typical brainwashing: guilt feelings are suggested into the subject and he is made to feel sick, bad, abnormal. This proves not only the need for change, but also the need for "treatment."]

He further pointed out the possibility of my having internal conflicts which would require much time to work out. Accusing other men of being women to hide feminine drives based on the

214

masculine protest, paranoid tendencies, and passive wishes toward him were all linked with my alleged unconscious homosexual wishes. This is the standard Freudian axiom, linking paranoia to unconscious homosexuality, which has been completely disproved.

Now all these interpretations were made from dreams and the associations supposedly related to them. The dream is, after all, a rather bizarre and ephemeral phenomenon upon which to base such serious diagnosis as catatonia, paranoid trends, homosexuality, and delusions. (It must be remembered, that at the time I had already practiced clinical psychiatry for some seven years.) Such terms applied to a person on such scant acquaintance indicate exceeding recklessness. The analyst had recorded little real information about me; all his conclusions were based on my dreams. (3:8-12)

A psychiatrist, capable of defending himself against distorting pressures upon his mind, Campbell was nevertheless brought to the brink of emotional disturbance through this "analysis." It is not difficult to imagine how powerfully the psychoanalytic technique might work on neurotically impaired patients.

The following sessions were marked by my anger and increasing subjectivity. Almost every event seemed to me tinged with ideas of reference, of persecution, and of someone prying into my business. Now it must be remembered that this irritability developed in a physician, but there is no difference between the training procedure and the therapeutic analysis of patients. Interpretations, procedures, and relationships are exactly the same in training physicians and in treating patients. The reactions of the subjects must therefore also be similar.

A recurrence of the hives brought on another interesting example of the analyst's interpretative art. An itching of my right hand was accompanied by what seemed like the beginning formation of an urtical wheel over the dorsum of the first phalanx. The analyst interpreted this allergic manifestation as the spreading of sexual feelings to my hand, in defiance of my mother.

One of the most distressing and annoying incidents of my training analysis was my detection of a horrible stench while lying on the couch. It was unbearable but the analyst denied emitting

215

flatus, though with quite evident embarrassment. At that stage, the transference (hypnotic) relationship was so prevailing, that I accepted his denial, in spite of the evidence of my own nose. This brought on a strong fear that I had suffered an olfactory hallucination, known to me as a serious symptom of damage to a brain lobe. (3:13-18)

In spite of his vigorous defense of the integrity of his mind, Campbell's armor showed serious chinks as he failed to resist fully the brainwashing pressure.

My notes [he writes] disclose a tendency to fall in line with psychoanalytic thinking, even to the point of anticipating the analyst's expectations . . . I was also somewhat aware of a desire to appease the analyst by submitting material in line with what I believed were his expectations. Since he had already established my "father transferences," dreams in which my father appeared were quickly reported. (3:16, 17, 18)

As Freud tried to assure himself that he was not imposing his views on Wortis through analysis, so Campbell's analyst tried to persuade himself and his trainee. "Interpretations will not be pushed," he said, "even when I am completely aware of the significance of your material." Campbell retorted: "I think you have already pushed interpretations pretty fast." (3:16) Apparently psychoanalysts practice a double deception: of the prisoner in analysis and of themselves. Verbally, they pretend to be dealing with him as an adult, while they reduce him to a dependent, regressed status in a concealed way. This hypocrisy has much less to commend it than the frank treatment of the newcomer to *Synanon* as practically an infant. (7)

The study of Campbell's report leaves the impression of psycho-analytic process being practically an exercise in "folie à deux" (also called induced insanity, imposed insanity, simultaneous insanity, by pre-Freudian psychiatrists). The training analyst appears to have been affected by developing a peculiar view of psychic reality, and in a paranoid fashion assumes that his view is superior and more correct because it coincides with Freud's fantasies. The analysand-trainee is led to assume a very humble role of an ignorant dude, who is to be inducted into mysteries of the unconscious psychic realms of which he supposedly knows nothing for sure. (See chapter X, 2 on the similar brainwashing pressures in ancient mystery religions.) The analyst proceeds unhesitatingly and authoritatively to proliferate fantasies along the lines of abundant Freudian traditions, assuming them to be right inasmuch as they show psychoanalytic flavor. There is also an implied expectation that the analysand will absorb the often non-sensical interpretations as revelations from on high. The adult analysand is reduced to the level of infantile irrationality, with analyst injecting his own irrational system into the subject's disorganized sense of reality.

The infantilization of analysands is also seen in other measures used to increase the dependence on the omniscient trainers. Campbell had to make long-distance calls, at his own expense, to his supervisor to draw upon the latter's esoteric insights about the cases handled by the practically imbecile trainee.

The control analyses acted as further conditioning devices, but this recalcitrant trainee again failed to accept the divinations of his master:

> My control analyses awakened me further to the realization that psychoanalysis is a delusional indulgence.
>
> The controls were undertaken with three different analyses over about two years. One of my cases was completed at a control seminar, and three others were continued as part of my training with control analyses. Some control sessions lasted for one hour each and were conducted by long distance telephone, at my expense. [4] At the termination of my control work, one of the "controllers" frankly told me I was posing. This accusation followed my criticism of the conclusions reached by training analysts in control seminars. At one such seminar, an inter-nationally famous analyst interrupted a presentation which included matter about a patient's writing a letter to his mother. Severely criticizing the analyst under control, he scolded: "Don't you know that writing a letter always symbolizes masturbation?" (3:19, 20)

Campbell's conclusions about his psychoanalytic misadventure are often expressed by other critics: "With the freedom to consider the concepts of Freud in a spirit of critical reflection, the same concepts which to those conditioned to belief by delusion appear so immutable,

217

will to those not conditioned assume the form and shape of a grotesque and bizarre system of rationalization." (3:22)

The insults to the personalities of these two trainees, help explain why Adler emphasized that he had not been and that he would not be psychoanalyzed.

3. *An angry ex-patient*

Maurice Natenberg was a medical writer who went into analysis upon recommendation of Dr. Paul Shilder, who sent him to a Freudian psychiatrist who had had analysis with Freud, the highest distinction imaginable in analytic circles.

Natenberg, like everyone entering analysis, started with high hopes of attaining valuable self-awareness and improving his emotional functioning. He endured the procedure for one hundred hours before he realized that he was not only getting nothing in return for the expense and trouble of psychoanalysis but was being psychologically abused in the process. He was outraged by irresponsible tampering with his mind, and he felt he was being subjected to the solemn fraud of a prolonged and disguised hypnotic experiment.

> For a time, these recollections almost completely unnerved me. It was sickening to consider my continuation in these fruitless sessions for one hundred visits without waking up to the fraud. Impressions formerly only vague became sharp and clear, enabling me to realistically appraise my experiences on the couch at last. While undergoing them, such capacity seemed entirely lost. In my disgust and resentment it was staggering to realize the futility and blindness of my experiment on the couch. (5:10, 11)

In the foreword to his book, *Freudian Psycho-Antics: Fact and Fraud in Psychoanalysis,* he says:

> The policy of inflicting physical brutalities on the insane has long disappeared because of the work of the late Clifford Beers and his mental hygiene movement. Today, however, there exists a new oppression imposed in the luxurious setting of the psycho-analyst's chambers. Instead of a physical, there is a psychological coercion carried out in the misapplication of hypnotic and

218

suggestive influences to further invalidate Freudian researches.

Free of regulation and supervision, analysts subject their patients to a merciless observation in the secrecy of their chambers, keeping them in an introspective trance for intolerable lengths of time, at exorbitant expense, and often with harmful results. All those considering an analysis should know the influences at work and the real goal of the treatment. The author hopes his work will help that end. (5:7)

Natenberg realized upon later reflection that a combination of his supine position and his concentration on free association led to the temporary befogging of his mind:

> . . . my experiences could be easily explained in the light of hypnotic phenomena. The prime necessity for inducing a hypnotic state is intense concentration on one idea. This had always been present in my psychoanalysis in my deep absorption with the process of free association. Consequently matters outside the scope of my concentration were hardly noticed and quickly forgotten, which accounted for my overlooking some very elementary considerations.
>
> In this absorption, reactions also became blurred and the memory clouded quickly. I had little capacity to understand the analyst when he did venture some opinion or interpretation, or to realize the implication of my own words. It was sort of mechanical performance, and at the end of each session a fog of amnesia enveloped everything. But it was free association and my addiction to it that had developed this fog. . . .
>
> . . . there is a gradual paralysis of the will and an inability to think clearly. Freud demanded a suppression of the critical faculties because thinking and acting on a rational, conscious level did not fit into his technique. Freud immobilized the capacity to reject foolish, irrelevant thoughts, just as a hypnotist can inhibit the ability to feel pain, see normal objects, or perform normal functions. (5:11, 12, 45)

Landis, a respected professor of psychology, and others undergoing psychoanalysis experienced a similar deterioration of their will in Freudian analysis. [See chapter IX of *Freud's Non-science* (9).] There is little to distinguish Natenberg's mental travail from that of

Americans subjected to Chinese brainwashing techniques. "My treatment is the most regrettable experience of my life and left me convinced that psychoanalysis is pure quackery," (5:19) Natenberg writes in retrospect. The Freudian claim to science is laughable to him:

> Psychoanalysis is . . . a novelty created by Freud by blending dashes of art, science, religion, philosophy and mysticism. His basic ingredient, however, was just pure authority, an unqualified demand for faith in the reliability of his data which he had gathered from purely verbal communications, and which he claimed could be constructed to form a science. (5:21)

Natenberg sees another element of fraud in psychoanalysis in its clandestine carrying on of research on patients under the pretense that this is therapy for them:

> A patient in analysis is not told he is contributing both his person and funds to a research project, but is permitted to either believe psychoanalysis is wholly directed towards healing, or that the aims of investigation and cure can be harmlessly combined in one procedure. This however, is strictly contrary to medical beliefs and practices which require written permission to conduct research on a patient. A surgeon must complete his work and sew up his incision as quickly as possible and limit himself to tried and proven methods. Experiments are conducted only on cadavers or research animals, except under very unusual circumstances.
>   It may now be understandable why Freud employed misleading comparisons to describe his system, for he could not describe it for what it really was. The influences that he and his disciples brought to bear in carrying out the hidden, unholy marriage of research and therapy, is probably the most sordid side of psychoanalysis. It needs careful critical examination.
>   Unofficially, he formed a research institution of his own, "The Sigmund Freud Foundation to Foster Psychoanalysis." Unfortunately, he neglected to inform the world or his patients of this very questionable action. Freud's experimentation, financed by his guinea pigs, is one of the most ingenious arrangements in the annals of human affairs. (5:30, 31, 37)

What revolted Natenberg most was the "unconditional surrender" to the analyst into which he was maneuvered by a subtle brainwashing on the couch. He traces this directly to Freud:

> His couch became an abyss, a strange, fantastic domain where he manipulated his patients like puppets on strings. . . . This complete surrender permitted Freud to secure acceptance of all his dogma.
>
> . . . Freud needed docile, willing subjects, he misapplied hypnotism by using it to prolong his treatments rather than work a cure. The same patient, formerly quickly treated by hypnotism and suggestion, was told the new psychoanalytic treatment had greater permanent value though it could take a long, long time. Certainly, this, too, is suggestion employed in this way to prepare the patient's mind for long courses of treatment. By stressing the uncertainties of his therapy in the very first interview, Freud believed he "deprived" his patients of the "right" to protest later on when the results were discouraging. His picture of a neurosis was gloomy and foreboding and gave it the character of a baffling, almost hopeless illness, possibly incurable.
>
> No other comparable professional relationship has ever existed on this earth. Such onesided terms amount to intellectual and emotional slavery, and reveal how indelibly Freud placed the stamp of his personality on every phase of his discipline. Only a dictatorial nature could demand such implicit surrender and such absolute authority. Analysts who follow Freud's teachings ape his methods by imposing the same conditions to manipulate their subjects at will (5:43, 46, 51)

His dismal experience on the couch left Natenberg perplexed for some time. His book became a catharsis from his Freudian adventure. He looked into the literature for other recorded experiences with psychoanalysis. One of them was a report full of praise, written under the pseudonym of J. Knight. His review of that book is found in the chapter of *Psycho-Antics* entitled "A Chemist Buys a Gold Brick." Of course, it was difficult for Natenberg to get over having bought the Freudian gold brick himself.

Natenberg discovered other professional opinions to support his experience of psychoanalysis as a destructive rather than a healing process.

221

Back in June of 1938, two psychiatrists (not to be confused with psychoanalysts), Doctors G. B. Jamieson and Edwin E. McNiel, presented a paper at the annual American Psychiatric Convention and discussed the dangers of psychoanalysis for patients with a predisposition for severe mental disorders.

The two psychiatrists had made a detailed study of seventeen psychotic patients admitted to their institution. Every one of these unfortunates had either had analysis at one time, or had succumbed to their psychosis while still on the couch. The periods in analysis varied from two years, with the majority tending toward the incredible duration of seven years of treatment.

"Psychoanalysis had not been of any particular value to any of these unfortunates," said Doctors Jamieson and McNiel, "and in a selected number had actually precipitated psychosis. . . . The free association and fantasy life without emotional integration tend greatly to lead this type of patient away from reality once he resigns himself to the treatment couch." (5:91, 92).

Such negative and devastating testimonials to the uselessness of psychoanalytic therapy to patients is echoed by hundreds of former patients and their families in the pages of the newsletter *Schizophrenia*. The column "Are the customers always wrong?" reflects hundreds of personal tragedies, of impoverishment of families through expensive "treatments," and of meager or no results.

Even some Freudian practitioners report to their confreres the psychotic trends which they developed or reinforced in their victims on the couch. Bychowski described several cases of psychotic episodes induced by psychoanalysis. An outsider to Freudian circles can be amazed at the theoretical blindness instilled in some Freudian healers. Bychowski talks about severe disturbances induced in the patients as if they have nothing to do with the peculiar method of "treatment" to which the patients are subjected. He talks about regressive reactions of patients, of increased irrationality, of emerging homosexual yearnings, without associating them to loosening of the ego strength through free association, and suggesting psychoanalytic verities of homosexuality and sexual perversions as allegedly latent in everyone. Even when he recognizes the association of psychotic symptoms with Freudian doctrines, he makes it appear impersonal, dissociated from analyst's operations, while in fact it is the "treatment" itself that induces deterioration toward psychosis:

[She] responded well to psychoanalysis and her symptoms melted with gratifying rapidity. Our gratification was interrupted in a most unpleasant way when she developed an acute catatonic psychosis with abundant hallucinations of a predominantly sexual character. She was hospitalized and successfully treated with insulin coma therapy, then a recent discovery.... [Regarding another patient:] It would appear that the psychoanalytic process, in addition to abolishing his defenses and laying bare the psychotic core, also stimulated his homosexual libido. ... The homosexual wish which was activated by the psychoanalytic situation assaulted the ego with vehemence. ... A weak ego was besieged by passive homosexual and destructive hostile impulses. (14:329, 331, 334)

4. *Two analysands see through Freudian games*

Martin Shepard, a psychiatrist, and Marjorie Lee, a psychologist, dutifully went through their own psychoanalyses and, judging by their book, were unconvinced. They wrote *Games Analysts Play,* rejecting the tricks of regular psychoanalytic training and therapy. Their book exposes the subtle frauds played on trainees and patients.

To begin with, Shepard and Lee see the main reason for therapeutic ineffectiveness in the basic insincerity of the psychoanalyst toward his patient. This insincerity had been trained into Freudian analysts by their own tedious indoctrination. Beside lectures, seminars and reading, many trainees are subjected from 600 to 900 hours (9:46) of personal analysis, which is considered the crucial experience by the trainers. On the basis of it the candidate is rejected or accepted into the ranks of the illumined.

The candidates are exposed to a veritable brainwashing process, which they are to apply to their patients in turn. (See chapter X on Freudwashing). The trainees are caught in an atmosphere of awe for the hallowed traditions and for the approved interpretations of the senior analysts and supervisors. The protracted and strenuous initiation is the "narrow door" through which candidates have to squeeze in order to join the ranks of the elect. They are put to severe tests which fill them with apprehensions. In a way they are at the mercy of their trainers, as these are in power to ruin their professional and psychological future. The trainees in "thought reform" camps in

Maoist China are no less threatened in proving their proper absorption of correct doctrines than are the physicians and psychologists trained into Freudian molds of thought.

A subject of Communist brainwashing is purposely kept in the dark about what is expected of him—in order to better oppress him. The brainwashers have in that way more of a chance to keep the subject off balance, to permeate him with apprehensions, to make him feel helpless, worthless, inadequate, and improper. The political trainee or prisoner cannot win the game till the trainer decides that the subject has squirmed enough, has yielded in the desired direction, and should be given respite. Shepard and Lee describe similar experiences in the Freudian "thought reform" establishments:

> C's [candidate's] challenge is to find his way to health. Should he by any chance dare, with S [supervisor] or CA [candidate's analyst] to presume health prematurely, he is brought up short with the old saw that "Everyone has problems, so what are you trying to deny?" Yet the acknowledgment of problems will not buy a certificate of health either, because "if you've got problems, then isn't it healthier to stay and work them out?" The logic is inescapable; the treatment proceeds. (9:30)

The Communist prisoners who are selected for brainwashing have to write new reports when those that they prepared are rejected by investigators, without getting any sure clues of what is the desired new response. The psychoanalytic subject is in no more enviable position. The trainer is always one up on the candidate:

> No matter how many ways in which a living situation is analyzed, there is yet another level of analysis possible. CA needs only to ask C "Why?" or "What do you make of that?" These questions can be used on C for any and all circumstances. For instance: C keeps telling CA of an intense dislike for one of his supervisors—a Dr. Brown. After several weeks of probing why-questions, he comes to a session with the following dream: *I went to Dr. Brown's office and there he was, sitting in a strangely familiar overstuffed armchair, eating chocolate bonbons, conveying them to his mouth with his pinkie extended . . . and on the pinkie was a large zircon ring.* CA, knowing that Dr. Brown never

munches chocolates in his office, and has no such ring or arm-chair, inquires as to whom C might really be dreaming of. Suddenly the Eureka Phenomenon occurs. C leaps up and shouts, "Uncle Joe, that old sonuvabitch!" And sure enough, the good uncle, long since deceased, was hooked on gooey chocolates, and possessed just such a ring and armchair. And was despised. But will that be enough to account for C's dislike of Dr. Brown? No. This is only the first year of training analysis. Rather than allow smug satisfaction to turn the head of the neophyte, CA counters with, "And what do you make of that?" Indeed, a good deal *can* be made of it. Why was Uncle Joe the object of a negative trans-ference? For whom was Uncle a misplaced surrogate? (9:30, 31)

Without admitting it officially, the trainers drill the candidates in subtle ways intended to make them into subjects unsure of their own minds. The Freudian system is so elastic and so well designed for disorganizing the normal mental functions, that it can be used in many tricks played on the patient and the candidate. One set of games played by trainers are the Snare Games, one of them being called *"Why Did You . . . ?"* It is sure at the outset that a candidate cannot win this game with his supervisor. It is a training trick to humiliate and deflate the trainee: " . . . the question is not an attempt to learn something; instead it is a studied plot to catch C with his therapeutic breeches down." (9:146)

Another game imposed on psychoanalytic subjects is that of *Opposites* [P=patient, T=therapist]:

The director of psychiatric training at a well-known metropolitan hospital, himself a nationally acclaimed analyst, once addressed his resident group as follows:

"When a patient tells you about a dream in which a log floats down a body of water, you'd do well to think about birth-trauma. If he tells you about birth-trauma, you ought to find out if he's had some recent experiences with water."

This man was a past-master at the game of Opposites. Yet considering the training ground T has traveled, it can be seen that very little additional gardening is needed to cultivate this therapeutically perverse attitude.

Here are verbal exchanges which illustrate the game in action:
(1) P: I really love my wife.

225

T: It seems to me that you are trying to hide the fact that you hate her.

(2) P: My mother was terrible and I hated her.

T: Perhaps what you are really trying to tell me is that you loved her too much. (9:60, 61)

The main thing is to induce insecurity, inadequacy and guilt in the trainee. The Communists use the sessions of self-criticism for that purpose as well as the threat to livelihood in a state where everything is controlled by the Party; the Freudian analysts hold over the prospective analyst's head the threat of pronouncing the candidate unworthy, killing his hopes of becoming a member of the elevated class of analysts, being classified as professional and personal failure, and wasting thousands of dollars already invested in training.

Most of the candidates, after a long (or very long) struggle, are given a reprieve:

Regardless of the school, at some point past the third year, the CA stops asking "Why?" or "What do you make of that?" and, by his silence, tacitly accepts what C says at face value. C, at first unnerved by this, gradually comes to believe that he has some answers, feels increasingly healthy and self-confident, has the idea that he has won CA's respect, and terminates. He has seen treatment work. He, as well as CA, has profited by it.

And so, several years from the day of beginning his training as a therapist, graduation occurs and a new analyst is launched upon the world. He has been bombarded by so many divergent dicta during his development that unless he is very careful he will lose sight of the forest for the trees. He may well forget what his job originally consisted in—namely, promoting behavioral change in a patient—and, instead, resort to playing games. (9:31, 32)

The candidates, now approved psychoanalysts, impose upon their patients the salutary methods through which they were molded. They have by now become "thoroughly trained," so much so that most of them do not dare be critical of the method. If they did, they would be punished by guilt feelings for showing such unseemly "resistance." Or, even worse, they can be crushed by pronouncing them "incompletely analyzed." Whichever way a free-thinking person may turn in psychoanalysis, he is not likely to find an escape; the trainers, not unlike their brainwashing counterparts, have insured it that the victims cannot escape the nets spread around them.

In the experience of Shepard and Lee, it is a simple thing to play the psychoanalyst. The scheme is easy and there is no one who can prove that anything said or done might be wrong:

> The therapeutic candidate learns of the irrevocability of early development: that having a mother inevitably means trouble, and that being toilet-trained compounds it. He learns that dreams are essential to personal understanding and that they can be interpreted in as myriad ways as there are numbers of dreamers and interpreters; and that no one, therefore, can invalidate his interpretation. (9:26, 27)

Part of the trick is to learn "the knack of translating the simple into the complex," (9:28) to mystify the innocents. In the *Game of Big Words* conscience is called superego; creative energy—libido; babyish—regressed; self-love—narcissism; eating pleasure—oral gratification; mother and father—archaic super-ego introjects, etc. (9:107) Any ordinary experiences of the patient are recast into serious revelations of ugly drives and criminal promptings. " . . . Nothing P said or did was ever taken at face value or interpreted as anything but of the utmost importance." (9:131)

The scared patient has to stay in treatment for years to overcome terrible features of his personality, which every Freudian analyst inevitably uncovers in every subject. Dreams are particularly useful in prolonging treatment, as they can be easily twisted into any terrifying or titillating content. The analyst can easily turn his patients into Sapphos, Hamlets, prostitutes, courtesans, unsuspected homosexuals, potential murderers—anything, just to provoke anxiety, dependency, guilt and self-concern, and manipulate them into submission. It is a devilishly clever scheme of climbing on patient's back, and staying there.

Whenever the analyst gets bored with interminable reciting of feelings by the patients, he can brighten things up by asking questions about sexual experiences or desires.

227

When P happens to be an attractive member of the opposite sex, her prone position, while perhaps not changing the monotonous content of her verbal productions, offers T many an enchanting hour during which to enjoy, unself-consciously, the sight of a heaving bosom or a particularly pretty pair of legs. T can, then, in all safety, resort to his own fantasy. (9:51)

When sexual stimulation brings about the "transference," the analyst can cool her off "by informing her that it is really her brother Erwin" (9:85) that she is erotically aroused about.

Psychotherapy or hoax?

5. *Who was sicker: the schizophrenic or his Freudian healers?*

The vicious games played by some Freudian psychotherapists are vividly illustrated in the sufferings induced by his healers in this mental patient during the prodromal stage of his schizophrenic breakdown. Gregory Stefan was in his late twenties when he started experiencing restlessness, irritability, and progressive personality disintegration. He had to turn for help and fell into the hands of a Freudian psychiatrist, whom he calls Dr. Gression. (Whether the name is a pun on the psychological aggression and disservice he suffered at the hands of the New York psychoanalysts, Stefan does not say.)

The first doctor played earnestly the games of creating confusion, inducing guilt and disorganizing further the already shaky personality of his patient. The pattern described by Shepard and Lee and by other observers of Freudian brainwashing to be quoted in chapter X was closely followed by Dr. Gression. The essence of brainwashing is to make the subject accept ideas formerly alien or repulsive to him as supposedly new and superior understanding.

Stefan's brainwasher used the normal tensions within married couples as the opening move to loosen up his remaining psychological anchors; thus he disarmed him and made it difficult for him to resist his thought reformer. The Chinese brainwashers of Korean prisoners used to feed them reasons for resentments: the people in the U.S. did not appreciate their sufferings anyway; their parents do not care about them, as they do not write (while they actually withheld mail from prisoners); the U.S. government has abandoned them to their doom; the stories about infidelities of wives in the U.S. were blown out of proportion. Hammering at confidence, hope, and trust, the wily brainwashers were filling the prisoners' minds with doubt, despair and bitterness. Dr. Gression started by fanning up the patient's resentment against his wife. He would lead him to disregard the patience, love, and self-sacrifice the good woman showed, and would inject the interpretation: "I think your problem is your wife." (10:29) Stefan was going to object, but the analyst skillfully excused himself by having to see another patient immediately. He apparently wanted the implant to grow between sessions. It worked, as it had in the lives of thousands of other Freudwashed patients:

> I thought about what Dr. Gression had said about our marriage as I walked home. Perhaps he was right. Perhaps the marriage had been a mistake. We had been supremely happy once, but now ... maybe it was a big mistake. Maybe the marriage had made me a milktoast. Maybe Laurie was castrating me. Whose idea was it to move to a bigger apartment? It hadn't been mine; Laurie had suggested it. Sure, it was her idea. Who the hell did she think she was, pushing me like that? There was nothing wrong with the apartment we had. (10:29, 30)

Upon coming home, where his wife had dressed specially for him, he only sullenly rejects her. He shows disdain for the sirloin steak she had prepared for him. He tells her rudely that they are not going to move. She is hurt, goes to the bedroom to cry. Stefan wakes up in the middle of the night, remorseful. The evil work of his demon has worn off and his deeper feelings of love for his wife break through. They recognize how much they love each other.

The doctor is not interested in these positive feelings. Through his own Freudwashing he was taught that all noble and good human feelings are shams, that the only "real" emotional reactions are hatred, passion, crudeness and ugliness. Stefan tells him how he was upset by his wife's crying. The doctor, out of his own bitter depths, brings a suggestion to his patient:

"Why didn't you tell her to go to sleep and stop bothering you?"

"What do you mean? She wasn't bothering me."

"Wasn't she?" Again the meaningful pause. He continued:

229

"Wives have all sorts of little tricks in controlling their husbands. Crying is one of them." (10:37)

Dr. Gression did not have to verify whether the patient noticed such tricks in his wife, for it is a Freudian axiom that love for one's wife is an uncertain and uneasy attachment, only a disguised and belated expression of the ungratified yearning for sexual intercourse with one's own mother. No well-trained Freudian would doubt that, as Freud the Great himself had taught it.

The poison was spreading through the personality of the patient. It showed in the disturbance of sexuality, an area which was untroubled in Stefan up to that time; the analyst's suggestions-interpretations were taking root, spreading the Freudian conceptual poisons through the psyche, and further incapacitating the patient:

> Last night Laurie wanted to make love. But I felt very strange. I became obsessed with the idea that my wife was my mother and that I would be making love to my mother. It crossed my mind that there was something incestuous or vulgar about making love to my mother. Neither of us was satisfied. Perhaps Gression was right. In not satisfying Laurie, I'm getting back at my mother for betraying me as a child. The Oedipus complex. That's it! Only, dammit, I *want* to satisfy Laurie. (10:37)

He *wanted* consciously, but his demonic healer was working in the more potent sphere of his person, the unconscious. To increase the feelings of insecurity and self-doubt in the patient, Dr. Gression had injected another solvent into Stefan's self-concept: he had enriched him with the Freudian illumination that we are all "bisexual." Taking this conjecture as a deep revelation about the alleged unconscious homosexuality present in everyone, Stefan starts wondering about himself. His paranoid suspicions of others are increased and his heterosexual functioning is even further handicapped. The Freud-washing was taking deeper root in him.

A month later, Stefan makes an entry about the generous and mature reactions of his wife: "Laurie continues to be sweet and obedient. I'm the dominant one now. She does everything I tell her to do; she doesn't push me or demand anything. I criticize her and she takes it. I blow up at her over small things. I'm unreasonable and she

230

still takes it." (10:47) But his doctor is blind to it. Three days later, Stefan describes the termite still burrowing in the foundations of his marriage:

Gression keeps hammering away at my relations with Laurie. I happened to mention today how envious I was of her because she was working so well on her play, while I couldn't even face a typewriter. "It's quite natural for you to resent your wife," he said. "You have a highly competitive marriage and, unquestionably, your wife has now assumed the dominant role. And you resent it deeply. How did she happen to decide that she was a writer?" "I thought she had a lot of talent," I said, "I encouraged her to write before we got married. She's a good writer and she enjoys . . . " "A better writer than you are, Mr. Stefan?" he interrupted me. "Are you sure you didn't create a Frankenstein in your own house?" I started to protest, but he continued: "Not only is your wife challenging you artistically, but she's also challenging you in every other way—intellectually, socially, sexually, and financially. Haven't you complained to me that your wife is now dominating conversations when you go to social gatherings?" I became angry. "That's because I feel so damn out of it, *way out*," I shouted, "I never feel much like talking. And, besides, I used to be proud of her mind—she's got a fine mind." "But how about now, Mr. Stefan?" he asked. "Do you enjoy staying at home while she works, even if it is part-time? Do you enjoy her usurping your function as the breadwinner?" "Hell, no!" I exploded. "I never wanted her to work—never." "That's the final blow, Mr. Stefan." he said. "Now she's the breadwinner." "She doesn't want to work," I said. "She's only doing it because she thinks we could use the money until I get on my feet again." "Are you sure that's the reason, Mr. Stefan?" he asked. "Yes . . . I don't know . . . oh hell," I said. "But *you're* the one who suggested I quit my job and rest. I hate sitting around the damn house. I wish I could function. I wish I weren't so damn nervous, so I could go out and get another job. Then she wouldn't have to work." A period of silence. "Mr. Stefan," he said, at length, "you are an intelligent young man. A sensitive young man. Now I'm certain you are intelligent enough to realize, by now, that your wife is the source of your difficulties. Certainly any man who is constantly challenged intellectually, artistically, and socially by his wife, any man who is forced to be idle while his

231

wife becomes the breadwinner of the family, will inevitably be unable to satisfy his wife sexually. Your sex problems are interwoven with these other factors." I wanted to argue. I wanted to tell him how proud I used to be of my wife's intellectual abilities, how often in the past I had helped her on her play with the same interest as though it had been mine. I wanted to tell him how much I had loved her cheerful conversation and her warm sense of humor. I wanted to tell him how much I appreciated her going to work while I was ill. I wanted to tell him how much her parents had done for me. I wanted to tell him how much I loved her. I wanted to tell him that I didn't believe in something invisible in my subconscious stirring up hate towards my wife, transforming my personality. But why did I feel so rotten? Why was I so exhausted? Why did I feel like an eunuch? There was a certain surface logic to Gression's analysis of my problems. "You're making me a schizophrenic," I said. He chuckled. "What's wrong with that? A friend of mine, a psychiatrist, is convinced he's a schizophrenic, and he has been going to another psychiatrist for five years." I wonder if he means himself. (10:47-49)

Perhaps we should beware of casting this psychoanalyst into the role of a despicable villain in the life of his patient. He had acted in good, if Freudian, faith. He was taught that there is in *every* marriage a mortal struggle for domination and he must have imagined that he was providing his patient with saving wisdom. It is Freudism as corrosive ideology rather than the psychoanalyst as its bearer that is to blame.

To break Stefan's loyalty to his wife, the doctor suggests that he have an affair. Stefan rejects it, steered by his decent promptings rather than by "therapeutic" proposals. He reads of another man made sicker by psychoanalysis, Tennessee Williams. The dramatist had said in the grand Freudian eloquence: "Love is the use of one person by another." "No," Stefan cries against this cynical distortion, "I love Laurie! I love Laurie!" The analyst, enlightened by Freud's "deep" understanding of human nature, dismisses this loyal clinging to his wife as only a reaction formation, a fooling of oneself. In the despair of the psychosis which was enveloping him, Stefan manifests how genuine his love is for Laurie: he gives up the intention of killing

232

himself in order to live for her. But the psychoanalyst is blind to that positive feeling, he still insists that the best thing for him would be to divorce his wife.

The patient was getting worse, but psychoanalysis was succeeding: Stefan was becoming progressively more confused. To his psychoanalyst this appeared as satisfactory completion of the first phase of Freudian indoctrination. Very few psychoanalyzed patients would deny the mental morass, a total uncertainty about anything, through which they had to pass following their Freudian guides. Stefan's mind reels:

> Christ, I'm confused! I'm beginning to doubt Gression, doubt what I'm telling him, what he's telling me. I tried to write a letter to my folks today, but somehow the letter disintegrated. There are no longer any casual relationships. What is cause and what is effect? What's the cause of what? Is my mother a cause? My father? My wife? Maybe I'm a cause. Can the past be a cause of the present? There's always a reason behind every reason, ad infinitum, so that, in the end, there's no reason at all. And every event has a half dozen or more interpretations and every thought a dozen meanings. And always there are profound symbols and something digging at me in the deep recesses of my subconscious. Come on out, you bastard! *Come on out!* (10:58)

He experiences a confusion regarding his wife, which is appropriate to psychoanalytic ideology:

> When I woke up this morning, I looked at Laurie who was still sound asleep beside me. Is this my wife? I thought. No, it's not my wife. It's my mother. No. Sometimes it's my father. And still other times my sister. And maybe even my brother. Who are you? Wife? Mother? Father? Sister? Brother? Gression says she reminds me of my mother, but yet she dominates me like a father. But I've always wanted a sister, and legally she's my wife. I'm going mad! (10:58, 59)

"With the gentle prodding of my Freudian psychiatrist," he could have added. He does however recognize that his doctor had coarsened up the responsible, socialized side of his person. He remarks to his wife: "You know. Gression had made me over into a well-adjusted bum." (10:63) He was sane enough to realize that this was "Gression's masterful brainwashing job." (10:103)

While his chief benefactor is on vacation, Stefan's state deteriorates and he has to seek help from a substitute suggested by his analyst. He sees a psychologist this time, but he proves no less naturally destructive to Stefan than the Freudian M.D. The psychologist reveals that he was no less than his patient caught in a similar sickness, the pessimistic, godless world-view of Freud. There was no hope with which he could help the patient overcome the demon of disenchantment:

> I rushed off first thing in the morning to see Dr. O'Conner, the tension building up unbearably. I sat in his office and cried and talked incoherently. "I'm going out of my mind!" I shouted, "I can't be right . . . no, I can't be right . . . is life really this rotten? . . . people lying all the time . . . lying to me . . . lying to each other . . . civilization just a pyramid of parasites . . . phony . . . nothing to live for . . . everything's futile . . . no meaning . . . I feel trapped . . . can't function . . . all I see is chaos . . . chaos all around me . . . am I right? . . . tell me! . . . am I right?" He hesitated a moment, taking a puff from his pipe. "Yes, Mr. Stefan," he said. "You are right. You are at last seeing life as it really is. It is phony and meaningless and chaotic. I regret that Dr. Gression is on vacation at this time. This is a critical point in your analysis. But I think that, now that you have this new insight, you should accept reality. Accept things as they are." "But I feel like I'm cracking up, doctor!" I said. He got up and extended his hand. "Nonsense," he smiled, "you're getting better." I ran home trembling, my mind spinning. (10:65, 66)

The patient is much worse for this bit of pessimistic and cynical "psychotherapy." Everything dissolves within his mind. If such hopelessness is the reality determined by his mind, his mind is then leading him to destruction. He concludes rightly: "My mind's a fraud, too. It can't be an instrument for my salvation. It reduces everything to a shambles. I keep crying. Why do I keep crying?" (10:66, 67) The "therapists" had infected him with their own sickness and had thrown him into unbearable depression. He sank into unawareness and found he was in a mental hospital when he dimly came to himself. He thanked God that in his madness, incited by his healers, he had not acted out his inflated rage at his wife and killed her, as he was on the verge of doing.

Later on, watching his fellow inmates, Stefan saw that the same sickening job was going on *en masse* in the personalities of other patients-victims. He also discerns clearly what a majority of Ph.D. clinical psychologists and M.D. psychiatrists fail to realize: the futility and nonsense of the game of discovering "causes" of mental illness. Any old guess is as good as any other; all of them serve equally well to mystify the patients with profound explanations and enable them to blame others for their own personality maldevelopments.

The patients parroted their analysts endlessly. In fact, each patient seemed to assume the world-view, philosophy and attitudes of his own psychotherapist. And it was curious to watch how quickly a patient's attitudes and beliefs changed when, as often happened, he was assigned another psychotherapist. He promptly assumed the convictions of his new doctor, which more often than not differed from the beliefs of his former doctor.

Everyone, meanwhile, brooded endlessly over his past. The patients talked of phallic symbols and Oedipus complexes and penis-envying women and castrated men and inward-directed anger and blurred identities and egos and ids and superegos. They talked of subconscious motives and conflicts and childhood traumas. And they wondered why they thought this, and why they felt that and why they did this. They wrestled constantly with their souls and chased the twin will-o'-the-wisps of cause and effect. Doctor Smith said this and Doctor Jones said that. And all the while they complained. When there wasn't anything to complain about, they invented things to complain about.

One would complain bitterly, as if that were the cause of his illness, about his mother who had slapped the hell out of him at the age of five. Another would complain about his father who had belted him at the age of nine. Another would blame everything on his wife because the woman wouldn't have intercourse with him more than twice a week. Another would blame her husband for not understanding her. Another would be convinced that he had suffered a breakdown because his niggardly boss hadn't offered him a raise. It never occurred to them that there are millions of people living happy, fruitful lives on the outside, who have bitches for mothers, bastards for fathers, who have

235

been slapped silly at the age of five, belted at the age of nine, who have frigid wives, who have unsympathetic husbands, and who have niggardly cantankerous bosses. It never occurred to them that millions of people on the outside survive wars, plagues, cranky mothers-in-law, poverty-stricken childhoods, drunken fathers, neurotic mothers, ax-wielding bosses, among other things without becoming psychotic.

Patients whose mothers had neglected them during their childhood were convinced that that was the cause of their illness. (One young woman patient I talked to traced her difficulties to a childhood trauma at the age of six when her mother refused to buy her a new dress to wear at a birthday party for one of her friends. Later, she confronted her mother with this discovery. "But, dear," the mother said, "I would have bought you the dress, but don't you remember, you weren't invited to that party?") Patients whose mothers had smothered them with love during their childhood were convinced that this was the cause of their illness. ("She spoiled me, that's what she did.") Patients whose fathers were business failures related that fact to their illness. ("I felt inferior to the other kids in the neighborhood.") Patients whose fathers were successful in business blamed them for being successful. ("He was always pushing me. I always felt driven to be better than the old man.") If their parents played favorites with the older brother or the younger sister, that was the cause of the patient's illness. If the patient himself was the favorite child of the parents, that was the cause of his illness. If it was a competitive marriage, that was the cause of his illness. If it wasn't a competitive marriage, then the patient figured that he had nothing in common with his spouse, and somehow that was the cause of his illness. If he had been a failure in life, he was persuaded that he subconsciously wanted to be a failure. If he had been notably successful, he was also persuaded that he subconsciously wanted to be a failure. There was no end to interpretations of similar as well as dissimilar backgrounds.

The fact was that all the patients, with the encouragement of the analysts, were striving desperately to find a psychological reason for their condition. And once their minds became fixed on what appeared to be a logical reason, they believed it unwaveringly. Again with the encouragement of their analysts, who called it "insight" and patted the patients on the head for agreeing with them. (10:132-135)

Stefan had not escaped the attack on his parents, a method used regularly by Freudians to dissolve another section of the patient's personality, his loyalty to his parents. The psychiatrist in the sanitarium, duly a Freudian, was strong with this weapon:

> Dr. MacLeod zeroed in on my parents. Who were you closest to, your father or your mother? Did your father punish you frequently? Did they suffocate you with love?
>
> I sat in a stupor and responded mechanically. Under the doctor's questioning I began to remember unhappy childhood scenes. I remembered my father, in a fit of temper when I hadn't come to dinner punctually, smashing to bits a model airplane I had built. I remembered my mother slapping my hand at the age of seven because I had attached her brassiere to the end of a stick and marched outside waving it like a flag. I remembered a lot of isolated instances of childhood unhappiness, but now I distorted them, exaggerated them, forgetting that they were just brief, passing rainstorms on the island of a happy childhood. I forgot that, after she slapped me, my mother laughed and took me inside and gave me a big dish of fruit salad with ice cream. I forgot all their love and generosity and sacrifices and all the wonderful times we had had together and how close as a family we had been. I forgot everything except what I was encouraged to remember. So I hated, hated the parents I had loved. For somehow they too were responsible for this hellish illness. (10:159, 160)

Even Stefan's interest in sports could be used as a "proof" of the ubiquitous Freudian motive in him. Hatred of the father, the Oedipus complex, is basic human reaction, as all Freudians know so well:

> "I notice you are quite athletic," Dr. MacLeod said. "And I understand that you used to participate in all kinds of sports when you were a teenager. Have you ever thought that it was probably your way a constructive way—of taking out your hostilities towards your father?"
>
> Why couldn't this guy accept the simple fact that I loved baseball, that I loved football and basketball and tennis? (10:160)

237

Stefan does not say that "this guy" could not think normally because he was indoctrinated into a specially twisted framework of thinking during his graduate Freudwashing.

Later on, when he became well through his efforts at moral and religious improvement and through dieting and treatment with mega-doses of Vitamin B, Stefan was able to take a more charitable view of his first psychiatric tormentor. He realized that the doctor was "a cynical bitter neurotic" (10:111), possibly sicker in this respect than his patients. Stefan blamed only himself "for having lived so foolishly that I fell into his hands." (10:223) He had to make a special effort to rid himself of the prejudices his Freudian "therapists" had injected into him: " . . . I also had to weed from my mind the resentments for my parents and my wife that had been planted there by my Freudian analysts." (10:223)

Their destructive work did not spare his wife either. Being disturbed by her husband's sickness and by the feelings of guilt for supposedly driving her husband to insanity, she had to seek support of another Freudian analyst. The result was that she became convinced that, in spite of the love she felt for her husband, she actually did not love him and should divorce him. This was the most painful of the hurts Stefan experienced at the hands of the Freudians. He had gotten better under shock treatment and was yearning to resume married and normal life with his wife. Then he learned that his and her therapists had decided they should be separated and had gotten his wife to agree to it. He felt that they had hurt him cruelly, "like helping a blind man across the street and then busting him in the teeth and stealing his wallet." (10:174)

Even though all these violations are done in secrecy of Freudian offices and under the cloak of medical practice, so that no records are available for inspection, it was not hard for Stefan to reconstruct the trail along which his wife was led:

> Turko [her psychoanalyst] would be brainwashing her in the same way that MacLeod was brainwashing me. He would be listening sympathetically to her complaining about me and the marriage and the whole goddamn mess. He'd help her isolate all the worst things she could think of and then put the marriage in an entirely new perspective—his own moldly perspective.

Forget everything that was beautiful and exaggerate the garbage. Suggest to her that we are incompatible. Tell her that I had ignored her sexually because I subconsciously hated her, not because I was so goddamn sick. Intimate that our marriage was too competitive. Question my motives in marrying her. Hint that the marriage is to blame, for my sickness and for hers.

Isn't there anyone in the whole goddamn world that will believe me when I cry out that my marriage had made me the happiest man in the whole goddamn world? Isn't there anyone in the whole goddamn world who will believe me when I say that my marriage didn't cause my sickness but it was my sickness that destroyed my marriage? (10:161)

There was no one, at least not in the Freudian world, who would heed Stefan's cry. The Freudians are too well protected by their professional immunity and secrecy to have to answer for the minds and lives they twist under the guise of healing.

After about a year of unsuccessful struggle against psychosis, Stefan commits himself to a VA hospital. There he meets the ubiquitous Freudians and they bruise him further:

The psychiatrists and psychoanalysts were still hard at work tracing all personality disorders to childhood difficulties, and blaming patients' fathers and mothers and treating everyone like children whose growth had been stunted by some sort of trauma. They were Freudians, most of them. Sex-obsessed, detached, cynical, egotistical father- and mother-hating Freudians: in short, a mirror of their patients. Some of them seemed to take pleasure in probing around a sick man's soul and reopening the wounds of a painful past.

In group therapy sessions, they looked you over with clinical eyes while the patients, in an orgy of self-examination, chopped each other up in little pieces. A thousand questions were asked and a thousand questions went unanswered as the patients struggled valiantly to comprehend and deal with the catastrophe that had befallen them. Each day the room would be filled with a mishmash of philosophical and psychiatric ideas, each one contradicting the other, so that in the end a patient did not know what to believe or what to do to improve his health. As a result, most stayed sick or, if they improved, often relapsed. I

239

could see no merit in group therapy, except perhaps the fact that a psychoanalyst could promote more confusion and ill-will among patients with less time and effort than was possible in individual therapy. (10:201)

Stefan tries to recover by turning to religious search. He feels a liking for the hospital chaplain, but is intercepted by his analyst, who as a true-blue Freudian, had bought wholesale the usual Freudian preconceptions about religion being unhealthy, a neurosis, and a "defense mechanism." Stefan had sensed that the existential meaning of his schizophrenic troubles was to lift his psyche to a more serene and spiritual level. His analyst was blind to the healing influence of genuine religious development, and he insisted on the outworn Freudian concept of "overstrict superego," telling him that he was sick because he was *too good* and *too moral*. This was the same delusion that Mowrer, the famous American psychologist who personally found psychoanalysis to be therapeutically worthless, fought to expose, through his books and lectures.

Like Mowrer, who in his autobiography (11) admits that he was far from being a moral purist (as psychoanalysts misperceived him, in interviews), Stefan knows that his VA analyst was only parroting the favorite theoretical cliches. He knows that his actual life was normally irresponsible, well within the sick cultural pattern considered normal by many of our learned people. He knows himself as idle, gluttonous, selfish, lazy, spoiled brat, sensualist, egotist, hateful, full of grudges, unforgiving, quick to condemn others, sluggish in doing good. He sees these faults as contributing to his psychosis. Fighting against them made his psychosis recede in proportion of his moral improvement, self-discipline and responsibility. He found sincere religious pursuit as a good antidote to personality disorganization. He sums up his rich contacts with the schizophrenic world:

> . . . in all that time, I never met one person who had a deep faith, either in himself or in a power greater than himself. Occasionally, I met a person who professed a religion, but I never met a person who was practising any more than the frills of his religion, and those who professed without practicing seemed to be worse off than the others. (10:238)

Through his personal effort Stefan arrived at what was always contained in the best wisdom of the ages. Many of his professional healers could not reach that far and that high, prevented by their proud and erroneous "knowledge."

An unbiased reader of Stefan's travails cannot escape the question which was finally forced upon Stefan as he was reviewing his sufferings: is this a new form of demon possession, in which a professionally sickened individual overpowers a supposedly mentally sick one? Stefan writes in his preface:

> ... I have also often pondered the contribution of my psycho-analysts to the illness which they were pretending to cure. I was born in the twentieth century and therefore was not raised to believe in demon possession. But I can bear testimony as to how completely one sick mind can overwhelm and possess another sick mind. And if that is not demon possession, it most certainly is not divine possession. (10:9)

Freud himself felt in the early phases of his psychoanalysis that he was caught in a demonic revival: "I am beginning to dream of an extremely primitive devil religion . . . a primitive sexual cult, which in the Semitic east may have been a religion (Moloch, Astarte)." (12:189) Dostoevsky, describing the cynical, depraved nihilists called them *"biessi,"* the evil spirits, the demons. It was rendered only in a mild form *"the possessed"* in the English title of the novel. The evil can become incarnate in various guises: a Nero or a Borgia, a Hitler or a Stalin, a Bluebeard or Mr. Hyde, an unscrupulous millionaire or a high-class prostitute, a Freud or any other active cynic. In another volume, *Freud's Phallic Cult* (13), I have dealt with demonic aspects of Freudian pseudoreligion, sapping the psychic strength of the Prophet himself, leading some of the followers to suicide, destroying the highest human functions in some of the deceived patients.

6. *This Freudwashing went smoothly*

Some readers may feel somewhat disconcerted by now with my presentation of several rejections of Freudwashing attempts. My account does not appear typical of the American psychiatric and cultural scene, with its plainly discernible Freudian ideological

241

domination. It is true that I have described the experiences and reactions of the rebels who refused to buy psychoanalysis on faith and on authority. These thoughtful and independent minds are certainly not typical of the majority of American professionals, not to mention laymen. To describe a more typical jump-on-the-bandwagon reaction and to exemplify the more commonly observed acquiescence to Freudwashing, I shall summarize a conformist experience.

The experience of Smiley Blanton is commonplace in the American psychiatric community. He had many virtues typical of educated and well-meaning Americans: he was energetic, enterprising, living outside the rigid strait jacket of social conformity; he was good-hearted, and involved with his community. He was compassionate, unaggressive, possibly overcivilized, and prone to naive, uncritical idealism and enthusiasm. He had that healthy American skepticism toward elaborate intellectual constructions which protected him from ideological extremism and dogmatism, so often exhibited by educated Europeans. This pragmatic aloofness from rationalistic and philosophical speculations also made him vulnerable to enticements of the superficially sophisticated Freudian views.

Blanton was already an established professional when psychological and career circumstances turned him toward Freud. He was in his late forties when he decided to go into private psychiatric practice, as he was displeased with his college teaching and child-guidance responsibilities. He had worked for ten years on the problems of schoolchildren and teachers, and had published a recognized textbook in that field. He was also a restless man, driven toward even more ambitious achievements. The Freudians had by that time (1929) established themselves as interpreters of superior psychological understanding and practitioners of the only deep and genuine psychotherapy. It was stated sometimes openly and certainly more often implied that no psychiatrist worth his salt could afford to miss "analysis." And the peak form of analysis was to arrange with Freud to shape the mind of the future analyst. Blanton was overjoyed when Freud consented to take him in.

Blanton's thinking was already Freudianized through reading Freud's works and going along with the whole-hearted approval that the leading psychiatrists accorded the professor from Vienna. However, the emotional involvement with Freudian thought and movement was lacking in his case. To become fully initiated, Blanton, like all other adherents, had to partake of the affective aspects of Freudwashing. As we shall see later on (chapter VII), many American professionals and patients, were well primed to see a deity in Freud even before they were ushered into his presence. Blanton was no exception. He suffered considerable intestinal upsets before he went to meet Freud for the first time and for several days after he began analysis. He was so terrified in the first meeting that Freud had to encourage him to uncramp and stretch himself on the couch. He hung reverently onto every word Freud said and felt depressed when he thought he was not winning Freud's approval.

The undertones of a religious conversion are discernible in the account of his analysis. He was brought up in the strict religious atmosphere of the South at the end of the nineteenth century, with the Bible as a most respected book for him. Later on, when he shook off the blighting influence of Freud, he wrote about the Bible: "It is the greatest textbook on human behavior ever put together. If people would just absorb its message, a lot of us psychiatrists could close our offices and go fishing." (16:722) Yet, under the distorting pressure of "transference" he loses his spiritual orientation and tells Freud in an ingratiating way that his *Interpretation of Dreams* had supplanted the old Book: "Yes, this is my bible. I carry it and reread it every year." (16:93) He tells Freud that he was awed to be in his presence: "Speaking in sober judgment, I think you have one of the greatest minds of the ages. At the present time, you and perhaps Einstein are the two greatest minds in the world." (16:78) Being in contact with what he imagined to be the greatest mind, Blanton reaped the gratification of such a belief. He felt inspired, uplifted: "One gets a feeling of increased power after these visits with the professor." (16:92) Not unlike devoted people feeling buoyant after a worship service or a prayer meeting. He realized temporarily that "analysis is a kind of religion," (16:46) and supplied Freud with the insight. For Blanton it was evidently a religion in which Freud had assumed the status of the infallible High Priest. When Freud shows that he believed that Shakespeare was not the true writer of dramas attributed to him—an opinion patently naive and faulty according to Blanton's convictions—his faith in the omniscience of his hero was so severely shaken that he felt like breaking off the analysis. The crisis he went through resembles the troubled state of mind which children suffer when disappointed in the infinite wisdom and strength of their father; or religious believers in the literal truth of the Bible when unable to reconcile a small, but obvious error with the infallible Book. Blanton, of course, recovered from his religious agony. He warmed up to Freud again, and remained steadfast in the faith, rejoicing in his lord and god unto the end of his long life.

All these dependency operations occur without reaching verbal or even fully conscious levels. As it ought to happen particularly in psychoanalytic situations, the real nature of inner promptings is only intimated, and usually presented in rationalized and not easily recognizable forms.

In the first meeting with Freud, Blanton, for instance, hastens to make clear to the master that he is already a staunch believer in Freud's ideas. He does not do it openly, but rather by expressing pointed disgust with Jung and Adler. He repeats this indirect attestation of allegiance in the following session. He evidently violates his former attitudes of respect for religious values by verbally embracing Freud's grim atheism. "My religion," he remarks to Freud, "is like yours as expressed in *The Future of an Illusion.*" (16:84) Yet, in fact, he was far from genuinely feeling Freud's hatred of religion. In spite of Freud's influence, he maintained a strong interest in religious healings at Lourdes, and went there to study them. Later on he started the American Foundation of Religion and Psychiatry together with pastor Vincent Peale, and wrote two books jointly with him on their experiences in treating mental troubles simultaneously by religious and psychiatric approaches. One of these books is titled *Faith is the Answer*—certainly not a Freud-inspired assertion, showing to what extent Blanton was denying his underlying beliefs in order to comply with Freud's views. He tells Freud that he dislikes Jung "because of the moral factor that he drags in." (16:23) Yet, with his view of love between human beings as the essence of his religion, Blanton could surely have been attracted to Jung's emphasis on "moral factor," if it were not officially disparaged by Freud. One can expect to uncover many such self-violations, enthusiasms for the ideological directors, and compliance with official doctrine, in the participants of Chinese "thought reform" camps, as we shall see in the last chapter.

Freud had developed a high level of skill in what was to become recognized as brainwashing. He tells Blanton just to relax and bring out whatever might come up into his awareness. Freud particularly encourages his subject that he should bring out what is in his unconscious mind. "It is necessary for the unconscious to express itself freely." (16:36) Freud never gives a hint that he knows why his payoff is in the unconscious levels of personality. He prevents the subject's understanding of the game by fixing his attention on "resistance." Resistance is in fact balking of the analysand at imposition of the analyst's preconceptions upon his psychic experience. The conscious attitudes are likely to bring about strong "resistance." The unconscious promptings, on the other hand, are not under the analysand's control and can therefore be more easily influenced by infantile drives in the subject and subtle suggestions implanted by the analyst.

The chief art of the professional brainwasher is gentle, but insistent pressure. Blanton finds Freud to be superb at it: "Again I am impressed by Freud's soft and easy manner. He does not push you. He does not make emphatic statements often. When he does, it is in a very undominating manner. I feel easy with him." (16:31) Five days later he notes again: "I am impressed with how little help Freud gives. He often says nothing for 10 or 15 minutes. It is a matter of growth, and I must go ahead and work it out as best as I can." (16:34) What Blanton omits saying is that "the matter of growth" has to be in compliance with the model announced by Freud and gently insisted on in analysis.

Freud subtly manipulates Blanton's "unconscious" reaction, covering it up with "transference" which supposedly arises spontaneously out of the analysand's psyche. One day Blanton remarks that he intends to buy Freud's complete works when he saves enough money. (He paid twenty-five dollars per hour for the treatment. That was a fabulous amount for European conditions at that time—many a worker had to support his whole family for a month on that sum). Freud reciprocated with a gift to Blanton of four volumes of his *Collected Papers,* mentioning casually that these contain "the foundation of psychoanalysis" and that it would be beneficial for him to read them. Blanton is overwhelmed by such a gesture of his deity and reciprocates with heightened production of dreams showing that his "unconscious" has become deeply devoted to Freud: the Professor becomes the cause for which he is ready to fight the bloody battles against infidels. Later on there is a scholarly discussion between them, drawing Blanton's attention to the undesirability of giving gifts in psychoanalysis. Freud cools off the situation somewhat by these technical exchanges, but the devotion was duly sunk in the analysand's "unconscious."

On another occasion, Freud just as subtly asserts himself over Blanton as his teacher. He gives him a copy of a symposium on psychopathology, published in the United States, with an introduction by Freud himself: "I thought you might like to just look this over. Don't take the trouble to read it." (16:55) Blanton took it as "an example of his thoughtfulness." The effect was perfect: Blanton bought more ideological goods gladly, and Freud could not be blamed for hard sell. (In chapter IX we shall look at some experimental data showing that a suggestion may be most effective if both the suggester and his subject are not aware of the transaction involved between them.)

Blanton shows both affective and intellectual effects of brainwashing. Emotionally, he develops a strong attachment and submission to Freud. He had three dreams and in all of them he recognized "childish wishes for love from the professor—to be passive in relation to him as my leader." (16:80) His wife, who also subjected herself to Freudian analysis, puts it more plainly: "Professor Freud became his beloved father figure." (16:131)

Intellectually, Blanton absorbed all doctrinal peculiarities of Freudism. He dreamed of himself defending, as a solider, the ramparts of psychoanalysis. He was interested in the study of stuttering before he underwent analysis, but now he makes fascinating "discoveries" that this speech defect is "an accentuation of the anal erotic impulses which [is] transferred to the oral erotic area." (16:74) He relates to Freud that one of his patients "seems to have anal penis." (16:65) Freud replies gravely that the size of the stool might not be pathogenically decisive, but rather the sensation in the clitoris. Such are the sublime intellectual delights experienced in psychoanalysis!

In compliance with Freud's "scientific" skepticism, Blanton shows further that he had interiorized the enlightened principles of the master, and assures him regarding his intended study of the miracle healings at Lourdes: "You must not think that I am becoming 'religious.'" He intends to be "coldly scientific." (16:86) He had apparently overlooked the Freudian dictum that psychoanalysis can be properly studied only by the analyzed, and that religious phenomena might not be any more amenable to "coldly scientific" approach than analysis. Such blind spots and compartmentalized thinking are characteristic of brainwashed individuals. In another session he told Freud of his wife's "saying that if he had had the psychological need to form a philosophy of his teachings, what a following he would have, what a cult would have grown around him." (16:94) Apparently this couple of analysands recognized the essential nature of Freudism as a quasi-philosophical cult, and then quickly reversed their conclusion into a denial of the original insight.

"The Freudian Pseudo-Science" is the matter of concern of the remainder of this volume, and Freudism as a pseudoreligion is considered in *Freud's Phallic Cult*.

Notes to Chapter Five

1. Havelock Ellis, the little-recognized predecessor of Freud in sexology, warned Wortis about this crucial religious aspect of psychoanalysis:

> About being psychoanalysed, my own feeling most decidedly is that it would be better to follow his [Freud's] example than his precept. He did not begin by being psychoanalysed (never was!) or attaching himself to any sect or school but went about freely, studying the work of others, and retaining always his own independence. If he had himself followed the advice he gives you, he would have attached himself to Charcot with whom he was working and become his disciple, like Gilles de la Tourette, an able man and now forgotten. If you are psychoanalysed you either become a Freudian or you don't. If you don't you remain pretty much where you are now; if you do—you are done for!— unless you break away, like Jung or Adler or Rank (and he has done it too late). (2:11)

Freud later confirmed the correctness of Ellis's insight about Rank: "Since leaving me, Rank has been having periodic fits of depression, and in between, sort of manic phases—periods in which he does a great deal of work, and others in which he cannot do any at all. He had this tendency before, but now . . . one could call him ill (*krank*)." (2:121)

2. Depending on circumstances and the availability of a suitable generalization, Freud was apparently able to admit the role of suggestion in his procedure. At a point earlier in analysis, Freud had been less defensive and could acknowledge his use of suggestion: "It's true that the analyst uses suggestion, but only to help psychoanalytic procedure." (2:64)

3. Kelman (6:9) mentions the conflict which Karen Horney had in her analysis with Abraham. Somewhat like Wortis and Campbell, she was brought up in an atmosphere of dissolution of that Victorian authoritarianism under which Freud and his contemporaries had been raised. She just could not see the manifestations of penis envy and feminine castration complex which Abraham found in her material. Again the selective distortion in analysis is evident. The analyst discovered findings which his theoretical preconceptions told him he must. Horney denied the existence of these supposedly universal traits in women, calling them only misconceptions created by masculine prejudices.

4. Similar delusional awe must be inculcated in some of the present-day trainees, who fly more than a thousand miles each week to expose their control cases to the august gaze of the enlightened teachers in the psychoanalytic institutes. Surely, these intelligent and capable physicians must find such ritual as rewarding to their faith as lowly monks once found their pilgrimages to famous spiritual fathers. Someone has said the capacity of modern man to believe is boundless. Here we find one of its unexpected confirmations. The educated can be conditioned as easily as the uninformed.

248

PART II

THE FREUDIAN PSEUDOSCIENCE

"Freud's work may in fact prove to be one of the great hoaxes of the century if it turns out that all the data obtained on the couch have been unwittingly fed into the patient by the therapist and then, unknowingly, given back to him by the patient. For instance Freud made no fewer than twelve consecutive women believe and confess to sexual interference by their fathers! This must have been brainwashing, as it occurred in 100 percent of the patients, and Freud himself finally realized that most of the confessions he had elicited were false."

William Sargant, M.D., in *The Atlantic Monthly*, July 1964.

"Freud . . . insisted that the information about the patient's past revealed by psychoanalysis had the status of scientific fact because it was elicited by an impartial, trained observer, the psychoanalyst. We now know, of course, that this was to some extent erroneous, because the patient's productions are so strongly influenced by the analyst's expectations."

Jerome D. Frank, M.D., Professor of Psychiatry, in *Persuasion and Healing*, p. 208, 209.

"Freud rightfully is entitled to be called fiction writer, but not a scientist."

Martin D. Kushner, M.D., in *Freud—A Man Obsessed*, p. 85.

"I rarely attend the meetings of the American Psychoanalytic [Association] (and then only as an amused observer) . . . "

Jules H. Masserman, M.D. (a trained psychoanalyst), in *A Psychiatric Odyssey*, p. 565.

249

Chapter VI

Psychoanalytic Pretenses at Science

Scientific precision has far too often been consciously excluded from classical psychoanalysis, because Freud rejected it. In consequence, classical psychoanalysis has assumed many of the trappings of a religion, and lost many of the essential characteristics of a science.

Nathaniel S. Lehrman, M.D. (72:1103)

... at the present time coming closer to phrenology and animal magnetism of another age, both from the standpoint of cult value and in success in erecting an imposing scientific facade, is that discipline which has come to be known as psychoanalysis.

H. K. Johnson, M.D. (1)

For at least a decade now, it has been known in scientific circles that psychoanalysis is a fiasco... that dubious art... impotence behind a facade of pretension.

O. Hobart Mowrer, Ph.D.,
Research Professor of Psychology (68:68, 84)

... America was highly sympathetic to both the goals and scientific pretensions of psychoanalysis, so that it was readily transplanted on the American soil.

Jerome D. Frank, M.D.,
Professor of Psychiatry (74:209)

Even though the Freudian movement took shape before the Madison Avenue experts consolidated the basic practices of their movement, the Freudians were never short on salesmanship. They knew how to toot their own horn, and they were not bashful about it in their struggle for recognition. They played the hoax earnestly.

1. *Assuming the scientific status*

In our technical age, one of the most successful promotional tricks is to get under the umbrella of science. The technical advances of the nineteenth and twentieth centuries, with their automobiles and air-planes, atom bombs and space vehicles, gadgets and antibiotics, have reduced the average man to religious awe before anything that calls itself a science. Many of our contemporaries, particularly those with superficial philosophical education, find it difficult to accept the tenets of traditional religion, but are ready to accept any preposterous idea offered in the name of "science." MacDougall (71) reports on dozens of "scientific" hoaxes.

Both true and false prophets of old gained influence by claiming: *"The Lord God saith,"* and today's true and false prophets also gain adherents by claiming: "The Lord Science saith." Educated modern man is as gullible as the savage listening to his medicine man, but he is impressed by the invocation of different idols. Allers correctly remarked that the gods of the marketplace, "the *idola fori* of Francis Bacon are today as powerful as they ever were, and there is a market place of science and one of general business which do not differ very much in their habits." (2:96)

The mystics of Mary Baker Eddy's persuasion call their movement Christian Science, and their rivals have adopted names like Spiritual Science, and Mental Healing Science. There is a Science of Hotel Management; Institutes of Sartorial Science advertise their services; and—yes, I saw it myself—a modest barbershop proclaims itself to be a Tonsorial Science Parlor. The Communists call their doctrines "Scientific Socialism," supposedly to distinguish their teachings from the bourgeois-tainted socialisms, which have departed from "science." [1] Little wonder, then, that there should also be a "Psychoanalytic Science."

In an incisive analysis of the Freudian propensity to assume the status of science, Breggin takes to task Freud and his followers for dissimulating about the true nature of psychotherapy. Breggin recognizes that psychotherapy is identical with "applied ethics" and he objects to the smuggling of therapists' implicit and explicit values under the guise of some misguiding label: "Freud hung onto the notion of 'biology' and Alexander the notion of 'medicine' to justify their theory and practice; Erikson has hung onto 'psychological insight' to bootleg his values." (69:66)

252

2. Freud's self-inflation

Freud took pains to emphasize in his lectures and articles that what he stood for was "science." A few examples from among many should suffice to illustrate Freud's insistence upon the scientific nature of his work.

Speaking of the young physician who had misused the psychoanalytic doctrine concerning the pervasiveness of sexuality, Freud says that he was "ignorant of a number of the *scientific* principles of psychoanalysis." (3:91, Freud's italics) In an article for an encyclopedia, Freud defines psychoanalysis as a "new scientific discipline based on its method of investigation and the application of therapy to neurosis." (4, v. 5:107)

In a lecture to his adherents at the Second International Psychoanalytic Congress at Nürnberg in 1910, Freud exhorts them in the final benediction to unshakeable "scientific" confidence:

> I will let you go, therefore, with the assurance that you do your duty in more than one sense by treating your patients psychoanalytically. You are not merely working in the service of *science,* by using the *only* and *irreplaceable* opportunity for discovering the secrets of the neurosis; you are not only giving your patients the *most efficacious remedy* for their sufferings . . . " (3:86, my italics)

Writing in 1925 about resistances to psychoanalysis, Freud unhesitatingly compares his troubles to the persecution Galileo suffered for the sake of another misunderstood science. (4, v. 5:164) On another occasion he pronounces his work more worthy of admiration than that of Einstein: "He had the support of a long series of predecessors from Newton onward, while I had to hack every step of the way through a tangled jungle alone." (6:17) Apparently it did not occur to Freud that some of the jungle was of his own making and that he had to hack his way through the tangle of his own illusions and preconceptions.

In 1919 the members of the Zürich Psychoanalytic Society rebelled against Sachs, who was sent from Vienna to oversee the activities. According to Freud, they considered him "an emissary of the High

253

Inquisition sent to keep a watchful eye on their orthodoxy." Freud assures Pfister that Sachs's mission was not political, that their assertion of "republican independence" was quite inappropriate. In Freud's words, they "might with equal propriety rebel against the tyranny of the logarithm tables." (7:10) The implication to the Zürich psychologists was that they had better stick to orthodox analysis which had the precision of logarithm tables. Knowing the low quality of Freudian science, one cannot help asking whether Freud was pulling the leg of recalcitrant members or was himself thoroughly deluded.

In 1926, when he was seventy and could be expected to have achieved a relative freedom from wishful thinking, Freud disclaims any similarity between psychoanalysis and philosophy, and finds instead a basic resemblance with physics and chemistry:

> Psychoanalysis [Freud claims] is not like a philosophical system which starts from a few strictly defined fundamental principles, uses them to embrace the totality of the world and, once perfected, has no room for new discoveries or improvements. On the contrary, it remains linked with the facts which are produced in its field of activity, it tries to solve the immediate problems of observation, tentatively continues its experience, it is always incomplete, always ready to correct or modify its theories. Like physics or chemistry it allows that its fundamental concepts are vague and its assumptions provisional, it does not expect a more rigorous definition than future work . . . (8:173)

A cursory consideration of Freud's assertions in the preceding passage reveals that psychoanalytic practice of "science" is the opposite of what Freud imagined it to be. [see *Freud's Non-science,* particularly chapter III (61)]

3. *Tireless promotion by his pupils*

Freud's pupils continued in the same vein, sometimes with more abandon. "Psychoanalysis," writes Bailey, "is certainly not a 'natural science' (Naturwissenschaft). Its followers, however try desperately to make it appear so, because of the prestige our society attaches to 'science.'" (9:93) "In looking over the literature," remarks Johnson, "one often has the feeling that the Freudian analyst is less concerned with results than with the fact that he is solely in possession of the one system of psychodynamics which purports to be thoroughgoingly scientific." (1:321)

> Probably the biggest factor contributing to the psychoanalytic hoax is that analysts strive so desperately to label their exploitation as a science without fulfilling any of the postulates set down and accepted by scientists the world over which would qualify it as being truly scientific. (54:70)

We have already encountered some of the wild statements about Freud's exalted position in science. Pfister considers Freud's science equal to the discovery of the new continents. (7:141)

Apparently the faithful followers combat their own unsureness and the suspicions of nonbelievers by making strong pronouncements about Freud's unexcelled scientific merits. Although psychoanalytic theorizing leaves much to be desired, Fenichel proposes "that science is its strong suit." "Its virtue of which all analysts are proud and which *belongs to psychoanalysis alone,* is that it is built upon scientific insight." (10, my italics) It is probably out of the same feeling of insecurity regarding their scientific status that the fanciful, philosophic and artistic discussions of the Vienna Psychoanalytic Society are consistently called "scientific meetings." (62)

Ferenczi labors the same point in speaking of what is actually a poorly elaborated portion of Freud's theory, his attempt to bridge the instinctual and thought processes: "As always, here once more Freud takes his stand on the sure ground of psychoanalytic experience and is extremely cautious in generalization." (12, v. 3:367)

Jones is even more emphatic about the scientific significance of Freud. His unsupported assertions about Freud's scientific merits could easily make him the number 1 salesman of Freudism:

> The future world may well speak of a Pre-Freudian and Post-Freudian era in thought. Man's conquest of nature has been proceeding for many thousands of years, and fumbling attempts have often been made in his more difficult task of self-conquest, but Freud's life work represents the first serious endeavor to apply to it the methods of science. . . . After all, Freud had been educated, not as a psychologist or mythologist, but in the tenets

of orthodox neurology. Undeterred by this bias, however, Freud determined to examine the facts themselves and let nothing but their evidence influence his conclusions. (13:121, 124)

Clara Thompson, even though a doubting believer, does not fail to pay homage to Freud's scientific acumen. Writing a foreword to Ferenczi's volume, she points out how much greater a scientist Freud was: "Ferenczi was essentially a dreamer, intuitive and capable of sudden flashes of insight. Freud on the other hand was the practical scientist, constructing carefully worked out theories around his observations." (12, v. 1:3)

The technique used by Freud's followers to smuggle psychoanalysis into science is similar to the one employed by Freud himself (4, v. 5:127, 129), *i.e.*, making broad claims to comparison between their "science" and physics or chemistry. Rickman, the translator of Ferenczi's volume, tries to influence the reader's view of psychoanalysis by comparing it with exact sciences:

> The understanding of psychoanalytical literature may be compared to that of mathematical science. Some things are comprehended in a flash, others only after long rumination. When in order to bring about an understanding, elaborate adjustments have to be made; in mathematical science these are almost entirely intellectual, in psychoanalysis almost entirely emotional, but in both adaptations it is an *unconscious process*. (12, v. 2:1)

A man with an M.A. and an M.D. should know better than to draw futile comparisons on the basis of the common unconscious adaptations to ideas. In this respect the Nazi doctrines or the cosmogonies of aborigines are also comparable to mathematics and physics. Rickman's illogical statement can, of course, be easily understood as the unwitting trick of a demagogue who colored the minds of his listeners by vague, positive, or negative associations. And Rickman apparently did not expect his readers to be bright enough to concude that if the adaptation to it has to be "almost entirely emotional," then psychoanalysis is more akin to religion or art than to science. Chemists and biologists do not have to change their emotional attitudes toward their subject matter.

This process of uncritical Freudian salesmanship is repeated even in our times. Hartmann, for instance, in a lecture in 1959, directed his listeners toward pious reverence from the beginning by asserting that a psychoanalyst's "objectivity is scientific objectivity, his truth is scientific truth." (14:10) Hartmann could not have been oblivious to the fatal objections to arbitrary Freudian theorizing which had been published in numerous studies. [see *Freud's Non-science*, ch. I (61)] Nevertheless, he remained faithful to his movement as "scientific." To show that he knew of the critics, though he despised their arguments, he adds cautiously: "This attitude [of considering Freudism a science] however, has frequently met with misunderstanding."

A similarly cavalier analogy between science and psychoanalysis appears in M. Sherwood's *The Logic of Explanation in Psychoanalysis*. After a painstaking exposition of the logical operations and pitfalls in scientific and other statements, Sherwood analyzes the clinical inferences made by Freud in the Lorenz case. Omitting the more outlandish postulates of Freud (Oedipus appears here in a desexualized version, libido is not eagerly erotic), Sherwood uses some of the general clinical processes and inferences to draw the parallel between Freud's logic and that used in some scientific theories. Although a trained logician, Sherwood does not mention a fact known to any educated individual; namely, that starting with mistaken premises we can use logical rules to reach "logical" conclusions, which may nevertheless be patently false or absurd. However, Sherwood, being a friend of psychoanalysis, does not fail to exort the readers in his final conclusion that "psychoanalysis can indeed stand on its own as a scientific discipline, and it can at least be on speaking terms with the natural sciences." (63:260)

Even currently, in spite of a serious decline in prestige, some Freudians hold steadfastly to the myth of Freudian science. A capable and tireless defender of psychoanalysis, Eissler, insists that it is a science. He believes that "... Freud presented the complete human cosmos scientifically... Freud's work contains a ... scientifically-correct presentation of the structure of the mind..." (56:181) He knows that there are other psychological theories, but he is sure that "none of these comprised a scientific psychological system that could compare with his [Freud's] in terms of completeness, depth and rationality." (56:181) Playing down Freud's utilization of contemporary philosophical and medical ideas, Eissler again states: "To be sure, psychoanalysis is a science, wherever it had its origin." (56:277)

4. *Medical status helped the hoax*

The fact that many of its supporters were physicians aided the general acceptance of Freudism. The public was confused by the stand taken by medical doctors (who were trusted as scientifically reliable), on the fantasy products of Freudism. These physicians were expected to be talking science, and Freudians obliged the uninformed by fostering that delusion. The medical status of most early Freudians was the Trojan horse by which they mastered their own and other people's doubts about their fantastic ideology.

La Pierre, a non-Freudian sociologist, analyzes the steps by which Freudism grew into a medical speciality:

> Since they were Doctors of Medicine before they became Freudians, and since they did not abandon their status of physicians in assuming that of Freudian psychoanalysts, they gave to the practice and advocacy of Freudianism the traditional authority of medicine.
>
> Thus had it not been for the fact that the Freudian doctrine was sponsored by men of medicine, the claim that it is "scientific" would no doubt have long since been brushed aside. And had not an increasing number of medical men come to accept and then to advocate the doctrine, there is little likelihood that it would ever have gained widespread acceptance among psychologists, anthropologists, social psychologists, political scientists, and sociologists.
>
> The emergence, then, of a class of physicians who were willing to specialize in the treatment of neurotics and who, moreover, possessed firm faith in their ability to probe into and then resolve the psychological difficulties of the neurotic fulfilled a vital professional function. The availability of psychoanalysts, who as members of the medical profession were presumably beyond reproach, enabled the general practitioner and the diagnostician to refer his neurotic patients to Dr. So-and-So with a reasonably clear conscience. Because the psychoanalysts served this function, rather than for any regard for the doctrine they represented,

the medical profession here and in England gradually recognized psychoanalysis—especially that of the Freudian variety—as a respectable and responsible medical specialty. (5:42-44)

It is obvious by now that physicians are no less prone to accept erroneous views than are other professionals. They are just as suggestible to authority figures as humans in any other profession. Physicists and chemists, biologists and geologists, psychologists and psychiatrists have uncritically bought a lot of nonsense from the elders in their professions. Physicians are as likely to accept suggestions from their authority figures as shaman's and *curandero's* trainees are apt to take from theirs. Temerlin and Trousdale (65) provide an experimental investigation of the suggestibility of psychiatrists even in a relatively objective matter of diagnosis. They constructed an imaginary interview with an individual showing no indications of psychological abnormality or weakness. They asked experimental groups of students, trained psychologists, and psychiatrists to diagnose the level of mental illness or health in the subject, mentioning in passing that a psychiatrist or two of considerable reputation had diagnosed this individual as psychotic. The psychiatrists led in suggestibility—twenty-five of them diagnosed this healthy individual as psychotic or neurotic. Clinical psychologists were no less gullible, 88% finding the "interviewee" mentally troubled. The three student groups testified to the general human suggestibility, with 84-90% finding the "interviewee" unhealthy.

I have already alluded to Masserman's (66) elegant demonstration of the gullibility of physicians brainwashed through psychoanalytic "deep" insights and ready to accept any nonsense couched in its mystifying terminology. He told his learned audience about the new psychosomatic syndrome of "onychoneurosis" (the stubbed toenail neurosis) which he had discovered by typical Freudian deduction. He used all the Freudian gobbledygook in jest, making fun of the unbridled fantasies which are passed for psychosomatic realities. His surprise was almost painful when he discovered that the audience had taken his playfulness seriously, and were convinced that they had heard a new revelation to be added to the series of other fantasies current among Freudian psychosomaticists.

Ordinary human gullibility was, in the case of physicians who accepted Freud uncritically, abetted by the skilled, though often unconscious, salesmanship of Freudian propagandists. These missionaries of psychoanalysis were unhampered by the usual scientific modesty, since it was necessary to spread the messianic news as assertively as possible. They made odd but assured pronouncements on all sorts of subjects, which the public accepted as the latest scientific conclusions on the human situation. La Pierre finds that the disciples

> ... are always ready to claim that Freudianism contains the key to an understanding of whatever problem happens to be newsworthy—the latest nasty crime, divorce, juvenile delinquency, the low quality of television programs, the rise or decline of dictators, or the continuing trend toward larger automobiles. Some, more responsible perhaps, produce a steady stream of articles, books, or public lectures in which they interpret in somewhat Freudian terms, the social past, the present, or the future. (5:44, 45)

Psychology, in its clinical application, also succumbed to Freudian assertiveness. Particularly, in so-called projective psychology, Freudians found an unoccupied ground on which to sow their fantasies and pretend to produce a scientifically ascertained crop of facts. To quote La Pierre again:

> The fact that "clinical psychology" was hardly more than a name proved no great deterrent. Freud, it was conveniently recalled, had favored lay, as distinct from medically trained, analysts; and the psychoanalytic approach to mental illness was already established and acceptable to the medical profession. Thus the clinicians, who took over Rorschach's ink blots, Murray's TAT, and other procedures that are supposed to provide inferential evidence of the state of the subject's unconscious, but who did not presume to take over the psychoanalyst's couch, were able to become preaching and practicing Freudians without encroaching upon the psychoanalyst's preserves. (5:46)

5. Tricks and promises

An illustration of effective oratorical evasion of the shaky scientific position of psychoanalysis might be taken from Kubie's lecture at the New York University Institute of Philosophy in 1958. (15) His topic was "Psychoanalysis and Scientific Method." After an unconvincing attempt to subsume psychoanalysis under science and a reluctant admission of some of the limitations of analysis, Kubie takes his listeners in a seemingly irrelevant direction, speculating about what computers might do to establish a psychoanalytic science. Although irrelevant to the topic, this strained ending succeeds in diverting attention from the miserable scientific results of psychoanalysis in its previous sixty years to the grand vista of general scientific technology. Although psychoanalysis has little to do with this achievement, Kubie thus manages to deflect some of the scientific glory to the Freudian would-be science. [see *Freud's Non-science*, chapter I (61)]

A similar skill in reflecting the glamor of science upon its poor cousin, psychoanalysis, continues to give a false impression to uncritical listeners and readers. Speaking of the intricate specialty of psychoanalysis, Thomas Mann, enchanted by Freudian fantasies, associates it with the exact sciences. For this purpose, he uses a statement by a biologist who confesses that science seems to be reaching a stone wall when considering the role of molecules in the central nervous system. Mann says that perhaps the "study of the nervous system is bringing us to the limits of human understanding, in that the brain cannot be capable, in the last analysis, of providing an explanation in itself." Mann generously shows a readiness to come to the aid of the troubled scientific discipline by implying that psychoanalysis has a "particular relevance" at this point! I could not help being reminded of the TV comedian I had watched playing the role of a sewer man. Having met the physician-chief of the city's health department through a mixup, he stretched out his hand to him fraternizingly: "Hi! Glad to meet you. We're in the same business, you know."

Many people, even psychologists who are supposed to be trained in thinking critically in scientific matters, are taken in by overconfident Freudian assertions about the status of their "science." Salzman's introduction provides an interesting example of these misleading

261

claims. In the first paragraph Salzman, who is definitely not one of those blind psychiatrists-adulators of everything Freud said, states confidently that "While almost every theoretical concept formulated by Freud has been altered or restated, his basic contributions have been reaffirmed and validated." (16:5)

Now, Salzman cannot be accused of spreading an untruth; but his statement is a qualified truth, and he fails to tell the reader that his assertion holds only in a limited way, *i.e.,* within the fellowship of Freudian believers. For them, certainly, Freud's contributions have been "reaffirmed and validated." Salzman does not say they have been reaffirmed in an objective way and validated in scientifically acceptable fashion, so we cannot accuse him of misrepresenting the facts; but the implication for many unwary readers is that Freud's fancies have been found valid by something more than an act of faith. Theories of art and literature, of politics and economics, of chiropractics and Christian Science, of philosophy and religion are all "reaffirmed and validated" to their believers in the same way as psychoanalytic propositions: by logical, rational validation, appropriate to dealing with values and opinions, but only acceptable within the circle of the faithful and on faith.

Salzman continues with the same argument, based on closed-circuit reasoning, to bolster respect for Freudian theory: "Freud developed a consistent and complete theory of personality development which was based on a set of hypothesis which were remarkably productive and capable of resolving almost all the questions in the psychopathology of human behavior." (16:5, 6) Such generalizations mislead the uninformed and innocent about the real state of Freudian psychopathology. Salzman asserts that Freud's hypotheses were "remarkably productive." Productive of what? Productive only of further Freudian speculative fantasies. Again, Salzman claims that they were "capable of resolving all the questions." How were these questions resolved? In the same way as in any philosophic discussion—by juggling previously stated assumptions, taking it for granted that they are proven, and building further theory on the basis of these unvalidated propositions.

Speaking of the enrichment of psychoanalytic technique which came with the concepts of resistance and transference, Kris adds encouragingly, "the verification of which by other methods of observation is now in progress." (17:22) Now, almost twenty years later, little has been heard of the results of these purported investigations. Those of us who remember the propaganda of World War II, may smile now at the memory of many morale-boosting announcements that were never realized. K. Colby, a colleague of Kris, engaged specifically in psychoanalytic research, does not mention these alleged verifications writing six years later. In his preface, he says only: "The training of psychoanalysts has been limited for the most part to the transmission of this system without encouragement of original work." (18:VII)

Seven years later, in 1967, Ford and Urban, two psychologists sympathetic to psychoanalysis, look at the field of Freudian therapy and find little worth reporting for the *Annual Review of Psychology:* "There is little substantive novelty in these writings ... the innovative steam is gone out of psychoanalytic movement. Major theoretical and technical advances will probably come from other orientations." (77:333) Future historians are likely to sum up their verdict on Freudian science: They talked big, they promised a lot, they wrote copiously, but it is hard to find scientific grain in the piles of chaff.

Of course, Kris is not the only one who had vain hopes of seeing Freudian fantasies and guesses verified by science. Thirty years ago, Rosenzweig (19) expressed the same bright hope that the opposition to psychoanalysis would be overcome by experimental proofs; very few have been made known up to this time. In 1968, a friendly reviewer of the scientific status of psychoanalysis, Rapoport, found that it "can be and ought to become a science." (67) Both terms of his statement indicate a friendly trust in the ability of a seventy-five-year-old adolescent to finally evolve into a scientifically respectable adult, but there is no indication that he found any scientific confirmation of Freudian fantasies.

The subscientific status of the psychoanalytic community as a whole is well demonstrated in an amateurish study (70) reported by the American Psychoanalytic Association in 1967. The "research" undertaken by the psychoanalytic professional association is so unsophisticated that its design would not have been accepted for even a master's thesis in a reputable department of psychology. If there are scientifically trained psychoanalysts, they must have become redfaced at the naive, undergraduate level of methods, assertions and conclusions.

Another way of smuggling Freudian doctrines into the scientific realm is by claiming psychoanalytic application of the laws of physics to the human psyche. Ellis takes Bellak and Ekstein (20) to task for going

> ... out of their way to contend that analysis makes use of scientific laws like the principle of causality, the law of conservation of energy, the biogenic law, and that therefore it is a most scientific doctrine. What they fail, however, to point out is that Freud took the law of conservation of energy, for example, and assumed that it strictly applied to human personality development. He thereupon constructed a theory of libidinal energies, cathexes, and counter cathexes which, while it may look imposing in the light of nineteenth century concepts of physics, has a most dubious reality for personality dynamics. (21:97)

We cannot deny that the persistent promotional efforts, deliberate or veiled and preconscious, have paid dividends. Most people in the mental health fields were properly impressed, and the faith was firmly established with anyone who counted. Even Einstein was misled to believe that Freud was a scientist in the field of personality by extravagant claims and messianic immodesty. When the League of Nations asked him in 1933, to select an expert with whom to discuss the problem of war, Einstein indicated Freud as his preference. Their discussions were published later in *Why War?* In it Einstein, with the humility of a scientist, takes Freud's scientific status for granted:

> ... this is the problem: Is there any way of delivering mankind from the menace of war? ... As for me, the normal objective of my thought affords me no insight into the dark places of human will and feeling. ... There are certain psychological obstacles whose existence a layman in mental sciences may dimly surmise, but whose interrelations and vagaries he is incompetent to fathom; you, I am convinced, will be able to suggest educative methods, lying more or less outside the scope of politics, which will eliminate these obstacles. (quoted in 22:12)

Apparently Einstein was not aware of the rickety foundations of Freudian "science," and the Freudians would not risk self-disillusionment by revealing them.

Strauss (60:48) suggests a comparison of Blake's mystical-poetic personality model with the one elaborated by Freud and labeled scientific. Blake's conceptualization is equally scientific; not unlike Freud's, it is even supplied with dignified names. A professor wrote the summary of Blake's scheme of *Four Zoas:*

> The Eternal Man who is "in the beginning" lives ideally in enjoyment of every aspect of his being. Of these aspects four are prominent: the imagination (Los), the reason (Urizen), the passions (Luvah), and the instincts or body (Tharmas). So long as these aspects are held in fluid interplay, all is well. But Man (Albion) is led astray by his passions, and begins to worship them. He permits himself to be dominated by Luvah, and only recovers in time to appeal to Urizen for help. But already the balance of consciousness has been disturbed—the excess in the direction of passion has to be remedied by an excess in the direction of reason. Urizen seizes all power into his hands, banishes Luvah, and initiates the egotistic universe of matter. Tharmas is precipitated in a material form as the ocean, and Los, separating from his emanation Enitharmon (inspiration), is engaged in an eternal struggle from now on to redeem man from the effects of his folly. This involves warfare with Urizen. (60:48)

On the whole, Freud and Freudians have acted more like representatives of Los and Luvah than of Urizen.

6. *Even Christians duped*

There always have been, of course, a few psychologists and psychiatrists who refuse to join the stampede and who will not accept assertions as proofs. The Freudians look down upon these rebels, for they represent such a minority that their radical opposition can easily be dismissed as erroneous and unworthy of attention; they are taken merely as illustration of what "resistance" can do even to intelligent people. For most professionals it was enough to note how many important people were on the Freudian bandwagon, to join the majority. It must have been misleading to see even good Catholics among them. Apparently they ignored that old conservative, Allers (2), who contended in the 40s that Freud's doctrines were mostly fallacies, irreconcilable to humanistic and Christian views. Now, for instance, twenty years after Allers, one can read in a book coauthored by a Catholic psychiatrist and priest: "In exploring the human mind Freud used the scientific method, objectively observing, recording, reducing data to common denominators and testing them meticulously over long periods." (23:54)

Catholic psychiatrists and psychologists, having been awed by the proliferation of Freud's clinical fantasies, misinformed a part of the Catholic world about the "scientific" worth of psychoanalytic constructions. Thus, even the venerable Catholic philosopher Jacques Maritain, who views Freud as a flounderer in philosophy ("like a man obsessed"), accepts him as "an investigator of genius" and "an admirably penetrating psychologist." (24:231)

As a philosopher, Maritain could not judge the validity of Freud's assertions in psychopathological and psychotherapeutic matters. He had to rely on Catholic clinicians, who, being human, were infected by the existing Freudian contagion and adopted the majority opinion, without critically investigating psychoanalytic notions. Freudian concepts were, thus, accepted by a number of Catholic intellectuals. The hoax spread in the way of fashion fads and political climates; it was assumed to be right because the majority seemed to follow it, and no one thought to question it. Freudism advanced under the guise of "scientific psychological findings," and even Catholics, usually resistant to secular fads, unwittingly honored the false Freudian coins of Gnostic psychological speculations under the name of "scientific discoveries" about the human soul.

As an informed Catholic scholar, Maritain must have known hundreds of fantasies entertained by mystics, alchemists, and heretics about the human psyche, but would hardly have thought of these dreamers as "investigators of genius" and "penetrating psychologists." These earlier "psychologists" lacked the outward manner of "scientists" and a quasi-scientific jargon, but more important, they lacked a host of living propagandists to spread the glow of "science" over their fanciful speculations. Speculative psychologists of old could not mislead Maritain and others as the promoters of Freudism did. Under their self-assured clamor, many Christians lost the critical

266

judgment by which they had scoffed at the twisted speculations of other pagan prophets.

Protestants, less well organized and less disciplined in church matters, seem to have been an even easier target for seduction by Freudians. And it was not only the working parsons, who could hardly be blamed for subjection to popular fallacies, who were misled. It is saddening to find that the independence of Christian thinking about Freudism is betrayed by a number of important Protestant names. Without trying to single out anyone, we might illustrate the trend with Niebuhr, a venerated Protestant theologian, and a thinker capable of considerable originality. Yet, even a man of his brilliant mind shares popular superstitions about the myths of Freudian psychology and psychotherapy:

> The position of Sigmund Freud as one of the great scientific innovators of our era is now generally acknowledged. The therapeutic efficacy of his disciplines and discoveries has been amply proved. By laying bare the intricate mechanism of the self's inner debate with itself, and its labyrinthian depths below the level of consciousness, he enlarged or indeed created new methods of healing "mental" diseases. (25:259)

Before the ascendance of Freudism as the dominant psychiatric fad, some Protestants dared depend on insights offered about human nature by Christian tradition. In the thirties, one of the leaders of the pastoral counseling movement, A. Boisen (26) sought to establish a non-Freudian view of psychopathology and psychotherapy, which was closer to traditional Christian insights into human nature. Boisen remained unappreciated by his pastoral colleagues, who preferred to join the Freudian professional throngs. In the sixties the pastoral counseling movement was so permeated by Freudian emanations that a large number of pastors could not readily accept Mowrer's (27) position which in many respects parallels the empirically derived conclusions of Boisen.

At one of Mowrer's workshops in 1965 I encountered a rather paradoxical situation. Mowrer, a learning theory psychologist, was arguing against the Freudian thesis that the "overstrict" superego is at the basis of neurosis and that the cure, therefore, consists in teaching the patient to take his conscience less seriously. Some ministers, conditioned by Freudian concepts, and some psychologists, even though sympathetic to religious values, were angry with Mowrer for threatening their comfortable integration into the current professional scene by thus questioning the dominant Freudian views.

Such thoughtless surrender to the imperial ascent of psychoanalysis as the alleged science of human depths did not occur among liberal Christians only in the United States. Runestam, former university professor at Upsala, and later a bishop of the Church in Sweden, wrote of his fellow-Protestants:

> Even within Christian camps one can find a dizzy ecstasy over psychology and psychoanalysis with the proclamation that the Christian soul care will please oblige by taking heed to and being guided by the findings of psychology. (Somewhere) I have read: "In so far as psychology is a science it is futile for the church to do otherwise than to interpret the gospel according to the new situation which has come about through this new knowledge about man." This is capitulation . . . (28:177)

The main reason for this betrayal of Christian insights into the depths of the human soul was apparently brought about by the false notion that psychoanalysis is a science, *i.e.* a body of verified knowledge. These Christians were duped like others into accepting as a new science what was only a collection of subjective guesses and fantasies born of Freud's philosophic and literary talent.

A touching example of the effects of Freudian propaganda upon unsuspecting Christians can be also seen in the case of Sanders. (29) Troubled about what loss to Christianity the spread of "scientific" Freudism might cause, he decided to write a book about it to warn other Christians against arrogant, yet empty Freudian claims. He wanted to support his weaker Christian brothers. In the course of his studies, he discovered that Freud's doctrines were only quasi-scientific assertions which need not carry much weight with any critically thinking and informed person. Yet, the Freudian hoax worked too well on Sanders. Apparently he remained emotionally impressed by the purported scientific standing of psychoanalysis, and he wrote the book anyway, more or less as an intellectual exercise that might help some naive Christian. The title he gave to his book—*Christianity After Freud*—seems to reveal his inability to shake off his sense of respect for Freudian "science." Otherwise he would have seen that his title in historical perspective could just as well have been *Christianity After Mesmer*, if the intention is to suggest that its topic concerns an adequate "scientific" challenge to Christianity.

7. An attempt at definition of science

Like many comprehensive concepts—religion, philosophy, mental health, morality, psychotherapy—"science" cannot be clearly defined. Definition is further confused by those who, because of its dignified connotations, apply the term "science" to almost any endeavor. Richfield points out the "eulogistic function, or emotive significance, of the term *science*. It seems to be assumed that to question the *scientific* status of an activity is equivalent to asking whether that activity is desirable, reliable, and valid." (30:434) The ambiguity is only compounded when two poorly defined terms, *"science"* and *"psychoanalysis,"* are yoked together.

It might be helpful to visualize a core of theories and practices which can indisputably be called science, a region that would encompass the established areas of physics, chemistry, biology, geology, astronomy, etc.

A recent observation illustrates that even natural sciences are riddled with uncertainties:

> Some scientists are hoping that unexpected clues in Apollo's samples will lead to new and more satisfying theories about the moon's origin. Complains Astrophysicist Ralph Baldwin: "There is no existing theory that gives a satisfactory explanation of the earth-moon system as we know it." Nobel Laureate Chemist Harold Urey wryly notes that it would be easier to prove that the moon did not exist than to get agreement on how it came to be. (58:27)

The speculative areas, the growing edges of these disciplines, would be placed farther from this core toward the region of would-be science or pre-science. Here one would find subjective theories, inspired suppositions, unconfirmed working hypotheses, and myths of science.

269

Proponents of would-be sciences, being human, sometimes lose their critical awareness and claim a scientific status for their still unconfirmed assumptions. Thus, *pseudoscience* is created.

Very small portions of the social sciences, as a whole, lie close to the core of the scientific realm. Only limited areas of psychology, sociology, anthropology, medicine, [2] physiology and allied disciplines represent undisputed and verified knowledge. The larger portions of these disciplines are still in the state of would-be science and, when propagated by insecure, ambitious workers, even assume the hues of pseudoscience. The disciplines of psychiatry, psychotherapy, social work, history, economics, politics, law, education and similar essentially subjective theories and practices lie even farther from the core of verified truth. [3] Psychoanalysis, for the most part, belongs to this prescientific region, with the nonscientific fields of literature, philosophy, mysticism, theology, aesthetics, and other products of intuition and effervescences of the unfathomable human spirit. The self-assertiveness of many Freudians, considering the poor scientific basis for their theories, places them often in the pseudosciences. Freud writes about psychoanalysis being midway between medicine and philosophy (4, v. 5:168), but one cannot rely on this as a final opinion, as he is liable to express another opinion in different circumstances. [4]

Speaking before the American Psychoanalytic Association in 1965, Engel tells the learned body that they have not even begun to assume the status of a science, that they are still at the level of pre-science, rich in unconfirmed clinical conjectures, but with no scientifically validated data.

> . . . unless such ideas can be subjected to rigorous testing, they remain only ideas. . . . The bulk of our literature consists of clinical reports, the great majority of which are poorly documented. . . . Our critics accuse us of relying too much on appeal to authority; unfortunately this criticism is too often justified. . . .
>
> What are the reasons that psychoanalysis as a science has failed in seventy-five years to progress significantly beyond the stage of observation, data collection and theory building. . . . Theoreticians and would-be theoreticians we have in abundance but not more than a handful of scientists skilled in and dedicated

to the critical examination of natural phenomena. (64:186, 198)

Responding to Engel's address, Walter Stein admits that he had touched "a raw nerve of the body psychoanalytic, the state of crisis in psychoanalytic research . . . our collective failure to live up to the enthusiastic overselling of our therapeutic promise that ushered in our sweeping acceptance by educated America but a generation ago. . . . Psychoanalytic research has never really gotten off the ground . . . " (64:215, 216)

8. Psychological sciences—not yet

The above requirements for full membership in the scientific club might appear stiff and disappointing to multitudes of learned men who would like to think of themselves as scientists and of their disciplines as sciences. On the other hand, there are psychologists and psychiatrists who do not care to delude themselves about the primitive scientific level of much of their discipline. Some of them refuse to evade the painful realization that psychology and psychiatry are in their infancy as sciences, somewhere at the stage of astronomy in Copernicus's time, or physics in Galileo's. Scientists, being human, have generally been reluctant to admit their deficiencies, preferring instead to proclaim as "science" hypotheses soon to be toppled. It is of such scientific salesmen that Lecomte de Nuoy remarks: "I deem it my duty to protest against the intellectual swindle that has tried to use science as an accomplice."

A majority of responsible psychologists and psychiatrists are aware of the subscientific status of their theories and practices. To enumerate some:

Jung, after thirty years of struggling with problems of psychology, wrote in 1929: "For the purposes of psychology, I think it best to abandon the notion that we are today in anything like a position to make statements about the nature of the psyche that are 'true' or 'correct.' " (40:334) Fromm, in his introduction to Mullahy's *Oedipus, Myth and Complex* (41), admits:

What we know about man, his motivations and the laws which govern his behavior, is pitifully little. Most of what we ought to know, we are ignorant of. We know much about the atom, we know less about the living cell, and we know even a great deal less about the mind. In fact, the preoccupation with the mastery of nature which has obsessed the Western World in the last few centuries has made us forget the considerable knowledge of human soul which, for instance, the Egyptians, the Indians, the Chinese had thousands of years back. It sometimes seems as if we had forgotten more than we discovered in the science of man. (41)

Gengerelli, a professor of psychology, echoes the same sense of humility:

Unfortunately there is very much we do not know; it seems we are ignorant of the more important things. We know very little for instance, about the sources of personality, ... the vacuum of sound scientific understanding of human thought, desire and action had provided an excellent arena for a conceptual Roman holiday. ... The measure of ignorance which surrounds the topic of psychology and the resulting babel of tongues about complexes, inhibitions, repressions, psychosomatic illness, fears, childhood traumas, Oedipus yearnings and maladjustments due to frustration have reduced many thoughtful adults to a helpless mass of disorganized and quivering apprehensions. (42:40)

Alexander, a research psychiatrist and teacher in a medical school, acknowledges the basic ignorance of psychiatry at the beginning of his *Objective Approaches to Psychiatry:* "The causes and nature of mental disease and mechanisms of response to therapy are unknown." (43:3) He does not deny that there are many opinions and guesses, better known under the dignified name of "theories," but he does not find any conclusive knowledge. Strupp, a professor of psychology and an experienced researcher in psychotherapy, recently made this unequivocal statement, " ... we do not as yet know how personality and behavior changes are achieved." (11:95)

Porteus, a professor emeritus of psychology, a researcher and test designer of considerable reputation, after more than fifty years in professional psychology writes: "Psychology is a very young science with more than its share of shaky hypotheses." (44:309)

A volume called *Integrating the Approaches to Mental Disease* (45), reporting the transactions of two conferences held under the auspices

272

of the New York Academy of Medicine, conspicuously belies its title. Many capable participants strove valiantly to make the best of their theoretical perspectives, using logical and polished verbalizations, but they failed to reach the announced goal of "integration." Even the ablest psychologists and psychiatrists cannot, apparently, go beyond present knowledge, permeated as it is by suppositions and theoretical guesses. The volume stands as a monument to the profession's lack of objective knowledge.

An example, selected at random, demonstrates that even some basic practical issues in psychiatry are subject to controversy, *i.e.,* open to the subjective interpretation of the practitioner. It is taken for granted by the majority of American psychiatrists that surgical interference for the purpose of obtaining psychological relief for the patient is undesirable because it tends to make him irresponsible, agitated, or stuporous. Frankl (57:45 ff), who certainly cannot be accused of contempt for human personality, argues from his own experiences and from reports in the literature that lobotomy should not be abandoned wholesale. He finds that in some intractable cases the lobotomized patient may find relief from compulsions and anxieties and an increased will to live responsibly. It is clear, then, that if psychiatry were a science, a body of securely validated knowledge, such diametrically opposed views would be impossible. The controversy over lobotomy has arisen lately with increased vigor. (73) Some well-known psychiatrists consider it a brazen interference with human beings, totally unjustified, crude and damaging. Others, equally renowned, firmly believe that psychiatric prejudices prevent many otherwise intractable cases from benefitting from surgical tempering of their brains.

When Berelson and Steiner published *Human Behavior: An Inventory of Scientific Findings* (46) in 1964, they announced that their purpose was to present "what we really know, what we think we know, and what we claim to know." Reviewing the book a year later, Worchel (47), symbolized the uncertainty of knowledge in the social sciences by using the revealing title "Necessarily Monumental and Controversial." In chemistry and physics, only a small part of scientific propositions are controversial; in the "science" of man, the greatest part are.

Pohlman provides an indirect demonstration of this point. He complains in a letter to the editor of *Contemporary Psychology* about the lack of objectivity in many reviews of books on psychology: "Most of us have seen the amusing contrasts that occasionally develop when the same book is reviewed independently for two different journals, and one review gives the book a halo and the other gives it horns." (51) Interestingly, Pohlman is speaking about American psychology, in which scientific demands are more stringent than in other fields of mental health.

A perusal of Eysenck's *Handbook of Abnormal Psychology* (50) can make any clinical psychologist or psychiatrist uncomfortable. An objective review of many diagnostic procedures shows them to be largely unvalidated, intuitive guesses, not far above the level of glorified folklore. [See chapter IV, "Rx for failure" (75).]

Some psychologists, disturbed by the lack of verified knowledge in their field, propose that what is scientific about psychology is not its content, but rather its method. This sounds like another rationalization by people who cannot bring themselves to admit: "We would like to be scientists, but for the time being we are only groping."

Eissler, an orthodox Freudian, considers psychoanalysis to be in its first post-Copernican phase (48:6), just struggling to establish its scientific status. Schmideberg writes of psychiatry as still in the Dark Ages. (49:245) Such a primitive level of psychiatry may have fatal consequences on patients. Not so long ago, four psychiatrists discussed deaths following treatment with psychiatric drugs. (52, 53)

A remarkably accurate appraisal of the current status of psychiatry was provided by a relatively recent article in the *Saturday Evening Post* entitled "Psychiatry: The Uncertain Science":

Psychiatry is a very young and imprecise science, and it has never found a workable definition of itself.... This untidiness is innate, for the simple reason that all psychiatry must start by defining man and his nature, and psychiatry has not one but many definitions of man. (55:37, 38)

The subtitle of the article—"A ... report on a remarkable profession surrounded by controversy, racked by dissension, unsure of its proper role in society and flourishing nevertheless"—points to the paradoxical social role of a science that does not possess even the definition of its principal object, man, and yet it is called upon to correct man's functioning both as individual and in relation to others.

It is not difficult to understand the paradox of a science that is not yet a science but which nevertheless purports to guide men out of the troubles of their minds. Secular civilization has thrown doubt upon the traditional sources of human inspiration: religion, philosophy, art. Deprived of these rich sources of inner life, many a post-Renaissance man tried to build new myths to live by: "science," political creeds, nationalistic pride. The same incontrovertible irrational psychic need has invested psychology and psychiatry with wisdom they do not possess. As we have seen in the foregoing chapter, Freudians have been particularly quick to seize upon this irrational need and to entrench themselves in the role formerly (and more adequately) filled by religious and philosophical thinkers. As students of the immature and unconscious functions in human beings, Freud and his disciples skillfully manipulated themselves into the position of leaders of opinion by claiming scientific status for themselves. Even if their fraud was not usually deliberate, impartial contemplation reveals their behavior as a hoax nevertheless.

Notes to Chapter Six

1. La Pierre compares the status of Marxist "science" with that of Freud's:

... the fact that the Freudian doctrine of man is unscientific has no real social significance. What is socially significant is whether man can and will give it social validity. The Marxian doctrine of social evolution was not, as Marx and all his disciples since have believed, derived from the empirical study of social history. Like Freud's doctrine of man, it was imposed upon facts, not deduced from them. Marxianism is, therefore, unscientific in the same sense that Freudianism is unscientific. Nevertheless, a great many men have for well over half a century been exceedingly busy in trying to give some social validity to Marxianism; and while they are still far from the Marxian goal of the prosperous classless utopia that Marx was confident would shortly follow the proletarian revolution, they are still presumably—or at least according to their claims—struggling to that end.

Freud presented the Western peoples a new and very radical idea of the nature of man, an idea of man that is in all respects the antithesis of that which was advanced by Luther; and to some extent the role of Freud in the twentieth century has been comparable to the role that Luther played in the emergence of the Protestant ethic. For upon the Freudian doctrine of man there has developed a new ethic, and this new ethic is being propagated by Freud's disciples in much the same way that the Protestant clergymen sanctioned and disseminated the Protestant ethic. And although the Freudian doctrine of man is hardly half a century old and the Freudian ethic somewhat less than this, already this new ethic is gaining considerable organizational representation and being made the justification for various changes in our social order. It is such social validation of the Freudian doctrine that gives to Freudianism its great significance. To question its scientific validity becomes, therefore, irrelevant. Freudianism, like Marxianism, is or will become just as valid as men make it.

The rise of the Freudian doctrine as the prevailing concept of the nature of man is at once a measure of the decline of the Protestant ethic, and a denial of the idea that man is a creature of reason. Freud's idea of man is one that in many respects resembles that which prevailed through the Middle Ages and which was sanctioned by the Medieval Church. In the Freudian concept, man is not born free with the right to pursue life, liberty, and happiness; he is shackled by biological urges that can never be freely expressed and that set him in constant and grievous conflict with his society. Life for him must be an unhappy and unending struggle to reconcile, both within himself and between himself and others, forces that are inherently antagonistic. Freud does not say, in the theological manner, that man fell from Grace and must therefore suffer in this life. But he does come to much the same concept of man; that man is by nature (or at least by virtue of the inevitable conflict between man's nature and society) a weak and irresolute creature without the stamina to endure the stresses and strains of living, and who cannot therefore hope to enjoy life on this earth. (5:60)

2. Some people, impressed by the general advance of medical knowledge, might feel that medicine is here denied its deserved scientific status. If they read Gross (31), they might be disquieted by some alarming reports. For instance, 60% of ailments are neither found nor labeled. Of the 40% that are discovered, one-half are diagnosed erroneously. A pathologist ventured to estimate that iatrogenic (doctor-produced) diseases about equal those produced by bacteria.

Grotjahn (32), a medically trained writer, recounts his tribulations with the famous specialists he consulted about a kidney stone. He was misdiagnosed and misadvised both regarding the state of his kidneys and their proper treatment. The professional medical men disagreed as much as artists about a work of art, on architects about urban planning.

On the occasion of the appearance of a long-overdue book on uncertainties of medical treatments, *Controversy in Internal Medicine,* edited by three Boston physicians, a columnist illustrates the prevalence of medical ignorance by the disagreements on how to treat three important diseases:

On ulcers:
The ulcer patient should watch his diet—Dr. James L. A. Roth, University of Pennsylvania Graduate School of Medicine. Let the ulcer patient enjoy his food—Dr. Franz J. Ingelfinger of Boston University School of Medicine.
On hardening of the arteries:
Both hardening of the arteries and blood clots are diet related —Dr. Jeremiah Stamler, Northwestern University Medical School. We need more convincing proof of the clinical usefulness of drugs in treatment of high blood pressure—Dr. William Goldring, New York University School of Medicine.
The death rate from high blood pressure has declined significantly since the introduction of drug treatment—Dr. William Hollander, Boston University School of Medicine. (76:20)

3. Selby expresses a similar view:

There is an underground notion, held by many behavioral scientists, that we can rate the subdivisions of social science on a scale of methodological rigor. Experimental psychology generally ranks up at the top end of the scale, and in descending order we find subfields of economics, hard-nosed sociology and so on, down to the bottom end where clinical psychology and anthropology are located. (59:315)

4. Here are some examples of Freud's contradictions and inconsistencies:
(1) La Pierre notes that Freud's writings, by virtue of their inconsistency are more in the nature of general and religious literature than scientific works:

Freud wrote with zest and considerable poetic license. As a result of all these factors, Freud's writings have little more internal consistency than does the Old Testament; anything that may be said about Freud's ideas can be contradicted by citations from Freud; and no one has yet been able to interpret Freud in a way that is acceptable to all Freudians. (5:34)

(2) Ludwig also finds that Freud changes his arguments according to the need of the moment. Ludwig illustrates his point through Freud's ambivalence regarding the sexual meaning of dreams:

Here again we see Freud on both sides of the fence. Here again he contradicts his own arguments, yet uses them. And so it is easy enough to quote him as either denying or affirming. But what is his essential doctrine?
At one place he declares firmly: "The assertion that all dreams call for a sexual interpretation is not to be found in my work *The Interpretation of Dreams.*" Yet on the same page he begins to retract, mentioning " . . . that dreams conspicuously innocent commonly embody crude erotic wishes" and "many dreams we might never suspect of any marked tendencies can be traced to unmistakable sexual wishes." Also, "dreams apparently innocent turn out to be the reverse if one takes the trouble to interpret them." In other words, the sex dream denotes sex, and the innocent dream denotes sex.
In speaking of "anxiety" dreams, for example, he cites one of the most commonly experienced dreams—that of falling. When a

woman has such a nightmare, he says, it is " . . . a circumlocution for giving way to erotic temptation."

Here we see Freud, who denies exclusive sexual interpretation, deliberately seeking it. (33:57-59)

(3) " . . . Freud broke with Rank. At that time Freud spoke of Rank's neurosis as being responsible for some of his deviations; but only eighteen months before, Freud had said that in fifteen years 'he had scarcely ever had the idea that Rank needed analysis.' " (34:136, 137)

(4) In 1912 Freud wrote to Pfister: "It is a pity that you did not meet or speak to Jung. You could have told him from me that he is at perfect liberty to develop views divergent from mine, and that I ask him to do so without a bad conscience." (7:56, 57) Yet at their next meeting, when Jung stuck by his ideas, Freud fainted in the intensity of conflict he experienced.

(5) Realistically evaluating the importance of psychoanalysis to psychological knowledge, Freud wrote: "Psychoanalysis has never pretended to give a complete explanation of the psychic life of man in general; it only asks that its data be used to complete the data gathered by other means." (Quoted in 35:30) However, Freud often implies that the only psychology worth anything is psychoanalysis. Freud also spoke of psychoanalysis as a "young science" (36:4) but in his zeal to gain acceptance for his theories he repressed such realistic modesty and misled himself and his followers into false assurance.

(6) Jones (37, v. I:163) informs readers that Professor Hammerschlag taught Freud the "Scriptures and Hebrew." Yet Freud denied any knowledge of Yiddish and Hebrew. Bakan puts it mildly when he considers such a dissimulation "strange":

In view of this evidence it seems strange indeed that Freud should deny knowledge of these languages in print. In an introductory statement to a Yiddish translation of one of his works he addresses the translator by saying that he was happy to have received a copy of the work and that he took it in his hands with great respect. It is unfortunate, he adds, that he can do no more with it. For, in the days when he was a student, they gave no care to the cultivation of the national tradition. He, therefore, did not learn either Hebrew or Yiddish, which he regrets very much. Nevertheless he still became a good Jew, although perhaps, not a believer. He makes a similar denial in the preface to the Hebrew edition of *Totem and Taboo*. (38:51)

(7) "Freud, as we recall, had attributed the original discoveries of psychoanalysis to Breuer. In his Clark University lectures he asserted quite forthrightly that Breuer was the originator of psychoanalysis, although he disclaimed this later." (38:57)

(8) Puner depicts the contradictions expressed by Freud: liberalism in verbalizations, dogmatism in behavior. No wonder that pupils were confused by the cues received:

He himself recognized the shortcoming of his theorizing and painstakingly and consistently worked on . . . [its] improvement.

When he spoke this way, with the voice of reason, he spoke accurately and well. But his psychoanalytic children reacted not so much to what he said as to what he did. He spoke of freedom to amend, revise and change his doctrines, but the emotional atmosphere that he generated for his followers was one of rigid, watchful authority under which any attempt to deviate was treated as heresy. So his followers have interpreted every tentative work he wrote as the ultimate crystallization of God-given truth. A pedantic and strictly defined conceptual system is exactly what has grown up among orthodox Freudians around the body of Freudian literature! (39:216)

(9) Stuart (75:55-57) lists several theoretical contradictions proposed by Freud at various times.

Chapter VII

A PSEUDOSCIENCE AT WORK

Nunberg [66] once made the statement that the place to study hypnosis is in the analytic transference situation. I was much struck by this seemingly paradoxical remark, since it pointed up the similarities between the two states or relationships.

Gill [67], MacAlpine [32], and Nunberg [68], discussing the similarities between the psychic states of the patient in hypnosis and the patient in analysis, describe them as states of induced regression that differ only in the degree and intensity of the regression. Among the factors that promote regression in the analytic situation, these authors mention the following: the couch position and the resulting reduction of external stimuli; the presence of an adult, who sits behind the patient; the reduction of reality cues; the refusal of the analyst to answer questions; the constancy of the environment; the fixed routine of the analytic ceremonial; the frustration of every gratification, and the simultaneous stimulation of needs.

Charles Fisher, Ph.D., M.D., a psychoanalyst (65:222-224)

Freud's so-called success with the transference neurosis is due simply to the charm of his personality and his powerful gift of persuasion and suggestion, affecting in a positive way the faith of his patients. In other words, it is not based on any scientific approach to the subject. It is just another form of hypnosis, based on faith, which he usurped from religious leaders and evangelists.

Martin D. Kushner, M.D. (52:14)

...analytic transference manifestations are a slow motion picture of hypnotic transference manifestations; they take some time to develop, unfold slowly and gradually, and not all at once as in hypnosis.

Ida MacAlpine, M.D., a psychoanalyst (32:519)

281

Freudism when weighed in the scales of science is found seriously wanting.

Joseph Jastrow, Ph.D.,
Professor of Psychology (1:74)

1. The quasi-scientific Freudian method of investigation

As one studies the writings of Freud and his close followers, one soon finds that it is vitally important to consider what is omitted from the descriptions of their procedures. Just as analysts seek out the pretenses of their patients by attention to what they leave unexpressed or only partially expressed, so the student of Freudian literature must carefully consider defensively slanted statements—slanted unconsciously perhaps, but no less slyly than those of hysterics on the couch. This evasive skill seems to develop as part of the trade, just as proverbially it takes a thief to catch a thief.

Now, what Freud told us he was doing was to sit unobtrusively behind the couch, let himself fall into a state of suspended animation, mentally "making no effort to concentrate attention on anything in particular—of 'evenly-hovering attention,' as I once before described it." (2:118) He chose to consider himself in the role of a neutral mirror reflecting the patient's free associations. He did not want his critics to think that he in any way influenced or interfered with the flow of associations. In 1904, when writing for Dr. Löwenfeld's *Psychische Zwangerscheinungen* (*Compulsive Psychological Phenomena*), Freud described his technique in such a way as to emphasize his neutral role as a mere recorder:

> The cathartic method had already renounced suggestion; Freud went one step further and renounced hypnosis as well. At the present time he treats his patients as follows: Without exerting any other kind of influence he invites them to recline in a comfortable position on a couch, while he himself is seated on a chair behind them outside their field of vision. He does not ask them to close their eyes and avoids touching them as well or any other form of procedure which might remind them of hypnosis. The consultation then proceeds as between two equally wakeful persons, one of whom is spared every muscular exertion and

every distracting sensory impression which might draw his attention from his own mental activity.

In order to secure these ideas and associations, he asks the patient to "let himself go" in what he says, "as you would in a conversation which leads you from cabbages to kings." In the task of collecting this material of otherwise neglected ideas Freud made the observations which became the determining factors of his entire theory. (2:56, 57)

Here, then, is an impartial scientist taking the utmost care not to interpose in the flow of data from the patient, "without exerting any other kind of influence." He explains elsewhere that he had taken up his position behind the couch not only because he could not stand to be stared at for eight or more hours a day, but also because he aimed at securing an immaculate experimental situation: "Since while I listen, I resign myself to the control of my unconscious thoughts, I do not wish my expression to give the patient indications which he may interpret or which may influence him in his communications." (2:146) The situation is set for a sterile operation, in which no germs from the surgeon's hands will infect the pristine material obtained from the patient. Many naive people, even psychologists and psychiatrists, took Freud at his word and marveled at the new discoveries that had supposedly welled up from hitherto unknown depths of the human unconscious—discoveries with which he shocked the uninformed and the philistines.

For the full picture of the situations Freud set up in his "investigations," it is necessary to take into account what Freud did not say, or said in a veiled way. He did not dwell carefully on the motivational state of his patient, and the influence of the couch, and he did not say much about how he deliberately and inadvertently steered the thinking of the patient.

The gist of my argument is this. Freud believed that the most important source of data in psychoanalysis is free association, which he called "the methodological key to its results." (49:403) This "methodological key" is so permeated by the analyst's comments and influences that it destroys the scientific validity of psychoanalysis. It makes Freud's findings of dubious scientific value; the contaminating

283

variables of the analyst's overt and covert suggestions render Freudian "findings" scientifically worthless.

As we shall see, the subject is in a highly unstable, suggestible state of mind; the couch reinforces the hypnotic state in the patient; and the analyst subtly imposes his theoretical or personal fantasies ("interpretations") upon the patient's weakened ego state, once suggestibility is enhanced through transference. These aspects will be dealt with in turn.

It is important at this point to grasp Freud's own basic delusion about what he was doing. Freud, like many researchers in the "unconscious," was duped by the mythopoetic (64:81) propensity of hysterical subjects to produce convincing fantasies, stories and pretenses while in trance or trancelike states. These beautiful fantasies can be spun in hypnosis, in somnambulistic states and mediumistic seances, in some dreams and certain psychotic delusions, by tortured witches and prisoners, and—on the Freudian couch. They all tend to impress therapists, torturers, hypnotists, and spiritistic audiences with expected statements, revelations, and discoveries. Early in his career as a psychologist, Freud was deluded by his hysterical female patients who neatly "confirmed" his suppositions about sexual "traumas" in childhood as alleged "causes" of neurosis. However, he was too deeply in love with his science to abandon building it on mythopoetic sands.

From the scientific point of view, the principal weakness of Freudism is that it had not advanced beyond its predecessor, Mesmerism. Anton Mesmer achieved some therapeutic benefits by placing his subjects in a state which was later to be known as hypnotic suggestibility. However, he had an arbitrary theory to explain his results. In accordance with the prevalent scientific notions at the end of the eighteenth century, he modeled his "explanations" on the lines of contemporary physics: the cures were thought of as being effected by "animal magnetism." Freud also achieved some therapeutic results and, like Mesmer, used a scientifically untenable theory of them. In his theoretical explanations he disregarded the actual suggestive operations in his treatment, and concentrated on the scientific fashion of his day, the imprecise biological concepts of instinct, sexuality, aggression, and psychological determinism. These terms may sound convincing to us, conditioned to contemporary scientific jargon as we are, yet they are no better founded than the concepts of "animal magnetism," influences of stars on human personality, or revelations of mediumistic seances or LSD trips.

2. *The unstable patient*

Freud mentions (2) that his patients usually came to him after other remedies failed. They were reduced to despair, their hopes alternating with anxiety and dark apprehensions. Most of them, particularly in the beginning of Freud's work, were labile hysterics, proverbially prone to suggestion, overemotionality, and immaturity. On one occasion Freud entertained his friend Fliess by observing how gullible some of his patients were, readily accepting the mystification of sexual etiology: "Meanwhile things have grown livelier in the usually struggling medical practice. The sexual business attracts people; they all go away impressed and convinced, after exclaiming: 'No one ever asked me that before!' " (3:77) (Note that Freud "asked," the patient did not bring out sexual material spontaneously.)

Garner states a commonplace observation of psychiatric literature: " . . . psychoneurotic patients are more easily conditioned than normal subjects." He mentions studies demonstrating "the greater responsiveness to suggestion of the psychoneurotic or the individual in a situation seeking help." (63:354)

One can wonder about Freud's character if he could exploit troubled people's sexuality for personal and professional gain. He knew how to hook and guide these sexually unstable women. Hypnotists have written, in the course of the previous hundred years, about sexuality inevitably pouring over into the hypnotic relationship. According to Ellenberger, the workers in that "First Dynamic Psychiatry" had clearly established these clinical facts:

> . . . Teste noted [in 1846] that the subject soon became able to detect the secret wishes of the magnetizer and warned against the dangers, not only of crude sexual seduction but of falling into a sincere and true love relationship. Reverend Debreyne, who was a medically trained priest and educator, remarked that the magnetizer was usually a healthy and strong man, the subject usually a pretty young woman (rarely an old or ugly one), and he

285

had good reason to believe that seduction occurred frequently ... Deleuze and the early mesmerists also described [how] this dependency could often take on a sexual slant. This well-known fact was rediscovered by Charcot, who gave an account of a woman who had been hypnotized five times within three weeks and who could think of nothing but her hypnotist, until she ran away from her home to live with him. Her husband took her back, but she fell into severe hysterical disturbances that necessitated her admission to a hospital. Meynert [Freud's colleague] based his opposition to hypnotism on the fact that the entire attitude of the woman toward the hypnotist was permeated with strong sexual undertones and the sexual emotions also played a part in hypnotized men. (60:118, 119)

Freud knew about the sexual obsession and suggestibility of hysterics and deliberately exploited it in the clandestine form of hypnosis, which he developed as psychoanalysis. He maintained the pretense that he had abandoned conventional hypnotic procedures, allegedly because of the unwanted sexual attachments of female patients to him. However, he was not scrupulously honest enough to abandon such charlatan "therapy"; instead, he used the insight long possessed by madames and pimps that "sexual business attracts people," as he put it. The reaction of another physician to the opportunity offered by hysterical females leaves Freud as a questionable character by comparison.

Axel Munthe, the physician-artist who was Freud's contemporary, and the author of the renowned novel *San Michele,* provides us with impressions of the hysterical patients of that period. Like Freud, Munthe had studied under Charcot, and for years the great master of suggestion and hypnosis referred patients to his good student, swelling his already large practice. This friendly relationship was broken off when Munthe tried to liberate a young woman from playing the role of exemplary hysterical patient *à la Charcot* and progressing into mental sickness in compliance with the doctor's expectations. (46:202-211) Unlike Freud, Munthe did not have to hang onto his patients, for he had more than he could handle; nor did he need to tie his patients to him by deliberately provoking an excessive emotional attachment or "transference" as Freud called it. Suggestible, immature women flocked to the fashionable Dr. Munthe in such multitudes that he

286

finally had to abandon his lucrative practice in Paris and resume it later under more controlled conditions in Rome. These childish, idle, rich women from France, Russia, and the United States developed such strong feelings for the male doctor, their father figure and their savior, that Munthe was often not only embarrassed but outright annoyed. They followed him to hotels and parties where they expected to see him, rented residences close to him, imposed upon him with all sorts of complaints and maneuverings for attention. Munthe could not shake them off. He tried to enlist the help of their families to get rid of them, but it was usually to no avail. The exalted hysterics clung tenaciously to their newly found hero. He tried to handle them in a stern, forbidding manner, and it did not help. A kindly, "understanding" manner was even less effective:

> It is easy to be patient with lunatics, I confess to a sneaking liking for them. With a little kindness one comes to terms with most of them as often as not. But it is not easy to be patient with hysterical women, and as to being kind to them, one had better think it over twice before being too kind to them, they ask for nothing better. As a rule you can do but little for these patients, at least outside the hospital. You can stun their nerve centres with sedatives but you cannot cure them. They remain what they are, a bewildering complex of mental and physical disorders, a plague to themselves and to their families, a curse to their doctors. Hypnotic treatment, so beneficial in many hitherto incurable mental troubles, is as a rule contraindicated in the treatment of hysterical women of all ages, hysteria has no age limit. It should in any case be limited to Charcot's suggestion à l' état de veille [wakefulness]. It is besides unnecessary, for these women are in any case already too willing to be influenced by their doctor, to depend upon him too much, to imagine he is the only one who can understand them, to hero-worship him. (46:283)

Apparently Freud thrived on fostering dependency in his immature patients, a procedure rejected by Munthe, a better physician than the famed psychologist from Vienna.

The neurotics in the offices of Freud and his followers were little different from those plaguing Munthe's practice. They suffered from excessive emotionality, their hopes rose high and sank low, they surrendered unconditionally to their therapist, to be molded into

287

beliefs arising from the wisdom of the Big, Big Daddy.

Some few examples might serve as illustrations of the weakened ego-strength of these people and their proneness to dependent surrenders, which are at the core of hypnosis. Knight (4) describes the disturbing struggle he experienced when the physician treating him for an ulcer suggested he go into psychoanalysis. He read avidly on the subject, invented meetings as excuses for not starting analysis, failed to keep one appointment with the analyst, suffered an anxiety attack, and experienced terror before being finally driven into contact with the analyst. He was an emotionally beaten man when he entered the psychoanalytic situation.

Maryse Choisy, a young and talented college graduate, experienced these feelings as she went to her first appointment with Freud: "Never did my heart beat for a lover as it did the day I walked up the Berggasse. Was that Vienna street a really steep climb? Or did it only appear so to me because I was at last going to see my God (at that time) who with some miracle had become accessible?" (5:1) Twenty-two at the time, she described her experience several years later, when she had earned her Ph.D. and had become president of the Association for Applied Psychoanalysis in France and editor of *Psyché*.

She was already caught in the irrational awe of Freud, the acclaimed genius of psychology:

> Didn't psychoanalysis harmoniously incarnate an infinite line of ancestors and an infinite line of scions in the finite substance of a living man? Wasn't Freud the last of the mechanists with a foot on the threshold of the cosmic force? His tragedy was to waver on the threshold, just as I was now myself wavering before stepping into the Holy of Holies. (5:2)

She is somewhat taken aback by the real Freud: The priest of this Holy of Holies, the all-wise prophet of the most profound truths, did not look the part painted by her anticipating enthusiasm. Yet she soon managed to discover the "radiance" in the commonplace:

> I had imagined Freud as a tall imposing hero. What? I and Freud—this old, bearded, bespectacled fellow? Would I have noticed him in the crowd? He looks as if he had a bulldog's

character and was full of fads. . . . Yes, it is Freud, this finely domed forehead, this noble forehead which seems to have no end. His dark brilliant eyes penetrate beyond your mortal flesh. From them a force rains down on me like some sacred dew. A radiance which it is impossible to resist . . . (5:3)

How much more impressionable and emotional need one be to show the plasticity of a good subject for a hypnotist or suggestionist? Freud did not even need to exert himself to impose hypnosis; the analysands were ready for hypnotic submission from the outset.

Freud asks Miss Choisy what she thinks of him. She is startled. "Yes, his tone was rude. Irony ran between the words. Or did I project this irony? But Freud *was* rude. Yes, this rude, bitter, misanthropic, utterly pessimistic outlook was Freud's business. It had nothing to do with my personal style." (5:3) She apparently did not realize that Freud was already working on her, getting the upper hand, covertly but expertly.

In the third session, Freud interpreted a dream of hers as a screen memory. Unknowingly, she had already reached an emotionally distraught state. "I jumped on the first plane back to Paris." She checked with her aunt who confirmed that the event of which she had dreamed had actually taken place in her childhood. The magic worked even at a distance.

> There was something uncanny about this dream interpretation. I did not return to Vienna. Freud now symbolized for me the magical father, the medicine-man. He saw through me. I felt as transparent as glass. I was scared. I was so scared that I would go to great lengths to avoid analysts. It took me eight years to overcome my panic. Freud did then what he later warned all his pupils to avoid: he interpreted too early, when analysand was still unable to accept what he was. This Freud called *wild analysis.* (5:7)

Apparently, Freud was oblivious to the patient's state in the analytic situation with him if he could so badly misjudge the unbearable build-up of emotionality in this beginning analysand.

The extreme proneness to suggestibility and the tendency to invest the psychotherapist with miraculous attributes is patent in the reactions of Joyce MacIver, who later wrote a novel, *The Frog Pond*, based on her travails with psychiatrists. She had been troubled with vague fears, inhibitions and masochistic trends all her life. She had reached a state of panic and did not dare let her friend Matthew leave her apartment, in terror of being left alone. He recommends his psychiatrist to her.

The minute the door closed on Matthew, I hurried upstairs and dialed the number. I had by then conceived a vague but thrilling image of Dr. Ramsey who had saved Matthew from the demons of the San Francisco Bridge and who was waiting at that moment a few buildings away to do the same to me. I pictured him as being extremely tall, about eight feet. I could not quite make out his features at that point, but I knew he was handsome without being showy, a cross between Cary Crant and Jesus Christ with the beard removed and with an enormous extra scuttle of masculinity thrown in. Say as if the Rock of Gibraltar should become a man, that would be about it. (6:33)

As could be expected, later in her contacts she was rudely awakened from the fairy tale she had spun out of her erotic yearnings and in the hope of becoming liberated from emotional discomfort.

The inner office was heavy with smoke. Through the smoke I saw a man with a long, soft, yellow face, and pale eyes and light straw-colored hair. There was weakness and pain in this face, but the deciding characteristic was pain. I noticed his tobacco-stained fingers and then his wiry neck. He looked something like a chicken, I thought. A depressed chicken. (6:36)

Dr. Ramsey was not a Freudian. He did not foster the transference deliberately, nor did he lead the patient toward regression and disintegration of personality through free-associating. He actually tried to prevent her from slipping into reveries of the past and held her to the present. Nevertheless—such is the nature of the psycho-therapeutic relationship, particularly if the healer and the patient are of opposite sex—a strong transference developed in spite of the initial setback.

290

By now Dr. Ramsey had become the center of the universe inside my head.

On one side he was the essence of maturity, benevolence and wisdom, on the other mysterious, frightening and unpredictable. Altogether a man possessed of infinite powers. Sometimes, remembering my first impression—he had looked so sallow I'd wondered if he mightn't have tuberculosis and felt some of the physical revulsion of the healthy toward the sick—I wondered how I could ever have felt so cold blooded. Now, seeing the long yellow face, I was conscious of wellsprings of compassion, tenderness and fear for his future. How was it possible that this same face, which had so recently resembled a cigarette left out in the rain for a month, now appeared beautiful? And outside in the daily routine of living I found myself turning from the healthy, sunburned males in favor of sickly, yellow people, convinced that all men who weren't yellow just hadn't mellowed. (6:55)

It does not take a psychological expert to discern that this woman was now in a quasi-hypnotic state and would be hypersensitive to any suggestions coming from her therapist.

The poetess Hilda Doolittle (7), in her forties when she met Freud, was even more capable of regressing to the level of an awestruck child. "I felt like a child summoned to my father's study or my mother's sewing room or told by a teacher to wait after school." (7:130) Of course, she was well brainwashed by the prevailing Freudian cultural fad of the mid-thirties before she met Freud. A great number of artists were deluded into the belief that psychoanalysis contained new revelations about everything: art, sexual life, anthropology, religion, human destiny. She refers with awe to the "growing body of doctors, psychologists, nerve specialists, who form the somewhat formidable body of the International Psycho-Analytical Association." (7:132) Freud is already among the demigods: "I was a student working under the direction of the greatest mind of this and perhaps many succeeding generations." (7:24, 25) Freud readily accepted the role to which she elevated him. He even condescends to tell her his well-guarded secret: "My discoveries are not a heal-all. My discoveries are the basis for a very grave philosophy. There are very few who understand this, there are a few who are capable of understanding

291

this." (7:25) Most of Freud's students, analysands, and readers never grasped this essential point.

It is doubtful if the mystical Indians, sitting humbly at their guru's feet, can reach the ecstasy of adoration of some Westerners infantilized through psychoanalysis. The incongruous religious trance grows stronger by the minute: "... finally he seats himself again, while from the niche rises the smoke of burnt incense, the smouldering of his mellow fragrant cigar." (7.32) In this atmosphere of irrationality, it is easy to comprehend what Moses must have felt when he approached the burning bush. There are pagan statuettes on Freud's desk and shelves. Earlier she had thought of Freud as "magician-analyst," as Moore calls him in the foreword to H.D.'s book. "But the Professor knew, he must have known, that by implication, he himself was included in the number of these Gods. He himself already counted as immortal." (7:46) She muses about Freud's "imposing desk (that it seemed placed there, now I come to think of it, almost like a high altar, with the Holy of Holies)." (7:103) Freud was seventy-seven by that time; he already had had surgical operations for cancer, but her imagination makes him into an invincible hero: "The old Professor doubles the part. He is Hercules struggling with death and he is the beloved, about to die." (7:112) She prays ardently for him, would give him some of her years to prolong his life. She was already in the trance, even without the help of the couch and the guided "free" association.

The patients need not be impressionable artists or hysterical personalities in order to make a demigod of their analyst. Fisher experimented with giving dream suggestions to garden variety of American homosexuals, alcoholics, character disorders, and depressives, and received the same adulation and submissiveness:

The initial anxious or suspicious attitude was always followed by a favorable one, in which the patient expressed the idea of feeling important, that he was the object of special interest from me, or the notion that the experiments represented an unusual therapeutic effort in his behalf. These latter attitudes were accompanied by strong conscious wishes to produce dreams in order to advance the treatment and please me, and marked disappointment when failure occurred. (65:229)

Even more emotionally stable individuals are prone to project omnipotent or succoring qualities upon their therapists. Even a machine-therapist can bring about such failures in reality testing, as all humans retain residues of their infantile stage of development. Beier supplies the following incident:

> Dr. Arnold Bernstein in New York, reported to us that he placed conventional responses such as "Hm, hm" and "Go on" on a tape and had an experimental volunteer patient alone in a room turn a switch which activated a tape recorder, whenever she wanted the therapist to respond. She was given the understanding that the therapist would be sitting next door. After six hours the patient was asked to describe the therapist and she said that she thought of him as "most understanding, warm, and considerate." (8:13)

In conclusion, it appears amply demonstrated that Freud had not, as he claimed in 1924 (48:195) and on earlier occasions, abandoned hypnosis for a supposedly different method of free association. He had abandoned hypnosis only verbally and outwardly while in practice he had found ways of evoking an even more potent suggestibility and subjection in the patient. The subjection was much more pervasive for being unconscious, certainly for the patient, but even largely for Freud himself. He rarely cared to expound on the essential similarity between transference and hypnotic dependence. Without announcing it clearly, he developed a more subtle way than hypnosis of sneaking into his patients' minds, creating regression and sometimes confusion in them. Then, having sickened them enough, he led them out of such induced disintegrations of personality as a savior, as a hero reminiscent of Orpheus rescuing Eurydice from Hades. The technique worked rather nicely, particularly for Freud as he needed some magic to build up his practice in the early stages, and to produce "proofs" for his sex-saturated theories.

3. *The couch as hypnotic reinforcement*

Freud tells us that the couch is the only historical remnant of the period when he struggled to impose hypnosis upon patients and that his purpose in retaining it was to relax the patient completely. This is at best a half-truth as it implicitly denies his later practice of an even subtler hypnosis. He believed the couch to be such an asset in handling patients ("treatment") that he never yielded to the pleadings of those who felt disturbed by lying on it, and he recommends analysts not to allow their patients to get away from it. (2) Here, again, Freud's unstated motives are as important as his declared purposes.

First, Freud neglected to mention that the couch gave him implied superiority, unconsciously sensed authority, and placed the subject in an inferior, manifestly sick role. It created a magical atmosphere, with the analyst hovering in the shadows like a priest of ancient oracles while the prostrate supplicant eagerly awaits mysterious revelations. Adolph Meyer, sympathetic to psychoanalysis, but not without critical reservations, noted the occult implication of the Freudian method of psychotherapy. "It struck Meyer that psychoanalysis was an ingenious way to practice medicine, by which he meant both the fee system and the mystical atmosphere created by the patient's facing away from the doctor." (10:131) A sensitive and honest practitioner of psychoanalysis, Choisy also remarks on the mystical implications of the couch:

> The only thing which remains from the hypnotic period is the couch. The analysand lies on the couch. Behind him is the silence of the invisible presence. It is often argued that Freud invented this situation because he could not stand his patients gazing at him the whole day. One may remember of course that the Israelites were not allowed to stare at Moses while he blessed them. It is even possible to ascribe a cause in keeping with analytic logic for the fact that for Jews and Muslims God must remain invisible. (5:125)

Apparently, Freud could not go to the lengths of Mesmer in order to overwhelm his patients; he could not bring himself to put on a lilac silk robe and darken the room for effect. The prone position on the couch and the odd ideas he delivered to patients from his niche proved sufficient to brainwash them into submission.

The couch effected another welcome benefit for the analyst, one which Freud did not describe either, but which could not have escaped his attention: the couch was conducive to a hypnoid state and the enhanced suggestibility resulting from it. Esquirol, one of the pioneers of medical hypnosis, called this twilight state between sleep and wakefulness "hypnagogic" and investigated the patient's suggestibility in that condition.

The hypnagogic state is one of the many and poorly defined Altered States of Consciousness (ASC). Vogel, Foulkes, and Trosman (51) have found through encephalographic studies and specific questioning of subjects brought back from this borderline state that the hypnagogic condition partakes of characteristics of both sleep and wakefulness. In general, uncontrolled thinking takes over, enabling the subject to experience his fantasies in a vivid and personally highly convincing manner. In a comprehensive review Ludwig (53) describes the common features of ASCs. These experiences tend to attain a special significance for the subject, as if they were important visions and revelations. This aspect must have been very useful in Freud's work. The experiences they reached or he helped induce in them were potent for those taking the couch cure, gave them the feeling that psychoanalysis provided them with great insights and an enlargement of their usual capacities. This illusion seems common to all ASCs, not only those induced by psychoanalytic procedures. It is obvious from the characteristics enumerated by Ludwig that in his use of the couch Freud had hit a rich gold vein of opportunities to mold the patient's mind in a mighty way, and yet get away scot-free from charges that he is using suggestions:

> In attempting to account for the dramatic feature of hypersuggestibility, I believe that a better understanding of this phenomenon can be gained through an analysis of some of the subjective features associated with ASC's in general. With the recession of a person's critical faculties there is an attendant decrease in his capacity for reality testing or his ability to distinguish between subjective and objective reality. This, in turn, would tend to create the compensatory need to bolster up his failing faculties by seeking out certain props, support, or guidance in an effort to relieve some of the anxiety associated with the loss of control. In his attempt to compensate for his failing critical faculties, the person comes to rely more on the suggestions of the hypnotist, shaman, demagogue, interrogator,

religious healer, preacher, or doctor, all representing omnipotent authoritative figures. With the "dissolution of self boundaries," which represents another important feature of ASC's, there would also be the tendency for the person to identify vicariously with the authoritarian figure whose wishes and commands are accepted as the person's own. Contradictions, doubts, inconsistencies, and inhibitions tend to diminish (all characteristics of "primary process" thinking), and the suggestions of the person endowed with authority tend to be accepted as concrete reality. These suggestions become imbued with even more importance and urgency owing to the increased significance and meaning attributed both to internal and external stimuli during alterations in consciousness. (53:17)

Alexander and Selesnick (11:28) describe how the Aesculapian priests used the hallucinatory possibilities of the hypnagogic state to induce dreams in those seeking cures in their temples. The two writers duly failed to describe the clinical effects and theoretical conveniences of the hypnagogic state in Freudian temples. It was undoubtedly easier for Freud to induce images, "memories" and associations in patients to confirm his favorite notions by letting them fall into a hypnagogic state. Could it be that Freud was caught in a sort of *folie á deux* with his patients, each reinforcing the delusions of the other?

Lest someone think that Freud was a victim of an impenetrable mystery of psychotherapeutic relationship and not of self-induced, wishful observational blindness, it would be useful to compare the opaque understanding of Freud with that of Sidis, a prominent American psychiatrist and a contemporary of Freud. In a paper published in 1909, Sidis reported in a clear way on the hypnoidal or subwaking state developed by patients relaxing under the instructions of the therapist. Freud, acclaimed as a most superior clinician, remained oblivious to the less easily recognizable influences of the couch. [1] Sidis, on the other hand, had been for years aware of the heightened suggestibility of patients in the twilight state of consciousness, similar to that of hypnotic states. In deference to the fashion of the times to refer mental phenomena to the theory of evolution, Sidis speculates that the hypnoidal state corresponds to the animal states of light sleep which precede the stage of deep sleep. Be that as it may,

Sidis saw clearly the benefits a suggester like Freud could reap from inducing the transitional state between wakefulness and sleep:

> ... in "The Psychology of Suggestion" I pointed out on the strength of a number of experiments that suggestibility can also be induced in the normal waking state. I have also shown that among the conditions of normal and abnormal suggestibility monotony and limitation of activity play an important role. Any arrangement tending to produce monotony and limitation of voluntary activity brings about a state of suggestibility termed by me *subwaking or hypnoidal,* a state in which mental life can be affected with ease. The induction of the state is termed *hypnoidization.* (61:152)

As we shall see in further exposition, the whole psychoanalytic procedure of indoctrination of trainees and patients could thus be subsumed under the term hypnoidization. Sidis observed the phenomena of ego regression and appearance of forgotten memories, which were often described by Freudians as exclusive benefits of psychoanalysis proper:

> In the hypnoidal state consciousness becomes somewhat vaguer than in the waking condition; memory is more diffused, so that experiences apparently long forgotten come in bits and scraps to the foreground of consciousness. Emotional excitement subsides, voluntary activity is changed to passivity, and suggestions meet with little resistance. The subwaking state is above all a rest-state, a state of physical and mental relaxation. (61:152)

Sidis saw the chief curative agent in this physical and mental relaxation, and not in the interpretations and suggestions given by the therapist. In this way Sidis comes very close to the views held by many contemporary psychotherapists. [see Introduction, *Direct Psychotherapy,* v. 3, 50] He also pierced through rationalizations about Freudian therapeutic rituals and perceived psychoanalysis as a special case of hypnoidization: " . . . it is highly probable that Freud's success in the treatment of psychopathic cases is not so much due to psycho-analysis, as to the unconscious use of the hypnoidal state."

(61:161) As a proof of his contention that relaxation, and not verbalizations, is the chief carrier of psychotherapeutic improvement, Sidis sites several cases of severe neurotics who were cured without a word about Freudian notions being suggested to them.

Orne points to another implicit benefit of the couch hoax to the analyst, *i.e.*, facilitating appearance of material threatening to the patient, as is achieved through hypnosis:

> ...in the case of obtaining material otherwise unavailable to consciousness, the therapist assumes the responsibility for patient's verbalizations; the patient feels, "because I'm in hypnosis, I'm not responsible for what I say." In some instances the function of hypnosis might be to legitimatize a change in behavior which the patient wishes to undertake but cannot without an appropriate excuse. As has been pointed out by others, we can ascribe a similar function to the psychoanalytic couch. Not only is the couch historically related to hypnosis, but it may also be related in the structural sense; in that it symbolizes an alteration of the situation which clearly delineates when a patient can feel without responsibility for his verbalized thoughts. The getting up from the couch is somewhat analogous to the hypnotist's waking up the patient when the shared expectation is that he is again to behave socially *i.e.* censor his speech as in everyday life. (12:1102)

4. Psychoanalysis as a concealed hypnotic practice

As Freud was wont to stress, he did not practice hypnotism as part of his later therapy. He did not, that is, use forceful, flamboyant, overt hypnotic techniques; but, in disclaiming the use of hypnotism, he exaggerated the technical differences between a hypnotic and nonhypnotic state.

Wolberg, a prolific writer on hypnosis with forty years of experience, shows that, contrary to Freud's views, hypnosis is far from being a rare state of consciousness. He considers that "hypnotizability is a normal trait, and everyone—healthy, neurotic, or psychotic—can be hypnotized if he is willing and able to focus his mind on the induction stimulus presented to him." (58:61) Wolberg estimates that about ninety percent of people can be hypnotized. Even more surprising is his belief that practically anyone can be a hypnotist:

"Hypnosis is a fantastically easy phenomenon to bring about; the technique is so simple that even a talented child can learn it in a few minutes." (58:87) He describes an eleven-year-old schoolgirl who created great concern among adults when she discovered she could put her grade-school friends in a trance by asking them to concentrate on jigsaw pieces of a vase picture.

Wolberg disposes of a number of misconceptions about hypnosis, which have prevented many observers from realizing that the operations on the couch in trained ("well-analyzed") subjects induce a form of hypnosis. First he points out that the depth of trance varies from light through medium to deep (somnambulistic), and that the criteria for judging the depth are arbitrary. For my thesis, it is important to note that Wolberg considers light trance as practically indistinguishable from the hypnagogic state, which is commonly experienced by subjects on the couch. "The average trance . . . is very much like . . . the normal 'hypnoidal' state." (58:77)

> In this state a person can hear, feel, smell, understand, reason, imagine, and remember quite actively, as readily and effectively as when he has full consciousness. He is fully aware of what is going on around him. He may be either critical and antagonistic or accepting and cooperative, and he may arouse himself if he does not desire to continue in the hypnotic phase.
>
> This may puzzle the person who is being hypnotized, because he usually has the idea that in hypnosis he becomes an automaton, completely at the mercy of the hypnotist. He believes he will simply follow commands and not engage in independent activities. He also has the idea that he is supposed to be "unconscious," as if he were asleep or anesthetized.
>
> It is important to understand that these are misconceptions about hypnosis. A person is never in a condition of unconsciousness during this state; the mind always functions actively.
>
> Yet, during the trance the subject undergoes psychological and physiological experiences that are characteristic of both waking and sleeping. The number of waking or sleep characteristics will depend upon how close to either state the person in hypnosis actually is. At one end of the hypnotic spectrum he is close to wakefulness, and his behavior—the quality and content of thinking and the physiological manifestations—is very similar to the waking condition. This is a light trance. (58:77)

299

Another characteristic of hypnotized subjects explains why very few Freudian subjects and Freudian operators-in-training caught on to what was happening to them while they lay on the couch: "Immediately after the first induction, most subjects—even those who have gone into a somnambulistic trance—will deny having been hypnotized." (58:83)

Wolberg also seems to demonstrate how difficult it is to view phenomena in a way different from what one has been trained to see in them. By circumscribing professional perception, analytic training appears to be analogous to posthypnotic suggestion: it compels the subject to only a particular understanding or action. Wolberg provides a table of therapeutic steps appropriate to various depths of hypnosis. He considers that in the prehypnotic (hypnoidal) stage, which in his view precedes the light trance, one could apply "supportive therapy (reassurance, persuasion, re-education, confession and ventilation) and hypnoanalysis (free association, fantasy induction.)" (58:106) Yet, he does not even suggest that there is a basic similarity between hypnoanalytic and psychoanalytic "free association." He actually postulates that the two are different processes for which different training of patients is required: "Therapists who practice psychoanalysis may *also* train a subject for hypnotic free association." (58:107, my emphasis) It appears that Wolberg, an experienced hypnotist and a professor of psychiatry, had accepted at face value the Freudian assertion that there is the widest possible difference between the states induced on the psychoanalytic couch and hypnotic states. A few pages later, he shows that he was not oblivious to the facts, but that he could not make an inference offensive to his Freudian colleagues; he writes:

There are few objective signs by which the hypnotic state can be differentiated from other states of consciousness. Laboratory studies reveal no reliable chemical criteria to distinguish hypnotic from "normal" physiological variables. Electrical brain (electroencephalographic) and muscle (myographic) tracings, and scrutiny of a wide range of physiological measurements yield ambiguous results. Even the subject's personal account of what he believes is happening to him may be fundamentally no different from what he describes in normal ego states. What is specifically characteristic of hypnosis is difficult to say, apart from the subject's avowal that there is something "different" about it. This cannot be considered too reliable a statement since all psychological states, from excitement to relaxation, may be interpreted by him as distinctive. It should not cause surprise, therefore, if, in surveying the happenings of hypnosis, we find that they do not come from another planet. (58:118)

Salter (13:chapters I, II) also shows that there are no important psychological differences between hypnotic trance and absence of it, and that even thinking is not greatly different.

Whether the eyes are opened or closed, does not represent a distinguishing feature of hypnosis; it can be employed as a coercive, crudely suggestive method leading to violation of the patient's individuality irrespective of eyes, or the posture of the subject. Erickson (55), a seasoned practitioner of hypnosis, describes his extraordinary explorations in hypnotic hypermnesia and amnesia with Aldous Huxley. In these experiments, the famous author would walk to open the door and perform other reactions usually associated with wakeful states, without breaking out of trance.

Freud, altogether, misconceived the hypnotic phenomena and then was pleased to announce that his method had nothing to do with such abuses and charlatanism. He deceived himself and misled others as to the breadth of hypnotic manifestations. We meet here an example of Freud's convenient repression of the undesirable implications of whatever view he currently held. At one point, he was aware of hypnosis as a state "which ranges from light sleepiness to somnambulism, from complete recollection to absolute amnesia." (quoted in 13:8) His later definition misidentifies outward stuporousness as a basic feature of hypnosis. In his determined avoidance of hypnosis, he fails to recognize some important aspects: the heightened perceptivity of hypnotized subjects; their capacity to move and converse while in hypnosis; and their use of it in individualized ways, in accordance with their personality pattern.

Considering the wider implications of hypnosis, it appears that Freud practiced a modified hypnotic procedure without wanting to fully realize what he was doing. It is not difficult to discern that he trained his subjects to attain a semihypnotic state in their interviews.

He induced regression in their ego controls by suggesting they relax bodily and renounce critical thinking while reporting what was passing through their minds without conscious interference. He suggested a state of reverie to them; yet, he wrote, with Breuer in *Studies of Hysteria* of reverie as the "prodromal stage of auto-hypnosis." Even without Freud's suggesting it, the couch and the prone position might be expected to induce autohypnosis, not to mention the hypnotizing effect of droning verbalizations and surrounding silence. Wiesenhütter (15) describes the "light sleepiness" which developed in Coué's subjects through the monotonous repetition of certain self-suggestive formulas. Marcuse points to the repetitive chanting of some mystics as an inducement to hypnotic states. (14:16) The repetitiveness of psychoanalytic procedure is likely to have similar effects, especially with renouncing the conscious controls of thinking.

Freud knew how easily some people are hypnotized. He reports of a woman who came for an eye examination and fell into a trance as soon as the light fell on her eyes. He also knew of Charcot's theory of major and minor hypnosis. Psychological phenomena aroused by psychoanalytic situations belong mostly to the minor hypnotic states. It is difficult to explain how a reputedly sharp observer like Freud could fail to notice his patients exhibiting these hypnotic manifestations after he had ostensibly renounced the practice of hypnosis. In all probability, his strong motivation toward maintaining the good reputation of his method led him to repress awareness of its underlying hypnotic aspects.

In the introduction to Bernheim's *Hypnosis and Suggestion in Psychotherapy*, Freud writes:

> Our natural sleep which Bernheim compares happily with hypnosis, behaves in a similar fashion. As a rule we bring on a sleep by suggestion, by mental preparation and expectation of it; but occasionally it comes upon us without any effort on our part as a result of a physiological condition of fatigue. So too when children are rocked to sleep or hypnotized by being held in a fixed position, it can hardly be a question of mental causation. (2:34)

He was evidently well aware that the kinesthetic stimuli by which sleep had previously been conditioned would lead to a hypnoid state, but he somehow dissociated this knowledge from what he was apparently doing to the patient by keeping him immobilized on the couch. Like his hysterical patients, Freud could, if need be, dissociate his observations.

Some less defensive workers with hypnosis do not blind themselves to these facts. As Freud and his disciples have spread much fog over the role of hypnosis in their procedures, I shall provide several comments and illustrations. Kline defines the regressive features common to hypnosis and Freudian analysis: "The concept of regression as evidence of the hypnotic state becomes rather striking when we review the diminished critical thinking and judgment present in all hypnotic states as well as the emerging hyper-suggestibility and lack of perceptual constancy." (9:82) Dalbiez reported that from session to session, and even within a session, the analysand's mental state "fluctuates between the level of logical thought and a level close to that of hypnosis or dreams." (17, v. 2:92) Dalbiez attributes the (assumed) memory of distant events on the Freudian couch to loosening of logical process and giving way to dreamlike productions: "Several of those whom I have myself analysed have told me spontaneously that they were conscious of being in a special condition distinct from the waking state; one of them had to make efforts to continue speaking, another was scarcely aware of my presence or regarded me as a half-dream-like figure." (17, v. 2:120) Dalbiez confirms his observations by those of Kretschmer, who wrote: "The more completely we relax into passivity, the more nearly does free association approximate to the psychic mechanism of dreams and hypnosis. Linkage by sentences begins to loosen, the verbal formation of thoughts yields noticeably to concrete imagery. . . . " (17, v. 2:92)

Thigpen and Cleckley speak about the clandestine nature of some hypnotic phenomena and their inevitable presence in the psychoanalytic situations:

As Barber has pointed out, hypnotic control (or something very similar to it) may occur in several other ways besides a sudden and dramatic induction into the familiar trance state. He also makes it clear that hypnosis in its less obvious and typical applications can indeed exert powerful influence upon the subject. Though the analytically oriented psychotherapist seeks to avoid exerting overt hypnotic influence upon his patient, it is difficult to see how some of the basic factors involved in hypnosis can be avoided. In ordinary hypnosis they are openly and quickly demonstrated, and are often spectacularly flourished. In prolonged psychotherapy such factors are certainly less overt. But who can say they do not operate insidiously, concealed behind the ostensible framework or the elaborate theoretical structuring of the program, whether or not they are consciously recognized by the patient or by the therapist? It has been said that only a very wise hypnotist can be certain as to who is being hypnotized during the imperfectly understood process that occurs between the practitioner and his subject. (18:105)

Out of his own experience on the couch, Johnson, a psychiatrist, found psychoanalysis to be a "hypno-suggestive process":

I must affirm that I have a most complete grasp and awareness of analytic procedure. For I underwent an analysis (orthodox) for over 10 months with the mounting conviction that the procedure was not scientific. For it soon became evident to me that the keystone of the process, the "free associations," was bogus. Let me emphasize that this is the bedrock of my argument which stands or falls with this thesis. I was soon made to understand by means of questions put to me, by means of "suggestion," emotional attitudes, eloquent silences and other cues, that certain of my productions were useless (resistance) and that other productions were good (*i.e.* had negative conditioning impact). ["He was quickly through with his associations; so the analyst tried to help him out. She suggested that perhaps . . . " (From French's *Integration of Behavior,* p. 81).] An analysis conducted by correspondence like an international chess game (or otherwise where cues were carefully screened out) would never work. This is because psychoanalysis is an active hypno-suggestive process, . . . (16:468)

In a nonpartisan view of Freudian free association, Ludwig classifies it as one of the many Altered States of Consciousness, together with meditative relaxation, "daydreaming, drowsiness, 'Brown study' or reverie; mediumnistic and autohypnotic trances (e.g. among Indian fakirs, mystics, Pythian priestesses, etc); profound esthetic experiences; . . . reading trance, especially with poetry; . . . nostalgia; music-trance . . . profound cognitive and muscular relaxation, such as during floating on water or sun-bathing." (53) In this context, the "free association" might appear degraded from an esoteric process to be attained through expensive lying on the couch to one of the mentally ineffective states enjoyed by beachcombers, effete esthetes and indolent daydreamers.

In concluding this section on psychoanalysis as a clandestine hypnotic operation, it is most important to grasp fully the potent indoctrinating influence of autosuggestion and heterosuggestion upon the subject's beliefs and reactions. Human suggestibility and the unconscious or deliberate unawareness of changes in mental content has been a most useful tool in Freudwashing both the patients and the public. The principal vehicle of deception is the susceptibility to react to symbols as if they were real objects ("reification"), and the tendency to ingratiate oneself with authority figures.

The extraordinary proneness to mistake symbols for reality might be illustrated by Wolberg's (58:117) allergic patient who showed a full-blown nasal and respiratory reaction to a plastic rose. He could not believe his senses when shown that the flower was artificial. His organism reacted to the representation of the flower as if it were the real thing, with plenty of troublesome pollen. In an analogous way, Freudian patients are genuinely convinced that they themselves have seen the deviant psychological forms when these are purportedly discovered by the analyst in their "free associations" and grafted onto them by interpretations.

The other component of psychoanalytic brainwashing is the common infantile compliant reaction to an assumed authority figure. Wolberg (58:126) made a posthypnotic suggestion to a patient that he would experience hives on forearm. The patient reported a few days later that he had indeed developed a case of hives. The form of his "hives" was not of regular appearance; it looked like scratches and skin irritation. The patient had no explanation except that he woke up with them that morning. Under hypnosis, however, he revealed that he had taken a walk through the forest and had rubbed ivy leaves against his forearm. Evidently he had repressed this event in his desire to please his therapist. Freudian analysands and subjects of Communist brainwashing conduct similar operations on their dreams and memories in order to get them in line with the wishes of the analyst and the brainwasher respectively. As we shall see later on, Freud was aware of compliant dreams and "free" associations of patients eager to supply the "evidence" for his pet theories, but he chose to rationalize them away.

Some psychoanalytic and hypnotic subjects show an extraordinary tenacity in trying to maintain the compliant fiction once they have accepted the covert or overt suggestions as genuine experience. "If, for example, an obsession or delusion is introduced into the mind of a normal subject, he will defend it vigorously with fabrications and rationalizations. Even absurd or foolish ideas may seem sound to the subject if it is suggested to him that he will remember them as true facts after he awakens from the trance." (58:136) Wolberg, suggested to a medical student in a demonstration experiment of hypnosis that he had attended the Kentucky Derby a few days earlier and had won a large sum of money. The trance was terminated and the student, upon a signal given by the experimenter, injected into the conversation his winning at the Derby. Other students pointed out that he could not have done it as the race took place several months after the date he quoted for the lucky event. He contrived an explanation about several races that were, by exception, run that year. His colleagues tried to dissuade him about the reality of his report, telling him how he had been with them in several classes at that time. He countered with additional "explanation" that he had taken a plane after classes to go to the Derby and had flown back the same night. He stuck to his "memory" in spite of all logical arguments. "Later on he had amnesia for this incident and was amused when informed of his behavior." (58:136) The numerous enthusiastic volumes of psychoanalytic subjects reporting the profound discoveries made on the Freudian couch might indicate that the analysands never recover from the particular amnesia about how they reached their illuminations.

It is also unfortunate regarding misdirections of psychological science by Freudian psychoanalysis, that the influencing of the subjects on the couch takes place in private chambers, without any witnesses to the experiments. The self-deception of both the operators and the analysands, could thus never be discovered. Freud, his patients, and his students remained convinced that their fantasies and fabrications were solid "scientific" facts.

The hypnotic experiments also throw light on the mechanism of pressure toward compliance on Freudian couch. Wolberg reports on artificial neurosis induced on a noncompliant subject. He had given him the suggestion that he would misspell his own name upon seeing the word "psychiatry." Wolberg had considerable difficulty in bringing him out of hypnosis. The subject shook and trembled violently. Trying to relieve him, Wolberg said that he need not comply with the original suggestion if he does not want. When he was finally wakened up, the student shook even more violently. He was re-hypnotized and direct suggestion was given to remove tremors. The shaking diminished, but he complained of nausea, tenseness and apprehensiveness. Wolberg wrote "psychiatry" on the blackboard, the subject reached for his pencil, then checked himself and brought the hand back. His discomfort grew worse. The hypnotist suggested that he had better write his name to gain relief from tension. He took the pencil, but the hand shook so violently that he could not write. With the utmost effort over several minutes he managed to write his name, and misspelled! After complying, his shaking disappeared. He explained that he was very sensitive to anyone misspelling his name and resisted doing it himself. As a consequence he suffered a bad case of artificial neurosis. The experience of the neurotic turmoil induced by psychoanalysts' pressure in Wortis, Campbell, Natenberg and others (chapter V) show plainly the weapon by which Freudians terrorize their patients into submission and enforced enlightenment.

5. Hypnosis, subtle and pervasive

Perhaps to avoid the suspicion of hypnosis and suggestion, Freud compared his method to "conversation." (2:57) Two French psychiatrists, Von Monakow and Mourgue, were misled into accepting the psychoanalytic situation as "conversation." Dalbiez criticizes them:

The term conversation to denote analytic investigation could not have been worse chosen; it is calculated utterly to mislead those who have not had personal experience of the obvious difference between waking thought and that which results from voluntary suspense of self-criticism and self-guidance. Our comparison between toxic, hypnotic and psychoanalytical inhibition enables us to form an exact idea of the nature of the last mentioned. (17, v. 2:93)

Other hypnotists and psychologists less famous than Freud, have seen the phenomenon more clearly and have been able to identify it without dissimulation. Arons (20) recommends using suggestions to relax completely as "the best and easiest disguised method of inducing hypnosis." Steiner (21) uses a similar method without disguise in her "Self-Hypnosis through Relaxation." In training his subjects in autohypnosis (which he distinguishes from self-hypnosis, where overt autosuggestion is used), Salter instructs them to repeat while relaxing "I feel very comfortable. My arms are so relaxed . . . my feet feel very relaxed and heavy . . . my whole body feels so comfortable and relaxed." (22:429) McCord (23) describes several cases of inducing hypnotic states in subjects seated on chairs who were instructed to resist hypnosis, but were told to relax and concentrate on tasks like reading, typing, and hand dexterity tests, while hypnotic suggestions were given. Evans (56) demonstrated in three studies involving 246 subjects that instructions to relax induce hypnotic states quite comparable in depth to those brought about by standard methods of hypnotic induction.

Wittels, one of the early psychoanalysts, describes various situations in which a hypnotic state may develop, even though it would not be recognized by uninformed observers:

Good mediums soon learn to hypnotize themselves. Many to this end gaze fixedly at an object; others succeed without aid merely through the will directed upon the end. Others resort to a living hypnotist, who frequently is unaware for what mischief he is being employed. An old man with sparkling cataract spectacles sits in a cafe and writes in a notebook. As he does so he moves his lower lip, as old people often do, and from time to time carries the pencil to his mouth to moisten it, in the manner of days of yore. A younger man, who has no acquaintance with the older one and to whom the old man pays no attention whatsoever, sits at a neighboring table and is unable to turn his glance away from the spectacles and the pencil which travels between lip and paper. He has fallen into a kind of hypnosis, which the old man, if it occurred to him, could intensify as he would.—An insurance agent calls upon a man and explains to him the advantages of a policy. After a short time the man no longer hears what is being said but slips into a twilight state, which is produced by the even murmur or the peculiar harshness of the agent's voice. In this state the man is far more at the mercy of the agent than were he to evaluate the advantages and disadvantages of the policy offered.—Many a man is almost completely unaware of what an attractive girl is saying, as he listens to the enchanting sound of her voice and watches the play of her lips and eyes. The girl holds sway and continues to hold sway without the content of her speech ever coming into question. One observes in such cases that everything is accomplished by the hypnotized person. The second person becomes a hypnotist against his will—apart from those not-so-rare cases where an agent, superior, or even a beautiful woman knows and consciously exerts her power over minds. (24:301, 302)

The whole secret is in concentration, with relaxation. Wittels also compares the state of lovers to that of hypnotic rapport. (24:312) The state of Freudian transference is often little different from the state of being in love, literally or figuratively.

One can see how easily hypnotic trance or trancelike states could be induced in a subject lying on a couch and concentrating on his associations. One such subject, Knight, describes his experiences:

As the average hourly session developed, my associations would become more dissociated from my current life. I would frequently lapse into a semi-dream state, a half-stupor from which I would arise with a start when Doctor Maxwell interjected a comment or question. During the half-dream state the associations would frequently revert, as do our dreams, to events of childhood, some almost forgotten, some completely repressed. (4:46)

Obviously he did not know, and the already conditioned analyst did not or could not tell him, that he was in a state of self-induced as well as situationally produced hypnosis.

One of my patients, who had tried psychotherapy in another city beforehand, used occasionally to fall into a state distinctly different from the usual conversational, alert posture which we maintained in the interviews. He would half-close his eyes, assume a droning voice, and begin free-associating. When, after observing him for about twenty minutes, I inquired about the change, he said that he had apparently fallen back into the habit established with the former therapist who used to hypnotize him and suggest free-associating. He was apparently so trained to fall into a trancelike state through repetitions in former interviews that he could induce it now even without being instructed to do so.

Why did Freud not mention such obvious changes in ego states that resulted from his procedures? Since he stood for much more unpopular causes on many occasions, it is hardly probable that he avoided these facts because hypnotism was in disrepute. Kline (94) finds a plausible explanation in Freud's emotional, unformulated reaction to the complications of the analyst-patient relationship which hypnosis fosters. Freud ostensibly gave up hypnosis after his servant happened to observe a woman patient embracing him as she awakened from a trance. This was probably merely the last straw in Freud's disappointments with the method. Kline suggests another dissatisfaction probably only partially recognized by Freud, *i.e.,* the potency of transference in hypnosis, which makes the patient more acutely aware of the emotional reactions of the therapist. Most psychotherapists could not tolerate such an openness to the patient, particularly Freud, who was in many ways an emotionally inhibited individual. He found it was easier to maintain his anonymity with the patient by keeping him in a less regressed, allegedly "wakeful" state. However, after finding a way to maintain a dominant position over the patient, Freud chose to believe that hypnotic aspects were completely eradicated, and he deluded himself and others into this false understanding.

Of course, this misperception was useful in his work with patients. Without realizing it, or at least without admitting it, Freud had hit upon a use of suggestion more powerful than hypnosis. Barber (25) finds in a review of research studies on the effects of hypnosis and motivational suggestions upon strength and endurance, that hypnotic induction, if not followed by suggestion, did not increase endurance; the suggestion, however, increased it, even without hypnosis. In continuation of research on suggestion and hypnosis, Barber and Calverley (26) demonstrated that permissive suggestions and suggestions to stimulate amnesia were more effective in influencing the mental operation of subjects than when hypnotic induction was added to the procedure.

Freud also made the most potent component of the hypnotic relationship, the transference, into the cornerstone of his thinking and practice of psychotherapy, without explicitly admitting that he was engaged in a hypnotic procedure.

6. Transference as a hypnotic state

The essence of the relationship between hypnotist and subject seems to be a profound, childlike dependency upon the dominant partner. There is an implicit trust like that of an infant for his mother or a parent figure. Accepting the role of a helpless individual, a good subject suspends his self-directiveness in favor of suggestions from the hypnotist. There is a temporary or lasting subjection of one individual to another. This description of the hypnotic relationship can hardly be distinguished from transference phenomena in psychoanalysis. Weitz, observing the much less intensive transference experienced in counseling, recognized its strong dependency features which lead to equating "permission" with "requirement": " ... this permits (requires?) the client to begin responding in new ways." (27:505) This is also a basic description of the state of transference relationship: the permission has the import of requirement. The trained and willing servant need not be told everything; he readily seeks and catches any clues from the master.

A number of writers have written on the common features of the hypnotic state and transference. Freud himself wrote in his autobiography: "We can easily recognize it [transference] as the dynamic factor that the hypnotists have named 'suggestibility' which is the agent of hypnotic rapport ... " (28:76) Dr. Loy writes to Jung in 1913: " ... from your three cases I cannot draw any ... distinction between

'susceptibility to the hypnotist' and 'transference to the analyst.' "
(29:262) Wolstein (30) notices that transference has sometimes the
quality of posthypnotic suggestion. Fisher (31) had the impression
that analyst and patient sometimes behave like hypnotist and subject.
MacAlpine (32), an experienced psychoanalyst, observed that
"analytic transference is a derivative of hypnosis," produced in a way
similar to hypnotic trance.

Another aspect of transference that parallels hypnosis is the
training necessary to achieve its full and efficient manifestation. A
common observation in hypnosis is that with repeated training the
subject becomes more and more conditioned to reach a trance sooner
and deeper. Charcot had left this preparation and implicit training to
his assistants and to expectations current among Salpêtrière patients
and doctors about hysterical symptoms, while he demonstrated only
with already perfected hypnotic subjects. Psychoanalysts, however,
must act as their own assistants in preparing patients for final
performance.

Psychoanalysis is a system of beliefs which the analyst needs to
graft on the patient. According to Harrington,

> He must create what a theologian might call the will to believe:
> he must produce in the patient a desire to see the things he would
> have him see and to believe the things he would have him believe.
> But how is he to do this? What force is there in the patient's mind
> which can be turned to account to produce such a result? (33:24)

How is this difficult feat of changing the beliefs of a patient to be
accomplished? By transference, Freud answers.

> But how does this transference or falling in love with the
> analyst help the patient to overcome his resistances and get cured
> of his neurosis? The answer is easy enough. If the patient is in
> love with the analyst, he wishes to find the things the analyst
> wishes to find and to believe the things the analyst wishes him to
> believe. (33:25)

In analysis, the modification of a patient's concepts through
interpretations does not even begin in a serious way until the subject

regresses and his ego organization is undermined by irrationality enhanced through free-associating and the infantile feelings revived in transference. Transference is to the analyst a symptom of the encroaching ego softening. "When shall we begin our disclosures to the patient?" asks Freud.

> When is it time to unfold to him the hidden meaning of his thoughts and associations, to initiate him into the postulates of analysis and its technical devices? The answer to this can only be: Not until a dependable transference, a well-developed *rapport*, is established in the patient. The first aim of the treatment consists in attaching him to the treatment and to the person of the physician. To ensure this one need do nothing but allow him time . . . such an attachment develops in the patient of itself . . . (2:152)

Johnson sees that transference is a gangway thrown to the patient's mind to get the analyst's notions over into the patient. It is a means of conversion to Freudian ideology, to the peculiar faith:

> The permanent personality changes which attend a successful psychoanalysis are brought about when the patient interprets the dynamisms in accordance with the conventions of the analytical system which is being used. . . . It would almost seem that the successful transference in all instances would depend upon the patient's acceptance of a special gnosis closely allied to the theological concept of faith (pistis), a complex system of philosophical fictions, the acceptance of which calls for something very close to religious conversion. (34:325)

When transference becomes evident, the analyst can be relatively certain that he can start to inject his more outlandish interpretations —suggestions—into the subject's mind, "to initiate him into the postulates of analysis and its technical devices." The conditioning process is likely to proceed relatively rapidly from that point on. Thus, Runestam wrote of a "radical interference with man's psyche which is characteristic of psychoanalysis." (35:175)

Many "successfully analyzed" subjects, patients and analysts alike, continue to be bound to their analysts in childlike ways. Anderson

(36:1) dutifully practiced what her elders had taught her until she grew to see the issues independently and differently. Campbell tried in vain to carry on "psychotherapy" in the way he had been taught during his personal Freudwashing. The majority of psychoanalysts, however, remain in a state of childish emulation of their training analyst or of a composite image of Freud and the classical analysts. Early analysts spoke of "father-hypnosis" and "mother-hypnosis" as continuations of parental influences in adults. (15) They failed to apply the concept to "analyst-hypnosis." Fleming, a staff member of the Chicago Institute for Psychoanalysis, testifies to the lasting transference mold created by the peculiar Freudian training:

> Most young psychiatrists who have had analysis or are in analysis during the course of their residency training tend to imitate their analyst. They tend to identify with him and to insist upon interpreting their own behavior and the behavior of their patients as if it has the same significance as their behavior with their analyst." (37:219)

Knight (4), reduced to a state of severe dependency, addresses Dr. Maxwell by name and title in practically every paragraph to the end of the analysis, just as a three-year-old boy, full of adoration for his "daddy," delights in pronouncing the glorious name. In these circumstances, an otherwise intelligent and rebellious woman, can ask the therapist questions as simple as those she might have asked her daddy when she was four. (38) Such infantilization of the patient is not the result of a "technical deviation" of American analysts. It is an inevitable consequence of Freud's method. Wolf-Man, analyzed by Freud in the period of 1910-1914, puts it quite plainly: "So I found in the person of Professor Freud a new father with whom I had an excellent relationship." (62:89)

Naturally, then, the analysis must be of long duration to reduce patients to an infantile state of dependency in Freudian transference, a supposedly therapeutic process. In fact, patients depend on the analyst as dope addicts and alcoholics depend on the source of their "life." Saul observes: " . . . patients become addicted to psychoanalysis as they become addicted to alcohol and drugs and for the same basic reason. Somewhere Freud said or wrote that at first he could not induce patients to come for analysis but later he could not get them to terminate." (39:179) (This is mentioned by Freud in 2:142.) Freud's method of regressing patients kept them longer in therapy, providing steady clients as well as guinea pigs for his enthusiastic "investigations." The hoax was played consistently and with dignity, even though at the patients' expense.

7. Patient's conversion to Freudism

Perls considers the growth toward maturity the main psycho-therapeutic goal and objects strongly to infantilizing the patients. He marvels at the blindness of psychoanalysts which lets them walk without concern into regular neurotic regressive traps.

> The neurotic cannot conceive of himself as a self-supportive person, able to mobilize his potential in order to cope with the world. He looks for environmental support through direction, help, explanations and answers. He mobilizes not his own resources, but his means of manipulating the environment— helplessness, flattery, stupidity and other ways of more or less subtle control in order to get that support. The psychoanalyst plays right into the hands of such behavior by disregarding the essence of human relationships and by turning any relationship into an infantile one, like father figure, incest, super-ego dominance. The patient is not made responsible, but the un-conscious, the Oedipus complex or whatnot receives the cathexis of cause and responsibility. (54)

Freud was not interested in the therapeutic aspects of his work. He confessed: "I became a therapist against my will." (5:8) His chief interest in working with patients was to condition them to produce for him "proofs" for his pet hunches. He kept this motive mostly out of his awareness. As we have already seen, he was a master at repressing any threats to his ambition to become the great and shocking psychologist of his era. Both Freud and his patients played blindly the roles in the scheme of Freud's messianic ambitions. It was not a wily fraud; it was a make-believe, a hoax.

Sargant, a British psychiatrist, provides an analysis of the Freudian game designed to convert the analysand by means of transference:

A patient under psychoanalytic treatment, for instance, is made to lie on a couch, where daily for months, and perhaps years, he is encouraged to indulge in "free association of ideas." He may also then be asked: "What does 'umbrella' mean to you?"—"Uncle Toby." "What does 'apple' mean to you?"—"The girl next door." These answers may perhaps also be found to be of sexual significance. He has to go back over his past sexual peccadilloes, and relive other incidents which arouse intense anxiety, fear, guilt, or aggression, especially in childhood. As the analysis proceeds, and emotional storms perhaps mount, the patient becomes more and more sensitized to the analyst. So-called "transference situations," both positive and negative, are built up psychologically; often assisted in the early stages of treatment by the fatigue and debilitation resulting from the anxiety aroused. The patient's tensions and dependence on the analyst may be greatly increased. A stage is finally reached when resistance weakens to the therapist's interpretations of a patient's symptoms, and he may start to accept them much more readily. He now believes and acts upon theories about his nervous condition which, more often than not, contradict his former beliefs. Many of the individual's usual patterns of behavior may also be upset by this process, and replaced by new ones. These changes are consolidated by making the patient's behavior as consistent as possible with the new "insight" gained. (40:77, 78)

One of my patients had a sister who was psychoanalyzed more than ten years earlier. However, the beliefs imposed by her Freudian indoctrinator proved to be stable in the subject. She inquired of her sister how her therapy with me was progressing. She asked her if we had gotten into castration anxieties and Oedipal troubles. As we were by that time in about fiftieth interview, and her sister told her that we had not touched on such matters, the Freudian convert expressed grave doubts about the value of such nontherapy for my patient.

Freud defined transference as the revival of childhood feelings in relationship to the analyst. This is only one meaning of the term. A meaning more realistic and to the point is that the analyst transfers his psychological and philosophical views upon the patient. This aspect of transference throws further light upon psychoanalysis as basically a process of conversion, an altering of the patient's mind.

That is why Freud maintained that there is no psychoanalysis without transference. (28) The patient's conversion to the therapist's views is possible only when the neurotic subject develops strong positive attachment to the analyst. Freud confirmed it himself:

> In so far as his transference bears a positive sign, it clothes the physician with authority, transforms itself into faith in his findings and his views. Without this kind of transference or with a negative one, the physician and his arguments would never even be listened to. Faith repeats the history of its own origin, it is a derivative of love and at first it needed no arguments. . . . Without this support arguments have no weight with the patients. . . . A human being is therefore on the whole only accessible to influence, even on the intellectual side, in so far as he is capable of investing objects with libido. (2:153)

The essence of psychoanalysis is revealed here by its author: *change by faith via libido.*

8. Glad headshrinking

"If a patient has a good and trusting relationship with an individual this increases his suggestibility. Suggestion is the process of influencing the patient to accept uncritically an attitude or idea." (59:557) One can imagine that in the induced states of pervasive reverence, the ideas expressed by the analyst, his overt or implied approval or disapproval, the bits of alleged revelation by interpretation, are taken as authoritative and often welcome suggestion. The therapist, as Meerloo warns, "must be continuously aware of the impact his statements and deductions have on his patients who often listen in awe to the doctor who is for them omnipotent and magic." (41:359) Soon there results a confusion in the peculiar Diad about who brought out what, and the subject's mind becomes molded more and more in the likeness of the analyst. It is a great comfort for the analysand to anticipate his analyst's expectations and produce discoveries, memories, observations, dreams, and fantasies to gladden the heart of his "daddy." Menninger admits: " . . . there comes a time when we (analysts) begin to observe that the patient is talking on,

317

telling us memories, fantasies, dreams, and experiences not so much to please himself . . . as for the reason that he wishes to please *us.*" (42:111)

Ehrenwald sees dreams produced in psychotherapy as mainly the products of "doctrinal compliance" to the theoretical position of the therapist:

> How can we be sure that it is not the effect of suggestion; empathic communication with his therapist, or operant reinforcement, or tele or telepathic leakage? In short, how are we able to rule out the basic methodological objection that his productions are not of the nature of genuine clinical data, but merely reflect the preconceived ideas of his therapist and, by indirection, of the school of thought to which he owes his allegiance? (45)

It is not hard to answer Ehrenwald's question: the objection cannot be "ruled out," since the data in analysis are not "genuine" but primarily products of the transference of the therapist's ideas upon the patient. Kennedy also sees the distorting effects of transference:

> When the analyst makes interpretations, the patient's unconscious may all too willingly comply by furnishing associations in the form of fantasies, dreams and selected memories which serve either submissively to corroborate the interpretation (though it may be wrong) or defiantly to corroborate the interpretation *because* it is wrong. And under the influence of the counter-transference the analyst himself may be seduced into accepting the patient's own subtly and indirectly proffered interpretations, or he may project his own unconscious conflicts on to the patient and end up by treating the wrong person. How is it possible to get out of this quagmire? (43:274)

Kennedy does not provide a solution, and most likely there is none. The analyst and his subject are bogged in the quagmire of the Freudian process of conversion.

The analysand is encouraged to proceed in the direction of "successful analysis" by the analyst's expression of agreement, confirmation, and subdued delight, none of which is unobserved by the sensitized dependent partner. Masserman describes this process of the patient's acquiring "insight" as "representing that mutually happy state in which the patient professes acceptance of the current formulations of his therapist." (44:324)

The infantilized subject goes on "freely" growing mentally into the enlightened state of his guru. And the guru is gratified by developments that verify his views by resulting in another enlightened human being, now capable of seeing through the maya veil.

One of the benefits of his otherwise futile Freudian analysis was for Johnson a clearer understanding of the shock therapy which is carried out on the couch by means of anxiety-arousing and guilt-arousing accusations or suspicions of ugly incestual desires, of latent homosexuality and any other depraved, shameful, and threatening promptings. They serve to scare a patient out of his wits by the awful things which the analyst "discovers" in him, and he clings for his dear (psychological) life to the only savior he knows who can deliver him from the beast within his breast. Johnson discerns behind the Freudian smoke screen of theoretical rationalizations the role which the guided "free" associations play in psychoanalytic headshrinking by shocking (deconditioning) the patient into a different, presumably less unhealthy way of thinking:

> For in psychoanalysis there are no "free" associations. The patient, if he desires to get better, quickly learns what he is to talk about, he learns that certain kinds of associations are worthless (resistance) while other associations have value, the most valuable in the Freudian scheme being the associations with the hardest hitting negative conditioning impact. . . . These valued associations in the Freudian method often are produced after long interludes of "resistance," and, in the cold light of scientific observation, are nothing more than a tissue of orthopsychiatric fictions (to use Vaihinger's term) which, in their deconditioning impact, bespatter the symptom of unwanted character trait with incest horror, emasculation phantasies, faeces-smearing, etc., until such symptom or character trait is broken up. Moreover only when the patient is convinced of the complete rationality of the process can he be said to have full "insight." What is more, in the Freudian method, only the bulls-eyes count; the tangential

hits such as the true cause-and-effect relationships between symptom and cause of symptom, causes which may be religious, sociological, vocational, or existential, have little value. This may be why the more reasonable, the more scientific derivatives of the Freudian method take longer to bring about results. One can go over the true causes of symptoms with neurotics at great length before results are obtained, whereas a few shots of incest horror or other necrotizing agent injected into the area of the symptom will work wonders. But this happens only when the patient is willing not only to handle his own syringe (under the expert guidance of the analyst) but also produces his own necrotizing agent. (34:37)

There could be no reasonable objection to such presumably wholesome influence upon a less mature human being, unless the procedures and contents were announced as new scientific discoveries about human nature, as Jones put it, "after thousands of years of fumbling." The mixture of the investigator's hunches and fantasies, called interpretations, with the subject's own productions, makes it look like the fumbling has continued, the protests of its supporters notwithstanding.

It has not been an easy matter for me to arrive at the conclusions expressed so far. It was a stunning experience to realize the enormous misrepresentation of the psychoanalytic process that is carried on in medical and graduate schools in this country, in Freudian textbooks, papers, and lectures. An amazing net of rationalizations and officially sanctioned views had mushroomed, preventing an objective appraisal of Freudian practices. The kind of self-deception and deception of others which is at the heart of psychoanalysis will be considered in the next chapter and remainder of this volume. The gist of it is that psychoanalysis is no analysis at all; it is rather an imposition of Freudian ideology upon patient's mind—a brainwashing, a hoax.

Notes to Chapter Seven

1. Sidis was also superior to Freud in recognizing that relaxation is one of the main curative factors in therapy and that the insight, on

which Freud laid so much store, was an unessential operation in psychotherapy. Sidis sounds quite modern in demoting insight from the position of major curative achievement:

> ... Important, however, as the following-up of the history or of the psychogenesis of the symptoms may be, both to the physician and to the patient, for an intelligent and scientific compre-hension of the case, *it does not cure,* as some are apt to claim, *the psychopathic malady.* The value of tracing the growth of the disease to its very germs lies entirely in the insight gained into the nature of the symptom-complex. *The tracing of the psychogenesis had no special therapeutic virtues,* as the Germans claim, but, like all theoretical knowledge, is of the utmost importance for a clear understanding of the causation of the psychopathic state, thus helping materially in the treatment of the case. (61:154)

Chapter VIII

SUGGESTION—A BASIC TOOL OF FREUDISM

. . . since the therapist as parent surrogate assumes a position of preeminence, and his every pronouncement comes to the patient from Mt. Olympus, he can influence the patient's feelings and behavior in many ways that have nothing to do with "pure gold of psychoanalysis."

Hans H. Strupp, Ph.D., Professor of Psychology (37:38)

The fundamental fallacy will be discovered in the concept of "free" associations, the basic concept upon which the entire superstructure is built and upon which all the scientific pretensions of psychoanalysis are based.

These "free" associations are in practice channeled into a definite and restricted range of categories and are guided and given value and stress by the system of preoccupations which the analysand quickly comes to perceive in the mind of the analyst.

H.K. Johnson, M.D. (1:335)

. . . the unconscious ideas of the patient are more often than not the conscious ideas of the therapist.

Erwin W. Strauss, M.D. (33:5)

1. Interpretation as suggestion

Bailey, in his customary straightforward and succinct way puts this issue in a nutshell: "Freud also boasted that he had abandoned suggestion but invented a very powerful form of suggestion which he called interpretation." (2:51) Kushner, an M.D. with his vision unencumbered by indoctrination through graduate schools of psychiatry and psychology, sees plainly that "free association" is just a screen behind which the analyst manipulates patients after they get caught in the trap of transference. He sounds angry at Freudian ability to confuse people by deft use of words:

322

In the hands of Freud, "free association" degenerates into just a meaningless babble, as the physician's mind is already made up before the patient's story begins. . . . Freud, who decried the methods of Liébeault and Bernheim of treating their patients by hypnosis and suggestibility, himself uses the method of suggestion but calls it "free association" and "transference"—just a different name for the same therapeutic method. (27:95, 96)

Janet, having no need to dissimulate, showed how omnipresent suggestion is in doctor-patient relationships, and why the Freudian undercover form of suggestion is apt to influence the patient even more potently than overt suggestion:

The International Society of Medical Psychology and Psychotherapy, when meeting at Brussels in 1910, devoted itself to the study of the nature of suggestion, but was unable to arrive at definite conclusions upon all points . . . Doubtless some suggestions have an imperative character, but it is no less certain that well-marked suggestions can be effected without anything like an order; in fact, suggestion by insinuation is often far more potent. . . . That is why, for some time past, the general tendency has been to avoid arousing attention when making suggestions. Many authorities have noticed that in certain patients suggestions made by insinuation, made gently without attracting attention, succeed better than imperative suggestions. I have myself written at considerable length about suggestions of this kind, terming them "suggestions by distraction." A great many subjects who are not ordinarily cataleptic will keep the arm raised if we raise it gently without complicated actions by standing behind them and suggesting the actions in low tones while they are talking to someone else. Let me recall the case of Ne., to whom the utterance of bad language was effectively suggested in this way. Suggestion by distraction is commoner than most people suppose; and in many instances, instead of associating suggestion with excess of attention, we should be inclined rather to associate it with distraction or absence of mind. (3:264)

Janet reported these experiences in the early 90s—and Freud knew about them. For seventy years Freudians have been turning their gaze away from these patent clinical facts. A decade ago, the topic of suggestion was still part of a collective repression of psychoanalysts. Commenting on a symposium held at New York University, Ducasse observes: "Strangely... suggestion was hardly mentioned at all... either in the papers presented at the symposium or in the discussions of them." (4:319)

By 1972 some Freudians appear to have learned nothing from the rich literature on suggestion, an attitude which is demonstrably present in all human relationships, particularly psychotherapy and psychoanalysis. Writing in an otherwise highly objective journal, a psychiatrist presents without bashfulness the official psychoanalytic thesis that the analyst only "digs" and "finds" the Freudian ores in the patient's psyche. In the light of perceptions of other discerning observers who knew that the analyst had previously "salted the mine," these assertions appear, to say the least, naive:

> The work of psychoanalysis is much like that of archeology. The archeologist digs in the sand carefully and diligently to discover what is underneath. No matter how patiently and carefully he digs, he can only unearth treasures if they are there. If the site is barren, he must fail. Some archeologists dig poorly, and others give up prematurely. These characteristics help to separate the mediocre from the gifted. A gifted analyst correctly identifies good sites and digs productively rather than destructively. (36:18)

In its early history, critics were more aware of psychoanalysis being essentially a suggestion procedure. [See, for example, Wolgemuth's clear perception of this issue in *Freud's Phallic Cult*, chapter III (25)] Later, when Freud's system gained ascendance, the originally sharp perception of observers was blurred. Most professionals became deluded, like the courtiers of Andersen's story who admired the emperor's nonexistent clothes. It took a child, with perception undistorted by suggestion, to see the factual situation. There were more clear-sighted children in the courts of psychology and psychiatry before the young Freudian emperor grew to be the haughty monarch he is today. Janet reports that at the beginning of this century:

> Aschaffenburg's idea is that Freud must question his patients regarding their sexual life in a peculiarly impressive manner; that he must influence them by suggestion in one way or another, so

that he gets from them the answers he wants; that he must take the patient's most trivial words concerning it, catch them on the wing, pin them down, put them into their places in the mental constellation he is manufacturing. (3:620)

Even Pfister, one of the few Christian fans of early psychoanalysis, hints at the same idea, *i.e.,* that the psychological data are largely colored by the preconceptions of the interviewer. In a letter written to Freud in 1912, Pfister speaks of dissension with Jung and expresses his allegiance to Freud. Then he adds: "I wonder what sort of technique he uses to arrive at such views." (5:58) On another occasion Freud confirmed indirectly that in this respect he is not different from Jung. He admits in 1908 that it is he who shapes the memories of his subjects: "Without an analysis, it is impossible to elucidate the childhood memories; for these memories are incorrectly focused by the individual himself." (23:282)

Two recent observers of psychoanalytic planting of ideas show what that "focusing" means. The game played in this section is called *Oedipus* (P=patient, T=therapist):

P: Today, when I was coming here, I dropped my umbrella.
T: How did that happen?
P: I had this big package to carry, and it was too much.
T: Very Oedipal . . .
By the time the session is over, T has successfully directed P to the insight that the umbrella, a phallic symbol, was really his father, whom he wished as a child, to "drop," or "get rid of"; that the package, being a container of something, was in truth the womb; and that the desire on P's part to "carry" this womb and not "drop it" proves his neurotic attachment to his mother. Since it is difficult to explain why any person in the rain, loaded with umbrella and large parcel, and rushing toward a destination might *not* experience some trouble, it is best to play a quick round of Oedipus in order to get the problem out of the way. Yet T has, by purely analytic standards, been impressive. (38:58)

Wiesenhütter (6), not particularly burdened by overreverence for Freudism, points to the additional suggestive effect on the analysand of the denial of suggestion by the analyst. Suggestion seems to work better if both the suggester and the subject are unaware of it, but especially the subject, as we shall see later.

2. *Both the analyst and the patient are fooled in psychoanalogy*

Harrington provides a clear analysis of patient reeducation through clandestine suggestion in psychoanalysis. Worth quoting fully, Harrington's exposition is basic to an understanding of psychoanalysis as a veritable brainwashing process. The patient is trained to use the primitive mode of thinking by analogies in which anything can pass for valid. The analyst does not have any guilt feelings about leading his patient down to an aboriginal level of logic, as that is the logic he uses continually in arriving at his "insights" and interpretations. After all, Freud achieved fame by building his theories largely on such a "logic." [see *Freud's Non-science,* chapter IV, (26)]

Harrington grasped with unusual clarity the process of subtle, mostly indirect, indoctrination through psychoanalytic practice; the gist of it being that the covert Freudian manipulator is in turn covertly manipulated by the patient, and both feel highly gratified with the game especially as it is carried out under the guise of science:

> ...when a girl makes a practice of stopping clocks and watches before going to bed at night, he (the psychoanalyst) observes the analogy between the ticking timepiece and the throbbing clitoris, and so is enabled to see that this act is due to a desire to avoid sexual excitement. [This is one of Freud's analogies—"interpretations."] Now, since in psychoanalytic procedure the discovery of unconscious desires is dependent on the perception of these analogies, the first thing necessary in educating a man to think psychoanalytically is to educate him to see and pay attention to them.
>
> In seeking to determine the meaning of the dream elements, the psychoanalyst falls back when necessary upon his permanent or stock interpretations, for which he is in no way dependent upon the patient and by means of which he can show practically any dream to be the expression of a sexual desire. More frequently, however, he gets the meaning of the dream element from the patient himself. This, we have seen, he does by the method of free association. The patient is required to let his mind drift, and mention everything that occurs to him which is suggested by the dream element, without regard to how trivial, indiscreet, or

indecent it may appear to be. If the first association given does not fill the bill, he calls for a second; if the patient says he cannot think of any more, he urges him to keep on trying; until finally one is produced which the psychoanalyst recognizes as the right one. Since probably every thought or memory bears some relationship, immediate or remote, to every other thought, there is of course no limit to the number or variety of associations which may be called up in connection with any dream element in this way; and so, if the patient is cooperative and the analyst sufficiently persistent, he is fairly certain, sooner or later, to get an association to his liking. The procedure is much like that in which a man decides a question by throwing up a coin, but allows himself the privilege of tossing it over and over again, until it falls as he wants it.

But this procedure not only enables the analyst to get from the patient the kind of associations which fit his theory, it also produces an inevitable effect upon the patient's own habits of thought. It does not take many repetitions of such a performance for the patient to get a fairly accurate idea of the kind of association the analyst is looking for, and when this happens, when he knows that the analyst, who is sitting beside him, urging him to let his mind drift, is only waiting for an association of a certain kind to come up to pounce upon it, his mind will inevitably drift toward associations of that kind. For example, I am quite sure that if I myself were being psychoanalyzed and the analyst were to ask me what a walking stick, an umbrella, or a chimney made me think of, my first association, if I were truthful, would be a penis, for I am sufficiently familiar with psychoanalytic thought to know what kind of thing the analyst is seeking, and that knowledge, under such circumstances, would afford a sufficiently powerful stimulus to determine the direction of my thoughts. And I am sure also that if, day after day, week after week, I kept calling up ideas of this sort in response to the demands made upon me in this so-called method of free association, the thing would presently become a habit. I would be seeing the symbolic expression of thoughts and desires in pretty nearly everything that came to attention.

And this, of course, is what actually does occur in the case of the psychoanalytic patient. Yielding up, in compliance with what is presented to him as a mere technical requirement, the voluntary control over his own thinking, letting his mind drift under the influence of those forces which the psychoanalyst brings to bear upon it, his thoughts flow along the channels in which the analyst wishes them to flow. Thus he develops new habits of association; that is to say, new ways of thinking. His mental processes come to resemble those of the psychoanalyst in whose hands he has placed himself.

When the patient has been sufficiently trained in the technique of drawing analogies as practiced by the psychoanalyst—psychoanalogist would be a more appropriate term—the next step, of course, is to encourage him, under the supervision of his mental trainer, to begin making interpretations of his own. As a rule the patient may be relied upon to throw himself into his work with a good deal of zeal; for not only is there to be found in it the satisfaction of doing something that he believes to be very clever and remarkable, there is also the added satisfaction that comes from winning the approval of his beloved master; a very important factor indeed, since, with most people, most of the pleasure to be found in doing something clever comes from having the right kind of audience.

The patient, having learned from experience just what kind of memories the analyst requires to substantiate his theories, sets himself with enthusiasm to the task of digging up memories of this kind. Infantile memories, he finds, are especially in demand, and the earlier the better, so he endeavors to recall the incidents of his early childhood. Here he encounters what under other circumstances might prove a serious handicap; he finds that his memory for these early experiences is extremely vague, so much so that he cannot be sure in many cases whether the pictures he calls up are memory images at all, or mere phantasies. In the world of psychoanalysis however, this inability to distinguish between the imaginary and the real is a matter of no consequence for, as Professor Freud says, "These phantasies possess psychological reality in contrast to physical reality, and so we gradually come to understand that in the realm of neuroses the psychological reality is the determining factor." As this understanding of which Freud speaks gradually penetrates into the patient's mind, as he comes to realize that in the eyes of the analyst his phantasies are of the same value as actual occurrences, so that there is no need of making any great fuss about distinguishing the one from the other, he naturally finds his task of recalling infantile experiences much simplified. As time goes on, as he becomes gradually emancipated from his old inhibitions or resistances, which hitherto have prevented him from giving his fancy rein, he is able to go back to the day when he was born, and back of that even into the time when he was nothing but a foetus in his mother's womb.

Professor Freud tells us that the man who has been psychoanalyzed is a changed man, and we can see that this is unquestionably true, in at least so far as his mental habits are concerned. For one thing, he has acquired the knack of perceiving analogies and his habits of association have been so altered that almost everything which comes to his attention tends to call up the thought of something sexual. Also his recognition of the line that should separate the real from the imaginary, which was probably none too clear to begin with, has been still further blurred by his psychoanalytic training, so that, looked at from the standpoint of its value as evidence, anything he may have to say about his infantile experiences must be taken as pure moonshine.

To appreciate the full significance of the changes in the mental habits of his patients which the analyst produces by his technique, it is necessary to remember how much belief and judgement depend on our habits of thought. If the judge in the court of law and the scientific worker in his laboratory frequently display a critical attitude toward the evidence presented to them which is not shown by the average man, it is due largely to the training they have received and the mental habits this training has given them. If to men of an earlier generation it appeared absurd to suppose that the world went around the sun, or that men were descended from monkeys, while to us these ideas seem quite reasonable, if in the United States of America it is believed to be a very wicked thing to have more than one wife, while in the Orient it is looked upon as quite proper, it is again due to differences in education and the differences in mental habits which these differences in education have produced.

Here, in the psychoanalytic technique, is, as we have shown, an instrument shrewdly fashioned for this work of breaking down the mental habits which would prevent a man from accepting the teachings of the psychoanalyst and for the building of more acceptable habits in their place.

329

The habits which the analyst must overcome in inducing a man to accept his theories are of three kinds: (1) there are the pre-existing habits of thought by reason of which he tends to explain psychological phenomena in other ways than those in which the analyst thinks they should be explained; (2) there is the pernicious habit of demanding proof, in support of any new theory, of a kind which the analyst is unable to give; and (3) there is the habit of turning one's back upon things which are unpleasant or disgusting. The analyst fixes his attention upon the third of these three sources of resistance and closes his eyes to the other two. He finds it more comfortable and satisfactory to believe, when he is breaking down his patient's habits of critical judgement and common sense, that he is merely helping him to overcome a pernicious tendency to turn his back upon the unpleasant. One would think from listening to the words of the psychoanalyst that resistance was a sort of mental impurity which was entirely eradicated by the process of psychoanalysis. As a matter of fact, a man has just as much resistance in his nature after psychoanalysis as he had before, only it takes a different form. Before analysis, it showed itself in the rejection of arguments in favor of psychoanalysis, and afterward, it shows itself in the rejection of arguments against it.

The new mental habits developed in the course of a psychoanalysis predispose the patient to look favorably upon the arguments and evidence presented by the analyst, but that is not all. They also lead the patient to discover for himself the evidence which proves the truth of psychoanalytic doctrine. At the beginning of the analysis, the analyst tells the patient that his dream elements have a certain meaning, that a walking stick means a penis, and that a decayed tooth stands for his father, and the patient must simply take his word for it, he cannot see for himself that these things are so. But, as the analysis progresses, the patient reaches a place where the evidence is before his eyes. He can see for himself that these things actually have for him the meanings which the analyst says they have. How is this fact to be explained? What does the perception of these truths really amount to?

He looks into his mind to see what thought or feeling is connected with the dream element, and this is its meaning. After an analysis, a man tends to discover in his mind the kind of meanings necessary to substantiate the theory of psychoanalysis but the reason he sees these meanings, that is to say, the reason he calls up the kind of associations necessary to achieve this result, is because of the new habits of association which have been formed in the course of the analysis. Neither the analyst nor the patient realize this, however. They assume that the patient's dream elements always had such meanings for him, only before the analysis his resistance prevented him from seeing them. Now that this resistance is overthrown, the meanings of these dream elements have become apparent. What the analyst really does, therefore, in developing new habits of association in the mind of his patient is to manufacture evidence in support of his theory.

Also, of course, the analyst is manufacturing such evidence when he leads his patient on to distort or call up from his unconscious, the memory of imaginary experiences which will serve to substantiate the doctrines of psychoanalysis. Freud, although he accepts these false memories as evidence, disclaims all responsibility for them on the grounds that "the same scattered childhood memories that the individuals have always had and have been conscious of prior to analysis may be falsified as well, or at least may contain a generous mixture of truth and error." That is to say, he sees proof that the psychoanalyst is not responsible for these falsifications which cannot be laid to his door. This is, as if a man accused of a certain crime were to offer as proof of his innocence, the fact that other similar crimes had been committed at other times of which he could not be held guilty. A truly Freudian piece of logic! (7:85-95)

Harrington's conclusion supports my basic thesis that psychoanalysis represents a gigantic hoax played on the public, professional and lay:

What this really means is that people are getting more credulous, at least in so far as psychoanalysis is concerned, and therefore more amenable to the suggestions on which the therapeutic value of psychoanalysis rests.

There would seem, then, to be some reason to suspect that perhaps after all psychoanalysis is not a new form of treatment, that on the contrary it is the very oldest kind of treatment known to man, the kind of treatment used by priests and witch doctors long before the birth of modern medicine. In olden days, witch doctors and divine healers explained to their patients that their ailments were caused by devils or evil spirits; then certain rites and ceremonies were performed, as a result of which, at least so the patients believed, the devils were driven out and, believing themselves to be rid of the causes to which they were due, the symptoms disappeared. Today, however, people have ceased to believe in these old-fashioned devils and, if mental healers are to continue using the same old-fashioned treatment, something else must be found to take their place, something scientific and up-to-date which will appeal to the present-day popular mind. (7:104, 105)

Ordinarily, we might accept the assertion that suggestion is an integral aspect of psychoanalysis and proceed straight to the main point of the argument, namely that interjection of interpretations and other remarks invalidates psychoanalysis as a method of investigation of the "natural" human mind. Unfortunately, however, the originator of psychoanalysis and his direct followers have thrown up such a smoke screen about suggestion, misleading themselves and others as well, making necessary some further documentation.

3. *Dr. Loy and Dr. Jung discuss suggestion*

Jung chose not to remain oblivious to the steering of the patient by clandestine, if unintended suggestion. He had an extended correspondence with Dr. Loy on this point. The discussion started with Loy's observation that faith in the therapist and the resulting suggestibility of the patient are the vehicle of all psychotherapies—faith cures, Christian Science, hypnotherapy and psychoanalysis:

... gradually, by means of frequent talks *apart from* light hypnosis, the patient gains such confidence in the analyst that he becomes susceptible to the direct suggestion that an improvement and then a cure, will follow. I go still further: in an analysis in the waking state, is not the patient's faith that the method employed will cure him, coupled with his growing confidence in the analyst, a main cause of cure? And I go still further: in every therapeutic method systematically carried out is not faith in it, confidence in the doctor, a main cause of its success? I won't say the only cause, for one cannot deny that physical, dietetic, and chemical procedures, when properly selected, have their own effect in bringing about a cure, over and above the striking effects produced by indirect suggestion. (8:255)

Jung agrees with Loy, although he shows certain reluctance in the whole discussion to recognize the everpresent effects of suggestion in his own method, at that time basically an orthodox Freudian approach:

> . . . light hypnosis and total hypnosis are simply varying degrees of intensity of unconscious susceptibility to the hypnotist. Who can draw sharp distinctions here? To a critical intelligence it is unthinkable that suggestibility and suggestion can be avoided in the cathartic method. They are present everywhere as general human attributes, even with Dubois and the psychoanalysts, who all think they are working on purely rational lines. No technique and no self-effacement avails here; the analyst works willy-nilly, and perhaps most of all, through his personality, *i.e.,* through suggestion. In the cathartic method, what is of far more importance to the patient than the conjuring up of old fantasies is the experience of being together so often with the analyst, his trust and belief in him personally and in his method. The belief, the self-confidence, perhaps also the devotion with which the analyst does his work, are far more important to the patient (imponderabilia though they may be) than the rehearsing of old traumata. . . .
>   The question as to how much the analyst involuntarily suggests to the patient is a very ticklish one. It certainly plays a much more important role than psychoanalysis has so far admitted. Experience has convinced me that patients rapidly begin to make use of ideas picked up from psychoanalysis, as is also apparent in their dreams. You get many impressions of this sort from Stekel's book *Die Sprache des Traumes.* (8:259, 260, 279)

Loy, reluctant to accept dogmatic Freudian assertions, anticipated by fifty years Ehrenwald's concept of "doctrinal compliance." He discerns the elements of hypnotic suggestion and transference of the therapist's views on the patient, which were supposedly eliminated from Freud's method:

But here another obstacle stands in my way, which I have already mentioned at our interview: You find the patient adopting the tone, language, or jargon of the analyst (whether from conscious imitation, transference, or plain defiance, so as to fight the analyst with his own weapon,—how then can you prevent his starting to produce all manner of fantasies as supposedly real traumata of early childhood and *dreams* which are supposedly spontaneous but in reality, whether directly or indirectly, albeit involuntarily, are *suggested?* (8:275)

Fifty years later Pinckney makes observations of the psychoanalytic process, practically identical with Loy:

. . . regardless of what analysts say to your face, once the psychoanalyst is behind your back (while you are on the couch) he deliberately directs your so-called "free association." No matter with what thoughts or problems you enter into an analyst's abode, you will, within a matter of minutes, find yourself being led down the path of infantile sexuality. (21:26)

4. *Freud in the webs of suggestion*

It is tragicomic to see those who proclaim their aim to be helping men to think more objectively trapped in their own self-fabricated webs. Freud, Ferenczi, and Jones in particular have spent a good deal of effort trying to prove that their operations have nothing to do with suggestion. Here we turn to Freud; in the subsequent sections to Ferenczi and Jones. The issue, of course, was and is vital and their concern justified. Harrington put it squarely:

If his technique (Freud's) is found to be sound and reliable, the alleged facts may be accepted as genuine, and then one may go on to consider the question of the validity of the conclusions which have been drawn from them; but if his technique is unsound, then his facts cannot be accepted as having any real existence and the whole theoretical structure which he has erected upon them falls to the ground. (7:16)

In 1904, Freud writes, "There is, actually, the greatest possible antithesis between suggestive and analytic technique." (9:67) He reiterates the same assurance on a number of occasions. In 1922 the issue was still alive, and Freud turned to it again to disclaim any taint of suggestion in his method:

> Psychoanalytic procedure differs from all methods making use of suggestion, persuasion, etc., in that it does not seek to suppress by means of authority and mental phenomenon that may occur in the patient.... the analyst respects the patient's individuality and does not seek to remold him in accordance with his own— that is, according to the physician's personal ideal; he is glad to avoid giving advice and instead to arouse patient's power of initiative. (10, v. 5:126, 127)

Presented this way, psychoanalysis appears as an ideal method of unfolding the patient's personality, without any contaminating influence by the therapist through advice, overt or covert suggestion, or pressure. Ferenczi echoes a similar, deceptive cant: "Analysis should be regarded as a process of fluid development unfolding itself before our eyes rather than a structure with a design pre-imposed upon it by an architect." (11, v. 3:90) Glover expresses the same preconception about suggestion. He tries to disclaim any presence of suggestion in psychoanalysis by alleging that the distinguishing mark of Freudian method as compared with general psychotherapy is precisely the lack of suggestion: "The conclusion seemed to me to be obvious: that when any two analysts or groups of analysts hold diametrically opposed views on interpretation, mental mechanisms, or content, one of them must inevitably practice the technique of suggestion rather than that of psychoanalysis." (34:140)

In struggling with the troublesome issue of suggestion in his procedures, Freud was facing an impossible task. He had to find ways of denying and pretending that what was patently there really was not. He had the thankless task of verbally camouflaging the painful truth. In following Freud in his meandering argument, I could not avoid a meandering discussion in this section.

As in the case of hypnosis, Freud causes confusion by assigning a special and narrow meaning to suggestion, and then assuming or asserting that other suggestive influences are also absent. He refuses to face squarely the basic issue of influence upon the subject, irrespective of whether the influence is conscious or unconscious, deliberate or fortuitous, verbal or unspoken.

In a statement on "revision of the theory of dreams," Freud admits the active role he plays in shaping the patients' thinking about his dreams. At this point Freud discusses the difficulty of obtaining associations to a dream; what he means in fact is that the patient balks at producing the symbols which can readily fit into psychoanalytic preconceptions. Instead of obliging with psychoanalytically fertile associations, the patient ". . . only touched them allusively. We now play a part ourselves: we follow up the indications, we draw inevitable conclusions and bring out into the open what the patient in his associations has only touched upon." (22:22) Freud realizes that his procedure is suspect scientifically as a form of coaching the patient, and he formulates the objection himself, as if that would disarm it. This is practically his standard trick in dulling the critical thinking of listeners and readers: "That sounds as if we allow our cleverness and our arbitrary imagination to play with the material which the dreamer has placed at our disposal, and misuse it to the extent of reading into his utterances what we have no business to find there; and indeed it is no easy matter to show the propriety of our behavior in an abstract exposition." (22:23) Instead of showing "the propriety of our behavior," Freud irrelevantly directs his readers just to try psychoanalytic procedure themselves, and they would become convinced by it the way he and his pupils were: ". . . if you try a dream-analysis yourselves, or make yourselves familiar with a well-described example from our literature, you will be convinced of the compelling manner in which such a process of interpretation unfolds itself." (22:23) The peddlers of patent drugs use the same "practical proof" in establishing their claims with the customers.

Such pretenses at objectivity took in many clever, but credulous students. In the scientific realm, one's reputation for objectivity is enhanced by conceding that things are not quite as ideally represented. This old demagogic maneuver to win the listeners' sympathy lends apparent credibility to the most exaggerated claims. Famous lawyers are masters of it; they learned it from ancient orators. Freud, undecided for a time about going into medicine or law, would certainly have done well at law, judging from his effective, if misleading presentations of the case for psychoanalysis. In the middle of the passage from Freud's paper in 1922 quoted earlier, in which he denied suggestion, Freud also conceded some suggestion in his method: "In psychoanalysis the suggestive influence which is inevitable by the physician is diverted on to the task assigned to the patient of overcoming his resistances, that is, of carrying forward the curative process." (10, v. 5:126) Many such contradictions and non sequiturs could be found in Freud's popular expositions. (See a partial list of Freud's inconsistencies in Note 4, chapter VI, pp. 276-278.) The tactics are simple: after denying the presence of suggestion in his work with patients he admits what he had denied: instead of going on with considering the consequences of suggestion in his system, he diverts readers' attention to a side issue—justifying suggestion by therapeutic need, which may be reasonable, but is also a point irrelevant to the issue under discussion. Freud switches attention from the fact that the theoretical status of psychoanalysis would be made even more precarious if suggestion were a part of its primary data to a separate matter of using suggestion as a means of overcoming . . . resistances." Freud does not explain that "overcoming resistances" is very largely a question of giving up one's ideas and molding one's views according to the analyst's preconceptions of so-called Oedipal complex, libido fixations, and the rest of the Freudian lore. As a skilled orator, Freud senses that he should give this aspect of his technique a lateral defense, and he continues with fine, if deceptive, words:

> Any danger of falsifying the products of a patient's memory by suggestion can be avoided by prudent handling of the technique; but in general the arousing of resistance is a guarantee against the misleading effects of suggestive influence. As you can see, there are safeguards against violating the person's integrity, which is sacred to the analyst, and even if the analyst pushed harder than the patient can take for the time being, the patient can take care of himself by developing resistances. (10 v. 5:126)

It sounds good, of course, if you believe that Freud can be trusted. However, the observations of other therapists (to be looked into presently) tend to make Freud appear unreliable and scandalously self-deluded and deluding for a reputed thinker and psychologist. The skeptic, after rereading the above quotation would remember, however, that the patient's ego has by this time been filled with childish admiration of the analyst or reduced to some highly dissociated, emotionalized or regressed state by the transference; a condition in which resistance is rather ineffectual. We saw that even mature, professionally trained individuals, Dr. Wortis and Dr. Campbell, felt their minds undermined by the pressures of analysis. What is to be expected of severely troubled neurotics who, Freud says (9), were sent to him after years of decompensating and other remedies had failed? Freud assures us that such patients are capable of opposing the analyst. True, even a wounded animal would fight against capture, but how long can it keep up the defense? And analysis is a dragged-out, patient process for both participants. What non-compliance the analyst cannot break down today, he can next month or next year. Time works in his favor. The patient's neurosis will assist in wearing down the resistance in the meantime.

It is not difficult to see that Freud had again defensively mis-represented the facts of psychoanalysis. Most patients do not put up a great deal of resistance anyway, they trust the analyst as a father figure and buy eagerly even the most preposterous interpretations. Garner (12) speaks of the patient's compliance as a regular feature of any psychotherapeutic process. Most patients readily help the analyst mold their mind. Grinker speaks of these patients as "the psycho-analyst's best collaborator," and sees through the myth of any significant resistance of the patient:

> Each interpretation may be a hypothesis according to Kubie, but there are not any alternatives and little possibility that the patient-collaborator will refute it, although theoretically much is made of the patient's behavior as an index of correction or refutation of interpretations. We have demonstrated that, in our experiments, attempting to provoke anxiety is frequently un-successful because the patient-subject interprets most everything that the psychiatrist states as having therapeutic meaning. (13:137, 138)

This tolerance of patients for the therapist's interpretations is not peculiar to the infantilized state of a Freudian analysand. I experi-mented for my doctoral dissertation (15) subjects, using ego-inflating interpretation with one half, and ego-deflating interpretations with

338

the other half of the group, for fifteen interviews. The subjects' opinions and feelings about me as therapist were the same in both groups as shown on the Q-tests I employed.

Landis, who undertook psychoanalysis when he was already a well-known professor of psychology, speaks of patient's emotional overvaluation of the analyst. He sees that the patient distorts the impressions of the analyst toward overcompetence. "The patient endows the analyst with extraordinary or supernatural wisdom and hopes that the analyst will be able to point out quickly the solution to his trouble—some thoughts and habits." (14:66)

Harrington depicts realistically the subdued state of the majority of patients caught by Freudian trickery:

> The patient of the psychoanalyst . . . sees himself as an ignorant and humble disciple sitting at the feet of his master. His business is not to criticize but to seek to grasp the truths offered to him. With such an attitude if certain conclusions drawn appear to be unwarranted by the evidence, he does not conclude that the logic of the analyst is at fault, but rather that his own mental limitations are such as to render him incapable of understanding the significance of the facts presented. Indeed, the more trivial the evidence, the more obscure the reasoning, and the more preposterous the conclusions, the more profoundly will he be impressed, for these things will simply serve to show what a marvelous science is psychoanalysis, and what a wonderful man the psychoanalyst who, by ways so devious and incomprehensible, can arrive at a knowledge of truths so astounding.

> But why should the patient have such a high regard for the psychoanalyst's judgement and such a low opinion of his own?

> There are three reasons that might be mentioned why the patient tends to form a very high opinion of the judgement of the psychoanalyst. (1) There is the psychoanalyst's professional prestige, the reputation which he had been at great pains to build up and maintain in the eyes of the public of being a man of marvelous understanding, deeply versed in the mysteries of the mind. Truly it would be an act of presumptuous folly for the patient to oppose his own puny judgement to the judgement of such a one. (2) There is the fact that the patient is a sufferer seeking relief from his suffering. Such people, as we know from

experience, are apt to be very credulous in their attitude toward those who hold out to them the promise of cure. The desire to be cured carries with it the desire to believe in the possibility of cure, which in turn carries an inclination or tendency to believe in the wisdom and veracity of him by whom the cure is promised. This tendency is in many cases a very strong one and had worked to increase the power and prestige of mental healers of all kinds in all ages, from the earliest times right down to the present. (3) There is the so-called transference, the personal attachment which the patient tends to form for the analyst during the analysis. Whether or not this attachment is always a sexual one, as the psychoanalyst would have us believe, it is at any rate an infatuation in which everything the analyst says or does seems wise and wonderful in the patient's eyes. It, therefore, to quote the words of Professor Freud, "invests the physician with authority and is converted into faith for his communications and conceptions." (7:75-78)

More than a hundred years ago, Braid reported how pliable patients are to suggestion. He used hypnosis combined with the phrenological theory that certain alleged bumps on the skull, when touched, would lead to manifestation of personality reactions corresponding to those bumps. See what wonderful results can be achieved with a subject and doctor ripe for suggestion:

> Under adhesiveness and friendship (that were supposed to be represented by certain protuberances of her skull) she clasped me and on stimulating the organ of combativeness on the opposite side of the head, with the arm of that side, she struck two gentlemen (whom she imagined were about to attack me) in such a manner as nearly laying one on the floor, whilst with the other arm she held me in the most friendly manner. Under benevolence she seemed quite overwhelmed with compassion. (quoted in 16:52)

Clearly, as in the case of hypnosis, which was supposedly abandoned by psychoanalysis, a semantic dissimulation is involved in disclaiming the role of suggestion in psychoanalysis. Because he does not use the crude, direct, forceful suggestion of Charcot or Bernheim and avoids using the term, Freud maintains that suggestion plays no appreciable role in his method. [1] Thus, an alcoholic can prove that he is no longer alcoholic because he has given up hard liquor and gets drunk on beer.

Dubois also denied that suggestion played any part in his moral treatment. He considered suggestion to be only a sly or forcible imposition of an idea upon the patient. He felt it injurious to the patient's human dignity to foist ideas upon him, either in a clandestine or in a direct fashion. He, therefore, could not consider his rational method of inspirational encouragement as suggestion. Equally mistaken, Freud did not admit of giving suggestions, because these were not deliberately introduced nor overtly made. What Dr. Bonjour of Lausanne said in criticizing Dubois is equally applicable to Freud: "It would be better when he uses suggestion to admit the fact frankly." (3:339)

Freud admitted it only in an oblique way, and rather in private than in public. He wrote to Fliess in 1897 about the weakness of his theory: "A severe critic might say that all this was fantasy projected into the past instead of being determined by the past." However, Freud quickly denied this realizaion by a brave statement: "The experimenta crucis would decide the matter against him [the critic]." (17:221) Yet, Freud's stance proved to be mere bravado. The *experimenta crucis* were never performed, yet later generations overlooked that fact and took to Freud's ideas uncritically. Freud remained genuinely deluded about the nature of his inventions. In 1922, he contrasts the psychological insights of his artistic "double" (23:333), the physician turned man of letters, Schnitzler, with his own ostensibly verified fantasies: "... you know through intuition—or rather from detailed self-observation—everything that I have discovered by laborious work on other people." (23:340) The wishes can obviously blind even as powerful a mind as Freud had. Masserman, who refused to stay in the role of a card-carrying Freudian, is amazed at Freud's oblivion regarding what he was doing to analysands. He quotes a paragraph from *Autobiography* in which Freud explains two ways in which the psychoanalyst can tell the patient about the meaning of his productions. Yet, in the next breath Freud writes that this "exposes the patient to the least possible amount of compulsion (and makes certain) that nothing will be introduced by the expectations of the

341

analyst." Masserman cannot help but conclude that Freud "demonstrated his utter inability to recognize how his own preconceptions affected his clinical data, skewed his observations, reinforced his predilections and thus greatly handicapped him as a research scientist." (28:386)

The uncertainty about the role of suggestion in patients and self-suggestion in Freud vitiates and invalidates (in the scientific sense) all of Freud's basic clinical writings and "demonstrations" of his theory. Of course some Freudians cannot concede this view. Eissler, for instance, calls Freud's report on his dream which proved to him that he had Oedipal hatred for his oldest son, "the greatest self-sacrifice a man has ever made in the service of science." (24:307) If Eissler had "psychoanalytic science" in mind there could be no objection, as that whole "science" consists of materials of ambiguous import. But he means science, *i.e.* propositions that are unequivocal and can be verified. Freud's interpretation can be understood in two mutually exclusive ways, and can therefore have the status of a mere opinion, but not of psychological fact. One of the meanings is what Freud and Eissler had in mind: the appearance of specific symbolic representations in the dream reveals the existence in Freud of primordial death wishes toward his son. This, of course, does not prove the Oedipal proposition that Freud hated his boy as a sexual rival for his wife; one can think of other possible motives for such hatred: the boy did not let him sleep during the night, worried him, or was adding to his financial burden, etc. It is true, of course that such murderous feelings toward the first son are encountered clinically in some immature, insecure, acting-out characters. We also have a confirmation of such a nasty fact from the world of biology: farmers are aware that some boars may eat up their progeny if not separated from them, and that sows have to fight them off and prevent the father from coming near his little ones. However, as a man is not an animal, the demonstration from biology is not binding for human behavior, for Freud's feelings. If Freud reported that he felt such a death wish consciously and when he was not angry with his son, we could accept that report as a genuine fact, but only for Freud, not for human beings in general.

The report is, on the other hand, open to another interpretation, even though it cannot be proven any more than Freud's own. That

342

other possibility is psychologically as feasible as Freud's: it is simply that, like his patients, Freud had a "compliant dream," this time to prove his pet theory. If patients can produce dreams to fit the psychoanalyst's notions, out of positive "transference," surely, the analyst has enough "cathexis" to his theories to produce dreams to "prove" them. Freud and other investigators have abundantly demonstrated that dreams include "day residues," *i.e.*, thoughts, feelings, and experiences of the wakeful state. Freud was certainly deeply enamored of his favorite postulates; he would be quite likely to carry them over into his dreams. In his wakeful life he had over-conditioned himself to the reality of Oedipal feelings, and such a notion could easily find expression in corresponding images, as happens with other experiences in wakeful states. We can think ourselves into perceiving our strongest concerns in wakeful reality, and by the same token can dream ourselves into our important concerns. As we have wishful thoughts, we can also have wishful dreams. In any case, science as verified knowledge cannot be built on materials brought forward by Freud, as they are contaminated by *bacillus psychologicus*, the suggestion.

Freud's role as suggester is plainly evident in his description of how he brought about Wolf-Man's conversion to psychoanalytic ideology.

5. *Freud brainwashes Wolf-Man*

One of Freud's famous patients, the Wolf-Man, demonstrated in his memoirs the suggestive operations that Freud performed on his subjects, and which Freud hid from himself, his pupils, his readers, and his patients. To begin with, Freud offered verbal expressions of friendly feelings to Wolf-Man, solidifying the already strong "transference": "And Professor Freud had a great deal of personal understanding for me, as he often told me during the treatment, which naturally strengthened my attachment to him." (32:89) Even fifty years later the patient is not free from the spell that Freud had a "great personality" and that his influence was "profound and lasting." (32:141) He retained the original awe over the years, feeling that "the attractive power of his personality was so great that there were certain dangers involved." (32:142) No doubt, Freud knew how

343

to get a firm grip on his patient's mind.

Far from being a neutral reflector of the patient's materials, Freud actively fostered a compliance with his views. He coached the Wolf-Man as good teachers train children into correct ways of thinking. He used abundantly both the direct instruction and the indirect motivation. He instructed him in his theories: "It was a revelation to me to hear the fundamental concepts of a completely new science of the human psyche, from the mouth of its founder." (32:138) He "often touched on . . . [the] theme" of repetition compulsion, which was the main controversial revelation by the master in that period of time. He provided a demonstration from Dostoevsky's novel of how his patient should interpret his own dreams " . . . in one of my analytic hours Freud made a psychoanalytic interpretation of a dream of Raskolnikov's." (32:145)

The patient was excited by the illuminations he was going to receive: "I perceived at once that Freud had succeeded in discovering an unexplored region of the human soul and that if I could follow him along that path a new world would open to me." (32:138) He soon adopted the Freudian mold for his thinking, believing that he had achieved a deeper understanding of himself: "Much that had been ununderstandable in my life began to make sense . . . " (32:83) He had been looking from his childhood for the undivided attention of someone having misperceived his own parents as rejecting him in favor of an older sister, and Freud provided the longed-for comfort: "It will be easy to imagine the sense of relief I now felt when Freud asked me various questions about my childhood and about the relationships in my family and listened with the greatest attention to all I had to say." (32:138) This gratification, naturally, steered the patient to produce the psychoanalytically required events, purportedly demonstrating the Oedipal complex, ubiquitous homosexuality, castration anxiety, etc. Freud obviously liked this gifted reproducer of correct materials and he rewarded (prodded) him by telling him that he had been a "thinker of the first rank" as a child. As could be expected, Wolf-Man responded even better with the desired fantasies. Only from time to time would Freud become manifestly active with suggestions, which the patient relished greatly as revelations from above: "Occasionally he [Freud] let fall some remark which bore witness to his complete understanding of everything I had experienced." (32:138) Apparently the Wolf-Man was adept at readily absorbing the psychoanalytic suppositions and Freud reinforced his pliable subject by open praise and promotion to the status of co-worker:

> ... In my analysis with Freud I felt myself less as a patient than as a co-worker, the younger comrade of an experienced explorer setting out to study a new, recently discovered land. ...
>
> This feeling of "working together" was increased by Freud's recognition of my understanding of psychoanalysis, so that he even once said it would be good if all his pupils could grasp the nature of analysis as soundly as I. (32:140)

The deception had thus become complete for both the analyst and the analysand—the one needed to remain oblivious to the fact that he was feeding the patient the approved views, and the other never realized it fully either. The patient is only dimly aware of being trained to think in the framework provided by Freud. He recognizes the training, but cannot penetrate beyond the terms and meanings imposed by the trainer. Wolf-Man writes that "When during the course of analysis resistances are overcome and repressed material is brought into consciousness, the patient becomes more and more accessible to the influence of the physician." (32:141) Apparently he could not realize that the actual influence of the analyst was imposed by analyzing "resistances" and that when the "repressed material is brought into consciousness" the brainwashing is already complete, as the "repressed material" is identical with Freud's notions.

It took years to build the psychoanalytic story into Wolf-Man. "... it was not, indeed, for several years that the story became any less incomplete and obscure." (32:159) Freud was determined to find the primal scene as the beginning of his patient's neurosis, and he finally convinced himself and the patient that all his troubles began when he suddenly woke up in his crib and saw his parents copulating. It was propitious for the development of neurosis that the baby boy (eighteen months) received the shattering impression of his mother's vagina as a castration wound resulting from cutting off the precious penis. And to make matters worse, Freud elaborated his construction in even more traumatic terms: the boy saw the penis disappear in the vagina and that convinced the poor kid completely of the reality of castration. The Freudian seed of neurosis was thus considered planted in the immature mind, to blossom later into a full blown obsessive-compulsive neurosis.

No doubt, Freud worked hard and long on it, till his subject produced the correct version; he describes the painstaking effort involved in shaping his patient's fantasies:

> I may remark that this interpretation was a task that dragged on over several years. The patient related the dream at a very early stage of the analysis and very soon came to share my conviction that the causes of his infantile neurosis lay concealed behind it. In the course of the treatment we often came back to the dream, but it was only during the last months of the analysis that it became possible to understand it completely, and only then thanks to spontaneous work on the patient's part. (32:177)

The reader should notice that Freud brought his patient "back to the dream," and that Wolf-Man yielded after repeated attempts, but that, nevertheless, everything happened "thanks to the spontaneous work on the patient's part." Freud obviously had tremendous powers of rationalizing if he could maintain such contradictory positions simultaneously.

Another obligatory Freudian discovery was achieved after a lot of diligent work of both the suggester and his subject. After much sweating and waiting, the subject produced enough hints in his associations for Freud to conclude that his sister (two years older than Wolf-Man) "seduced" him when he was four years old. By all signs Freud could smell out what he "had already divined," (32:164) that sister must have playfully handled her brother's penis, and this "seduction" contributed another fatal thrust toward neurosis. Again what was in Freud's mind as theoretical presupposition became part of patient's "spontaneous" communication out of his "unconscious." Freud did not have to prod the Wolf-Man into compliance, as "One day the patient began to continue with the interpretation of the dream." (32:179)

Freud now writes ardently about the conjectured copulation as if he personally witnessed it. Of course, the patient was caught in the trainer's enthusiasm and they collaborated in refining Freud's original hunch: "It gradually became possible to find satisfactory answers to all the questions that arose in connection with this scene; for in the course of the treatment the first dream returned in innumerable variations and new editions, in connection with which the analysis produced the information that was required." (32:181)

Freud did not limit himself to subtle implanting of the desired contents of "analysis." He admits that he also coached his subject by telling him of his theoretical conjectures, giving hints about what would be psychoanalytically proper form and content of his "free associations," dreams, and other communications. Freud admits that "these scenes from infancy are not reproduced during the treatment as recollections, they are the products of construction," (32:194) that is, the theoretical content that the analyst injects into his subject.

One can easily realize from the preceding quotation that the patient's communications are not important at all, as the analyst can put the cloak of his constructions over any materials, using analogies, and other imprecise verbal operations. Freud states that these recollections, which are not recollections, "have to be divined—constructed—gradually and laboriously from an aggregate of indications." (32:194) Notice the imprecise process of "divining" from "an aggregate of indications," *i.e.,* theoretical speculations of the analyst.

Freud gets himself even farther out on a limb of unreason. He tells us that "there is no danger at all in communicating constructions of this kind to the person under analysis; they never do any damage to the analysis if they are mistaken; but at the same time they are not put forward unless there is some prospect of reaching a nearer approximation to the truth by means of them." (32:163, 164) Again Freud attempts to encompass two irreconcilable views at the same time. In other writings and under different conditions he maintained that the productions by the patient are uninfluenced by him; now he tells us that he implants constructions in the patient's mind. He may be right in claiming that such coaching does not do "any damage to the analysis." Of course, if "analysis" is the imposition of the analyst's views upon the analysand, then telling the analysand how to think does not do any harm, and it actually speeds up the indoctrination. Freud calls this indoctrination somewhat deceptively "a nearer approximation to the truth." The "truth" mentioned here is psychoanalytic doctrine, which only the analyst knows with any degree of authority. In the subsequent sentence Freud tells what effect this instruction in the "truth" had on Wolf-Man: he produced some dreams which could then be used by Freud to prove to him that he must have gone through the shock of witnessing the copulation of his parents. Here we find one of the many examples of circular reasoning in Freud: he implants a hint in patient's awareness; the hint produces dreams which can be manipulated to appear to prove that there was reality to the hint. The dreams are, then, proposed as proofs of validity of the original hint.

Only about thirty pages later, but still in the same paper, Freud proposes to his readers that "the physician feels himself entirely blameless" for "spontaneous recollections" during the "successful treatment." (32:194) However, a Freudian treatment is considered successful only if the patient adopts the analyst's suggestions and produces them back as a "spontaneous" welling-up of the psychological truth from within him. Freud pretends that the repeated dreams of the kind he could use in building up his constructions are the proof of the truth of the hunch he planted in the patient: "It is this recurrence in dreams that I regard as the explanation of the fact that the patients themselves gradually acquire a profound conviction of the reality of these primal scenes, a conviction which is in no respect inferior to one based on recollection." (32:195) "Inferior" in what way? An imaginary travelogue may be richer than an actual description of a country and yet we need hardly argue that, as a source of objective knowledge the former is inferior to the latter.

In the next paragraph Freud surprises the reader by admitting that "it is well known that dreams can be guided." (32:195) He compares the therapist using suggestion and the analyst implanting constructions in the patient, and the differences, as far as influencing the patient's mind is concerned, do not appear great: "The old-fashioned psychotherapist, it might be maintained, used to suggest to his patient that he was cured, that he had overcome his inhibitions, and so on; while the psycho-analyst, on this view, suggests to him that when he was a child he had some experience or other, which he must now recollect in order to be cured." (32:195)

It appears that Freud never found a steady view of the role of suggestion in his kind of treatment. He denied it when needing to prove that his findings were produced by the subjects without his nurturing their thinking, he admitted injecting his views into patients' minds as part of his therapy. He attempts once more to state clearly the case both of the critics and of the analyst. It seems that Freud could muster no better argument than to "comfort himself" by asserting that the slowness of the process proves that the analyst is innocent of shaping the mind of his patient:

> ... what is argued now is evidently that they are phantasies not of the patient but of the analyst himself, who forces them upon the person under analysis on account of some complexes of his own. An analyst, indeed, who hears this reproach, will comfort himself by recalling how gradually the construction of this phantasy which he is supposed to have originated came about, and, when all is said and done, how independently of the physician's incentive many points in its development proceeded ... (32:196)

As we shall see later, the brainwashing also works slowly, till the brainwasher's truth shapes up in the mysterious recesses of a mind under duress.

Freud concludes in a futile way that there is no reconciliation between the detractors of psychoanalysis and himself. "On the one side there will be a charge of subtle self-deception, and on the other of obtuseness of judgement; it will be impossible to arrive at a decision." (32:196) For me the decision is not impossible: Freud did suffer from self-deception, glaring rather than subtle, as he put it.

6. *Ferenczi also worried about suggestion*

Ferenczi, uneasy about the problem of suggestion, follows an argument similar to Freud's. Ferenczi's discussion is given at some length for it illustrates defensive vacillations between attempts to idealize psychoanalytic procedures and the piling up of verbiage to conceal unpleasant, but honest realization that suggestion does indeed play a troublesome role in them.

> Many people from lack of information regard psychoanalysis as a therapy that acts suggestively. But those who have perhaps read something of analytic literature are inclined if they have not

349

experience of their own to refer to scientific and therapeutic results of analysis, on analytical grounds, as "suggestive." To define the meaning of the word "suggestion" is perhaps difficult, but everyone knows what the word implies: it is the deliberate smuggling of sensations, feelings, thoughts and decisions into another person's psychic world, and in such a way that the person influenced cannot of himself modify or correct the suggested thoughts, feelings or impulses. Put briefly, suggestion is the forcing upon, the unquestioning acceptance of, a foreign psychic influence. The setting aside of all criticism is therefore the precondition of successful suggestion; by what means, however, can this be achieved? On the one hand by impressiveness, by intimidation, on the other by bribery, by means of friendly, kindly talk. [Wortis and Campbell could easily mistake a part of the description of suggestion in the above passage as a definition of psychoanalysis as they experienced it.] . . .

Suggestion artificially encourages the narrowing of consciousness, and therefore . . . is an education in blindness. [Psychoanalysis also narrows consciousness.] . . .

Suggestion, therefore, is a palliative treatment, analysis desires to be called a "causal process of healing." [An example of magical thinking not infrequent in psychoanalytic writings: I wish to give it this name, and it is already truly as the name states!] . . .

As I have already said, there have been people who declared that analysis itself is nothing else but a form of suggestion. The analyst was much preoccupied with his patient, he "put it to him" that the symptoms were caused by this or that and the suggestion had a curative effect.

As I said, in suggestion, the patient's belief is the precondition of success. Now in analytic treatment we begin by explaining to the patient that the absolute skepticism on his part is permitted, nay, necessary. We permit him to control all our statements, he may laugh at us, scold us, and criticize whenever anything we say seems to him incredible, laughable, or unfounded. [An example of hoodwinking himself and others by partially describing the situation. But his honesty comes quickly to the fore, denying that he was really serious about the fanciful statement, and describing his real experience with patients.] I cannot say that at the beginning of treatment patients make much use of this permission; to the contrary, they show great propensity to take all our statements for revelation. In such cases we recognize the suppressed skepticism even from slight mistakes, slips of the tongue on patient's part, and compel him to acknowledge this disbelief to himself and to us. [*i.e.,* subduing the patient.] Many a patient is seized after the very first explanation with an extraordinarily strong tendency to proselytize; he preaches constantly and everywhere about psychoanalysis, can talk about absolutely nothing else and always wants to gain new adherents. [Similar "conversion" phenomena are reported in the victims of communist brainwashing.] To such people we must then ourselves prove that all this ado only serves to shout down certain of their own doubts. In a word, in contrast to the suggester who desires only that the patient should believe him, we are constantly on our guard that the patient should believe nothing of which he has not convinced himself. [The brainwashers play the same game. Some prisoners had the impression that their trainers believed themselves to be neutral in the whole business of "thought reform." The reform just happened freely on the subjects' own conviction!]

Could there, however, be a less fertile ground for the evocation of suggestion than a relationship in which a person is at liberty to entertain himself in every conceivable way at his doctor's expense, to disparage him—if it occurs to him—and to humiliate him. [Again Ferenczi falls into fantasy. Have you ever heard of a sensible patient rebelling against the way the dentist pulled his tooth? How many novices in a monastery would risk their souls by laughing at their spiritual director? The suffering and credulous neurotics hoping for a cure, paying $30 or $50 an hour can be counted on to have retained enough sanity not to risk what they imagine are their vital psychic interests.]

If the patient fights tooth and nail against so unpleasant an insight, the analyst takes care not to talk about it, and finally even concedes the possibility of an error on his side. Only when the patient of himself brings up memories and ideas that strengthen the analyst's suspicions that is to say after the patient's self-correction, can one count on an advance in psychoanalytic knowledge and also an improvement in the condition. [The brainwasher does not argue either; he mostly waits.]

The suggester has other weapons besides impressiveness at his command. As regards the patient, he can simulate interest and selflessness. [Some brainwashers and psychoanalysts are reported to do it too, until the prisoner violates his own mind.]

351

A similar inclination to unquestioning submission on the part of the patient certainly manifests itself also in analysis, and so far the presence of suggestive factors in analysis must be acknowledged, but this "suggestion" in analysis is only a transitional stage, and no patient can analytically be held to be cured who has not sobered out of this condition. [The brainwashers reject the first enthusiastic declarations of their victims. They wait for the "reformed thought" to sink in and take deeper root in their human animal. Some weary brainwashers must also be tempted to come out more strongly with their implied wishes, but they are usually reported as not abusing their power but behaving patiently, as prescribed by their rule book.]

In what I have said, I have only wanted to show that not only is analysis not any kind of suggestion, but constant battle against suggestive influences, and that the technique of analysis uses more protective measures against blind belief and unquestioning submission than any methods of teaching and enlightenment that have ever been used in the nursery, the university, or in the consulting room. (18:v. 2:55-66)

The chief weakness in Ferenczi's argument is that he defines suggestion in a circumscribed way, as direct teaching or pressuring of the patient. In this way he absolves himself from discussing the use of other suggestive methods in psychoanalysis which are more potent because they act outside the awareness of the patient, and probably of the analyst too.

Compare Ferenczi's frantic defenses against the presence of suggestion in analysis with Kelman's frank admission:

The therapist thus takes a most active part in the analytical process. He observes and examines the patient's every move.... Through his interpretations, explanations and questions, he influences the course of analysis.... The analyst actually conducts the analysis. And this is as it should be. For while analysis is a co-operative enterprise between patient and analyst, it is the analyst who for many reasons must carry the greater responsibility. (19:15)

Garner speaks unabashedly of the "therapeutic implant" (12), *i.e.,* various suggestive procedures in his confrontation technique.

The issue seems to resolve basically into the therapist's willingness to take responsibility for the patient, while that is necessary, instead of playing a game confusing to himself and the patient. Beier puts it unequivocally:

> Not all individuals are willing to accept their wish of influencing others with their message. It is through the covert cues attached to a given message that such messages serve to hide the sender's intent. The person's intent to influence others can become hidden even from himself; the message camouflages this information from the respondent. The extent to which a message can be understood for its intent to influence others represents the degree of responsibility the sender wants to accept for having sent this particular message. Responsibility in communication, then, has to do with accepting one's own wish to influence others. (20:280)

7. Jones winces at suggestion

In 1910, Jones, the future chief biographer of Freud, almost stumbled onto the terrible discovery. He came close to realizing that Freud had been blinded by his wishful thinking and had deluded himself, his patients, his pupils, and the public at large, into believing that his data were new "discoveries" of psychic secrets. Jones hovered dangerously at the brink from which he could see, if he dared, that the psychopathological materials gathered on the couch were mostly recitations of notions previously implanted in subjects by the "analyst." A closer look at what Freud was doing would reveal that rather than analyzing he was clandestinely feeding his subjects the responses he wanted from them by direct coaching through interpretations and indirect suggestions through the tricks of transference. Freud and later psychoanalysts have become adept at seizing from patients' productions any vague intimations of their brand of complexes and anxieties, and skillfully presenting them as "demonstrations" of the validity of Freudian theory. With equal adeptness Jones manipulated his rational abilities and succeeded in not seeing the glaringly present suggestions in psychoanalytic work on the patient. He had started with the intention of proving that no suggestion was ever employed by a good Freudian analyst, not to speak of the master, and he maintained his single-minded intention to

353

the end of his paper (29) presented to the First Annual Meeting of the American Psychopathological Association. He was at that time a Demonstrator of Psychiatry at the University of Toronto, and he ably demonstrated that in matters of reasoning "where there is a will, there is a way." He demonstrated that anything can be seemingly proved by juggling words and concepts.

Jones starts with an objective recognition of the role of suggestion in every therapy. He accepts the definition of other writers of two forms of suggestion: one is verbal, open, direct, what Bernheim called "the act by which an idea is introduced in the brain and accepted by it"; the other one Jones calls "affective suggestion," "the acquirement by a person of a given affective state, such as when one person responds to the 'personal influence' of another." (29:218) He then "illustrates" how logically obtuse some of the critics are, who "with no knowledge of the subject" assert that Freudian "cures are due to suggestion." The implication of his paper is that the critics should despair of their ignorance. The real import of the criticism he intends to refute does not escape him, as he admits that, if proven, the imputation of suggestion would invalidate the data gathered in psychoanalytic chambers. He pretends that he does not want to scandalize his listeners with such "preposterous" claims:

In this phrase [that "cures are due to suggestion"] at least two different criticisms are evidently confounded: it is at one time meant that the memories evoked during psychoanalysis are false, having been merely "suggested" to the patient, and at another time that, whether the recovered memories are true or false, the improvement of the patient's condition is brought about through the personal influence of the physician; sometimes the two are fused, as when it is alleged that the physician's influence compels the patient to accept the suggestion that evocation of memories will be followed by improvement. It is, I hope, unnecessary to take up the time of the members of this society with discussion of the first of these criticisms, which is even more preposterous than the second, but it will presently be found pertinent to the main theme of this paper briefly to consider the latter one. (29:219)

So Jones lightly dismisses the first and very damaging criticism of psychoanalysis (that Freud and Freudians inject their notions into patients) and goes rather to deal with a more tangential question (of psychoanalysts and other therapists cajoling patients toward improvement by convincing them overtly or covertly that they are being "cured"). Jones then deftly conscripts Bleuler into an ally for his cause by quoting him, "Die Suggestion ist ein affectiver Vorgang" [Suggestion is an affective process]. As a way of deflecting the thinking of his listeners from applying it to psychoanalysis, Jones hastens to limit the connotation of Bleuler's statement to only verbal direct suggestion. Such limiting the concept of affective suggestion to conscious processes obviously intends, as in Ferenczi's case, to gloss over the unconsciously induced suggestion. In this form the concept does not make much sense coming from a Freudian, whose expertise and emphasis is supposedly in the area of unconscious reactions. However, that is exactly the direction in which Jones does not want his and his listeners' thought to stray, as it would let the cat out of the bag. He drags in another subject to mislead himself and others about the shadowy and risky zone of psychoanalysis which he was treading: he deflects attention to "the most perfect form of suggestion, namely, hypnotism." (29:220) And, again, he deals largely with conscious aspects of hypnotic relationship and behavior, skimming over the more important affective, unconscious processes, of which he had read in the eighteenth and nineteenth century masters of hypnotism whose works he cites in his papers. He deals at length with hysterical symptoms (paralyses, anaesthesia, hallucinations, ecstasies, etc.) occurring spontaneously or through hypnotic influence. He even makes the precipitous excursion into "the peculiar *rapport* between the operator and the subject" (29:222), but he never lets himself grasp clearly the point of essential similarity between *rapports* of Freud and mesmerists with their patients. He even ventures the comparison of posthypnotic suggestion and what Freud had described in his patient as "nachträglicher Gehorsam" [subsequent obedience] (29:222) to suggestions of others who maintain their grip on the neurotic until the liberator-psychoanalyst breaks the spell (by establishing his own grip on the patient's mind). Jones then traces the origins of such slavery to transference of some feelings and relationships from childhood to adult stages of individual development. He describes the essentially childish reactions of the subject to his newly found mighty father, the hypnotist. Together with Freud, Jones admits the difficulty of dis-

355

tinguishing between hypnotic rapport and Freudian transference, both being motivated by sexual and dependent drives. He takes recourse to the traditional mystification of uninitiated outsiders, saying that only the psychoanalyzed illuminati can know "the nature and origin of the affective processes underlying transference and suggestion." (29:233) He quotes a number of writers to the effect that hypnotic *rapport* means complete subservience of the subject to hypnotizer, a complete preoccupation with the ideas and wishes of the beloved hypnotic master. He even mentions the appearance of "sexual affection" [2] and of special attention and docility to the hypnotist. Contemporary readers, acquainted with Freudian descriptions of transference, may feel that there is little difference between hypnotic *rapport* and the attachment and affective infatuation of psychoanalytic patients. (We have seen some of these ecstasies in chapter VII.) Jones, warned by the special Freudian reflex, avoids making that small but critical step of identifying transference and hypnotic dependence, as it would devastate the cobwebs Freud had spun fifteen years earlier when he invented psychoanalysis and which Jones and Ferenczi, as his adjutants, tried to protect from harm.

Jones even takes into consideration Janet's reports of his experiences with hypnosis, showing that there is a marked influence on the subject between *séances:* the initial fear of hypnosis is replaced by addiction to it; the patient forgets her symptoms, feels better, senses an approaching cure; the therapist assumes a disproportionate role in patient's thinking and feeling; when not hypnotized (analyzed?) the patient feels at a loss. Antedating the Freudian experience, Janet honestly described how the subject "experiences affection mixed with awe for a being much more powerful than he is." (29:241) Ferenczi had no trouble recognizing the nature of such dependent and adoring feelings, when they concern patient's father, and he called such a mental state "paternal hypnosis." Ferenczi might have inadvertently supplied us here with a designation properly applicable to the form of hypnosis induced on the Freudian couch.

However, such irreverent insights are far from Jones. He still hovers on the threshold of full discovery by quoting further from Janet on hypnosis:

> . . . "The subject feels happy when he sees his hypnotizer, when he speaks to him, he experiences pleasure when he thinks of him,

356

and consequently soon comes to the point of feeling a strong love for him." Referring to hysterics he says: "As soon as the physician shows an interest in them, he ceases to be, in their eyes, an ordinary man; he stands for them in a predominant position that no one else can occupy. But in return for this they are extremely exacting; they desire their physician all to themselves; he must not attend equally to any one else; he must come to see them at any moment, remain a long time with them, and take their smallest concerns to heart." [Jones interprets further] This exacting jealousy is a very frequent and well-known occurrence; it was commented on by many of the old magnetizers. Janet finds that his patients' attitude towards him is frequently that of a child towards its elders: "most often the subjects feel themselves humble and small, and compare themselves to children before their parents." Again, a sense of guilt or shame was commonly met with: "Je suis, dit Berthe, comme un enfant qui a fait quelque sottise et qui a peur que sa mère le sache." [I am, Berthe says, like a child who had done something foolish and who is afraid that mother may know about it] (29:242)

What does Jones do with all this? It apparently does not occur to him to apply it to psychoanalysis, as it comes naturally to anyone not affected by special Freudian astigmatism. Instead, Dubois Jones turns to other inferior therapies of the hypnotists' and of Dubois's persuasive method and applies Janet's remarks to them, preserving for psycho-analysis the special status as allegedly free from suggestive contamination. Even the thought of any presence of suggestion in the Freudian method is repulsive to him: "The criticism sometimes made of psycho-analytic treatment, that its brilliant results are brought about merely by suggestion, betrays a complete ignorance of what actually happens, and is easily answered by the following objective consideration." (29:245)

What is the "objective consideration"? It is the experience which Jones had with both suggestive and psychoanalytic treatments, which in his thinking he had placed worlds apart. Forgetting all the unconscious processes and clinging to the logic of consciousness, which Freudians, regularly and rightly consider deceitful, Jones hangs onto this despised "logic" for the dear life of his theories. "It would be absurd," he states victoriously, "to infer that suggestion is the influence at work in both instances, and that it is more successful

357

when it is deliberately observed and neutralized, than when it is the sole mode of treatment." (29:246) What Jones assumes to be a preposterous supposition, turns out to be true, as we shall see in the next chapter.

Jones brings in the authority of Freud and Ferenczi to reinforce his self-deceit. He tells us that they

> ... hold that transference of unconscious sexual affects plays the most important part in all forms of treatment of the psycho-neuroses, with the exception of the psycho-analytic. In the latter it is merely a stage passed through in the cure, but in the other—electro-therapy, massage, sanatorium treatment, persuasion, etc.—it is not only the main agent in bringing about improvement, but it often remains as a more or less lasting effect of the treatment. (29:246)

True to the form of an intellectual acrobat, Jones reverses the tables: in the enumerated treatments, which contain sexual stimulations to a minimum, he sees a major role of affective elements; in the Freudian treatment, notorious for deliberate, "therapeutic" fanning of sexual preoccupations, he sees a minimal role of such unworthy elements. He admits only parenthetically that sexual attachments to the psychoanalyst may play a role—but only temporarily and unimportantly, till he succeeds in "analyzing" them, and supposedly resolving them. It is an incongruent spectacle to witness a leading psychoanalyst, bound to disparagement of reason, express a belief that a tenuous rational operation can budge the mighty "instincts." Yet such an incongruent belief is essential if the whole structure of psychoanalytic assumptions is to be considered more than sheer net of speculations and delusions. So Jones duly finds no suggestion operative in the Freudian shaping of patient's mind.

Four years later Jones does not show any more ability to face objectively the role of suggestion in psychoanalysis. It appears impossible for most people infected with Freudian preconceptions to break out of them. In 1914 Jones (30) set out to rebut the famous attack of Janet (31) on plagiarism of his theoretical propositions by Freud. The chief thrust of the attack is, besides allegations regarding the appropriated or renamed concepts by Freud, that he is a very sloppy investigator, indiscriminately mixing up his own hunches with productions suggested into patients and receiving them back as confirmation of these hunches. Jones deals in his rejoinder with some minor inaccuracies and misunderstandings committed by Janet, but avoids tackling the major criticism that the analyst's suggestions vitiate the whole fanciful structure of Freudian doctrine.

8. *A seeing psychoanalyst confronts suggestion*

A paper by British psychoanalyst Ida Macalpine is almost unique in Freudian literature in dealing with suggestion in a straightforward manner. Even here the discussion of suggestion in Freud's therapy is veiled by the title "The development of transference." It apparently would have been too much of a shock for her colleagues to title the paper "The basic role of suggestion in psychoanalytic treatment," as would have been proper according to its contents. In the twenty years since its publication, Macalpine's clear realization was obliterated by more conventional Freudian conceptualizations which traditionally shied away from suggestion.

In the introductory portion, Macalpine draws attention to the avoidance of the topic, which would have otherwise forced Freud and subsequent analysts to recognize the clandestine suggestion in their work with patients. They avoided it by not considering seriously the theory about how "transference" is brought about. She quotes from a paper by a major theoretician of psychoanalysis, Fenichel: " . . . it is amazing how small a proportion of the very extensive psychoanalytic literature is devoted to psychoanalytic technique . . . and how much less to the theory of technique." (35:501) Macalpine illustrates the avoidance of a closer look at a process most widely talked about among Freudians, the transference, by using Fenichel's large volume on treatment of neuroses, "which, containing more than one thousand six hundred and forty references, quotes only one reference in the section on Transference." (35:501) She adds succinctly: "It seems tacitly to be assumed that the subject is fully understood." She almost recognizes that she was dealing with a Freudian "no, no" topic, the skeleton in the closet, which was avoided by all prudent members of the family.

Macalpine traces Freudian shying away from "the factors which

359

produce transference," to threefold causes: "historical, inherent in the subject matter, and psychological." (35:502) Among the historical causes, the chief is the embarrassment which Freud and his followers felt about the forerunner of their method, hypnosis. They strove to present the phenomena of transference, already well known in hypnosis, as "an entirely new phenomenon peculiar to psychoanalysis, and altogether distinct from what occurred in hypnosis." (35:502) The hypnotists used suggestion in a direct and open fashion in order to create their kind of relationship, their "transference," with the subjects; Freud decided to use suggestion indirectly and furtively, and therefore created an inhibition in his thinking, which was later trained into the disciples.

In his early paper on Bernheim's book on hypnosis and suggestion, Freud had seen suggestion clearly as a "mental influence" and he described it as "an idea . . . aroused in another person's brain which is not examined in regard to its origin but is accepted just as though it had arisen spontaneously in that brain." (35:503) This definition of suggestion is equally valid for hypnosis, psychoanalysis and brainwashing. In the same "preanalytic" paper, Freud recognized the two kinds of suggestion, direct and indirect, and that the difference between them is that in the indirect form "the mental processes . . . are no longer exposed to the full light of consciousness which falls upon direct suggestions." In this way Freud described not only what happened in his early subjects, but also what was to happen in his later career as a clandestine suggester and a self-deluded theoretician of his own procedures. He created a convenient misinterpretation, Macalpine writes, equating the indirect suggestion with autosuggestion and presenting the subject as responsible for continuing the process started by the suggester, instead of admitting to an ongoing interaction between the subject and his mentor.

Macalpine discerns that the matrix within which the psychoanalytic suggestive activity takes place is the emotional infantilization of the patient, so-called therapeutic regression, covered up by the vague term, transference. She reviews the bits of information scattered through Freudian literature depicting the submissiveness of the subject to hypnotist and psychoanalyst as a state of extreme suggestibility. She brings in some of the relatively rare admissions of Freud that he operated by suggestion. In his *Autobiographical Study* Freud wrote, for instance: "Transference is equivalent to the force which is called 'suggestion.'" In his often practiced maneuver of admitting and denying a statement at the same time, Freud first equates the transference and suggestion, and then confuses the issue by asserting that they are "not the decisive factor." At other times, of course, he had asserted that transference, alongside with resistance, are the basic processes of psychoanalysis. A number of years later, Freud had not achieved a greater degree of clarity on the subject. In his *Group Psychology and the Analysis of the Ego* he writes "Having kept away from the riddle of suggestion for some thirty years, I find in approaching it again that there is no change in the situation." In view of the facts already reviewed, it seems that it would have been more appropriate for Freud to refer to not "the riddle of suggestion," but to his own confusion regarding it.

As to the influence of the subject matter of transference and suggestion in creating a confusion among psychoanalysts, Macalpine offers a twofold explanation. She observes first that psychoanalysts sidetracked themselves by concentrating on mechanisms of transference as manifested by the subjects on the couch, and, second, that they blinded themselves to their own role in arousing these phenomena.

Macalpine sees the analyst's anxiety about recognizing his own role as suggester as the psychological cause for Freudian blind spots about suggestion in psychoanalysis. Here lies the explanation of why, after a thorough survey of Freudian literature, Macalpine found "no clear-cut definitions and many differences of opinion as to what transference is." (35:508)

Macalpine shows more daring than is commonly found among Freudians. Starting with Freud's statement that psychoanalysis is "above all an art of interpretation," she reaches the bold conclusion that analysis is actually no analysis at all, but rather implantation of Freudian thought forms in patient's mind. She observes that the Freudian operations take place first in the analyst, and only subsequently in the analysand. Using the paradigm of "analysis" of children, she points out that

The interpretation is not from current material backward to Ucs content, but from the allegedly presented unconscious material to

361

an alleged immediate transference significance. This, it should be noted, is a mental process of the therapist and not of the patient; hence in the strict scientific sense, it is a matter of countertransference rather than of transference. (35:515)

She considers the classical Freudian method little different from child "analysis," except that it uses interpretation more "sparingly and never until the transference neurosis is well established, and analysis has become a compulsion." (35:516)

Macalpine assails the deceptive presentations of transference as supposedly arising "within the analysand spontaneously." Freud is shown as the chief dissimulator in this respect; other analysts only reiterated the master's self-imposed delusions:

"This peculiarity of the transference is not, therefore," says Freud, "to be placed to the account of psychoanalytic treatment, but is to be ascribed to the patient's neurosis itself." Elsewhere he states: "In every analytic treatment, the patient develops, without any activity on the part of the analyst, an intense affective relation to him ... It must not be assumed that analysis produces the transference ... The psychoanalytic treatment does not produce the transference, it only unmasks it."

And Freud further states: "The fact of the transference appearing, although neither desired nor induced by either physician or patient, in every neurotic who comes under treatment ... has always seemed to me ... proof that the source of the propelling forces of neurosis lies in the sexual life." (35:517)

Macalpine illustrates the process, to which I have alluded a number of times in this volume, of Freud seeing correctly the analyst's role with the corner of his eye and quickly reverting the gaze elsewhere as if he had observed nothing important. She would not let Freud get away easily with his contradictory assertions:

There is, however, a reference by Freud from which one has to infer that he had in mind some other factor in the genesis of transference apart from spontaneity—in fact, some outside influence: the analyst "must recognize that the patient's falling

362

in love is induced by the analytic situation . . . " "He (the analyst) has evoked this love by undertaking analytic treatment in order to cure the neurosis; for him, it is an unavoidable consequence of a medical situation . . . " (35:517)

Macalpine remarks with tongue in cheek: "Freud did not amplify or specify what importance he attached to this casual remark." (35:517)

She would rather clear the deck of the accumulated pretenses and present the Freudian transference as only an instance of rapport between hypnotist and his subject: " . . . both hypnosis and psychoanalysis exploit infantile situations which they both create." (35:535) She quotes Freud's indiscretion: "theoretically and therapeutically, psychoanalysis is the trustee of hypnotism." (35:518) She points to some parallel psychological processes in both analysis and hypnotism: hysterical dissociation between emotional and cognitive processes; an unbounded love of the subject for the hypnotist-analyst; occasional negative transference; similarity of personality reaction (hysterical) in both hypnotic and Freud's subjects; infantilization of the subject and induction of regression.

Macalpine destroys another favorite Freudian misrepresentation: that the couch is used to reduce the patient's anxiety. She points out that the couch is likely to only increase the insecurity as it contributes to the disorganization of patient's mature coping patterns. She sees the couch as part of the "infantile setting to which the analysand is exposed." (35:522) She reasons correctly that if the couch were meant to allay anxieties, it would not lead to regressions which occur when the subject is exposed to "stress, frustration, and insecurity."

Macalpine then takes a closer look at the ways by which the analyst shapes the mind of his patient, without either of them becoming aware of the technique. She stresses the fact that these ways of unconscious influencing have all been described in the Freudian literature, but have "never been described as amounting to a decisive outside influence on the patient." (35:523) In her analysis (35:524-528) she comes at many points to conclusions I have elaborated in previous sections:

1. "The position on the couch approximates the infantile posture": external stimuli are reduced, the subject is left alone as a baby in its crib, with analyst outside the field of vision. "The fixed routine of the

analytic 'ceremonial' . . . is reminiscent of a strict infantile routine."

2. "The constancy of the environment, which stimulates fantasy."

3. Receiving no reply from the analyst replicates the infantile situation. "Interpretations on an infantile level stimulate infantile behavior."

4. "Ego function is reduced to a state intermediate between sleeping and waking," and suggestibility is correspondingly increased. "Free" association leads to a larger role of fantasy and a reduction of critical, rational functions.

5. The dependency on analyst is fostered; "this relationship in itself contains a strong element of magic, a strong infantile element."

6. As psychoanalyst does not respond in supportive ways to the patient, "disillusionment is quickly followed by regression." "The analysand is thus forced to fall back on fantasy." And the analyst occasionally injects his interpretations to grow in that exuberating fantasy.

7. Deliberate frustration of the analysand leads to deeper regression and disorganization of mature personality integrations. "Under these influences the analysand becomes more and more divorced from the reality principle, and falls under the sway of the pleasure principle," comparable to an infant.

Macalpine then inevitably concludes that Freudians have been giving false information to themselves and to the public about their alleged "neutrality" and "passivity": "It is evident that all these factors working together constitute a definite environmental and emotional influence on the analysand. He is subjected to a rigid environment, not by any direct activity of the analyst, but by the analytic technique. This conception is far removed from the current teaching of complete passivity on the part of the analyst." (35:525)

As to the poor guinea pig of Freudian procedures, she admits: "It is quite true, assessing the process as a whole, that the analysand is misled and hoodwinked as analysis proceeds." (35:527)

At the end of this astute analysis of the case against psychoanalysis, Macalpine performs what amounts to an intellectual somersault, an unexpected *non sequitur:* "To have created such an instrument of investigation may well be looked upon as the most important stroke of Freud's genius." (35:526) Such acrobatic feats are known ordinarily among the oppressed penitents of authoritarian regimes who have to save their lives by obeisance to the dictator, boss, or other kind of Big Brother. Brainwashing and Freudwashing will be dealt with in the last chapter.

Notes to Chapter Eight

1. *Introductory Lectures,* chapter 28, p. 373. Denials of suggestion are also made in *Autobiographical Study,* p. 77, *Problems of Lay Analysis,* p. 129, and elsewhere.

2. Jones expends a great deal of effort in describing the unmistakable sexual movements and facial expressions present in hypnotic trance, which did not go unnoticed by medical observers who made the report to the king on the reactions of Mesmer's patients. The fact that the hypnotic state is in many subjects only a veiled expression of sexual passion was known to all informed students of hypnotism through two hundred years of its history before Freud. The intent of these discussions is not clear; they seem calculated to deflect attention from the utilization of sexuality in Freudian analysis. Jones appears ambivalent about it, he speaks of the "possibility, or as is usually expressed, the danger of erotic manifestations or complications" (29:237) in hypnotism. It was not easy for him to make up his mind and say openly that sexuality is an opportunity ("possibility") in both hypnotic and Freudian treatment. He apparently tried to avoid embarrassment before the public, who might see a "danger" in utilizing sexual tensions as a vehicle of therapy. Of course, in private Jones must have found "sexual business," as Freud lovingly called it, quite useful in maintaining a lucrative practice.

365

Chapter IX

SUGGESTION, NOW IN, THEN OUT

Evocative therapies may influence patients as much as directive ones. The powerful influencing effects of psychoanalysis and other "permissive" therapeutic methods have long been noted, ... To recapitulate, the contents of the patient's utterances in nondirective therapy follow the therapist's unwitting leads, and the patient's values shift toward those of the therapist in the course of successful treatment.

> Jerome D. Frank, M.D.,
> Professor of Psychiatry (68:212)

Although it is vigorously denied today, Freud admitted the process of psychoanalysis puts thoughts as well as words in the patient's mind and mouth. You cannot apply the scientific method to test a hypothesis where you create your own evidence out of words, discard whatever evidence displeases you, and then say that your concept is correct simply because you say so.

> Edward R. Pinckney, M.D., and Cathey Pinckney (53:76)

Freud ... his 'free association' or fishing expedition.

> Martin D. Kushner, M.D. (64:78)

For purposes of studying the processes of suggestion 95 dream suggestions were given to six patients under analysis. A positive result was obtained in 68% of the experiments, in the sense that a dream was produced.

> Charles Fisher, Ph.D., M.D., a psychoanalyst (75:252)

1. *Some empirical and experimental findings on suggestion*

Some less renowned, but perhaps less biased, psychiatrists and psychologists have seen clearly what Freud preferred to see only out of the corner of his eye, *i.e.*, that both deliberate and inadvertent suggestions are unavoidable in psychotherapy. Verbalizations represent only a portion of that influence. Even when there are no

366

appreciable verbalizations, two therapists evoke different responses. Pilowsky and Spear (1) found that with one of the therapists seven out of twelve patients spoke longer than eight minutes on their own, while with the other only two of the patients spoke to that extent. "Among humans," writes Beier, "the exchange of information involved in the therapeutic hour is based largely on verbal cues. It is the fashion to think of verbal behavior as essential in the therapeutic process, but the chances are that its role is not quite so significant." (2:4) Research in communications has uncovered the influence of such overtly insignificant response as saying "huh" (3), or "mm-humm" (4), or nodding, to some types of the subject's verbalizations. (5) Schlicht and her associates (6) demonstrated that subjects could be influenced to increase references to the therapist by commenting "good," leaning toward the patient, moving the head, or saying "mm." Salzinger (7) and his co-workers induced their subjects to talk more and increase the proportion of self-referring words by flashing a red light before them. Schlicht also showed that normal subjects condition better than schizophrenics, a finding with definite implications for psychoanalytic procedures since they are employed primarily with nonpsychotics.

Surveying the pertinent literature, Beier (2) reports that the unconscious transfer of messages in the interview and even outside of it (*e.g.*, in advertising) seems to be most successful when the subject is not aware of it. "He must be made to feel, not to think" (2:10), exactly what is done in psychoanalytic situations. This is the "Permissive Message." In the "Evoking Message," neither partner is aware of what is transmitted, as often happens in Freudian and nondirective practice.

Fisher and his associates (8) have verified through experimental research what Freudian analysts and various brainwashers have been practicing all along in changing people's beliefs without ever telling them openly about it. They have shown that subjects yield to the prestige figure in the course of time, even though they may resist in the beginning. Somehow plausibility increases for subjects as they stay exposed to invisible pressure. Fischer (9) has also demonstrated that plausibility of a statement for the subject is greater when the interpretations give the impression of depth—a weapon which Freudians have used quite skillfully.

Quay demonstrated that emotionally charged verbalizations can be

367

manipulated by flat grunts of "uh-huh" by the experimenter. The subjects, university sophomores, were told that the experiment concerned recall of early memories. Subjects were seated facing away from the experimenter, analogous to psychoanalytic situation. In the experimental group the production of memories associated with their family was reinforced by "uh-huh"; in the control group the verbalizations of "non-family" memories was similarly reinforced. Both groups showed an increase in the reinforced type of memory. Quay reasons that

> . . . if a response that minimal [flat, conversational "uh-huh"] could influence verbal behavior, then almost any remark of a psychotherapist would be reinforcing.
> . . . several considerations lead one to predict that the effect would appear with even greater magnitude over a series of psychotherapeutic interviews. For example, a psychotherapist would have much more time in which to respond selectively, his verbal participation in psychotherapy would be considerably greater than the very minimal reinforcing verbalization used in this study, and it seems very likely that he would have more prestige (Verplanck, 1955b) with his patients than the graduate-student investigator in the role of E [experimenter] had with the Ss [subjects] in this experiment. (69:255, 256)

It is of interest in understanding the unawareness of analysands regarding their being manipulated by their analysts, that Quay sent questionnaires to subjects of this experiment, checking on their ability to catch onto what transpired in the experiment. Only one of thirty respondents realized the connection between the reinforcing stimulus (uh-huh) and his responses. However, in spite of this awareness, he was one of the subjects most highly influenced by the inarticulate reinforcer.

Bach (70) discovered that not only verbal responses, but also expressive productions, supposedly revealing (projecting) the subject's unconscious or preconscious tendencies, were influenced by the therapist's ideology, *i.e.*, his theoretical orientation. Bach was intrigued to find that human figure drawings produced during psychotherapy with him were different from the drawings of patients shaped by his office mate, a Freudian psychoanalyst.

A most important series of researches uncovering the concealed and unexpected influences of the unconscious intentions of the experimenter upon the unconscious behavior of his subjects was performed by Rosenthal (10) and his associates. In the main, the experiments demonstrate that the experimenter's hypothesis and expectation influence his subjects, sometimes in an uncanny way.

Not only human, but even infrahuman subjects respond to the experimenter's ideas, or more exactly, the experimenter is able to guide them unconsciously in the direction of his expectations. Even planaria, an invertebrate organism low on the phylogenetic scale, can be influenced to produce different results with different experimenters. (11) When the experimenters (laboratory assistants) were told that one strain of mice was more intelligent and the other dull, even though the mice did not differ in this respect, the experiments produced results in line with the experimenters' beliefs. When those who experimented with "dull" mice were later told their animals were not dull, they simply could not accept the information as correct. To them, the mice remained "really dull." Pavlov had observed in his laboratory that subsequent generations of mice appear more intelligent than earlier ones, but that this may be a function of the improved ability of experimenter to teach the animals.

In experiments with humans, the experimenters' bias is almost regularly demonstrated. In one experiment, using 30 experimenters and 375 subjects, the experimental task was to rate a series of photographs taken from newspapers as being "successes" or "failures." The experimenters were divided into two groups: one was told that these photos represented "successes," the other "failures." The results obtained showed that the experimenters influenced the subjects by their preconceived belief about the photographs without ever telling the subjects what hypothesis they privately held.

In twenty experiments, with 250 experimenters and about 1700 subjects, it was shown that "experimenter internal-orientation bias is both fairly general and a fairly robust phenomenon." (10:271)

Rosenthal quotes Ebbinghaus, who described in his book on *Memory* (1885) the trends which become established and influence results after expectations are set in experimenters. Ebbinghaus was himself experimenter and subject. He observed that if an initial value of a series of experiments was average, his subsequent repetitions of

369

these experiments would tend to be in the average range; if "especially large or small numbers are expected, it would tend to further increase or decrease the values." Rosenthal found that even the computational errors of the experimenters were in the direction of their expectations.

Vikan-Kline (12) found that experimenters with higher status produced greater effects on their subjects. Experimenters rated as looking more "professional" also have a greater influence upon their subjects. If experimenters are privately acquainted with their subjects, their influence is also greater. Females are found to be more "biasable" as subjects than males. (Let us remember that the majority of Freud's early subjects were hysterical females seeing a handsome physician for months on end.) The influence of the experimenter's bias was demonstrable even when he did not work directly with the subject but had assistants do this and did not convey to the assistants what kind of bias he had. In this way we can readily understand the ability of supervisors of training analysts to influence the trainee's patients without ever coming in contact with them. The trainee is thus manipulated into awe of his supervisor, who could "predict" so well some of the patient's psychological reactions without ever seeing him. This must be a fascinating experience for the naive trainee, and ego-inflating for the Freudian scientist.

The implications of these findings for the transfer of the theoretical biases of a psychotherapist are rather obvious.

> ... perhaps the most compelling and the most general conclusion to be drawn is that human beings can engage in communication with one another. The subtlety of this communication is such that casual observation of human diads is unlikely to reveal the nature of this communication process. (10:279)

It surely has fooled many clever people. Friedman (55) developed further the serious implications of Rosenthal's research for psychological investigations. It invalidates many experimental findings which did not take into account the experimenter's influence upon the variability of responses.

Orne (13) draws similar implications for behavioral bias introduced in human contacts by the dominant partner. He experimented with the influence of the subject's expectations upon his behavior in hypnosis, or "the demand characteristics of the experimental situation," as he called it. He instructed one class of students, prior to demonstrating hypnosis to them, that there would be "catalepsy of the dominant hand" as one of the hypnotic phenomena. The students did not know that if catalepsy takes place, it regularly affects all limbs, and they showed the irregular, but expected phenomenon. The control class was not given the erroneous instruction, and its members did not exhibit the suggested form of catalepsy. Orne comments:

> The problem of recognizing which elements ascribed to hypnosis are artifactual or epiphenomenal is extremely difficult. The nature of hypnosis is such that any expectation the hypnotist entertains may unwittingly be communicated to the subject who then acts in a way that demonstrates the validity of the expectation. Thus, we have the potentiality for the occurrence of self-fulfilling prophecies without the investigator being aware of his role therein.
>
> It is generally recognized that unwittingly detailed and accurate communications may take place in the form of implicit and non-verbal cues. Clearly the subject does not respond merely to the verbal suggestions but rather to the totality of the situation from which he actively attempts to ascertain the behavior which is desired.
>
> ... the interlocking motivations of subject and experimenter will thus lead to a pact of ignorance. (13:1098)

2. The fiction of neutrality

Orne points out that the experimenter is influenced by the role he thinks he should play no less than the subject. "Particularly striking is the behavior of the hypnotist with a subject in age regression. His speech becomes altered from that customary in addressing an adult to that typically used when addressing a child." (13:1101) The hypnotist apparently regresses too.

Perceiving the subtle suggestive influences in narcoanalysis ("truth serum"), Frankl denies the possibility that the "pure truth," *i.e.*, reality uncontaminated by the observer's presence and questions, can ever be found about human beings:

371

... If we turn to the discovery of unconscious, repressed, or simply concealed facts, we have to emphasize that in any attempt to uncover them we get neither full nor pure truth. Why not the full truth? Because the patient or, let us say, the subject remains, as can be experimentally demonstrated, at least partially capable of concealing the truth, even in the narcoanalytic situation. And why not the pure truth? Because man is patently suggestible in narcoanalysis, that is, he can be influenced to give the required answer merely through the way questions are put to him. The experimenter will, without knowing, obtain in the answer only an echo of what he had placed into the subject by his questioning. (54:94, 95, my translation)

The biasing influence of interviews has been noticed in public opinion surveys; the respondents often comply with the questioner's expectations. (14) Masling (15) has demonstrated that the assessor's behavior with those whose personality is being evaluated influences the personality assessment obtained.

Truax (16) discovered the influence of subliminal guidance of the subject where it would be least expected—in the classical nondirective interviews of Rogers. He analyzed the interviews for nine client behaviors and found that Rogers, without being aware of it, responded differently to five of them. Of these five, four behaviors were increased as therapy progressed, and these are attributable to inadvertent reinforcement by the therapist.

Any human relationship is replete with unconscious and preconscious influences. Marcuse writes of physicians:

While denying suggestion entrance by the front door, physicians often admit it by the back door in the form of pills, medicine, or bedside manner. Negatively it has been reported that incautious or casual remarks, untimely silence or vocal inflection of the examining physician may by suggestion cause or accelerate disease." (17:124, 125)

Meerloo (18) sees that even doctors are unconsciously subject to suggestive influences of manufacturers, ads, etc. in making their prescriptions. They in turn play the same game with their patients:

Every physician practices psychotherapy, frequently without knowing it. He prescribes valerian drops or orangeblossom tea. He often injects ineffective preparations which he draws with a shining syringe from a small glass retort while the nurse, garbed in snowy white and with profound seriousness, assists him. In sanatoria his patients must undergo obscure treatments. All this is psychotherapy, which since Braid (1840) has been called suggestion, a word as popular as it is misapprehended. The gravity with which a physician surrounds himself, the Latin unintelligibility of his prescriptions, his spectacles, his self-assurance, are all suggestive. I prefer to call this kind of psychotherapy veiling psychotherapy. (18:316)

What can be said about the neutrality of the Freudian analyst? Marmor writes about this fiction:

It has become increasingly clear that such neutrality is actually a fiction; that in the transactional relationship that exists between patient and therapist, the very effort to be impersonal or neutral is an active attitude which must affect the patient either positively or negatively, depending on his needs. Thus, Mandler and Kaplan [19] have demonstrated in an interesting experimental study that the same mm-mmm on the part of a therapist may be interpreted as approval by some patients and disapproval by some others, thus influencing some positively, others negatively. (20:292)

Whether the therapist likes it or not, the patient experiences him as a "reinforcing machine" (21): whether the therapist talks or refrains from talking, shifts in the chair or sits without moving, is tense or relaxed—everything is taken as a clue, given some meaning by the patient. That is why Skinner represents the therapist on the model of general reinforcer. Garner (22) points out that the therapist is a social reinforcer even by his selective attention to some of the patient's statements and disregard of others. Grinker recognizes that the analyst shaped the patient's responses: "These are loaded operations and determine a priori the contents of communications between patient and therapist." (23)

373

A psychiatric discussion reveals insights about the subtle, steering role of the psychoanalyst. The participants seem to agree that instead of representing the analyst's work as active or passive, it would be more realistic to define it as covert or overt:

Dr. Hayes brought up Albert E. Scheflen's characterization of the analyst's role as covert instead of overt, rather than as either active or passive. Scheflen had said that the analyst spends four or five years learning not to say anything in gestures—the way he breathes, moves in his chair, etc. Scheflen listed about seven modes of sensory symbolic communication that the analyst uses, consciously, in every session, continually conveying approbation and disapprobation and thus also expressing moral judgements. Even though in the purest form of analytic technique the therapist says practically nothing, except occasionally to give a classical kind of interpretation, the patient is attuned to pick up the meaning of the covert communication. (24:16)

An exponent of orthodox psychoanalysis, Hendrick, testifies unwittingly that the Freudian analyst interferes with spontaneous flow of data more than a priest confessor, who is expected to instruct and exhort the believer:

Merely listening to all that some of his patients know of their own problems, duplicating in some ways the role of the Roman Catholic confessor, would not, of course have led to psychoanalysis; for it was necessary to learn also what patients did not and could not know of their own unconscious selves. (25:14)

The analyst had to tell them what he imagined was in the statements of his obtuse patients. It is the interference with subject's self-awareness that invalidates psychoanalysis as a method of investigation, reducing Freudism to a remarkable experiment in suggestibility.

The rich matrix of suggestions in which every human relationship is embedded is described by Anderson (26), who shows that implicit meanings are far more numerous than explicitly stated ones. Cain (27) illustrates the subtleness of suggestion by showing how Phoebe, the long-suffering, loving wife of the "Senator" implanted the idea of another alcoholic bender in his mind when he had barely recovered from one: "Don't even think about it, dear; it might make the spell come even quicker." The "Senator" flinched as the idea was suggested. The suffering wife would have been offended if anyone had told her that she was unconsciously motivated to preserve her noble role of the dominating savior.

Freud must have had trouble bringing himself to overlook what seems plain to any practicing therapist. One case from my own experience may illustrate how easily the therapist may deliberately or unintentionally structure the patient's mind by his interpretations (suggestions). A highly anxious, agitated, and impulsive patient in his early forties had started psychotherapy with me after brief hospitalization on a psychiatric ward for depression and suicidal tendencies. His agitation subsided by the tenth interview, then flared up again. One morning he was excited, desperate, at the point of tears. He wanted to give up his job which he considered his main source of trouble. Actually, the job was to terminate in four months anyway, and it was the uncertainty of change that often troubled him; the job itself was undemanding, and his superiors were not pressuring him.

There was an agreement between us that he would openly discuss any suicidal thoughts if they started to appear in him. Just to make sure, I asked him about any such notions. He denied them. He had no trouble with his wife either. He went on for twenty minutes with his panicky talk, filled with self-condemnation. I had a distinct feeling that he was scared about something other than he was talking about. "What have you been worrying about lately?" He again went back to his job, his fear of failure and his sense of letting his family down. I expressed disbelief: "You do not seem to be getting at the source of your recent agitation. You had the fears you speak about all along, and you lived with them for years. You seem to be hedging about something."

He paused, made a trial of probing into the shadows of his mind, got up from his chair, walked nervously about the room. In the meantime, I struggled to get a glimpse of the emotional developments that were leading to a deterioration of the patient's condition. A hunch presented itself: last week we had spoken about his need to see some counselor to investigate the possibility of a new job. I decided to follow this hunch: "You didn't tell me anything about visiting those counselors?"

He was startled. "You think it might be it?"

I hesitated for a moment about whether to lead the patient to consider his agitation in this light. It was clearly more advantageous to this patient to break out of his squirrel cage by taking some appropriate action. "Did you do anything?" I inquired.

"No, I did not. I was afraid, though I was trying to force myself."

By this time, I had decided that it would be useful to handle his troubles in this way, whether it was the "true" source of his upsets or not. In order not to impose an opinion upon the patient, I asked: "Do you have any other explanation for being swept over by these fears?"

"No. By golly, you might be right."

I tried to reinforce the lesson once begun: "Were you so scared about doing anything regarding your future job that you misled yourself to concentrate on your familiar fears, about which you cannot do anything at this time anyway?"

The patient nodded, untensed his body, and relaxed his facial muscles for the first time in forty minutes. "Yes, I see what I was doing."

I had led the patient to a certain pattern of thinking. The patient apparently accepted it, and the certainty made him less agitated. Who could know the objective truth in this case? I could not know any more than the patient, and it does not matter so long as the patient is helped. But it would be quite a different matter if I were to develop out of this situation a general rule that, let us say, patients are agitated because they are afraid of taking action about something they are not talking about. This would parallel Freud's method in developing many of his theoretical "discoveries": he would suggest an idea to himself or to the patient and would then indulge in speculative reasoning to "prove" that his notion was right because it seemed so to him and to his patient. He would then generalize it upon all psychological reactions of that class.

3. *Some unwilling admissions*

Suggestion to patients, a common operation in therapy, has become "a complex" for Freudians. Strupp, otherwise a relatively objective observer of psychoanalysis, tries to get around this difficulty of recognizing suggestion as an inherent component of every therapeutic relationship, by constructing a rationalization. He admits the presence of suggestion in psychoanalysis, but places it outside the formal operations on the couch, as supposedly occurring only in the informal communications between "the couch and the door." The passage amply illustrates the indecision of even nonorthodox Freudians about seeing the full picture and admitting the subtle coaching of the patient that takes place even during the "free" associating; Strupp seems to draw back from the unpopular conclusion to which a cursory consideration of the outcomes of experiments with subliminal suggestions would have compelled him. He retreats upon a version acceptable to the Freudian establishment:

> The therapeutic situation provides plentiful opportunities for more or less subtle advice, suggestions and guidance. It has been said that Freud, following his own recommendations, never gave advice to an analysand on the couch but did not stint with the commodity from the couch to the door. It has taken decades for us to accept the glaring fact that this aspect of therapy is as much a part of analysis as interpreting the unconscious from free association. In their zeal to protect the purity of the analytic situation, Freud and his followers have shown a strange blindness on this subject. Analysts, beginning with Freud, have not denied that they use suggestion, but they claim that they direct it at resistances that act as roadblocks in the treatment. The truth probably lies somewhere in the middle: the therapist strongly encourages independence and autonomy; he takes pains not to suggest courses of action to the patient. At the same time, he cannot prevent himself from offering powerful hints about the general directions of solution. (71:40)

Psychoanalysis certainly is not the bland process Freud and other defenders wished themselves and their naive readers to believe. Occasionally, Freud himself thought that, as interviewer, he was "like a mirror, reflect nothing but what is shown to him." (72:331) At other times he was aware that "we serve the patient in various functions as an authority and a substitute for his parents, as a teacher and educator. . . . " (73:77) On another occasion he admitted that "the personal influence of the analyst . . . does exist and plays a big part in

377

analysis. . . . This personal influence is our strongest dynamic weapon . . . " (74:25, 82)

It seems that, not unlike an apprehensive neurotic who tries to foresee and forestall future difficulties, Freud gives hints here and there in his writings of how he might twist the arm or make things emotionally rougher for an uncomplying patient, but he treats these as occasional measures, not to be associated with the pure doctrine and the ideal treatment. [1]

In *An Autobiographical Study* Freud admits in a vague way that "free association is not really free. The patient remains under the influence of the analytic situation." (65:76) If the topic were not embarrassing to Freud he would have stated more plainly that by "situation" he meant the analyst who molds the patient's mind into Freudian forms. In another statement, Freud reveals indirectly that he is aware that others do not know to what extent he intervenes in the patient's productions to bring them in line with his theoretical suppositions. On this occasion, he denies that his method is as simple as some imagine it, *i.e.*, just sitting and listening. Freud writes,

> . . . among my colleagues there is a widespread and erroneous impression that this technique of searching for the origins of the symptom and removing the manifestations by means of this investigation is an easy one and can be practiced off-hand, as it were. I conclude this from the fact that not one of those who show an interest in my therapy and pass definite judgements upon it has ever asked me how I actually go about it. (29:67, 68)

Is that not partly his fault, for he described himself in an earlier quotation given here as merely sitting behind the couch and "collecting neglected ideas"? Apparently, believers took Freud at his word.

Freud goes on to ridicule the naivete of a would-be, untrained analyst: "His expectation therefore must be that the patient will offer him his secrets as a present, as it were, or perhaps he looks for solution in some sort of confession or confidence . . . for it is not easy to play upon the instrument of the soul." (29:68) That is apparently the important point: the instrument does not play itself; the analyst has to energize it.

Freud explains further:

There is, however, another point of view which you may take up in order to understand the psychoanalytic method. The discovery of the unconscious and the introduction of it into consciousness is performed in the face of a continuous *resistance* on the part of the patient.

The process of bringing this unconscious material to light is associated with pain (*Unlust*) and because of this pain the patient again and again rejects it. It is for you to interpose in this conflict in the patient's mental life. If you succeed in persuading him to accept, by virtue of a better understanding, something that up to now, in consequence of this automatic regulation by pain, he has rejected (repressed), you will have accomplished something toward his education. For it is an education even to induce a person who dislikes leaving his bed early in the morning to do it all the same. Psychoanalytic treatment may in general be conceived of as such a *re-education in overcoming internal resistances*. (29:73, Freud's italics)

Now the picture becomes clearer: the analyst not only collects "free" associations, he also struggles with the patient's mind to change it, to reeducate it, to "interpose" himself into the patient's mental life, to persuade him about the meaning of his associations, "by virtue of a better understanding."

On another occasion Freud spells out unambiguously the teaching he imposes upon his patient:

... the patient knows nothing of these elemental motives or not nearly enough. Now we teach him to understand the structure of these highly complicated formations in his mind; we trace the symptoms back to the instinctual impulses which motivate them; we point out to the patient these instinctual motives in his symptoms of which he has hitherto been unaware ... (29:182)

A rather convincing proof that analysts impose their theoretical biases upon their patients is obtained indirectly by considering the

379

numerous interviews published by therapists of the nondirective approach. In the thousands of interviews held, Rogerian counselors have not uncovered the special Freudian pathologies in their patients. Oedipus complex or castration anxiety, anal character or id demands, are not reported by the client-centered counselors. The nondirective counselors scrupulously try to avoid any overt influences and suggestion to their patients. If Freudian categories were really part and parcel of the human psyche, they would be present in the relatively undisturbed flow of verbalizations of the nondirective subjects. Since they do not appear in the content of non-Freudian interviews, it is likely that their appearance in psychoanalytic interviews is due to suggestions given by the analyst, who subtly indoctrinates his analysands. Nagel, a philosopher of science and a logician, recognized this clearly: " . . . although in the interview the analyst is supposedly a 'passive' auditor of the 'free association' in point of fact the analyst does direct the course of the narrative." (31:49)

Analysts train their subjects about *what* to think, even though they do it without obvious instruction. They educate their analysands, though neither educator nor student is fully aware of the hidden persuasion.

Hollingworth, a well-known American psychologist, his vision unclouded by later Freudian dominance, rendered forty years ago a practically identical verdict of the fictional nature of psychoanalytic concepts:

> We can dispense with the "unconscious" and the "Oedipus complex" and "projection" as easily as we can dispense with fairies, demons, and "Santa Claus." . . . The "psychoanalogy" is all in the explanation, in the theory of the analyst, not in the material of the case. This indeed is quite opposed to the assumptions and quite explicable without them. . . . All these "literary analogies" are dangerous. The unsophisticated may take them to be accounts of something supposed really to happen. . . . Rational explorations with simpler concepts may take the place of the mysticism and demonology of psychoanalysis. (32:281)

4. *A valiant defense*

Ehrenwald seems to be having difficulties in arriving at a decided position regarding suggestion in Freudian analysis. His struggle is typical of many intelligent Freudians. Early in his discussion, he shows a clear grasp of the problem of suggestion in the body of Freudian "evidence," but he proposes a less clear term for the process, namely "doctrinal compliance," since both the therapist and the patient are unaware of the game in which they are caught. He cites examples of the operation of doctrinal compliance in hypnotism rather than psychoanalysis. The hypnotic patients produced "animal magnetism" and hysteric phenomena for Mesmer, "somnambulistic trance" for Marquis de Puysègure, and "lucid sleep" for hypnotists who were influenced by the Platonic ideas of Abbé Faria. He correctly concludes that "it is now difficult to tell which was first, the chicken or the egg," the phenomena or suggestions that molded the phenomena, and were in turn molded by them. Here he comes to the brink of a genuine uneasiness by realizing vaguely that Freudian-dominated psychiatry may have no valid data whatsoever:

> ... if it is indeed possible for the therapist's unconscious or pre-conscious wishes and expectations to enter unawares into his personal equation with the patient, we are confronted with several perplexing questions. What are the criteria of valid ob-servational data in the field of psychotherapy, and in situations of the type of clinical interview in general? How are we to rule out the methodological objection that the patient's responses are psychological artifacts reflecting the therapist's preconceived ideas, his countertransference or his narcissistic desires and inclinations? How can we be sure that the therapist's conclusions are not based on his own self-fulfilling expectations and, by indirection, those of the school of thought to which he owes his allegiance? The fact is that each one of the contemporary schools by psychotherapy has evolved a well ordered, coherent and well-nigh self-sealing system of thought. Each one can claim consider-able measure of success in its therapeutic approach. Each has developed a set of logically consistent hypotheses whose validity is borne out over and over again, by their findings. Yet, the overall picture is one of a variety of conflicting, if not mutually exclusive theoretical positions and "basic principles." (33:55, 56)

Ehrenwald appears unprepared to take the final step and recognize clearly that Freudians, as well as less influential schools, have led psychiatry into a glorious mess, not unlike the situation of someone who believed he had a large sum of money in his savings account and who has suddenly learned that the bank had gone bankrupt.

Ehrenwald then seems to retrace his steps towards reaffirming his faith. He points to Sophocles, drawing parallels to Hamlet, to Schreber's diary, to Freud's autoanalysis, etc. as supposed independent confirmation of Freudian guesses. The whole discussion is contaminated with Freudian preconceptions and distorted in the desired confirmatory direction.

> ... in going back to the creative work of the playwright, Freud could once more feel to be on safe ground. In these instances, suggestion or other forms of doctrinal compliance with their therapists's preconceived ideas could safely be ruled out. From the onset they disposed of most objections which were to be raised by Freud's critics in the ensuing years. This is why the discovery of the Oedipus complex had become one of the cornerstones of the psychoanalytic system of thought. (34:112)

This kind of argument is typical of those who want to accept Freud on faith. A well-informed psychiatrist like Ehrenwald had simply to repress discussions often met in non-Freudian literature that Freud distorted the real meaning of Sophocles' drama. He freudianized the Greek hero, reading into the fate-decreed incest his own prejudices. [see *Freud's Phallic Cult,* chapters III, V (61)] The study of other "supportive evidence" enumerated by Ehrenwald ("interpretations" of Hamlet, shaping of Schreber into a paranoiac homosexual, Freud's self-analysis) will also show that all of them have serious flaws. They are all contaminated with Freudian interpretative preconceptions. It is hard to imagine that such a well-read and thoughtful man would not be aware of the shoddiness and contrived nature of the Freudian interpretation of those "data." Ehrenwald is, however, convinced that such wishful distortion of historically available material was Freud's "stroke of genius." As a believer, Ehrenwald appears to treat as simply inadmissible the realization that Freud's biased "factual evidence" may be invalid. To make the confusion worse, he confounds for example, the first-order observations on emotional ambivalence or inferiority feelings with Freud's second-order imaginative derivations of Oedipus and castration complexes.

Ehrenwald also mentions Rorschach, TAT, and other projective tests as supportive sources for the tottering Freudian structure. Again, it is hard to imagine that Ehrenwald is not aware that, like dream interpretations or other Freudian operations, one gets out of these tests what one has put into them by preconception, and that they are not independent sources of validation.

Ehrenwald shows irresoluteness and vacillation between critical and uncritical attitudes to Freudian theoretical fantasies. In some portions of his book (34), he seems to exempt Freud from the usual reliance on myth in psychotherapy, taking Freud at his word about producing an allegedly scientific psychology. At such times, Ehrenwald considers that "as a consistent system of scientific thought, . . . [psychoanalysis] has gone far to purge itself of the vestiges of magic and myth." (34:77) It is in such a mood that Ehrenwald presents Jung as a "mythophylic" theorist, and Freud he alleges to be a "mythophobic" one. He fails to see that both Jung and Freud dealt largely in myths, except Freud liked to pretend that his myths were "scientific." At other times, when he regains his critical objectivity, Ehrenwald sees that psychoanalysis is as permeated by myths as other therapeutic approaches: "It is true that these paraphernalia of analytic technique are based on thoroughly rational dynamic principles. But they are overdetermined at the same time by vestiges of magic and myth in the analytic approach." (34:169)

After making the above shaky argument in favor of Freudian validity, Ehrenwald has recourse to what we have seen earlier as a favorite play of Freudian apologists, *i.e.,* a comparison to physical science.

> Certain findings of quantum physics are particularly relevant at this point. Quantum theory has led to the conclusion that all methods of observing physical objects involve definite interference with the actual physical state of the object observed; conversely, the object invariably affects the physical state of the measuring instruments and ultimately the sense organs of the observer. (34:113)

There follows a more elaborate discussion of statements by various physicists, which would probably mislead an uncritical reader into thinking that psychoanalysis is on at least the same scientific level as atomic physics, if not higher. [Ehrenwald had much earlier in the book asserted, "But even when measured by the self-validating standard of science, orthodox analysis tends to be more scientific than science itself." (34:75)] Yet the whole argument is built on a false premise: When the physicist studies the movement and position of atomic particles or molecules, he takes the experimental distortion into account as an extraneous variable; when Freudians register the productions of their patients, they treat the extraneous variable, *i.e.,* their suggestions, as the supposed spontaneous response of the subject.

Following this defensive excursion, Ehrenwald comes to less partisan considerations, but still without drawing the inevitable conclusions about the invalidity of Freudian "findings":

> This leads to a further parallelism between the modern psychological and physical approaches. The "causal anomalies" suggested by the occurrence of doctrinal compliance in psychotherapy indicate that we cannot be sure whether our findings represent genuine productions of an individual patient or merely reflect our own preconceptions. We do not know whether our interpretation was made to fit the forthcoming evidence, or whether our evidence was called forth by the interpretations looming in the back of our minds. We cannot tell which came first—the therapist and his theories, or the patient and his neurotic symptoms. However, the fact is that, irrespective of the therapist's allegiance to one or the other of the rival schools, and regardless of the apparently inescapable epistemological difficulties in assessing their respective merits, psychotherapy—scientific and prescientific—has from time immemorial been a going concern: it has stood the test of application in practice. It has met the emotional needs of countless generations even though it has done so on the basis of inadequate theoretical presuppositions. (34:114)

In this way, the argument about the self-fulfilling nature of Freudian "research" remains suspended in the air. All we can do is accept it on faith or reject it. Seemingly uncomfortable about drawing a bold conclusion, Ehrenwald has recourse to his faith in the ultimate validity of Freudian productions. He takes a look at the heap of Freudian fantasies and suggestions and takes courage from the impressive pile: " . . . comparable research data supplied by the rival

384

schools—including attempts at various conditioned reflex or behavior therapies—still lag behind the evidence amassed by Freudian analysis in the past decades." (33:56)

What "research data" and what "evidence"? He had just thrown those out of scientific court as a hopeless mixture of the "process of circular feed back" in which the patient and therapist succeed in confusing each other. Ehrenwald is, of course, right about the huge volume of Freudian writing output. But what does that prove? Philosophers, literary men, politicians have also flooded the libraries with their productions. Their prolificacy does not make them into science any more than psychoanalysis. A psychologically oriented reader would easily grasp that Ehrenwald is searching for a peg on which to pin the faith he needs.

We cannot begrudge Ehrenwald's flight to faith for safety, since we need certainty, even if it is irrational, to cope with the anxieties of the big, real world. For my part I prefer to seek this certainty regarding suprascientific matters in the faith of the Christian Church, refined and confirmed through centuries, than to have recourse to "scientific" delusions. But, each one to his taste.

Ehrenwald's final conclusion remains, naturally, quite inconclusive:

> Viewed in this light, even the apparent artifacts derived from doctrinal compliance appear in a new light. They are joint productions of the patient and the therapist, meaningful and psychologically significant in their own right. Once they have made their appearance in the psychoanalytic situation, they tend to establish a circular pattern of feedback: they may become legitimate idioms in an existing system of communication. Indeed with the widening ripples on the surface of such a system, they qualify as cultural, or subcultural, events in the making. Before long, they are likely to be adopted as new modes of psychological expression: as myths or archetypes in statu nascendi, as it were,—as neo-types, if you like. They become the "myths of our time" and derive their ultimate "existential validation" from the concensus of those who are ready to accept them as authentic statements of scientific truths. (34:116)

In the end, it appears that Ehrenwald comes to essentially the same conclusion I reached earlier about the hopelessness of verifying

Freudian propositions and basing their acceptance upon the consensus by faith of indoctrinated believers. Freudian truths were contaminated with Freudian hidden persuasion right from their beginnings in Freud's chamber, and the contamination was compounded by infecting the public with deceptive claims for their self-evidential value. The "Freudian dust" has spread everywhere, and we breathe it unavoidably.

5. *Browbeating the child-patient*

In the article discussed earlier in this chapter, Freud mentions that the patient must be "educable," (29:70) that is, willing to adopt the analyst's views as a schoolchild adopts the views proposed by his teacher. This method of "interposing" his "better" ideas into the patient's uncertain mind, Freud considers a definite advancement, as he writes six years later, in 1910:

> At the beginning, psychoanalytic treatment was inexorable and exhaustive. The patient had to say everything himself, and the physician's part consisted of urging on incessantly. Today things have a more friendly air [1]. The treatment is made up of two parts, one of what the physician infers and tells the patient, and out of the patient's work of articulation, or working through what he hears. The mechanism of our curative method is indeed quite easy to understand; we give the patient the conscious idea of what he may expect to find [*bewusste Erwartungsvorstellungen*] and the similarity of this with the repressed unconscious... (29:78)

This, then, is the gist of the Freudian process of reeducation: the subject is told what to look for, and lo and behold, he finds it in his unconscious! Freud uses the misleading phrase "more friendly" for such more open indoctrination of his patient. Perhaps he expected that "more friendly" readers would not recognize what he was saying in the quoted passage, *i.e.,* that he coaches the patient what and how to think about his troubles.

Simply telling the patient the meaning of his dreams and other productions is not enough: already by 1897, Freud had found that giving an unadorned interpretation is wrong, that it does not pressure the patient sufficiently to accept the analyst's views; so he turned his attention to convincing the patient:

> At that time I was of the opinion (recognized later to be incorrect) that my task was limited to informing patients of the hidden meaning of their symptoms. Whether they then accepted or did not accept the solution upon which success depended—for that I was not responsible. I am grateful to this error, which, fortunately, has now been overcome... (35:197)

The patient evidently is not told that he is quarrying in "salted mines"; Freud conveniently chooses to disregard this aspect of his procedure.

The imposition of Freudian ideology upon the patient by subtle training and suggestive interpretations did not, however, escape the notice of uninvolved observers. Hilgard, a seasoned experimenter with hypnosis, points to the connection between the sexually colored relationship in psychoanalysis and the sexuality so richly represented in dreams of Freudian patients:

> Subjects, for example, interpret dreams differently for a familiar hypnotist than for a strange one. Classical psychoanalysis interprets the transference situation as essentially a sexual one. It may be that this interpersonal relationship accounts also for the sexual emphasis of dream interpretations within the analytic period. (62:14)

La Pierre describes even more pointedly the clandestine conditioning process:

> The process of interpretation presumably runs throughout the entire analysis. It is, ordinarily, made piecemeal and gradually, and it involves inducing the patient into the Freudian way of thinking about psychic matters. In effect, then, the patient is gently schooled in Freudian doctrine; or, as non-Freudians would be inclined to say, converted to the Freudian faith. Even in Freudian theory, it is quite essential to therapeutic success that the patient come to accept as valid the Freudian concept of him

as a person. He must learn to think of himself as composed of id, ego, and superego; and a victim of the Oedipus, castration, and other complexes; as one whose behavior has obscure implications; as one whose natural self and socially imposed self are unceasingly engaged in an unresolvable conflict; and as one who is, as a consequence, psychologically frail. For only if he does come to see himself in this way will the analyst's interpretation of the causes of his mental distress be acceptable to him. And it is, presumably, through this accepting the analyst's interpretation that he is absolved from the mental consequences of those causes. (36:69)

Freud explains his particular method of brainwashing further: "Psychoanalysis was then first and foremost an art of interpreting. Since this did not solve the therapeutic problem, a further aim quickly came in view; to oblige the patient to confirm the analyst's construction from his own memory." (37) It is this "obliging the patient" to find the analyst's fantasies in his psyche that disqualifies Freudian findings (or rather "puttings-in") from scientific status in investigations of unadulterated psyche.

In 1926, Freud describes how he *told* a patient what was the "secret of his neurosis" and the patient got worse, struggling against imposition of Freudian meanings upon his troubles:

With our lad A.B. things are going very strangely. My belief as a physician that he is on the verge of a paranoid dementia has increased. I was again very near the point of giving him up, but there is something touching about him which deters me from doing so; the threat of breaking off the treatment has made him gentle and amenable again, with the result that at present a good understanding prevails between us. The great deterioration during which the letter to you was written was connected with my telling him the apparently real secret of his neurosis. The immediate reaction to that revelation was bound to be an enormous increase in the resistance. (38:101)

Of this kind of coaching, Nacht, a French psychoanalyst, had said fifty years later: "The associations of the patient are literally 're-thought' by the analyst." (39:90)

Other Freudians have also tried to maintain the make-believe of objectivity. For instance, the pretense of a noninterfering analyst seems to be intended in Menninger's diagrams in which the psychiatrist is described as "examines—councils [sic]—organizes treatment" while a psychoanalyst only "suspends judgement—interprets." (40:32, 28)

6. *Hopelessly contaminated Freudian data*

There are, objectively speaking, no Freudian *data*. No hard facts, that is. What we find are imaginative speculations, inextricably mixed with effects of autosuggestion on the analyst and suggestion on the patient. It is usually taken for granted that Freud's self-analysis and interpretation of dreams, many of them his own, are cardinal sources of Freud's science. And it is here that contamination began. Freud and Freudians do not apparently want to grasp the fact that dreams can be molded by the dreamer's wishes. Freud himself taught that dreams are wish fulfilments. Of course he did not suspect consciously that his intellectual ambitions could steer his own wish fulfillments through dreams. He intimated his partial insight into sources of his dreams only indirectly, in order not to topple the house of cards he had built with his writings and subsequent fame. In that period, when he was struggling to overcome his own neurosis by self-analysis and create the basis for his later views on psychic life, Freud writes to Fliess that he knew in advance what dreams he would have during the coming night. Apparently his mind was obliging him to produce custom-made dreams. Van Eedem, a Dutch psychiatrist, Freud's contemporary, and a more astute student of dreams than Freud, reported at the Fourth International Congress of Psychology in 1900 in Paris, that "a person could train himself to direct his dreams at will." (66:780)

After having deluded himself about his "data," Freud proceeded to delude his students and his readers. The contamination of observed data with the analyst's suggestions is clearly seen in the analysis of Little Hans, which is hailed by many Freudians as strong confirmation of a number of cherished psychoanalytic doctrines. Freud admitted that Hans had to be told how to think according to psychoanalytic postulates, and excused this coaching by the supposed therapeutic

389

effects of the interpretations. One might question the therapeutic value of interpretations that explain to a five-year-old boy that what he really wants is to copulate with his mother, but it is beyond doubt that Freud and his psychoanalysts prefer to remain blind to the effects of their participation in their patient's psychic productions, so that they can later quote these as the alleged proofs of the validity of the Freudian imaginations. Sensing that weakness, Kubie proposes that conclusive validation is "possible chiefly with the material from uninformed children, naive psychotics, and subjects under hypnosis. In the literature there are many examples from these three sources where the patient sounds as though he had written the textbooks." (41:63) In view of Kubie's assertion, it is surprising that other reviewers of Freudian writings have not found such examples; Kubie gives no reference for it either, although he provides sources for many of his other assertions. What the reviewers do find is contaminated material coming from directly or indirectly coached persons.

Freud himself never found the material provided by naive subjects gratifying. "Even in the most deep reaching psychoses," he wrote, "the unconscious memory does not break through, so that the secret of infantile experiences is not revealed even in the most confused states of delirium." (42:45) Yet though the unconscious does not yield its secrets even under conditions of severe personality breakdown, Freud and Freudians talk of their conjectures regarding the unconscious as if they were objective findings. The vast accumulation of Freudian literature can be schematically presented in four stages:

1. Freud fantasizing about himself and about the psyche of his patients, and purportedly proving his hunches by productions of his self-analysis and analyses of his indoctrinated patients.
2. Patients confirming these fantasies upon the direct or subtle coaching of Freud and the early analysts. (The "thought-reform camps" provide a similar "proof" of the truth of Communist doctrines in the subjective convictions of converted future party propagandists.)
3. Freudian pupils taking up the alleged findings on faith, being indoctrinated by reading and personal analysis, and spreading the faith to the unsuspecting public.
4. Freudian mythology becoming part of the public lore and acquiring the status of self-evident truth.

In view of this realization, it seems almost incredible that a professionally educated man like Kubie should be able to assert that the flimsy Freudian data outlined above "carry the validity of precise experimentation." What is worse, a great many well-trained psychologists and psychiatrists also cannot see the incoherence of such assertions.

I do not at this point object primarily to psychoanalytic technique as reeducation, though I shall protest against such reeducation on the grounds that it is harmful to moral and religious values. [2] I should also point out that I do not consider Freudian therapy as coarse an interference with personal dignity as brainwashing. What concerns us here primarily is the scientific unreliability of the psychoanalytic method of investigation. Freudians, we discover, offer "proofs" which are not that at all since they are vitiated through the suggestive effect of interpretations. The analyst meddles with the psychic productions of his patients, contaminating them with his intervention and making them worthless as objective psychological materials. "If the double blind experiment," writes Grinker, "is necessary for the study of potent drugs to avoid the effects of suggestion, how much more necessity is there for the objective observers when only words and attitudes are used and a psychiatrist himself is the drug!" (43:369)

Garduk and Haggard (67) showed in a controlled investigation that interpretations have a potent influence in shaping patients' verbal and behavioral reactions. They compared the patients' responses after interpretations (explanations of "unconscious" meanings) and non-interpretations (getting or giving information, etc.) from the recordings of four psychoanalytic treatments. The interpretations were shown to bring about significant increases in the patient of transference-related responses, understanding and insight (of course, in terms of Freudian teachings), affect, and passive dwelling on the message provided by the analyst.

One of Freud's delusions which has also misled many psychotherapists into naive thinking is that the improvement in the patient's condition supposedly proves that the interpretation made was the correct one. This is one more example of the unwarranted misuse of logic by Freud and his followers. Sargant (44:24) reports that patients improved as much or more when they abreacted to *imaginary*, suggested, affect-laden situations as to the ones which were known to have traumatized them. In the light of these experiences, another Freudian shibboleth must be discarded.

Just two years before his death, Freud proposed that interpretations should more correctly be called "constructions," and he explained why:

> The analyst furnishes a piece of construction and communicates it to the subject of the analysis so that it may work upon him, deals with it in the same way and proceeds in this alternating fashion until the end. If, in accounts of analytic technique, too little is said about "constructions," that is because "interpretations" and their effects are spoken of instead. But I think that "constructions" is by far the more appropriate description. (45, v. 5:362)

His followers did not adopt Freud's suggestion, probably because the new term shows too plainly that the analyst constructs in the patient's mind the weird concepts of psychoanalysis. The method of analysis would thus appear close to those of suggestion, persuasion, and brainwashing.

Freud had realized also that the procedures of "constructions" would throw doubt on the validity of theoretical material supposedly gathered objectively from patients' associations. He was aware that this was a fatal flaw in the evidence for his imaginative theories, and he reassured his possibly worried listeners at the Second International Psychoanalytical Congress:

> ...in speaking to you I need not rebut the objection that the way we practice the method today obscures its testimony to the correctness of our hypotheses; you will not forget that this evidence is to be found elsewhere and that a therapeutic procedure cannot be performed in the same way as a theoretical investigation. (29:78, 79)

Quite true, but where, then, is the evidence?

Probably, he was alluding to *The Interpretation of Dreams* as his *magnum opus*, articles on infantile and adult sexuality, and some previously published clinical papers. Unfortunately for Freud, all these are suspect. They are riddled by the usual Freudian method of proving one assertion by referring to a previous unproven assertion as a "fact." If it is to *The Interpretation of Dreams* that Freud sends his listeners to find proofs for his current practice, he sends them to a book that discusses one of the most illogical and arbitrary procedures of his whole "science." [see *Freud's Non-science*, chapter VII (30)]

If Freud refers to his personal analysis as the basis for his theory, he courts an even greater fiasco. In 1909, Freud tells a group of American students: "The analysis of myself . . . I carried out by the aid of a series of my own dreams which led me through all the happenings of my childhood years." This is scientifically the least acceptable source of Freudian data. Freud overlooks here what was otherwise known to him, that dreams can be induced hypnotically or by suggestion in wakeful state. This practice was a European psychotherapeutic tradition, developed more fully later on by a French psychologist (56) and an Italian-American psychiatrist. (57) The only difference between their methods of induced dreams and Freud's appears unessential: instead of producing dreams through hetero-suggestion, Freud induced them on himself by autosuggestion, as I have already pointed out.

Freud made another scientific blunder on this occasion. He naively trusted his and his patients' recall of dreams as if it were on the level of facts, overlooking the untrustworthiness of human memory. Objective investigations of details of even recent occurrences show wide distortions, according to the subject's biases, not to speak of the distortion which Freud, eager to build his theory, would introduce *not* into his own and his patients' childhood memories, but into reconstructions of the supposed childhood events from dreams! This is as much science as an old wives' tale. Even in hypnosis, Orne (46) found that the information produced was unreliable because the subjects wanted to produce data which they expected would please the hypnotist. Even a drugged person in narcoanalysis cannot be trusted in his productions. (18:358) Wolberg protests against the naive reliance on "truth" obtained from criminals under hypnosis:

Frequently hypnosis is employed as a tool to authenticate motives or to restore amnesic episodes. As a professional who has hypnotized thousands of individuals, I can attest to the fact that there is nothing virtuous about the material divulged in the trance state. It is subject to as many distortions and secondary elaborations as ideation in the waking state. Indeed the material elicited is even more untrustworthy since phantasy formation is more intense, and the hypnotized person quickly picks up from verbal and nonverbal cues what the hypnotist wants him to say. The suggestive element is so strong that the subject will feed back to the hypnotist material the subject believes is expected of him.

I have some interesting examples of this from my practice, subjects bringing out in stark detail presumably authentic past activities that investigation has proven false, even though the subject sincerely believed, at the time the pronouncements were made, and even later on in the waking state, that his divulgences were truthful. (58:558)

It remains wholly uncertain how Freud's theoretical biases and needs influenced his self-analysis. In 1909, Freud complains to Pfister that people think of his ideas as psychological fantasizing: "If only one could get the better people to realize that all our theories are based on experience (there is no reason, so far as I am concerned, why they should not try to interpret it differently) and not just fabricated out of thin air or thought up over the writing desk." (38:27)

It is true that Freud's ideas are based on *his* experience, but that experience is so distorted by his personal pathology, his wishful thinking, and the suggestions by which he manipulated his patients on the couch, that what he reconstructed writing later on at the desk was vitiated to the extent that it had no objective and comprehensive psychological application. It was the record of the personal neurotic peculiarities of the doctor and the reflection of these in patients and readers influenced by suggestion and persuasion. When, in 1910, Freud points out to Pfister that "If my friends are now ready to accept what I say, that is only because they have found so much of it to be borne out, and a natural compensation for the incredulity which I encountered for ten years," (38:45) he forgets that they had accepted it on faith from him, even as he had accepted the "nose neurosis" concept of his friend Fliess in the previous decade.

Perhaps, though, we are taking Freud too seriously on this point. He may only have wanted to exhort his adherents gathered at this congress and allay their self-doubts by alluding to these "proofs." [3]

Freud hints in a passage quoted earlier that he had not, in his initial practice, used interpretations to mold the patient's psychic productions. However, the inspection of Freud's clinical papers reveals that he had never paid attention to the basic requirement of any impartial psychological investigation, *i.e.*, not to influence the flow of data by overt or covert suggestions. In spite of reassuring his disciples about other alleged sources of his information, Freud obtained his data as they came from patients unconsciously trained by him to produce them. In that early period in 1895, he writes to Fliess: "Confirmation from neurotics' material keeps pouring in on me . . . one of the two cases has given me what I was waiting for (sexual shock, *i.e.* infantile abuse in a case of male hysteria!) . . . the few remarks on paranoia arise from a recently begun analysis . . . " (42:130, 132, 141)

He could not just sit back and wait for the expressions to come spontaneously from the analysand. He directed the process actively, obstinately "feeding up" for months till he got what he was after—sexuality all over the place:

> . . . the connection between obsessional neurosis and sexuality does not always lie so near the surface. I can assure you that in my case II (compulsive micturition) it was not so easy to find. If it had been sought for by anyone less obstinately wedded to the data, it would have been overlooked. And in this case, which I have been studying carefully over months of feeding up, sexuality quite simply dominates the whole scene. (42:81)

Again, Freud reveals privately what he would not admit publicly: that he badgered his patients till they produced what he wanted. As Rank reports, patients start producing the required dreams when they are threatened by discontinuance of sessions. Little wonder, then, that Skinner concluded that "Freud did not discover the mental apparatus but rather invented it." (48:425) He discards as worthless the personality model so painstakingly built by Freud and his disciples as "fictitious or metaphorical apparatus which Freudians feel they observe in the organism. So far as I'm concerned, these are versions of some sort of primitive animism." (63:7)

In one of the previous quotations, Freud says that he used to "urge" the patient to produce associations. We can only guess what this "urging" consisted of. Coming from a former user of old-fashioned hypnotism and suggestion, Freud's "urging" is enough to make his data scientifically suspect, despite his protestations of innocence. We know that Freud pushed his opinions upon his patients with some determination. After one of his early cases, Dora, interrupted analysis because of the insistence of Freud's interpreting, he vowed to press his interpretations more gently in the future. The experiences more than twenty years later of Wortis and Miss Choisy show that this was only a superficial rational decision, while his more deeply determined drives kept him rushing ahead with enlightening interpretations.

The process of contaminating evidence with the analyst's suggestions has gone on unchecked among Freud's pupils:

> Schaffer, among others, has noted that a serious danger of analysis is its being based on unreliable data. Where other scientists may rely on fairly objective observations, analysts have relied almost exclusively on data gained through introspections whose reliability is questionable. Not that there is anything intrinsically unscientific about the use of introspective methods, but where introspection is employed in psychological research, special care must be exercised to see that the personal biases of the observer or experimenter do not infiltrate or unduly influence the gathering and the reporting of the introspective evidence. This special care, however, has frequently not been taken by analytic investigators. Thus, Wittels candidly admits that Freud's specific method of investigation ... was not suitable for setting up boundaries and strict definitions. Through insight into himself he came to understand a psychological phenomenon and from the beginning his discoveries carried a strong inner conviction of certitude. While an inner conviction of certitude is a fine trait for a prophet to possess, its liabilities for the scientist should be sufficiently obvious to warrant any further comment. (49:96)

The naive attitude to the contamination of data with the analyst's suggestions is exhibited, for example, by Jones. He claims that the odd Freudian ideas are valid because they have been confirmed in analysis. He is oblivious to the fact that the content of analyses is shaped by the analyst's coaching of the analysand, as his "footnote" reveals:

The desire to manipulate the product (viz. of defaecation) further and to create out of it leads to various sublimations, beginning with the usual fondness of children for moulding and manipulating plastic material, putty, plasticene, etc. The commonest sublimation is in the direction of cooking, which may later be replaced by an aversion from cooking, or continued as a passion for it. It finds extensive application in two other spheres of life, the industrial and the artistic; good examples of the former are metal moulding, building, carpentry, engraving, etc.; examples of the latter are sculpture, architecture, wood-carving, photography, etc. Footnote—lest it may be thought that any of these conclusions are speculative, I may say that every one is based on the data of actual analyses, as are all the conclusions presented in this paper. (50:685)

Even a psychiatrist who was exposed to canons of scientific objectivity demanded of researchers in this country, fails to see the scientific hopelessness of the chief Freudian tool of investigation, the "free association." Pumpian-Mindlin, summarizing a symposium convened to evaluate the scientific worth and liability of psychoanalysis, takes great pains in justifying Freudian confusion of data from patients with fictions of the investigator. He proposes the view that unconscious material investigated in psychoanalysis is so peculiar that it cannot be investigated by accepted scientific techniques. The main reason for adopting the nonscientific Freudian technique is that their instrument, free association, is "useless in the presence of other observers," (59:136) which might mean that it would embarrass the analyst to manipulate the patient in customary ways in front of an observer.

There are at least two serious fallacies in his argument. First, he overlooks the possibility of noninterfering forms of free association as one might practice in Rogers's classical approach to nondirective counseling or in the type of unloading of preoccupations present in the brain in the cathartic procedures developed within Autogenic Training (60), in which the therapist does not inject any comments. The second fallacy is so patent that it is a wonder how Pumpian-Mindlin could have missed it: if, as he says, the instrument is useless in the presence of other observers, how does it become useful in the presence of the standard observer who guides subjects' association into Freudian channels?

In striving to give scientific respectability to Freudian free association, Pumpian-Mindlin cites an experiment in support of his thesis, without apparently realizing that the same experiment, objectively interpreted, denies scientific status to psychoanalytic findings. The experiment was carried out by Luria in a series investigating the influence of hypnotic suggestions upon the source of associations. The subjects were asked to associate to certain words which were later to be used under hypnosis to induce a conflict of guilt in them. Posthypnotic suggestion was given to not remember the suggested reprehensible deeds. When the free associations were obtained after hypnosis, there was a decided difference on conflict-connected words from prehypnotic series. So far, the experiment proves that subjects can be suggested into conflicts, that artificial induction of psychic discomfort is possible. "However, a further test was done which was most significant," (59:141) claims Pumpian-Mindlin. The subjects were asked to free-associate to neutral words and ultimately the chain of associations led to the conflict induced in earlier hypnotic sessions. Pumpian-Mindlin proposes that here we find "experimental evidence for the validity of the technique of free association." (59:141) By a rather broad interpretation of Luria's experiment, one can admit the possibility of unconscious conflicts emerging through free association. But that is not the point which bothers the scientist about psychoanalysis. The real question is not about the possibility of bringing out unconscious conflicts through *genuine* free association, but whether the material brought out of *Freudian* free association may not be only an artifact of analyst's injecting his ideas into subjects, as Luria did with his hypnotic suggestions.

The hoax is subtle and sometimes not easy to discern. A tragic analogy to the blindness of the analysts to what they contributed to the situation is seen in the stubborn refusal of doctors, whose maternity cases were dying from puerperal fever, to believe that these deaths had anything to do with materials carried on their hands from dissections of cadavers.

It is ironical to read Freud's description in his *Autobiographical Study* of how he discarded electrotherapy, then in vogue, as worthless, misleading of both the patient and the doctor. Freud's explanation seems to parallel the exposition given here of suggestion as the basic process in psychoanalysis:

> My knowledge of electrotherapy was derived from W. Erb's textbook (1882), which provided detailed instructions for the treatment of all the symptoms of nervous diseases. Unluckily I was soon driven to see that following these instructions was of no help whatever and that what I had taken for routine, if exact observation was merely the construction of phantasy. The realization that the greatest name in German neuropathology had no more relation to reality than some "Egyptian" dream-book such as is sold in cheap book-shops, was painful, but it helped to rid me of another shred of the innocent faith in authority from which I was not yet free. So I put my electrical apparatus aside, even before Moebius had saved the situation by explaining that the successes of electric treatment in nervous disorders (insofar as there were any) were the effect of suggestion on the part of the physician. (51:16)

Freud's experience with Erb's method is repeated in the experiences of many psychologists and psychiatrists who went into psychoanalysis hopefully, only to be disillusioned. Freud's derogatory remarks about the fad of electrotherapy, describe psychoanalysis equally well: " . . . no more relation to reality than some 'Egyptian' dream-book, such as is sold in cheap book-shops." We might use Johnson's insight into psychoanalysis as a summary to the foregoing discussion:

> Certain essentials of the method: the necessity for skill in handling the counter-transference; the darkened room; the couch; "free" associations, which as we have seen actually cloak an active role on the part of the analyst and are anything but free; the passivity; but, most of all, the emphasis on dreams stamp the Freudian method as basically unscientific, suggestive or rather, hypnosuggestive psychotherapeutic technique. (52:336)

Notes to Chapter Nine

1. Lossy (28), a contemporary defender against the charge of suggestion in psychoanalysis, explains it away in typical Freudian fashion by ascribing it to the patient's "resistance." He speculates further that the patient even derives some benefit from protesting against the suggestion, for he can bring into the open his unwelcome thoughts, and also indulge in passive libidinal satisfactions, which are assuredly homosexual. It would be of interest to read what ingenious explanation Chinese brainwashers must have made about the perverse resistance of their American victims.

2. See *Freud's Phallic Cult* (61), particularly chapters 6, "The Corrosive Philosophy of Freudism," and 7, "Some Pathogenic Emanations of Freudism."

3. Kubie (47) seems to follow closely the example of the master in this respect. He promises to deliver scientific data on neurotics, primitives, etc. He even disparages the "science-fiction of Melanie Klein." Yet, what one finds in his own article is no less a science fiction. The "data" are made of speculation, deductive reasoning from the unproven Freudian theory, loose rationalizations, and a dearth of references to experimental work supposedly supporting psychoanalytic theory.

Chapter X

Freudwashing: Psychoanalysis As Camouflaged Brainwashing

When a set of delusions is well organized, the whole thing
becomes logical if we buy one or two crazy ideas.
>
> Hugh Storrow, M.D.,
> Professor of Psychiatry (17:73)

... the patient is constantly brainwashed into accepting analytic
interpretations even when they seem to have a far-fetched
relationship to the facts of his life.
>
> Albert Ellis, Ph.D.,
> Clinical Psychologist (1:17)

Wagner-Jauregg, Professor of Psychiatry at the University of
Vienna and Nobel Prize winner, asked a patient of Dr. Helene
Deutsch, then his assistant, later famous Freudian analyst: "Has
Dr. Deutsch put in your mind that you want a child from your
father?" (31:73)

The answer to this puzzle [why Communism did not become as
popular in America as Freudism] lies in the fact that psychoanalysis is not an impartial medical or psychological therapy. The
method of psychoanalysis requires that the patient be persuaded,
or trained, to accept fully and unreservedly the Freudian philosophy. Using the popular term of brainwashing, we may say that
it is the base of psychoanalytic therapy. Again and again in his
numerous seances, the psychoanalyst impresses on his patient the
basic ideas of Freud. At the end of one or two years of psychoanalysis, the patient becomes convinced of the greatness of the
Freudian doctrine. And in most cases of psychoanalysis, he
declares himself a faithful Freudian follower. And incidentally,
that was exactly the "promotion" plan of Freud himself. Here, he
would say to his adepts and students, is the only way to introduce
his postulates to large masses of the population: through close

personal contact and repetitious implantation of the ideas in individuals. Freud used the "conditioned reflex" method of Professor Pavlov in his promotion campaign.

Boris Sokoloff, M.D., Ph.D. (35:34, 35)

For some readers it may come as a minor shock to discern features of brainwashing in psychoanalytic practices. Through training, reading, and other culturally determined indoctrination and Freudian promotion, they have adopted the view that psychoanalysis is a benign medical procedure. It may be somewhat unexpected or even offensive to some to see a purported psychological healing method compared with hideous mental distortions produced in Soviet prisons, or Red Chinese "thought reform" camps for "reeducation" of politically unreliable and uninstructed citizens, or in the dungeons of the Inquisition.

There is one aspect, however, which reveals a basic similarity between Freudwashing and other kinds of brainwashing. It is the introduction of beliefs in the subject (novice, patient, prisoner) without instructing him openly and directly about the correct or desirable views he is expected to express or confess. The whole mental reorientation through brainwashing comes ostensibly from within the subject, with the brainwasher (psychoanalyst, police investigator, inquisitor, political reeducator, guide to the mystery) passively hanging around as a benevolent, if overpowering presence.

1. *Brainwashing—old and new*

Brainwashing, *i.e.,* clandestine implantation of beliefs under imposed physical and/or emotional pressures and strains in a somewhat disoriented and regressed subject, has been practiced in various forms in ancient and contemporary cultures. The physiologically and psychologically strenuous initiation of novices into ancient Egyptian or Greek mystery cults is in its psychological import hard to distinguish from the "reeducation" processes in Communist corrective camps and prisons. The rough and stressful maturity rites of African and New Guinea tribes are essentially based on the same psychological principles as the introductory phases of membership into the Mafia and Cosa Nostra: painful or fearful experiences are imposed on subjects as an alleged introduction to maturity, or secret knowledge,

402

or membership in an elite group or restoration to an approved social status in an authoritarian state.

The basic operation of brainwashing is to regress the subject to the immature, nonassertive level of functioning, to undermine his self-reliance and supplant it by feigned or genuine submission. It seems that this reaction of complete subservience of the weak organism to the overwhelmingly more powerful one is a biological heritage in human beings. I remember in this connection the behavior of a small dog I observed when it could not escape the menace of a big one. The small dog turned itself on its back, with all fours in the air, completely surrendering its body and its destiny to the mercy of the bristling, growling big brute. Its gesture seemingly meant: "I am not going to fight back. You do with me what you please." The gesture was apparently an effective way of coping with mortal danger. The big dog inspected the little one at leisure and then walked away to more interesting things. The little one stayed on its back for a while and then moved in the opposite direction.

The ordeal of applicants to some of the ancient cults and the severe stress placed upon both their mind and body is vividly described by a writer of a hundred years ago. (34:27, 28) He had reconstructed from ancient sources the strain imposed on the subject who is learning new beliefs in ways never to be forgotten. The procedure to be summarized here concerns initiation into the ancient Zoroastrian religion, and is basically similar to practices in other pagan cultures, though perhaps more elaborate.

The candidate for initiation into the mysteries of the Zoroastrian religion was routinely exposed to grievous strains, both physical and emotional. As a novice he was already accustomed to stresses of obedience, effort, and danger which the already initiated imposed upon him. His most distressing trial was to place him in a sub-terranean cave in total solitude for fifty days of fasting and medi-tating. Some died during this ordeal, others went insane. Those who emerged alive and with their wits about them were pronounced worthy of partaking in the unfathomable and mighty mysteries.

The candidate was placed in a cavern with a guide to begin his initiation. This enlightened brother was there to accompany the novice through grisly experiences till he finally reached the cave of blessed illumination. The companion gave him the enchanted armor and talismans to protect him from vicious demons he was told to expect on the arduous journey of the seven stages of initiation. He also assured the candidate that he, the guide, was a representative of Simorgh, one of the demonic monsters of Persian mythology. The candidate was led to the first chamber; he was brought there to the edge of a yawning chasm. A single wrong step could throw him down to the "throne of dreadful necessity," which was interpreted as a crushing revelation of the basic principles of nature. Moving further with his silent guide through the dark cave, it was arranged that the candidate receive the encouragement of seeing occasional sacred fires in the distance. The roaring of ravenous beasts reached him from the direction in which the companion was nudging him, saying nothing. They arrived at the den of beasts, which was dimly lit by a lamp, filled with demonic noises of the initiated disguised as dangerous animals. They viciously attacked the candidate, who tried to fight them back as well as he could. Then he passed into another chamber filled with thunder and flashes of lightning. He was enabled to notice the ghostly shapes of genii who were resolved to prevent the candidate from learning their secrets. At this point some relief was provided to the sorely strained man, and he was led into a chamber with melodious music and delightful perfumes. When he had recovered sufficiently, he gave the sign to his guide that he was ready to proceed. Three priests appeared, one of whom thrust a living serpent into the candidate's bosom; the serpent being the symbol of regeneration, the shocked candidate was assured that he was gaining in spiritual strength. To test him further he was greeted with howlings and groanings of Hades, in which the unregenerated souls were being tormented. Escaping narrowly from perils of hell, the candidate finally reached the Sacellum, the Holy of Holies, brightly illuminated, with gold and precious stones glistening in the dimly lit vaults. The archimage was on his golden throne, with diamonds in his diadem; he was encircled by other priests, guardians and dispensers of mysteries. The novice was received warmly, congratulated on his persistence and courage. He was enjoined to keep the secrets to be revealed to him at pain of death and eternal damnation. Secret words were then entrusted to him, the chief being the name of the god, through whom the now initiated member would earn victory in life and in death.

404

The readers might have already noticed the parallels between these ancient practices and the Freudian initiation into those particular mysteries of the psyche. The neurotic or mentally ill candidate has already experienced severe strain and turmoil. He comes to the priest of the Freudian cult, the psychoanalyst, to be saved from ignorance and peril. Freud had succeeded in asserting himself as the revealer of eerie or unexpected truths about the psyche. His students and many other willing promoters of his doctrines had firmly established themselves in the American culture as guardians of salutary psychological mysteries. The patient becomes a candidate and travels through psychic mysteries by falling in trances on the couch. The psychoanalyst discovers all kinds of depravities in the patient, revealing many demons residing in him: the sexual lust for the parents and other incestuous wishes; homosexual and other perverse strivings; vicious aggressiveness; a basic bestiality and insane foundations of the psyche. Only a faithful adherence to the hallowed principles and practices announced by Freud can save the patient from becoming a victim to the hell that threatens to overwhelm him from within. The shadows of the evil genii of the unanalyzed and the blessed memories of the saved, "fully analyzed," show the true path of salvation. The guide through these psychological travails, like his Zoroastrian counterpart, is taciturn and insists on progressing toward deeper revelations of genitality and other stages of Freudian illumination. In the main the companion leaves the patient to struggle alone with the monsters within him; sometimes he helps by explaining (instructing, interpreting) the profound psychological secrets and saving names and concepts to the bewildered novice of the cult; occasionally he provides respite from the arduous journey by indicating implicit or explicit praise of the patient, which is music to the tortured soul. Some candidates never complete the journey, struggling forever in the dim labyrinths of Freudian ideology; others perhaps more intelligent or more gullible, are sold the supreme mysteries of the psyche, and are established as official or unofficial priests and promoters of the psychoanalytic cult.

Pursuing further this analogy between brainwashing in the ancient cults and the Freudian pseudoreligion, we might remember that in some ancient mysteries the deity to be revealed to the novice after so many tribulations was represented in the form of a sculpted lingam

405

(usually male sexual organ). The Freudian analysand is also illumined with a similar ultimate revelation, *i.e.*, that at the basis of all human psychological striving is an assumed creative force—sexualized libido—with phallus as its most appropriate symbol. On the way to this revelation, the candidate for this particular mystery cult learns that there are many signs of pervasive sexual problems in him, with perversions and crazy promptings allegedly uncovered in associations, dreams, and interpretations of transference. He is gradually led to accept Freud's mystical realization that sexuality is the cornerstone of all human action and desiring.

The essential thrust of brainwashing is to induce the subject to consider himself immature as an adolescent, unenlightened as a novice expecting vital revelations in ancient mystery cults, or as a deviant from what social authorities hold as correct or desirable thoughts and attitudes under a totalitarian regime. To begin with, the subject is put under emotional and physiological strain, he is made bodily weaker and psychologically perplexed. Without being expressly disapproved of, the subject is induced to feel guilty about being different, inferior, or uninformed. If he does not feel so at the outset, the representatives of the cult (dictatorship) put the subject under threat or stress in order to increase his feelings of inadequacy and confusion in the preparatory stages. The novice of a mystery cult or the new prisoner of secret police is led to regress and decompensate toward feeling like a helpless child, by physical weakening or exhaustion, through fasting or poor diet, lack of sleep and privacy, cold cell or glaring hot lamps, fear of death and apparitions of phantoms. In Communist prisons the breakdown is speeded up by disturbance of spontaneous elimination processes through lack of opportunity or by purgatives. As the powerful lights glare at the prisoner, he is able to hear the groans and screams of other prisoners being tortured or executed. In different brainwashing procedures, anxieties about the coming events are aroused in him either by supposed demonic noises and fearful apparitions, or frequent and extended interrogations, or prolonged abandonment or suspense and grim apprehension of a Communist prison. This infantilization and destruction of self-confidence and of previously achieved personality organization is apparently an essential step in preparing the way for acceptance of new mystical illuminations or unquestioning adoption of authorized political doctrines or producing the desired confessions.

2. *Psychodynamics of ancient cults and psychoanalysis*

Frank, a psychiatrist capable of unorthodox professional perceptions, likens the whole approach of Freudian psychotherapy to another kind of experience, designed to reorganize inner functions. He compares it with the intricate, sensitive preparations of the faithful visiting miracle shrines. The patient of a contemporary Freudian clinic is referred by a professional counselor and given explanations that raise his hopes as well as his insecurities. Then he goes through a preliminary interview or interviews, and some psychological testing may be added to it. Again his worthiness for psychotherapy is brought into focus. "In this sense it may not be too far fetched to liken the intake procedure to the preparatory rites undergone by supplicants at faith healing shrines, with the social worker in the role of acolyte and the psychiatrist as the high priest." (2:129)

Freud had apparently stumbled upon some of the ancient practices of psychological handling, influencing, and strengthening of weakened people without allowing himself to become more than dimly aware of his remote predecessors in the priest-magicians of ancient Egypt, Babylonia and Greece. We saw in chapter VII that some of his patients experienced an awe in his presence which would have been appropriate to a sick Egyptian or Greek communing with a priest in the temples of Isis or Asklepios two or three thousand years ago. It might be instructive to depict in some detail the parallels of psychological shaping of patients by ancient sages and contemporary psychologists, particularly Freud and psychoanalysts.

Magician-priests	*Freud and Freudians*
If one had psychological malaise, unhappiness, anxiety, sickness or misfortune, the only wise and efficient helper one could turn to was the priest. Illumined	When suffering from neuroses or psychosomatic troubles contemporary Americans are referred to psychiatrists or clinical psychologists, who, more

by secret knowledge of mysteries of life and death, acquainted with the will of gods and the secrets hidden within the psyche, the priests themselves were subjected to arduous training before being allowed to practice.

The brainwashing influence of the culture had established as a fact that the healing god would help the sufferer only at a particular temple or shrine, and not in his home or community.

likely than not, are Freudians. It is expected that these experts have become illuminated by their previous training, and enabled to repeat the wondrous cures attributed to Freud.

This brainwashing influence of American culture has created the conviction that psychological troubles can be treated in a "deep" and "dynamic" way only in the offices of trained Freudian psychoanalysts or "psychoanalytically oriented" professionals.

Effects of promotion

The priests and the cured believers spread the fame of the potency of their deity throughout the country. The sufferers were primed in that way to expect much from their pilgrimage to the shrine, and the suggestive effects were assured and enhanced thereby. On festival days the priests would announce the miraculous cures of the previous period.

The American equivalents of magician-priests have taken care to present their treatment as superior through indoctrinating physicians and graduate students of social sciences, producing a voluminous literature of self-praise, aggrandizing the chief prophet, belittling other prophets and their shrines. The great cures of psychoanalysis are publicly announced in "scientific" papers at the conventions of the movement and on numerous other occasions.

Material sacrifice

The supplicants to the deity were expected to bring gifts in money and kind (animals, cakes, products of the land). If deity cured them, they were expected to be even more generous. If unable to pay immediately, they could make a pledge to be fulfilled within a year. If they reneged on the pledge, dire consequences were threatened. The grateful supplicants erected steles or plaques or even statues of gods and new shrines.

Deity being proscribed from Freud's thinking, he placed himself in the role of old gods. Those who are "cured" write books on the untold benefits of psychoanalytic treatment, or at least testify to it by word of mouth. They send friends and relatives to their analyst, increasing thereby his earnings and his local fame. If they do not comply with implicit and explicit instructions of the healer, the analysis will fail and dire consequences of personality breakdown ensue.

Training

The Egyptians had seminaries, called "houses of life," to insure the uniform practices of their priesthood and proper indoctrination and discipline. The Greeks had colleges for priests-physicians, to disseminate the correct practice and skill at the healing temples.

Psychoanalytic institutes try to stamp all physician-trainees with as strong orthodox indoctrination as they would submit to. Minute technical considerations are given an exaggerated emphasis in order to preserve precepts as close to Freud's practice as possible and to create awe in the trainee.

The patient status

Supplicants at the pagan shrines were filled with apprehensions about the outcome of their illness and with hope that their pilgrimage would bring relief and cure to them. They were oppressed by a feeling of guilt, as it was known that illness, mental or physical, is brought about by gods or spirits angry at the sufferer for some indiscretion.

Psychoanalytic patients suffer for years in mind and/or body and are afraid of a final dissolution of their personality. The visit to the Freudian shrine is their last hope. They believe that if the reputedly most powerful and "deep" treatment does not cure them, their prospects are hopeless. They also feel guilty about developing such serious maladjustments that they have to go to a mind-doctor to save them from encroaching doom.

Preparatory phase of treatment

The readiness for treatment by magic suggestions was enhanced by purification rites and fasting. The supplicants had to bathe in the sea or the sacred springs according to the prescribed ritual. This brought them closer to a decision to change their ways and live more faithfully according to the principles of health, *i.e.* avoiding the wrath of spirits and gods. In this phase, at least in some shrines, the priest would tell them if they were to be accepted for treatment or should go elsewhere. Prayers were also offered

Being avowedly atheistic, Freud could not use religious enhancement in treatment. Instead, he instituted a period of trial analysis to check on the pliability of the patient to his method, *i.e.,* willingness to endure the stressful treatment and comply with demands of the rigid therapist. The patient also had to decide if he would change his ways of thinking and behaving in order to become a satisfactory patient and reach the state of psychological health as defined by psychoanalysis. As to dreams, Freud had no problem,

to deity to "order it [dream] right, according to your loving-kindness to men." (46:280) A number of writers have observed similarity of these ancient procedures to those of therapists using suggestion and hypnotism. (46:281)

as we have seen, to induce the "right" ones.

We have already covered the common features of psychoanalysis and suggestive and hypnotic procedures. (chapters VIII and IX)

Psychological handling

Once purified and promised the interest of deity, the supplicant could enter with hope the temple precincts, where he would sleep and be visited by deity in the dream. This was the incubation sleep, the crucial point of the pilgrimage. The divine message about healing method or solution to a thorny problem was expected to come in the dream and the 'attending priest did not fail to reassure his subject that the dream would most likely come to him. The prayers for a blessed dream would further fortify the supplicant in his expectations.

Deity being supplanted by Freud's authority, he relegated messages of salvation and resolution of psychological problems to the no-better-defined region of the unconscious. Interpretation of dreams has become a hallmark of psychoanalysis, and the patient fervently hopes that his dreams will be in a form acceptable to the analyst and interpretable through Freudian theory. The benign expectation of the analyst reinforces the proper dreams and assures their appearance. Freud himself knew of the compliant dreams of patients eager to please. As we saw, he was able to order his own dreams in self-analysis too.

Dreams being a confusing medium for messages in ancient cultures no less than in our own, the priests were trained and skilled in drawing necessary

Interpretation of dreams is no problem to the analyst or for that matter to any intelligent individual. There are bound to be words, images, and shapes

interpretations out of the blurry materials. The interpretations were easy to make as the priest knew both the wishes of his subjects and the general tenor of messages of the deity to the dreamers at that shrine.

The message having been interpreted, it was up to supplicant to determine what he would do with it. The priest did not see it as his role to get involved in supplicant's life.

Some supplicants could not dream interpretable dreams. The priest or a relative would then dream for them and supply them with the divine message. At some shrines the supplicants were allowed to repeat their purification rites and try incubation sleep a sufficient number of times to get the desired message. A kind of group therapy took place in the morning as others told gleefully of their visitations with the deity during their sleep; this enhanced the readiness to produce better dreams later on.

which can be easily fitted into Freudian preconceptions, taking into account the wishes and problems of the patient. Once one learns the rules of the interpretative game, their application to any patient situation is a cinch, and there is no one to contradict the interpretations anyway.

Once the dream or defenses are interpreted, it is of no concern to the analyst what the patient does with them. As a rule, the analyst stays out of patient's real problems.

Even though Freudian analysts do not offer to dream outright for the patients who produce poorly usable dreams, they let their "unconscious" play on patient's associations and produce interpretations. They strenuously and imaginatively interpret even the slight clues from dreams, slips of tongue, and any loose materials floating into "free" associations. And if one session does not produce the desirable materials, there are hundreds of interviews to be held till the pieces fall in place nicely. Patients can also model their dreams according to those published in various Freudian books.

Considering the above analogies, it becomes clear that psycho-analysis may not be such a completely new discipline in its basic practice as Freud and his disciples imply. They only disguise an ancient psychological art by theoretical verbiage.

An even more surprising methodological closeness is that of psychoanalysis and brainwashing of witches in the Inquisition inter-rogation chambers. Freud himself, as we shall soon see, confided this insight in private correspondence to Fliess, which, of course, was not intended for publication. Posterity should be grateful to Fliess for preserving the letters in spite of Freud's suggestion that they should be burnt, as without them we would have no way of getting glimpses into the shadow side of Freud's operations.

3. *Witch-making and Freudwashing*

Freud was apparently unembarrassed by his insight that the revelations on his couch suspiciously resembled the self-accusing "confessions" of tortured witches. He could not discern that his method of playing with his patients' minds by instructing them covertly, while denying it overtly, is basically a degradation, an invalidation of human personality, as Szasz called it. In this way Freud continued the humiliating activity over human beings for which Szasz damns the whole psychiatric caste before and after Freud:

> Although Freud's "therapeutic" methods differed from those of his colleagues, his enthusiastic endorsement and use of a psychiatric vocabulary for denigrating people place him in the mainstream of psychiatric thought: By reclassifying witches as neurotics, he helped to replace theological by psychiatric methods of invalidating human beings. The result—which is contemporary history—is a justificatory rhetoric legitimizing man's inhumanity to man not by appeals to God but by appeals to Health. (43:69)

Freud almost chuckles in telling Fliess about his startling discovery:

> By the way, what have you got to say to the suggestion that the whole of my brand-new theory of the primary origins of hysteria is already familiar and has been published a hundred times, though several centuries ago? Do you remember my always saying that the medieval theory of possession, that held by the

413

ecclesiastical courts, was identical with our theory of a foreign body and the splitting of consciousness? But why did the devil who took possession of the poor victims, invariably commit misconduct with them and in such horrible ways? Why were the confessions extracted under torture so very much like what my patients tell me under psychological treatments? (3:187, 188)

Evidently, Freud had little awareness of the extent of personality disintegration that his method induces in some patients, particularly hysterics. Otherwise he would not have been surprised that some of his patients pour out self-accusing material in a way similar to that of the wretched victims of the Inquisition who "proved" they were intimate with Satan, undeterred by the coming punishment and in compliance with inquisitor's notions. Apparently Freud could not fully grasp the significance of these phenomena for his "treatment." He was tricked by the irrationality and suggestibility in both the patients and himself.

Ehrenwald also recognizes similarities between "brainwashing" of witches and Freudian psychoanalysis:

All this was exactly what the exorcist wanted to hear and the hysterical nun, subjected to many weeks of brainwashing, obliged. It is impossible to decide whether or not a telepathic element was involved in such a performance. Nor is it permissible to describe the procedures of the inquisitors in terms of anything like modern psychotherapy. But there are three ingredients of the therapeutic situation which can be recognized in the ecclesiastic setting: the patient's profound emotional disturbance, reminiscent of hysteria in our sense; a "healer" seeking to effect her "cure" by psychological means; a "transference relationship" between the two, however warped and distorted this may have been. The result was unmistakable: the grafting of a new, iatrogenic neurosis upon the existing mental disorder. As it happened, the new syndrome seemed to be just what the doctor ordered. It amounted to a perfect corroboration of the exorcist's expectations, and met the needs of his own selfish or frankly sadistic countertransference. (4:107)

Maybe Ehrenwald is too lenient in saying that "it is not permissible to equate" psychoanalytic and allied therapies with the psychological methods of the inquisitor. Apart from physical torture and burning at the stake, the psychological process of obtaining confirmation for the "healer's" presuppositions is identical in both settings, as Freud had himself intimated.

Another psychiatrist, Meerloo, a sensitive and knowledgeable student of brainwashing, is even clearer than Ehrenwald about the transfer of inquisitor's views upon the crazed witch, a process essentially similar to elicitation of "transference neuroses" in Freudian analysis and grafting of psychoanalytic thought forms onto the mind of the analysand. Meerloo sees the "masochistic pact" operating between the inquisitor or brainwasher and his subject: there is an unconscious readiness to submit to punishment and accept the patently false accusations as true. The victim is caught in the mechanisms of the child-parent dependencies and ambivalence toward authority figures: under pressure, the victim takes over the unreasonable and destructive demands of the oppressor. Freud recognized this subtle operation and called it "identification with the aggressor." However, he did not discern it in the relationship between him and his psychoanalytic victims; he would not conceive of analysis as a subtly aggressive and overpowering relationship, and of himself as basically a mental aggressor against the neurotic's personality.

In elucidating the psychological commonalities of "modern mental torture" and inquisitorial practices, Meerloo finds "a peculiar spiritual relationship and mental interplay between the victim and the rest of the community." (33:26) The repentant witches took over all the fantasied sins imputed to them by the inquisitors as representations of authority (the Pope) and science (theology) of that time. They agreed with their judges and executioners that it would be best for them to be burnt in order to be separated from the devil and enter the eternal rest.

Both Meerloo and Szasz see the public witch-burnings as a purification rite for the onlookers. The spectacle of sinners being strangled and burnt at the stake or incinerated alive, enabled the watchers to assuage their guilt feelings and join the comfort of being counted among the just.

In our own culture the role of such vicarious purification and assurance of psychological health is played by popular versions of psychoanalytic lore and therapy. Like the witches, the analysands take upon themselves all the Freudian ugliness and depravity, expiating in long analyses for the sins others would rather deny than admit.

A further survey of inquisitors' and Freud's psychological effects reveals common features of the two treatments. A reading of the principal manual of medieval inquisitors, *The Malleus Maleficarum* (*The Witch Hammer,* 44) can be quite instructive in this respect.

The manual was prepared by two Dominican monks, Heinrich Kramer and James Sprenger, and published at the end of the fifteenth century. It was so well argued and exhaustive that it served for three hundred years as the main handbook in dealing with witches, sorcerers, and heretics. Both of the writers were active and zealous inquisitors in Germany and Austria. Their insights and recommendations grew out of a working relationship with "patients" and general theoretical presuppositions, as was the case with Freud. A contemporary historian of psychiatry, Zilboorg, found it pertinent to modern practice: " . . . the Malleus Maleficarum might with a little editing serve as an excellent modern textbook of descriptive clinical psychiatry of the fifteenth century, if the word witch were substituted by the word patient, and the devil eliminated." (45:68)

The cultural context contributes to brainwashing effects as much as to techniques of the brainwashers and I shall take both into account.

Inquisitors	*Freud*

Philosophical presuppositions

The two inquisitors start out with the Christian faith of their times. They believed that God ran the world in a sovereign way, with devils exerting a limited sway over human beings, as much as God permitted it. They were convinced that human beings, particularly women, could relate to devil and receive from him the power to perform extra-	Freud starts out with the atheistic faith of his times, a now outmoded "scientific" materialism. He believed that there is no God in the universe and there are no spiritual forces to influence humans. He was confined to anthropocentric perspective. Human beings were conceived as utterly alone in the mechanistic universe, with only

416

ordinary deeds and to harm other human beings as well as animals. They were believed able to bring about physical and mental illness, using the tricks and powers bestowed upon them by the devil.

"natural forces" playing upon them and within them. He called these forces environmental "vicissitudes" and "instincts." He was convinced that these "instincts" and environmental pressures "cause" mental illness or lead to mental health, harming or benefitting the particular individuals and persons in their environment.

Cultural background and reactions

The inquisitors lived in a time of transition. At the end of the fifteenth century, medieval religious certainties were undermined by revival of classical pagan ideas (Renaissance) and the ecclesiastic and feudal authorities were losing ground to some extent. Many wild superstitions were rampant, sometimes smothering the rational and scientific gains. In such an atmosphere of uncertainty many preposterous ideas can be accepted if they fit with prevalent general beliefs, which at the time were theologically colored and ecclesiastically controlled.

Freud lived in another time of transition. At the end of the nineteenth century the values and authority of the Christian Church were further questioned by many "free thinkers," Freud being one of them. The stability of the social order was challenged by the rise of nationalism overthrowing monarchies, and of socialist movements threatening the bourgeois democratic institutions. In such a transitional period many unproven and irrational notions (political, social, religious, or "scientific") can be palmed off on the public. Freud passed his ideas under the guise of prevalent secular belief, controlled by the "scientific" establishment and its dogmas.

In spite of proneness to super-

Freud presented his precon-

stition, many contemporaries, even ecclesiastics, scoffed at the idea of witches, devils, and particularly of believing that witches and sorcerers could harm other human beings. Pope Innocent VIII had to send out a special bull against those indifferent to the grave peril, which he believed witches represented for civilized humanity. He recommended heartily that both churchmen and secular powers, aid the inquisitors in their important task of reestablishing right beliefs and practices by weeding out the witches.

ceptions about the decisive role of sexuality in human psyche, and most contemporaries thought he was out of his mind. They just could not see how the new witches, the sexual frustrations, could have such decisive influence on mental illness, neurosis or psychosis, as Freud was asserting. His opinions were and still are scoffed at by most educated Europeans. His popularity was strongly reinforced in post-World War II Europe by the prelates of the Freudian sect from the United States, as that country gained some ascendancy over Europeans following the two World Wars.

The theoretical system

The two inquisitors argued very cogently, if mistakenly, for their assumptions. Their book reads well in a logically convincing manner about the grave offenses of the witches. Their method is basically rationalistic, philosophical, theological, deductive, *i.e.*, only remotely scientific. Their assertions could essentially neither be proved nor disproved, being based only on seemingly logical postulates.

Freud, too, argued with apparent cogency for his assumptions. His well-written books seemed to prove beyond doubt that sexuality is the basic function of human beings and that its frustration leads to grave psychological consequences. His argument is indistinguishable from the philosophical deductions. His assertions are essentially neither provable nor disprovable, being founded on ra-

The main logical trap for inquisitors was their reliance on formal reasoning. Once they accepted a groundless assumption, they could build a seemingly irrefutable scholastic system on it. Their chief unprovable assumption was that there are, in fact, devils, and that human beings can become possessed by them. Once this was accepted, the other assumptions flowed easily and "logically" from them. The undergirding cultural orientation, at that time still strongly religious, made the whole system appear credible.

tional, logical, postulates, *i.e.* a barely scientific structure.

Freud relied on popular, if often false, reasoning. He assumed at one point in his career that sexuality is the root problem in neuroses and psychoses, and the rest of his arguments flowed, seemingly correctly, out of that basic and unprovable proposition. He found "demonstrations" for his hunches in his own psychic experiences (an example of self-brainwashing) and in the communications of his patients, whom he subtly converted to his views. He provided credence for his hunches by giving them the surface look of scientific propositions, e.g. "psychic determinism," and they were bought wholesale by the credulous.

The subjects

The inquisitors' subjects were individuals deviant from the prevailing culture. Their personality make-up and their outward behavior placed them apart from the majority. Many psychologically sophisticated historians believe that witches were a part of the underground movement

Freud's subjects were for the most part misfits in their particular situations. Their neurotic or prepsychotic personalities and their disturbed behaviors set them apart from the majority of the Viennese. Many of them were Jews, alienated from the dominant population both by

419

against the ruling feudal class, a sort of "anticulture" movement of their time, mostly containing uneducated searchers. Many economically dispossessed and socially disadvantaged people flocked into secret societies with other religiously and emotionally alienated individuals. Others could not accept the demanding moral and religious discipline of a theocratic society, and reverted to the more congenial pagan mores, or what might in our day be euphemistically called "personal morality" and "situational ethics." The witches, being typically hysterical or paranoid characters, were searching for unusual and titillating experiences, just like many of our contemporaries who flock to esoteric cults. Sorcerers, also tried as witches, were usually criminals, poisoning or otherwise dispatching victims for money. Other witches were deluded individuals who genuinely believed in their magic powers, this belief being strongly reinforced by prevailing superstitions. Like our modern witches, some of the medieval ones hoped to gain extraordinary powers of money, long life, influence over others. Some of the heretics, inasmuch

differences in traditions and prejudices of the ruling groups of Christians. Freud himself suffered all of his life from being a misfit (to some extent by his own choice) in Vienna. He joined the rebels, identifying himself with anti-Christian trends. He remained a rabid atheist to the end of his life, and stamped his psychology with atheistic hues. He molded his students and his patients into the philosophical-cultural forms of his own likeness. Most of his patients, like those of the inquisitors, were hysterical females, ready to align themselves into behavior expected by the authority. Other people, exposed to similar stresses of living, had found a modicum of peace of mind, by immersing themselves into views and behaviors of the dominant group; the neurotics had to seek their own forms in esoteric or provocative views and experiences; they were ready to put on the particular coloring of Freud's psychological notions.

as they were not falsely accused, were misfits in their culture, striking out with their own beliefs because they were incapable of identifying with and trusting the majority and accepting the prevalent views.

The inquisitors provide these personality assessments of their subjects: " ... since they are weak, they find an easy and secret manner of vindicating themselves by witchcraft ... as they are very impressionable they act accordingly. ... " (44: 44) They were easily defeated by inquisitors. They yielded readily to them as they yielded readily to fantasies about the pact with the devil." ... three general vices appear to have special dominion over wicked women, namely, infidelity, ambition, and lust." (44:47)

In his case histories and in general descriptions of neurotics, Freud shows that he worked with similar type of personality maladaptations: hysterical, tense, weak, impressionable, phobic, immature, overdependent, sometimes overdemanding. In their general personality weakness they were unable to cope with life stresses; they readily submitted to neurosis as they readily yielded to Freud. Freud surmised that his patients' chief problems were with marital or extramarital frustrations, and thwarted needs for pleasure.

"Psychodynamics" of "treatment"

The final outcome of treatment was decided by the treater even before the process began: the witch had to be brought around, by threat and kindness, to confess all the heinous deeds of which the inquisitors suspected her. The inquisitors were

Freud had no doubt what the outcome of analysis had to be even before he began it: the neurotic patient had to be brought around in innumerable sessions, paid for by the patient, to confess to all the psychopathology of which he, Freud, suspected

421

fully convinced that the fact of her being in their hands was proof enough that she was a witch and must have done many of the fiendish misdeeds which other witches had confessed in the past. As there could be hardly any witnesses to those secret events, the technical thrust of treatment was to get the witch to accuse herself: "the expert testimony of the witches themselves has made all these things credible." (44:111). The witch was finally brought around to speak the language and the wishes of her tormentor.

The witch was a challenge to professional and personal integrity of the Inquisitor. If he did not extract her confession of the guilt he imputed to her, then he would be a poor Inquisitor. He would be threatened by personal and religious guilt feelings and a sense of inferiority. He was therefore bound to find her guilty, and if persuasion did not help, then torture was available for the recalcitrant sinners.

her. He was stern, impersonal, detached, threatening enough for what he needed to accomplish. The fact that the wretch was on his couch proved that she was neurotic; therefore she must have done all the things from his psychopathological list that neurotics do or get done to them in order to make a mess of themselves. He coached the patient how to think and talk, by giving her interpretations of dreams, free associations, and other "materials." The analysis was considered to be going well when the patient "demonstrated" on her own what Freud had expected to discover in her beforehand.

The neurotic is a personal and professional challenge to the analyst (the caution against "therapeutic zeal" notwithstanding). If he does not get the patient to produce at least a semblance of the proper Freudian psychopathology, his skill in analysis would be proven inadequate. The analyst is, therefore, bound to find all the fine points of abnormalities in this or that production of the patient. If the patient balked at complying with the analyst's expressed or implied demands, she would be

The inquisitor was, of course, a terrifying challenge to the witch. Her life, or rather death, was in his hands. She was "altogether uneducated" (44:97), usually of lowly origin, facing abject immediate and probably even worse eternal prospects. He was learned, a member of the highly respected clerical caste, with a secure immediate future and an even more glorious eternity. These differences in status, even apart from the power to deliver her to torture, created a subservient attitude in the scared and depressed woman. Her resistance crumpled and she came over to the aggressor's side, complying, cooperating, keeping the good will of her judge, even if it was ephemeral. She started telling him what he wanted to hear, incriminating herself more deeply with every question. The pleased Inquisitor nudged her gently to paint herself as black as she could. Here the inquisitorial process ended. The Inquisitor had achieved his noble purpose of saving a soul by leading the witch to contri-

accused of "resistance" and the threat of failure and termination of analysis would face the unyielding neurotic.

The difference in status between the analyst and the patient is great. Even if she be educated and of higher social class, she feels inferior for developing her stupid neurotic symptoms. She feels sick, hopeless, more or less depressed. He is a Doctor, a member of a highly respected class in the community. As a psychiatrist, and especially as an analyst, he is reputed to know the deep secrets of the psyche, and can ferret them out of anyone by his "analysis." He is healthy, trained and wise; she mentally sick, ignorant, and foolish. She comes begging for help for delivery from neurosis, and her psychological well being, a miserable or trouble-free future, is in his hands. The only choice she has is to comply and be attentive to his suggestions of how she should think of her neurotic difficulties. The great doctor shows progressively more approval the closer she comes to resemble the ideally mentally sick according to his book, and as a result she comes to find in

tion and confession. Now he could "relax her," *i.e.* deliver her to secular authorities to burn her body for her misdeeds, while her redeemed soul went to heaven. The witch was also in a better frame of mind as she had come to believe these things herself, or could look to her death as a delivery from the inescapable misery of her life.

The unrecognized or unadmitted but emotionally tangible side benefit of the whole inquisitorial process was that it was supercharged with sexuality. There were plenty of thrills in it for both participants. Some of the crimes imputed to witches were those of aggression (harm) to people, animals, or crops. However, much more impressive were the lurid sexual perversions. What the "repressed" sexuality of the monk-inquisitor could not even dream about, the witch "forced" the celibate judge to hear about and visualize. There was some vicarious thrill in the monk's disgust of devil's debaucheries. The inquisitors repeat several times that

herself most aspects of Freudian psychopathology. The Freud-washing is completed for both the doctor and the patient, and both are happy about "successful analysis." The patient can look forward to a life without former neurotic upsets, and the analyst is delighted with the benefit his skill has evidently brought about. The productions of his "expert witness" have again vindicated the Great Method, and proven it beyond any reasonable doubt.

The hallmark of Freud's psychology is its thorough sexualization. To the end of his life he refused to accept suggestions of more balanced psychologists that the psychic force "libido" could consist of other drives than the sexual. For Freud it remained adamantly and exclusively sexual, so that the whole drama of psychotherapy was drenched with sexual implications. We have seen that early in his career Freud had discovered that "sexual business attracts people" to him as a psychoanalyst, and he could catch and retain more patients by that bait. We can also speculate that, being sexually inhibited, he could have a few vicarious sex-

"all witchcraft comes from carnal lust." (44:47) Many witches enjoyed shocking their torturers and regaling themselves by telling of the "venereal pleasure" and "carnal delectations which are procured for the witches by the devil." (44:112) They spoke so convincingly, that the sexually undergratified monks could have no doubt about the "abominable coitus." Various witches had reported that the devil had a scaly penis, that naturally, heightened the sinful delight. Others went further in perverse imagination, describing his forked penis, which provided them with a double bonus, simultaneous vaginal and anal penetration. Even the aggressions of witches were structured in a sexually titillating direction. They were accused of causing impotence in men or increasing the carnal lust in others; some were accused of making women barren, others of seducing virgins or chaste wives into illicit experiences.

ual thrills to break the customary monotony of his therapeutic technique. There was, of course, a definite methodological advantage to overuse of sexual categories, as it was the easiest way to stir up guilt feelings in the patient and keep her in therapy for a long time. The patient could learn from Freud or from his books, that even as a baby she was a "polymorphous perverse," bent on getting sexual pleasure from all bodily orifices, about equally "erotogenic" for the infant, according to Freud's understanding. Hacking backward through long analysis, the patient was expected to find memories of other proofs of early depravity. If they did not find such proofs of their guilt themselves, Freud would kindly interpret any past events or memories as indicative of the hurtful witnessing of the "primal scene" (parents copulating), of Oedipal entanglements, puzzlement over sexual organs, infantile masturbation. Particularly easy is to "demonstrate" to the patient the "bi-sexuality" and homosexuality. A skilled analyst can construe these out of anything.

Both participants had a double payoff in this game of make-believe. The witch enjoyed vicarious and exhibitionistic thrills and staying of the torturer's hand; the inquisitor had a chance of legitimate, "professional" delving into pervert sexual practices, and the subsequent benefit of strengthening his chastity by seeing the witch's "abomination" as the sexual work of the devil. Even when the inquisitor thought that the witches were inventing stories to get off the hook, he still counted them as real misdeeds, because they were fantasies inspired by the devil. It was the old game of "tails, I win; heads, you lose"; the witch could never win.

The game of Freudian make-believe has also payoffs built into it for both the patient and the analyst. The patient is sexually stimulated by "discovering" her "deep" sexual drives, which were there in abundance even in infancy. She is also awed by getting such profound glimpses into the secret nature of her psyche. The analyst is thrilled by his skill in obtaining the "correct" materials. His conviction about the worthwhileness of his method is enhanced accordingly. Even when Freud found that his patients were inventing their stories in order to comply with his theoretical expectations, he still used these fabrications as supposed demonstration of sexual libido anyway. Neither the patient nor the reader could win with Freud. He had arranged his system of rationalizations in such a way that he could always win; at least in his own imagination.

If someone suggested to the inquisitors that there might be some unhealthy personal pleasures in carrying out the Inquisition, there would be a hurt look and protestation of sheer profes-

If someone wondered for whose benefit the "analysis" is carried out—patient's or analyst's?—ignorance would be imputed to the questioner. As far as the analyst is concerned, the

Inquisitors	*Freud*
sional interest in serving God, the community, and the witch.	patient's needs and interests are superbly protected by analyst's training to control his "counter-transference."

4. *Totalitarian and Freudian brainwashing*

Meerloo carried out a masterful psychological study of subtle aspects of totalitarian brainwashing in his book *The Rape of the Mind: The psychology of thought control, menticide, and brainwashing.* (33) He was imbued with the usual respect for Freudian psychoanalysis and did not intend to draw any parallel between it and contemporary brainwashing. He, in fact disagrees so strongly with my perception of psychoanalysis as clandestine brainwashing that he refused the permission to quote his passages, and I had to resort to paraphrasing. The discernment of similarity between the two conditionings is thus entirely mine. Being unintended by Meerloo, my comparison gains an additional validity as psychological processes involved are rather strikingly alike. Meerloo analyzes the brainwashing procedure in four phases:

Brainwashing	*Freudwashing*

Phase I. Artificial Breakdown and Deconditioning

The inquisitor, whether of Middle Ages or in Communist detainment, uses many stresses to weaken the ego of his prisoner. Sometimes physical torture (hunger, cold) is used; however, as bodily suffering may increase stubbornness, subtler pressures are found to be more efficient in breaking down the	The Freudian analyst also tries to weaken the ego of his prisoner. He insists on free association as the only important way of communicating. This amounts to training in irrationality, weakening of logical thinking, flooding by emotions, loosening of previously established personality reactions fall-

427

subject. When torture is used, it is more with a view to implant fear into onlookers' imagination, and to soften the other prisoners by anticipated pain. (33:90) The brainwasher does not need to act crudely with the victim, as the subject had been alerted to this possibility by what is common knowledge.

The modern inquisitor uses many devices: "intimidating suggestion, dramatic persuasion, mass suggestion, humiliation, embarrassment, loneliness and isolation, continued interrogation, overburdening the unsteady mind, arousing more and more self-pity. Patience and time help the inquisitor to soften a stubborn soul." (33:90) We shall see in the next section examples of these subtle methods.

ing back upon childish patterns. In Freudian jargon this is "therapeutic regression."

Physical torture is, of course, not practiced in psychoanalysis, but mental threat is prominent. Whether the analyst reinforces it or not, the patient lives in terror of a psychotic disintegration or a more troublesome neurotic maladjustment. This makes him endure the rigor of frequent interviews, silences, the stress of talking when nothing sensible comes to mind. The specter of a failing analysis or termination of treatment by a displeased analyst is ever present with analysand, just as sentencing and disgrace are with a political brainwashee.

One of the regularly used "intimidating suggestions" by Freudians is accusation of resistance, of endangering the analysis and of hating the analyst. "Dramatic persuasion"—there are overpowering dramatic moments in Freudian analysis, when the passive and taciturn analyst delivers the revelations about what he has allegedly discovered in the patient's unconscious. "Mass suggestion"—

there is a host of successfully analyzed patients invisibly present to the patient's unconscious in every session; they act as pressures toward conformity on the couch and reshaping oneself into the illumined (analyzed) models of those who had gone on before. "Humiliation"—a powerful dose of it is in store for the patient, who is expected to develop erotic transference toward the analyst, homosexual or heterosexual. "Embarrassment"—as the analyst obligatorily discovers nasty sexual schemes the patient had toward his parents, or uncovers many mean traits in the analysand, he cannot help feeling embarrassed before analysis is completed if there is any decency left in him. "Loneliness and isolation"—in fostering the regression of the patient, the analyst leaves his prisoner to sometimes excruciatingly painful loneliness on the couch; the patient is also enjoined against sharing his concerns with anyone but his analyst. "Continued interrogation" —Freudian interrogation continues for hundreds of hours, implying that there are important secrets the patient has not yet confessed, and that his psychological salvation depends on squeezing the correct Freudian pathology out of his own soul. "Overburdening the unsteady mind"—the analyst increases the stresses on the patient, already a weakened personality, by his passivity and by imputations of resistance, homosexuality, transference distortions, etc. "Arousing self-pity"—the analyst leads his patient to reject other authority figures, increasing thereby the dependency on the newly found perfect and permissive parent-figure in the analyst.

The totalitarian agents, Meerloo points out, prepare the victim to accept the official ideology by humiliating him in various ways; some of the crude old religions used the same method. The victim may also consciously give in simply out of intellectual opportunism, as a way of avoiding further tensions. (33:90)

Freud and other analysts described in chapter V and elsewhere in this book, demanded a humble attitude of trainees or patients toward them; they had to accept the inferior status of ignorant learners, or they would be eventually branded by the awful stigma of being failures in analysis. It is easier to pretend conversion than to stick to what one's judgment indicates.

Phase II. Submission to and Positive Identification with the Enemy

The submission to the brainwasher's demands often occurs suddenly. The resistance is supplanted by surrender and acceptance of the implied "line." To the inquisitor this looks like a conversion to right views and achievement of inner illumination. Meerloo remembers that psychoanalysts have already uncovered this process; they called it "identification with aggressor" and "a parasitic superego," which impels the victim to speak the voice of his master. In Meerloo's experience (he was imprisoned by Nazis) this surrender to the master is sometimes followed by hysterical laughter and crying, not unlike small children surrendering after temper tantrums. The brainwasher manipulates the victim into such regressive behavior by playing a paternal role. Meerloo mentions that POWs in Communist hands are cajoled by gifts, sweets at birthdays, and subtle promises of better things to come. (33:91)

Every successful Freudian psychoanalysis carries a connotation of conversion. The interpretations the analyst has tended to his subject become revelations of deepest truths. There is an enthusiasm to convert friends to the newly found wisdom. The analyst is established as the arbiter of values and guide through perplexities of life—"the parasitic superego" of Meerloo. The conversion is accompanied by elation, as we have already seen in some of Freud's patients (chapter VII). The patient casts the analyst into the parental role and the analyst obliges by playing it benevolently. Whether this state would be called autohypnosis, as Meerloo does, or couchhypnosis as I described it (chapter VII), is irrelevant; the important fact is that the patient is placed in a hypnotic state, unknown to himself and the analyst.

431

Phase III. Reconditioning to the New Order

The newly adopted views and attitudes are reinforced daily in the victim. The brainwasher subtly trains the subject in how to think about the official ideology and how to defend it. The subject is repeatedly supplied with new arguments and "reasoning." (33:91)

The surrender to the analyst and finding the appropriate Freudian pathology in oneself, is only the beginning of molding oneself into a "good" patient. Hundreds of interviews will be carried on in the attempt to fix Freudian thought forms in the patient by overlearning.

Phase IV. Liberation from the Totalitarian Spell

If the subject returns to a full democratic society, the "hypnotic spell" is usually broken. (33:91) If the victim remains under the surveillance and mass brainwashing of a totalitarian society, the spell may hold for years.

The Freudian spell is not that easily broken. Social incentives are different for totalitarian brainwashing and Freudwashing. The prisoner returns to a society discouraging the continuance of attitudes grafted through brainwashing. The Freudian patient has his Freudwashed mentality reinforced by cultural approval of a freudianized community. There are exceptions to usual effects of both brainwashing and Freudwashing; I have described the latter in chapters III, V and elsewhere in this volume wherever unsuccessful analyses are described.

Meerloo also depicts other aspects of brainwashing that are reminiscent of Freudian analysis:

1. The dangers of non-compliance

The totalitarians spread the "myth of an imaginary world conspiracy" in order to bring their subjects into an attitude apprehensive before the unseen dangers. This leads to unconscious identification with dictatorship—by hating the alleged enemy they participate in totalitarian community. The increased fear and guilt lead thus to deeper allegiance to the regime. The subject abdicates his individual judgment to join the crowd. The continuously raised specter of plotters drives the citizens into dependency and immaturity. Only the dictator, it is asserted or assumed, can protect them from the perils of external enemies, and they had better remain loyal suppressing the occasional doubts. (33:132)

Freud and his faithful have built a distorted image of human psyche. They have played up the psychopathological possibilities and played down the functions of health and strength present in most, even neurotic, human beings. They represent every individual as besieged with sickening propensities, as if humanity were a vast mental hospital. This overemphasis on pathology serves a useful purpose in diverting attention from meager therapeutic results of Freudian treatment. It also makes patients huddle around the Freudian gurus as the only enlightened guides out of prevailing mental abnormalities. The Freudians maintain in this way their positions of prominence in society, with corresponding economic benefits, which are due to the assumed keepers of mental health.

433

2. "The strategy of criminalization."

The usual tactic of totalitarian manipulation is to encourage subject to betray his friends and even his parents. This is a proof of loyalty to the regime and it helps put into action the repressed angers and immature resentments. The subject is thus freed to act out his primitive impulses. The regime removes his feelings of guilt by supplying him with numerous "justifications" for yielding to sadistic impulses. Catchphrases, such as "historical necessity," help the individual to rationalize immorality and evil into morality and good. "We see here the great corruption of civilized standards." As the result of such mass criminalization the totalitarian agents destroy the conscience of their subjects, just as they had destroyed their own. (33:133)

It is a standard Freudian practice with patients to dissolve their loyalties to parents, spouses, or traditional ideals. Parents and spouses are cast into the roles of tyrants or exploiters, mothers being most often the scapegoats of Freudians winning the patients to their ideology. Hostility and divorce are encouraged. We have seen (in chapter III) that a number of observers consider Freudians the termites of the moral structure of our society. Justifications for irresponsibility are offered to patients by presenting psyche as driven by animal impulses, teaching them that human decency is only skin-deep. What had been considered traditionally as immorality is rationalized as "new morality." Having lost the traditional concepts of morality through their training, the Freudians now loosen the consciences of their patients. Civilization and goodness are shams to them; they cynically debunk the values still held in esteem in the larger part of the world which does not yet have the "benefit" of the Freudian revolution.

3. "Verbocracy and semantic fog—
talking the people into submission."

Totalitarians use the power of words ("verbocracy") deliberately in enhancing their power. Fraudulent catchwords, propagandistic Big Lies, and phoney slogans serve the purpose of confusing and dulling the subjects. This makes the victims more ready to buy official myths of happiness. The continual drumming of totalitarian "truths" leads to the expected results: the subjects start seeing their world in ways suggested by the trainers and develop a sort of reflex reaction to official mythology. (33:135, 136)

Freudians have also established their own verbocracy. Their theoretical fictions of Oedipus complex, castration anxiety, death wish, ("Freudian") slips of tongue or pen, pleasure principle, etc., have become norms not only in professional jargon, but in common parlance, journalism, and general literature. The guesses have become reified into psychological facts. Both professionals and laymen have accepted the oft-repeated and solemnly presented Freudian myths as truth and reality. The "citizenry" no longer "see and hear with their own eyes and ears but will look at the world through the fog of official [Freudian] catchwords." (33:136) They innocently use Freudian concepts in understanding themselves and others.

In the beginning the subject may dismiss the propaganda barrage as nonsense and double-talk. Yet, the human mind being an easy prey to suggestion, the denial and refusal leave traces of the rejected ideology nevertheless and these accumulate over a period of time

Americans initially showed a sensible disbelief in Freudian categories, and sometimes made fun of them. In time, however, the "inherent suggestion" worked and befogged the original discernment; people, particularly the educated sector, gave up verifying the peculiar Freud-

435

in the mind under attack. This is the subtle trick of double-talk —the unwitting buying of a viewpoint. The difference between rationale and rationalization becomes blurred, and objective reasoning is lost. The subject finally finds himself able to believe anything and "retreats into sullen dullness." (33:137)

ian propositions, and accepted them as established verities, and made it their unofficial religion. Less educated individuals still reject Freudian oddities, but being powerless to combat it, they retreat "into sullen dullness"—a noncommittal, skeptical attitude about the learned nonsense.

4. The soft and hard touch of brainwashing

Meerloo draws attention to an important mechanism of brainwashing. Apparently people accept more easily any peculiar suggestions in the relaxation following a period of tension. During this respite from stress the subjects let down their guard, reduce their alertness, and fall more readily into the totalitarian webs that are continually spread around them. The modern dictators therefore alternate masterfully the periods of terror and of breathing spell. When the pressure seems to be over, the subjects let their defenses down and are ready "to swallow any strong suggestions." (33:168)

The Freudian analyst refrains from making any interpretations till the apprehensiveness and tension of the initial phase is quieted down. When the trust and relationship is built up ("transference") he starts with "deep" interpretations, *i.e.* imposing upon the subject the Freudian ideas about what is allegedly shown in patient's unconscious. With his watchfulness ("resistance") relaxed, the patient is ready to buy even the most preposterous suggestions of the psychoanalyst.

5. Unobtrusive coercion

Man is subject to cultural and ideological contagion. They have a "constant psychic exchange with one another." (33:204) "Our feelings and thoughts are conditioned and coerced by various social influences." (33:193)

Contemporary psychoanalysts in the United States have a relatively easy time in imposing their ideology upon patients, who come into therapy prepared by an American culture saturated with Freudian concepts.

5. *He saw that the emperor had no clothes*

Meerloo, as we saw in the previous section, ably analyzed the totalitarian brainwashing processes, but categorically disagreed with my discernment of "thought reform" features in Freudian psychoanalysis. Another psychiatrist, Frank (38), a professor of psychiatry at Johns Hopkins University, was apparently not imbued with conventional deference for Freudism, and was capable of iconoclastic perception of underlying similarities between brainwashing methods on the couch and in Communist "reeducational" prisons and camps. A study of his 1961 text (2) and its 1973 revision shows that his discernment sharpened in the ensuing years and his outspoken attitude grew bolder. In the early edition he drew parallels between psychotherapy in general (which at that time was practically all Freudian anyway) and "thought reform" manipulations of subjects; in later study he narrows his comparisons to specific Freudian operations on the couch, on both trainees and patients. The earlier text had no statements like these from the later edition: "Similar confabulations are known to occur in intensive long-term psychotherapy. See p. 174 below." (38:100) On that page he discusses Freud's discovery that his hysterical patients had misled him by inventing sexual traumas in childhood to comply with his pet hunches. Frank compares such inventions with that of a Communist prisoner who accused himself in all sincerity that the previous night he had tried to attract attention of a representative of his country, when in fact no such representative could have been anywhere near the prison.

Another example of clearer focus Frank attained in the revised text, might be the analogy he drew between the zeal for conversion of Chinese indoctrinators and the Freudian therapists' subtle imposition of their ideology upon patients. Frank explains it by need to bolster the shaky faith by obtaining confirmation from converts. He makes this restrained comment: "These considerations may have some pertinence for some current American psychotherapeutic training programs. See p. 176 below." (38:89) The reference here is to the "analyst's dogmatic adherence" to ideology with which he was indoctrinated in training institutes and "the energy devoted to the propagation of analytic doctrines."

What enabled Frank to exercise independent perception seems to have been his unconventional scheme of viewing all psychotherapy as a process of convert or overt persuasion. Seeing through this prism, it is not hard to discern that psychoanalysis and "thought reform" rely on the same psychological process—clandestine persuasion. Discussing the Freudian assertion of the neutrality of the therapist, Frank puts "neutrality" between inverted commas; he sees the myth of neutrality as basically a rationalization to firm up the therapist's faith in his theory by obtaining "confirmation" from patient's verbalizations.

Frank provides a subtle and sophisticated analysis of affinities between brainwashing and psychoanalytic pressures for attitudinal changes along the lines of Freudian "mental health." It suffices for the discussion here to mention only the salient insights, some of them implicit and developed further by me, others explicitly stated in Frank's discussion:

1. Communist brainwashers present their society as more progressive, standing for justice, equality, and other official myths. American society is depicted as corrupt, unjust, sick. The deprivations suffered by American POWs were presented as results of American bombings, and the victims were induced to feel guilty about their own plight. (38:96)

The traditional Freudian stance has been that their ideology stands for a better, freer, healthier psychological experience. The Freudians believe themselves to be the bearers of a better humanity. They denounce the traditional Judeo-Christian morality as hypocritical, unsound and reactionary. Psychological troubles are interpreted as coming from the unenlightened adherence to established mores, and the patient is made to feel guilty and inferior about the values and views he had absorbed from his family and schools.

2. "The focal point of indoctrination process was the interrogation, which had individual and group forms." (38:96) The victims of "thought reform," both American and Chinese, had to prepare "confessions," which mainly consisted of life histories. The more self-accusatory the "confessions," the more approbation by authorities would be expressed and the wretched status of the victim would be slightly improved. The "confessions," to be proper, had to contain not only the wrongdoings, but also wrong thoughts from the past life. And all of the statements had to be couched in the "correct" terminology, with a zestful appreciation of the Communist world view.

The Freudian parallel is not hard to discern. The analysand, be he trainee or patient, has to streamline his life history with doctrines announced by Freud and popularized by his adherents. From one hour to another, for hundreds of interviews, the patient is expected to remember real or hallucinated events, all in order to prove Freud's presuppositions of human nature. The analyst, like his brainwashing counterpart, sits there awaiting the "right" confessions, implying by his very presence that the authorized doctrines are infallible, and that the subject must have deviated in doctrinally expected ways. If he does not produce the desired confession, the subject is accused of resistance, and a deterioration in his status is threatened: the prisoner would undergo further strains, the trainee would be deprived of becoming an analyst, and the patient would face return to neurotic miseries.

3. The chief trick of the brainwasher is to induce guilt in the victim in order to subdue him. Frank quotes from a westerner who spent *Four Years in a Red Hell* (40) about this basic demand: "Just confess your crimes and all will be forgiven! No one is clearly told what crimes he is charged with ... but he must confess the crimes he is charged with." (38:97) Finally the victim "voluntarily" comes around and prepares his own accusation. An American woman, who was thus converted to the Communist viewpoint, recalls the procedure in her book. (41) She felt she had emptied her mind of all her non-

439

Communist transgressions and says so to the interrogator, who nudges her gently:

"Well, we feel there are some points you have missed, and we would like you to go on thinking a bit more . . . it is to the interest of both of you [the prisoner and her husband, also a prisoner, but separated from her] that you get all possible details cleared up. We will not force you in any way, but we would like you to think about your history and your activities some more. Is there any-thing in your history that you have failed to make a clean breast of?"

I stared at him hopelessly for a moment. "But I have thought and thought these past few weeks and there just isn't any more. Can't you give me a hint, or some line toward which to direct my thoughts?"

"That would be no help. You just think if there is anything at all that should be cleared up. . . . "

For the next six weeks I sat and thought. . . .

(I) began to look at our actions from the standpoint of the Chinese. . . . I tackled the problem from the standpoint of what I felt they wanted about us and not from what I considered wrong myself. (41:114)

Frank comments: "The interchange is not too dissimilar from what might go on in long-term psychotherapy. Ostensibly the procedure is completely permissive—responsibility for producing pertinent material rests entirely with the prisoner." (38:97) And, we should add, with a Freudian analysand. As we saw in previous examples in this volume, victims on the couch were led to aggravated guilt feelings about all of the shameful thoughts and actions that they "discover" in their life with the help of analyst, through "free" associations and dreams. Like the brainwashed American woman, the analysands begin "to look at our actions from the standpoint of the Chinese," in this case, the Freudians.

4. The brainwashers are past masters in twisting small utterances and gestures to suit their purposes. Any insignificant word or past event could be forced into an accusatory threat against the bewildered victims. In this way they led these persons, disorganized by stresses, to build a case against themselves.(38:99)

As we saw in the experiences of many professionals on the couch, they found their analyst always ready to produce big interpretations from minute clues. Maybe only paranoiacs can outdo Freudian analysts in producing "interpretations" out of thin air or barely perceptible signs. All this clever sophistication impresses deeply the prostrate subject, and encourages him, if analysis is "successful," to produce thousands of case histories, and sometimes publish them, showing a beautiful congruence of Freudian theory with what they "discovered" on the couch.

5. Frank expresses doubt about the Freudian promotional myth about the "deep changes" and "reconstruction" of personality that is supposed to occur almost exclusively in "psychodynamic" treatment. On the example of unstable conversions of most Americans under Chinese brainwashing pressures, he asserts:

> These findings raise some doubts about the claims of certain schools of psychotherapy to produce fundamental personality change. From this perspective, such changes may be analogous to false confessions. That is, the person has not changed fundamentally, but rather has learned to couch his problems and to report improvement in the therapist's terms. (38:102)

6. Frank attributes changes in victims of brainwashing to "participation and repetition." (38:99) The potency of participation is demonstrated by some laboratory experiments. In one of them (42), three groups of students read a purportedly factual statement that a majority of students would be drafted and that the period of service would be extended by one year. A hardly less welcome piece of news could be given to the students. One group was given the task of role-playing an advocate of the alleged change in conscription. The other two groups read the statement, one loudly, the other silently. The only positive shift in attitude occurred in the group that actively argued for the draft threat. The other two groups were unaffected.

Both Chinese and Freudian brainwashers reap the benefits of "participation." The subjects cannot avoid active role-playing of the parts assigned by those in control of them, and their verbalizations change in the direction imposed by the brainwasher. The practice of repetition leads to overlearning, which is essential for embedding the new attitudes as firmly as possible in subject's mind. That is why the subjects of indoctrinations have to remain for months in the re-educational camps, or for hundreds of sessions on the Freudian couch.

7. As other observers whose opinions we reviewed in earlier chapters, Frank points out that "the training analysis is a powerful method of indoctrination...which in some respects resembles thought reform." (38:171, 170) The ostensible purpose is to make the candidate a better therapist by pressing him through Freudian therapy; the real purpose is conditioning to psychoanalytic ideology.

> It involves a detailed review of his current thoughts and feelings in relation to his life history, interpreted consistently by the training analyst in terms of the doctrines of the institute. Since the initiative in the production of material resides with the candidate, the method fosters improvisation and participation. Training analysis lasts for several years, with the same material being reviewed repeatedly. As we have seen, improvisation, participation, and repetition are important in producing attitude change. The training analysis, furthermore, is not complete until the candidate produces memories, thoughts, and feelings in a form that confirms the doctrines of the institute.
>
> At this point the full significance of the term "candidate" becomes clear. (38:172)

The candidate is kept in an insecure position during the years of training; the threat of being accused of "resistance" to being molded into a true believer in official ideology plays viciously on the trainee, no less than in "thought reform" subjects.

The brainwashing is greatly facilitated by the models of other more "advanced" subjects in the camp who are rewarded for producing the precious fruits of indoctrination. A similar process occurs in the hothouse atmosphere of psychoanalytic institutes.

> The conceptual scheme is reinforced by the trainee's colleagues, who are also in the process of becoming indoctrinated. The more deeply they become immersed in their training, the more they tend to confine their professional and social contacts

to each other. This may be partly because they learn a specialized vocabulary, the terms of which are fully grasped only by members of the same school, partly through the development of a common body of shared experience. The cohesiveness of each group is heightened by the lack of sympathy of rival groups and of large segments of the medical profession. (38:175)

6. *Brainwashers at work*

The stereotype of totalitarian brainwashers is that they are brutal, crude torturers. Basically they are, especially in Soviet prisons. Their Chinese counterparts have, however, learned that honey catches more flies than vinegar, and they overpower their victims by calculated dosage of faked permissiveness, keeping most of the time their big stick behind their back.

The priests of a pagan cult training novices or secret police reeducation agents are stern, but not violent as a rule. They play the role of solicitous, patronizing friends, who are trying to save the subject from some terrible experiences in the future. Inquisitors expressed concern about saving heretics and witches from eternal sufferings; Communist brainwashers believe that they really want to elevate the wretched reactionary into a redeemed member of their glorious "socialist" society. The Communist Chinese "educators" of American GIs in Korean POW camps were often surprisingly mild, considerate, and seemingly reasonable with their subjects, at least on the surface. It was a part of the calculated psychological shock to the naive GI, who expected the brutalities of the Japanese POW camps of World War II. The Russian examiner of the Polish prisoner Stypulkowski, who is struggling against an impending total personality breakdown, assures the tortured man:

> I am sorry for you. I see how tired you are. I am happy to inform you, on behalf of the authorities, that the Soviet Government has no wish you should lose your life, or spend thirty years rotting in some labor camp in Siberia. On the contrary the Soviet Government wants you to live and work as a free man.
> You must decide today which path your future is to take. You could be a cabinet minister, one of the leaders of the new world order, and work for your country; the alternative is to depend on

Anglo-Saxon protection, rot in prison and await the result. (5:277, 278)

The distraught person coming to an analyst faces a similar dilemma. If he is to liberate himself from painful neurotic ways, he has to identify himself with "healthy" Freudian ways of looking at himself and the world. By the allegiance to Freudian truths, and abdication to the analyst's odd way of thinking, the patient hopes to gain relief from emotional difficulties. The analyst is there to offer him the saving truths, but the patient has to make them his own if they are going to benefit him. His choice is, then, either to thrust his mind in the indicated Freudian mold or to return to the dreaded sickness. It is not surprising that the patient chooses to accept the Freudwashing.

The main point of the brainwashing endeavor, as I intimated earlier, is to manipulate the deviant to reach the desired way of thinking supposedly on his own. The American officer Marlin, who gave testimony about the alleged germ warfare by Americans in the Korean War, was deeply grateful to his brainwasher, Ling. Although Ling and his colleagues may have known little of Freud and his methods, their techniques show a strange resemblance to certain psychoanalytic procedures. Later, in the United States, Marlin related some of the methods:

> "I'm not supposed to be helping you prepare for our reporters this way," Ling confided one day. "I'm only supposed to question you. The last thing we want is for you to think we're trying to influence you in what you've got to say."
> "You're a swell fellow, Ling, and I'm terribly thankful how you're helping me out," Marlin hastened to reply.
> All Ling wanted was to help him. Marlin knew this well. Hadn't Ling often told him? "You're your own boss," he always said. He kept telling Marlin that he didn't have to make a move or open his mouth until he wanted to, until he believed it himself. That was the right way, the "people's way." Ling had told him that too. Ling told him everything. Good old Ling! He was always so patient, and he always tried to do just what Marlin wanted, even to anticipate his wants. Marlin had never met anyone in the U.S. military service who was that patient and thoughtful. (5:46-48)

Apparently Marlin experienced a full-blown transference neurosis relationship to Ling. Many patients speak proudly of the dear man as "my analyst." The masochistic pact between Ling and his "patient" Marlin was in evidence.

Another prisoner describes the cunning ways of the Red brain-washers:

He said he now understood how the Reds had laid their trap for him and how he hadn't noticed it until he was caught in it. "The Communist tactic, when they want a certain action taken, is not to say so at all," he said. "One by one, they make every alternative move impossible. They put you in a position where you have no other possibility but to act voluntarily. They don't tell you what they wish, but wait for you to find out for yourself, no matter how long it takes. You're trapped like a rat. You've perfect freedom to choose, they say. You try one way and find it's impossible, because perhaps money is lacking. You try another method and it does not work for some other reason. They make sure of it. Finally you have to take the line they've wanted all along, though nobody told you. (5:63)

Sargant draws on the experiences of a British officer to make a comparison between the brainwashing cat-and-mouse game and psychoanalytically prescribed procedures:

Major A. Farrar-Hockly gives an apt description of the techniques by which ideas can be implanted without the use of strong, direct and obvious suggestion. He learned these as a result of his experiences as a British prisoner-of-war in Korea. The same principles obviously apply in some psychotherapeutic disciplines and in police examinations where strong direct suggestion is also denied: The Chinese are past masters at this technique. They wouldn't tell me what they really wanted. Whenever we got near to something substantial, they would immediately come back to it from another angle and we'd go all round it, but I'd never find out what it was. And then they would go away and leave me—thinking. I believe if the interrogator went on long enough with someone who is in a very weak state, and then sprang the idea suddenly on him, the chap would seize on it and become obsessed by it. He would begin to say, "Well, by Jove, I wonder whether in fact it's all really true, and this is what I was thinking in the first place." Every time they went away I spent hours saying, "Now was it that? No, it couldn't have been that. I wonder if it was so and so?" and that's what they were trying to do. They were trying to get me to a state when the idea would suddenly come Bingo, and I would begin to wonder whether I'd thought of it or they had. As regards the means of bringing one to a point of confession some imaginary crime spontaneously, he also says:

Now another method is to gradually suggest something by talking round it and getting a little nearer each time and just giving a fragment so that you build up the idea in your own mind, and eventually you say something (this presupposes you are in a pretty weak state of mind, which I wasn't at the time, at least I don't think I was). And then you say something and they say, "But you said this, you produced this, we didn't" and you begin to say after a time, "My God, I did produce it—where did I get it from?" Here the resemblances of modern brainwashing and some methods of psychotherapy are obvious. (6:197, 198)

The indoctrinators of the Korean prisoners of war were not pushing their views strongly upon some of their victims. The pressure was relatively gentle. They could wait for the prisoners to absorb the only correct views and reject the wily capitalist misinformation. The prisoners could not well afford postponing the conversion, as they were severely tried by demoralization, loneliness, confusion, and despair; their need to ease their lot pushed them toward relinquishing the loyalties which brought only disadvantages to them. If they joined these benevolent enemies they could receive mail, get cigarettes or other important privileges and, what was most desirable, free themselves from unbearable inner tension.

This method of getting the prisoner to come over to the oppressor's side "voluntarily," to build a case against himself by self-accusing confessions, is technically known as the Yezhov Method in the Soviet brainwashing technique. The name is derived from the period of the infamous NKVD chief who perfected it so that persons would without apparent coercion confess to the most heinous crimes, condemning themselves to death or brutal imprisonment as alleged traitors to the regime.

Sargant (6:170, 171) quotes a London *Times* report of the case of a Chinese owner of a modest drugstore and chemist shop. The constant drumming of the official propaganda machine about the evils of capitalism had created a guilty feeling in him, as if he were himself an ugly exploiter. In order to redeem himself, he went to the local authorities, telling them that he wanted to give his property over to the state and become a decent citizen. His offer was not accepted at that time; he was upbraided for possible ulterior motives and sent back home to meditate further on the issue. The authorities emphasized that sincere motives alone could make such a gift acceptable. A month later he returned entreating them even more fervently to take his property away from him. After much deliberation, the party authorities decided to grant his request if he could get his shareholders to agree to the transaction. He arranged a meeting of shareholders and won them over to the idea. They all enthusiastically relinquished property rights to the state and were delighted with the reciprocal generosity of the Party authorities, who allowed them to continue working in the store and sharing in some of the profits. Only a few preachers and even fewer psychotherapists could boast of such marvellous results.

Sargant points out that the delusions of the brainwashing process may be mutual. The secret service examiner or, for that matter, even the police investigator in democratic societies may be caught in the brainwashing process himself. While he leads the subject toward the confession that appears only reasonable and right in his view, he ignores the role of his own implicit suggestions, offered through questions, suppositions, and his own partially revealed beliefs. The process of brainwashing is tedious, and the examiner is subject to human fatigue and reduced alertness. The subject is also in a confused, strained state of mind, unable to distinguish his own thoughts from those directly or subtly implanted by the examiner. When the subject starts coming around to the expected views, neither the trainer nor the trainee can be sure about how they arrived at the resolution of the struggle—anyway, they need not waste time on such minute considerations, when there is the satisfying result to enjoy. The brainwasher is satisfied with a job well done, the brainwashed is relieved for the time being from extreme psychological and physical

447

distress, and his guilt feelings and possibly masochism are assuaged. I touched on these mutual delusions in discussing the psychoanalytic transference and countertransference.

A classical example of the delusions into which even astute psychoanalytic observers like Freud can fall is seen in his being taken in by his early hysterical patients. In those early days of his psychological career, Freud was enthusiastic about proving that hysterical disorders were the consequence of early sexual traumata. He presented a lecture before the medical society of Vienna and published a paper dealing with cases in which subjects had confided to him, after much dramatic hesitation and a proper display of emotion, that they had been molested sexually in their childhood. The etiology of hysterical disorders seemed proved without doubt; Freud thought that he had reached the source of the Nile. Yet he began to have his doubts. He finally realized that he had brainwashed his patients by leading them with suggestive questions, in turn deluding himself by what they produced for him. He faced a veritable emotional crisis and entertained the idea of giving up his psychoanalytic labors and turning to something less tricky and self-deluding. However, he had invested so much hope and effort in his system, that he finally constructed a rationalization and shored up the shaken structure.

There is little doubt about the efficacy of brainwashing in reconstructing the thinking of many subjects. Chinese propagandists exhibit a continued missionary zeal for causes which they are assigned to serve, whether in the army or among civilian workers, at home or abroad, as recognized officials or clandestine revolutionary agents. Most of them show no desire to return to their prebrainwashing selves. That some of them may have doubts and inner struggles is shown by occasional defections, but on the whole they avoid the turmoil which awaits those who slip toward "sick," socially disapproved attitudes. It is a matter of self-protection and avoidance of conflicts that holds them in line; if they retain their enthusiasm for directions implanted through arduous brainwashing schools, they gain emotional and social security.

Political brainwashers insist on changing the subject's values and attitudes. The psychoanalytic brainwashers also strain at separating the patient from traditional values, which are supposedly unhealthy, and implanting the atheistic and hedonistic ethical orientation. They

448

try to loosen the previous loyalties of their patients and establish new loyalties common to psychoanalytically enlightened people. Perhaps the need to dissolve a person's previous loyalties partially explains why Freudian analysands uniformly see their mothers and fathers, their teachers or preachers as the supposed main villains of their neuroses and the stumbling blocks to their growth into (psychoanalytically defined) maturity. First, it is necessary to relinquish the views and feelings that bind the patients to the mental and emotional framework in which they grew up. Then, when the ties to the patient's early values are weakened, the new psychoanalytic values can be grafted in place of the discredited, supposedly immature or incorrect ones. This process is also carried on in the indoctrination of youth in Communist countries. Family ties and traditions are disparaged and loyalty to party doctrines established instead. The Chinese indoctrinators call this process appropriately "the tail-cutting," meaning the disruption of ties with family and former friends and separation from previous values.

7. Freudwashing in slow motion

For those who are even superficially familiar with the process of psychoanalysis, the implications of the preceding discussion of brainwashing are rather plain. The common features of the two are in fact striking. There is, first, the general psychological situation. In brainwashing the correct view is determined in advance. Other ways of thinking are dismissed a priori as erroneous, biased, and "unscientific." The brainwashing expert is also quite convinced that the views he forces upon the "trainee" are the highest form of truth, approved by the Party and its almighty and all-wise leader (Stalin, Mao). Those who dare to have different opinions are reactionaries, antiparty, deviationists, showing a misguided resistance. The reeducator is sure that he has a socially creative role in bringing the resisters to health. To think and behave in ways approved by the party is by definition considered healthy. The politically enlightened agent knows that there are different, even diametrically opposite views existing outside his party, but he confidently dismisses these as nothing more than lies, errors, incorrect interpretations, deviationism.

Now, little of the above definitions needs to be changed to read them as an adequate statement of Freudism; the nouns employed might readily be replaced by "Freud," "psychoanalytic movement," "Freudian theory," "analyst." Consider, for instance, how easily an American patient slips into the ideological thought forms of her analyst. Mabel Dodge imagined she was discovering something herself and was delighted to find so many weird things in herself. She describes the "game" in *Movers and Shakers:*

Mabel Dodge began to be psychoanalyzed by Dr. Smith Ely Jelliffe, one of the leading psychoanalysts in America. At first she loved it. She enjoyed Jelliffe's "amusing intuition." She said: "It became an absorbing game to play with oneself, reading one's motives, and trying to understand the symbols by which the soul expressed itself. Psychoanalysis was apparently a kind of tattle-taling. . . . I longed to draw others into the new world where I found myself: a world where things fitted into a set of definitions and terms that I had never even dreamt of. It simplified all problems to name them. There was the Electra complex and Oedipus complex, and there was the Libido with its manifold activities, seeking every chance for outlet, and then all that thing about Power and Money!"

She did not find this entertaining tattle-taling "at all dangerous. It was interesting," she said, "to watch my soul provide exciting subjects to discuss with Jelliffe. Whenever things got dull, something would turn up from down below to keep the ball rolling—and he chased it about. He told me more strange and fascinating oddities and now I have forgotten them nearly all!" (quoted in 7:310, 311)

Then, there is the vulnerable Freudian subject. For a number of years he has faced emotional turmoil and conflicts with those around him. He is anxious, irritable, depressed, tired of life, at odds with himself. Those who know him say or imply that something is wrong with him, that he is heading toward unhappiness, nervous breakdown, or institutionalization. He does not know what to do with himself but cannot endure his inner agitation any more. Someone might suggest that he go to see a witch-doctor, a priest, or a psychotherapist, depending upon the society or social level to which he belongs. In our society, if he can sacrifice a large sum of money and if he is lucky enough to find what is purported to be the most efficient healer of souls, he will go to the office of a psychoanalyst.

The myths of Freudian wonder-cures are spread far and wide as part of the superstitions of the educated classes:

> A Puerto Rican or Haitian patient in New York City, still committed to his native voodoo creed, will have little faith in the analytic couch. But the middle or upper class urban intellectual will take to it like Tarzan to the trees. He is likely to enter the treatment situation with the proper expectations and reasonable confidence in the psychoanalytic approach. (4:169)

The subject is apprehensive, alternating between hope and doubt, hating the discomfort and expense of an interminable series of sessions four or five times a week, yet desiring the new person he is to become when the travail is over. The analyst plays it cool. Although he wants to add the subject to his sources of income, he does not try to rope him in by crude methods. He tells the subject that it is all up to him: he may begin therapy, but there is no guarantee of improvement, not to speak of a cure (if the patient only knew how realistic this caution is). It all depends, the analyst tells the patient, on how strenuous an effort the subject is willing to make to abide by what the analyst calls the cardinal rule: not to hide any thoughts that come to him, but to speak them without self-censoring. The subject's common sense tells him that it is doubtful whether he can straighten out his longstanding personality quirks merely by talking freely, but he reassures himself that the profound healer must know what he is talking about. After all, this particular order of lay priests is reported to have discovered some tremendous and unbelievable mysteries about human beings. It is true that they have some odd ideas about the human mind, but the more peculiar they are, the more profound they must be. So the subject decides to begin the unwelcome bother, just as the prisoner or political trainee decides to let himself be influenced by his interrogator.

American POWs in the Korean War were also asked to be "frank," to discuss matters in an open fashion, to confess even trivial matters of which they were supposedly guilty. It seemed quite harmless to play the silly game, and the prisoners often complied in a joking manner. The long-suffering brainwashers seemed pleased even with the farce,

451

as they knew well what they were after. Through resistive talking and farcical "confessing," the prisoner's minds began to fall in line with the schemes of the experts in "thought reform": the animal was induced to play around the trap. The more willing talkers were selected as hopeful prospects for more serious "treatment." (5:144, 238)

The subjects of both psychoanalysis and brainwashing are in this way preselected for the process. The prisoner is selected from a group as being more talkative, more "liberal" or more compliant; the analysand is interviewed, and his readiness to yield to the analyst is determined in the trial interviews. The prisoner is "softened" by long periods of waiting, uncertainty, anxious searching for the mysterious "crime" he is held for; the analysand comes into analysis a confused and suffering person, deflated and threatened, at the end of his tether.

The analyst continues to play it cool. He sits in the shadows, like secret police investigators or instructors in thought-reform camps, following the mysterious healing rite as revealed to him. The investigators or political instructors have almost absolute control over the subject; the Freudian analyst is more subtle, but no less authoritarian. He increases his control over the subject not only by positioning him on the couch and enjoining him to reveal every thought, but also by issuing other prohibitions: not to talk about his analysis with others; not to meet with other analysands; not to make any major decisions except with the consent of the analyst; not to read psychoanalytic literature; not to fail with payment. In spite of all these rules and interferences, the psychoanalyst maintains his pretense of being uninvolved with the patient, convincing him that revelations will arise out of his own mind, uncontaminated by any influences of the analyst. After all, the semblance of scientific impartiality must be preserved at all costs.

In the meantime the patient squirms in discomfort. He feels his mind dissolving, for he is being trained to abstain from using it critically, normally. That does not bother the analyst, who has been taught that discomfort promotes the breakdown of the old personality organization, or, better to say, it promotes "treatment." A British psychiatrist suspects that "thought disorder in a psychoanalytic session is . . . the disordering of the patient's thoughts and perceptions by the analyst." (32:325) Freud himself had agreed with Ferenczi that emotional pain speeds up the transformation into a "successfully analyzed" patient. [1] Freud had said no "cossetting" of patients: *"Analytic treatment should be carried out, as far as possible, under privation—in the state of abstinence."* (8:185, Freud's italics)

What this "privation" means in the initial phase was described by Landis, a professor of psychology at Columbia University who undertook psychoanalysis more for academic reasons than because of any serious emotional trouble:

> After about ten or twelve hours of analysis (one hour a day, five days a week) I found that I was possessed by a thoroughgoing anxiety which pervaded all my thinking and inter-personal relations. At first there was no tendency for this apprehension to attach itself specifically to any event, person or class of relationship. Rather it colored my existence in the same way that colored glasses tint the visual field. I was never puzzled by this anxiety, although I was bothered by its persistence. (9:4, 5)

The dissolution of the previously better-functioning ego goes on as "therapy" proceeds:

> An interesting development in this anxiety experience in later stages of the analysis was its tendency to dissociate from the original circumstances which set it up and which I myself was satisfied had set it up. The apprehension entered into all kinds of judgements and behavior. Because it took constant conscious effort to discount the effect, at times an interesting mental state of semi-dissociation intervened. I would watch myself behaving or talking in an anxious fashion, yet not seeming to care sufficiently to correct them. (9:5)

Sargant recognizes that repeated insinuation of supposed sexual traumata is one of the chief ways of keeping the patient off balance: "Though it is now generally admitted that not all mental illnesses are due to sex trauma, they still in practice encourage the patient to harp on early sexual excitements and associated sex guilt feelings, and thus help to arouse in him the emotions necessary for successful abreaction." (6:77)

Freudian therapy is contrary to the healing processes of nature. The Pinckneys speak unequivocally of the wanton Freudian disrespect for delicate personality balances:

Nature has graciously given us the ability to forget, or at least to ameliorate with time, the agonies and sorrows in our lives, so that it is easier for us to go on in spite of unhappy experiences. However, analysts say you must remember and verbally relive each of these painful experiences. Childhood memories, animosities, fears, frustrations and humiliations mushroom in importance when they are revived in later life, endowed with sexual interpretations, and then interminably discussed. This sort of muddying of the waters of the past is more than enough to create a really depressed attitude in the most normal, healthy person.

The technique, therefore, deprives the patient of as much of his freedom of thought as is possible while sustaining vegetative life and activity during the instillation of the thoughts and ideas of Freud, along with the analyst's sexual interpretations of the patient's every word and movement.

The need for the analyst to interpret for the patient what is in his unconscious, is described by Freud thusly, "What is in your mind is not identical with what you are conscious of; whether something is going on in your mind and whether you hear of it, are two different things." Therefore he considered it essential that the analyst tell you what is going on in your mind, because you may not "hear of it," though how a total stranger can know this better than the possessor of the thought, is a mystery. By such devious methods, the analyst achieves the patient's complete dependence upon him. It is hard not to compare the method to that of brainwashing. (28:48, 49)

This process of breaking down a patient's will can be quite successful with many patients. One of Freud's analysands told Sargant:

For the first few months I was able to feel nothing but increasing anxiety, humiliation and guilt. Nothing about my past life seemed satisfactory any more, and all my old ideas about myself seemed to be contradicted. When I got into a completely hopeless state, he (Freud) then seemed to start to restore my confidence in myself, and to piece everything together in a new setting. (6:78)

There are, apparently, two stages of psychoanalytic brainwashing: first, intensifying the disturbance in a patient by making him tense, unstable, unsure of himself, apprehensive; then, instilling indifference and mild depression, necessary to reduce resistance to the trainer's suggestions.

After about forty or fifty hours of analysis, Landis relates a dream. The analyst seizes the occasion to convince the patient that he is sick. "That's one aspect of your neurosis," he tells Landis, who takes over:

> I asked, "Have I a neurosis?" "Why certainly." That set off a long soliloquy on normality and neurosis. I asked, "What is normality?" He replied, "I do not know. I never deal with normal people." I asked, "But suppose a really normal person came to you." He interrupted, "Even though he was normal at the beginning of analysis, the analytic procedure would create a neurosis." (9:11)

So here it is: the analytic treatment, parallel to its brainwashing counterpart, creates neurosis. "This is a dawning admission. Psychoanalytical treatment may thus cause the appearance of what was not there before, or the direct result of treatment may be a neurosis." (10:46)

The reason for this abuse of the patient is supposedly to lead him to a new personality organization, defined by Freudian preconceptions. Landis sees that he was made neurotic all right: "Then I realized he was absolutely right on that point. I have described anxiety, apprehension, irritation, resistance and mental befuddlement that the process of enforced free association set up, and these are all cardinal symptoms of neurosis." (9:11) Apparently, Landis saw clearly the nature of the weapon with which the analyst disorganizes the patient's ego: it is the hallowed "first rule" of psychoanalysis, free association. It forces the analysand to decompensate, to become flooded by the primitive forces of his personality. "Psychoanalysis is the sickness it professes to heal" was the insight of a Viennese satirist, Karl Kraus. An American satirist, the cartoonist Berry, caught this feature of

Freudian "therapy" quite well in one of his cartoons. He pictures two fellows sitting at the bar, with one of them saying: "I'll be so glad when my psychoanalyst goes on vacation so I can get back to 'normal'!"

The brainwashers are less subtle in their methods at this point. They go straight toward befogging the mind of their victim. Hunter describes the process:

> The entire mechanism of brainwashing, so as to condition the patient and indoctrinate him, particularly to accomplish the latter, is geared to putting his mind into a fog. That is the purpose of all the sly and harrowing pressures used. Brainwashing is a system of befogging the brain so a person can be seduced into acceptance of what otherwise would be abhorrent to him. In brainwashing, fog settles over the patient's mind until he loses touch with reality. Facts and fancy whirl around and change places, like a phantasmagoria. Shadow takes form and form becomes shadow, inducing hallucinations. However, in order to prevent people from recognizing the inherent evils in brainwashing, the Reds pretend that it is only another name for something already very familiar and of unquestioned respectability, such as education or reform. (5:202, 203)

Psychoanalysts, too, call their method reeducation and consider regression (11:50) an essential step in the treatment before the patient becomes able to absorb ideas abhorrent to him.

Hunter held discussions with Dr. Leon Freedom, a psychiatrist intensely interested in how the procedure of brainwashing attained such success with a great many American POWs. One of Dr. Freedom's impressions was that "the entire process was similar to the familiar clinical practice known as *free association*." (5:252, Freedom's italics) He also points out another similarity between psychoanalytic practice and brainwashing: delving with dreams to undermine inner security. The brainwashers express interest in their victims' dreams, as many analysts do; they would even order guards to watch any signs of restlessness and dreaming in the prisoner, and the subsequent interrogation would contain inquiries about the dreams, which could uncover secrets not yet ferreted out.

We might well ponder the intensity of the loosening of the ego that occurs in psychoanalysis. If Landis, who did not need psychoanalysis, slipped into the partial disintegration he describes above, what can be expected to happen to a person less stable, in real need of psychological help? Mlle. Choisy sensed the abyss to which she was drawn and took the first plane out of Vienna. Knight (12), midway in treatment, felt like leaving his satisfactory job as a chemist and running away from the artificial turmoil which analysis brought him. He could no more do so than the trainees in a thought-reform camp. The patient's disintegration is viewed as a step in bringing him closer to the "maturity" toward which the analyst presumably guides him. One is reminded of Janet's story about one of Mesmer's patients who died while his letter of gratitude was being published. The papers wrote: "Monsieur Court de Gebelin has just died, cured by animal magnetism."

If the patient balks at the pressure that is being put upon him, he is accused of "resistance" by the analyst. He is made guilty by the implication that he is uncooperative and sabotaging his own treatment. This in turn makes him even more guilty and more compliant with the healer's pressures. Suggestions are made by the analyst that the patient is probably withholding some ugly secrets of an Oedipal, anal, or other dirty nature. These insinuations are put forward as vague hunches regarding dreams or various lapses, but they are often sufficient to bring the patient into submission.

Harrington describes the Trick of Resistance and its mystical implications:

> The confusion and uncertainty which this problem tends to produce in the mind of the patient, the psychoanalyst has utilized very cleverly. The psychoanalyst has so stressed the pernicious effects of resistance, and has attributed to it such subtlety and cunning, that he has come to envisage it as a sort of evil spirit which is forever putting doubts and objections into people's minds in order to prevent them from understanding or accepting the great truths of psychoanalysis. As a matter of fact, practically all of the opposition he encounters, whatever its nature or from whatever source it may come, he attributes to this cause. This conception of resistance as a tricky enemy against whom one must wage a constant war, he is at great pains to impress upon his patient, and every time the patient's doubts are awakened by

those "difficulties and improbabilities" which, as Freud tells us, "a normal yet uninstructed thinking is bound to find in the theory of analysis," that is to say, every time the analyst tries to shove something down the patient's throat which the latter finds it particularly hard to swallow so that he is moved to offer criticism or objections, the analyst disposes of these objections by pointing out that they are simply another manifestation of the pernicious activities of the arch-enemy, Resistance, against whom we must be constantly on guard and whom we must be ever striving to overcome. (13:80, 81)

Brainwashers do the same with their victims. One of the POWs describes the trick:

> The Reds were constantly on the watch for some excuse to charge you with having a hostile attitude, and when they got the slightest chance, squeeze every bit of advantage they could out of it. . . . When anyone would say something to them with conviction and they could not refute it otherwise, they were quick to retort "You have a hostile attitude." This took them off the hook and put you on it. (5:17)

When the prisoner or member of a political discussion group did not make the desired "confessions," and self-criticisms, he was rebuked for subtle resistance: "Comrade, you are not frank." The victim is not approved of until he produces confessions in the form desired by his interrogator, trainer, or Freudian analyst.

To return to the analyst. He continues his august role of apparent noninvolvement. He watches his rules, the first of which is "play it slow." He abides by the rationalization that the patient's pupa should break out of its cocoon by all appearances on its own. He is wary of giving "suggestions" because that kind of activity belonged to the prescientific phase of psychotherapy. Of course, the analyst has no doubt what the trouble with the subject is since the genius of Freud provided all the necessary revelations. But the analyst will remain in the shadows both literally and symbolically in order not to interfere in the "independent" discoveries of the subject. The occasional suggestions need not be considered anything serious because they are not suggestions at all; everyone calls them interpretations, quite a different matter from suggestion. When applied to brainwashing, this method is known as "suggestive interrogation" (5:73), for the questions imply the expected answers. Similarly, if analysis is successful, the analysand is considered to have discovered his own truths.

Since many patients come to psychotherapy in a state predisposing them to interpret their feelings in terms of environmental cues, and since the psychotherapist-patient relationship in some ways resembles the parent-child one, the interesting possibility arises that the therapist's name for patient's emotions may affect the emotional experience itself. Perhaps a patient's vague unrest becomes castration fear, anger towards his mother, or lustful feelings towards her, because the therapist labels them. (14:31)

"If only the psychologist insists that will occur to the patient, the latter often produces thoughts which are in accord with the psychoanalytic interpretation of the symbol." (15:142) The implanting of the analyst's ideas into the thinking of the analysands was plain in the cases of Wortis, Campbell, Natenberg, and others (chapter V).

Frankl calls such indoctrination of patients plainly "brainwashing." He tells how he helped an elderly physician overcome grief, describes the aggravatingly insensitive cynicism of a Freudian indoctrinator, and recalls his own protest against imposition of psychoanalytic dogmas upon patients.

... An old doctor consulted me in Vienna because he could not get rid of a severe depression caused by the death of his wife. I asked him, "What would have happened if you had died first and your wife would have had to survive you?" Whereupon he said: "This would have been terrible for her—how she would have suffered!" I then added, "Well, your wife has been spared this suffering and it was you who spared her. But now, as it were, you have to pay for it, by surviving and mourning her." The old man suddenly saw his plight in a new light, re-evaluating his suffering in the meaningful terms of a sacrifice for the sake of his wife.

Even if this story is well-known to you, what is unknown is a comment which was given by an American psychoanalyst some months ago. After hearing this account, he stood up and said, "I understand what you mean, Dr. Frankl; however, if we start from the fact that obviously your patient had only suffered so deeply from the death of his wife because unconsciously he had hated her all along ... "

If you are interested in hearing my reaction, here it is: "It may well be that after having the patient lie down on your couch for 500 hours, you will have brain-washed and indoctrinated him to the point where he confesses, like the Communists behind the iron curtain in the course of what they call self-criticism: "Yes, Doctor, you are right, I have hated my wife all along, I have never loved her at any time ... " "But then," I told my discussant, "you would have succeeded in depriving that old man of the only precious treasure he still possessed, namely, this ideal marital life they had built up, their true love ... while I succeeded, within a minute, in bringing about a significant reversal of his attitude, or let me frankly say: in bringing consolation." (27:56, 57)

"An experiment in approximation of thought reform," devised and carried out by Harsch and Zimmer (16) shows that even when the subjects are unaware of the wishes of the interviewer, they can be induced to change the trends in their talking through subliminal cues. The experiment was designed as an analogue to the practice of Communist "trainers" who return the confessions to be rewritten without giving any reasons.

The subjects were students, both male and female. The plan of the experiment was to investigate the possibility of changing the intro-punitive and extrapunitive trends in the subjects without any communication, verbal, gestural or any other. The "interviewer" sat in the adjoining room, operating the electrical apparatus without being seen by the subject. The task of the subjects was to talk on about fifteen topics for two minutes each in the three sessions. If the subject stopped talking, a moderately painful shock was administered to his calf. If the subject kept talking, only the light was used either to encourage him (rewarding him with points to raise his grade in psychology) to proceed or to signal him to change his direction. The hidden purpose of the light signals was to lead the subjects to take a direction opposite from that of their dominant trend. The subsequent interrogation showed that the subjects caught no glimpse of what brought either reward or punishment. Nevertheless, the students got the message subconsciously or unconsciously, for they changed the intrapunitive trend toward the extrapunitive, and vice versa, without any understanding of the pattern of the cues given them.

One can imagine the suggestive power of the clearer cues of the psychoanalytic situation if the quite vague signals of this "brainwashing" experiment could produce ascertainable changes in verbalizations.

Psychoanalysts undoubtedly possess more potent means than subliminal cues to brainwash their patients without necessarily making a deliberate decision to do so. Beside the influences which I reviewed in the preceding discussion, Freudwashing is greatly facilitated by the freudianized cultural climate. Not unlike Hindus and Moslems living in monolithic cultures, who are continuously reinforced in particular viewpoints, educated Americans are prepared for thinking Freudian thoughts, and adopting Freudian molds, by their experiences in schools, groups, literature and communication media. Thomas Mann, an admirer of Freudism, notes that we become Freudians imperceptibly, just as some grow to be Christians of sorts: "One could be influenced in this sphere without any direct contact with [Freud's] work, because for a long time the air had been filled with the thoughts and results of the psychoanalytical school." (47:77) Indeed, a hitherto unsuspected source of air pollution.

Further points of similarity between brainwashing and psychoanalysis need be noted only briefly. Just as the brainwashing agent rejoices when the subject comes to the right views without overt imposition, so the analyst confirms, in measured expressions, his approval when the subject discovers in himself any of the revealed truths of psychoanalytic science. The subject's progress only confirms the validity of the truths propounded by the master and his gifted disciples. The fact that the patient might be guiding himself by the popular spread of Freudian notions and by the covert clues received in the sessions stirs no doubts in the analyst. He himself was brainwashed in the same way, and, like his totalitarian brainwashing counterpart, the analyst believes that the truth is known; his role is to help in the "moral regeneration" of the subject, as the Chinese call it, to open his eyes to reality as defined by the illuminated members of

461

the healer's community. The "confession" of correct views is considered the criterion for discharge from both the brainwashing installation and from didactic or therapeutic psychoanalysis. Like his brainwashed brother, the analysand should also feel pleased for he is now considered a member of the right-thinking society, an achievement which gives him relative peace of mind and a reduction of inner tensions.

The criticism leveled by Train at Szasz's autonomous therapy is even more applicable to Freudian therapies: "With 'success' both players, psychoanalyst and his patient-victim, are duped into a spurious feeling of gratification by the cunning of the unconscious." (18:13)

In concluding this section, we might point out that psychoanalysis can hardly be considered a science when it is so permeated with vague procedures and gross unawareness about the basic processes involved.

8. *An impious view of psychotherapy*

In all fairness to psychoanalysts, whom I have depicted as inadvertent brainwashers, it should be said that some brainwashing, because of the influence of one person upon another within a cultural context, is involved in both psychotherapy and "thought reform." In this respect, the difference between psychotherapy and psychoanalysis is that most psychotherapists overtly recognize their purpose to be a guided change in the subject's attitudes and beliefs, a therapist-inspired adaptation to the inner and outer reality that enables the subject to live in greater ease with himself and others.

"Medical therapy and psychotherapy are the subtle sciences of human guidance in periods of physical and emotional stress." (26:359) This is the basic psychotherapeutic work. Some theoretical superstructures, depending on the biases of various leaders or schools, serve only to block the clear view of both the therapist and his patient of the sometimes unpalatable psychotherapeutic task. Only a minority of American therapists dare see the point clearly, abide by it, and admit it. Marmor, trained as a Freudian, but apparently unorthodox in his stand, testifies that the therapist molds the patient's mind by building "insights" into him according to the model preexisting in the therapist:

462

But what is insight? To a Freudian it means one thing, to a Jungian another, and to a Rankian, a Horneyite, an Adlerian or a Sullivanian, still another. Each school gives its own particular brand of insight. Whose are the correct insights? The fact is that the patient treated by analysts of all these schools may not only respond favorably, but also believe strongly in the insights which they have been given. Even admittedly "inexact" interpretations have been noted to be of therapeutic value. (Glover) Moreover, the problem is even more complicated than this; for, depending upon the point of view of the analyst, the patients of each school seem to bring up precisely the kind of phenomenological data which confirms the theories and interpretations of their analysts! Thus, each theory tends to be self-validating. Freudians elicit material about the Oedipus complex and castration anxiety, Jungians about archetypes, Rankians about separation anxiety, Adlerians about masculine strivings and feelings of inferiority, Horneyites about idealized images, Sullivanians about disturbed interpersonal relationships, etc. The fact is that in so complex a transaction as the psychoanalytic therapeutic process, the impact of patient and therapist upon each other, and particularly of the latter on the former, is an unusually profound one. What the analyst shows interest in, the kinds of questions he asks, the kind of data he chooses to react to or ignore, and the interpretations he makes, all exert a subtle but significant suggestive impact upon the patient to bring forth certain kinds of data in preference to others. (20:289, 290)

Some psychotherapists find it hard to accept the full import of this stress on their role as mind-changers. Others see it as their proper function. Marmor, for instance, considers this changing of the patient to the model provided by the therapist as "the central aspect of the psychoanalytic process." He quotes Strachey, who wrote in 1934 that superego modification through introjection of good objects is the essence of the patient's alteration by psychoanalysis. Freud expressed a similar view in *An Outline of Psychoanalysis*. Mowrer (21), writing from a diametrically opposite viewpoint, stresses modeling as basic to psychotherapeutic progress.

However, many therapists, preferring their myths of neutrality and nondirectiveness, will reject this view of their work with patients.

Frankl (19:76) considers that many American therapists suffer from a phobic ailment of avoiding at all price the prescription of values to the patient. He contrasts it with logotherapeutic principle of inculcating or developing values in the patient. It is obvious that in the States, it has become opprobrious to influence anyone's mind in candid ways, particularly in the contemporary democratic society of the United States, with its emphasis on freedom and dislike of social restrictions and controls.

Skinner argued this point with Rogers in a symposium in 1956: "We hesitate to admit, even to ourselves, that we are engaged in control, and we may refuse to control, even when this would be helpful, for fear of criticism." (22:1057) He sees it as an overreaction to the selfish, unscrupulous control of others. But some control of others is unavoidable. Censure or admiration exercise controls in personal contacts. Early training, society at large, and various relationships exercise control over the patient's choices, even if the therapist consciously relinquishes control.

Skinner criticizes the myth of the therapist's neutrality in the patient's decisions:

> What evidence is there that client ever becomes truly self-directing? . . . Even though the therapist does not do the choosing, even though he encourages "self-actualization"—he is not out of control as long as he holds himself ready to step in when occasion demands—when, for example, the client chooses the goal of becoming a more accomplished liar or murdering his sons. . . . Fear of control, generalized beyond any warrant, has led to misinterpretation of valid practices, and the blind rejection of intelligent planning for a better way of life. (22:1063, 1065)

Wiesenhütter (23), a German psychiatrist, comments on the adaptation of the statements of psychotherapeutic theory to prevalent cultural trends. In Europe, where a greater degree of authoritativeness is acceptable, these statements are more frankly authoritative, while in the United States, they pay tribute to libertarian shibboleths.

In the United States, even educators, whose duty of molding immature minds is obvious, shy away from such clear statements of purpose, and prefer attractive, but nebulous, locutions like "self-expression" and "freedom to grow," and other popular half-myths. The majority of American conventional (Freudian) psychotherapists, playing their role in a socially acceptable fashion, also shy away from defining their goal in realistic terms, *i.e.*, as the guidance of misguided minds toward some modicum of conformity to the demands of their conscience or community. Psychoanalysts are likely to persist in this confusion in the most pious ways, holding to their illusion of permissiveness, moral and scientific neutrality, passive reflection of the client's expressions, and other accumulated rationalizations. They provide, together with the so-called nondirective therapists, a good example of the brainwasher being brainwashed in the same process.

Compare this sanctimonious pretense of disclaiming responsibility for the changes which the patient makes with the unabashed, frank way in which a European psychiatrist describes himself as a "leader of men":

> The psychotherapist must have empathy and be able to establish trust . . . the psychotherapist should be a leader and an educator, too. In his need for dependency the emotionally disturbed is looking for an authority. The pedagogue tries to lead his client to self-government by energetic suggestive procedures. (25:136, my translation)

Anderson, liberated from Freudian and cultural superstitions of her country, does not shirk the responsibility of leadership in psychotherapy: "I need to know if he [the patient] thinks and reasons the way I do or if he is mouthing meaningless cliches. I have to be the measuring rod of the adequacy of his thinking. The leader has to lead." (36:282) Another American therapist, Garner, summarizes the frank observations of Lesse about the leading role of the professional: "The therapists, at least in America, are shown to have a relationship with patients in which the therapist expects to dominate and the patient to be dominated." (37:345) Masserman, with characteristic disregard for psychiatric shibboleths, states unabashedly: "Whether he admits it or not, the psychiatrist is an officer of the social order, duly commissioned and licensed to yield important powers. . . ." (48:349) However, such unsanctimonious admissions of leadership are very much an exception on the American scene.

465

Jaspers, a European therapist, similarly finds little need to pretend that psychotherapy is an objective or noninterfering procedure. He states plainly that any psychotherapist has to rely upon his own values in guiding the patient to what seems to the therapist to be a desirable way of behaving:

> Where general attitudes to life are concerned, everything depends on the personality of the psychiatrist and his own philosophical outlook. This raises so many difficulties and conflicts that the individual psychiatrist has to reach his decisions simply on the basis of instinctive conviction rather than by any process of scientific reasoning. . . .
> Cure becomes linked inseparably with what we call faith, general philosophical outlook or personal morality although the relationship is a highly ambiguous one (containing both truth and falsehood). It is pure fiction to believe that the doctor only confines himself to what has been thought healthy and objectively desirable by philosophy and religion. (30:5, 23)

Social myths are powerful in the United States as they are in the Soviet Union or a tribal society. In the American liberal circles it is a strong tradition that we should consider ourselves bound by no tradition at all. That is also why psychotherapists have to pretend that they operate outside any frame of values, as that is supposedly characteristic of authoritarian societies. This kind of tradition against tradition is accepted without questioning. It is not popular in an individualistic society to recognize that we are bound by societal values and limitations, whether we like it or not. Neither the therapist nor the patient can be "free" and self-determining except in a socially limited way. On important issues, it is the community which decides whether we are right or wrong though we might pout against such abrogations of individual choice.

According to the community, neurotics and psychotics are wrong in their self-centeredness and avoidance of responsibilities, and psychotherapists are given an open mandate to help the aberrant members to live more acceptably with others and, to some extent, for others. The amount of change will depend on the ability and willingness of the patient to integrate into his behavior the explicit and mostly implicit suggestions of the therapist. In vain do psychotherapists deny this expectation of change by the community and by the patient. Of course, they may fail their charge by subscribing to the popular myth of maximal freedom from obligations. The moral maturity of the therapist and his understanding of unavoidable tensions between reality and the wishful myth will largely determine his efficiency with the patient. One therapist, Black, has summed up the dilemma of a peculiar cliché in psychotherapy:

> The client or patient must, it is true, feel that he can express any thought without endangering his acceptance by the therapist, but it is unnecessary that the therapist pretend to be an amoral, acultural being without beliefs, opinions and attitudes. The therapist's value to the client stems partly from the fact that he *is* a member of society and possesses or is familiar with the mores and morality of the culture. . . . It is nonsense for the therapist to pretend that he does not make, in general, the same moral judgements as society at large, for the client infers that he does anyway. (29:303, 304)

The Freudians, sharing their master's ambivalence and confusion on moral and community living, have contributed greatly to the role-diffusion of many contemporary psychotherapists.

Notes to Chapter Ten

1. Ferenczi, an irrepressible innovator and eager therapist, had tried more frankly persuasive methods of working on patients, but after a few years recanted. Perhaps such strong techniques are impractical with paying patients since they might seek another, more permissive therapist, or Ferenczi had gone too far in his strong-arm methods. A timid patient of Ferenczi's was pressed to produce "forced fantasies" of aggression against the therapist, until the poor fellow broke into a cold sweat. (24, v. 2:72) Apparently, Ferenczi was tired of the slow brainwashing that is the first fundamental rule of psychoanalysis.

POSTSCRIPT

We have seen that Freudian claims are built on pretenses and specious reasoning and they end in a process that greatly resembles brainwashing in its essential features. Freudism has usurped psychological and psychotherapeutic authority, without furnishing scientific proofs of its assertions. It has denigrated its critics and accorded unbounded praise to its adherents, even idolizing its founder. It denies suggestion, but uses it as its chief tool to manipulate the patient into accepting the broad beliefs and preconceptions of the analyst. Misrepresenting its method as free association, Freudism attempts to conceal its use of the couch as hypnotic reinforcement and transference as a quasi-hypnotic state.

Misusing its medical auspices, Freudism has established a virtual dictatorship in American psychiatry, and, to a large extent, in clinical psychology. With its speculative and scientifically unreliable methods, it has impeded progress toward verification of the abundant hypotheses of the mental health field. The unscientific science of Freudism will be considered in the next volume, *Freud's Non-science: Pitfalls in Clinical Practice and Thinking*. The misleading influence of the pseudoreligion of Freudism, its harmful effects upon the lives of patients and its reinforcement of popular trends toward irresponsibility, will be considered in another volume, *Freud's Phallic Cult: A Pseudoreligion Posing as Superior Psychology*. The implication of Freud's atheistic presuppositions for the Christian community will be dealt with in a final volume, *Freud and Christ: Irreconcilable Adversaries*.

In view of its unscientific foundations, its misrepresentations and its manifold ill effects, Freudism can be considered as basically a gigantic hoax.

INTRODUCTION: REFERENCES

1. Committee on Evaluation of Psychoanalytic Therapy. *Bull. Amer. Psychoan. Assoc.,* 1950, 6.

2. Zilboorg, G. *Sigmund Freud: His exploration of the mind of man.* New York: Scribner, 1951.

3. Putnam, J.J. Dream interpretation and the theory of psychoanalysis. *J. abn. soc. Psychol.,* 1914-1915, 9, 36-60.

4. Bonaparte, M., Freud, A., Kris, E. *The Origins of Psychoanalysis. Letters to Wilhelm Fliess, Drafts and Notes: 1887-1902 by Sigmund Freud.* New York: Basic Books, 1954.

5. Ludwig, E. *Doctor Freud: An analysis and a warning.* New York: Hellman, Williams, 1947.

6. Bakan, D. *Sigmund Freud and the Jewish Mystical Tradition.* Princeton: Van Nostrand, 1958.

7. Grollman, E.A. *Judaism in Sigmund Freud's World.* New York: Bloch, 1965.

8. Eissler, K.R. *Talent and Genius. The fictitious case of Tausk contra Freud.* New York: Quadrangle Books, 1971.

9. Bottome, P. *Alfred Adler: A Biography.* New York: Putnam, 1939.

10. Frankl, V.E. *Pathologie des Zeitgeistes: Rundfunk Vorträge über Seelenheilkunde* (Pathology of the Spirit of Our Times: Radio lectures on psychotherapy). Wien: Deuticke, 1955.

11. Frankl, V.E. *Das Menschenbild der Seelenheilkunde: Drei Vorlesungen zur Kritik des dynamischen Psychologismus* (Human Image in Psychotherapy: Three critical lectures on psychodynamic psychologism). Stuttgart: Hippocrates Verlag, 1959.

12. Maslow. A. *The Farther Reaches of Human Nature.* New York: Viking, 1971.

CHAPTER I: REFERENCES

1. Jastrow, J. *The House That Freud Built*. New York: Greenberg, 1932.
2. Grinker, R.R. The science in psychiatry; fields, fences and riders." *Arch. Gen. Psychiat.,* 1965, 122, 367-376.
3. Frank, J.D. *Persuasion and Healing: A comparative study of psychotherapy*. New York: Schocken Books, 1963.
4. Eysenck, H.J., ed. *Behavior Therapy and the Neuroses*. New York: Pergamon Press, 1960.
5. Salter, A. *The Case against Psychoanalysis*. New York: Holt, 1952.
6. Haugen, G.B., Dixon, H.H., Dickel, H.H. *A Therapy for Anxiety Tension Reactions*. New York: Macmillan, 1960.
7. Allers, R. *The Successful Error: A critical study of Freudian psychoanalysis*. New York: Sheed & Ward, 1940.
8. Ludwig, E. *Doctor Freud: An analysis and a warning*. New York: Hellman, Williams and Co., 1948.
9. Vanderplas, J. M. Psychoanalytic theory. In J. M. Vanderplas, ed. *Controversial Issues in Psychology*. Boston: Houghton Mifflin, 1966.
10. Ellis, A. An introduction to the principles of scientific psychoanalysis. In S. Rachman, ed. *Critical Essays on Psychoanalysis*. New York: Macmillan, 1963.
11. Orlans, H. Infant care and personality. In S. Rachman, ed., *Critical Essays on Psychoanalysis*. New York: Macmillan, 1963.
12. MacIver, Joyce. *The Frog Pond*. New York: Braziller, 1961.
13. Bowman, K. Opinions of contemporary teachers of psychiatry. In F. Alexander, *Psychoanalysis and Psychotherapy: Developments in theory, technique and training*. New York: Norton, 1956.
14. Thigpen, C.H. Multiple personality. In S. Rachman, ed. *Critical Essays on Psychoanalysis*. New York: Macmillan, 1963. Reprinted from *The New Physician,* 1960, by permission.
15. Bailey, P. The Great Psychiatric Revolution. In S. Rachman, ed. *Critical Essays on Psychoanalysis*. New York: Macmillan, 1963.
16. Braceland, F.J. *Faith, Reason and Psychiatry: Sources for a synthesis*. New York: Kennedy, 1955.
17. Thigpen, C.H. and Cleckley, H.M. Some reflections on psychoanalysis,

hypnosis and faith healing. In J. Wolpe, A. Salter, L.J. Reyna, eds. *The Conditioning Therapies: The challenge in psychotherapy.* New York: Rinehart and Winston, 1964.

18. Eysenck, H.J. Psychoanalysis—Myth or Science? In S. Rachman, ed. *Critical Essays on Psychoanalysis.* New York: Macmillan, 1963.

19. Anderson, Camilla. The pot and the kettle. *J. Amer. Med. Woman's Assoc.,* 1963, 18, 293-298.

20. Grinker, R.R., Sr. A struggle for eclecticism. *Amer. J. Psychiat.,* 1964, 121, 451-457.

21. Low, A.A. Mental health through will training. In R.M. Jurjevich, ed. *Direct Psychotherapy,* vol. 2: *Twenty-eight American Originals.* Coral Gables, Fla.: University of Miami Press, 1973.

22. Grinker, R. R. Sr. A philosophical appraisal of psychoanalysis: Psychoanalysis as a science. In J. Masserman, ed. *Science and Psychoanalysis.* vol. 1 *Integrative Studies.* New York: Grune and Stratton, 1958.

23. Rieff, P. Introduction, *Collected Works of Sigmund Freud,* ten vols. New York: Collier, 1963.

24. Kaplan, S.D., Pain, Auld, and Kisker. *Contemp. Psychol.,* 1965, 10, 542-543.

25. Cowles, E.S. *Conquest of Fatigue and Fear.* New York: Holt, 1954.

26. Brandwin, M.A. Review of Fierman, L.B., *Effective Psychotherapy: The contribution of Hellmuth Kaiser. Contemp. Psychol.,* 1966, 11, 544.

27. Grazia, A. de. *The Velikovsky Affair: The warfare of science and scientism.* New York: University Books, 1966.

28. Appel, K.E. Opinions of contemporary teachers in psychiatry. In F. Alexander. *Psychoanalysis and Psychotherapy: Developments in theory, technique and training.* New York: Norton, 1956.

29. Johnson, H. K. Psychoanalysis: Some critical comments. *Amer. J. Psychiat.,* 1956, 113, 36-40.

30. Bing, J.E. and McLaughlin, F. Correspondence: Psychoanalysis. *Amer. J. Psychiat.,* 1956, 113, 466-467.

31. Johnson, H. K. Reply to the foregoing. [Reference 30, above.] *Amer. J. Psychiat.,* 1956, 113, 467-469.

32. Harms, E. Carl Gustav Jung—Defender of Freud and of the Jews. *Psychiat. Quart.,* 1946, 20, 199-230.

33. Lemon, R. Psychiatry: The uncertain science. *Saturday Evening Post,* 1968, August, 37-54.

34. Abroms, G.M., Miller, H.M., Greenfeld, N.S. American academic psychiatry and organized psychoanalysis. In I. Galdston, ed. *Psychoanalysis in Present-Day Psychiatry.* New York: Brunner/Mazel, 1969.

35. Adelson, R.R. Orthodoxy and Enthusiasm: A reconciliation. *Contemp.*

471

Psychol., 1968, 13, 456-458.

36. Jurjevich, R.M. *Freud's Phallic Cult: A pseudoreligion posing as superior psychology* (in manuscript).

37. Jurjevich, R.M., ed. *Direct Psychotherapy vols. 1 and 2: Twenty-eight American originals.* Coral Gables, Fla.: University of Miami Press, 1973.

38. Jurjevich, R.M. *Direct Psychotherapy vol. 3: International Developments.* Coral Gables, Fla.: University of Miami Press, 1974.

39. Strauss, E.B. *Reason and Unreason in Psychological Medicine.* London: Lewis, 1953.

40. Mann, J. The place of psychoanalysis in present-day psychiatry. In I. Galdston, ed. *Psychoanalysis in Present-Day Psychiatry.* New York: Brurner/Mazel, 1969.

41. Samra, K. A classic study in censorship. *Schizophrenia, Newsletter of the Amer. Schiz. Assoc.,* 1969, 3, 1 and 10.

42. Rogow, A.A. *The Psychiatrists.* New York: Putnam's Sons, 1970.

43. Sargant, W. Psychiatric Treatment: Here and in England. *The Atlantic Monthly,* July 1964, 214, 88-95.

44. Spiegel, H. Is symptom removal dangerous? *Amer. J. Psychiat.,* 1967, 123, 1279-1282.

45. Jacobson, E. Addiction to ideas. *Insight,* 1966, 4, 40-43.

46. Ellenberger, H.F. *The Discovery of the Unconscious: The history and evolution of dynamic psychiatry.* New York: Basic Books, 1970.

47. Brody, L.S. Harassed! A dialogue. *Intern. J. Gp. Psychother.,* 1966, 16, 463-500.

48. Green, J.C. Thought Disorder. *Intern. J. Psycho-Anal.,* 1966, 48, 525-535.

49. Millar, T.P. Who's afraid of Sigmund Freud? *Brit. J. Psychiat.,* 1969, 115, 421-428.

50. Wilson, Louise. *The Stranger, My Son: A mother's story.* London: Murray, 1969.

51. Shakow, D. *Clinical Psychology as Science and Profession.* Chicago: Aldine, 1969.

52. Brody, B. The conventional elite. *Psychother. Soc. Sci. Rev.,* 1971, 5, (10), 22-25.

53. Marmor, J. The current status of psychoanalysis in American psychiatry. *Amer. J. Psychiat.,* 1968, 125, 679-680.

54. Challenge in psychoanalysis: Impact of "personality attitudes." *Roche Report: Frontiers of Clin. Psychiat.,* 1970, 7, 5-8.

55. Freeman, E.K. Theodore Reik: A conversation. *Psychol. Today,* 1972, 5, (11), 47-50, 86-92.

56. Elkind, D. Demythologizing Freud. *Contemp. Psychol.*, 1972, 17, 56-59.

57. Meerloo, J.A.M. *The Rape of the Mind: The psychology of thought control, menticide, and brainwashing.* New York: Grosset and Dunlap, 1971. (first edition, 1956).

58. Lehrman, N.S. Precision in psychoanalysis. *Amer. J. Psychiat.*, 1960, 116, 1097-1103.

59. Meyerson, A. The attitude of neurologists, psychiatrists and psychologists towards psychoanalysis. *Amer. J. Psychiat.*, 1939, 96, 623-641.

60. Kopp, S.B. *Guru: Metaphors from a psychotherapist.* Palo Alto, Calif.: Science and Behavior Books, 1971.

61. Eissler, K.R. *Talent and Genius: The fictitious case of Tausk contra Freud.* New York: Quadrangle Books, 1971.

62. Glover, E. *Freud or Jung?* New York: Meridian Books, 1956.

63. Fromm, E. *The Crisis of Psychoanalysis.* New York: Holt, Rinehart, Winston, 1970.

64. Efron, E. *The News Twisters.* Los Angeles: Nash Publications, 1971.

65. Efron, E. *How CBS Tried to Kill a Book.* Los Angeles: Nash Publications, 1972.

66. *Human Events* (folder). Washington, D.C., 1973.

67. Anderson, Camilla. Assumptions-centered psychotherapy. In R.M. Jurjevich, ed. *Direct Psychotherapy,* vol. 1: *Twenty-eight American Originals.* Coral Gables, Fla.: University of Miami Press, 1973.

68. Yablonski, L. Synanon. In R.M. Jurjevich, ed. *Direct Psychotherapy,* vol. 2: *Twenty-eight American Originals.* Coral Gables, Fla.: University of Miami Press, 1973.

69. Frank, J.D. *Persuasion and Healing: A comparative study of psychotherapy.* Baltimore: The Johns Hopkins University Press, 1973. (Revised edition)

70. Masserman, J.H. *A Psychiatric Odyssey.* New York: Science House, 1971.

CHAPTER II: REFERENCES

1. Zilboorg, G. The changing concept of man in present-day psychiatry. In B. Nelson, ed. *Freud and the 20th Century*. New York: Meridian Books, 1957.

2. Gross, M. L. Dirt, injection, error and negligence: The hidden death threats in our hospitals. *Look*, 1966, 30, 27-30.

3. Hoch, P. *Failures in Psychiatric Treatment*. New York: Grune and Stratton, 1949.

4. Marcuse, F. L. *Hypnosis: Fact and Fiction*. Penguin Books, 1963.

5. Duffey, F. D. *Psychiatry and Asceticism*. St. Louis, Mo.: Herder, 1950.

6. I, 1.

7. Ellis, A. *Reason and Emotion in Psychotherapy*. New York: Stuart, 1963.

8. Alexander, F. G. *Psychoanalysis and Psychotherapy: Developments in theory, technique and training*. New York: Norton, 1956.

9. Jurjevich, R. M. *No Water in My Cup: Experiences and a controlled study of psychotherapy of delinquent girls*. New York: Libra, 1968.

10. Alexander, F. G. and Selesnick, S. T. *The History of Psychiatry*. New York: Harper and Row, 1966.

11. Ellis, A. Rational-Emotive Psychotherapy. In R. M. Jurjevich, ed. *Direct Psychotherapy vol. 1: Twenty-eight American Originals*. Coral Gables, Fla.: University of Miami Press, 1973.

12. Glasser, W. Reality Therapy. In R. M. Jurjevich, ed. *Direct-Psychotherapy vol. 2: Twenty-eight American Originals*. Coral Gables, Fla.: University of Miami Press, 1973.

13. I, 67.

14. King, A. *Seven Sinners*. New York: Harcourt, Brace and World, 1961.

15. Mowrer, O.H. Conscience and the unconscious. *J. Communic. Disorders*, 1967, 1, 109-135.

16. Mowrer, O.H., ed. *Morality and Mental Health*. Chicago: McNally, 1967.

17. Storrow, H. Verbal behavior therapy. In R.M. Jurjevich, ed. *Direct Psychotherapy, Vol 1: Twenty-eight American Originals*. Coral Gables, Fla.: University of Miami Press, 1973.

18. Menninger, K. *The Theory of Psychoanalytic Technique*. New York: Basic Books, 1958.

19. Storrow, H.A. Psychotherapy as interpersonal conditioning. In J.H. Masserman, ed. *Current Psychiatric Therapies*. New York: Grune and Stratton. 1965.

20. Meng, H. and Freud, E.L., eds. *Psychoanalysis and Faith: The Letters of Sigmund Freud and Oskar Pfister*. New York: Basic Books, 1963.

21. Post H. Putting a lid on the id. *Psychoan. Quart.*, 1966, 40, 472-481.

22. Ellis, A. Is psychoanalysis harmful? *Psychiat. Opinion*, 1968, 5, 16-24.

23. Wortis, J. *Fragments of an Analysis with Freud*. New York: Simon and Schuster, 1954. Also published in paperback edition by Bobbs-Merrill Co., 1968.

24. I, 8.

25. Jurjevich, R.M. *Freud's Non-Science: Pitfalls in clinical thinking and practice* (in manuscript).

26. Shepard, M. and Lee, Marjorie. *Games Analysts Play*. New York: Putnam's Sons, 1970.

27. Grinker, R.R. A transactional model for psychotherapy. *Arch. gen. Psychiat.*, 1959, 1, 132-148.

28. Frankl, V.E. *Theorie und Therapie der Neurosen*. München: Reinhardt, 1968.

29. Frankl, V.E. *The Doctor and the Soul: From psychotherapy to logotherapy*. New York: Knopf, 1965.

30. Marmor, J. *Sexual Inversion*. New York: Basic Books, 1965.

31. Treffert, D.A. Psychiatry revolves as it evolves. *Arch. Gen. Psychiat.*, 1967, 17, 72-74.

32. Parlour, R.R., Cole, P.Z., and Van Vorst, R.B. Treatment teams and written contracts as tools for behavior rehabilitation. *The Dis-Coverer*, 1967, 4, 1-6.

33. I, 45.

34. Salome, Lou A. *The Freud Journal of Lou Andreas-Salomé*. New York: Basic Books, 1964.

35. Quoted in Jones, E. The action of suggestion in psychotherapy. *J. Abn. Psychol.*, 1910, 5, 217-254.

36. I, 36.

37. McGuire, M.T. and Sifneos, P.E. Problem solving in psychotherapy. *Psychiat. Quart.*, 1970, 44, 667-673.

38. Müller-Hegemann, D. The problem of prolonged psychotherapy. *Amer. J. Psychother.*, 1968, 22, 233-244.

39. Haley, J. The art of being a failure as a therapist. In H.H. Barten, ed. *Brief Therapies*. New York: Behavioral Publications, Inc., 1971.

40. Ziferstein, I. Psychotherapy in USSR. In R.M. Jurjevich, ed. *Direct Psychotherapy, vol. 3: International developments*. Coral Gables, Fla.:

University of Miami Press, 1974.

41. Lazarus, A.A. Science and Service. *Psychol. Reports,* 1968, 23, 48.

42. Schmideberg, Melita. Iatrogenic disturbance. *Amer. J. Psychiat.,* 1963, 119, 899.

43. Chapman, A.H. Iatrogenic problems in psychotherapy. *Psychiat. Digest,* 1964, 25, 23-29.

44. Stein, A. Causes of failure in psychoanalytic psychotherapy. In B.B. Wolman, ed. *Success and Failure in Psychoanalysis and Psychotherapy.* New York: Macmillan, 1972.

45. Strupp, H.H. Ferment in psychoanalysis and psychoanalytic psychotherapy. In B.B. Wolman, ed. *Success and Failure in Psychoanalysis and Psychotherapy.* New York: Macmillan, 1972.

46. Saul, L.J. Some problems in psychoanalytic technique. In B.B. Wolman, ed. *Success and Failure in Psychoanalysis and Psychotherapy.* New York: Macmillan, 1972.

47. Wolman, B.B., ed. *Success and Failure in Psychoanalysis and Psychotherapy.* New York: Macmillan, 1972.

48. Riess, B.F. The working-through phase—Failure to focus. In B.B. Wolman, ed. *Success and Failure in Psychoanalysis and Psychotherapy.* New York: Macmillan, 1972.

49. I, 61.

50. I, 37.

51. I, 38.

52. Goodall, K. Tie line. Sex on the couch: A negative view, with questions. *Psychology Today,* 1972, 6 (5), 16.

53. Weinberger, G. Some common assumptions underlying traditional child psychotherapy: Fallacy and reformulation. *Psychother.: Theory, Res., Practice,* 1972, 9, 149-152.

54. Ferman, D. The psychoanalytical joy ride. *The Nation,* Aug. 26, 1950, 183-85.

55. Wertham, F. What to do till the doctor goes. *The Nation,* Sept. 2, 1950, 205-207.

56. Zilboorg, G. Ignorance—Amateur and professional. *The Nation,* Sept. 2, 1950, 207-209.

57. Mendelssohn, M. Book Review of Wechsler, J.A., Wechsler, N.F. and Karpf, H.W. *In a darkness.* New York: Norton, 1972. *Huxley Institute News,* 1972, 1, 3.

58. Ferber, A. Critique of Philip Guerin and Thomas F. Fogarty: The

Family Therapist's family. *Psychother. Soc. Sci. Rev.,* 1973, 7, (4), 16.

59. Nierenberg, M.A. Critique of Philip Guering and Thomas F. Fogarty: The Family Therapist's Family. *Psychother. Soc. Sci. Rev.* 1973, 7, (4) 16.

60. (No author given) Even the sane are labeled insane. Denver, Colorado: *Rocky Mountain News,* Jan. 18, 1973, p. 78.

61. I, 59.

62. I, 50.

CHAPTER III: REFERENCES

1. Lehrman, N.S. Moral aspects of mental health. *The Humanist,* 1963, 22, 58-61.

2. Mowrer, O.H. Even there, thy hand. *Chicago Theol. Sem. Register,* 1962, 52, 1-17.

3. Phillips, E.L. *Psychotherapy: A modern theory and practice.* Englewood Cliffs, N.Y.: Prentice-Hall, 1950.

4. Smith, V.H. Identity crises in conversion hysteria with implications for Integrity Therapy. *Psychother.: Theory, Res., Practice,* 1966, 3, 120-124.

5. Landis, C. Psychoanalysis and experimental psychology. In L. Salzman and J.H. Masserman, eds. *Modern Concepts of Psychoanalysis.* New York: Philosophical Library, 1962.

6. La Pierre, R.T. *The Freudian Ethic.* Des Moines, Iowa: Duell, Sloan and Pierce, 1959.

7. Pinckney, E.R. and Cathey Pinckney: *The Fallacy of Freud and Psychoanalysis.* Englewood Cliffs, N.J.: Prentice Hall, 1965.

8. Andriola, J. Correspondence: Psychoanalysis. *Amer. J. Psychiat.,* 1956, 113, 467.

9. I, 8.

10. II, 28.

11. Wertham, F. In W. Wolff: *Contemporary Psychotherapists Examine Themselves.* Springfield, Ill.: Thomas, 1956.

12. II, 7.

13. I, 67.

14. I, 36.

15. Kushner, M.D. *Freud—A Man Obsessed.* Philadelphia: Dorrance & Co., 1967.

16. I, 32.

17. Haronian, F. The ethical relevance of a psychotherapeutic technique. Reprint 13. New York: Psycho-synthesis Research Foundation, 1971.

18. II, 12.

19. I, 59.

20. I, 60.

21. I, 61

22. Sokoloff, B. *The Permissive Society.* New Rochelle, N.Y.: Arlington House, 1971.

23. I, 7.

24. Brody, B. Review of N.G. Hale, *Freud and the Americans. Psychol. Today,* 1972, 6, (2), 8.

25. I, 31.

CHAPTER IV: REFERENCES

1. Wohlgemuth, A. *Critical Examination of Psychoanalysis*. London: Allen and Unwin, 1923.

2. Dunlap, K. *Mysticism, Freudianism and Scientific Psychology*. New York: Mosby, 1920.

3. II, 10.

4. Nelson, B. Preface. In B. Nelson, ed. *Freud and the 20th Century*. New York: Meridian Books, 1957.

5. Ehrenwald, J. *Psychotherapy: Myth and Method—An integrative approach*. New York: Grune and Stratton, 1966.

6. Jones, E. *Sigmund Freud: Four Centenary Addresses*. New York: Basic Books, 1956.

7. Ruitenbeek, H.M. *Freud and America*. New York: Macmillan, 1966.

8. Puner, Helen W. *Freud: His life and his mind*. New York: Howell, Soskin 1947.

9. Cohen, M. R. *Reflections of a Wondering Jew*. Boston: Beacon, 1950.

10. Kazin, A. The Freudian Revolution analysed. In B. Nelson ed. *Freud and the 20th Century*. New York: Meridian Books, 1957.

11. Janet, P. *Psychological Healing: A historical and clinical study*, 2 vols. New York: Macmillan, 1925.

12. Dalbiez, R. *Psychoanalytical Method and the Doctrine of Freud*. 2 vols. New York: Longman and Green, 1941.

13. Riese, W. The pre-Freudian origins of psychoanalysis. In J.H. Masserman, ed. *Science and Psychoanalysis*, vol. I. New York: Grune and Stratton, 1958.

14. Bry, Ilse and Rifkin, A. H. Freud and the history of ideas; primary sources, 1886-1910. In J. H. Masserman, ed. *Psychoanalytic Education*. New York: Grune and Stratton, 1962.

15. Harms, E. Simon-Andrea Tissot (1728-1797): The Freudian before Freud. *Amer. J. Psychiat.*, 1956, 112, 744.

16. I, 7.

17. Taylor, W. S. Psychoanalysis revised or psychodynamics developed. *Amer. Psychologist*, 1962, 11, 784-788.

18. Whyte, L.L. *The Unconscious Before Freud*. New York: Basic Books, 1960.

19. Bailey, P. The Great Psychiatric Revolution. In S. Rachman, ed. *Critical Essays on Psychoanalysis.* New York: Macmillan, 1963.

20. Rosenzweig, S. The Ellisian view. *Contemp. Psychol.,* 1966, 11, 182-190.

21. Zilboorg, G. *Freud and Religion: A restatement of an old controversy.* Westminster, Maryland: The Newman Press, 1961.

22. Freud, S. The History of Psychoanalytic Movement. In A.A. Brill, ed. *The Basic Writings of Sigmund Freud.* New York: The Modern Library, 1938.

23. Dorer, M. *Historische Grundlagen der Psychoanalyse.* Leipzig: Meiner, 1932.

24. Freud, S. Autobiographical Study, (1925). In *Standard Edition,* v. XX. London: Hogarth.

25. Bonaparte, Marie, Freud, Anna and Kris, E. *The Origins of Psychoanalysis: Letters to Wilhelm Fliess, Draft and Notes, 1887-1902, by Sigmund Freud.* New York: Basic Books, 1954.

26. Robert, Marthe. *The Psychoanalytic Revolution: Sigmund Freud's life and achievement.* New York: Harcourt, Brace and World, 1966.

27. Bailey, P. *Sigmund the Unserene: A tragedy in three acts.* Springfield, Ill.: Thomas, 1965.

28. II, 1.

29. Fromm, Erika, Review of the C.M. and Silvia Grossman's *The Wild Analyst: The life and work of Georg Grodeck. Contemp. Psychol.,* 1966, 11, 137.

30. Kline, M. V. *Freud and Hypnosis.* New York: Julian Press, 1958.

31. Erikson, E. The first psychoanalyst. In B. Nelson, ed. *Freud and the 20th Century.* New York: Meridian Books, 1957.

32. Weiss, E. and English, O.S. *Psychosomatic Medicine.* Philadelphia: Saunders, 1943.

33. Dejerine, J. and Gauckler, E. *Les Manifestations Fonctionelles des Psychoneuroses.* Paris: Masson, 1911.

34. Tuke, H. *Influence of the Mind on the Body.* Philadelphia: Lee, 1884.

35. Sweetser, W. *Mental Hygiene: An Examination of the Intellect and Passions.* New York: Langley, 1850.

36. Sorokin, P.A. *Fads and Foibles in Modern Sociology and Related Sciences.* Chicago: Regnery, 1956.

37. I, 8.

38. Methods for revising Freud's theory proposed by A. Kardiner. *Roche Report: Frontiers of Clin. Psychiat.,* 1967, 4, 5-6.

39. Herberg, W. Freud, the revisionists and social reality. In B. Nelson, ed.

Freud and the 20th Century. New York: Meridian Books, 1957.

40. Bailey, P. Sigmund Freud: Scientific period (1873-1897). In J. Wolpe, A. Salter, and L.J. Reyna, eds. *The Conditioning Therapies: The challenge in psychotherapy.* New York: Holt, Rinehart and Winston, 1964.

41. Menninger, K. Recent trends in psychoanalytic theory and practice. *Bull. Menn. Clinic,* 1944, 8, 14-17.

42. Rado, S. *Psychoanalysis of Behavior.* New York: Grune and Stratton, v. I, 1956; v. 2, 1962.

43. Murray, H.A. What should psychologists do about psychoanalysis. *J. Abn. Soc. Psychol.,* 1940, 35, 150-175.

44. Hendrick, I. *Facts and Theories of Psychoanalysis.* New York: Knopf, 1958.

45. Fromm, E. *Sigmund Freud's Mission: An analysis of his personality and influence.* New York: Grove Press, 1963.

46. III, 2.

47. Zilboorg, G. *Sigmund Freud: His exploration of the mind of man.* New York: Scribner, 1951.

48. II, 18.

49. Lief, A. *The Common Sense Psychiatry of Dr. Adolph Meyer.* New York: McGraw-Hill, 1948.

50. Harrington, M. *Wish Hunting in the Unconscious.* New York: Macmillan, 1934.

51. Kepecs, J.G. Psychoanalysis today: A rather lonely island. *Arch. Gen. Psychiat.,* 1968, 18, 161-167.

52. Jaspers, K.: *Einführung in die Philosophie.* Munchen: Piper, 1966.

53. Lief, H.I. Psychoanalysis and psychiatric training. In I. Galdston, ed. *Psychoanalysis in Present-Day Psychiatry.* New York: Brunner/Mazel, 1969.

54. I, 62.

55. I, 39.

56. Choisy, Maryse. *Sigmund Freud: A new appraisal.* New York: Philosophical Library, 1963.

57. I, 36.

58. Nunberg, H. and Federn, E., eds. *Minutes of the Vienna Psychoanalytic Society,* vol. I:1906-1908. New York: International University Press, 1962.

59. Hitschmann, E. *Great Men: Psychoanalytic studies.* New York: International Universities Press, 1956.

60. Veith, Ilza, On "the loneliness of Freud's achievement." *Bull. Menn. Clinic,* 1965, 29, 245-255.

61. Roazen, P. *Brother Animal: The story of Freud and Tausk.* New York: Knopf, 1969.

62. Fadiman, C. Report. *Book-of-the-Month Club News,* June, 1971.

63. Stone, I. *The Passions of the Mind.* New York: Doubleday, 1971.

64. Dorrach, B. The Great Destroyer. *Time,* April 5, 1971.

65. I, 46.

66. *Roche Report: Frontiers of Clin. Psychiat.,* 1970, 7, 3.

67. Kovel, J. Interpreting the literary unconscious. *Psychother. Soc. Sci. Rev.,* 1971, 5, 20-27.

68. Stekel, W. *Impotence in the Male: The psychic disorders of sexual function in the male,* 2 vols. New York: Liveright, 1959.

69. Stekel, W. *Frigidity in Woman: In relation to her love live,* 2 vols. New York: Grove Press, 1962.

70. Moreno, J.L. Editor's Foreword. In J.L. Moreno, ed. *International Handbook of Group Psychotherapy.* New York: Philosophical Library, 1965.

71. II, 25.

72. Hartmann, H. Sigmund Freud. *Encyclopaedia Britannica,* v. 9. Chicago, Ill.: 1970.

73. Österling, A. Presentation address. *Nobel Prize Library: Hermann Hesse.* Del Mar, Calif.: CRM Publishing, 1971.

74. III, 22.

75. I, 53.

76. I, 52.

77. Sherman, M.A. Theodore Reik and the crisis in psychoanalysis. *Psychother. Soc. Sci. Rev.,* 1971, 5 (12), 15-20.

78. MacDougall, C.D. *Hoaxes.* New York: Dover, 1968.

79. I, 61.

80. Astley, M.R.C. Comment on Dr. Lorand's Paper. *Intern. J. Psycho-Anal.,* 1962, 43, 56-58.

81. Stengel, E. Hughlings Jackson's influence in psychiatry. *Brit. J. Psychiat.,* 1963, 109, 348-355.

82. Strupp, H.H. Freudian analysis today. *Psychol. Today,* 1972, 6 (2), 33-40.

83. Mousseau, J. Freud in perspective: A conversation with Henry F. Ellenberger. *Psychol. Today,* 1973, 6 (10), 50-60.

84. Roeckelein, J.E. Eponymy in psychology. *Amer. Psychologist,* 1972, 27, 657-659.

CHAPTER V: REFERENCES

1. Johnson, H.K. Psychoanalysis—a critique. *Psychiat. Quart.*, 1948, 22, 321-338.

2. II, 23.

3. Campbell, C.H. *Induced Delusions: The psychopathy of Freudism.* Chicago: Regent House, 1957.

4. IV, 50.

5. Natenberg, M. *Freudian Psycho-Antics: Fact and fraud in psychoanalysis.* Chicago: Regent House, 1952.

6. Kelman, H., ed. *New Perspectives in Psychoanalysis.* New York: Norton, 1965.

7. Yablonski, L. Synanon. In R.M. Jurjevich, ed. *Direct Psychotherapy,* vol. 2: *Twenty-Eight American Originals.* Coral Gables, Fla.: University of Miami Press, 1973.

8. II, 25.

9. II, 26.

10. Stefan, G. *In Search of Sanity: The journal of a schizophrenic.* New York: University Books, 1965.

11. Mowrer, O.H. *Abnormal Reactions or Actions? An autobiographical answer.* Dubuque, Iowa: Brown, 1966.

12. IV, 25.

13. I, 36.

14. Bychowski, G. Psychosis precipitated by psychoanalysis. *Psychoan. Quart.,* 1966, 35, 327-339.

15. I, 43.

16. Blanton, S. *Diary of My Analysis with Sigmund Freud.* New York: Hawthorn, 1971.

17. Burrows, G.W. Spiritual Therapy with Alcoholics. In R.M. Jurjevich, ed., *Direct Psychotherapy,* vol. 2: *Twenty-Eight American Originals.* Coral Gables, Fla.: University of Miami Press, 1973.

18. I, 70.

19. Heckethorn, C.W. *The Secret Societies of All Ages and Countries,* vol. 1. New York: University Books, 1966.

CHAPTER VI: REFERENCES

1. V, 1.
2. I, 7.
3. Freud, S. *Therapy and Technique.* New York: Collier, 1963.
4. Freud, S. *Collected Papers,* 5 vols. New York: Basic Books, 1959.
5. III, 6.
6. Hartmann, H. Psychoanalysis as a scientific theory. In S. Hook, ed. *Psychoanalysis, Scientific Method and Philosophy.* New York: New York University Press, 1959.
7. II, 20.
8. IV, 26.
9. IV, 40.
10. Fenichel, O. *The Psychoanalytic Theory of Neurosis.* New York: Norton, 1945.
11. II, 45.
12. Ferenczi, S., *The Selected Papers,* 3 vols. New York: Basic Books, 1950, 1953.
13. IV, 6.
14. Hartmann, H. *Psychoanalysis and Moral Values.* New York: International Universities Press, 1960.
15. Kubie, L.S. Psychoanalysis and scientific method. In S. Hook, ed. *Psychoanalysis, Scientific Method, and Philosophy.* New York: New York University Press, 1959.
16. Salzman, L. Modern concepts of psychoanalysis. In L. Salzman and J.H. Masserman, eds. *Modern Concepts of Psychoanalysis.* New York: Philosophical Library, 1962.
17. IV, 25.
18. Colby, K. M. *An Introduction to Psychoanalytic Research.* New York: Basic Books, 1960.
19. Rosenzweig. S. The experimental study of psychoanalysis. *Character & Personality,* 1937, 6, 61-71.
20. Bellak, L. and Ekstein, R. The extension of basic scientific laws to psychoanalysis and to psychology. *Psychoan. Rev.,* 1946, 23, 306-313.
21. I, 10.
22. Grazia, S. de, *Errors of Psychotherapy.* New York: Doubleday, 1952.

23. Braceland, F.J. and Stock, M. *Modern Psychiatry: A handbook for believers*. Garden City, N.Y.: Doubleday, 1963.

24. Maritain, J. Freudianism and psychoanalysis: A Thomist view. In B. Nelson, ed. *Freud and the 20th century*. New York: Meridian Books, 1957.

25. Niebuhr, K. Human creativity and self-concern in Freud's thought. In B. Nelson, ed. *Freud and the 20th Century*. New York: Meridian Books, 1957.

26. Boisen, A.T. *The Exploration of the Inner World*. New York: Harper, 1952.

27. Mowrer, O.H. Learning theory and neurotic fallacy. *Amer. J. Orthopsychiat.*, 1952, 22, 679-689.

28. Runestam, A. *Psychoanalysis and Christianity*. Rock Island, Ill.: Augustana Press, 1958.

29. Sanders, B.G. *Christianity after Freud: Interpretation of the Christian experience in the light of psychoanalytic theory*. London: Bless, 1949.

30. Richfield, J. The scientific status of psychoanalysis. In J.M. Vanderplas, ed. *Controversial Issues in Psychology*. Boston: Houghton Mifflin, 1966.

31. Gross, M.L. *The Doctors*. New York: Random House, 1966.

32. Grotjahn, M. A psychoanalyst passes a small stone with big troubles. In R.A. Baker, ed. *Psychology in the Wry*. New York: Van Nostrand, 1963.

33. I, 8.

34. Fromm, E. Psychoanalysis—science or party line? In *The Dogma of Christ: And other essays on religion, psychology and culture*. Garden City, N.Y.: Doubleday, 1963.

35. Gemelli, A. *Psychoanalysis Today*. New York: Kennedy, 1955.

36. Sarason, I.G. *Science and Theory in Psychoanalysis: An enduring problem in psychology*. New York: Van Nostrand, 1965.

37. IV, 6.

38. Bakan, D. *Sigmund Freud and the Jewish Mystical Tradition*. New York: Schocken Books, 1965.

39. IV, 8.

40. Jung, C.G. *Freud and Psychoanalysis. The Collected Works*, v. 4. New York: Bollingen Foundation, 1961.

41. Fromm, E. Introduction to P. Mullahy, *Oedipus, Myth and Complex*. New York: Hermitage Press, 1948.

42. Gengerelli, J.A. Limitations of psychoanalysis: Dogma or discipline? *Sat. Rev.*, March 23, 1957, 9-11, 40.

43. Alexander, L. *Objective Approaches to Psychiatry*. Springfield, Ill.: Thomas, 1958.

44. Porteus, S.D. Review of H.J. Eysenck's *Fact and Fiction in Psychology*. *Contemp. Psychol.*, 1966, 11, 309.

45. Kruse, H.D., ed. *Integrating the Approaches to Mental Disease*. New York: Hoeber-Harper, 1957.

46. Berelson, B. and Steiner, G.A. *Human Behavior: An inventory of scientific findings*. New York: Harcourt, Brace, World, 1964.

47. Worchel, P. Necessarily monumental and controversial. *Contemp. Psychol.*, 1965, 10, 294-295.

48. Eissler, K.R. *Medical Orthodoxy and the Future of Psychoanalysis*. New York: International Universities Press, 1965.

49. Schmideberg, M. Values and goals in psychotherapy. *Psychiat. Quart.*, 1958, 2, 233-265.

50. Eysenck, H. J., ed. *Handbook of Abnormal Psychology: An experimental approach*. New York: Basic Books, 1960.

51. Pohlman, E. *Contemp. Psychol.*, 1967, 12, 252.

52. Brauchitsch, H. von and May, W. Deaths from aspiration and asphixiation in a mental hospital. *Arch. Gen. Psychiat.*, 1968, 18, 137-148.

53. Leestma, J.E. and Koenig, K.L. Sudden death and phenothiazines: A current controversy. *Arch. Gen. Psychiat.*, 1968, 18, 137-148.

54. III, 7.

55. I, 33.

56. I, 61.

57. Frankl, V.E. *Der Unbedingte Mensch*. (*The Unconditional Man*). Wien: Deuticke, 1949.

58. *Time*, July 18, 1968.

59. Selby, H.A. The healer. *Contemp. Psychol.*, 1969, 14, 315-316.

60. I, 39.

61. II, 25.

62. IV, 58.

63. Sherwood, M. *The Logic of Explanation in Psychoanalysis*. New York: Academic Press, 1969.

64. Engel, G.L. Some obstacles to the development of research in psychoanalysis. *J. Amer. Psychoan. Assoc.*, 1968, 16, 195-229.

65. Temerlin, M.K. and Trousdale, W.K. The social psychology of clinical diagnoses. *Psychotherapy: Theory, Res., Practice*, 1969, 6, 24-29.

66. Masserman, J. Faith and delusion in psychotherapy. *Amer. J. Psychiat.*, 1953, 11, 324-333.

67. Rapoport, A. Psychoanalysis as science. *Bull. Menn. Clinic*, 1968, 32, 1-20.

68. Mowrer, O.H. *The New Group Therapy.* New York: Van Nostrand, 1964.

69. Breggin, P.R. Psychotherapy as applied ethics. *Psychiat.,* 1971, 34, 59-74.

70. Hamburg, D.A., Bibring, Grete, L., Fisher, C., Stanton, A.H., Wallerstein, R.S., Weinstock, H.I., and Haggard, E. Report of Ad Hoc Committee on central fact-gathering data of the American Psychoanalytic Association. *J. Amer. Psychoan. Assoc.,* 1967, XV, 841-861.

71. IV, 78.

72. I, 58.

73. *Roche Report: Frontiers of Clin. Psychiat.,* 1972, 2, 16-17.

74. I, 69.

75. Stuart, R.B. *Trick or Treatment: How and when psychotherapy fails.* Champaign, Ill.: Research Press, 1970.

76. Snider, A.J. Opinions vague on treatments: Physicians agree to disagree. *The Denver Post,* 1966, June 19.

77. Ford, D. H. and Urban, H. B. Psychotherapy. *Annu. Rev. Psychol.,* 1967, 18, 333-372.

CHAPTER VII: REFERENCES

1. I, 1.
2. VI, 3.
3. IV, 25.
4. Knight, J. *The Story of My Psychoanalysis.* New York: Pocket Books, 1953.
5. Choisy, Maryse, *Sigmund Freud: A new appraisal.* New York: Philosophical Library, 1963.
6. I, 12.
7. D., H. *Tribute to Freud.* New York: Pantheon Books, 1956.
8. Beier, E.G. *The Silent Language of Psychotherapy: Social reinforcement of unconscious processes.* Chicago: Aldine, 1966.
9. IV, 30.
10. IV, 49.
11. II, 10.
12. Orne, M. Implications for therapy from current research on the nature of hypnosis. *Amer. J. Psychiat.,* 1962, 118, 1097-1103.
13. Salter, A. *Conditioned Reflex Therapy.* New York: Capricorn, 1961.
14. II, 4.
15. Wiesenhütter, E. Suggestive and autosuggestive methods. In R.M. Jurjevich, ed. *Direct Psychotherapy,* vol. 3: *International Developments.* Coral Gables, Fla.: University of Miami Press, 1974.
16. I, 31.
17. IV, 12.
18. I, 17.
19. Freud S. *A General Introduction to Psychoanalysis.* New York: Perma-books, 1955.
20. Arons, H. *The Best and Easiest Disguised Method of Inducing Hypnosis. (Indirect Method).* Irvington, N.J.: Power Publishers, 1954.
21. Steiner, Lee B. *Sounds of Self-hypnosis through Relaxation.* New York: Folkways Records, FX 6104.
22. Salter, A. Three Techniques of Autohypnosis. *J. Gen. Psychol.,* 1941, 24. 423-438.
23. McCord, H. Trance induction under unusual circumstances. *Intern. J. Clin. Exp. Hypn.,* 1965, 13, 96-102.
24. Wittels, F. *Freud and His Time.* New York: Grosset & Dunlap, 1931.
25. Barber, T.X. The effects of hypnosis and motivational suggestions on

strength and endurance. *Brit. J. Soc. Clin. Psychol.,* 1966, 5, 42-50.

26. Barber, T.X. and Calverly, D.S. Toward a theory of "hypnotic" behavior: Experimental analyses of suggested amnesia. *J. abn. Psychol.,* 1966, 71, 95-107.

27. Weitz, H. Problem-centered guidance. In R.M. Jurjevich, ed. *Direct Psychotherapy,* vol. 1: *Twenty-eight American Originals.* Coral Gables, Fla.: University of Miami Press, 1973.

28. IV, 24.

29. VI, 40.

30. Wolstein, B. *Transference: Its meaning and function in psychoanalytic therapy.* New York: Grune and Stratton, 1957.

31. Fisher, C. Studies on the nature of suggestion. Part II. The transference meaning of giving suggestion. *J. Amer. Psychoan. Assoc.,* 1953, 1, 406-437.

32. MacAlpine, Ida. The development of transference. *Psychoan. Quart.,* 950, 19, 501-539.

33. IV, 50.

34. V, 1.

35. VI, 28.

36. I, 67.

37. II, 8.

38. Freeman, Lucy. *Fight against Fears.* New York: Pocket Books, 1953.

39. Saul, L. J. *Techniques and Practice of Psychoanalysis.* Philadelphia: Lippincott, 1958.

40. Sargant, W. *Battle for the Mind: A physiology of conversion and brain-washing.* Garden City, New York: Doubleday, 1957.

41. Meerloo, J.A.M. The essence of mental cure: The manifold principles active in psychotherapy. *Amer. J. Psychother.,* 1958, 12, 42-63.

42. II, 18.

43. Kennedy, Gail. Psychoanalysis: Protoscience and metapsychology. In S. Hook, ed. *Psychoanalysis, Scientific Method and Philosophy.* New York: New York University Press, 1964.

44. VI, 66.

45. Ehrenwald, I. Doctrinal compliance: A history of error in psychotherapy. *J. Hist. Behav. Sci.,* 1966, 2, 51-57.

46. Munthe, A. *The Story of San Michele.* London: Murray, 1968 (83rd printing).

47. I, 29.

48. Freud S. A short account of psychoanalysis. *Standard Edition,* vol. 19.

49. Freud, E. L., ed. *The Letters of Sigmund Freud.* New York: Basic

Books, 1960.

50. I, 38.

51. Vogel, G., Foulkes, D. and Trosman, H. Ego functions and dreaming during sleep onset. In C.T. Tart, ed. *Altered States of Consciousness*. New York: Wiley, 1969.

52. Kushner, M.D. *Freud—A man obsessed*. Philadelphia: Dorrance, 1967.

53. Ludwig, A.M. Altered states of consciousness. *Arch. Gen. Psychiat.*, 1966, 15, 225-234.

54. Perls, F.S. Unpublished draft of a manuscript, 1966.

55. Erickson, M. H. A special inquiry with Aldous Huxley into the nature and character of various states of consciousness. *Amer. J. Clin. Hypn.*, 1965, 8, 17-33.

56. Evans, F.J. An experimental indirect technique for the induction of hypnosis without awareness. *Intern. J. Clin. Exp. Hyp.*, 1967, 15, 72-85.

57. IV, 61.

58. Wolberg, L.R. *Hypnosis: Is it for you?* New York: Harcourt, Brace, Jovanovich, 1972.

59. Linn, L. Clinical manifestations of psychiatric disorders. In A. M. Friedman and H. I. Kaplan, eds. *Comprehensive Textbook of Psychiatry*. Baltimore: Williams and Wilkins, 1968.

60. I, 46.

61. Sidis, B. The psychotherapeutic value of the hypnoidal state. *J. abn. Psychol.*, 1909, 4, 151-171.

62. Gardner, M., ed. *The Wolf-Man By the Wolf-Man*. New York: Basic Books, 1971.

63. Garner, H.H. Confrontation Problem-solving Therapy. In R.M. Jurjevich, ed., *Direct Psychotherapy*, v. 1: *Twenty-eight American Originals*. Coral Gables, Fla.: University of Miami Press, 1973.

64. I, 46.

65. Fisher, C. Experimental induction of dreams by direct suggestion. *J. Amer. Psychoan. Assoc.*, 1953, 1, 222-255.

66. Nunberg, H. In discussion of paper by Brenman, M., Gill, M., and Knight, R.P.: Spontaneous fluctuations in depth of hypnosis and their implications for ego-function. Read before the New York Psychoanalytic Society, Nov. 22, 1950. Abstract in *Psychoan. Quart.*, 1951, 20, 340-341.

67. Gill, M. Paper read before the Psychiatric Forum Group. New York, 1951.

68. Nunberg, H. Transference and reality. *Intern. J. Psychoan.*, 1951, 32, 1-9.

491

CHAPTER VIII: REFERENCES

1. V, 1.
2. I, 15.
3. IV, 11.
4. Ducasse, C.J. Psychoanalysis and suggestion: Metaphysics and temperament. In S. Hook, ed. *Psychoanalysis, Scientific Method and Philosophy.* New York: New York University Press, 1959.
5. II, 20.
6. VII, 15.
7. IV, 50.
8. VI, 40.
9. VI, 3.
10. VI, 4.
11. VI, 12.
12. VII, 63.
13. I, 22.
14. Landis C. Psychoanalytic Phenomena. In S. Rachman, ed. *Critical Essays on Psychoanalysis.* New York: Macmillan, 1963.
15. Jurjevich, R.M. *The effects of Ego-inflating and Ego-deflating Responses of the Psychotherapist.* Doctoral dissertation, University of Denver, 1958.
16. IV, 5.
17. IV, 25.
18. VI, 12.
19. V, 6.
20. VII, 8.
21. III, 7.
22. Freud S. *New Introductory Lectures on Psychoanalysis.* New York: Norton, 1933.
23. VII, 49.
24. I, 61.
25. I, 36.
26. II, 25.
27. III, 15.
28. Masserman. J. Sexuality re-evaluated. *Can. Psychiat. Assoc. J.,* 1966,

11, 379-388.

29. II, 35.

30. Jones, E. Professor Janet on psychoanalysis: a rejoinder. *J. Abn. Psychol.*, 1914, 9, 400-410.

31. Janet, P. Psychoanalysis. *J. Abn. Psychol.*, 1914, 9, 1-35, 153-187.

32. VII, 62.

33. Strauss, E.W. Quoted in May, R. *Existence.* New York: Basic Books, 1958.

34. Glover, E. Remarks on success and failure in psychoanalysis and psychotherapy. In B.B. Wolman, ed. *Success and Failure in Psychoanalysis and Psychotherapy.* New York: Macmillan, 1972.

35. VII, 32.

36. Cancro, R. Critique of Harold M. Voth: Some effects of Freud's personality on psychoanalytic theory and technique. *Psychother. Soc. Sci. Rev.*, 1973, 7, (4), 18.

37. IV, 85.

38. II, 26.

CHAPTER IX: REFERENCES

1. Pilowsky, I. and Spear, F.G. The psychiatrists's role in the interview situation. *Amer. J. Psychother.,* 1964, 18, suppl. 1, 174-183.

2. VII, 8.

3. VII, 27.

4. Matarazzo, J.D., Wions, A.N., Saslow, G., Allen, Bernadene, V. and Weitman, M. Interviewer's "mm-hmm" and interviewee's speech durations. *Psychother.,* 1965, 1, 109-114.

5. Leitenberg, H., and Agras, W.S. Behavior therapy: Operant conditioning and related methods. In R. M. Jurjevich, ed. *Direct Psychotherapy,* vol. 3: *International Developments.* Coral Gables, Fla.: University of Miami Press, 1974.

6. Schlicht, Joan, Gwynn, W. and Peoples, C. Verbal conditioning of schizophrenics and normals in a situation resembling psychotherapy. *J. Consult. Psychol.,* 1963, 27, 223-227.

7. Salzinger, K., Portnoy, S. and Feldman, R.S. Experimental manipulation of continuous speech in schizophrenic patients. *J. Abn. Soc. Psychol.,* 1964, 68, 508-615.

8. Fisher, S., Rubinstein, I. and Freeman, R.W. Intertrial effects of immediate selfcommittal in a continuous social influence situation. *J. Abn. Soc. Psychol.,* 1956, 52, 200-207.

9. Fisher, S. Plausibility and depth of interpretation. *J. Consult. Psychol.,* 1956, 20, 249-256.

10. Rosenthal, R. On the social psychology of the psychological experiment: experimenter's hypothesis as an unintended determinant of experimental results. *Amer. Sci.,* 1963, 51, 268-283.

11. Rosenthal, R. and Hala, E.S. Experimenter effect in the study of invertebrate behavior. *Psychol. Rep.,* 1962, 11, 251-256.

12. Vikan-Kline, Linda. The effect of experimenter's perceived status on the mediation of experimental bias. Master's thesis, University of North Dakota, 1962.

13. Orne, M. Implications for therapy from current research on the nature of hypnosis. *Amer. J. Psychiat.,* 1962, 118, 1097-1103.

14. Hyman, H. H., Cobb, W. J., Feldman, J. J., Hart, C. W. and Stember, C. H. *Interviewing in Social Research.* Chicago: Chicago University Press, 1954.

15. Masling. J. The influence of situational and interpersonal variables in projective testing. *Psychol. Bull.,* 1960, 57, 65-85.

16. Truax, C. B. Reinforcement and non-reinforcement in Rogerian psychotherapy. *J. Abn. Psychol.,* 1966, 71, 1-9.

17. II, 4.

18. Meerloo, J.A.M. Medication into submission: The danger of therapeutic coercion. *J. Nerv. Ment. Dis.,* 1955, 122, 353-360.

19. Mandler, F. and Kaplan, W. K. Subjective evaluation and reinforcing effect of a verbal stimulus. *Science,* 1956, 124, 582-583.

20. Marmor, J. Psychoanalysis at the crossroads. In J. H. Masserman, ed. *Science and Psychoanalysis.* New York: Grune and Stratton, 1966.

21. Krasner, L. The therapist as a social reinforcement machine. In H.H. Strupp, and L. Luborsky, *Research in Psychotherapy.* Washington, D.C.: American Psychological Association, 1962.

22. VII, 63.

23. Grinker, R. R. A transactional model for psychotherapy. *Archives Gen. Psychiat.,* 1959, 1, 132-148.

24. Academy of Religion and Mental Health. *Moral Values in Psychoanalysis: Proceedings of the sixth Academy symposium,* 1963. New York: Academy, 1965.

25. IV, 44.

26. I, 67.

27. Cain, A.H. A program of recovery for the alcoholic. In R.M. Jurjevich, ed. *Direct Psychotherapy,* vol. 2: *Twenty-Eight American Originals.* Coral Gables, Fla.: University of Miami Press, 1973.

28. Lossy, F.T. The charge of suggestion as a resistance in psychoanalysis. *Intern. J. Psycho-anal.,* 1962, 43, 448-467.

29. VI, 3.

30. II, 25.

31. Nagel, E. Methodological issues in psychoanalytic theory. In S. Hook, ed. *Psychoanalysis, Scientific Method, and Philosophy.* New York: New York University Press, 1959.

32. Hollingworth, H.L. *Abnormal Psychology: Its concepts and theories.* New York: Ronald Press, 1930.

33. VII, 45.

34. IV, 5.

35. Freud, S. *The Interpretation of Dreams.* In A.A. Brill, ed. *The Basic Writings of Sigmund Freud.* New York: Modern Library, 1938.

36. III, 6.

37. Freud, S. *Beyond the Pleasure Principle.* New York: Liveright, 1950.

38. II, 20.

39. Nacht, S. *Psychoanalysis of Today.* New York: Grune and Stratton, 1959.

40. II, 18.

41. VI, 15.

42. IV, 25.

43. I, 2.

44. VII, 40.

45. VI, 4.

46. VII, 12.

47. Kubie, L.S. The neurotic process as the focus of physiological and psychoanalytic research. *J. Ment. Sci.,* 1958, 104, 518-536.

48. Skinner, B.F. Critique of psychoanalytic concepts and theories. In J.M. Vanderplas, ed. *Controversial Issues in Psychology.* Boston: Houghton Mifflin, 1966.

49. I, 10.

50. Jones, E. *Papers on Psychoanalysis.* London, 1918.

51. IV, 24.

52. V, 1.

53. III, 7.

54. Introduction, 10.

55. Friedman, N. *The Social Nature of Psychological Research: The psychological experiment as a social interaction.* New York: Basic Books, 1967.

56. Desoille, R. *Le Rêve Eveillé en Psychothérapie.* Paris: Presses Universitaire, 1945.

57. Sacerdote, P. *Induced Dreams.* New York: Vantage Press, 1967.

58. Wolberg, L.R. Notes and Comments. *Amer. J. Psychother.,* 1969, 23, 558.

59. Pumpian-Mindlin, E., ed. *Psychoanalysis as Science.* Stanford: Stanford University Press, 1952.

60. Luthe, W. Autogenic Therapy: Methods, theories, research and clinical applications. In R. M. Jurjevich, ed. *Direct Psychotherapy,* vol. 3: *International Developments.* Coral Gables, Fla.: University of Miami Press, 1974.

61. I, 36.

62. Hilgard, E. Experimental approaches to psychoanalysis. In E. Pumpian-Mindlin, ed. *Psychoanalysis as Science.* Stanford: Stanford University Press, 1952.

63. Evans, R.I. *B.F. Skinner: The Man and His Ideas.* New York: Dutton, 1968.

64. III, 15.

65. IV, 24.

66. I, 46.

67. Garduk, E.L. and Haggard, E.A. *Immediate Effects on Patients of Psychoanalytic Interpretations.* New York: International Universities Press, 1972.

68. I, 69.

69. Quay, H. The effect of verbal reinforcement on the recall of early memories. *J. Abnorm. Soc. Psychol.,* 1967, 59, 254-257.

70. Bach, G.R. Some diadic functions of childhood memories. *J. Psychol.,* 1952, 33, 87-98.

71. IV, 85.

72. Freud, S. Recommendations for physicians on the psychoanalytic method of treatment. In *Collected Papers,* vol. 2. London: Hogarth Press, 1956.

73. Freud, S. *An Outline of Psychoanalysis.* New York: Norton, 1949.

74. Freud, S. *The Question of Lay Analysis.* New York: Norton, 1950.

75. VII, 65.

CHAPTER X: REFERENCES

1. II, 22.
2. I, 3.
3. IV, 25.
4. IV, 5.
5. Hunter, E. *Brainwashing: From Pavlov to Powers.* New York: Farrar, Straus and Cudahy, reprinted by Bookmailer, Inc., 1961.
6. VII, 40.
7. IV, 8.
8. VI, 3.
9. VIII, 14.
10. VI, 35.
11. II, 18.
12. VII, 4.
13. IV, 50.
14. Frank, J.D. Emotions and the psychotherapeutic process. In J.H. Masserman, ed. *Current Psychiatric Therapies.* New York: Grune and Stratton, 1964.
15. Herzberg, A. *Active Psychotherapy.* London: Research Books, 1963.
16. Harsch, Q.H. and Zimmer, H. An experimental approximation of the thought reform. *J. consult. Psychol.,* 1965, 29, 475-479.
17. II, 19.
18. Train, G. J. Towards an appropriate psychotherapy. *Psychiat. Opinion,* 1968, 5, 5-14.
19. Frankl, V.E. *Das Menschenbild der Seelenheilkunde: Drei Vorlesungen zur Kritik des dynamischen Psychologismus* (Image of Man in Psychotherapy: Three critical lectures on psychodynamic psychologism). Stuttgart: Hippocrates Verlag, 1959.
20. IX, 20.
21. Mowrer, O.H. The Behavior Therapies with special reference to modeling and imitation. *Amer. J. Psychother.,* 1966, 20, 439-461.
22. Rogers, C.R. and Skinner, B.F. Some issues concerning the control of human behavior. A symposium. *Science,* 1956, 124, 1057-1066.
23. VII, 15.
24. VI, 12.

25. Stransky, E. Der Psychotherapeut als Menschenführer. *Acta Psychotherapeutica et Psychomatica,* 1962, 10, 129-139.

26. IX, 18.

27. Frankl, V.E. The philosophical foundation of Logotherapy. In E.W. Strauss, ed. *Phenomenonology: Pure and applied.* Pittsburgh, Pa.: Duquesne University Press, 1964.

28. III, 7.

29. Black, J.D. Common factors in patient therapist relationship in diverse therapies. *J. Clin. Psychol.,* 1952, 8, 302-306.

30. Jaspers, K. *The Nature of Psychotherapy.* Chicago: University of Chicago Press, 1965.

31. IV, 61.

32. I, 48.

33. I, 57.

34. V, 19.

35. III, 22.

36. I, 67.

37. I, 46.

38. I, 69.

39. I, 70.

40. Rigney, H.W. *Four Years in a Red Hell.* Chicago: Regnery, 1956.

41. Rickett, A. and Rickett, Adele. *Prisoners of Liberation.* New York: Cameron Associates, 1957.

42. King, B.T. and Janis, I.L. Comparison of the effectiveness of improvised versus non-improvised role-playing in producing opinion changes. *Human Relations,* 1956, 9, 177-186.

43. Szasz, T.S. *The Manufacture of Madness: A comparative study of the Inquisition and the mental health movement.* New York: Harper and Row, 1970.

44. Krämer, H. and Sprenger, J. *The Malleus Maleficarum.* New York: Dover, 1971.

45. Zilboorg, G. *The Medical Man and the Witch during the Renaissance.* Baltimore: Johns Hopkins Press, 1935.

46. Jayne, W.A. *The Healing Gods of Ancient Civilizations.* New York: University Books, 1962.

47. IV, 47.

NAME INDEX

Abraham, K., 248
Abroms, G. M., 28, 471
Adelson, R. R., 471
Adler, A. 6, 10, 21, 29, 53, 141, 165-71, 187-8, 191, 195, 247
Agras, W. S. 494
Alexander, F., 34, 82, 126, 127, 164, 166, 191, 252, 296, 474
Alexander, L., 272, 486
Allen, Bernadene V., 494
Allers, R., 17, 149, 265-6, 470
Allport, G. W., 167
Alvarez, W. C., 59
Andersen, C., 324
Anderson, Camilla, 143, 314, 374, 471, 473
Anderson, S., 173
Andrèas-Salome, Lou, 90, 475
Andriola, J., 478
Angel, 181
Appel, K. E., 471
Aristotle, 165, 166
Arons, H., 308, 489
Artemidorus, 179
Aschaffenburg, G., 31, 324
Asklepios, 407
Astley, M.R.C., 154, 483
Auld, F., Jr., 56, 57, 471

Bach, G. R., 368, 497
Bacon, F., 252
Bailey, P., 6, 31, 183, 188, 190-91, 193, 254, 322, 470, 481, 482
Bakan, D., 5, 7, 469, 486
Baker Eddy, Mary, 252
Baker, R. A., 486
Baldwin, R., 269

Balint, M., 37, 38
Bandura, A., 165
Barber, T. X., 303, 310-11, 487, 490
Bartemeister, L., 32
Beers, C., 218
Beethoven, L., 57, 58
Beier, E. G., 293, 353, 367, 489
Bellak, L., 264, 485
Benedikt, M., 162, 181, 183
Berelson, B., 273, 487
Berne, E., 22
Bernheim, H., 180, 323, 340
Bernstein, A., 293
Berry, 455
Bibring, Grete L., 488
Billings, J. P., 160
Binet, A., 165
Bing, J. E., 171
Black, J. D., 467, 499
Blake, W., 265
Blanton, S., 242-6, 484
Bleuler, E., 165, 357
Boisen, A. T., 267, 486
Bolivar, S., 58
Bonaparte, Marie, 184, 469, 480
Bonjour, Dr., 341
Bottome, Phyllis, 469
Bowman, K., 28, 29, 470
Braceland, F. J., 32, 470, 486
Braid, J., 340, 373
Brauchitsch, H. von, 487
Brand, M., 60, 61
Brandwin, M.A., 57, 58, 471
Bray, A., 13
Breasted, J., 192
Breggin, P. R., 252, 488
Breuer, J., 177, 187, 280
Brody, B., 39, 200, 472, 479

501

* As the whole book deals with S. Freud, only reference pages are provided here, and other mentions are to be found in Subject Index.

504

505

506

507

SUBJECT INDEX

Addiction, to ideas in intellectuals, 17; to psychoanalysis, 86, 116, 314, 362

Aggression, main human drive for Freud, with libido, 10

Alchemists, compared with Freud, 194

American psychiatry, usurped by Freudians, 3; and dominated by them, 7, 13, 15-17, 28, 33-34, 38, 43, 56, 107; people duped by Communists, 155; psychologists misled about Freud, 166; psychology, misdirected by Freudians, 15, 17, 33, 40, 261, 306

Analysand, reduced to first-grader, 207; Freud pushes opinions on, 207-210; intimidated by Freud, 210; homosexuality imputed to subdue the, 214-215, 222-223; is hoodwinked, 354; indoctrination of, 380, 401, 454; humiliation of, 216, 224

Anthology, 11

Autogenic Training, allows objective free associations, 397

Autosuggestion, Freud victim of, 3; molding Freud's dreams, 4

Awareness, unimportant in shaping verbalizations, 368

Bisexuality, as Freud's philosophical fancy, 10, 57; as erroneous concept, 107

Book burning, The Freudian way, IV, 61-63

Book censorship, the Freudian way, 55-61

Brainwashing, aspects of Freudism, 2, 8, 36, 205, 208, 221, 223-224, 227- 228, 234, 238, 244-247, 249, 305-306, 320, 326, 349, 351, 365, 367, 388, 392, 400-403, 449, 454, 459-461, 467; or conditioning, 2; pressures of Freudism, 8, 208, 211; most efficient in psychoanalysis, 35, 99, 211; of psychiatrists, 107; of Americans by Communists, 202; on Freudian couch, 221, 294; of physicians, 259; through prevailing culture, 291; of Wolf-man by Freud, 343-349; old and new, 402-407; in ancient mystery cults, 402; regressing the subject, first step in, 402-406; based on biological propensity, 403; Freudian and totalitarian, 427-437; faked permissiveness in Freudwashing, 443-447; procedures, 443-449; masochistic pact in, 444-447; cat-and-mouse game in, 445-447; implantation of ideas in, 445-447; Yezhov method in, 446; befogging the mind in, 456; misrepresented as education and reform, 456

Castration anxiety, overgeneralized by Freud, 10

CBS, accused of suppressing information, 64

Circular reasoning, by Freud, 348

Charlatanism, imputed to Freud, 52, 186, 204

Children, pretend unawareness in psychotherapy, 113; can intimidate parents, 113

China, as police state, 2; "thought reform" in, 3

Christ, and Freud, 1
Christians, duped by Freudism, 265-269; 325
Communism, conversion to, 439-440
Conditioning, or brainwashing, 2; used by Freud in analyses and promotion, 402, 441-442
Conversion, to Freudism, 36, 243-244, 313, 315-317, 401, 438
Couchhypnosis, in Freudwashing, 431

Dependency, fostered by psychoanalysis, 83, 98, 117, 454, 459
Depression, brought about by psychoanalysis, 74, 93, 116, 125, 208, 455
Diagnostic, farce, 109; vagaries of Freudism, 106-109
Divorce, fostered by Freudians, 116-120, 133-138, 144
Doctrinal compliance, molds free association, 306; in psychoanalysis, 318, 333, 381; in Freud's dreams, 342-343, 389
Dreams, symbols of, doubted 208; easy sexualization of, 326; covertly suggested in psychoanalysis, 334; induced 366, 393; inner security undermined by delving in, 456; patient regresses when preoccupied with, 456-457

Educators, avoiding identification with guidance and authority, 466-467
Ego regression, in psychoanalysis, 100, 297, 302, 314-317, 364, 455-456
Ego strength, undermined by "free" association, 222
Eros, as Freud's mythological and philosophical concept, 10
Eroticism, not discovered by Freud, 163
Experimenter's attitude, influences animal and human subjects 369-371; and even his own inferences, 369; and errors, 370

Expression of feelings, as Western delusion, 141; fostered asocially by Freudians, 149

Faith, of Freudians, 35-36, 317, 384-385, 438; demanded by Freud for his doctrines, 207; cures like psychoanalysis, 332
Family, preconceived as sick by Freudians, 112; disrupted by Freudians, 116, 128, 133-138; disturbed by Freudian "treatment", 122, 125, 130-138
Fiction of neutrality, of experimenter, 367-371; in narcoanalysis, 372; in public opinion surveys, 372; in personality testing, 372; in non-directive counseling, 372; in medicine, 372-373; of psychoanalyst, 373-374, 377, 463, 465; of therapist, 375-376
Fraud, of Freud, iv
"Free" association, as alleged therapeutic tool, 11; is impossible, 206; as a farce, 209, 214, 216; leads to befogging of mind, 219, 290; precipitates psychosis, 222; reduces ego strength, 222; is bogus, 304; influenced by doctrinal compliance, 306; Freud is smoke screen of, 319, 322; fundamental fallacy about Freudian, 322; psychoanalyst directs, 334; as Freud's fishing expedition, 366; subtle coaching in, 377; as scientifically hopeless method of investigation, 397-398; Autogenic Training allows objective, 397; leads to mental befuddlement, 455-456;
Freud, as fraud, iv; fallacy of, iv; and Christ, 1; indulged in delusions, 1; suffering from "middle-age neurosis," 3; as victim of his patients, 3; victim of autosuggestion, 3; borrowed from Jewish mystics, 5; es-

512

it, 335, 349; claimed scientific status for psychoanalysis, 249, 253-254; called a fiction writer, 249; rejected scientific precision, 251; compared with Galileo, 253; tangled in own illusions, 253-254; liberal in verbalizations, dogmatic in behavior, 280; compared to revivalist preachers, 281; used persuasion and suggestion, 281; covertly steered patient's thinking, 283; deceived by mythopoetic hysterics, 284; finds that "sexual business attracts people," 285; as poor physician as compared to Munthe, 286-287; hysterics counter-exploiting, 287; patients in irrational awe of, 288; misconceived hypnosis, 298, 301; faking about hypnosis, 302-303; misnames psychoanalysis a "conversation," 307; equates transference with suggestibility, 311; "a therapist against my will," 315; in the webs of suggestion, 334-343; admits shaping patient's thoughts about dreams, 336; scandalously self-deluded, 337, 341-342, 389-390; claims "laborious work," not suggestion, in his "findings," 341; a complaint dream of, 342-343; brainwashing Wolf-Man, 343-349; building up a transference, 343, 345; coached patient in his theories, 344, 347; built psychoanalytic pathology into patient, 345-347; on a limb of unreason, 347; circular reasoning by, 348; blinded by wishful thinking, 353; as sloppy investigator, 358-359; dissimulating about suggestion, 360-362; overgeneralizing, 376; admits personal influence of analyst, 377-378; admits teaching his patient, 379, 386; began contamination of psychoanalytic "data," 389; custom made dreams of, 389; renames interpreta-

tions "constructions," 392; trusted the untrustworthy human memory, 393-394; invented, not discovered, mental apparatus, 395; rejected electrotherapy, yet continued suggestion therapy, 399; used conditioned reflex method in promoting psychoanalysis, 402, 441-442; priest-magicians as remote predecessors of, 407-413; *See Also* Freudian, Freud's, Psychoanalysis, Psychoanalytic

Freudian, Inquisition, iv; book burning, iv, 61-63; fallacious logic, 1; corrosive influences, 1; speculations, presented as "insights" and "research," 1; kind of persuasion, 3; indoctrination grew in U.S., 4, 39; reductionism (dynamic psychologism) 6, 10; undemocratic manipulations, 7; Mafia, 13; crooks, 13; establishment, 13, 67; metapsychology and jargon rejected, 18; pretences at science, 20, 251-271; humiliating treatment of a psychiatrist, 22-23; arrogance with colleagues, 22-28, 30-31, 195, 201; intimidation of psychiatrists, 23, 56, 172, and families, 87; worshipful training, 25; misunderstanding of Synanon, 27; pseudoreligionists, 30; oppression of psychiatrists and psychologists, 28-34, 35, 38, 59; intolerance for nonbelievers, 31; "rubbish cluttering the minds of young doctors", 33; terrorism, 34-38; dogma, 35-36; faith, 35-36; converts intolerant of other approaches, 36; usurpation of medical schools, 37, 41-42; deifying of Freud, 37; cult of personality, 40; theoretical misperceptions, 41; persecution of unbelievers, 41; smearing of Jung, 47-55; censorship, 55-61; influence on publishers, 47; and selection of library books, 58; paranoid intolerance to new

515

ference as hypnotic state, 311-315, 355-356; indoctrination via transference, 312-313; indoctrination is durable, 316, 343; aboriginal level of logic, 326, 331; manipulator manipulated by patient, 326; smoke screen around suggestion, 332, 358-359, 377, 380-386; trickery to subdue patient, 339; glossing over unconsciously induced suggestion, 355, 359, 363; special astigmatism, 357; "no, no" topic and skeleton in the closet (suggestion), 367; special pathology not uncovered by non-Freudian investigators, 380; psychiatry has no valid data, 381, 389-399; hidden persuasion, 386; browbeating the child-patient, 386-389; ideology imposed on patient, 387; hopelessly contaminated data, 389-399; shibboleth to be discarded, 391-392; initiation compared with that of ancient cults, 403-406; analysands' psychodynamics and of witches, 421-426; gurus, 319, 433; faith strengthened by obtaining converts, 438; authorized doctrines as infallible, 439; training analysis as powerful indoctrination, 442; uprooting of patients from tradition, 448; wondercures are broadcast, 451; Trick of Resistance, 457-458; indoctrinator cynical and insensitive, 459-460; role diffusion, 467; *See* Freud's, Psychoanalytic

Freudian couch, and suggestible hysterics, 8; as substitute for mother's apron strings, 118; ritual, 121; a futile experiment on, 218-222; subtle brainwashing on, 221, 294; as hypnotic reinforcement, 293-299; provides superiority over patient, 294; occult implications of, 294; enhances suggestibility, 294-295; conducive to monotony essential for hypnosis, 297; 303; as part of psychoanalytic hoax, 298; has a durable effect, 306; disorganizes mature reaction patterns, 363; conducive to infantilization, 363; for moderns like trees for Tarzan, 451; increases control over patient, 452

Freudian denigrating of Jung, 21, 47-55; Adler, 21, 168-169; Rank, 21, 37; Stekel, 21; Ferenczi, 37-38; Dr. Wertham, 120-123; Mrs. Ferman, 120, 123-124

Freudian hoax, as practical joke, 1; reminiscent of propaganda, superstitions, myths, brainwashing, 2; as clandestine conditions, 3; begun with Freud's self-analysis, 3; is unwitting, 4; as concealed pseudoreligion, 5; medical aspects of, 7; losing ground, 202; played earnestly 251, 255; played on Christians, 265-269; helped by the couch, 298; as make-believe, 315; of psychoanalysis as no analysis, 320; gigantic, 331; is subtle, 398

Freudians, usurping positions in psychiatry, 3; glossing over Freud's Kabbalistic sources, 7; suppress opponents, 7; intimidate opponents, 13, 17, 56; Jung's psychology maligned by, 21; smug superiority of, 25; bound in conventronal therapy, 26, 27; psychiatrists duped by, 28; claim to be innovators, 31; suffer from ignorance of history, 31; established a corner on rich foundations, 37; more prophets than scientists, 44; retaining irrationalities, 51; sexual exploitation of patients by, 74; enamored of psychopathology, 109, 112, 122, 124, 142; weave fantasy into theory, 111; discard the obvious and the rational, 111, 114; preconceive family as sick, 112; make scapegoats of society, 113; intimidate parents, 114; foster divorce, 116, 133-138; as compulsive reformists, 129; likened to sociopaths, 129; condone marital infidelity, 131; make immorality more comfortable, 132; as moths of moral fabric, 138; encourage expression of hostility, 138-142; oblivious to self-cure, 143; enslave patient to symptoms, 143-144; astoundingly gullible, 154; compared to Epicureans, 166; sectarian narrow-mindedness of, 202; disregard positive personality aspects, 229, 233, 238-239; undermine responsible behavior, 233; inject their views into patients, 235; induce brooding over the past, 235; twist lives as supposed healing, 239; ubiquitous in USA, 239; sex-obsessed, 239; promote confusion and ill-will among patients, 240; oblivious to psychotherapeutic value of religion, 240; usurped scientific status, 252; psychologist duped by, 261; asserted themselves as opinion leaders, 275; like to stay oblivious to suggestion, 324; parading as bearers of a better humanity, 438; like brainwashers, produce big interpretations from minute clues, 441

Freudism, futility of, 1; fraud of, 1; pretense of, 1; as secular sect, 1, 4, 17, 43-45; indoctrination aspect of, 2, 29; as substitute for religion, 4, 41; as psychological and moral epidemic, 4; reinforcing, hedonism, 4; immaturity, 4; and irresponsibility among Americans, 4; Ludwig concerned with contamination by, 4; as "monstrosity of the Jewish spirit", 6; humanistic correction of, 6; as militant sect, 7, 43-44; why preferred to "Freudianism," 8; impossible to define precisely, 8; even by Freud, 10; tentatively defined, 9; has many faces, 9-11; as materialistic philosophy, 11; as nontheistic religion, 11; as naturalistic and rationalistic presuppositions, 11, 20; debilities of, 11; like food fads, impervious to criticism, 11, 18; claims superiority, 11; denigrates opponents, 11; critical look at, 15; harmful professional effects of, 15, 33, 40; its demise would allow the use of better approaches, 17; as intellectual contagion, 17-18; as addiction to ideas, 17; dominates American psychiatry, 17; better psychologies to supplant it, 18; is anathema at Oxford, 18; considered a disease, 19, 20; a personal equation to, 19; as part of anti-Christian movement, 19; close to Marxist and Nazi concepts, 19; as part of "Comptean" (positivistic) revolution, 20; as a scientism, 20; as intellectually closed world, 32; undesirable effects of training in, 32, 34, 40; oversold, 32; hampering psychiatric research, 33; propounded as scientific gospel, 33; tyrannizes American psychiatry, 33; as dictatorial system, 34, 38; some won freedom from, 41; anti-scientific effects of, 42; as a sexual church, 44; opposition to, branded as unAmericanism, 56; as atheistic and mysanthropic ideology, 57; as psychiatric sect, 57; retarded progress of mental hospitals, 91; psychiatrists overtrained in, 107; as indoctrination in mythology, 107; as antireligious religion, 128, 139; as cult, 128; two fundamental scientific errors of, 132; sanctions return to jungle law, 138; as revolution led by Jews and foreigners, 148; permeated social sciences, 148, 150; creates poorly integrated personalities, 152; reduces women to sexual objects, 153; enabled homosexuals to gain influence, 153; utilized propaganda techniques, 154-155; as promotional success, 154; as esoteric system, 196; as theocratic sect, 196; spread like a hoax, 196; built on crowd behavior, 198; compared to fads and follies, 199; weird delusions of, 211; corrosive ideology of, 232; as quasi-philosophical cult, 247; as covert religion, 248, 436; fantasy products in, 258; physicians gullible about, 259; asserting wide relevance of, 260; Christians duped by, 265-269; as "new ethic," 276; denies men's rationality, 276; man pictured as unfree by, 276; conversion of patient to, 313, 315-317; suggestion, a basic tool of, 322; the allegedly scientific psychology of, 381-383; quasi-data of, 382; gentle schooling in doctrines of, 387; phallus, as ultimate revelation of, 406; *See* Psychoanalysis, Psychoanalytic, Psychoanalysts

Freudophile, incited against mother, 142; blames others for his actions, 145

Freud's nonscience, 1, 11, 71; phallic cult, 1, 5, 7, 11, 39, 91, 406; neuroticism, 3, 203; ambitiousness, 3; self-analysis as beginning of his hoax, 3; uncritical pupils, 4; psychopathological hangups, made into universal model, 4; ideas taken from Zohar, 5; waning sexuality and creation of psychoanalysis, 5; ideas dehumanizing and degrading, 6; customary repression of sources of ideas, 6; false amnesia, 6; concept of libido rejected by Jung and Adler, 10; needs misdirected his therapy, 11; speculations rejected by European psychiatrists,

18, 19; soulless materialism, 54; fantasies about bisexuality, 57; "research" turned into therapy, 73; followers are of low order, 128; pernicious influence, 128; Messianic complex, 128; cynical moral negativism, 129; theories uncritically accepted, 174; pretended modesty, 184-189; neurotic straining for "science," 184; famous blunder about sexual "traumas," 184, 249, 284, 448; sexual etiology of neuroses, 187; armchair speculations, 193; works, as the new covenant, 196; predetermined interpretations, 206-207; arbitrary and dogmatic interpretations, 206-207; authoritarian manner, 206-207, 220-221; dream symbols doubted, 208; clinical fantasies, 266, 268; and Marxist "science" compared, 275-276; doctrine of man is imposed upon facts, 275; contradictions and inconsistencies, 278-280; sexual overinterpretations, 278; evasive skill, 282; false claim of renouncing hypnosis, 282, 293; findings have dubious scientific value, 283; exploitation of sexuality, 285; misanthropic, pessimistic outlook, 289; messianic ambitions, 315; semantic dissimulation about suggestion, 340, 360-362; bravado about suggestion, 341; tremendous power of rationalization, 346; fishing expedition in "free" associations, 366; illusion about analyst as a reflecting mirror, 377; wish fulfillments in own dreams, 389; misuse of logic, 391; old wives tale, 393; "months of feeding up" the patient, 395; operations compared with Inquisitors', 416-427; and Inquisitors' patients compared, 419-420; self-brain-washing, 419

Freudwashing, in U.S., 4, 154, 291;

106-110   215   169   214-216   222-223   145   223

through press, 4; only a minority escaped it, 8; docile submission to, 8; defined, 8; parallel with Communist brainwashing, 8, 28, 116, 208, 427-437; parallel with secret cults, 8, 403-413; of teaching and training psychiatrists, 24, 143, 223, 238; of children, 112-115, 152; of parents, 114; of patients, 116, 144, 223, 229, 317-320; of public, 151; subjects balking at, 205-241; a smooth, 241-247; of ministers, 268; based on suggestibility, 305; in Freud's description, 388; as camouflaged brainwashing, 401-467; as clandestine implantation of Freudian beliefs, 402; compared with witch-making, 413-427; a psychiatrist views brainwashing and, 437-443; faked permissiveness in brainwashing and, 443-447; accepted by defeated subject, 444; in slow motion, 449-462; "truth" is known beforehand in, 449-450, 461; delving in dreams helps regress patient in 456-457; accusations of resistance soften patient in, 457-458; facilitated by freudianized culture, 461; go slow, the first rule of, 467

Games, in psychoanalysis, 84, 103, 115, 205-228; in brainwashing, 445-447

Guilt feelings, deliberately induced in psychoanalysis, 72, 78, 137; stirred up in Freudian analysands and witches, 425, 434

Gullibility, helps the hoaxers, iv, of Freudians, 154; is widespread, 155-161; equals suggestibility, 155; explanations of, 156; based on childishness, 160; of modern man, 252; of physicians regarding Freudianism, 259

History, as an area of Freudian ignorance, 31; distorted by Freudians, 164-172

Hoax, thrives on gullibility, iv; attains gigantic proportions, iv; refuses to die, iv; liked by people, iv; defined, 1; many kinds of, 155-161; artists particularly prone to, 156-157; played on medical men, 160

Hoax of Freudism, The, iv; how it came about, 3; thesis of, 3;

Homosexuality, overdiagnosed, 106-110, 215; imputed irresponsibly to Leonardo, 109; imputed to analysand, 214-215, 222-223; incited by psychoanalysis, 145, 223

Hostility, urged toward expression by psychoanalysis, 138-142; expression of, discouraged by Reality Therapy, 141

Humanistic psychology, repudiates Freud, 6, 176

Humiliation, of subjects in brainwashing and Freudwashing, 430, 454; by Freudians, of a psychiatrist, 22-23; of analysands, 216, 224

Hypnosis, Freud not skilled in, 190; ostensibly abandoned by Freud, 218-219, 221, 281-282, 293, 298-311, 363; reinforced by Freudian couch, 293-298, 299, 303; psychoanalysis as light, 295-297, 299, 301-302, 304, 308, 310-314; misrepresented by Freud, 298, 301; is a normal state for human mind, 298, 308-309; concentration and relaxation chief factor in, 309; doctrinal compliance in, 381; misconceived by Freud, 302-303

Hypnotist, is also hypnotized, 304; his expectations influence subject's behavior, 371; regresses with subject, 371

Iatrogenic (doctor-induced) sickness, 70, 72, 75, 87, 92, 108, 277

Immaturity, reinforced by Freudism in US, 4

Improvement, in therapy is no proof of

519

291, 324, 329-332, 334, 342, 354, 359, 383, 390-391, 393-400, 462

Oedipus complex, overgeneralized by Freud to all humans, 10; in Freud, 10; supposedly basic to psychopathology, 103; Freud, a prisoner of, 141; not construed into patient, 146; suggested into patient, 230; playing a quick round of, 325; theoretical fiction of, 435; overlearning, in Freudwashing and brainwashing, 432, 441-442

Parents, scapegoated, by Freudians, 83, 94, 103, 113, 116, 122, 139, 227, 237, 239, 434, 449

Patients, infantilized in psychoanalysis, 97, 117, 119, 313-315, 360, 363-364, 459; sickened by psychoanalysis, 92, 115-120, 228, 232, 241, 293; regressed by the couch, 100, 127, 363; psychoanalyst sets bad example to, 103; psychoanalysis becomes religion for, 103, 118; taught mistaken theories in psychoanalysis, 105; intimidated by Freudians, 114; swallow Freudian line, 144, 235, 387, 395; Freudian hypocrisy with 216; manipulate Freudians, 326; subdued by Freudian trickery, 339, 452; browbeat in psychoanalysis, 386-389; in psychoanalysis, handled like witches, 421-426; directed away from tradition, 448; Freudwashing of, 116, 144, 222, 229, 444; worship psychoanalysts, 119, 292, 339; psychoanalysis deteriorates the character of, 139, 145; enslaved to symptoms by Freudians, 143-144; covertly inoculated with Freudian values, 252, 312, 325, 366; reeducated in psychoanalysis, 326, 386; trained in drawing analogies, 328-329

Pavlov, and Freud contrasted, 71-72

Permissiveness, faked in Freudwashing and brainwashing, 443-447

Phallic cult, of Freudism, 1, 5, 7, 11, 39, 91, 406

Philistines, spited by Freud, 10

Plagiarism, imputed to Freud, 173, 358

Prestige, enhances suggestion, 367-368, 370

Projective tests, built on shaky Freudian foundations, 382-383

Psyche, Freudian animalized model of, 130

Psychiatric, sect of Freudism 57; dogma irrelevant, 87; power is dangerous, 119; theories are self-validating, 463; shibboleths about authority role, 465

Psychiatrist, sect of Freudism 57; dogma irrelevant, 87; power is dangerous, 119; theories are self-validating, 463; shibboleths about authority role, 465

Psychiatrist, idealized by patient, 290-291; patient reflects preconceived ideas of his, 318; treatment as function of morality and philosophy of the, 468

Psychiatrists, Freudism rejected by European, 18-19; intimidated by Freudians, 23, 56, 172; oppressed by Freudians, 28-35, 38, 59; show human weaknesses, 119; playing social prophets, 200; as spoiled priests, 200; vicious games of Freudian, 228; phobic reaction to a stand on values by American, 464; shying from open controls, 464; do not like facing the mandate to change neurotics and psychotics, 466-467

Psychiatry, swallowed by Freudism, 154; basic ignorance in, 272; still in the Dark Ages, 274; does not have even a definition of man, 275; assumed the role of secular religion,

275; no valid data in Freudian, 381, 389

Psychoanalysis, fallacy of, iv; lack of scientific validation of, 1; "inimical to welfare of mankind," 6; harmful effects of, 7, 92, 95, 307; as poor therapy, 7; as futile therapeutic ritual, 11, 120; undeserving of scientific status, 15-16; injurious to mental welfare, 15; dominates American psychiatry, 15, and psychology, 21; accused of dogmatism, 16; trailing behind behavioral science, 16; its assumptions unverified, 16; maintains strangle hold on American psychiatry, 16; refuses to yield to better approaches, 16; French psychiatrist's aversion to, 18; classified as extra medical cult, 19; rejected by European psychiatrists, 18-19; claims to be "deep" psychology, 20; is like surveying road with microscope, 27; cripples reality contact, 27; as quackery, 28; as most efficient form of brainwashing, 35, 99, 211; has purely philosophical tenets, 35; is akin to religious conversion, 35; as poor treatment or worse, 36, 71, 96, 104-105, 211, 218-223, 228-241; as ticket to power and wealth, 40; as the highest of therapeutic churches, 43; personality maldevelopment through, 45; has no final answers in psycho-pathology, 56; as detrimental psychology, 57, 68; leads to suicides, 57; as a therapeutic failure, 68-110, 115-122, 131-138, 144-145; patients sacrificed to dogma and ritual of, 69, 95; harmful to professional development, 69; unmentioned dangers of, 70, 222; needs to induce guilt, 72, 78; psychological vivisections in, 72; patients seek sexual thrill in, 74; in-creases suicidal tendencies, 74, 93; plight of victims of, 77, 115-120; designed for psychotherapeutic failure, 77-79; concentrates on unreal, rather than real world, 78; five guarantees of failure in, 79; unclear focus on therapeutic goals in, 79; fosters dependency, 83, 98, 117, 454, 459; travesty of psychotherapy in, 83; as practise of no-therapy, 83; criticized for passivity, 83, 103; as costly futility, 86; as addiction, 86, 116, 314; as years of confabulation, 86; victimizes parents, 87, 103, 122; better ways of psychotherapy than, 88-104; enhances abulia (lack of will), 90, 219; protected by medical immunity, 91; as senseless psychological torture, 92; countertherapy needed to undo, 98; sickens patient by focusing on unconscious, 93, 96, 98, 105; infantilizes patients, 97, 117, 119, 313-315, 364, 459; therapeutic nonsense of, 100-101; ego deterioration through, 100; misguides patients, 101, 135; supplants patient's pathology with Freudian one, 101; sidetracks patients, 101; becomes religion for patient, 103, 118; as a mode of "positive thinking," 103; utterly disillusioned patients of, 104; as execrable synthesis, 104; does not touch fundamental problems, 104; is exceptionally superficial, 104; teaches patient mistaken theories, 105; has antimedical effects, 105; abnormalizes patients, 105; undermines social values, 105; warps personality, 106; brings about depression, 116, 125, 208, 455; overvaluation of, 116; leads to psychological hypochondriasis, 117; as a nostrum, 119; is socially wasteful, 120; weakens, not strengthens pa-

training, 84; sets bad example to patient, 103; plays "therapeutic games," 103; provides patients with irrationalities, 103; drives patient into transference, 103; as patient's demon, 117-118; worshipped by patient, 119; gives advice covertly, 119, 137; ruins six lives, 136; little knowledge needed to be a, 197, 202; proliferates fantasies, 217; trained in tedious indoctrination, 223, 461; it is easy to be a, 227; as a demigod to patient, 292; analysand anticipates expectations of, 317; as parent surrogate, 322; his conscious ideas turn into patient's "unconscious" ideas, 322; trains patient in drawing Freudian analogies, 328-329; "free" association directed by, 334; is overvalued by patient, 339; influences the course of analysis, 352, 356, 391; suggestion viewed by a seeing, 359-365; indoctrinates the analysand, 380, 401, 454; obliges patient to confirm his constructions (Freud), 388; streamlines patient's psyche with Freudism, 439; plays it cool 451-452; pretends uninvolvement during Freudwashing, 452; "cunning of the unconscious" fools both patient and, 462

Psychoanalysts, of America, called crooks by Freud, 13; classified as quacks, 19; as a new kind of aristocracy, 43; as an exclusive guild, 46; as a professional union, 46; as character assassins, 47; interfere unscrupulously in patient's lives, 73; irritating, not healing emotional wounds, 74; neglect patient's real trouble, 77; do not work to change the patient, 78; play games with subjects, 84; as pseudophilosophers and emotional historians, 84; as anti-

action therapists, 84; forget about their role as doctors, 85; magnify incidents to fictitious significance, 86; reinforce, not cure neurosis, 90, 455; considered to be of low order, 128; aggravate guilt, then "cure" it, 137; as adherents of a peculiar cult, 196; are vociferous, 197; as elitist group with heterodox ideology, 200; overlook other emotions, 214, 320; practice double deception, 216; are awed by their tradition, 223; do not see forest for the trees, 226; bluff by making simple into complex, 227; manipulate analysands into submission, 227; delusional awe among, 248; smuggle own values into patients, 252, 312, 366; infantilize patients, 314-317; fall into traps of neurotics, 315; patients ascribe magic to, 317; plant ideas into patients, 325; magical thinking among, 350; as lay priests, 451; as inadvertent brainwashers, 462

Psychoanalytic, institutes damned, 15, 39, 40; rejection of vigorous thinking, 16; dust breathed by everybody, 18; superstitions about what is therapeutic, 25; brainwashing, 36; overattention to ugly and immoral promptings, 72; exploration a menace, 73; misdirection of patient, 76, 90; treatment has deleterious effects, 92; hypotheses are only assumptions, 103; butchery, 71-77; myth of superior worth, 115; joy ride, 115-124; overemphasis of old grievances, 116; patients never graduate, 117; misguiding of public, 121; decadence sold as enlightenment, 121; infiltration of social work, 121; indoctrination, 145; octopus, 153; blinders, 211; trainer injects himself into analysand's psyche, 212; solemn farce of interpretations, 213; interpretation opportunistically swallowed, 213; humiliation of analysands, 216; conditioning into belief, 217; abuse of patient, 218; oppression of analysands, 224; meetings are amusing, 249; pretences at science, 251-271; hoax played earnestly, 251, 255; quagmire, 318; thinking becomes a habit, 327-328; patient as humble disciple, 339; juggling words and concepts, 354; self-deceit, 358; intellectual acrobatics, 358, 364; ideology influences human figure drawings, 368; work characterized as covert or overt, rather than active or passive, 374; method of investigation is scientifically unreliable, 391-399; dogmas imposed upon patients, 459-460; myths of neutrality, 373-377, 463, 465

Psychodynamic, interpreters of psyche, 3

Psychology, still in subscientific phase, 271; shaky hypotheses of, 272; is full of controversial propositions, 273; is not far above folklore; 274

Psychopathology, Freudian obsession with, 109, 112, 122, 124, 142; the artifact of Freudian, 380; psychoanalysis increases patient's, 57, 68, 70-72, 74, 76-79, 90, 92, 105, 115-120, 117, 122, 219, 222-223, 225, 234, 241, 453-455, 457

Psychosis, recedes with moral and religious growth, 240; precipitated by "free" association, 222

Psychotherapist, as baby-sitter, 88; encouraged or guided by patient, 89; encourages facing symptoms, 89; must look for results, 92; a machine, 293; as "reinforcing machine," 373; "loaded operations" between patient and, 373; as mind-changer, 463

Psychotherapy, psychoanalysis as poor, 7, 11, 25, 36, 83-86, 91-92, 95-96, 104-105, 100-101, 211, 218-223, 228-241, 307, 319; failure guaranteed if following Freudian preçepts in, 77-79; as collaborative problem-solving, 80, 126; analytic and writer's contrasted, 79-83; Freud-aping in, 83-88; Freudian travesty of, 83; resulting in suicide, 87-88; deemphasis of emotions in, 88; should change behavior pattern, 92; theories and techniques are secondary in, 92; speculations are luxury in, 92; should strengthen values, 97; does not foster sickly transference, 97; discourages dependence, 97; Freudian oddities in, 100; must require effort of patient, 104; as overt and covert persuasion, 438; some brainwashing unavoidable in any, 462; as human guidance, 462; modeling as a basic process in, 463

Rational Therapy, 93

Reality Therapy, more effective than psychoanalytical, 115

Regression of personality, as first phase of brainwashing, 402-406

Religion, Freudism, as a nontheistic, 11, 128, 139; Freudism as substitute for, 1, 4, 17, 35, 41, 43-45, 103, 183, 196, 200-201, 247-248, 251, 262, 292, 380, 436, 451; undervalued by Freudians, 240

Science, an attempt at definition of, 269-271; natural, ridden with uncertainties, 269; myths of, 269; would-be or pre-, 269-270

Secret cults, and Freudwashing, 8, 403-413

Self-fulfilling prophecy, in experimentation, 371; in psychoanalysis, 381

Sexuality, considered basic drive by Freud, 10, 31; passed as Eros by Freud, 10; equated with libido by Freud, 10; Freudian obsession with, 74, 93, 106-110, 113, 129, 184, 215, 239, 249, 278, 284, 448; exploited by Freud, 74, 285; incited by hypnosis and psychoanalysis, 285-286; as seen by madames, pimps, and Freud, 286; psychoanalytic fanning of, 358, 361; looming large in Freud's and Inquisitors' thinking, 419, 424

Shock Therapy, in psychoanalysis, 319-320

Social immaturity, of Freudians, 121-122, 129, 131-133, 136, 138-142, 153, 232

Social scientists, suffering from a historical malady, 190; as businessmen of science, 101, 252; as *docta ignorantia*, 191; duped by Freudians, 148, 150

Stoics, 166-167

Soviet Union, as police state, 2; Stalin's purges in, 2

Sublimation, reduced to "instincts" by Freud, 10, 31

Suggestion, in Freudism, 2, 8; as *bacillus psychologicus*, 8, 343; unsuspected and pervasive, 8; mental acrobatics of Freud, Jones, Ferenzi about, 8, 334-343, 349-359; Freudian undercover form of, 197, 323, 333; through interpretation, 230, 322, 367; Freud admits using it, 249, 337, 361, and denies it, 335, 349; enhanced by couch, 294-295; defined as uncritical acceptance of an idea, 317; by distraction and insinuation is more potent, 323, 352, 367; Dr. Loy and Dr. Jung discuss, 332-334; Freudian smoke screen around, 332, 355, 358-359, 363, 377, 380-386; Freud in webs of, 334-343 vitiates

and invalidates all Freudian "data," 342, 354, 395-396; as smuggling thought and feelings into a mind, 350; verbal and affective kind of, 354; as Freudian "no, no" topic and skeleton in the closet, 359; emotional infantilization is basic to Freudian, 360; Freud dissimulating about, 340-341, 360-362; empirical and experimental findings on, 366-371; is unavoidable in psychotherapy, 366-367; nonverbal cues more important for, 367; is enhanced by suggester's prestige, 368-370

Superstition, defined, 2; aspects of Freudism, 2

Transactional Analysis, humiliating treatment of the founder of, 22

Transference, not abused by therapist, 146; as hypnotic state, 216, 281, 309, 311-315, 332-334; equated to suggestibility by Freud, 311; compared to posthypnotic suggestion, 312; as medium of Freudian indoctrination, 312-313, 316-317; as analyst-hypnosis, 314; childish relationship to analyst in, 315; as means of converting patient, 315; as sexual attachment, 340; built by Freud, 343; of Freudians and rapport of Mesmerists, 355; "paternal hypnosis" and Freudian, 357; discovered in Freudian, 359-365; falsely ascribed to patient, 360, 362

Unconscious, patient sickened by focusing on the, 93, 96, 98, 105; psychoanalysis as wish-hunting in the, 209; exploited by Freud, 245; attitudes influence experimental subjects, 369; both doctor and patient fooled by the cunning of the, 462